Twentieth-Century British Social Trends

Twentieth-Century British Social Trends

Edited by

A. H. Halsey
Emeritus Fellow
Nuffield College, Oxford

with

Josephine Webb
Research Officer
Nuffield College, Oxford

First published in Great Britain 2000 by
MACMILLAN PRESS LTD
Houndmills, Basingstoke, Hampshire RG21 6XS and London
Companies and representatives throughout the world

A catalogue record for this book is available from the British Library.

ISBN 0–333–72148–9 hardcover
ISBN 0–333–72149–7 paperback

First published in the United States of America 2000 by
ST. MARTIN'S PRESS, INC.,
Scholarly and Reference Division,
175 Fifth Avenue, New York, N.Y. 10010

ISBN 0–312–22706–X

Library of Congress Cataloging-in-Publication Data
Twentieth-century British social trends / edited by A.H. Halsey,
Josephine Webb.
p. cm.
Rev. ed. of: British social trends since 1900. 2nd completely rev.
ed. 1988.
Includes bibliographical references and index.
ISBN 0–312–22706–X (cloth)
1. Great Britain—Social conditions—20th century. 2. Great
Britain—Economic conditions—20th century. 3. Great Britain–
–Politics and government—20th century. 4. Social structure—Great
Britain—History—20th century. I. Halsey, A. H. II. Webb,
Josephine. III. British social trends since 1900.
HN385.B759 1999
306'.0941'0904—DC21   99–15879
                                                                        CIP

First edition (*Trends in British Society since 1900*) 1972
Second edition (*British Social Trends since 1900*) 1988
Third edition 2000

This book is printed on paper suitable for recycling and made from fully managed and sustained
forest sources.

10   9   8   7   6   5   4   3   2   1
09   08   07   06   05   04   03   02   01   00

Printed and bound in Great Britain by
Antony Rowe Ltd, Chippenham, Wiltshire

Contents

List of Tables

List of Figures

Acknowledgements

The authors and publishers wish to thank all of those who have kindly given permission for the use of copyright material.

An estimate was made of the use in the book of Office for National Statistics material and, after negotiation, permission to reproduce it was agreed.

Particular acknowledgements of the sources and thanks to the people who have provided relevant information have been made in each individual chapter.

Every effort has been made to trace the copyright holders, but if any have been inadvertently overlooked, the publishers will be pleased to make the necessary arrangement at the first opportunity.

Preface to the Third Edition

This is neither the beginning nor the end. *Trends in British Society Since 1900* was first published in 1972. A second enlarged version came out in 1988. Now here we go again for a third round. It takes us to the end of the century and to the threshold of the third millennium. Continuity is represented by the fact that Macmillan remains our publisher; change is denoted by funding from the Gatsby Foundation, affording us the collaboration and authorship of Josephine Webb and the secretarial help of Sarah McGuigan. I am grateful to all four sources of sustained support. It has meant that I have had time to laugh at the idiosyncrasies of our contributors, and at my own. Jo Webb and I think the third edition improves on its predecessors.

Some change of authorship may be seen from the contents page. Contributors to the first edition and more to the second edition are still aboard. We also welcome newcomers – A. B. Atkinson, Ray Fitzpatrick, Duncan Gallie, Jonathan Gershuny, Brian Harrison, Anthony Heath, Alan Holmans, Roger Hood, Amanda Root and George Smith. With them there are some new co-authors and other helpers. They are all welcome. Such a book as this entails much arduous labour.

Three aims have survived all three editions:

(a) To trace major developments in British social institutions – productive, reproductive, authoritative and communicative – in the course of the twentieth century
(b) to have these developments interpreted in relation to each other by leading social scientists and synthesized by the editor
(c) to show students how to use official and unofficial statistical sources so as to avoid the pitfalls of definition and procedures of collection.

The significance of the study is that it provides a guide to the main statistics and social change in a particular country – 'the first industrial nation' – over the whole of the twentieth century. The method is largely the collection of statistical trends from official (census and survey) and unofficial (birth cohorts and ad hoc investigation) sources, a careful check of changing definitions, and interpretation in terms of established theses.

One of our predecessors in the long tradition of 'political arithmetic', Daniel Defoe (1660–1731), wrote late in life:

How little repining there would be among Mankind, at any Condition of Life, if People would rather compare their condition with those that were worse, in order to be thankful, than be always comparing them with those which are better, to assist their Murmerings and Complainings.

Robinson Crusoe, 1719

Readers of this book may compare British 'Conditions' in 1900 with those in 2000 and decide whether the nation should be thankful or complain.

A. H. Halsey
Oxford, 1999

Notes on Contributors

A. B. Atkinson is Warden of Nuffield College, Oxford.

Peter Brierley is Executive Director, Christian Research, London.

David Butler is Emeritus Fellow of Nuffield College, Oxford.

Jackie Carter is the Data Visualization Support Officer at Manchester Information Datasets and Associated Services, University of Manchester.

Judith Chance is Lecturer in Geography at Oxford Brookes University.

Tarani Chandola is Prize Research Fellow, Nuffield College, Oxford.

David Coleman is Reader in Demography, University of Oxford.

Patricia Daley is University Lecturer in Geography at the University of Oxford and Fellow of Jesus College, Oxford.

Andrew Dilnot is Director, Institute for Fiscal Studies, London.

Carl Emmerson is Research Economist, Institute for Fiscal Studies, London.

Kimberly Fisher is Research Officer, Institute for Social and Economic Research, University of Essex.

Ray Fitzpatrick is Professor of Public Health and Primary Care, University of Oxford, and Fellow of Nuffield College, Oxford.

Duncan Gallie is Professor of Sociology, University of Oxford and Nuffield College, Oxford.

Jonathan Gershuny is Director of the Institute for Social and Economic Research and Professor of Sociology, University of Essex.

A. H. Halsey is Emeritus Professor of Sociology, University of Oxford, and Emeritus Fellow of Nuffield College, Oxford.

Brian Harrison is Professor of Modern British History, University of Oxford, and Fellow of Corpus Christi College, Oxford.

Anthony Heath is Professor of Sociology, University of Oxford and Fellow of Nuffield College, Oxford.

Alan Holmans is the former Chief Housing Economist, Department of the Environment.

Roger Hood is Professor of Criminology, Director of the Centre for Criminological Research, and Fellow of All Souls College, Oxford.

Julia Parker is a former Lecturer in Social Administration, University of Oxford.

Clive Payne is Director of the Computing and Research Support Unit, Social Studies Faculty Centre, University of Oxford, and Fellow of Nuffield College, Oxford.

Ceri Peach is Professor of Social Geography, University of Oxford, and Fellow of St Catherine's College, Oxford.

Andrew Roddam was statistical advisor to the Oxford Centre for Criminological Research while completing his doctorate in the Department of Statistics. He is now Statistical Advisor, Wellcome Trust Centre for the Epidemiology of Infectious Diseases, University of Oxford.

Alisdair Rogers is College Lecturer in Geography, St Catherine's and Keble Colleges, Oxford.

Amanda Root is Research Officer, Transport Studies Unit, University of Oxford.

George Smith is University Research Lecturer, University of Oxford.

Josephine Webb is Research Officer, Nuffield College, Oxford.

Bruce Wood is Dean of the Faculty of Economic and Social Studies, University of Manchester.

1
Twentieth-century Britain

A. H. Halsey

We were among the last of the Utopians or Meliorists as they are sometimes called, who believe in a continuing moral progress by virtue of which the human race already consists of reliable, rational, decent people ... The view that human nature is reasonable had in 1903 quite a long history behind it.

J. M. Keynes, *My Early Beliefs*, 1938

the belief in historical destiny is sheer superstition, and ... there can be no prediction of the course of human history by scientific or any other rational method ...

Karl Popper, *The Poverty of Historicism*, 1957

Introduction

No two theorists have had more influence on liberal social thought in the twentieth century than Keynes or Popper. Keynes died in 1946 before our first edition, Popper in 1995 before our third.

Within a few years of our first edition in 1972 the post-war period came to an end. Dates are somewhat arbitrary and periods only become clear in retrospect, but perhaps the winter of 1973/74 can be taken as the turning point of a 30-year economic boom into a period of recession and readjustment affecting the whole of the 'first world' and not least the United Kingdom. The long-run context of a switch of social consciousness from the Victorian Empire through the Attleean Welfare State to Europe is widely known. But soon after our second edition in 1988 it became clear that 'Thatcherism' was laying claim to serious changes in British ideology and politics (Skidelsky, 1988). In fact the evidence from opinion polls like the British Social Attitudes Surveys or the British Electoral Studies suggests that Mrs Thatcher's crusade to change social values largely failed; for example, on the family or the National Health Service: there was no obvious transformation of public ideology though institutions were undoubtedly changed as was the language of public discussion. Words like 'competition', 'private enterprise' and 'individual choice' became more frequently heard and displaced ideas about socialism, cooperation, national-ized industry and the comprehensive school which had dominated political discussion in the 1940s and 1950s.

With Major's succession to the premiership in 1990 and the abrupt decline of Jenkins' attempt in the 1980s to reshape the traditional mould of British politics, it became clear that argument about citizenship and the Welfare State was no more than a modernized revival of nineteenth-century disputes about pauperism and the Poor Law. Christian socialism (Dennis and Halsey, 1988), somewhat surprisingly, again confronted economic liberalism in a new age of technological affluence. Then the collapse of European communism and the Marxist states, the fall of the Berlin Wall, and the rise of the European Union re-transformed the life of Britain. Manufacturing, trade unions and the tradi-tional family waned while lawyers, supermarkets, the Internet and education waxed.

The task for a third edition is therefore to put the new developments of the most recent decades into the perspective of the experience of the three previous generations. We must connect what Eric Hobsbawm (1994) calls the Age of Catastrophe (1914–45) and the Golden Age (1945–74) to the evolving new age of uncertainty of the 1990s, and the dawn of the new millennium. Our method is numerical: the result is a series of statistical trends with comments on their sources, guidance against their misuse, and suggestions for their interpretation. Ideas, hypotheses and concepts are measured as numbers. Numbers make up trends, and trends represent the history of British institu-tions in the twentieth century. Nothing could be more straightforward. Or could it?

Theories

The facts, it is sometimes held, especially in the form of numbers, speak for themselves. But neither life nor sociology are so happily simple as that. The very concept of a trend may generate unintended misrepresentation. In this book we take it to refer to consequences and not to causes. Trends may be held by some theorists to have explanatory value; we see them as phenomena to be explained.

Trends are in any case absurdly easy to find. If a series of observations between two points in time yields neither random fluctuation nor absolute stability, there could be a trend. But what follows? Stability may be equally significant. A zero rate of population growth would have momentous social implications in most countries in our time. Facts have to be interpreted. Bias may come in subtle forms from contentious, unproven or false theories of history. Our sociology, by contrast, and in agreement with Popper's, holds that there are no established laws of historical development or decline. The view that social institutions evolved and culminated in Victorian liberal society – the so-called Whig version of British history – could be said to be an extravagant preference for graphs moving upwards to the right. It is now regarded with scepticism. The underlying theory, as Keynes reminds us, is a belief in progress and, we might add, in the superiority of European civilization, especially the activities of British men. In complementary fashion the Marxist theory of history, at least for 'capitalist' societies, looks for downward trends; for example, in the rate of profit or the income of proletarians, towards a revolutionary crisis. It fell from academic grace along with the Berlin Wall in 1989.

The statistics of trends in British society in the twentieth century which are collected together in this book are vulnerable in the same way – a theory of social structure and social change must underlie them. To describe is also, however imperfectly, to explain. Statistical compilations of the kind made here can all too easily inform the student only to deceive. They may appear, or even purport, to 'speak for themselves'; but this is never completely so, and often very far from so, for two broad reasons. First, there may be difficulties about the meaning of the numbers which arise from the manner of their collection and classification. Second, more fundamentally, the chosen collection may reflect a partial or distorted view of what is significant in social structure and change.

The first type of difficulty is the lesser: it can, admittedly laboriously, be avoided by careful description of the sources and of the method of collection and definition of the data. Thus one aim of each of the following chapters is to guide students in the use of the statistical sources and to point out the dangers in interpreting statistics which are typically collected for administrative purposes rather than to answer questions in the social sciences. Illustrations of this kind of difficulty recur in every chapter. The Central Statistical Office (CSO) may evolve into the Office for National Statistics (ONS) or, more importantly, the conceptual definitions may change as in the example of the disputed occupational classifications used by the Registrar-General in successive censuses. Or the administrative basis of data collection may change; as, for example, in the statistical series on unemployment, the basis of which has shifted during the century with the extension of unemployment legislation.

The second type of difficulty, which merges into the first, is more intractable. It is revealed if we reverse the logical procedure implied by a table of bare social statistics (that is, to infer a conception of change from the facts), and start instead from a conception of social structure and deduce what facts should be collected. Any conception of social structure is inevitably selective: it is a way of not seeing as well as a way of seeing.

What notion of structure and change would be adequate to prescribe the scope and character of statistics to be collected, either officially or academically? This question is the first to confront anyone who tries to devise a book like this. What T. B. Bottomore wrote in 1962 is still true, 'The fundamental conception, or directing idea, in sociology is that of *social structure*', but while many useful distinctions have been made, an adequate classification of societies, social groups and social relationships has still not appeared. Perhaps the nearest approximation is by James S. Coleman (1990). This immediately raises the problem of what is a society? What are the limits in time and space which can be used meaningfully in order to specify British society as a more or less circumscribed network of social relationships?

The timespan must be arbitrary because neither evolution nor revolution ever totally transform all the institutions of a society, its language, its kinship structure, its economy. We have chosen to confine our attention to the twentieth century, but for particular reasons we might just as reasonably have begun with, say, the first census in 1801, or the Education Act of 1870, or the beginning of World War I in 1914. Though there would be general agreement that Britain in 1700 was a different society in its fundamental institutions and culture from Britain in 2000 – the former early-modern or agricultural and the latter industrially advanced or post-industrial – there could be no agreement on a unique date for any transition.

Runciman (1997) argues for the importance of World War I and its aftermath as predominant in twentieth-century Britain. Peter Clarke (1996), in his social history up to 1990 is more inclined to see the closing years of the century as crucial, in decisions about European union, in the transformation of Imperial Victorian Britain, and in preoccupation with relations with the rest of Europe. Taking a global perspective, Hobsbawm (1994) points to the third quarter of the century which 'marked the end of the seven or eight millennia of human history that began with the invention of agriculture in the stone age ...', and he goes on to a new transformation, 'the disintegration of the old patterns of human social relationships and with it, incidentally, the snapping of the links between generations, that is to say, between past and present'. This new state of human affairs, Hobsbawm argues, has been particularly evident 'in the most developed countries of the western version of capitalism' to which Britain belongs. The logical end of capitalism, as this leading exponent of Marxism would persuade us, would be to destroy even those parts of the pre-capitalist past, which it had found convenient. The result has been 'the most profound revolution in society since the stone age ... and [s]ince the middle of the century this has been happening' (pp.9, 15–16). Hobsbawm's view is expounded in the *Age of Extremes*; Runciman's argument is detailed in Volume III of his *Treatise on Social Theory*. We shall suggest a different interpretation. History cannot be reduced to historicisms, nor is it possible to accept the form of mechanical functionalism which is implied by the search for periodization of all the institutions of a country.

The partial social integration of England, Scotland, Wales and Northern Ireland as well as the regions within them raises another question. The main focus of this book is on England and Wales, each author having decided whether it would make more sense to use Great Britain or the United Kingdom as the aggregate unit for analysis in the light of knowledge of national variations in the structure of the social relationships with which he or she is concerned, and in the light of the availability of statistics. So, though we may begin with the intention of defining the data collection in terms of sociological concepts, there will be ambiguities in theory and obstacles in practice which result in a variety of compromises.

These problems of delimiting a society in time and space are likely to restrict the picture gleaned from the statistics in this book. The period in question is one in which the relations between Britain and the rest of the world have changed radically; and the consequences are not only external but ramify throughout the indigenous structure of British life. During the century Britain has lost a vast empire which once

> meant that India and Africa and parts of the Middle and Far East were also in a sense the lower strata of British society. The dissolution of the Empire and increasing real independence of the English-speaking dominions have contracted the size of the society over which the British elite – and British society as a whole – were superordinated. (Shils, 1964)

Neither the pattern of migration nor the course of immigration nor the statistical trends reported in the chapters on housing, health and welfare can fully express the changes in class structure which have accompanied the transition of British society to its post-imperial position. Even the polarization of capital and income, which Atkinson discusses in Chapter 10, has to be set in the context of the shrinking of the traditional working class throughout the century.

What then can be expected for social theory of the statistical series which comprise this book? We hope they will cover the essential institutional framework of the society for the chosen period. Certain institutions and groups are easily identifiable in all societies. We may list them here as four institutional systems:

- Institutions of *production*
- Institutions of *reproduction*
- Institutions of *power and authority*
- Institutions of *communication*

All societies must produce goods and services and reproduce appropriate social personalities if they are to maintain themselves; if not, like the Soviet Union, they collapse. Hence the necessity for a division of labour, work organizations and familial and educational institutions. Institutions of production and reproduction form the basis of social arrangements for the distribution of life-chances (for food, shelter and opportunity) which 'work' through a system of power and authority. At least in societies with a complex division of labour, life-chances are distributed unequally and the society is composed of groups which are stratified by class, status and power. Social cohesion is then further reinforced through institutions serving to assert and reassert values and to offer social recognition to personal events such as birth or marriage. Finally, society presupposes communication and hence requires institutions of language and organizations for storing and transmitting information.

None of these elements is expected, in modern as distinct from function-alist theory, to fit together like some efficiently lubricated machine. But each demands to be covered in the following chapters according to the special form of social structure which has emerged in modern Britain. It is here that our own emphases and interpretations have entered. We have paid little attention to the institutions of language. The British population is almost universally literate in a common language, though in earlier centuries dialects and illit-eracy would have to be taken into account, and in any case it is open to debate how far the existence of the Welsh language, of class-linked linguistic structure and usages, and of non-English-speaking communities among the ethnic minorities can be disregarded. Chapters 2, 5, 6 and 7 are concerned with those aspects of social structure which determine the reproductive character of the society. The productive system is dealt with in Chapters 8, 9 and 10.

Though we have already characterized twentieth-century Britain as a contracting society because of its transition from the position of a dominant imperial power, it is none the less important to note the expansion of its produc-tive system. The gross domestic product (GDP) has risen sevenfold between 1900 and 1995. This increase in available goods and services has, of course, to be discounted in terms of inflation and population increase but, even allowing for these two forces, the growth has been more than fourfold. These figures cannot be wholly satisfactory to the sociologist because of the methods used in calculating them. They exclude a wide range of social exchanges (for example, between friends and spouses) which are not defined as 'economic' and they include economic exchanges such that, for example, the employment of more warders to guard more prisoners would count as economic progress and a reduc-tion in the staff of tuberculosis clinics would count as economic regression. None the less, the amelioration of material conditions, emphasized by Dilnot and Emmerson in Chapter 9, must be taken as a central fact of this century and especially of the period since World War II in Britain.

Hence the interest of trends concerning the distribution of national income and wealth which give us an indication of changes in the structure of classes, gender and ethnic minority groups. Again there are difficulties in interpreting the data; for example, the probability that tax avoidance is positively correlated with income and therefore inequality may be underestimated. Inequality remains the outstanding feature of both income and, especially, wealth distributions. As may be seen from Figure 10.6, there has been a marked fall in the share of wealth held by the richest 5 per cent of the population since 1922 when it was over 80 per cent. Taking occupational and state pension rights into account reduces the inequality in wealth distribution. In 1994 the share of the richest 5 per cent was 25 per cent. On the other hand, as Atkinson writes in Chapter 10, 'we are ending the century just as we began with a widespread concern about poverty'.

The changing class structure appears from another point of view in Chapter 8 where the development of the division of labour is traced by Gallie. White-collar workers are now in a majority, and within their ranks the growing number of managers and professionals, especially in the most recent decades, reflects the development of an increasingly complex division of labour on the basis of an increasingly scientific and capital-intensive technology. As a proportion of the labour force, manual workers fell from three-quarters to under a half between 1911 and 1981 and further to not much more than a third by the mid-1990s. Table 8.4 shows the trend. The productive life of the working class has been gradually transformed in the process. Hours of work have been reduced and paid holidays dramatically increased. Moreover, a sombre aspect of the same phenomenon, the number (though not the rate) of unemployed in the late 1970s and 1980s, returned to, or exceeded, the levels of the 1930s though they were reduced in the late 1990s (Figures 8.3 and 8.4). Men (not women) also figure less prominently on the work scene for the double reason of extended education and increased longevity.

Meanwhile, corporate organization of working men in occupational or industrial unions has increased sevenfold since the beginning of the century – peaking in the 1970s – so the proportion of actual to potential male union membership (or density) rose from 16.7 per cent to 54.4 per cent in 1979. Trade union membership and density fell with the rise of unemployment from 1980, and so loosened its grip on the employed population. Over the century, however, the interests of groups included in the productive process have become highly organized. Nevertheless, this should not be interpreted as evidence for growing proletarian solidarity. The most dramatic recent rises of unionization have been among white-collar workers and in the 1970s among women. The interests of 'the proletariat' have become divided by a complex of competing occupational groups within the broad stratum of employed workers. Perhaps the most telling reflection of advancing material affluence in statistics concerning working-class living standards is that of the progressive shift of the definition of a 'cost of living' from its narrow and normative focus on the 'necessities of life' towards a retail price index reflecting the consumption patterns of the general population. These patterns have changed, especially since World War II, towards greater emphasis on the purchase of leisure, private transport and consumer durables. The rise of government spending is traced by Dilnot and Emmerson in Chapter 9, of private transport and communication by Root in Chapter 13, and of leisure pursuits by Gershuny and Fisher in Chapter 18. Together they constitute a vast social transformation from a static, industrious and poor country to a mobile, leisure-seeking and opulent one.

In the second half of the century huge strides have been made towards transforming the life of women. Feminism has taken advantage of changes in the economy to narrow gender gaps in health, welfare and educational opportunity. The upward trends in women's participation in paid employment are the opposite of those of men. There was, as Gallie makes plain in Chapter 8, a post-war surge in paid employment for women. By 1981 they formed 39 per cent of the total occupied population, and by 1998 over 46 per cent. Women have contributed especially to the growth of white-collar, especially clerical and sales, employment. This is all the more remarkable in the light of developments in the institution of marriage. In the first half of the century, domesticity was the norm for women after marriage. But especially since 1951, the increasing participation of married women is the most outstanding factor in the changing balance between employment and non-employment – a fact which raises many questions about the changing character of family life, and particularly for the Parsonian functionalist analysis of the relation between marriage, kinship and economy in an advanced industrial society.

Similarly, we must note that, in addition to the growth of Britain as a productive enterprise, there were profound twentieth-century changes in the reproductive system. The demographic details are set out by Coleman in Chapter 2. Britain began in 1900 as a leading example of the Western European system of kinship based on the nuclear family with high fertility and also high mortality, checked further in Malthusian terms by delayed marriage, relatively high bachelordom and spinsterhood, and virtually non-existent (though harshly punished) divorce and illegitimate births. Government largely left all this to the severe customs of 'civil society' and the moral surveillance of religion. At the same time Britain had also moved into the first demographic transition of falling fertility without any sign of weakening kinship; indeed the popularity of marriage subsequently increased with ever higher proportions marrying and at earlier ages. Only after World War II did divorce, separation, cohabitation and lone motherhood begin to rise against the background of a net reproduction rate of less than population replacement. Thus Britain ended the century as a

European leader of extramarital and teenage births, rising divorce and cohabitation – the hallmarks of the second demographic transition.

Government in the later decades spasmodically, and on the whole ineffectually, intervened in society's arrangements for reproduction but it did transform the education system, making secondary schooling universal and enlarging the coverage of university education from less than 2 per cent to over a third of the nation's young men and women.

A visible consequence of the new demographic regime, apart from the increasing presence of old people and the disappearance of children, is that the patterns of imperial migration inherited from the nineteenth century and continuing into the twentieth to give a net outflow of migrants numbering over a million, has been reversed. As Coleman concludes, 'immigration from the indigenous populations of former colonies ... comprises half the country's growth and has permanently transformed major cities into racially mixed populations unimaginable in 1950, let alone 1900'. Caribbean, African and Asian minorities made up 5.5 per cent of Britain's total population in the 1990s.

The ethnic minorities are vividly described by Peach et al. in Chapter 4. Rates of assimilation have varied. Though the 'ethnic penalty' persists over the generations, even for the Irish and Western Europeans, Peach's measures of segregation show that ethnic ghettos are much less marked than in the cities of the United States and there is evidence of black British and British Asian identity as well as of mixed households. On the other hand there are pockets of high unemployment and still widespread racist attitudes. Jews are most firmly established in the professional and entrepreneurial classes. Bangladeshis are the most deprived of ethnic minorities. There is serious discussion of a 'Jewish' future for Asians and an Irish (proletarian) one for Caribbeans. At all events the Britain of the twenty-first century seems destined to be multi-ethnic.

Chapter 11 on the electorate and the House of Commons, as well as Chapter 12 on urbanization and local government, may be seen as more or less satisfactory statistics on the distribution of power and authority. We then look at three aspects of the distribution of life-chances – housing (Chapter 14), social services (Chapter 15), and social security (Chapter 16) in the context of the so-called Welfare State. Chapter 19 on religion deals in part with the system of persuasion, but Chapter 20 on crime may also be thought of as concerned with those coercive institutions which maintain social cohesion. However, this classification of the content of chapters is somewhat arbitrary since all groupings and institutions tend to have multiple functions; for example, churches and chapels are also part of the system of communication, the economy, and the socialization process as well as the distribution of authority and power.

Where, then, in the statistical record are the crucial turning points to be found, separating the life, work, leisure and pleasure of British generations? Is there a single turning point in twentieth-century Britain, dwarfing all other

periods of change and transforming society? Runciman thinks there is. He might summarize our purpose as an attempt to describe a 'descent with modifications' from nineteenth-century industrialization towards, in his phrase, 'a sub-culture of capitalist, liberal-democratic society'. Capitalism is a type of economy, the mode of production, liberalism a tradition of ideology 'the mode of persuasion', and democracy a variant of 'the mode of coercion'.

'At the turn of the century', English society was in the middle of what I shall continue to call its 'late-Victorian and Edwardian' evolutionary stage. After the First World War, it became capitalist, liberal, and democratic in a qualitatively different sense, which, however it should be labelled, and however it was seen by the people who lived through it, made the institutions of the pre-war era irrecoverable even for those who were most determined to restore them and most reluctant to accept that the world, and England's place in it, would not be the same again. (Runciman, 1997, p.10)

And he adds that

The changes which took place in, or in the aftermath of, the Second World War did undoubtedly make England a better place to live in for many of its citizens. But those changes were in no sense fundamental to its modes of production, persuasion, and coercion, and they can in any case be traced back to selective pressures which antedated the outbreak of war. English society did undergo an evolution from one to another sub-type of capitalist liberal democracy between 1915 and 1922, despite all the contemporary rhetoric about 'normalcy'. But after 1945, it did not, despite all the contemporary rhetoric about a 'social revolution'. However the changes which followed the Second World War are to be explained, described, or evaluated, they cannot be reported as an evolution out of one into another sub-type, let alone mode, of the distribution of power. (1997, p.11)

Runciman writes of Britain, or rather of England, with an aristocratic pen. His preoccupation is with the decline of the nineteenth-century nobility in terms of wealth, political power and administrative influence. No reader of David Cannadine could deny the waning potency of this class from the death of Queen Victoria at the dawn of the twentieth century. It was, as Cannadine observes, marked by the virtual disappearance of the Irish grandees, the death rate of upper-class sons in World War I (higher than that of other classes and exceeding that of any conflict since the Wars of the Roses), and the sale of its land between 1910 and 1922 (a volume of transfer equalled in the second millennium only by the Norman Conquest and the dissolution of the monasteries) (Cannadine, 1990, p.704).

Yet we must also listen to another voice, that of Francis Beckett in his biography of Clement Attlee who led the British government from 1945 to 1951 in creating the National Health Service, a first and serious attack on poverty, and the essential elements of the Welfare State.

I was born in 1945, four days after VE day and a month before Clement Attlee became Prime Minister. I had my childhood illnesses in NHS hospitals. My tonsils rest, no doubt carefully preserved, in Mount Vernon Hospital, Northwood, Middlesex. When I got polio (from which I made a complete recovery) my parents did not have to worry about enormous hospital bills, as their parents would have done.

At the age of eleven I went to Rickmansworth Grammar School, less than a mile from my home. It was a monument to the Attlee government: purpose built and newly opened at the start of the 1950s to cope with the new customers created by the swift implementation of the 1944 Education Act and the raising of the school leaving age, and typical of its kind: light, airy and modern, with young and idealistic teachers who enjoyed what they did. A fine and civilized place it was too, with a wealth of cultural activities ... (Beckett, 1997, p.ix)

I could not decide between these two views, the one patrician and the other plebeian, so I circulated a quotation from Runciman to the other authors writing their specialist chapters for this book asking for comments on Runciman's thesis and suggesting three other possible periods as candidates for the disputed dominance of transformation, namely:

1 World War I and its aftermath   1915–22
2 World War II and the boom   1940–75
3 Mrs Thatcher's governments   1979–90
4 New Labour   1995–2000

Which, I asked, from the point of view of the author's chapter, was most important in the transformation of twentieth-century Britain? In sum the replies support Runciman in that the institutional framework was laid down at the beginning of the century but the distribution of life-chances only began to change rapidly in the 1960s. No one voted unequivocally for World War I, though David Butler 'wobbled between (1) and (2)', pointing specifically to the expansion of the electorate in 1918 and the arrival of the Labour Party, as the main opposition – these two events were 'surely key'.

Some opinion tended to favour World War II and its subsequent economic boom. Duncan Gallie stressed two crucial shifts in this period – the upsurge of

female participation in paid employment and the expansion of the modern service industries. Bruce Wood was more cautious, though confident in 'the personal mobility revolution' after the war. From the point of view of crime, Roger Hood was uncertain between (2) and (3) but clear that the upsurge of recorded crime from the mid-1950s to the mid-1990s, with its effects upon the criminal justice and penal systems as well as on public perceptions and fear of crime, was the outstanding trend of the century. Brian Harrison came down confidently in favour of Mrs Thatcher as far as voluntary or non-state activity ('civil society') is concerned. 'Throughout the twentieth century the trend was against voluntarism, and the two world wars accentuated that. 1979 turned the whole thing round and "New Labour" merely followed the path that Thatcher had laid down.' He has in mind Frank Field's emphasis on self-help and duty. Perhaps other readers may remember R. H. S. Crossman's (1973) death-bed repentance in favour of the volunteer, the voice of 'old labour' as early as 1973. Julia Parker was altogether more doubtful and struck by the 'change of rhetoric' in the late 1940s, about welfare and social security. She sees Thatcherite 'choice' as an expression of anti-statism and also as an extension of the growing tendency of government and administration to ask people what they want.

Amanda Root similarly doubted the periodization offered especially as, arguably, the information revolution is the biggest change that has affected twentieth-century Britain but cannot be accorded to New Labour. She observes that 'the development of the railways was obviously massively influential in opening up travel opportunities (and linked social change such as regularly exposing the rich to the sight of the urban poor alongside railway lines[1]), but this was largely a late nineteenth-century phenomenon and so it is not appropriate. The period 1940–1975 was 'when "motorization" happened: cars became commonplace, motorways were built etc., bringing in their wake the huge changes, pleasures, opportunities and horrors which we know about, and the consequences of which are still unfolding'.

So there are no agreed periods for all of the separable facets of society. Each facet has to be reported according to the logic of its own particular development: and it will vary according to the standpoint of the author and according to the multiple roles of the social actors involved. Moreover, there are distinctive theories to which the available data have a more or less indistinct fit. Yet the collective effort of compiling a century of statistics and pointing to both their trends and their pitfalls is eminently worth while, not least in opening the way to further analysis and debate.

The reader will find many twentieth-century transformations dealt with in great detail in the chapters below. But we should also note a different kind of transformation – a shift of interpretative stance that has penetrated the intellectual circles for which we write – one form or another of relativism. My

colleagues and I, in assembling the first and second editions, ignored relativism. We saw ourselves as inheritors of the political arithmetic tradition rooted in the Enlightenment and modernity. That tradition is now widely castigated as positivistically scientistic and even inhumane by a mounting opposition of postmodernists.

The relativist view, essentially that no objective truth is possible, has since made massive inroads, not only in newspapers but in universities, not only in literature and cultural studies but in the social sciences. What could once be dismissed as the ignorant posturings of ethnomethodologists has since become entrenched in the formal curriculum of undergraduate social scientists. Of course it is understood and is often a problem that, for example, the same television programme will mean different things at different times for different social groups and different individuals, but Eric Hobsbawm (1997) is worth quoting in this connection:

> relativism will not do in history any more than in law courts, whether the accused in a murder trial is or is not guilty depends on the assessment of old-fashioned positivist evidence, if such evidence is available. Any innocent readers who find themselves in the dock will do well to appeal to it. It is the lawyers for the guilty ones who fall back on post-modern lines of defence. (p.viii)

Similarly, the chapters which follow are based on the methods advocated by Karl Popper, not those employed by Professors Derrida, Lacan and Baudrillard, which may be traced in Paris or Frankfurt to origins preceding the 1960s. This book, like a law court, is based on the commonality of judgement among the human race which, as Keynes believed, 'already consists of reliable, rational, decent people'. Thus Atkinson follows the same tradition when he tells me that 'Each person has a particular idea of what is meant by "poverty" and where the line is drawn, but there is enough agreement that half average income is "not too high" for statistics on this basis to be of value [in public discussion].'

Methods

In the face of theoretically inadequate statistics, social scientists may, of course, resort to the academic sociological survey which can be designed in explicit relation to theory. Direct sociological investigation is a powerful tool, and 'panel' or longitudinal studies in which a cohort of respondents is followed over a long period of time can yield information on trends; but such studies do not constitute more than a tiny if growing fraction of the numerical data available, the bulk of which is collected and published by governmental agencies. The measurement of social mobility is a case in point which is dealt with in Chapter 7. Knowledge about rates of mobility depends on direct sociological enquiry with the resulting difficulty that trends are difficult to establish without exact replication of a given study at later points in time. Incidentally, the method used by Heath and Payne in the search for trends in social mobility is to compare the same birth cohorts within a series of (electoral) surveys. Theoretically informed statistical surveys have been repeated by sociologists only recently, partly for reasons of academic organization (survey data only began to be stored systematically in the 1960s), partly because of expense, partly because the 'laboratory' (that is, the world) changes and partly because theoretical interest in the social sciences and definitions of concepts are influenced as much by fashion as by cumulation.

More generally it is in the nature of scientific progress that more adequate measures are devised to cope with the changing questions put by social scientists or by governments, or with the changing character of society itself. The classic case is measurement of, in Adam Smith's terms, the wealth of nations. Yesterday's realities remain with us as today's concepts. There is a tired old joke used by lecturers to social science beginners about the man who reduced the gross national product (GNP) by marrying his housekeeper. Measurement is fraught with conceptual difficulty. The Victorians, even Alfred Marshall, judged that national income could be adequately measured without reference to the vast labour of women in the domestic economy. Economists knew, of course, that the total of goods and services exchanged was thereby underestimated. But they thought that trends would make the phenomenon less and less important.

Over the past two decades, and under the influence of economists like Sen (1987), Maddison (1995) and Crafts (1997), there have been sustained attempts to define an index of human development. The Human Development Reports give details of progress in the movement towards comparable statistics. They refer mainly to industrial countries, though they tell us the numbers for the world as a whole and for categories and regions within it; they also indicate both current performances (1990) and trends (1960–90) of life expectancy, real GNP per capita, and child welfare in various ways. Obviously they could be improved, and there is good technical discussion of roads to improvement in the 1993 report. We could use them to indicate progress in terms of the major values sought by both liberals and democratic socialists as follows:

1   Freedom or extent of individual choice
2   Equality of access to essential capabilities
3   Social solidarity or belonging to the country in question.

Point (1) can be measured by longevity and income, (2) by the distribution of income, education and health, and (3) by the incidence of suicide, drug abuse, family break-up, and so forth. No doubt we could do better. But we can catch a glimpse of trends in the United Kingdom from such data.

While clarification of the measurement problems remains incomplete at the end of the twentieth century, few can doubt that the family as an institution is in trouble. Parliament and people are now casting around for solutions to what is seen as a problem of widespread disorder – rising divorce, lone parenting and child poverty, endemic crime, intrusive squalor, spreading welfare dependency, collapsed community. Chapters 14, 15 and 16, on housing, social services and social security, all describe an optimistic and deter-mined intrusion by the state in the first half of the century, a golden interlude after World War II, and a series of retreats from the mid-1970s, paradoxically coinciding with crucially enhanced national and individual income. Can we then conclude that what essentially has happened is that the past generation has failed to bring up its children to observe traditional civilities, and that the cure is political – to strengthen traditional families? Such inferences are essen-tially contentious. We must first identify the causes, correlates and consequences of changes in family structure (or more accurately, if pedanti-cally, the circumstances of upbringing and the adolescent and adult behaviour that issues from them). If we get these wrong we can only prescribe good and effective policy by accident.

In practice, meanwhile, the problem remains largely that of adapting statis-tics which are a by-product of administrative and organizational activity to social science ends. The authors of this book have had to wrestle with this problem in every chapter. One example is Wood and Carter's attempt (in Chapter 12) to use a sociological definition of urbanism in addition to the legal definition in terms of local government boundaries. Thus, in examining the increasing interdependence of town and country they use such indicators as the journey to work, shops, and centres of entertainment.

Again, in tracing twentieth-century improvements in health in Chapter 3, Fitzpatrick and Chandola rely ascetically on mortality measures and so produce a tidy and on the whole encouraging trend picture. But, had they used the much less reliable morbidity statistics, the continuing miseries of mental ill health would have come into view to give us a less cheerful picture.

Part of the drive towards more precise measurement comes from the indi-vidual and organized initiative of social scientists: but motive also has its origins in popular preference or in political reaction to crises or problems. Take, for example, the environmentalist movement. Accelerated by an inter-national conference in Rio de Janeiro in 1992, the British government committed itself to a strategy of sustainable development and to targets for reducing pollution (DoE, 1996). The outcome was 120 measures of the envi-ronment which could be monitored in progress towards the declared aim. Collection of the necessary data was put in train. In 1998 the Deputy Prime

Minister published a consultation paper (DETR, 1998) specifying 12 indicators to be pursued by government. Another example comes from health. The publication of hospital waiting lists was introduced by Major's government. Labour's 1997 manifesto promised their reduction. A public controversy ensued refining the measuring of the waiting times.

A third example pertains to social stratification. The drive in this case can again be traced to dissatisfaction with the classifications by social class used in many governmental publications. At the beginning of the century, long before sociometrics were invented, T. C. Stevenson offered and the government accepted a division of the British population into five classes. As the century advanced the old rough and visible class categories, popularly and properly thought of as an unequal hierarchy of ways of life tied to virtually hereditary occupations, became more blurred, more challenged as to their legitimacy and more blessed with opportunities for people to rise out of the class of origin through secondary and even higher education. By the end of the century millions of the children of manual workers had risen into non-manual jobs and many thousands had become the graduate grandchildren of butchers, bakers and candlestick-makers, following professional careers. The class structure had shifted. In 1900 the vast majority of Britons were elementarily schooled proletarians: by 1970 Stevenson's classification divided the employed half and half between white- and blue-collar jobs. By 2000 the balance had been tipped decisively to form a button-pushing majority dominating a minority of the remnants of the former working class.

The ONS noticed that the traditional class causes of inequality in voting, health, income and education were now challenged by new sociologies of gender, ethnicity, region and the Right. It therefore asked the Economic and Social Research Council (ESRC) to revise the old (Stevenson) fivefold classification. The ESRC set up a committee (Rose and O'Reilly, 1998) to produce a new 'socio-economic classification' (SEC) which, it is hoped, will carry us through the twenty-first century and improve our understanding of society in 'its more opaque and subtle stratification processes'. Precisely because social classes have become less sharply differentiated and less obvious to the eye of common sense, sociologists have exerted themselves towards clearer definitions and measurements. They have analysed the concept of class, distinguished it from status and from power and clarified employment relations and conditions. Under the old scheme, ownership, skill and scale of organization were paramount in drawing up stratification categories. Now the further concept of 'the labour contract' contrasted with 'the service bargain' takes precedence over more traditional elements such as skill. The labour contract is a short-term market exchange of supervised effort in return for weekly or hourly pay. The service relationship is a long-term exchange of service to the aims of the employer in return for a secure salary, extended tenure and the associated features of a career, including present autonomy, future possibilities of promotion and a comfortable working environment.

The classical professions have constituted the purest form of the service relationship, unadulterated, as so many intermediate occupations are, by the elements of insecurity in a labour contract. For example, the twentieth-century history of teaching is a story of advance towards an organized and unified profession: recruitment has gradually eliminated the uncertificated and raised the qualifications of entrants, salaries are monthly, the pay scale is recognized, notice of leaving is a month or more, there are opportunities for promotion, hours are negotiated, and the design of work (though constrained by the national curriculum) is largely left to the individual teacher. Nevertheless, the increasing use of 'supply teaching' has added to the insecurity of employment at the end of the century – and contract employment is spreading; for example, among nurses where temporaries are recruited from agencies to meet emergency shortages.

These and many more examples show the modern interaction of government and social science: the latter adapting to the former and the former deriving economic and social policies from the political arithmetic of academic social science. This book is, in effect, a resumé of the state of the social science art. It is, on the whole, a progressive story of advances in method. Official statistics have without doubt improved in the twentieth century. Surveys like the General Household Survey are now important data sources for academic research, as are the other official surveys outlined in Appendix 2. The GHS covers nearly 30 years and provides reliable national estimates on a wide range of behaviour. However, official statistics, quite apart from their deficiencies as a record of objective experience, seldom offer data on the subjective experience of actors in social systems. The census, and most surveys undertaken for Royal Commissions, eschew 'opinion'.[2] Replicated surveys (or panel studies) yield trends. But again the theorist may be thwarted in that the surveys may not bear directly on the question he or she wishes to put. In this sense the survey is never more than historical evidence, albeit precise and quantified, to be used like any other historical evidence as a servant which may not be adequate to its theoretical master. Britain is the international leader in birth cohort national studies. Two of the three, those of 1958 and 1970, are occasionally used in the pages which follow. A convenient source of information about this developing field is the *Data Archive Bulletin* published at the University of Essex.

Substance

We have distinguished four institutional systems. Comparing 1900 with 2000 in Britain, we can summarize empirically that:

1 the productive system expanded
2 the reproduction system diversified ethnically, contracted to yield an older population, and moved from being a net exporter to a net importer of people
3 power and authority were democratized early in the century and bureaucratized thereafter. The two principles of authority – democracy and bureaucracy – were in complicated interaction at the end of the century, developing involvement with the European Parliament in Strasbourg and its bureaucracy in Brussels at one end and devolving power to Scotland, Wales and Northern Ireland at the other. Many further problems of power and authority are left for the twenty-first century including not only further devolution but also European integration. In short there is an uncertain prospect for the United Kingdom. All forms of authority faltered in the second half of the century – parents, politicians, priests and police as well as scoutmasters and schoolteachers all became less trusted, less popularly admired as the century wore on. In party terms the rise of the Labour Party dominated the House of Commons after World War I, mostly at the expense of the Liberals but leaving the Conservative Party in office for 58 of the 82 years from 1918 to 2000 (see Chapter 11). Nevertheless, the general thrust of Labour policy, aided by the two world wars, was towards centralization. Belief in the power of politics became commonplace after World War I. Government accordingly challenged 'civil society' until Thatcher came into office and the battle continued to the end of the century (Chapter 17)
4 the system of communication was spectacularly elaborated with growing wealth, the private motor car, enlarging labour markets, radio, television, telephone, and finally the computer and 'the World Wide Web'.

We have treated Britain in this book for the main part as if it were a self-contained island. But two forces – empire and globalization – make our restriction somewhat distorting. Imperialism belongs to the past, global economics and politics to the future. Indeed, under neither condition can home be separated from abroad, as we saw briefly in our reference to social stratification.

International awareness is the distinctive mark of British life as the century draws to its close. It manifests itself diversely: the debate over European integration, the 'special relationship' with Washington, our indecision over immigration and a 'multi-faith' society, the economic competition from the changing global market. So I invited all contributors to include a brief comparison with other countries at the end of the century. Here we can use the Human Development Reports to anticipate the detail of subsequent chapters.

In 1995 the UK was ranked 14th in human development among the 174 countries distinguished by the United Nations Development Programme. Ten countries are chosen in Tables 1.1 and 1.2 to bring Britain into focus. It is ranked 4th among the ten. In terms of life expectation at birth it is also 4th. In terms of adult literacy it shares top place with most other industrialized countries and, in terms of educational enrolment, only France and the US are ahead. The lag appears to be economic. France, the US, Japan, Germany and Italy enjoy a higher GDP per capita. Yet Britain remains a rich country, well above the average of industrialized countries, 3.5 times the world average and 19 times that of the least developed nations.

Table 1.1   Britain in international perspective, 1995

	HDI[a] Rank 1995	Life expectancy at birth 1995	Adult literacy rate 1995	Educational enrolment ratio	Real GDP per capita (PPP$)
UK	14	76.8	99.0	86[b]	19 302
France	2	78.7	99.0	89[b]	21 176
US	4	76.4	99.0	96[b]	26 977
Japan	8	79.9	99.0	78[b]	21 930
Germany	19	76.4	99.0	81[b]	20 370
Italy	21	78.0	98.1	73[b]	20 174
Hungary	47	68.9	99.0	67[b]	6 793
Russia	72	65.5	99.0	78[b]	4 531
China	106	69.2	81.5	64	2 935
India	139	61.6	52.0	55	1 477
Industrial countries		74.2	98.6	83	16 337
Least developed countries		51.2	49.2	36	1 008
World		63.6	77.6	62	5 990

Notes: [a] Human Development Index Rank. The Human Development Index has three components – longevity, knowledge and income. Longevity is measured by expectation of life at birth and is unadjusted. Knowledge is measured by two variables – the adult literacy rate and the gross enrolment ratios at primary, secondary and tertiary level. Income is measured by real GDP per capita in purchasing power parity (PPP) terms: a logarithmic transformation is used. The HDI is a simple average of these three indices (UNDP, 1998, p.107). The HDI has evolved since 1990 and is much discussed. A good summary of the discussion may be found in the 1993 report (pp.100–14). [b]Carried over from UNDP, 1997.

Source: United Nations Development Programme (1998), *Human Development Report 1998*.

It is, in short, a highly privileged country by any standards of longevity, knowledge and income. Between 1960 and 1990 the expectation of life at birth rose in the United Kingdom from 70.6 years to 75.7 years, whereas Japan began lower and ended higher at 78.6. In the industrial world as a whole, life expectation was 74.5 years, and in the world as a whole 64.7. The British real GDP per capita also rose, and was above average in both the European Union and among OECD (Organization for Economic Co-operation and Development) countries. Britain's total health expenditure constituted 6.1 per cent of GDP by 1990, compared with 12.2 per cent in the US, 8.6 per cent in Sweden and the Netherlands, 9.1 per cent among OECD countries, and 7.7 per cent in the EU. The relation, or rather non-relation between expenditure and mortality is recorded by Fitzpatrick and Chandola in Table 3.15.

Table 1.2   Trends in human development, 1960–95, human development index numbers

	1960	1970	1980	1992	1995
UK	0.857	0.873	0.892	0.919	0.932
France	0.852	0.871	0.895	0.927	0.946
USA	0.865	0.881	0.905	0.925	0.943
Japan	0.686	0.875	0.906	0.923	0.940
Germany	0.841	0.856	0.881	0.918	0.925
Italy	0.755	0.831	0.857	0.891	0.922
Hungary	0.625	0.705	0.838	0.863	0.857
Russia					0.769
China	0.248	0.372	0.475	0.644	0.650
India	0.206	0.254	0.296	0.382	0.451
Industrial countries					0.911
Least developed countries					0.344
World					0.772

Source: United Nations Development Programme (1998), *Human Development Report 1998*.

Looking at signs of weakening social fabric, it may be repeated that Britain is high with respect to live births outside marriage which were 25 per cent between 1985 and 1989, compared with 15 per cent in the EU; and there were 41 per cent divorces compared with 27 per cent in the EU. On the other hand, Britain records less murder or suicide than its European neighbours. Other indicators of human distress suggest that the UK bears a family resemblance to other European nations with respect to unemployment and inequality of income distribution; but the Nordic countries do better from both points of view. The rise in crime and fear of crime in the second half of the century was historically unprecedented, but did not make British experience internationally exceptional (Chapter 20).

At the beginning of the century, Britain, though markedly smaller in population, was arguably the greatest and more certainly the greatest imperial nation in the world. At the end of the century all that is left territorially, quite apart from the subtraction of Eire, are a few small islands and promentories like St Helena and Gibraltar which once guarded the passage of world-wide British shipping. At the beginning the Union Jack flew over one-fifth of the world's people and territory. At the end its fluttering was confined to one-thousandth of the world.

Accordingly, the story must be one of rapid decline, and so it would be if nothing else had changed to offset our nineteenth-century notions and means of empire. In fact the whole structure of human life, the world over, has been transformed. Mr Blair presided at the end of the century over a country totally different from that over which the third Marquis of Salisbury was prime minister in 1900. Economies have grown; communications have accelerated; kinship, friendship, power and authority have changed fundamentally. Some economic, political and social institutions are no longer British or national but international and global. Britain has thus become much less distinctive. George Orwell, writing as late as 1940, could still observe that 'when you come back to England from any foreign country, you have immediately the sensation of breathing a different air … The crowds in the big towns, with their mild knobby faces, their bad teeth and gentle manners, are different from a European crowd' (Orwell, 1941).

It is doubtful whether he could say so in 1999. What would strike him perhaps would be the rapidity of change from his death in 1950 and the degree of assimilation of life in Britain to that of the other advanced industrial countries in Europe, Scandinavia and North America. He would certainly notice the upward shift of income and life expectancy: income multiplied by four since 1900, average age of death risen from 50 to 80 during the same 100 years. Looking more closely, the period after World War II probably brought the most rapid improvements in the wealth of nations, the elongation of individual life, and the advance of women towards freedom in occupation, in sex and in politics.

Detailed study of our assembled statistics will convince readers that no simple story of better or worse will suffice. For example, despite many advances, the life of women has not become unequivocally more leisured. As Gershuny and Fisher show in Chapter 18, hours of paid employment have been shortened and domestic chores eased by affluence, but sharing of domestic labour has moved glacially and at the end of the century remained in favour of men; women did 260 minutes a day of unpaid work, men 172. Nor is the record of an elongation of life a simple gain. There remain debates about how far the longer average life is marred by elderly infirmity.

So, at least for some observers, the story of decline nevertheless predominates. Divorce, birth outside marriage, crime, traffic congestion and atmospheric pollution all rose while probity and church attendance fell. These commentators are pessimistic traditionalists and they are opposed by optimistic liberals who can point to such advances as the occupational liberation of women, rising educational attainment, tolerance of homosexuals and ethnic minorities, and greater leisure, better housing, and more freedom of movement. Again, debate rages over the distribution of chances in life between traditionally privileged and deprived groups. Is society more open in 2000 than it was in 1900? In absolute terms mobility chances have carried several million Britons from working-class origins to careers in the salariat, especially in the second half of the century. And Heath and Payne produce evidence (in Chapter 7) of an equalization of *relative* chances in the same period. On the other hand, the distribution of income and wealth, having shown a tendency towards less inequality for the first three-quarters of the century is now shown by Atkinson (Chapter 10) to have reversed direction towards polarity in the final decades.

It has been an eventful century of progress and barbarism throughout the world, with paradoxical movements towards both a longer and fuller life and towards unprecedented genocide and slaughter, towards democracy and towards dictatorship. For the aristocrat, perhaps a century of dispossession. For the old and the ill, perhaps a rather more comfortable 100 years. For the homeless and dispossessed, a time of persistent degradation accentuated by surrounding opulence. For women, the young, and the fit and ordinary citizens, perhaps the greatest century in the whole history of human kind.

Notes

1 The graphic description is by George Orwell. See his *The Road to Wigan Pier* (1937) pp.29–30. 'I had time to see everything about her – her sacking apron, her clumsy clogs, her arms reddened by the cold. She looked up as the train passed and I was almost near enough to catch her eye'.
2 Systematic surveys of opinion have been conducted annually since 1984 by Roger Jowell and his associates at Social and Community Planning Research. See Appendix 2 for more information.

References

Beckett, Francis (1997) *Clem Attlee*, Richard Cohen Books, London.
Bottomore, T. B. (1962) *Sociology – A Guide to Problems and Literature*, Allen and Unwin, London.
Cannadine, David (1990) *The Decline and Fall of the British Aristocracy*, Yale University Press, London.
Clarke, Peter (1996) *Hope and Glory: Britain 1900–1990*, Penguin, London.
Coleman, James S. (1990) *Foundations of Social Theory*, Harvard University Press, Cambridge, Mass.
Crafts, N. F. R. (1997) 'The Human Development Index and changes in standards of living: Some historical comparisons', *European Review of Economic History*, 1, pp.299–322.

Crossman, Richard (1973) 'The Role of the Volunteer in the Modern Social Service', in
    Halsey, A. H. (ed.) *Traditions of Social Policy*, Blackwell, Oxford, pp.259–85.
Dennis, N. and Halsey, A. H. (1988) *English Ethical Socialism*, Clarendon Press, Oxford.
Department of the Environment (DoE) (1996) *Indicators of Sustainable Development for the
    UK*, HMSO, London.
Department of the Environment, Transport and the Regions (DETR) (1998) *Sustainability
    Counts*, The Stationery Office, London.
Hobsbawm, Eric (1994) *Age of Extremes: the Short Twentieth Century 1914–1991*, Michael
    Joseph, London. Quotations are taken from the Abacus edition, 1995.
Hobsbawm, Eric (1997) *On History*, Weidenfeld and Nicolson, London.
Maddison, A. (1995) *Monitoring the World Economy, 1820–1992*, OECD, Paris.
Orwell, G. (1937) *The Road to Wigan Pier*, Victor Gollancz, London.
Orwell, G. (1941) *The Lion and the Unicorn: Socialism and the English Genius*, Secker and
    Warburg, London.
Rose, D. and O'Reilly, Karen (1998), *Final Report of the ESRC Review of Government Social
    Classifications for the Office for National Statistics*, ESRC Research Centre on Microsocial
    Change, University of Essex.
Runciman, W. G. (1997) *A Treatise on Social Theory*, vol. III, *Applied Social Theory*,
    Cambridge University Press, Cambridge.
Sen, A. K. (1987) *The Standard of Living*, Cambridge University Press, Cambridge.
Shils, Edward (1964) in Hall, P. (ed.) *Labour's New Frontiers*, Andre Deutsch, London.
Skidelsky, Robert (ed.) (1988) *Thatcherism*, Chatto and Windus, London.
United Nations Development Programme (annual from 1990) *Human Development
    Report*, Oxford University Press, New York.

Part I
Demography

2
Population and Family

David Coleman

'... and multiply ...'
Genesis 1: 28

Introduction

Two hundred years ago Robert Malthus wrote his 'First Essay on the Principle of Population'. Fated to be right in his interpretation of centuries past but rendered obsolete by the advent of new modes of production which he imperfectly understood, he is in other respects now being vindicated. The end of population growth, and the possibility of population decline, is now in sight. However new developments unthought of in his time now dominate the demographic agenda. The debates above all about population ageing and pensions, inner cities, the frailty of the family, health and asylum-claiming have all brought demography on to the front page and occasionally into the tabloids. Ten years ago the previous version of this chapter noted the growing awareness of demography. In the last decade the subject has earned the final accolade of popularity, that is vulgarization. 'Demographics' now trips readily off the tongues of market researchers, admen and politicians, and even those who should know better.

Sources of data

British demographic data are among the most complete and comprehensive in the world. Since the reorganization of the General Register Office (GRO) as the Office of Population Censuses and Surveys (OPCS) in 1973, analysis and presentation has been among the best too, with the publication of the admirable volume of data analysis and commentary, *Population Trends*. A further chapter, not initially welcome to all demographers, occurred in 1996 when the OPCS was swallowed up in an enlarged government statistical service, the Office for National Statistics (ONS). More recently, mortality analysis has been removed from *Population Trends* into a new ONS publication, *Health Trends Quarterly*, another retrograde step.

A great advance has been made, however, in the availability of machine-readable anonymized household and individual records from the 1991 census, and access to the entire series of Labour Force Surveys and General Household Surveys from the ESRC data archive, the Household Panel Survey (Buck, 1994) and the Longitudinal Study (Hattersley and Creeser, 1995). These, together with other new sources such as the European Household Panel Survey, go some way to compensate for the ruinous prices charged for special census tabulations. The ONS provides a variety of new services and data; best obtained from the ONS Website http://www.ons.gov.uk

In Britain there are two main kinds of demographic data. The first relates to the number and condition of the people at any given point in time. The census has collected these 'stock' data compulsorily from all residents every ten years since 1801 (except 1941). Since 1841 the census has been based on the household, not the individual (except for institutions). Surveys of various kinds, noted below, provide data more regularly but on a voluntary basis. The other data relate to events as they occur. Most important of these 'flow' data are the vital events (births, marriages and deaths, and details about them) recorded compulsorily since 1837. Put these together and we can calculate the rates at which events occur, or, put another way, the annual risk to the individual. The stock data provide the denominator (the population at risk), the flow data are the numerator (the number of vital events).

The history of the collection of these data and the struggle to overcome initial resistance to their collection mirrors the development of state interest in the welfare of the people from the eighteenth century onwards, and the habit of intervention to improve conditions. In earlier times collected to assess the basis for taxation or militia service or to monitor religious conformity, demographic data have been transformed into the basis for public services in education and health (Glass, 1973; Alderson, 1983; Mills, 1987; Swerdlow, 1987) and increasingly to help marketing decisions for the sale of products and the location of services and outlets. Controversies continue, however; some suggest that the limits of data collection have been reached if not passed. Others question the propriety of new forms of data collection (on racial or ethnic or even religious characteristics), however praiseworthy their ostensible intention may be.

Since 1841 the basis for the census has been a return for each private household; the group of people (or single individual) sharing the costs of living in the same dwelling. Individual returns are only provided for the inmates of institutions (barracks, colleges, prisons, hospitals). The census forms for each household are confidential to the OPCS and are not available for study (or even to other government departments) for 100 years (Bulmer, 1979) although this ruling is challenged from time to time by eager researchers. Topics, questions and analysis change from census to census but there is usually a core of questions which do not change much from year to year. Any changes make the demographer's job tiresomely difficult as time-series are disrupted. The 1911 census was a particular landmark, with the first questions on fertility and child survival, and the beginning of social class analysis. That of 1981 was particularly thin, omitting questions on fertility and an expected question on ethnicity. The 1991 census asked that question for the first time (Coleman and Salt, 1996) and also reintroduced questions on disability, formerly asked in the nineteenth century but dropped as the responses were then of little use.

The 2001 census will go further, not only including questions on ethnicity but also, following pressure from Asian immigrant groups, a question on religion. This topic was formerly considered to be a private matter, not one for compulsory questions in the census. In the apparently inexorable growth of questions on ethnicity, language and religion we see the influence of American-style pressure group lobbying from minorities and the unchecked momentum of official statisticians interested in pursuing such topics.

A third way exists in demographic statistics, although the British have not yet favoured it – a system of continuous registration. Records held on individuals and households (usually at municipal level) are continuously updated through births, deaths, marriages and migration (and registered cohabitation in the case of Denmark). The population and its basic characteristics are thereby known for all local areas at all times and, through aggregation, for the whole country. However, the data kept in such registers tend not to be comprehensive. Demographers in some countries which have given up censuses (for example, the Netherlands, where the census was last held in 1971) are asking for their return. The final development of continuous registration is the person-number system, where an individual number, allotted at birth, is used not just for a population register but also as a key for tax and welfare codes and entitlements. In Sweden, for example, it is possible to change one's spouse, any or all of one's names, or one's sex, but never one's person-number. Britain almost gave itself the basis for a system of registration in 1753, only the measure ran out of time in Parliament (Glass, 1973).

National summary tables provide comprehensive tabulation of age structure, marital status, occupation, migration and birthplace, journey to work, Welsh language, car ownership, housing tenure and other topics (OPCS, 1977; Pearce and White, 1994) Local authorities are the biggest consumers of census data and aggregate data are published in great detail on a county basis down to ward level. Small area statistics are available to order, down to enumeration district level (about 200 households) since 1971, and since 1991 anonymized samples of individual and household data have been available in machine-readable form (online, or tape/disk) for limited public use for the first time on the US model.

Registration of birth collects information about the age of the mother (and father where appropriate), their occupation and address and marital status, and (only in the case of marital births) the number of previous births. As over one in three births are now illegitimate, the lack of direct data on births by true birth order, an important dimension of fertility analysis, is becoming embarrassing. Data on true birth order can, however, be estimated from the General Household Survey which, not being part of the compulsory civil registration system, does not need a change in the law to ask such questions. Death certificates record date and place of birth of the deceased, occupation and cause(s) of death in a complex hierarchical fashion.

Cause of death is recorded in detail for important legal and medical reasons. Most epidemiological research depends on their accuracy, but only a third of deaths are certified by autopsy which sometimes reveals important discrepancies in diagnosis (Royal College of Physicians, 1982). Least information is collected about marriage and divorce. Because no date or place of birth is recorded, these events cannot be linked to other records to create life-event histories, and that collected is often sketchy. Divorces as legal proceedings are the responsibility of the Lord Chancellor's Department, but, like adoptions, notifiable diseases and the migration records of the NHS Central Register, the figures were published through OPCS and more recently through the ONS.

The old Registrar-General's *Statistical Review* ceased in 1973, when the General Register was reorganized as the Office of Population Censuses and Surveys. Its tables and analysis continued and were developed through a regular series of annual OPCS publications (now ONS) with commentary on fertility, marriage, mortality and migration and other topics. The most up-to-date information used to be presented through Monitors in the same series, although that series has been seriously curtailed in recent years. Commentary (to which Volume III of the *Statistical Review* used to be devoted), further analysis and quarterly demographic summary comes in the journal *Population Trends* as well as other more detailed occasional publications. Census volumes are likely to be increasingly supplemented – maybe replaced – by Internet access and online data capture.

One of the highlights of each census is the publication of a detailed set of analyses of mortality by geographical area, occupation and social class. These analyses are made possible because only the census can provide the detailed data of the population at risk by occupation, age, marital status and other characteristics both at national and at local level, for matching to the numbers of deaths occurring around the census year. These Decennial Supplements on Occupational and on Regional Mortality, published every ten years since 1851 (OPCS, 1978; 1986; 1995) comprise the best and most comprehensive series of social analysis of differential mortality anywhere in the world. In recent years other decennial supplements have been published on a variety of other topics.

Separate series of data on international migration come from the International Passenger Survey (ONS, 1998a) and the Home Office (1998a). For different reasons, neither is demographically very satisfactory. There is no direct record at all of internal migration as it happens, unlike some continental countries which maintain population registers. Surrogate data from changing doctors' registration from the NHS Central Register are used instead, together with census and survey questions.

The biggest post-war innovations were the development of longitudinal studies and regular official surveys. See Appendix 2 for more on these. The General Household Survey instituted in 1971 (ONS 1977) includes data available nowhere else; on income and household size, or remarriage and occasionally on family intentions, cohabitation, contraception, perceived illness, and smoking and drinking habits. Interviewers' assessments of colour were tabulated up to 1986; ethnic self-identification was used from 1983. The Labour Force Survey (LFS) is big enough to be called a microcensus. It is now part of an EU-wide operation, providing comparable data (plus some additional national questions) across the whole EU. Until the 1991 census it provided the only population denominators for ethnicity in Britain, and intercensal ones for occupation and marital status. Researchers can conduct their own analysis on tapes of these surveys, available from the ESRC Data Archive. The British Household Panel Survey instituted in 1990 (Buck, 1994) is part survey, part longitudinal study. The UK also takes part in Eurostat surveys across the whole of the EU, such as the European Household Panel Survey, and British demographic data is published in common with those of other member states in the annual demographic yearbooks of Eurostat (1998) and of the Council of Europe (1998).

Enormous strides have been made in analysing the cumulative effect of life-experiences and age upon the demographic behaviour of individuals. Four major cohort studies, all still running, have been started since World War II and provide information not available from any other source. They are the Medical Research Council's (MRC) National Survey of Health and Development study of a cohort of babies born in the same week of 1946 (Wadsworth, 1987), the 1958 National Child Development Study (Fogelman, 1983) and the 1970 Child Health and Education Study (Butler et al., 1986). The biggest of all is the Longitudinal Study, a record linkage study based initially on the 1971 census (Hattersley and Creeser, 1995). Unlike the three surveys, which require contact to be kept with an inevitably diminishing proportion of the original sample, this sample from the 1971 census of 530 000 persons born on four selected dates is kept in play through computer linkage of records of subsequent births of offspring, cancer registration, death, and so on – linked

by date of birth (which thereby excludes marriages which lack this information) (Fox and Goldblatt, 1982; Fox and Leon; 1988; OPCS, 1988). The data are
linked to successive censuses in 1981 and 1991 and permit the wealth of data
on personal circumstances in the census to be linked to the probabilities of
child-bearing, mortality by cause and cancer registration. The volume of data
this yields has required a special unit to be set up for its analysis and to permit
access by researchers, initially at the City University and now the Centre for
Longitudinal Studies at the Institute of Education in London. This innovation
has been copied in other countries.

One major drawback with UK population statistics is their division between
no less than three Registrars-General: for England and Wales, Scotland, and
Northern Ireland. Data are usually published separately and at different levels
of detail. The census schedules differ slightly, as do the resources available for
analysis and publication. Data for England and Wales are by far the most
abundant and most comprehensively analysed and commented upon. Data for
Great Britain (England and Wales, and Scotland) can quite easily be found.
Those for the UK (Great Britain plus Northern Ireland) tend to be more rudi-
mentary and less up to date. The recent trend towards dismantling the United
Kingdom will no doubt make this problem even worse, and may provoke
demands for Wales to have an additional set of its own data, for example. The
deficiencies of information from Northern Ireland make it impossible to
compute the total fertility rate for the whole of the UK before 1961. A number
of the statistics published by Eurostat under the heading 'United Kingdom' in
fact only relate to England and Wales, despite warnings from government
statisticians. 'UK' is the normal and only logical level of analysis for international migration. Northern Ireland does in fact have some rather distinctive
characteristics of fertility and mortality which deserve special attention.
Unfortunately, there is insufficient space here to do other than note them in
a few of the tables. A comprehensive analysis is given by Compton (1996).

Background to twentieth-century demographic trends

The old demographic regime in Western Europe, of which Britain was a good
example, preserved since at least the sixteenth century unusual patterns of
moderate birth and death rate, delayed marriage and frequent lifetime spinsterhood, and a household usually based on the nuclear family (Hajnal, 1965;
1982; Macfarlane, 1986). From about 1750, however, this pattern became
destabilized with a slow decline in the death rate and in the severity and
frequency of mortality crises, and by a rise in fertility around the turn of that
century, following a reduction in the average age of marriage. Together these
initiated a prolonged period of population growth; first to 0.5 per cent per
year, then to a peak of 1.3 per cent per year by the 1830s. Although rates of

population growth of this magnitude had probably been reached before in the thirteenth and sixteenth centuries, never before had they been sustained for so long, for 200 years of uninterrupted growth; never before had the British population managed to break decisively through the barrier of a population size of about five million.

The industrial world has shared similar demographic trends for the last century or more. British and other industrial or post-industrial nations in the earlier twentieth century were dominated by the later phases of the 'demographic transition' from high to low birth and death rates (Chesnais, 1993). Most developed societies are now emerging from the far end of this transition, having achieved a birth rate not exceeding two children on average and a death rate equivalent to an expectation of life of about 80 years for women and 75 years for men. A birth rate equivalent to less than two children was established as early as the 1930s, and we have returned to that position after the transient excitements of the 'baby boom' period. The population of Britain, like the rest of the developed world, is now at the beginning of a new and unprecedented 'post-transitional' demographic regime of low birth rates, low and falling death rates and low or negative growth. Its final form is still unclear, except that it brings inevitably with it a period – presumably permanent – of minimal population growth, demographic ageing and its attendant problems of demographic maturity.

Fertility

By 1900 a hitherto unprecedented decline in family size within marriage was well established (Tables 2.1–3; Figure 2.1). In this new development Britain was ahead of some of the rest of Europe and the English-speaking world, but well behind France. There, married couples had begun to limit their children, especially third and subsequent births, from the 1780s onwards. By the 1900s contraception had been firmly established in most British families (Banks, 1954; Fryer, 1964; McClaren, 1978; Leathard, 1980; Mason, 1994; Szreter, 1996). The General Medical Council succeeded in preventing family planning being taught in medical schools until 1928. By then, many 'patients' knew more than their own doctors about it, thanks in part to the tireless efforts of early enthusiasts such as Marie Stopes (1918), who founded Europe's first birth control clinic in 1921. There were working-class pioneers in contraception too; especially those in service jobs working close to middle-class people, and also women working in textiles with one of the most pressing reasons (preserving their incomes) for limiting their fertility. Miners and agricultural workers in their isolated communities, with little opportunity for women to work, retained high fertility until later.

Table 2.1 Crude birth rate, crude death rate and rate of natural increase, 1901–96, England and Wales, and Scotland, and Northern Ireland (per 1000 population)

Year[a]	England and Wales			Scotland			Northern Ireland		
	CBR	CDR	RNI	CBR	CDR	RNI	CBR	CDR	RNI
1901–05	28.2	16.0	12.2	29.2	17.1	12.2			
1906–10	26.3	14.7	11.6	27.6	16.1	11.4			
1911–15	23.6	14.3	9.3	25.4	15.7	9.7	24.0	17.7	6.3
1916–20	20.0	14.4	5.6	22.8	15.0	7.8	22.5	18.0	4.5
1921–25	19.9	12.1	7.8	23.0	13.9	9.1	23.1	15.6	7.5
1926–30	16.7	12.1	4.6	20.0	13.6	6.4	21.2	14.8	6.4
1931–35	15.0	12.0	3.0	18.2	13.2	5.0	20.0	14.3	5.7
1936–40	14.7	12.2	2.5	17.6	13.5	4.0	19.8	14.3	5.5
1941–45	15.9	12.8	3.1	19.4	13.8	3.7	22.7	13.4	9.3
1946–50	18.0	11.8	6.2	20.0	12.6	7.4	22.0	11.9	10.1
1951–55	15.3	11.7	3.6	17.9	12.1	5.8	20.8	11.3	9.5
1956–60	16.4	11.6	4.8	19.2	12.0	7.0	21.7	10.8	10.9
1961–65	18.1	11.8	6.3	19.7	12.2	7.4	23.0	10.8	12.2
1966–70	16.9	11.7	5.2	17.9	12.1	5.8	21.0	10.6	10.4
1971–75	14.0	11.9	2.1	14.5	12.2	2.3	18.7	11.0	7.7
1976–80	12.3	11.9	0.4	12.7	12.3	0.3	17.5	10.9	6.6
1981–85	12.8	11.6	1.1	12.9	12.4	0.5	17.5	10.2	7.3
1986–90	13.6	11.3	2.3	12.8	12.3	0.5	17.3	9.9	7.4
1991–95	13.1	10.8	2.3	12.4	12.0	0.5	15.4	9.4	6.0
1996	12.5	10.8	1.7	11.6	11.8	–0.2	14.8	9.1	5.7

Note: [a]Up to 1975 the 5-yearly data are weighted averages. After 1975 they are unweighted averages.

Sources: Registrar-General, ONS/OPCS, *Birth Statistics*, Series FM1, Table 1.3; Registrar-General, *Annual Report*, Scotland, Table 1.1; Registrar-General, *Annual Report*, Northern Ireland, Table A1 / 1.1.

The average Victorian family size was about six children ever-born (one would die in infancy, another before maturity), but the average for all women, taking into account the proportion who never married (most of whom remained childless), was about five. Fertility since 1900 declined considerably and was in a state of rapid change. The average family size of all ages of women at all durations of marriage at the time of the 1911 census (the first to ask questions about reproductive histories) was 3.5 children. The rate of child-bearing in 1901 among all ages of women was equivalent to a family size of 3.5 (Table 2.2). This is the total fertility rate (TFR), calculated by summing the age-specific rates for ages 15–49. It gives the average number of children that a woman would have if she experienced through her life the birth rates at each age in the year in question. By the end of their child-bearing career (conventionally by their 50th birthday), women married in 1900–09 had on average 3.4 live-born children (surviving or otherwise) (Table 2.3). Subsequent marriage cohorts continued the plunge into low fertility for a further 20 years, an almost linear decline except for the disruption of World War I. The low fertility of 1914–18 represents a birth deficit of about 600000, not entirely restored by the short but massive baby boom which followed the end of the war. This short boom was none the less bigger than the much better known one which followed the end of World War II, in 1946–48. 1933 ended the trend begun in 1870. That year saw a nadir of fertility (TFR = 1.72) unmatched for a further 45 years.

Table 2.2 Trends in total fertility rate and net reproduction rate, 1901–97, England and Wales, Scotland, and Northern Ireland

Year	England and Wales		Scotland		Northern Ireland
	TFR	NRR	TFR	NRR	TFR
1901–05	3.50	1.20			
1911–15	2.80	1.10			
1921–25	2.40	1.00			
1931 35	1.80	0.80			
1941–45	2.00	0.90	2.40	1.00	
1951–55	2.20	1.00	2.50	1.10	
1961–65	2.80	1.30	3.00	1.40	3.54
1971–75	2.10	1.00	2.20	1.00	3.02
1976–80	1.80	0.90	1.80	0.80	2.70
1981–85	1.77	0.85	1.73	0.83	2.51
1986–90	1.81	0.88	1.66	0.80	2.35
1991–95	1.77	0.86	1.62	0.79	2.02
1996	1.73	0.84	1.55	0.74	1.95
1997	1.73		1.58	0.76	1.93

Sources: Registrar-General, *Annual Reports* for Scotland up to no. 92 (1946); Scottish data from 1951: Registrar-General, *Annual Report*, Scotland, no. 131, Tables S1.2, S1.7 and S1.8, then Tables 3.4, 3.6; ONS/OPCS, *Birth Statistics*, Series FM1, Tables 1.1b and 1.4; *The Health of the Public in Northern Ireland*, *Annual Report* of the Chief Medical Officer, Table 5A (up to 1995); Registrar-General, *Annual Report*, Northern Ireland, Table 1.6 (1996 onwards).

The total fertility rate had therefore fallen substantially below the level required to replace the population in the long run (a population TFR of about 2.1; the number required to replace the two parents with a small allowance for mortality). The actual completed family size of real cohorts of women then at the peak of their child-bearing at this time was eventually about 2.0 – just about replacement level (Figure 2.1). It is typical of 'period' measures of fertility such as the TFR that they exaggerate the effects of the current fertility trend. Any delay in the beginning of child-bearing – that is, an increase in the mean age at first birth – will for a while depress the level of the TFR even if the final actual completed family size remains unchanged, and vice versa. As changes in tempo (say, a delay in the timing of fertility) usually accompany a change in the quantum (say, a reduction in the final achieved family size), period measures such as the TFR conflate the two effects, exaggerating (or underestimating) the outcome as measured by cohort rates. Cohort and period rates are not attempting to measure the same thing, even though they may appear to be similar. The period TFR has great value in showing the immediate implications of current fertility patterns. It correctly indicates a change in the number of births at a given time and the extent to which the reproductive age groups are replacing themselves in a given year. Cohort rates, formerly granted excessive veneration, give correct information about completed family size usually in time to be of interest mainly to historians. The relative merits of the two have provoked some lively recent debate (Ni Bhrolchain, 1993).

Table 2.3   Births to marriage cohorts, 1889–1965

(a) Marital fertility		(b) All births[a]	
Great Britain		England and Wales	
Period of marriage	Completed family size	Year of birth of mother	Completed family size
up to 1889	5.14		
1890–99	4.34	1902	1.96
1900–09	3.53	1906	1.81
1910	3.11	1913	1.98
1915	2.61	1918	1.97
1916–20	2.46	1923	2.11
1921–25	2.18	1928	2.25
1926–30	2.04	1933	2.41
1931	1.99	1938	2.37
1936–40	1.97	1942	2.28
1941–45	2.15	1947	2.11
1946–50	2.20	1952	2.02
1951–55	2.29	1957	1.95
1956–60	2.27		
1961–65	1.89		

Note: [a]Year of birth is aligned with year of marriage assuming mean age at marriage at about 25. This is only approximate, so fertility data do not quite match. Birth cohort data include births outside marriage.

Sources: Up to 1915, Glass and Grebenik (1954); 1946 *Great Britain Family Census* Volume 1, Table 9, London, HMSO; 1916–65, 1971 *Census Fertility Report*, Series DS No. 5, Table 1 (England and Wales); 1965, ONS/OPCS *Birth Statistics*, Series FM1, Table 10.4 (England and Wales).

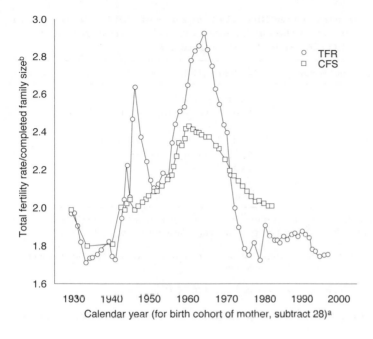

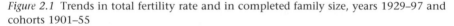

Figure 2.1 Trends in total fertility rate and in completed family size, years 1929–97 and cohorts 1901–55

Notes: [a]The cohort (CFS) data are positioned on the graph such that the calendar year given corresponds to mothers at age 28, which is approximately the mean age of child-bearing. Thus the completed family size of women who were aged 28 in 1940 is graphed at calendar year 1968, and so on.
[b]Completed family size is given for women at age 40 up to the birth cohorts of 1955. Beyond that cohort, women have not yet completed their fertility and the (incomplete) data cannot be graphed.

Source of data: ONS/OPCS *Birth Statistics*, Series FM1.

In the 1930s fears of the 'twilight of parenthood' (Charles, 1936), future under-population and of 'race suicide' became lively topics (Keynes, 1937). The fertility decline was given added bite by the earlier decline of middle-class fertility, compared to working-class fertility (Tables 2.4(a) and (b)), and of European fertility compared to that of other continents (Hogben, 1938). The spur it gave to demographic analysis included the widespread use of such calculations as the net reproduction rate (NRR). This shorthand projection shows how far the current fertility as measured by the total fertility rate (of female children only), discounted by the mortality of children up to the age of their mother, will enable the present generation of mothers to replace themselves – or not – and by extension the whole population. Thus a net reproduction rate of 1.0 implies long-term population replacement (other things being equal); 0.9 a reduction by 10 per cent per generation (about 28 years), and 1.1 an increase of 10 per cent per generation (see Table 2.2).

Table 2.4 (a) Comparative fertility, 1911: number of children ever-born to married women by social class of husband (at 20–25 years duration of marriage, age in 1911 less than 45) (standardized)

Class	Rate per woman	Nature of class
I[b]	4.24	Upper and middle
II[b]	5.02	Occupations intermediate between I and III
III[b]	5.86	Skilled occupations
IV[b]	5.99	Occupations intermediate between III and V
V[b]	6.54	Unskilled occupations
VI[a]	5.37	Textile workers
VII[a]	7.25	Miners
VIII[a]	6.5	Agricultural workers

Notes: [a]Classes VI to VIII do not form part of a series in that they are not ranked in descending order of social position. These occupations were thought sufficiently important to warrant separate identification.
[b]Classes I to V are not unlike the present Registrar-General's social class scale, but the categories here do not distinguish employers from employees.

Source: *1911 census*, volume XIII, *Fertility of Marriage*, Pt II, Table 25.

Table 2.4(b) Comparative fertility, 1931: number of infants under age one enumerated with fathers

Class	No. of infants (average = 100)
I	64.5
II	66.5
III[a]	97.2
IV	114.8
V	132.2

Note: [a]In 1931 male clerks were transferred from Social Class II to Social Class III – about 500 000 people.

Source: Registrar-General's *Decennial Supplement 1931*, Part IIb, *Occupational Fertility*, Table E (p.42).

Elsewhere in Europe, fear of this population decline with its economic and military implications unleashed population policies designed to prevent abortion (which in the late 1920s exceeded live births in Germany), prevent the dissemination of contraceptive knowledge and encourage family building, (Glass, 1942; Winter and Teitelbaum, 1985). In Britain the more decorous response was to appoint a Royal Commission on Population. Its report (1949) was a pioneering work in demography, and it conducted the first British official inquiry on family planning in 1946. The Population (Statistics) Act 1938 enabled voluntary questions to be asked at the registration of births, on the date of marriage, and the number and age of previous children. This enabled fertility to be analysed in a more sophisticated way than was previously possible, and has helped us to avoid repeating some of the errors of demographic judgement of the 1930s. Private concerns had set up the National Birth Rate Commission in 1916. The Eugenics Society (now the Galton Institute), among its many pioneering activities in demographic work, set up the Population Investigation Committee (PIC) in 1935, appointing D. V. Glass to be its Research Secretary. The PIC is now incorporated in the London School of Economics (Langford, 1988) and is responsible for the premier journal *Population Studies*, which recently celebrated its 50th birthday.

This reduction in fertility – reached by most industrial countries at about the same time in the 1930s – had no historical precedent. A new regime of low fertility was about to begin, the basic outlines of which have lasted to the end of the century. The variability of this new fertility regime has yet to be settled. From the 1930s up to the 1970s it was characterized, in almost all developed societies, by a wholly unprecedented volatility in fertility, especially in its timing. That was made possible by the new power enjoyed by parents to adjust the pace of their child-bearing through family planning to their perceived circumstances and personal wants, with a precision hitherto impossible. That generated bigger swings in fertility over a short time than had previously been possible through the old Malthusian regulator of the delay or avoidance of marriage. The erratic course taken by fertility since the 1930s, with its troughs and booms of births, has dominated the age-structure of the populations of the industrial world for the rest of the twentieth century and will do so well into the next . From the 1970s a different picture has emerged in different parts of Europe. For Britain, north-west Europe in general and the English-speaking world overseas, the last 25 years have been the quietest of the whole century, with TFRs staying at approximately 1.7–1.8 (Britain and France) or 1.8–2.0 (parts of Scandinavia and the English-speaking countries overseas). Elsewhere the turmoil is not over. After about 1980 the birth rates in southern Europe fell quickly to much lower levels. By the late 1990s Italy and Spain were vying for the position of the country with the lowest birth rate in the world (1.2–1.3). The twentieth century continued to spring surprises right up to the end. The collapse of communism in the East brought with it an even faster collapse of the birth rate in some countries of Eastern Europe and most of the European parts of the former Soviet Union.

In Britain, fertility rose gently up to World War II – a predictable Malthusian response, through the relaxation of checks on births including earlier marriage, to gently rising prosperity at a time when men's wage-packets still dominated household income. The war itself first depressed fertility, with births rising to a sharp peak after the end of the war in 1946 (TFR = 2.69 in 1947). Most European countries had a short post-war baby boom – even the vanquished and the neutrals. It seems likely that fertility would have continued to rise in the early 1940s had it not been for the distraction of the war. Mean age at marriage had already started to fall in the late 1930s – somewhat later than on the continent

– and in the two neutral continental countries (Sweden and Switzerland) birth rates began to rise in the early 1940s.

After the war, and the short-lived spike of births in 1946–48, the late 1940s seemed like the 1930s revisited. Fertility was apparently drifting down again towards replacement rate (in 1951 TFR = 2.14; NRR = 1.00). Official projections made even in the early 1950s assumed continuing low fertility and consequent slow population growth (Figure 2.2). Fluctuations in fertility have been subverting official projections ever since.

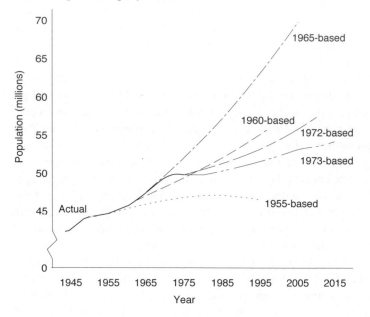

Figure 2.2 Actual and projected population 1945–2010, England and Wales

Source: Registrar-General, *Quarterly Return*, no. 501, 1st Quarter 1974, Chart 2, p.50.

The most interesting feature of the post-war fertility in the developed world was the great boom in births from the early 1950s until the late 1960s, peaking in 1964 in the UK with a TFR of 2.94. This baby boom, shared by most of the industrial countries of the free world, added about two million births to the number that would have occurred had fertility remained at its 1955 level through to the 1970s. It put heavy pressure on the primary schools, secondary schools, higher education and the employment and housing system in turn. From the early decades of the twenty-first century it will put great pressure on the sustainability of pensions systems and old-age health care throughout the West. It caught demographers quite by surprise. So did its end. Projections made at the height of the boom looked forward to a UK population of 60 million in

1980 and 70 million in 2000. The actual population in 1980 was 56 million, and in 1997, 59 million. These projections (Figure 2.2) were an important reason why so much high-density local authority housing, which now causes so much trouble, was put up – to avoid the countryside becoming covered with houses. They also gave added impetus to regional policy to divert population away from the already crowded south-east and provoked a rash of private and public warnings against the harmful effects of continuing population growth (see, for example, Taylor, 1970; Select Committee on Science and Technology, 1971).

The most recent phase of fertility change has lasted from the early 1970s to the present. No longer declining, fertility as measured by the TFR has remained stubbornly below replacement rate ever since 1972, not varying much between the temporary nadir of 1.66 in 1977 and a peak of 1.89 in 1980. In the 1990s there has been a slight downward trend, so that TFR reached 1.73 in 1997 and in the first quarter of 1998. Cohort rates in Britain are about the same, although the latest birth cohort of women whose fertility is complete are those born around 1955 (Tables 2.5 (a) and (b)), who are aged 44 at the time of writing. This also stimulated further interest in the problems of an ageing or even declining population, although in a more demographically and economically informed context where zero population growth is no longer automatically regarded as a problem (Central Policy Review Staff, 1973). But within this sub-replacement average level, now maintained for almost a quarter of a century, much change is taking place in the pattern of child-bearing.

Table 2.5(a) Total number of live births per woman by woman's year of birth and age, England and Wales

Woman's year of birth	Mean number of children per woman achieved by successive ages, up to 1996					
	Age of woman					
	20	25	30	35	40	45
1921	0.14	0.74	1.44	1.82	2.01	2.05
1926	0.15	0.87	1.52	1.94	2.14	2.18
1931	0.19	0.94	1.70	2.16	2.32	2.34
1936	0.22	1.10	1.93	2.29	2.39	2.40
1941	0.30	1.28	2.00	2.27	2.32	2.34
1946	0.36	1.22	1.82	2.08	2.17	2.19
1951	0.36	1.02	1.61	1.91	2.02	2.04
1956	0.29	0.90	1.50	1.86	1.99	
1961	0.23	0.78	1.39	1.77		
1966	0.20	0.71	1.28			
1971	0.22	0.65				
1976	0.21					

Source: ONS/OPCS. *Birth Statistics*, Series FM1 Table 10.2.

Table 2.5 (b) Total number of live births per woman by woman's year of birth and age, Scotland

Woman's year of birth	Mean number of children per woman achieved by successive ages, up to 1996					
	Age of woman					
	20	25	30	35	40	45
1921	0.10	0.78	1.67	2.20	2.47	2.56
1926	0.09	0.74	1.51	2.06	2.34	2.41
1931	0.11	0.81	1.67	2.25	2.48	2.51
1936	0.11	0.97	1.92	2.39	2.54	2.56
1941	0.16	1.09	1.96	2.32	2.41	2.43
1946	0.21	1.11	1.83	2.13	2.24	2.25
1951	0.24	0.93	1.57	1.90	2.01	2.03
1956	0.22	0.79	1.40	1.76	1.90	
1961	0.16	0.67	1.26	1.66		
1966	0.14	0.58	1.13			
1971	0.15	0.50				
1976	0.14					

Source: Registrar-General, *Annual Report*, Scotland, Table 3.7.

Components of fertility trends

What do these average measures mean in terms of the variety of experiences of couples and of individual women? There have been radical changes in the timing of births, in the proportion of women delaying having children until their thirties. Teenage fertility none the less remains a striking British peculiarity. Childlessness is increasing to levels not seen for decades, while one in three births is now outside marriage.

Up to the late nineteenth century, trends in marriage – in its timing and its avoidance – determined trends in births (Wrigley and Schofield, 1981). In the nineteenth century illegitimacy was low and falling, although in Britain contraception within marriage was little practised until the 1870s. Now, contraception is paramount in determining fertility trends. But marriage patterns – and increasingly cohabitation patterns – still have a significant effect on births. This is a two-way relationship – couples marry when they are prepared to have children, although that relationship in cohabitation is more ambiguous. From the 1930s until the 1970s marriage became much more popular and occurred earlier in life than ever before, especially among women. This general advance of marriage from the 1930s, and its retreat since the early 1970s, are broad social changes and are discussed below.

The advance of marriage in the 1950s and 1960s increased age-specific fertility rates among younger women (Table 2.6). Particularly striking increases were evident in birth rates of women in their early twenties and among teenagers – initially at least because a much higher proportion were married (Glass, 1976). These rates at least doubled from 1938 to 1964. In theory, the rise of family planning would have allowed couples to enjoy the consolations of married life without the need to acquire its burdens in the form of children straightaway. From 1900-09 to 1930–34 the median interval from marriage to first-born (in two-child families) increased only modestly from 18 months to 19 months. But rather surprisingly, this interval remained relatively constant well into the post-war period: it was just 20 months in 1971, unlike the continental experience. But since then it has lengthened considerably. However, family planning has allowed women to compress their child-bearing into a shorter space of married life. By the 1960s, most families of two children were completed within the first ten years of marriage. Irrespective of family size, the interval between first and last birth was getting shorter into the 1980s. It is more difficult nowadays to make generalizations about timing using routine data. More than one in three births occur outside marriage, and there is no marker to date the beginning of cohabiting unions. The Longitudinal Study, however, can provide data on birth intervals and marital status.

Table 2.6 General fertility rate, age-specific fertility rates and total fertility rate, all live births to married and unmarried women, 1938–96, England and Wales

| | | | | Age of woman | | | | | |
| | General fertility rate | | | | Age-specific fertility rates | | | | TFR |
Year	15–44	15–19	20–24	25–29	30–34	35–39	40–44	45–49	
1938	62.2	14.7	92.3	113.2	82.9	47.3	16.1	1.5	1.83
1940	58.7	15.3	90.7	108.4	75.2	43.0	14.8	1.4	1.74
1945	68.8	17.2	102.9	117.6	93.6	57.7	18.5	1.4	2.04
1950	73.0	22.2	126.3	136.2	89.4	48.3	14.2	1.1	2.18
1955	72.8	23.5	137.0	141.7	84.3	44.2	12.4	0.8	2.22
1960	86.7	34.0	165.5	171.9	100.8	46.4	13.8	0.8	2.66
1965	92.1	45.4	179.5	180.8	102.6	48.1	12.6	0.9	2.86
1970	84.3	49.4	156.1	154.7	80.1	34.7	8.6	0.6	2.41
1975	63.0	36.5	114.7	123.2	58.5	20.0	4.8	0.4	1.79
1980	64.2	30.9	114.1	135.7	71.3	22.6	4.3	0.5	1.88
1985	61.0	29.4	94.6	127.4	76.4	24.1	4.6	0.4	1.78
1990	64.2	33.3	91.4	122.6	86.9	31.1	5.0	0.3	1.84
1995	60.4	28.5	76.8	108.6	87.3	36.2	6.5	0.3	1.72
1996	60.5	29.8	77.5	106.9	88.6	37.2	6.9	0.3	1.73

Sources: Registrar-General, *Statistical Review*, Vol. II, *Population*, Table EE(b); ONS/OPCS *Birth Statistics*, Series FM1, Table 3.1b.

Table 2.7 Intervals between marriage and last birth, and first and last birth: marriages 1931–60, England and Wales, women married once only under 45 years

| Year of marriage | Two children born by 1971 | | Three children born by 1971 | |
	Marriage/ last birth (years)	First birth/ last birth (years)	Marriage/ last birth (years)	First birth/ last birth (years)
1931–35	8.6	6.0	11.5	9.8
1936–40	8.1	5.0	10.9	8.7
1941–45	7.5	4.6	10.6	8.4
1946–50	7.1	4.5	10.2	8.2
1951–55	7.0	4.0	9.5	7.4
1956–60	6.1	3.4	7.8	6.0

Source: *1971 Census, Fertility Report*, Table 7.3.

With the exception of teenage births (discussed below), all these trends towards early child-bearing were reversed in the early 1970s and have been in retreat ever since. 1972 was the record year for low mean age at first birth, as it was in most of the rest of Western Europe. Since then mean age at first birth has increased to 26.5 (1996) from 23.9. Except for teenagers, birth rates for women aged under 30 have been falling for about 20 years; those for women aged over 30, and particularly for those over 35 and over 40, have been increasing, having previously been on a downward trend. By 1996, 41 per cent of births were to women aged 30 years or over, and that is relatively low by the standards of some countries in north-west Europe, such as the Netherlands.

This delay in child-bearing is associated with marked increases in women's workforce participation (as detailed in Chapter 8) and in their economic independence generally, and is assumed to be here to stay. It is, however, raising a number of problems. While most births are now trouble-free for mother and for child, none the less the biologically optimum age for first birth is not in the thirties. Births delayed too long may become births cancelled, as sterility increases more rapidly after the age of 30. Involuntary childlessness afflicts about 5 per cent of married couples, but this may increase as couples begin child-bearing later. Congenital malformations increase sharply after the late thirties. These are issues quite separate from the increase in voluntary childlessness.

Childlessness is becoming interestingly prevalent. At the beginning of the twentieth century it was, as in previous centuries, relatively high (at least 15 per cent) thanks primarily to the relatively high proportion of women who never married. Of women married in 1926–30, 19 per cent were still childless in 1961, probably the highest level recorded in our history. By the middle of the century all that was changing. Only 10 per cent of those married in the late

1940s and 1950s were still childless by 1971. Since then the proportions childless at given ages have increased, and the popularity of marriage has fallen to an all-time low. We cannot yet say how many of today's young women will be voluntarily childless. About 17 per cent of the women born in 1955 were still childless in 1996 and therefore likely to remain so. About 25 per cent of women born in 1961 had not had a child by the age of 35, which is leaving child-bearing quite late. Projections based on the rate of increase of childlessness, with regard to intentions revealed in surveys, suggest that at least 20 per cent of women now in their thirties will never have children. The priorities behind voluntary childlessness have been studied seriously only recently. Some research suggests that the voluntarily childless have a surprisingly ordinary social and psychological profile (McAllister and Clarke, 1998).

The fall in the number of families with over three children continued from the previous century. This may be regarded as a longer-term trend whereby knowledge of family planning and the ideal of a small family have become familiar even to many of the poorest and least-educated families. By the 1970s family size had become more concentrated around two children than previously. Since 1971 the valuable census question on fertility has been dropped, to be replaced with others of lesser but more modish value. We have some up-to-date knowledge from the small sample of the General Household Survey. But even though two-child families resulted from only 22 per cent of the marriages of 1911–15 and comprised 44 per cent of the marriages of 1961–65, they were still not quite the majority of families. Almost a quarter (24 per cent) were larger; almost a third comprised one or no children. Because of the social distinction in fertility whereby upper-class households seem more prone to slightly larger families than average, and the tendency for the growing immigrant and ethnic minority population to have larger than average families, the decline in the larger sibship has probably halted.

In 1938 there were 25 000 teenage births, of which 81 per cent were legitimate and 3 per cent were premaritally conceived. The number of teenage births doubled by 1960 primarily because of the novel popularity of teenage marriage – the proportion illegitimate scarcely changed at all. But after the 1960s the position reversed. Teenage births peaked in 1966 at 87 000 (93 births per 1000 teenagers) and declined to 58 000 in 1976 and to 45 000 in 1993 at which level it has remained relatively constant (44 700 in 1996). However, the reduction in the total since the mid-1970s simply arises because there are fewer teenagers; the rate per 1000 females aged 15–19 is scarcely changed, from 32.2 per 1000 in 1976 to 29.8 per 1000 in 1996, representing about 7 per cent of all teenage births. But the number of legitimate births has collapsed as teenage marriage has become relatively rare – only 12 per cent of teenage births were legitimate in 1996. The British teenage fertility rate is about four times the Western European average and twice as high as any other individual Western

European country. Most of these children are born to single mothers, mostly without partners, mostly with low levels of education, no skill and no job, and dependent upon welfare and subsidized state housing. Prospects are not good for mother or for child. Alone of all components of the birth rate, the reduction of teenage pregnancies to a lower target figure has been made a policy priority of both the previous and the present government (DoH, 1992).

Contraception and abortion

It is often supposed that the general decline in fertility since the 1960s follows from the much improved contraceptive methods (for example, the pill) which became available in that decade or to the Abortion Act of 1967, which greatly widened the grounds for termination. This apparently common-sense view has distinguished support (Murphy, 1993). Many children of the 1960s have testified to the sexually liberating effect of more dependable contraception under a woman's control. But the whole post-materialist sexual and ideological revolution was underway in that decade, affecting many other aspects of life. It seems more logical to attribute the ups and downs of the birth rate to changes in the desire of couples to have children, implemented with greater precision with modern methods, rather than to ups and downs in the methods (except for pill scares; see below).

Total abortions only account for about a third of the birth deficit of the present day compared to 1964; in any case, most are to unmarried women or to older married women. And, of course, legal abortion must to a great degree replace the level of illegal abortion before the 1967 Act – variously estimated at between 30 000 and 100 000 per year. Better contraception merely allows family intentions to be translated more accurately into reality. The birth 'famine' of the 1930s was achieved with decidedly old-fashioned means of contraception – such as withdrawal, the condom, or sexual abstinence (Mason, 1994) – while the baby boom of the 1950s occurred at a time of progressively wider use of family planning.

Marie Stopes was the first to amass information on family planning early this century, although her extensive correspondence (Peel, 1997) does not comprise a systematic survey. The first major family planning inquiry of 1946 by Lewis-Faning (1949), in conjunction with the 1946 Family Census, covers couples married in the first half of the century. Knowledge of family planning in the nineteenth century comes from other sources, including statistical inference from the results of the 1911 census (Banks, 1954; Matras, 1965). Since the Family Census of 1946 there have been a large number of surveys of contraceptive knowledge, attitude and practice, and sexual behaviour (see, for example, Langford, 1976; Cartwright, 1978; Dunnell, 1979; Wellings, 1994; Bridgwood, 1996). Some of the results are summarized in Tables 2.8–2.10. Questions on contraception feature from time to time in the General Household Survey. However, little was known about family planning in Northern Ireland before a major survey in the 1980s (Compton and Coward, 1989).

Table 2.8 Family planning and contraception (women married 1941–65): ever-use of family planning by social group, Great Britain

Year of marriage	Manual (%)	Non-manual (%)	All (%)
1941–45	76.8	88.7	82.1
1946–50	86.4	88.2	86.7
1951–55	86.3	95.8	89.7
1956–60	89.3	93.3	90.6
1961–65	91.3	92.7	91.4

Source: Glass (1971), Table 3.

Table 2.9 Trends in ever-use of contraception by method, 1941–65 marriage cohorts

Year of marriage	% ever-use	Pill	IUD[a]	Condom	Cap	Withdrawal	Safe period	Spermicide	Other
				Method used by ever-users					
1941–50	84.6	6	<1	59	15	47	9	27	5
1951–60	90.2	22	2	65	22	47	12	29	4
1961–65	91.4	31	4	60	17	36	13	22	3
All	88.2	18	2	61	18	45	11	27	4

Note: [a]IUD = intra-uterine device.
Source: Langford (1976), Table 4.1.

Contraception among most age-groups of women has become as widespread as it is likely to be, with 73 per cent of women aged 16–49 currently using some form of family planning in 1995, and over 90 per cent ever having done so. The two measures of current use and ever-use are of course always different, as some women will want to become pregnant, others are not in sexual relationships, and others know themselves to be infertile. In general, older methods of contraception such as withdrawal and the sheath have become much less popular, especially the former. In the 1970s the pill and to a lesser extent the IUD (intra-uterine device) became predominant. The pill remains number one (25 per cent of users) with unmarried younger women, but its use has declined among older women with wider knowledge of health risks and even wider unfounded fears of them. Condom use has revived as a result (18 per cent of users in 1995), initially among older women; since 1991 there has been a (somewhat transient) increase among the partners of younger women, possibly related to HIV (human immunodeficiency virus) concerns.

The most spectacular increase is in sterilization, with a sixfold increase in the proportion of women protected by sterilization from 1970 (4 per cent) to 1995 (23 per cent) of all women aged 16–49. This has become the predominant form of contraception for couples over the age of 30. In 1983, only 9 per cent of women aged 25–29 were protected in this way compared with 31 per cent of women aged 30–34 and 44 per cent of women aged 35–39 (28 per cent in all). In 1995, this had risen to 24 per cent of women aged 16–49. Other new methods, such as injectables (Depo-Provera, Norplant), have made little headway, although there is growing interest in 'emergency contraception' which may be regarded as a form of very early abortifacient; used at least once by up to 5 per cent of women (Bridgwood, 1996), or 7 per cent according to the 1995 GHS. No serious progress in male contraception has been made so far.

Table 2.10 Married/cohabiting women: current use of contraception by method, Great Britain, 1970–95

| | Ever-married women aged 16–40, England and Wales | | All women aged 16–49, Great Britain | | | | | |
	E&W Family Planning Services Survey		GHS	GHS	GHS	GHS	GHS	GHS
Form of contraception	1970[a]	1975[a]	1983[a]	1986[b]	1989[b]	1991[b]	1993[b]	1995[b]
Pill	19	30	29	23	22	23	25	25
IUD	4	6	9	7	5	5	5	4
Condom	28	18	15	13	15	16	17	18
Cap	4	2	2	2	1	1	1	1
Withdrawal	14	5	4	4	4	3	3	3
Safe period	5	1	1	1	1	1	1	1
Abstinence	3	1	1	(no longer included as contraception)				
Spermicides		3	1	1	1	1	1	2
At least one non-surgical	71	63	58	49	46	46	48	49
Female sterilization	4	13	12	12	11	12	12	12
Male sterilization			12	11	12	13	12	11
Total at least one	75	76	81	71	69	70	72	73
Not using any	25	24	19	29	31	30	29	28
Sample base	2520	2344	2850	5866	5802	5571	5203	5067

Notes: [a]Data refer to ever-married women aged 16–40
[b]Data refer to all women aged 16–49. Levels of use are consequently lower from 1986 onwards.

Sources: General Household Survey (1983), Table 5.5; General Household Survey (1995), Table 11.1.

Despite all this apparatus, high proportions of pregnancies are still unintended. Estimates vary in part depending on definition (those unplanned in relation to timing may have been intended at some time) and are as high as 50 per cent in 1989 (Allaby, 1989; 1995). Some of these unwanted pregnancies follow contraceptive failure (either of method or user) (Lewis, 1996); others result from failure to take any precautions at all. Some of the unplanned pregnancy clinics surveyed in these studies reported 48 per cent of clients complaining of condom failures and 25 per cent using no method. The 'Health in England' survey of 1995 (Bridgwood, 1996) reported that 86 per cent of respondents had used some form of contraception on the first occasion of sexual intercourse, but this seems difficult to square with the teenage pregnancy figures. The shape of the British fertility curve is certainly distorted out of the expected symmetry by the high rate of births to teenagers (Chandola et al., in press), which is by far the highest in Western Europe.

Among adolescents, some groups of immigrant and ethnic minority women, and others, contraceptive use is still at a low level. There has been some success in the US in reducing teenage pregnancy and child-bearing (Ventura et al., 1998), where rates are even higher than those in the UK. Among several initiatives, the use of the injectable contraceptive Depo-Provera, initially developed for the Third World, appears to have been effective and has been recommended for use in Britain, for uneducated teenagers and others inept at taking a daily pill. Repeated scares about the safety of oral contraception in the 1970s, mostly unjustified in relation to long-term effects (Beral et al., 1999), have persuaded women, especially older and more educated women, to move to less effective forms of contraception (such as the sheath) or to be sterilized. This continues today (Wood et al., 1997), with clumsy announcements, most recently by the Committee on the Safety of Medicines, unnecessarily frightening women into actions that lead to unplanned pregnancies.

Most conceptions (perhaps as many as 75 per cent) abort spontaneously, mostly because of genetic defects and in most cases without the mother being aware of it. However, therapeutic termination of a known pregnancy is a legal process and annual abortion statistics are published (see, for example, Filatki, 1997; ONS, 1998c). Unlike Eastern Europe, abortion is not generally a front-line method of contraception in Britain except for certain groups such as teenagers and women aged over 35. Since the 1967 Abortion Act its impact has been concentrated on pregnancies outside marriage (56.3 per cent in 1971, 67 per cent in 1981, 77.4 per cent in 1991) or pregnancies of married women aged over 35. Overall, the number of abortions and the abortion ratio (ratio of abortions to 1000 live births per year) in Britain remains about average by Western European standards. Abortions under the Act on resident women increased slowly in the 1970s, from 95000 in 1971 (12 per cent of all conceptions) to 129 000 in 1981 (16 per cent of all conceptions). Following an increase in the 1980s, the annual number of abortions in the 1990s has been relatively steady at about 160 000. In 1997 the total was 168 000, about the same as in 1991, representing 21 per cent of known pregnancies (Table 2.11). Most abortions are performed on the 'social' grounds C or D of the Act (risk of physical or mental injury to the woman or to existing children: 136 928 and 13 051 respectively in 1995; together, 97 per cent of the total). In that year only 1671 (1.1 per cent) were carried out on ground E alone (risk of serious foetal handicap), mostly on older women. Methods are improving and a higher proportion of abortions are now carried out early in pregnancy. The Human Fertilization and Embryology Act 1990 (effective 1 April 1991) reduced the time limit for legal abortion from 28 to 24 weeks' gestation on grounds C and D of the 1967 Act; that is, risk of injury to the health of the woman or of existing children.

Table 2.11 Legal abortions on women resident in England and Wales, 1968–96 (000s)

Year	Total	All women Under 16	16–19	20–34	Single women	Married women	Widowed/ divorced	Total births	Abortion ratio[a]
1968	22.1	0.2	3.6	13.5	10.1	10.1	1.9	819.3	27
1970	75.4	1.7	13.5	45.5	34.1	34.3	7.0	784.5	96
1971–75[b]	105.9	3.0	22.4	61.5	50.8	44.7	10.4	685.6	154
1976–80[b]	113.2	3.5	27.2	64.4	58.1	41.9	13.2	608.8	186
1981–85[b]	132.4	3.9	32.3	77.9	76.7	39.5	16.2	636.6	208
1986–90[b]	163.3	3.6	35.7	105.9	106.8	38.3	18.2	686.0	238
1991–95[b]	159.1	3.1	26.9	109.9	104.8	35.4	18.8	675.0	236
1996	166.4	3.6	28.5	112.9	113.1	33.9	19.4	649.5	256

Notes: [a]Abortion ratio is the number of abortions per 1000 live births per year.
[b]Weighted averages.

Sources: *Population Trends*, Tables 16, 17; OPCS *Abortion Statistics*, Series AB, Table A; OPCS *Birth Statistics*, Series FM1, Table 1.1a (for the total live births figure).

The proportion of pregnancies terminated by abortion among unmarried teenagers almost doubled from 1971 to 1981. The 1980s saw no further tendency for extramarital pregnancies to end in abortion; in fact the tendency is downwards, in association with the higher proportion of births outside marriage. About 35 per cent of teenagers' pregnancies were terminated in

1995, little changed from earlier years. The proportion of pregnancies terminated in that year was at its lowest (about 12 per cent) among women in their younger thirties and rose to almost 40 per cent among women over the age of 40 (among whom pregnancies are relatively rare, of course). These figures compare badly with some continental countries, notably the Netherlands, where teenage pregnancies and abortions alike are rare.

Births inside and outside marriage

One of the major trends of the latter part of the twentieth century in Britain has been a reduction in the importance of marriage as a setting for births. Birth control within marriage, and illegitimate births outside it, have displaced marriage from its old function as the regulator of fertility. Much of the recent increase in illegitimacy has been to cohabiting couples who see no religious or secular need for marriage formalities. The timing of marriage and the timing of births are still related, but the connection is weaker than it was.

Until the 1950s, less than 5 per cent of births were illegitimate. Illegitimacy had been declining throughout most of the nineteenth century in Western Europe (Shorter, et al., 1971) and this decline continued into the early twentieth century. After the inevitable war-time increases the rate became particularly low in the 1930s and the 1950s. From the 1960s the trend in illegitimacy changed radically. Since that time the rate has been resolutely increasing (Figure 2.3). Britain is now top of the European league outside Scandinavia. Meanwhile 'illegitimate' births paradoxically disappeared; legal changes effectively ended the formal distinctions between being born outside and inside marriage, although not necessarily the attendant disadvantages, even though they are more numerous than ever. In England and Wales in 1996 more than one child in three (233000 of the total of 650000, or 35.8 per cent) was born outside marriage. Proportions in Scotland are almost as high, and those in Northern Ireland, traditionally much lower, are catching up fast. Of this total in England and Wales, 39 300 births outside marriage were to teenagers (88.0 per cent of all births at that age), 71 100 to women aged 20–24 (56.5 per cent), and 62 300 to women aged 25–29 (29.5 per cent). The rate remains high among women aged 35 and over (23.9); slightly higher than that of women in their younger thirties, a pattern evident for most of the post-war period. Some of these older unmarried women are divorcees living with new partners, some of them still awaiting divorce (many couples living together include at least one partner who was formerly married to someone else, and in the case of separated couples, still is).

Table 2.12   Teenage births and illegitimacy, 1938–96, England and Wales (all data refer to women aged under 20)

Year	Total live births	Rate per 1000 women	Legitimate live births	Rate per 1000 married women
1938	25410	14.7	20680	519.6
1940	26270	15.3	21683	330.5
1945	25437	17.2	16779	289.8
1950	30847	22.2	25492	455.2
1955	32947	23.5	27407	402.7
1960	51645	34.0	41957	442.6
1965	81611	45.4	62325	523.3
1970	80975	49.4	60112	464.5
1975	63507	36.4	43015	307.9
1980	60754	30.4	34894	340.4
1985	56929	29.4	20057	358.8
1990	55541	33.3	10958	277.0
1995	41900	28.5	5623	444.0
1996	44700	29.8	5365	445.2

Source: OPCS/ONS *Birth Statistics*, Series FM1, Tables 3.1, 5.2.

The greater part of the post-1960s increase in these births was to couples living together in some form of informal union (Table 2.13). This can be inferred from the joint registration on birth certificates of illegitimate births (Haskey and Coleman, 1986). This increased from 38.3 per cent (of a much smaller number) in 1966 to 58 per cent in 1981 and to 78 per cent in 1996. Just over half the registrations of illegitimate births are not only jointly registered but give the same address for both parents (58.1 per cent in 1996). Correspondingly, the more 'traditional' type of unmarried motherhood where the mother registers the child only in her own name has fallen from 61.7 per cent of the total (41 400 births) to 21.9 per cent in 1996. However, this is still an increase in absolute numbers of babies registered without a father, from 41 000 to 51 000. A disproportionate number of these are teenage births. Many of the parents of these children subsequently marry so that later births to the same parents are within marriage. However, others clearly do not, or they go on to have other children once their marriages are over. Over 20 per cent of all births to women over the age of 30 are outside marriage. Parents of births outside marriage who jointly register the birth of their child and who give the same address – just under 60 per cent – are usually and correctly deemed to be

Pre-maritally conceived	% of legitimate live births pre-maritally conceived	Illegitimate live births	Rate per 1000 non-married women	% illegitimate of all live births to women under age 20
13768	66.6	4730	2.8	18.6
12782	58.9	4587	2.8	17.5
8031	47.9	8658	6.1	34.0
13995	54.9	5355	4.0	17.4
15456	56.4	5540	4.2	16.8
23567	56.2	9688	10.4	18.8
35610	57.1	19286	11.5	23.6
34815	57.9	20863	14.0	25.8
21940	51.0	20492	12.8	32.3
17768	50.9	25860	13.7	42.6
10010	49.9	36872	19.7	64.8
4856	44.3	44583	27.4	80.3
1860	33.1	36315	24.9	86.6
1783	33.2	39302	26.4	88.0

cohabiting and therefore in what is usually called a 'stable informal union' and thus considered a functional substitute for marital births. The circumstances are different from those of ordinary unmarried motherhood unsupported by a co-resident male. However, informal though these unions may be, stable they are not, as we will see below.

Statistics are unclear about the number of illegitimate children born to continuing marriages: they have more social than demographic consequence. Reports on blood group matching some time ago suggested that up to 30 per cent of births within marriage might be illegitimate (that is, the husband is not the father) but later data suggest a smaller proportion (Coleman, in press).

There is no doubt that sexual activity before marriage has become more popular and has started at an earlier age as time has gone on. Malthus' axiom, 'towards the lessening of the passion between the sexes, no progress has hitherto been observed', has never been more true. In 1974–75, 42 per cent of single girls aged 16–19 had experienced sexual intercourse compared with 17 per cent in Scotland in 1976. Scottish girls were still more reticent in 1982 than the English in the 1970s; 26 per cent of teenagers had experienced intercourse (Bone, 1986). The 1990 Sexual Attitudes and Lifestyles Survey and the 1995

Health of England Survey confirm that these trends continue. However, they are not matched by trends in conceptions. Extramarital conceptions in 1970 were likely to lead to marriage; by 1980, most ended either in abortion or in an illegitimate birth, a position which remained into the 1990s.

Table 2.13 Illegitimate live births according to registration by mother or by both parents, 1975–96, England and Wales

		All ages No. (000s)	All ages	Age of mother at birth Under 20	20–24	25–29	30–34	35+
				Percentage sole/joint in each age group				
1975	Total	54.9	100.0					
	Sole	28.0	51.0	65.8	50.7	35.6	31.8	32.5
	Joint	26.9	49.0	34.2	49.3	64.4	68.2	67.5
1977	Total	55.4	100.0					
	Sole	26.1	47.1	60.8	46.4	34.2	29.5	31.1
	Joint	29.3	52.9	39.2	53.6	65.8	70.5	68.9
1979	Total	69.5	100.0					
	Sole	31.1	44.8	57.1	44.3	33.9	29.4	31.8
	Joint	38.3	55.2	42.9	55.7	66.1	70.6	68.2
1981	Total	81.0	100.0					
	Sole	33.8	41.8	51.7	41.6	33.4	29.7	29.9
	Joint	47.1	58.2	48.3	58.4	66.6	70.3	70.1
1983	Total	99.2	100.0					
	Sole	38.4	38.7	47.2	38.5	32.5	28.6	30.3
	Joint	60.8	61.3	52.8	61.5	67.5	71.4	69.7
1985	Total	126.2	100.0					
	Sole	44.5	35.2	43.0	34.5	30.4	27.8	26.7
	Joint	81.8	64.8	57.0	65.5	69.6	72.2	73.3
1987	Total	158.4	100.0					
	Sole	50.5	31.9	40.0	31.4	27.1	25.3	24.9
	Joint	108.0	68.1	60.0	68.6	72.9	74.7	75.1
1989	Total	185.8	100.0					
	Sole	53.5	28.8	37.1	28.5	24.8	23.1	22.7
	Joint	132.3	71.2	62.9	71.5	75.2	76.9	77.3
1991	Total	211.3	100.0					
	Sole	54.1	25.6	35.0	25.3	21.7	21.0	20.3
	Joint	157.2	74.4	65.0	74.7	78.3	79.0	79.7
1993	Total	216.5	100.0					
	Sole	50.2	23.2	32.8	23.3	19.9	19.0	19.8
	Joint	166.3	76.8	67.2	76.7	80.1	81.0	80.2
1995	Total	219.9	100.0					
	Sole	47.9	21.8	32.7	22.4	18.2	17.5	17.6
	Joint	172.0	78.2	67.3	77.6	81.8	82.5	82.4
1996	Total	232.7	100.0					
	Sole	51.0	21.9	32.9	22.9	18.2	17.2	18.0
	Joint	181.6	78.1	67.1	77.1	81.8	82.8	82.0

Source: ONS/OPCS *Birth Statistics*, Series FM1, Tables 3.9, 3.10.

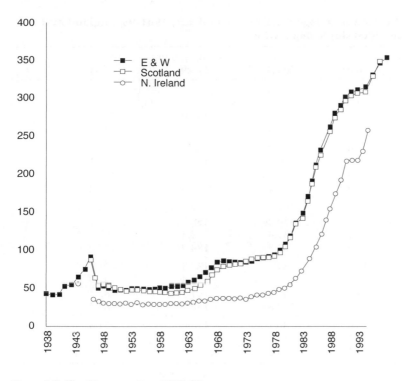

Figure 2.3 Illegitimacy ratios, 1938–97

Sources of data: ONS/OPCS *Birth Statistics*, Series FM1, Registrars-General Scotland, *Annual reports*, Registrar-General Northern Ireland, *Annual reports*.

Marriage, cohabitation, divorce and remarriage

From the sixteenth until well into the twentieth century, marriage in Britain conformed to the long-established West European pattern of delayed and frequently avoided marriage (Hajnal, 1965). The earlier data come from the parish registers, since 1837 annual statistics have been published by the Registrar-General in the annual *Marriage and Divorce Statistics*, Series FM2 (ONS, 1998d). Average age at first marriage in 1931 was 27 for men and 25 for women; figures not much different from what they had been 300 years before. Starting from the marriages of the late 1930s, marriage became earlier and more popular for both sexes, especially for women, beginning a trend towards younger, and more popular marriage. This continued for more than 30 years, reaching its peak in 1972, some years after fertility had begun to decline (for a general account see Leete, 1979; Coleman, 1980). First marriage rates for teenage bachelors changed little before World War II, then increased sixfold by the early 1970s. Marriage rates of men in their early twenties doubled; those of young women almost

Table 2.14 First marriage rates by sex and age, 1901–95, England and Wales, per 1000 single population[a]

Bachelors Year	16–19	20–24	Age group 25–29	30–34
1901–05	3.0	82.8	128.0	
1906–10	2.7	78.2	124.7	
1911–15	3.1	81.0	144.0	102.7
1916–20	4.2	82.3	153.1	121.6
1921–25	3.6	89.0	165.8	122.1
1926–30	3.7	79.4	160.8	108.5
1931–35	3.9	72.3	162.9	129.5
1936–40	4.9	94.4	210.6	156.3
1941–45	9.5	109.9	148.8	114.4
1946–50	7.1	110.2	180.3	132.1
1951–55	8.4	131.8	174.4	107.3
1956–60	14.0	152.8	184.9	100.9
1961–65	17.5	159.6	187.3	92.1
1966–70	23.5	170.0	179.4	91.0
1971–75	24.1	154.1	161.9	87.4
1976–80	16.0	112.8	136.5	84.7
1981–85[b]	8.8	80.1	115.0	71.3
1986–90[b]	5.1	57.4	94.8	73.7
1991–95[b]	2.6	34.6	71.9	54.0

Spinsters Year	16–19	20–24	Age group 25–29	30–34
1901–05	15.4	103.4	90.5	
1906–10	14.2	100.8	91.1	
1911–15	16.0	104.7	116.4	65.3
1916–20	15.8	107.0	113.6	66.0
1921–25	16.7	108.6	116.7	60.3
1926–30	18.6	107.2	117.7	57.8
1931–35	21.0	109.7	127.6	62.3
1936–40	33.1	154.4	171.3	78.7
1941–45	45.6	171.6	132.2	62.6
1946–50	47.6	205.2	153.5	81.4
1951–55	55.5	231.9	157.2	75.1
1956–60	72.7	261.6	164.4	75.9
1961–65	76.4	260.2	161.3	73.8
1966–70	85.0	260.9	159.4	72.7
1971–75	86.2	228.2	167.8	83.4
1976–80	58.3	177.3	139.3	83.7
1981–85[b]	33.8	123.1	116.3	65.6
1986–90[b]	20.4	95.2	103.0	69.1
1991–95[b]	11.1	62.2	86.9	60.2

Notes: [a]The population estimates by marital status were re-based at the census of 1981 and 1991 and consecutive rates are not completely comparable.
[b]Averages are unweighted.

35–39	40–44	45–49	50–54	55+	First marriage rate/1000 over 15
	44.3		14.8	3.4	59.6
	44.1		14.6	3.5	58.0
62.7	36.7	21.8	12.5	4.5	61.8
80.2	52.1	32.7	17.8	5.8	64.7
67.7	37.0	21.2	12.6	5.3	63.5
62.3	34.9	20.8	13.1	5.9	61.1
65.8	34.1	19.5	11.7	5.2	62.6
83.8	38.8	22.5	13.5	5.3	78.7
76.0	44.4	26.5	15.4	4.9	71.2
73.8	39.6	23.6	15.6	5.2	75.6
60.7	35.6	21.7	14.1	5.1	75.9
52.8	31.0	20.6	11.7	4.8	78.7
47.7	27.3	17.6	11.2	4.6	75.6
43.7	24.7	15.8	10.3	4.1	82.1
45.0	24.9	16.4	11.3	4.5	76.6
42.6	22.2	13.0	8.9	3.6	60.0
37.9	19.5	11.4	7.0	2.8	48.1
39.7	20.5	11.4	7.2	2.6	43.1
37.7	19.7	11.1	6.9	2.4	34.6

35–39	40–44	45–49	50–54	55+	rate/1000 over 15
	25.1		8.9	1.4	57.4
	24.5		8.7	1.6	55.8
34.0	18.7	11.6	6.6	1.9	58.7
37.1	21.4	13.4	7.1	2.1	57.4
29.1	15.7	10.1	6.0	2.0	55.2
27.6	14.9	9.9	6.2	2.4	54.8
27.8	15.1	9.6	5.8	2.3	57.3
34.7	18.2	11.0	6.4	2.1	73.3
32.0	19.1	12.1	6.9	1.9	67.6
41.4	22.0	13.5	8.3	2.2	75.7
38.6	21.2	12.8	7.9	2.1	76.8
36.1	22.0	12.7	7.9	2.1	82.6
38.0	21.8	13.5	8.2	2.2	83.6
37.2	20.4	13.6	8.5	2.1	94.2
42.2	23.7	16.3	11.6	2.6	91.9
42.4	21.8	13.4	8.7	1.9	74.7
34.8	18.6	10.7	6.7	1.4	59.9
35.7	19.1	11.7	6.9	1.2	54.1
35.6	18.0	11.4	6.8	1.2	44.0

Source: Registrar-General, *Annual Review* Part II, OPCS/ONS Series FM2, *Marriage and Divorce Statistics*, Table 3.3.

trebled (Table 2.14). These rates greatly increased the proportions of men and women ever-married in their twenties, to levels not seen for centuries. By 1971, 37 per cent of men aged 20–24 had been married. By the same year 60 per cent of women in their early twenties had been married, compared to about a quarter before the war, and 87 per cent by their late twenties. These post-war birth cohorts broke all records for marriage as they aged. Before the 1940s about 15 per cent of women remained single throughout their lives, and about 8 per cent of men. But only about 5 per cent of women and 7 per cent of men in the imme- diate post-war birth cohorts have remained single, although as we will see plenty have also by now been divorced.

These marriage records are likely to stand for a long time, because since 1972 the trends have gone into reverse. For a quarter of a century now, mean age at marriage has risen and proportions married at each age have fallen for both sexes. The number of marriages has fallen from a total of 404 700 in 1971 to 283 000 in 1995. In England and Wales, mean age at marriage has increased from 24.6 years for bachelors and 22.6 for spinsters in 1971 to 28.9 years and 26.9 years respectively in 1995. Married women under the age of 25, who numbered 1.25 million in 1971, 66 per cent of the female population aged 16–24, are now a rarity: there were just 250 000 in 1996. The implications of the current retreat from marriage can be shown further in an index derived from age-specific rates of marriage. Cumulating age-specific first marriage rates gives us a 'total first marriage rate' (TFMR) for men and women, which shows the number of first marriages that a person is likely to have by age 50, or more intuitively, how many single persons per thousand will marry by that age. This is calculated in the same way as the TFR and ranges in theory from 1.0 – everyone married at least once, and zero – no one ever marries. Like the TFR, it is vulnerable to changes in the pace of the process. When marriage is becoming popular it can give an impossible figure of over 1.0 first marriages per individual. But because of its simplicity, this measure is widely used for comparative purposes (Haskey, 1992b). In England and Wales it has declined from over 0.9 for men and women in the 1970s to about 0.6 today – still higher than in some Scandinavian countries where it has fallen below 0.5. A more subtle calculation, applying the first marriage rates of the single popula- tion to a life table, gives an index known as 'nuptiality', which cannot exceed 1.0. Calculations of nuptiality indicate that the chances of ever-marrying to age 50 have fallen from about 0.95 in the 1960s and 1970s to about 0.65 for bachelors and 0.69 for spinsters in 1995 (Table 2.15). For the first time in centuries women have a higher chance of marrying than men.

On the face of it, current trends mark a return to the earlier pattern of later and less popular marriage, but in fact the pattern is a new one. Unlike in the past, marriage is now normally preceded by two or three years cohabitation in which, as we have seen, many children are born. Many such cohabitations occur without being followed by marriage at all. The effective mean age at first entry into a sexual union is therefore considerably younger than the mean age at first marriage.

Table 2.15 Gross nuptiality to age 49, England and Wales, 1900–95

Year	Bachelors	Spinsters
1900–02	880	816
1911–15	898	843
1921–25	932	832
1931–35	925	844
1941–45	934	915
1948–50	949	949
1951–55	935	946
1956–60	941	960
1961–65	938	958
1966	939	957
1971	930	960
1976	858	917
1981	831	873
1986	793	836
1991	719	742
1995	654	687

Sources: Coleman (1980); ONS/OPCS Series FM2, *Marriage and Divorce Statistics*, Table 3.8.

Cohabitation

Cohabitation first started to attract statistical attention in the 1970s (Brown and Kiernan, 1981). Its study is of course greatly complicated by its very informality and sometimes by problems of definition. However, its importance led to questions relating to cohabitation before marriage being introduced into the annual General Household Survey; the Labour Force Survey includes them with marriage. These of course are voluntary enquiries, but a question on cohabitation was also introduced into the 1991 census schedule. We still lack knowledge about the formation and break-up of such unions. The data available have shown that, as early as 1979–82, 24 per cent of first married couples had lived together before their marriage, and 65 per cent of remarrying couples. The duration of such pre-marital cohabitation has increased, from about one year before the marriages of the 1970s to about two years in the early 1990s (Haskey, 1995). What proportion then lived together but did not marry is uncertain, but according to the General Household Survey in 1996, 11 per cent of all women aged 18–49 and 16 per cent of all women aged 16–24 were currently cohabiting, including over 25 per cent of all non-married women (Table 2.16). Up to the 1980s cohabitation tended to delay marriage but did not replace marriage as a stated expectation of most young people (Eldridge and Kiernan, 1985). More recently, with cohabitation continuing to increase and with it the proportion of births outside marriage, it is assuming a different status of 'nubile cohabitation', to some extent replacing the formal arrangement (Kiernan and Estaugh, 1993; McRae, 1993).

Table 2.16 Percentage cohabiting by legal marital status and age, 1995 and 1996 combined, Great Britain, women and men aged 16-59[a]

Legal marital status

Women	16-24	25-34	35-49	50-59	Total
Married	–	–	–	–	–
Single	17	34	22	9	23
Widowed	0	–	6	5	6
Divorced	–	35	27	18	27
Separated	9	9	9	7	9
Total non-married	17	31	21	12	22
Total	16	14	6	3	9
Men					
Married	–	–	–	–	–
Single	9	36	21	7	19
Widowed	0	–	18	7	10
Divorced	–	50	36	28	36
Separated	–	20	22	17	20
Total non-married	9	36	27	17	22
Total	8	18	7	3	9

Note: [a]Dashes mean the base was too small for a reliable analysis to be made.

Source: 1996 General Household Survey, Table 12.4.

The position in the late 1990s is that cohabitation precedes about 60 per cent of first marriages and over 75 per cent of remarriages. The proportion currently cohabiting has greatly increased to exceed the proportion married under the age of 35. For example, 39 per cent of women in Great Britain in 1996 aged 25-34 were cohabiting compared with only 19 per cent who were married. The equivalent proportions for men at the same age were 48 per cent and 15 per cent respectively. It is still difficult to construct a lifetime pattern for cohabitation, to show what proportion are likely to cohabit during their lifetime, for how long and how often, and what the rate of break-up is. Estimates for the latter suggest that cohabitations are between three and four times more likely to break up than marriages at equivalent ages, even when children are present. About 50 per cent of women who have their first births in a cohabiting union are likely to find themselves as lone mothers within ten years. Furthermore, marriages preceded by cohabitation are about twice as likely to end in divorce than otherwise, contrary to popular expectation (Haskey, 1992a). The mechanisms for this are unclear, but cohabitation is essentially a compromise state of low commitment to the partner, even if there is a desire for a child (Kravdal, 1997).

The differential advantage of women follows in part from a shift in their favour in the sex ratio (Leete, 1979). The nineteenth and early twentieth centuries had an excess of women thanks to warfare, seafaring and emigration. These factors have diminished; men are in surplus. Changes in marriage behaviour affecting both sexes are due more to the socio-economic changes arising out of the enhanced opportunity for women to follow careers and for married women to continue to work. The widely perceived impermanence of marriage shown by the startling increase in divorce figures makes it a less certain lifetime option; cohabitation may be regarded therefore as a cautious compromise (Ermisch, 1983). Professional women have always been least likely to get married; women with fathers in unskilled manual occupations are the most likely (the reverse is true of men). However, there does not seem to be a marked social gradient in cohabitation (Haskey and Coleman, 1986), although there is with respect to the chance of having a child when in a cohabiting union.

Divorce

Divorce is also fast eroding marriage, as it were from the other end. More than any other 'demographic' event except for abortion, divorce depends upon legal provisions. It is, if anything, attracting more attention than marriage as a barometer of the health of the institution of marriage, showing 'changeable, if not stormy times' (Haskey, 1996a, p.25). Before 1858 a civil divorce was effectively impossible without a private Act of Parliament. None the less, in the nineteenth century marital breakdown was common, marriages being broken by death of one or other partner almost as often as they break through divorce in the 1980s – that is, about a third by 25 years' duration (Coleman, 1980; Haskey, 1982) with an average 'expectation of life' of about 15 years. While the risks of premature mortality have receded, successive legislation has broadened the availability of divorce in terms of grounds and access; equalizing the grounds (1938), granting Legal Aid (1948), changing the cases for divorce from 'facts proven' to 'irretrievable breakdown' and introducing divorce by mutual consent (1969, effective in 1971), and shortening even further the minimum duration of marriage before divorce (1985 and 1995). The Law Commission and successive Lord Chancellors have taken steps to meet – sometimes, it seems, to encourage – what appears to be an unlimited demand for easier divorce. Each measure has stimulated an upward movement in frequency (Leete, 1979), although the increase in divorce has also preceded each new legal stage and has occurred within most of them (see Schoen and Baj, 1984), especially in the unsettled conditions during and after both world wars (Table 2.17). There were in fact declines in divorce in the 1930s and 1950s (after peaks following each world war), which can be regarded both in respect of statistics on family stability and the level of illegitimate births, as 'golden ages'. At that time, because of the much-reduced chances of dissolution by death and the scarcely awakened threat from divorce, marriages enjoyed at least an external stability without precedent in history – and one which is unlikely ever to be revisited (Anderson, 1983).

Table 2.17 Petitions for divorce, 1901–95, England and Wales, and decrees granted, Scotland

Period	Number of petitions filed during period	Average per year	Percentage by: Husbands	Wives	Number of decrees; divorce dissolution and nullity of marriage	Average per year
England and Wales					Scotland	
1901–05	4062	812	53	47	905	181
1906–10	4043	809	48	52	975	195
1911–15	5167	1033	45	55	1320	264
1916–20	14768	2954	67	33	2655	531
1921–25	14240	2848	41	59	2135	427
1926–30	20260	4052	41	59	2390	478
1931–35	23921	4784	45	55	2535	507
1936–40	37674	7535	47	53	3750	750
1941–45	80373	16075	56	44	7065	1413
1946–50	194503	38901	55	45	12175	2435
1951–55	160841	32168	44	56	11370	2274
1956–60	137392	27478	45	55	8960	1792
1961–65	188283	37657	42	58	11265	2253
1966–70	285449	57089	37	63	20280	4056
1971–75	608891	121772	34	66	33020	6604
1976–80	812403	162481	28	72	45340	9068
1981–85	884845	176969	27	73	59710	11942
1986–90	761801	152360			60335	12067
1991–95	797822	159564			63045	12609

Sources: OPCS Series FM2, *Marriage and Divorce Statistics*, Tables 4.7, 4.8; Registrar-General, *Annual Report*, Scotland, Tables R1.1, 8.1.

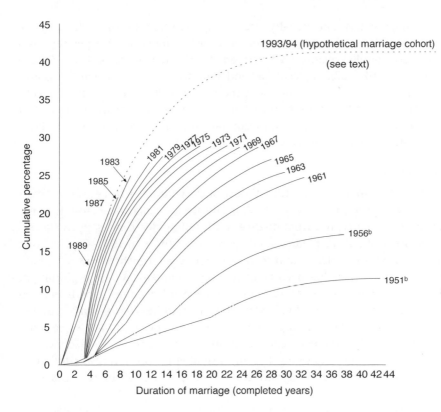

Figure 2.4 Cumulative percentages of marriages which ended in divorce,[a,b] by marriage cohort and duration of marriage, England and Wales

Notes: [a]Includes those divorces in 1994 which complete the total number of divorces in each duration of marriage.
[b]Estimated.

Source: Haskey (1996a), p.35.

Until World War II there were fewer than 10 000 divorces per year in England and Wales. After war-time excitements the total in the 1950s had risen to about 40 000 per year but was declining. As with so many other indicators of the national sexual and personal life, everything changed after the 1960s. By 1971 divorces were almost 80 000 per year, by 1981 over 156 000, and by 1993 the number had peaked at about 183 000. Divorces in 1996 numbered 154 000, the third year running of a decline. This respite, however, follows mostly from a reduction in marriages over the last 20 years – there are simply fewer at risk. Divorce rates have remained more or less constant during the 1990s.

Only 2 per cent of the marriages of 1926 had ended in divorce after 20 years, only 6 per cent of the marriages of 1936, and 7 per cent of the marriages of 1951 (Figure 2.4). The casualty rate has rapidly increased since then. By the marriages of 1956, the risk of dissolution had doubled to 11.4 per cent and more than doubled again to 24 per cent by the marriages of 1966. Of the marriages in 1971, 27.5 per cent had ended in divorce after 20 years. This is as much as we can say at present about the risk over 20 years. But more recent marriages have failed at an even higher rate; 29 per cent of the marriages of 1978 had failed after 15 years, for example, and 24 per cent of the marriages of 1983 after just 10 years (Haskey, 1996a, Table 1, p.28).

Remarriage

Earlier in the nineteenth century almost one wedding in three was a remarriage for one or both partners. The opportunity for remarriage arose through premature mortality, not from divorce. With falling death rates, at the beginning of the century most marriages (88 per cent of those in 1901–05) were first marriages for both partners, and even 83 per cent as recently as the late 1960s. Since then remarriage has become increasingly frequent. At the beginning of the 1990s, over 40 per cent of weddings involved at least one formerly married person; in 12 per cent, two divorced persons. Remarriages increased in number until the 1980s (95 000 in England and Wales in 1986) and have since stabilized at about 85 000 per year. As death rates continue to decline, the remarriages of widowed persons become a smaller proportion of the total (9.2 per cent of the remarriages of men in 1995; 8.9 per cent of the remarriages of women in 1995).

Age-specific remarriage rates are much higher than those of single people at all ages. Divorced persons have much higher remarriage rates than widows at all ages; in many cases an alternative partner has already been lined up (Coleman, 1989). Men remarry faster than women, especially after the age of 35, and a much higher proportion of formerly married men eventually remarry compared to women, competing with bachelors for younger women.

Remarriage rates themselves (as opposed to the number of remarriages) have declined, as part of the general retreat from marriage. The breakdown of first marriage is very often followed by cohabitation, which also precedes about three-quarters of remarriages. The increase in remarriage has occurred only because there are more divorced people available to be remarried. Remarriage and divorce are connected in another way; many partners divorce in order to marry or to live with another person.

It is not obvious that there is a natural maximum level to divorce, except possibly that determined by ability (of individuals or the state) to afford the costs. The UK divorce rates remain the highest in Europe, even though, as we have seen, they have not increased further during the 1990s. It is unlikely that divorce will become substantially less frequent, although Britain may have some unusual predisposing factors which might be remedied. It is a universally common phenomenon in modern industrial society, although individual countries do show major differences, only partly for legal reasons. While family size remains small, while women remain able and willing to go out to work when married, while traditional religious observance declines or remains relatively weak, relatively high divorce rates are here to stay (Kunzel, 1974).

Migration

Migration has tended to be rather ignored as a demographic process, but its importance has increased in recent years. In this book international migration is considered in detail in Chapter 4; here, its measurement and its effects upon population growth will be described only briefly. UK gross migration flows are a third or a quarter of the total number of births or deaths in a year; net migration is about half of that (Table 2.18). Migration matters partly because of its increasingly substantial direct demographic effects on population growth, especially at sub-national level, and additionally because post-war migration flows create new ethnic minority communities which previously did not exist. The concentration of immigrant populations in urban areas, and their subsequent growth through high fertility, radically changes the social, economic and ethnic character of urban areas in a highly visible way, notably London and the south-east. Growing immigration at a time of low natural increase affects overall population change at the margin, and now accounts for about half the UK's population increase.

In the UK there was no comprehensive direct measurement of international migration of any consequence before the 1905 Aliens Act. Under the Navigation Acts, statistics were gathered on emigrating passengers in the nineteenth century (Coleman, 1987). Effective series of immigration data on foreign citizens only (not British or Commonwealth subjects) date only from the Aliens Order of 1920, which instituted the basic system of immigration control and work permits. Commonwealth immigrants did not come under immigration control until the Commonwealth Immigrants Act of 1962; statistical series for them date only from 1964. Migrants from the Irish Republic are subject neither to control nor to counting, so no information at all is available directly on their migration flows (see Garvey, 1985), although estimates are published from various indirect sources (ONS, 1998a). Statistics derived from the Home Office control of immigration apply in detail only to inward-bound persons granted leave to settle (either on arrival or after arrival – in recent years, almost all the latter). These statistics follow non-demographic definitions derived from immigration law (see Home Office 1998a). Consequently, numbers can change radically following political decisions on immigration law. For example, the decision by the present government (Home Office, 1998b) to eliminate the four-year qualifying period for permanent settlement to persons granted asylum, and to reduce that for persons granted 'exceptional leave to remain' from seven years to four years – is expected to increase the annual numbers of those accepted for settlement to over 100 000 in 1999 (Home Office, 1998c), the highest ever recorded. However, these are persons who are already in the country. The other major source, the International Passenger Survey (IPS), a voluntary sample survey of all arriving and departing passengers (except to and from the Republic of Ireland) provides more demographically useful information of less certain accuracy (see ONS, 1998a). The decennial census also provides information on birthplace and, up to 1961, on nationality, while microcensuses such as the annual Labour Force Survey provide information on both, although only for a sample of the population. Both censuses and surveys have under-counted New Commonwealth immigrant and ethnic minority populations to varying degrees from the earliest times (Peach and Winchester, 1974; Hollis, 1982; Coleman, 1985; Simpson, 1996).

The twentieth century continued two existing contrary trends in migration. Traditionally the UK has been an exporter of people, particularly in the nineteenth century with young men leaving for North America, the Antipodes and the colonies. Family migration was less common. In all, about three million people were lost from the UK to North America in the nineteenth century (more left, but, as in all migration streams, some came back). It was encouraged as a means of strengthening the colonies and their ties with the UK, and for this reason continued to attract government sponsorship and interest until the 1960s (Oversea Migration Board, 1954). Emigration had earlier been seen as one solution to rural poverty, although most of the migrants in fact came from towns.

The old pattern of migration of single men was lost after the 1920s. The war changed much, liberal attitudes to migration in the US ended with new restrictive legislation, and the Depression of the late 1920s was easier to weather at home. Immigration dried up, and many migrants returned, to create the first net gain from migration this century. The new pattern was of family migration; more to Australia, New Zealand, Canada and South Africa. It still continues on a smaller scale, although no longer subsidized and diminished by the policies of the Dominions themselves. Migration with South Africa has gone into reverse; mostly of whites escaping increasingly lawless conditions. It has been estimated that about 800 000 of the South African white population of about three million are entitled to enter the UK. Dominions' immigration policies no longer give preference to people of British origin or nationality. The encouragement of immigration from elsewhere has made their populations much more ethnically and racially heterogeneous than they were; their links with Britain have been made deliberately weaker.

For almost a quarter of a century now, migration from the continental European Community has usually been relatively modest, balanced between substantial but approximately equal flows in each direction, despite the free entry of European Union (EU) citizens since 1973, made easier by the provisions of the Single European Act 1985. In the 1990s there has been an influx of young French people and others to London, where about one in ten of the workforce is now foreign. Migration for purposes of work, regulated by the work permit system in relation to the demands of the economy for non-EU citizens, increased to about 30 000 per year in the early 1990s (EU citizens are of course allowed to enter freely for work and other purposes). The long-term work permit migrants, admitted initially for one to four years, are for the most part highly skilled, many of them being moved by their companies ('inter-company trans-fers'). In recent years Americans and Japanese have been the most numerous of the many nationalities involved (Salt and Ford, 1993; Salt, 1995; 1998).

About half of all the gross migration flow into the UK since the 1960s has been from the New Commonwealth. Despite attempts to limit it, it has always been reasonably substantial and always positive. None the less, thanks to the outflow of British citizens, it is only in 1962, 1973 (Ugandan Asian refugees), and from 1983 to the present that immigration from all countries together has exceeded emigration. However, the composition of gross inflows and outflows by ethnicity and citizenship has been very different: mostly non-British citizens arriving; mostly British citizens leaving (net flows respectively +126 300 and –34 300 in 1997). Net migration of British citizens has been about –30 000 per year in the last decade, while immigration of non-British citizens has been high and generally rising.

According to the 'ordinary' official figures, net immigration increased unevenly over the 1990s to 62 000 per year in 1994 and was 60 000 in 1997, including 28 000 from the New Commonwealth – back to the levels of 20 years ago. However, if the 'visitor switchers' (see below) are included, the corrected official total rises to about 100 000 net additions to the population: 109 000 in 1994 and 92 000 in 1997. These large totals mean that UK immigration control has become, to a considerable degree, ineffectual (Coleman, 1997) (Table 2.18). Revised totals are reported in the preliminary tables (Tables A1–A3, 1.1 and 1.2) of the recent OPCS/ONS Series MN, *International Migration* annual volumes. But the bulk of the detailed published tables (Tables 1.3–3.20) in the same publica-tions continue to be based on uncorrected data which represent about half the actual figure of immigration from a demographic viewpoint – that is, of persons entering the country intending to stay permanently or for a substantial time. It is difficult to see how their continued publication can be justified.

It has often been claimed by the Home Office, the Commission for Racial Equality and by immigrant groups that 'primary' immigration from the New Commonwealth – that is of heads of household – has effectively ceased. This is both incorrect and irrelevant. Regular entry of males from the New Commonwealth under work permit is indeed modest. Instead, large numbers of

Table 2.18 Immigration trends to the UK, 1966–97 (000s)

| | Home Office acceptances for settlement | | International Passenger Survey | | |
	All countries	NC[b]	All countries Inflow	Outflow	Net
1966			219.2	301.6	−82.4
1971	72.3	44.0	199.7	240.0	−40.4
1976	80.7	55.0	191.3	210.4	−19.1
1981	59.1	31.0	153.3	232.8	−79.4
1986	47.8	22.6	250.3	213.4	36.9
1991	53.9	27.9	266.5	239.0	28.0
1996	61.7		272.0	216.0	56.0
1997	58.7				

Notes: [a]Asylum totals include dependants.
[b]NC = New Commonwealth.

males enter for marriage, as asylum claimants or illegally. Others enter legally on short-term pretexts as tourists, family visitors or students and then 'switch' to long-term stay through marriage or post-entry asylum claiming. The queue of dependants entitled to enter once considered to be (theoretically) limited, instead grows with every male migrant admitted. Previous estimates have been long overtaken. The problem is exacerbated by large and complex families, lack of vital registration and different attitudes towards the state and its officials.

Marriage as a source of immigration has been growing rapidly in importance. The practice of arranged marriages for women from the Indian Subcontinent has proved quite resilient in Britain. Spouses from the area of origin at home are preferred. Right of entry conferred on a fiancee or spouse to join a partner already settled in the UK makes such partners attractive on the Indian marriage market, where these advantages are widely advertised. The number of persons entering for purposes of marriage has been increasing, although not as fast as the age structure of the Asian population (Jones, 1982; Coleman, 1987) despite various attempts to curtail it by the government. This privilege had to be applied equally to husbands and wives following a decision in 1985 by the European Court of Human Rights. The decision in 1997 by the present government to remove the 'primary purpose rule' whereby such intending entrants had to show that the intention was marriage, not migration, has already substantially raised the level of inflow for marriage, from 22 000 in 1996/97 to 32 000 in 1997/98 (Home Office, 1998c). By 1991 the cumulative effects of New Commonwealth immigration had given to the UK

Net corrected	NC Net	NC net corrected	Home Office acceptances of spouses (all countries)		Asylum claims including dependants[a]
			Husbands	Wives	
	35.0				
	27.0				
	36.0		11.1	19.8	
	27.1		6.7	16.8	2.9
58.2	32.2	29.8	6.8	14.1	5.7
73.3	31.0	45.3	11.6	19.0	67.0
93.1	23.0	38.9	12.5	21.5	37.0
			11.3	20.4	41.5

Sources: Home Office, Control of Immigration Statistics; OPCS/ONS International Migration, Series MN.

a net gain of about 1.6 million New Commonwealth immigrants, and in addition their 1.5 million UK-born descendants.

Recent population projections have abandoned the assumption that net immigration is likely to be reduced to zero. Instead it is recognized as an important component of future growth in population and household, with an estimate of an annual and permanent net immigration of 65 000 persons now built into the population projections (ONS, 1998a, Figure 2). For example, the increase in immigration and its recognition in the household projections accounted for about a third of the increase in the now notorious forecast projections of housing in Britain from 1991–2016 (DoE, 1995). The most recent national population projections, based on 1996 (ONS, 1998e), project a population in 2001 which is 150 000 bigger than that projected in 1994, and a population in 2021 which is 1.1 million bigger (almost 2 per cent). These changes are mostly due to the more realistic assumption that immigration will not, as previously supposed, decline to zero. An additional immigrant population of 764 000 is assumed by that date, with the rest of the increase arising from the additional births to the new immigrants (Shaw, 1998). The biggest fertility differences between groups in Britain are those between the native British population and some of the immigrant groups from the New Commonwealth and other parts of the Third World. Along with continued immigration and a youthful age-structure, these fertility patterns, discussed further in Chapter 4, contribute substantially to the rapid growth of the ethnic minority populations.

Total population and age-structure

What does all this add up to in terms of effects on the British population and its age structure? Fertility decline in the twentieth century has disconnected the main engine of British population growth. Such natural increase (excess of births over deaths) that the population still enjoys follows from population momentum – the inheritance of the higher birth rates of 20–40 years ago; especially in the baby boom period, the babies of which now comprise today's parents. All potential mothers for the next 15 years or so have already been born. Thus population growth rates do not just reflect today's vital rates; they also depend on those of the previous 100 years, which created the present age-structure.

Moreover, the continued reduction of death rates at all ages except for early adult life is making an increasingly important additional contribution to population growth, only recently fully recognized in population projections (Murphy, 1995). Low fertility is the main reason why populations are getting older. In most populations, except those with very low death rates already, mortality reduction typically makes populations younger. It has had this counter-intuitive effect on the British population for the first half of the twentieth century, preserving infant life and allowing more mothers to complete their child-bearing career. But now that the average new baby has a 98 per cent chance of survival to age 50, that effect is all but played out. For the last few decades, further falls in mortality have had the effect that common sense would always expect them to have had; that is, to make the population older on average, thus reinforcing the similar effects of low fertility in making the population age. On aggregate, international migration has had a negative effect on British population size for most of the twentieth century, even if it has created new immigrant populations. The position of the last decade or more, of growing net immigration having an increasingly powerful effect upon the relatively modest level of overall population growth, is a new development in Britain's twentieth century history.

Table 2.19 shows how the population growth inherited from the nineteenth century continued into the twentieth, but at a declining rate. In 1977 the population declined in peace-time for the first time since the middle of the eighteenth century. The decennial increase from 1971 to 1981 was the smallest since the census began in 1801. It looked then as though the population was reaching the asymptote long predicted by devotees of the logistic curve (Raeside, 1988). However, in the 1980s and 1990s population growth has revived, partly because of the effects of lower mortality and partly through renewed immigration. On the most recent (1996-based) projections the UK population is not expected to begin to decline until it reaches 63 million in about 2031 (ONS, 1998e). This projection is based upon the assumption of a stabilization of the TFR at 1.8 (approximately the level in 1998), a constant net immigration of 65 000 persons (less than the latest 1997 estimate of 92 000), and life expectancy for men increasing from 74.6 to 77.8 and from 79.5 to 82.5 for women by 2021. Births are expected to be exceeded by deaths at some time around 2026. When this natural decrease is no longer compensated by net immigration, the population will begin a relatively gentle period of population decline (Shaw, 1998). However, the reader will not need to be reminded of the difficulty of forecasting events so far into the future. These changes in total population will be accompanied by more important changes in the age-structure of the population and in dependency ratios.

The age-structure

In 1901 the age structure was youthful, reflecting the previous century of slow declining mortality and (until 1870) relatively even and high fertility. Neither nineteenth-century mortality nor fertility before 1870 had shown any great fluctuations. The day of the mortality crisis had gone and the period of fertility fluctuations of the later twentieth century was still to come. The 1921 age-structure (Table 2.21) shows more clearly the effects of falling fertility and the direct mortality effects of World War I, the birth deficit during the war and the baby boom which followed. The 1961 figure is more mature: 40 years of low fertility had aged the population to create a more parallel-sided shape. But it is also more uneven: the demographic damage of two world wars shows up in excess male mortality, the deficit of births of both sexes and the subsequent baby boom. It also shows the effects of new mid-twentieth-century peace-time fertility fluctuations, arising from the new control of fertility – in the birth deficits of the 1930s, 1950s, and the beginning of the 1960s baby boom. The age-structure of the 1990s (Figure 2.5) shows the maturing of that boom and the moderate fertility since. It is apparent why today's low fertility does not immediately reverse population growth. Today's mothers, born 20–30 years ago, belong to older, larger birth cohorts. Figure 2.2 shows the contrast between the track of births since 1890 and their survivors in the age-structure of 1981, left after the effects of mortality and of net migration (including, of course, the addition of people not born in the UK).

The mean age of the population is estimated to rise from 38.4 years in 1996 to 41.9 years by 2021 and will continue to rise thereafter. Elements of the age-structure can be projected with more confidence than the total because in some future age-groups all the members have already been born, thus eliminating the influence of future birth rates which are the greatest source of uncertainty in projections. Thus we can be confident that children 0–14 years old will decline only slightly in numbers up to about 2011 (by about 490 000, falling from 19.3 per cent to 17.2 per cent of the UK total). Projected decline after that is expected to be much more modest: a TFR of 1.8 is not much below the replacement rate

Table 2.19 Natural increase, and net gain or loss by migration, 1901–97, England and Wales, Scotland, and Northern Ireland, and the UK

	Years	Population at start of period	Average annual change Births	Deaths
England	1901–11	32528	929	525
and	1911–21	36070	828	584
Wales	1921–31	37887	693	469
	1931–51	39952	673	518
	1951–61	43758	714	516
	1961–71	46196	832	560
	1971–81	49152	638	585
	1981–91	49634	664	576
	1991–94	51100	683	565
	1995–96	51820	640	569
	1996–97	52010		
Scotland	1901–11	4472	131	76
	1911–21	4761	118	82
	1921–31	4882	100	65
	1931–51	4843	92	67
	1951–61	5096	95	62
	1961–71	5184	97	63
	1971–81	5236	70	64
	1981–91	5180	66	63
	1991–94	5107	65	62
	1995–96	5137	59	61
	1996–97	5128		
Northern	1901–11	1237	31	23
Ireland	1911–21	1251	29	22
	1921–31	1258	30	21
	1931–51	1243	28	18
	1951–61	1371	30	15
	1961–71	1427	33	16
	1971–81	1540	28	17
	1981–91	1538	27	16
	1991–94	1601	25	15
	1995–96	1649	24	15
	1996–97	1663		
United	1901–11	38237	1091	624
Kingdom	1911–21	42082	975	689
	1921–31	44027	824	555
	1931–51	46038	793	603
	1951–61	50225	839	593
	1961–71	52807	962	638
	1971–81	55928	736	666
	1981–91	56352	757	655
	1991–94	57808	773	642
	1995–96	58606	723	646
	1996–97	58802		

Source: *Annual Abstract of Statistics* 1996, Table 2.2; *Population Trends*, Table 5.

Natural increase	Net migration	Actual increase (+) or decrease (−)
404	−50	354
244	−62	182
224	−17	207
155	38	193
197	47	244
272	23	296
53	−5	48
89	58	147
119	55	174
71	110	
54	−25	29
36	−24	12
35	−39	−4
25	−22	13
34	−25	9
34	−30	3
6	−11	−6
3	−10	−7
3	6	8
−2	−6	5
8	−6	1
7	−6	1
9	−11	−2
10	−4	6
15	−9	6
17	−6	11
11	−11	0
12	−5	6
10	3	13
9	6	14
467	−82	385
286	−92	195
268	−67	201
190	22	213
246	12	258
324	−14	310
69	−27	42
103	43	146
132	64	196
77	110	196

of about 2.07. However, the population aged over 60 (all of whom have already been born for the period of the projection) will increase both in absolute numbers and as a percentage; from 12.0 million in 1996 (20.4 per cent of the UK population) to 15.9 million (25.6 per cent) in 2021. This rapid increase of almost four million represents a combination of two factors: the natural process of population ageing from low birth rates and longer survival, strongly reinforced after the second decade of the twenty-first century by the movement into old age of the baby boom cohorts of the 1950s and 1960s. The problems created by these age-structure changes will be considered further below.

Table 2.20 Broad age-groups as a percentage of the total population, 1901–95, England and Wales, Scotland, Northern Ireland, and the UK

	Year	0–14	15–64	65+	Overall dependency ratio[a]	Youth dependency ratio[b]	Aged dependency ratio[c]
England	1901	32.4	62.9	4.7	59.0	51.5	7.5
and Wales	1911	30.6	64.2	5.2	55.8	47.7	8.1
	1921	27.7	66.2	6.0	50.9	41.8	9.1
	1931	23.8	68.8	7.4	45.3	34.6	10.8
	1939	20.6	70.2	9.2	42.5	29.3	13.1
	1951	22.1	66.8	11.0	49.6	33.1	16.5
	1961	23.0	65.1	11.9	53.6	35.3	18.3
	1971	23.7	62.9	13.3	58.8	37.7	21.1
	1981	20.3	64.4	15.2	55.1	31.5	23.6
	1991	19.0	65.1	15.9	53.6	29.2	24.4
	1995	19.3	64.8	15.9	54.3	29.8	24.5
Scotland	1901	33.4	61.7	4.8	61.9	54.1	7.8
	1911	32.3	62.3	5.4	60.5	51.8	8.7
	1921	29.5	64.5	6.0	55.0	45.7	9.3
	1931	26.9	65.8	7.3	52.0	40.9	11.1
	1939	24.1	67.2	8.7	48.8	35.9	12.9
	1951	24.6	65.4	10.0	52.9	37.6	15.3
	1961	25.9	63.5	10.6	57.5	40.8	16.7
	1971	25.9	61.8	12.3	61.8	41.9	19.9
	1981	21.2	64.5	14.3	55.1	32.9	22.2
	1991	18.8	66.2	15.1	51.1	28.4	22.8
	1995	18.9	65.9	15.1	51.6	28.7	23.0
Northern	1901	30.7	63.2	6.1	58.3	48.6	9.6
Ireland[d]	1911	30.4	60.8	8.8	64.5	50.0	14.5
	1926	29.0	62.9	8.1	59.0	46.1	12.9
	1937	27.1	63.9	9.0	56.6	42.4	14.1
	1951	27.6	62.5	9.8	59.9	44.2	15.7
	1961	28.9	61.0	10.1	64.0	47.4	16.6
	1971	30.6	58.7	10.8	70.5	52.1	18.4
	1981	26.8	61.2	12.0	63.3	43.8	19.6
	1991	24.4	62.9	12.7	58.9	38.8	20.2
	1995	23.7	63.5	12.9	57.5	37.2	20.2

	Year	0–14	15–64	65+	Overall dependency ratio[a]	Youth dependency ratio[b]	Aged dependency ratio[c]
United	1901	32.5	62.8	4.7	59.3	51.8	7.5
Kingdom	1931	24.3	68.3	7.4	46.4	35.6	10.8
	1951	22.5	66.6	10.9	50.2	33.8	16.4
	1961	23.4	64.8	11.8	54.2	36.1	18.2
	1971	24.1	62.7	13.2	59.6	38.4	21.1
	1981	20.6	64.4	15.0	55.3	32.0	23.3
	1991	19.1	65.1	15.7	53.6	29.4	24.2
	1995	19.4	64.9	15.7	54.1	29.9	24.3

Notes: [a]Overall dependency ratio = population (0–14) + (65+)/population (15–64)
[b]Youth dependency ratio = population (0–14)/population (15–64)
[c]Aged dependency ratio = population (65+)/population (15–64)
[d]Northern Ireland comprises six of the nine counties of the ancient province of Ulster: Antrim, Armagh, Down, Fermanagh, Londonderry,Tyrone

Sources: Census of Ireland 1901, 1911, Miscellaneous tables, Table XV, Registrar-General (Northern Ireland); *Statistical Abstract* of the United Kingdom up to 1931; National Register 1939, *Annual Abstract of Statistics*, Table 2.3; *Population Trends*, Table 6.

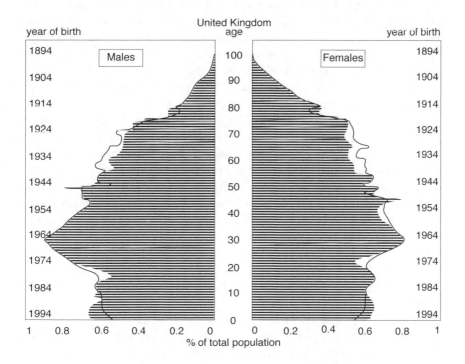

Figure 2.5 Population pyramid for the 1990s

Source: Eurostat (1996) *Demographic Statistics*, p.57.

Household and family structure

Family and household are at the root of European demographic distinctiveness. Their radical change this century is accordingly interesting and important. In the absence of continuous registration, however, we must rely on the decennial census and on annual surveys such as the GHS and the LFS to keep us informed about their development. For centuries average household size was around 4.7 persons (Laslett, 1983). This century the average household began to shrink; from 4.6 persons in 1901 to 3.0 in 1961 to 2.4 in 1994. Correspondingly the number of households, and therefore of dwelling houses, has increased much faster than population growth.

Partly this is thanks to the modern decline in fertility and the rarity of very large families. It is also due to the departure of one of its more distinctive features, domestic servants and lodgers. In previous centuries residential 'husbandry' or 'life-cycle' servants accounted for up to 17 per cent of the entire population. Even in 1861, 14 per cent of households had at least one residential servant, compared with just 1 per cent in 1951 when the species appeared to be nearly extinct. Only 2192 persons were recorded as domestic servants in 1981 – including nannies and au pairs. This must be a substantial underestimate as, in 1994, 9400 au pairs alone were given leave to enter the UK (excluding any from the EU, whence many come) and in the mid-1990s there were estimated to be about 25000 in the country. A revival in domestic service is now under way, it seems, although much of it is not residential. That is a necessary complement to the increase in educated high-earning mothers who pursue careers, an essential adjunct to their child-bearing.

Decline in household size has not been due to any great change in the residential pattern of different generations of the same family. Contrary to popular sociological myth, there never was any time in recorded history when co-residential 'extended' families were very common in Britain, either vertically extended (three or more generations) or horizontally (relatives outside the nuclear family). In 1861, 47 per cent of Victorian households consisted of one or both parents with their children but no other relatives, exactly the same size as in 1961 and 1966 (Hole and Pountney, 1971). In 1861, 15 per cent of households contained relatives of the household head, the same as in 1951, although this fell to 10 per cent in 1966.

These changes in average size conceal even more striking changes in distribution, especially in the number of people living alone. The distribution of household sizes is first available for England and Wales from the census of 1911. Then, 5 per cent of households were one-person households (Table 2.21). In 1911 there were more unmarried adult men and (particularly) women than today. There were more widows, and almost no divorced persons. Many of these unmarried people lived alone; others with their siblings. Old people often lived alone then, as they do now.

Table 2.21 Distribution of size of private households, 1911–91, England and Wales, and Scotland

Year	1	2	3	4	5	6	7	8–9	10+	Total
	Proportion of households with given numbers of persons									
England and Wales										
1911	5.3	16.2	19.3	18.1	14.4	10.4	6.9	6.9	2.4	100
1921	6.0	17.7	20.8	18.6	13.9	9.4	6.0	5.7	1.9	100
1931	6.7	21.9	24.1	19.4	12.4	7.3	4.1	3.2	0.9	100
1951	10.7	27.7	25.3	19.0	9.6	4.3	1.9	1.2	0.3	100
1961	11.9	30.2	23.4	19.1	9.1	3.8	1.5	0.9	0.1	100
1971	18.1	31.8	18.9	17.2	8.2	3.5	1.3	0.8	0.2	100
1981	21.7	32.1	17.0	18.1	7.3	2.5	0.7	0.4	0.1	100
1991	26.1	34.0	16.5	15.7	5.5	1.6	0.4	0.2	0.1	100
Scotland[a]										
1951	11.1	24.1	23.7	18.9	10.8	5.6	2.9	2.1	0.7	100
1961	11.8	26.5	22.8	19.7	10.5	5.0	2.1	1.4	0.3	100
1971	18.4	28.3	18.7	17.1	9.4	4.6	1.9	1.3	0.3	100
1981	21.9	29.4	17.5	18.3	8.2	3.2	1.0	0.5	0.1	100
1991	28.2	32.0	16.8	15.7	5.4	1.5	0.3	0.1	0.0	100

Year	1	2	3	4	5	6	7	8 9	10+	Total
	Proportion of persons in households of different sizes									
England and Wales										
1911	1.2	7.4	13.3	16.6	16.6	14.3	11.2	13.2	6.3	100
1921	1.5	8.6	15.1	17.9	16.7	13.6	10.1	11.5	5.0	100
1931	1.8	11.8	19.4	20.8	16.7	11.8	7.8	7.2	2.7	100
1951	3.4	17.3	23.7	23.8	15.0	8.1	4.3	3.1	1.2	100
1961	3.9	19.6	22.9	24.8	14.7	7.5	3.4	2.4	0.8	100
1971	6.3	22.2	19.7	24.0	14.2	7.2	3.2	2.4	0.7	100
1981	8.1	23.8	18.9	26.9	13.5	5.6	1.9	1.1	0.3	100
1991	10.5	27.3	19.9	25.2	11.1	3.9	1.1	0.7	0.2	100
Scotland[a]										
1951	3.3	14.2	21.0	22.3	15.9	10.0	6.0	5.1	2.2	100
1961	3.6	16.4	21.1	24.3	16.1	9.3	4.5	3.5	1.2	100
1971	6.1	18.8	18.6	22.6	15.6	9.2	4.5	3.5	1.1	100
1981	7.9	21.2	18.9	26.4	14.8	6.8	2.4	1.3	0.3	100
1991	11.5	26.2	20.6	25.7	11.1	3.6	0.8	0.4	0.1	100

Note: [a]1901–31 census volumes for Scotland give number of persons by house, not distinguishing separate households sharing a house.

Sources: Census 1911, Summary Tables, England and Wales; Census 1951, Vol III, Scotland; Census 1961 Household Composition Tables, England and Wales; Census 1971, England and Wales, and Scotland, Household Composition Tables, Part 1; Census 1981, Household and Family Composition, England and Wales, and Scotland; Census 1991, Household and Family Composition, Great Britain, Table 1.

Table 2.22 Household type, 1979–96, Great Britain

Year		One person	Two+ adults unrelated	Married or cohab. couple with dependent children
1979	Households	23	3	31
	Persons	9	2	49
1981	Households	22	3	32
	Persons	8	3	49
1983	Households	23	3	30
	Persons	9	3	47
1985	Households	24	4	28
	Persons	10	3	45
1987	Households	25	3	28
	Persons	10	3	44
1989	Households	25	3	26
	Persons	10	3	42
1991	Households	26	3	25
	Persons	11	2	41
1993	Households	27	3	24
	Persons	11	3	41
1995	Households	28	2	24
	Persons	12	2	40
1996	Households	27	3	25
	Persons	11	3	42

Source: 1996 General Household Survey, Table 2.3.

Since then there has been an enormous growth in single-person households at both ends of the age range – young people leaving home, and elderly people. Much of this change has occurred since the 1960s. In 1961 the proportion of households with only one person had just doubled since 1911, to 11 per cent. By 1971 they comprised 18 per cent; by 1991, 27 per cent, almost as many as married couples with no children (27 per cent) and married couples with dependent children (30 per cent) (Table 2.22). This increase is almost equally due to an increase in pensioners living alone and of younger people living alone.

At the other end of the scale, only 3 per cent of households (comprising 7 per cent of people) included six or more people in 1983; a decline from 6 per cent and 13 per cent respectively in 1971. The decline of large households, however, has been moderated by the growth of the immigrant and ethnic minority population; among Asians, household size is twice the national average.

Almost half the population – 42 per cent – live in households of a married couple with dependent children, and only 11 per cent of people live by themselves (although another 8 per cent are single-parent families with dependent

Married or cohab. couple with non-dependent children	Married couple with no children	Lone parent with dependent children	Lone parent with non-dependent children	Two+ families
7	27	4	4	1
9	20	5	3	2
8	26	4	4	1
10	19	5	3	2
8	27	5	4	1
11	21	5	3	2
8	27	4	4	1
11	21	5	4	1
9	27	4	4	1
12	21	5	4	2
9	27	5	4	1
12	22	6	3	2
8	28	6	4	1
11	23	7	3	2
7	28	7	3	1
9	23	8	3	2
6	29	7	3	1
9	25	8	3	1
6	28	7	3	1
9	24	8	3	1

children). (These families comprised 13 per cent of all families with dependent children, compared to 8 per cent in 1971–73 – Table 2.23.)

Some categories of household have remained roughly constant for decades. Married couples with no children comprised 26 per cent in 1961 and 27 per cent in 1994. However as might be expected from the rise of cohabitation, married couples with dependent children have fallen from 38 per cent in 1961 to 25 per cent in 1994, while lone-parent households with dependants have increased from 2 per cent to 7 per cent of all households, and up to 25 per cent of all households with dependent children. Up to the mid-1980s, much of the increase in single-parent families was due to the effects of rising divorce rates. After that time, the even more rapid increase of illegitimacy became statistically more important. Of all one-parent families with dependent children in 1983, 39 per cent were headed by divorced women – a category almost non-existent in 1901 – and 15 per cent by separated women, while 23 per cent were headed by single women. By 1992 there were about 1.4 million one-parent families with dependent children. Of these, 35 per cent were unmarried mothers, 52 per cent were divorced or separated, 4 per cent were widows and 9 per cent were lone fathers (Haskey, 1996b, p.11). Of families with dependent children in 1994, 22 per cent lived in lone-parent families and another 7 per cent lived in cohabiting-couple families. Of the married-couple families, step-families accounted for 5 per cent and 'step-cohabiting' families about 2 per cent (Haskey, 1996b). These proportions of children being brought up in historically unconventional family backgrounds are the highest in Europe.

Table 2.23 Families with dependent children:[a] family type and marital status of lone mothers, 1971–96, Great Britain

	Family type (%)							
Year	Married or cohab. couple	Lone mother total	Lone mother single	Lone mother widowed	Lone mother divorced	Lone mother separated	Lone father	All lone parents
1971	92	7	1	2	2	2	1	8
1975	90	9	1	2	3	2	1	10
1979	88	10	2	2	4	3	2	12
1981	87	11	2	2	4	2	2	13
1983	86	12	3	2	5	2	1	14
1985	86	12	3	1	5	3	2	14
1987	85	12	4	1	5	2	1	14
1989	83	15	5	1	6	3	2	17
1991	81	18	6	1	6	4	1	19
1993	78	20	8	1	7	4	2	22
1995	78	20	8	1	7	5	2	22
1996	79	20	7	1	6	5	2	21

Note: [a]Dependent children are under the age of 16, or aged 16–18 if in full-time education and living in the household.

Source: 1996 General Household Survey, Table 2.4.

Population trends and their consequences

These demographic changes suggest a number of ways in which population trends matter (Joshi, 1989). Changes over time in the relative size of groups relying on different aspects of 'intergenerational' transfer payments are particularly important; that is, instant transfers of money through the tax system from younger earners to older spenders. Figure 2.6 shows the relative sizes of the age groups in the past and projected into the future. The projections are reasonably secure as far as they relate to people already born. The mid-twentieth-century pattern of unstable fertility has brought this sharply into focus. It has meant rapid increases and decreases – up to 30 per cent in ten years – of cohort size of births, who then need medical care, education and employment. Policies on teacher recruitment, school building or, more recently, closure and the like, need to anticipate these changes, but it was only in the 1970s that detailed attention began to be paid to demographic trends in planning their provision (see Central Policy Review Staff, 1978).

From the late 1960s – five years after the peak of the 'baby boom' – until the early 1980s, primary school enrolment fell, ending up about 200 000 per year fewer from peak (1969) to trough (1982). The secondary school population experienced similar decline five years later although the drop in potential candidates for tertiary education (and workforce entry) did not affect 15–19 year olds until the early 1990s. Following later trends in the numbers of births, primary school entrants increased somewhat up to about the mid-1990s, with a small increase in secondary schools following later. The whole school-age population will reach a modest peak around the turn of the century. At the level of the school catchment area, local migration is much more important than the trends in births and deaths which dominate the national scene; emptying some inner-city schools even faster than the falling birth rate by itself, and in some areas – immigrant areas in the inner cities, growth areas in suburbs – creating demand for new schools.

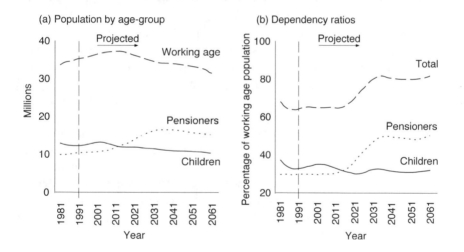

Figure 2.6 Actual and projected number of children, population of working and pensionable age, and dependency ratios, United Kingdom, 1981–2061

Source: OPCS (1993).

All radical upsets in the age-structure cause problems as the crests and troughs progress through life: for example, the baby boom of the 1950s and 1960s showed that the ability of the British economy to 'create' jobs was easily exceeded by the ability of the British people to create babies. UK unemployment in the 1980s was not helped by the increase of 30 per cent in the annual supply of young people seeking jobs each year compared with the 1960s. While the situation eased to a similar extent from the mid-1980s onwards, it had by then provoked a pressure to encourage early retirement which is now highly inappropriate with the growth of problems of pensions adequacy and old-age dependency. For the foreseeable future, entry to the workforce will be dominated by the declining size of the birth cohorts of the 1970s and the relatively stable or modestly increasing ones of the 1980s and 1990s. Most of such growth as occurs in the workforce at the end of the century, and for the foreseeable future, will come from increased levels of female workforce participation (Chapter 8).

One of the most powerful demographic consequences of a declining birth rate, and latterly increased survival, is the ageing of the population. Population ageing causes a deterioration of the balance between the economically productive parts of the population and a non-working old-age population which includes a high proportion of dependants, many in declining health. These, which upset the demographic assumptions behind welfare states, affect all countries in the developed world to a varying degree (Johnson, et al., 1989; Stolnitz, 1994) and, with the world-wide reduction in fertility, will become a global problem in the twenty-first century.

In Britain in 1931 there were 9 people aged 15–64 to every 1 aged 65 and over. Falling fertility and the consequent ageing of the population, together with improvements in survival at old ages, brought that ratio to 4.3:1 in 1981, corresponding to a ratio of persons of working age to persons of pensionable age of 3.4:1. Then it will stay constant for the rest of the twentieth century and for a short time into the twenty-first (Table 2.24). Now is the good time for pensioners and indeed the dependency ratio is becoming generally more favourable for a while. The workforce is inflated by the baby boom and by the high workforce participation of women, while pensioner recruitment is low. The birth rate in 1931 was low and declining so there will be little growth in the number of new pensioners for the next decade or so, even though the numbers of the elderly over 75 and especially over 85 will increase – they were born in the higher fertility years at the beginning of the century.

Problems start next century when the baby boom starts to age. Then pensioner numbers will increase sharply and their needs will have to be met by a reduced working population based on the modest birth cohorts of the 1970s, 1980s and 1990s. As all the old-age population for the next 60 years are already born and death rates are not very volatile, this problem can be predicted with confidence. The deterioration of the crucial ratio of taxpayers to pensioners is even more severe than the demographic ratios; a high proportion of persons of nominal working age are not economically active through participation in higher education, early retirement, unemployment or permanent illness. At the present age of entitlement to the old-age pension in the UK

(65 for men; 60 for women) the ratio of persons of working age to pensioners will fall below 3:1; that of actual National Insurance contributors to pensions recipients below 2:1 by around 2020.

Table 2.24 Ratio of pensionable population to population of working age, 1994–2061[a]

Year	Working-age population (000s)	Pensionable-age population (000s)	Ratio of working-age to pensionable-age population
1994	35689	10630	3.36
2001	36715	10703	3.43
2011	37737	11619	3.25
2021	38582	11746	3.28
2031	36140	14104	2.56
2041	34417	14863	2.32
2051	33102	14175	2.34
2061	31167	13848	2.25

Note: [a]These projections assumed the continuation of current ages of pensions entitlement; that is, 60 for women and 65 for men. These will be unified at 65 early in the twenty-first century.

Source: ONS/OPCS Series PP2, 1994-based *National Population Projections*, Table 7.2.

These ratios are particularly important in respect of pensions because state pensions do not operate in the UK (or in most other places) on a funded basis. Occupational and private pensions schemes do so: in that system, the individual's contributions plus profits, are used to pay the subsequent pension. Instead, a pay-as-you-go scheme operates through the direct transfers of tax payments from workers directly to pensioners. Such a scheme depends on population growth preserving a relatively helpful ratio between taxpayers and dependants, and on the absence of fluctuations in this ratio (funded schemes are not invulnerable to this either, as a more adverse dependency ratio will affect the productivity of the whole economy and thus the yield from invested funds).

Throughout the industrial world, governments are attempting to adjust pensions and welfare arrangements to meet this challenge. Some steps have been controversial. The attempt of the Conservative government to moderate the effects of the State Earnings Related Pensions Scheme (SERPS) which they inherited from their predecessors, is but one example (DHSS, 1984; Kay, 1988). More recently, the requirement on other grounds to unify the age of pensions entitlements of men and of women (DSS, 1991) has led to both being unified at the current men's age of 65. In nominal terms at least, this adjustment, to be introduced gradually between 2010 and 2020, will increase the working age population by about 1.5 million compared with the present prospect and reduce the 2021 pensioner population by about 2.0 million. These nominal changes may not at all correspond with the number who choose to remain in work, of course, but they are in line with increases in life expectation and in active life. Other adjustments to pensions systems and retirement will also be needed in order to accommodate population ageing, discussed in detail elsewhere (Johnson and Falkingham, 1992; Daykin, 1997).

Table 2.25 Projections of future households and population, England, 1991–2016 (000s)

Household types	1991	1993	1996	Year 2001	2006	2011	2016
Married couple	10547	10458	10341	10217	10118	10037	9945
Cohabiting couple	1222	1298	1377	1447	1499	1549	1579
Lone parent	981	1045	1122	1202	1243	1259	1257
Other multi-person	1350	1425	1512	1671	1852	2051	2240
One person	5115	5394	5824	6509	7185	7875	8577
All households	19215	19620	20177	21046	21897	22769	23598
Increase from 1991	–	405	962	1831	2682	3554	4383
Private household population (000s)	47490	47805	48321	49255	50029	50658	51135
Average household size	2.47	2.44	2.39	2.34	2.28	2.22	2.17

Source: DoE (1995), *Projections of Households in England to 2016*, HMSO, Table 1.

All developed countries will also experience a fall in average household size. Consequently the modest rate of population growth is greatly exceeded by a much faster rate of growth of households. This contrast has become marked at the end of the twentieth century, and is predicted to become more so, thanks to the high rate of household formation caused by the numbers of the older old, the exceptional high rates of divorce and lone parenthood in the UK, and the recent increase in immigration. Household forecasts of an additional 4.4 million dwellings required between 1991 and 2016 – a 23 per cent increase – (DoE, 1995) – have caused great controversy, not the least in the light of their implications for town and country planning policy. These forecasts, having taken on board the evidence of longer survival, higher immigration and household fragmentation, are considerably higher than the previous 1991-based projections (Table 2.25). However, it should be remembered that a large part of the projected growth was for the 1990s – now almost over – and that not all components of the growth are inevitable (see Holmans, 1987). The new set of household projections in 1999 (DETR, 1999) incorporate the higher level of immigration, especially from asylum-claiming, which has become apparent in the 1990s. This is now projected to stabilize at 65 000 net inflow per year. These projections and the new sub-national projections (ONS, 1998f) show that internal and international migration will cause significant population growth and housing demand in the south-east. However, the new projections suggest an overall increase of only 3.8 million households from 1996 to 2021, less than the 4.4 million from 1991 to 2016 noted above. This is partly because some of the 4.4 million extra households had already been set up by 1996. On the same time-base (1991–2016) the new projection was for an additional 4.1 million, or 300 000 fewer than the previous one. Otherwise, the main reason for the reduction – or lack of further increase – in projected households is the revision of the marital status projections: more cohabitation, and fewer widows living alone thanks to further reductions in male mortality.

Conclusions

1900 and 2000 are but arbitrary markers in demographic and historical processes but they do encompass the beginning of the end, and the termination of many aspects of the old demographic regime. At the beginning of the twentieth century, Britain had only recently begun its fertility transition. Average family size was almost four children. Expectation of life at birth was about 50 years. Population was still growing at about 1 per cent per year, almost 30 per cent were under the age of 15, and the elderly over the age of 65 scarcely numbered 5 per cent. Poor infant survival and child and maternal welfare were prominent problems. In a racially homogeneous population, social class differences in birth and death, then first beginning to be measured in a modern way and emerging statistically as the sea of fertility ebbed, were salient issues. Apart from the earlier departure of husbandry servants, household structures were not that different from previous centuries – no decisive break with the past had become apparent. While it was still common for families to be disrupted by widowhood in 1900, illegitimacy was rare and declining, divorce was almost unheard of and cohabitation the exclusive and rare pursuit of the lowest social classes and of the more adventurous radicals and bohemians.

Now all that has changed. Problems of high child and infant mortality have been as well resolved as anywhere in Europe, with 98 per cent of children being expected to survive to the age of 50. An average expectation of life of 85 years may be in sight. A century of low fertility has made us worry about aged dependency, not large families; about second childhood rather than childhood. If fertility falls much lower than its present level of 1.7 then the concerns which our early-twentieth-century forebears had over low birth rates might be revived. Instead of a substantial proportion of young people expecting to emigrate to North America and to welcoming dominions and colonies, immigration from the indigenous populations of former colonies and other parts of the Third World comprises half the country's population growth and has permanently transformed major cities into racially mixed populations unimaginable in 1950, let alone 1900. Most dramatic of all, households have become smaller and simpler, but also more varied and disrupted. Britain has become an enthusiastic participant in the 'second demographic transition', becoming Europe's leader in divorce and in lone-parent families with substantial demands upon welfare support and housing subsidy. Whether this will be a sustainable position given its cost to the taxpayer and its effects upon a quarter of our children, remains to be seen.

Where does the UK belong in Europe? Britain's fertility and mortality, divorce rate and illegitimacy ratio place it in a distinct Scandinavian/Northern European cluster. Despite devolution, the UK (even with the high fertility of Northern Ireland) is one of the most demographically homogeneous countries in Europe in respect of geographical variation in its birth rate; in England and Wales regional variation in fertility is by far the lowest of any major country for which data are available.

The British position in the European demographic space has shared many recent trends. Where it is distinctive in recent years is in respect of unfavourable rather than favourable characteristics. Britain is now exceptional in Western Europe in respect of high teenage births, lone-parent families, and divorce and upward trends in immigration and asylum-seeking (Coleman and Chandola, in press). Few of these changes are neutral. They reflect, over the last 30 or 40 years, a failure to maintain previously higher relative standards of health and of family stability. The trends in teenage births suggest that important sections of Britain's population have experienced the sexual revolution in a less responsible or educated fashion than the teenagers on the continent – problems which we appear to share with the English-speaking countries overseas. To an extent which is (to this author) rather alarming, Britain's distinctiveness in European demography, which once mirrored a leading position in Europe's society and economy, instead now reflects Britain's disadvantage.

Acknowledgements

I am most grateful to Jo Webb for updating tables in this chapter.

References

Alderson, M. (1983) 'William Farr's contribution to present day vital and health statistics', *Population Trends*, vol. 31, pp.5–8.

Allaby, M. A. (1989) 'Risks of unintended pregnancy in England and Wales 1989', *British Journal of Family Planning*, vol. 21, pp.93–4.

Allaby, M. A. (1995) 'Contraceptive services for teenagers: do we need family planning Clinics?', *British Medical Journal*, vol. 310, pp.1641–3.

Anderson, M. (1983) 'What is new about the modern family: an historical perspective', in British Society for Population Studies Conference Proceedings 'The Family', OPCS Occasional Paper no. 31, OPCS, London, pp.1–16.

Banks, J. A. (1954) *Prosperity and Parenthood*, Routledge and Kegan Paul, London.

Beral, V. (1999) 'Long-term effects of pill use', *British Medical Journal*, 8 January 1999.

Bone, M. (1986) 'Trends in single women's sexual behaviour in Scotland', *Population Trends*, vol. 43, pp.7–14.

Bridgwood, A. (1996) *Health in England 1995: What People Know, What People Think, What People Do*, HMSO, London.

Brown, A. and Kiernan, K. (1981) 'Cohabitation in Great Britain: evidence from the General Household Survey', *Population Trends*, vol. 25, pp.4–10.

Buck, N. (1994) *Changing Households: The BHPS 1990 to 1992*, ESRC Research Centre on Micro-Social Change, University of Essex, Colchester.

Bulmer, M. (ed.) (1979) *Censuses, Surveys and Privacy*, Macmillan, London.

Butler, N. P., Golding, J. and Howlett, B. (1986) *From Birth to Five: A Study of the Health and Behaviour of Britain's Five Year Olds*, Pergamon, Oxford.

Cartwright, A. (1978) *Recent Trends in Family Building and Contraception*, OPCS Studies in Medical and Population Subjects, no. 34, HMSO, London.

Central Policy Review Staff (Population Panel) (1973) *Report of the Population Panel*, Cmnd 5258, HMSO, London.

Central Policy Review Staff (1978) *Population and the Social Services*, HMSO, London.

Chandola, T., Coleman, D. A. and Hiorns, R. W. (in press) 'Patterns of recent European fertility data: fitting curves to distorted distributions', to be published in *Population Studies*.

Charles, E. (1936) *The Menace of Under-Population: A Biological Study of the Decline of Population Growth*, Watts & Co., London.

Chesnais, J.-C. (1993) *The Demographic Transition* (translated by Kreager, E. and Kreager, P.), Clarendon, Oxford.

Coleman, D. A. (1980) 'Recent trends in marriage and divorce in Britain and Europe', in Hiorns, R. W. (ed.) *Demographic Patterns in Developed Societies*, Taylor and Francis, London, pp.83–125.

Coleman, D. A. (1985) 'Ethnic intermarriage in Great Britain', *Population Trends*, vol. 40, pp.4–10.

Coleman, D. A. (1987) 'UK statistics on immigration: development and limitations', *International Migration Review*, vol. 21, pp.1138–69.

Coleman, D. A. (1989) 'Patterns of remarriage in contemporary Britain', in Grebenik, E., Hohn, C. and Mackensen, R. (eds) *Later Stages in the Family Life Cycle*, Clarendon, Oxford.

Coleman, D. A. (1997) 'UK immigration policy: "Firm but Fair", and failing?', *Policy Studies*, vol. 17 (3), pp.195–213.

Coleman, D. A. (in press) 'Male fertility: theories in search of some evidence', in Bledsoe, C., Lerner, S. and Guyer, J. (eds) *Male Fertility in the Era of Fertility Decline*, Oxford University Press, Oxford.

Coleman, D. A. and Chandola, T. (in press) 'Britain's place in Europe's population', in McRae, S. (ed.) *Population and Household Change*, Oxford University Press, Oxford.

Coleman, D. A. and Salt, J. (eds) (1996) *Ethnicity in the 1991 Census, Volume One: Demographic Characteristics of the Ethnic Minority Populations*, HMSO, London.

Compton, P. (1996) *Demographic Review Northern Ireland 1995*, Northern Ireland Development Office, Belfast.

Compton, P. A. and Coward, J. (1989) *Fertility and Family Planning in Northern Ireland*, Avebury, Aldershot.

Council of Europe (1998) *Recent Demographic Trends in Europe*, Council of Europe, Strasbourg.

Daykin, C. D. (1997) *A Crisis of Longer Life: Problems Facing Social Security Systems Worldwide and Options for Reform*, Government Actuary's Department, London.

Department of the Environment (DoE) (1995) *Projections of Households in England to 2016: 1992-based Estimates of the Numbers of Households for Regions, Counties, Metropolitan Districts and London Boroughs*, HMSO, London.

Department of the Environment, Transport and the Regions (DETR) (1999) *Projections of Households in England to 2021, 1996-based*, DETR, London.

Department of Health (DoH) (1992) *The Health of the Nation: A Strategy for Health in England*, HMSO, London.

Department of Health and Social Security (DHSS) (1984) *Population, Pension Costs, and Pensioners' Income*, HMSO, London.

Department of Social Security (DSS) (1991) *Options for Equality in State Pension Age*, Cm 1723, HMSO, London.

Dunnell, K (1979) *Family Formation 1976*, HMSO, London.

Eldridge, S. and Kiernan, K. (1985) 'Declining first marriage rates in England and Wales: a change in timing, or a rejection of marriage?', *European Journal of Population*, vol. 1 (4), pp.327–45.

Ermisch, J. (1983) *The Political Economy of Demographic Change*, Heinemann, London.

Eurostat (1998) *Demographic Statistics, 1997*, Office for the Official Publications of the European Communities, Luxembourg.

Filatki, H. (1997) 'Trends in abortion 1990–1995' *Population Trends*, vol. 87, pp.11–19.

Fogelman, K. (ed.) (1983) *Growing Up in Great Britain. Papers from the National Child Development Study*, Macmillan, London.

Fox, A. J. and Goldblatt, P. O. (1982) 'Socio-demographic mortality differentials', *OPCS Longitudinal Study 1971–75*, Series LS no. l, HMSO, London.

Fox, J. and Leon, D. (1988) 'Disadvantage and mortality: new evidence from the OPCS Longitudinal Study', in Keynes, M., Coleman, D. A. and Dimsdale, N. (eds) *The Political Economy of Health and Welfare*, Macmillan, Basingstoke, pp.221–40.

Fryer, P. (1964) *The Birth Controllers*, Secker and Warburg, London.

Garvey, D. (1985) 'The history of migration flows in the Republic of Ireland', *Population Trends*, vol. 39, pp.22–30.

Glass, D. V. (1942) *Population Trends and Policies*, Oxford University Press, Oxford.

Glass, D. V. (1971) 'The Components of Natural Increase in England and Wales', Memorandum submitted to the First Report of the Select Committee on Science and Technology, HMSO, London.

Glass, D. V. (1973) *Numbering the People*, Saxon House, Farnborough.

Glass, D. V. (1976) 'Recent and prospective trends in fertility in developed countries', *Philosophical Transactions of The Royal Society*, B 274, pp.1–52.

Glass, D. V. and Grebenik, E. (1954) *1946 Great Britain Family Census Vol. 1*, HMSO, London.

Hajnal, J. (1965) 'European marriage patterns in perspective', in Glass, D. V. and Eversley, D. E. C. (eds) *Population in History*, Edward Arnold, London.

Hajnal, J. (1982) 'Two kinds of preindustrial household formation system', *Population and Development Review*, vol. 8 (3), pp.449–94.

Haskey, J. (1982) 'The proportion of marriages ending in divorce', *Population Trends*, vol. 27, pp.4–8.

Haskey, J. (1992a) 'Pre-marital cohabitation and the probability of subsequent divorce: analyses using new data from the General Household Survey', *Population Trends*, vol. 68, pp.10–19.

Haskey, J. (1992b) 'Patterns of marriage, divorce and cohabitation in the different countries of Europe', *Population Trends*, vol. 69, pp.27–36.

Haskey, J. (1995) 'Trends in marriage and cohabitation: the decline in marriage and the changing pattern of living in partnerships', *Population Trends*, vol. 80, pp.5–15.

Haskey, J. (1996a) 'The proportion of married couples who divorce: past patterns and current prospects', *Population Trends*, vol. 83, pp.25–36.

Haskey, J. (1996b) 'Population Review: (6) families and households in Great Britain', *Population Trends*, vol. 85, pp.7–24.

Haskey, J. and Coleman, D. A. (1986) 'Cohabitation before marriage: a comparison of information from marriage registration and the General Household Survey', *Population Trends*, vol. 43, pp.15–17.

Hattersley, L. and Creeser, R. (1995) *Longitudinal Study 1971–1991: History, Organization and Quality of Data*, OPCS Series LS no. 7, HMSO, London.

Hogben, L. (ed.) (1938) *Political Arithmetic*, George Allen and Unwin, London.

Hole, W. V. and Pountney, M. T. (1971) *Trends in Population, Housing and Occupancy Rates 1861–1961*, Department of the Environment (Building Research Station), HMSO, London.

Hollis, J (1982) 'New Commonwealth ethnic group populations in Greater London', in Coleman, D. A. (ed.) *Demography of Immigrants and Minority Groups in the United Kingdom*, Academic Press, London.

Holmans, A. E. (1987) *British Housing Policy*, Croom Helm, London.

Home Office (1998a) *Control of Immigration: Statistics United Kingdom 1997*, Cm 4033, The Stationery Office, London.

Home Office (1998b) *Fairer, Faster and Firmer – A Modern Approach to Immigration and Asylum*, Cm 4018, The Stationery Office, London.

Home Office (1998c) 'Control of immigration: statistics United Kingdom, first half 1998', *Home Office Statistical Bulletin 24/98*.

Johnson, P., Conrad, C. and Thomson, D. (eds) (1989) *Workers versus Pensioners: Intergenerational Justice in an Ageing World*, Manchester University Press, Manchester.

Johnson, P. and Falkingham, J. (1992) *Ageing and Economic Welfare*, Sage, London.

Jones, P. R. (1982) 'Some sources of current immigration', in Coleman, D. A. (ed.) *The Demography of Immigrants and Minority Groups in the United Kingdom*, Academic Press, London.

Joshi, H. (ed.) (1989) *The Changing Population of Britain*, Blackwell, Oxford.

Kay, J. (1988) 'The welfare crisis in an ageing population', in Keynes, M., Coleman, D. A. and Dimsdale, N. H. (eds) *The Political Economy of Health and Welfare*, Macmillan, Basingstoke.

Keynes, J. M. (1937) 'The economic consequences of a declining population', *Eugenics Review*, vol. 29.

Kiernan, K. E. and Estaugh, V. (1993) *Cohabitation: Extra-marital Child-bearing and Social Policy*, Family Policy Studies Centre, London.

Kravdal, Ø. (1997) 'Wanting a child without a firm commitment to the partner: interpretations and implications of a common behaviour pattern among Norwegian
cohabitants', *European Journal of Population*, vol. 13 (3), pp.269–98.

Kunzel, R. (1974) 'The connection between the family cycle and divorce rates. An analysis
based on European data', *Journal of Marriage and the Family*, vol. 36 (2), pp.379–88.

Langford, C. M. (1976) *Birth Control Practice and Marital Fertility in Great Britain*,
Population Investigation Committee, London School of Economics, London.

Langford, C. M. (1988) *The Population Investigation Committee: A Concise History to Mark
its Fiftieth Anniversary*, Population Investigation Committee, London School of
Economics, London.

Laslett, P. (1983) *The World We Have Lost*, third edition, Methuen, London.

Leathard, A. (1980) *The Fight for Family Planning*, Macmillan, London.

Leete, R. (1979) 'Changing patterns of family formation and dissolution in England and
Wales 1964–76', OPCS Studies in Medical and Population Subjects no. 39, HMSO,
London.

Lewis, C. (1996) 'Unplanned pregnancy: is contraceptive failure predictable?', *British
Journal of Family Planning*, vol. 22, pp.16–19.

Lewis-Faning, E. (1949) *Report of an Enquiry into Family Limitation and its Influence on
Human Fertility during the Past Fifty Years*, Papers of the Royal Commission on
Population Vol. I, HMSO, London.

McAllister, F. and Clarke, L. (1998) *Choosing Childlessness: A Study of Childlessness in
Britain*, Family Policy Studies Centre, London.

McClaren, A. (1978) *Birth Control in Nineteenth-Century England*, Croom Helm, London.

Macfarlane, A. (1986) *Marriage and Love in England 1300–1840*, Blackwell, Oxford.

McRae, S. (1993) *Cohabiting Mothers: Changing Marriage and Motherhood?*, Policy Studies
Institute, London.

Mason, M. (1994) *The Making of Victorian Sexuality*, Oxford University Press, Oxford.

Matras, J. (1965) 'Social strategies of family formation: data for British female cohorts
born 1831–1906', *Population Studies*, vol. XIX (2), pp.167–82.

Mills, I. (1987) 'Developments in census taking since 1841', *Population Trends* vol. 48,
pp.37–44.

Murphy, M. (1993) 'The contraceptive pill and women's employment as factors in
fertility change in Britain 1963–1980: a challenge to the conventional view',
Population Studies, vol. 47, pp.221–43.

Murphy, M. (1995) 'The prospect of mortality: England and Wales and the United States
of America, 1962–1989', *British Actuarial Journal*, vol. 1 (II), pp.331–50.

Ni Bhrolchain, M. (1993) 'Period paramount: a critique of the cohort approach to
fertility', in Ni Bhrolchain, M. (ed.) *New Perspectives on Fertility in Britain*, Studies on
Medical and Population Subjects no. 55, HMSO, London, pp.1–16.

Office for National Statistics (ONS) (1997), *Living in Britain: Results from the 1995 General
Household Survey*, The Stationery Office, London.

Office for National Statistics (1998a) *International Migration*, Series MN no. 23, The
Stationery Office, London.

Office for National Statistics (1998b) *Abortion Statistics 1997*, Series AB no. 24, The
Stationery Office, London.

Office for National Statistics (1998c) *Birth Statistics 1996*, Series FM1 no. 25, The
Stationery Office, London.

Office for National Statistics (1998d) *Marriage, Divorce and Adoption Statistics*, Series FM2
no. 23, The Stationery Office, London.

Office for National Statistics (1998e) *National Population Projections: 1996-based*, ONS Series PP2 no. 21, The Stationery Office, London.

Office for National Statistics (1998f) *1996-based Sub-National Population Projections*, Series PP3 no. 10, The Stationery Office, London.

Office of Population Censuses and Surveys (OPCS) (1977) *Guide to Census Reports, Great Britain 1801–1966*, HMSO, London.

Office of Population Censuses and Surveys (1978) *Occupational Mortality 1969–1972*, Series DS no. 1, HMSO, London.

Office of Population Censuses and Surveys (1979) *Fertility Report from the 1971 Census*, Decennial Supplement Series DS no. 5, HMSO, London.

Office of Population Censuses and Surveys (1986) *Occupational Mortality: The Registrar-General's Decennial Supplement for Great Britain 1979–80, 1982–83*, Series DS no. 6, HMSO, London.

Office of Population Censuses and Surveys (1988) *Census 1971–1981. The Longitudinal Study: Linked Census Data*, Series CEN 81 LS, OPCS, London.

Office of Population Censuses and Surveys (1993) *Nationbal Population Projections: 1991-based*, HMSO, London.

Office of Population Censuses and Surveys (1995) *Occupational Health Decennial Supplement*, Series DS no. 10, HMSO, London.

Oversea Migration Board (1954) *First Annual Report of the Oversea Migration Board*, HMSO, London.

Peach, G. C. K. and Winchester, S. W. C. (1974) 'Birthplace, ethnicity and the under-enumeration of West Indians, Indians and Pakistanis in the census of 1966 and 1971', *New Community*, vol. 3, p.386.

Pearce, D. and White, I. (1994) '1991 Census of Great Britain: summary of results', *Population Trends*, vol. 78, pp.34–43.

Peel, R. A. (ed.) (1997) *Marie Stopes, Eugenics and the English Birth Control Movement*, The Galton Institute, London.

Raeside, R. (1988) 'The use of sigmoids in modelling and forecasting human populations', *Journal of the Royal Statistical Society* A, vol. 151 (3), pp.499–513.

Royal College of Physicians/Royal College of Pathologists (1982) 'Medical aspects of death certification', *Journal of the Royal College of Physicians of London*, vol. 16 (4).

Royal Commission on Population (1949) *Report*, Cmnd 7695, HMSO, London.

Salt, J. (1995) 'Foreign workers in the UK labour market', *Department of Employment Gazette*, pp.251–67.

Salt, J. (1998) *International Migration and the United Kingdom: Report of the UK SOPEMI Correspondent*, Migration Research Unit, Department of Geography, University College London, London.

Salt, J. and Ford, R. (1993) 'Skilled international migration to Europe: the shape of things to come?', in King, R. (ed.) *Mass Migration in Europe: The Legacy and the Future*, Belhaven, London, pp.293–309.

Schoen, R. and Baj, J. (1984) 'Twentieth century cohort marriage and divorce in England and Wales', *Population Studies*, vol. 38 (3), pp.439–50.

Select Committee on Science and Technology (1971) *First Report: The Population of the United Kingdom*, HMSO, London.

Shaw, C. (1998) '1996-based national population projections for the United Kingdom and constituent countries', *Population Trends*, vol. 91, pp.43–9.

Shorter, E., Knodel, H. and van de Walle, E. (1971) 'The decline of non-marital fertility in Europe 1880–1940', *Population Studies*, vol. XXV (3), pp.375–93.

Simpson, S. (1996) 'Non-response to the 1991 census: the effect on ethnic group enumeration', in Coleman, D. A. and Salt, J. (eds) *Ethnicity in the 1991 Census. Volume 1: Demographic Characteristics of the Ethnic Minority Populations*, HMSO, London.

Stolnitz, G. J. (ed.) (1994) *Social Aspects and Country Reviews of Population Aging: Europe and North America*, United Nations, New York.

Stopes, M. (1918) *Married Love*, Fifield, London (1995 edition with introduction by Peel, J., Victor Gollancz, London).

Swerdlow, A. J. (1987) '150 years of Registrar-General's medical statistics', *Population Trends*, vol. 48, pp.20–6.

Szreter, S. (1996) 'Falling fertilities and changing sexualities in Europe since c. 1850: a comparative survey of national demographic patterns', in Australian National University Research School in Social Sciences Working Papers in Demography no. 62, Australian National University Research School of Social Sciences, Canberra.

Taylor, L. R. (1970) *The Optimum Population for Britain*, Academic Press, London.

Ventura, S. J., Mathews, M. S. and Curtin, S. C. (1998) *Declines in Teenage Birth Rates, 1991–97: National and State Patterns*, National Vital Statistics Reports vol. 47 no.12, National Center for Health Statistics, Hyattsville, Maryland.

Wadsworth, M. E. (1987) 'Follow-up of the first national birth cohort: findings from the Medical Research Council National Survey of Health and Development', *Paediatric and Perinatal Epidemiology*, vol. 1, pp.95–117.

Wellings, K. (1994) *Sexual Behaviour in Britain: The National Survey of Sexual Attitudes and Lifestyles*, Penguin, Harmondsworth.

Winter, J. M. and Teitelbaum, M. (eds) (1985) *Fear of Population Decline*, Supplement to *Population and Development Review*, The Population Council, New York.

Wood, R., Botting, B. and Dunnell, K. (1997) 'Trends in conceptions before and after the 1995 pill scare', *Population Trends*, vol. 89, pp.5 –12.

Wrigley, E. A. and Schofield, R. S. (1981) *The Population of England 1541–1871: A Reconstruction*, Edward Arnold, London.

Further reading

This chapter has outlined the main demographic events and trends during the whole of the twentieth century and has attempted to guide the reader to the sources available for their further study. Their causes, significance and likely future development are only lightly sketched. For a more extensive treatment the reader is referred to *The British Population: Patterns, Trends and Processes*, by D. A. Coleman and J. Salt (Oxford, Oxford University Press, 1992). The quarterly journal *Population Trends* produced by the Office for National Statistics and published by The Stationery Office provides in each issue a summary of the latest demographic statistics and a series of articles on current demographic trends. *Regional Trends* provides more data on a sub-national basis. For further details the reader is referred to the annual volumes on demographic statistics provided by the ONS published by The Stationery Office; Series FM1 *Birth Statistics*, Series DH1 and DH2 *Mortality Statistics*, *Key Statistics* from the 1991 census and several others. The annual *Key Population and Vital Statistics* and the *Annual Abstract of Statistics* give basic data. The General Household Survey provides data and commentary on family and household, smoking, contraception, and other topics related to demographic change.

There are several works on the analysis of demographic data, of which the most user-friendly are *The Methods and Materials of Demography* by C. Newell (London, Belhaven, 1988) and *Demographic Methods* by P. R. A. Hinde (London, Edward Arnold, 1998).

For the UK in a European context, the annual demographic volumes *Recent Demographic Developments in Europe* (Strasbourg, Council of Europe) and Eurostat's *Demographic Statistics* (Luxembourg, Publishing Office of the European Communities; also in disk form) are now more widely available in bookshops. For analysis see *Europe's Population in the 1990s* (ed. D. A. Coleman, Oxford, Oxford University Press, 1996) and 'Britain's place in Europe's population' by D. A. Coleman and T. Chandola, in *Changing Britain: Population and Household Change in the 1990s*, edited by Susan McRae for Oxford University Press (forthcoming).

ONS website: http://www.ons.gov.uk
ONS e-mail: info@ons.gov.uk
ONS and other publications available from:
The Data Shop, National Statistics, 1 Drummond Gate, London SW1V 2QQ 0171 533 5678

Other government publications:
http://www.official-documents.co.uk

and for the Home Office:
http://www.homeoffice.gov.uk/index.htm

Council of Europe catalogue website:
http://book.coe.fr

Eurostat Publications available from:
European Data Shop (address as for ONS data shop above)
http://europe.eu.int/eurostat.html

3
Health

Ray Fitzpatrick and Tarani Chandola

> There is no health, physicians say that we
> At best, enjoy but a neutralitie
> And can there be worse sickness, than to know
> That we are never well, nor can be so!
>
> John Donne (1572–1631)

Introduction

At the end of the twentieth century it is increasingly common for discussions of health to begin with the World Health Organization's (WHO) definition of health as 'physical, mental, and social well-being, and not merely the absence of disease and infirmity'. This rather broad emphasis upon well-being realistically reflects both the aspirations of citizens of Britain when they consider health and the purposes and objectives of formal health services. The expansion of definitions and expectations of health that has occurred in recent years in many ways is the most striking testament to the improvements in health status that have taken place in Britain and other Western societies in the last 100 years. To a large extent Britain at the beginning of the twentieth century still experienced such high death rates that the absence of death and its accompaniments of serious disease may have been a more appropriate and understandable definition of health for the time.

However, for the most pragmatic of reasons, this chapter mostly considers health in terms of mortality. Mortality is virtually the only dimension of health for which we have reliable and consistent data over the last 100 years. Because of compulsory registration of deaths, mortality data became comprehensive in England and Wales from 1841 onwards. The reliability of causes of death even now is imperfect and changing fashions in medicine mean that consistency of disease-specific mortality cannot be assumed for this time period.

Table 3.1 Expectation of life by sex and selected ages, England and Wales, Scotland, and Northern Ireland

Year	Birth		Age 1		Age 65	
	Males	Females	Males	Females	Males	Females
England and Wales						
1901–10	48.5	52.4	55.7	58.3	10.8	12.0
1910–12	51.5	55.4	57.5	60.3	11.0	12.4
1920–22	55.6	59.6	60.1	63.0	11.4	12.9
1930–32	58.7	62.9	62.3	65.5	11.3	13.1
1950–52	66.4	71.5	67.7	72.4	11.7	14.3
1960–62	68.1	74.0	68.8	74.4	12.0	15.3
1970–72	69.0	75.3	69.4	75.4	12.2	16.1
1980–82	71.0	77.0	71.0	76.8	13.0	17.0
1990–92	73.4	79.0	73.0	78.5	14.3	18.1
1993–95	74.1	79.4	73.6	78.8	14.6	18.3
Scotland						
1890–1900	44.7	47.4	51.1	52.7	10.5	11.5
1910–12	50.1	53.2	55.8	57.8	10.9	12.2
1920–22	53.1	56.4	58.4	60.4	10.9	12.5
1930–32	56.0	59.5	60.7	63.1	11.0	12.6
1942–44	59.8	64.6	63.6	67.6	11.7	13.6
1950–52	64.4	68.7	66.2	69.9	11.4	13.2
1960–62	66.2	72.0	67.3	72.7	11.5	14.2
1970–72	67.3	73.7	67.8	73.9	11.6	15.4
1980–82	69.1	75.3	69.0	75.1	12.3	16.1
1990–92	71.3	77.1	71.0	76.6	13.2	16.9
1996	72.0	77.7	71.5	77.1	13.8	17.3
N Ireland						
1900–02	47.1	46.7	–	–	10.5	10.4
1910–12	50.7	51.0	–	–	12.1	12.8
1925–27	55.4	56.1	59.9	59.5	11.9	12.7
1936–38	57.8	59.2	–	–	11.6	12.4
1950–52	65.5	68.8	67.5	70.3	12.1	13.5
1960–62	67.6	72.4	68.7	73.2	12.2	14.4
1970–72	67.6	73.7	68.3	74.1	12.0	15.2
1980–82	69.3	75.7	69.3	75.4	12.4	16.1
1990–92	72.2	78.1	71.8	77.5	13.6	17.4
1993–95	72.7	78.3	72.3	77.8	14.0	17.6

Sources: Registrar-General for Scotland (1997); Registrar-General for Northern Ireland (1996); ONS (1997a).

The chapter relies heavily on mortality data from registration. It is also possible, for the latter part of the century, to draw on a small number of cohort studies initiated for the purposes of understanding causes of ill-health and

Table 3.2 Deaths and death rates for England and Wales, Scotland, and Northern Ireland: 1901–95

Year				England and Wales		
		Deaths			Crude rates per 1000 living	
	Persons	Male	Female	Persons	Male	Female
1901–05	2671566	1379931	1291635	16.0	17.1	15.0
1911–15	2598719	1344171	1254548	14.3	15.4	13.3
1921–25	2336270	1189865	1146405	12.1	12.9	11.4
1931–35	2426435	1232370	1194065	12.0	12.7	11.4
1941–45[a]	2497073	1301357	1195656	12.8	15.1	11.1
1951–55	2571153	1325747	1245406	11.7	12.5	10.9
1961–65	2766372	1415447	1350925	11.8	12.4	11.2
1971–75	2914762	1474783	1439979	11.8	12.3	11.4
1981–85	2896974	1443291	1453683	11.7	11.9	11.4
1991–95	2830033	1370879	1459154	11.0	10.9	11.1

Note: [a]Data relates to civilians only.

other social problems (such as the Office for National Statistics (ONS) Longitudinal Study). Such studies, unlike registration data, link diverse information about individuals to their mortality and other risks. In addition, in the last 40 or so years other survey data (such as the General Household Survey (GHS)) have also added to our understanding of trends and social patterning of self-reported health.

This chapter uses few technical devices to report trends in mortality. For the most part deaths are expressed as rates (per 1000, or whatever the denominator). In addition the standardized mortality ratio (SMR) is frequently used. Essentially it relates an observed number of deaths (in a group) to the expected number of deaths as a ratio. The expected deaths are calculated from a relevant whole population. SMRs above 100 indicate poorer than expected death rates in a group. The chapter also uses the more familiar concept of life expectancy to summarize the average number of years an individual can expect to live from birth, given prevailing death rates. A very similar expression is occasionally reported which is life expectancy at any given age; that is, the average number of further years that may be expected from that age.

Overall trends in mortality and life expectancy

In many ways the trends in mortality and life expectancy in twentieth-century Britain have been continuations of improvements that began in the nineteenth century. In the middle of that century, life expectancy for men was 41, and for women, 43. By the beginning of the twentieth century improvements

| Scotland | | N.Ireland | |
| Deaths | Rates | Deaths | Rates |
Persons	Persons	Persons	Persons
77313	17.1		
74466	15.7	21929	17.7
67652	13.9	19594	15.6
64839	13.2	18026	14.3
66302	13.8	17478	13.4
61838	12.1	15557	11.3
63309	12.2	15628	10.8
63808	12.2	16948	11.1
63723	12.4	15972	10.3
61171	11.9	15228	9.4

Sources: Registrar-General for Scotland (1997); Registrar-General for Northern Ireland (1996); ONS (1997a).

in life expectancy were already occurring. In the first decade of the twentieth century men could expect to live 49 years and women 52 years (Table 3.1).

However, in the twentieth century these gains in life expectancy have been far greater. By 1991, the life expectancy of men at birth was 73, and for women, 79 years. The trend of improvement has been steady and consistent throughout the century (Charlton, 1997).

Table 3.3 Standardized mortality ratios and infant mortality rates: 1901–95

| Year | SMR[a] 1950–52 = 100 | | | Infant mortality rate | | |
	Persons	Male	Female	E&W	Scotland	N.Ireland
1901–05	249	234	264	138	120	–
1911–15	205	195	215	110	99	–
1921–25	157	147	166	76	92	–
1931–35	134	127	141	62	81	–
1941–45	112	110	113	50	68	–
1951–55	97	98	95	27	33	46
1961–65	90	95	87	21	25	31
1971–75	84	89	80	17	19	18
1981–85	75	78	73	10	11	10
1991–95	67	67	67	6	7	7

Note: [a]Standardized Mortality Ratio (England and Wales only).

Sources: Registrar-General for Scotland (1997); Registrar-General for Northern Ireland (1996); ONS (1997a).

Table 3.4 Death rates by sex and age–group: England and Wales, 1901–95

	All ages	under 1	1–4	5–9	10–14	15–19	20–24
Females							
1901–05	15.0	124.0	19.2	3.8	2.2	3.0	3.7
1911–15[a]	13.3	97.0	15.7	3.4	2.1	2.8	3.3
1921–25	11.4	66.0	9.7	2.4	1.7	2.6	3.1
1931–35	11.4	54.0	6.2	2.1	1.4	2.2	2.8
1941–45[a]	11.1	44.0	3.3	1.3	1.0	1.7	2.4
1951–55	10.9	23.0	1.0	0.4	0.3	0.5	0.7
1961–65	11.2	18.0	0.8	0.3	0.3	0.4	0.5
1971–75	11.4	15.0	0.6	0.3	0.2	0.4	0.4
1981–85	11.4	9.0	0.4	0.2	0.2	0.3	0.3
1991–95	11.1	6.0	0.3	0.1	0.1	0.3	0.3
Males							
1901–05	17.1	151.0	20.1	3.7	2.1	3.2	4.4
1911–15[a]	15.4	121.0	16.7	3.4	2.1	3.0	4.0
1921–25	12.9	86.0	10.6	2.6	1.7	2.7	3.5
1931–35	12.7	70.0	6.9	2.3	1.4	2.5	3.2
1941–45[a]	15.1	56.0	3.7	1.7	1.2	2.2	5.0
1951–55	12.5	30.0	1.2	0.6	0.5	0.9	1.2
1961–65	12.4	23.0	0.9	0.5	0.4	1.0	1.1
1971–75	12.3	19.0	0.7	0.4	0.3	0.9	1.0
1981–85	11.9	11.0	0.5	0.3	0.3	0.8	0.8
1991–95	10.9	7.0	0.3	0.2	0.2	0.6	0.8

Note: [a]Data relate to civilians only.

Improvements in mortality began at different times for different age-groups. As a broad generalization, improved mortality rates began earlier in the century for younger age-groups and life expectancy rose for older age-groups as the twentieth century progressed (Tables 3.2–4; Figure 3.1). The first marked improvement in mortality took place around 1860 and occurred in the young age-group – 5–24. This effect is quite striking because for the later part of the nineteenth century, mortality rates deteriorated for older age-groups, above the age of 45.

Infant mortality began to fall steadily from the beginning of the twentieth century. This improvement was accelerated in the period immediately after World War II, but further marked gains occurred in the 1970s. One graphic way of conveying changes in infant mortality is to note that in 1900, one-quarter of all deaths in the population occurred in the first year of life. By the last decade of the century, less than 1 per cent of deaths occurred in this age-group.

Death rates in the age-range 15–44 have steadily improved over the course of the twentieth century, although the 1918 influenza epidemic and the two world wars produced peaks of mortality in this age-group.

25–34	35–44	45–54	55–64	65–74	75–84	85 and over
5.0	8.1	13.1	25.4	54.8	119.9	249.4
4.1	6.5	11.4	22.7	51.7	117.5	245.4
3.6	5.0	8.8	18.7	45.5	112.9	241.2
3.1	4.3	8.0	17.0	42.8	108.9	245.0
2.5	3.3	6.4	14.0	36.0	93.5	206.6
1.1	2.1	4.9	11.8	33.1	92.4	222.0
0.7	1.8	4.4	10.6	29.8	83.6	206.7
0.6	1.6	4.4	10.2	26.4	74.5	188.9
0.5	1.2	3.6	9.6	24.1	64.4	175.9
0.4	1.1	2.7	7.7	21.6	57.7	152.0
5.9	9.7	17.0	32.4	65.3	137.6	274.6
5.2	8.2	14.9	30.2	64.1	139.2	281.6
4.1	6.5	11.6	24.9	58.2	135.5	272.7
3.3	5.4	11.2	23.6	56.7	135.2	278.9
4.2	4.8	9.9	23.1	51.7	121.6	226.1
1.4	2.7	7.9	22.5	54.6	126.7	265.9
1.1	2.5	7.4	21.7	54.0	121.3	253.2
1.0	2.2	7.2	20.1	51.1	115.1	237.1
0.9	1.7	5.7	17.4	45.2	103.5	220.8
0.9	1.7	4.2	13.0	37.1	91.0	196.4

Source: ONS (1997a).

Death rates at older ages, above 45, had been static throughout the nineteenth century. Overall, the pattern for older individuals has been for improvements to begin later in the century the older the age band. In broad terms, at age 45–54, falls in mortality started at the beginning of the twentieth century; for those aged 55–74, mortality began noticeably to decline in the 1920s, and for those aged over 74, mortality declines began after World War II. For older age-groups the most marked improvements in mortality have occurred since the 1970s.

It is worth underlining the fact that modest but real increases in life expectancy continued to occur at all ages in the last part of the twentieth century. Thus, in the period from 1961 to 1991, both men and women aged 75 could expect to live a further two years. It is not easy to think in terms of a clearly defined biological limit to life expectancy in these circumstances (Wilmoth and Lundstrom, 1996).

The result has been to create a population with a higher proportion of older individuals. This 'ageing' of the population is in turn associated with a pattern in which death tends to occur at older ages. At the beginning of the

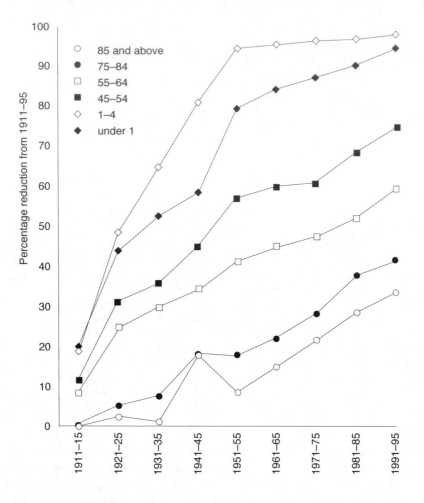

Figure 3.1 Percentage reduction in mortality in England and Wales by age-groups, 1911–95

Source: ONS (1997a).

century only 12 per cent of all deaths were of individuals aged 75 or over. By the end of the century, over 59 per cent of all deaths occur in this older age-group.

In general terms females have benefited more than males from the reductions in mortality in the twentieth century; whereas males have gained 28 years in average life expectancy over the century, for females this gain is 30 years. Most of this relatively greater benefit for women has occurred since World War II. However, in the last 20 years, from 1971 to 1991, in the age-group 45–74, whilst in absolute terms still having worse mortality rates, men have enjoyed a greater proportional reduction in mortality rate than women.

Changing patterns of mortality

It is not easy to give a very precise account of changes in the causes of death over this period because methods of diagnosing and recording health problems have constantly changed. Nevertheless, there is broad agreement about the main trends (Figure 3.2). From the beginning of the twentieth century infectious diseases have been responsible for a diminishing proportion of all deaths. Instead, the so-called degenerative diseases, particularly heart disease, strokes and cancer, have become the major causes of death.

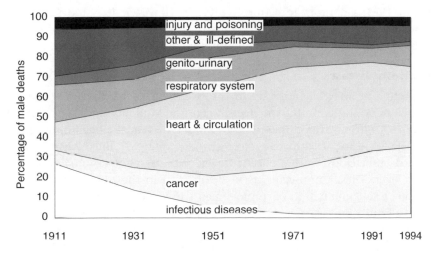

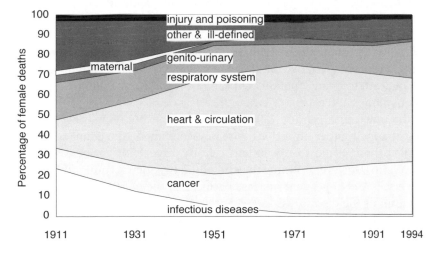

Figure 3.2 Causes of male and female deaths in England and Wales, 1911–94

Source: Charlton and Murphy (1997).

The declining significance of infectious diseases was the single main reason for the dramatic increase in life expectancy described in the previous section. Conversely, the main reason for the increase in heart disease, strokes and cancer has been that individuals were increasingly likely to reach the older ages at which these diseases typically, although not exclusively, occur.

These changes have been described as being the final stage of a three-stage 'epidemiological transition' that Western populations generally have experienced: (stage 1) the age of pestilence and famine; (stage 2) the age of receding pandemics and (stage 3) the age of degenerative and man-made diseases (Omran 1971; Charlton and Murphy, 1997). However, it is too simple to summarize the twentieth century as this third stage and trends for different causes of death need to be considered in more detail.

Infectious diseases

The decline of infectious diseases in the twentieth century was a continuation of a trend started in the nineteenth century. Mortality rates began to fall in the 1870s, from over 20 per 1000 to 16 per 1000 at the beginning of the twentieth century. Death rates for a wide range of infectious diseases declined: tuberculosis (TB), enteric fever, typhus, cholera, smallpox and scarlet fever. These improvements in death rates in the nineteenth century were due to a combination of improvements in standard of living, especially improved nutrition, cleaner water supplies, and better personal hygiene and sanitation, partly related to reduced overcrowding from smaller family sizes. In the twentieth century these trends have continued so that whereas at the beginning of the century infectious diseases were responsible for 20 per cent of all deaths, by the end of the century they caused only 0.5 per cent of deaths.

Mortality in infancy was dramatically reduced during the course of the twentieth century. A range of infectious diseases became unimportant as causes of death to infants: poliomyelitis, diphtheria, tetanus, whooping cough, measles, mumps and rubella (German measles).

In the nineteenth century tuberculosis was probably responsible for more deaths than all other infectious diseases combined. Its dramatic decline continued through most of twentieth century, except for an increase during World War II. However, towards the end of the twentieth century, this decline has reversed. An 8.5 per cent increase occurred in the notification of the respiratory form of the disease, associated with poverty and homelessness. A small proportion of this recent increase in tuberculosis may have arisen in individuals with human immunodeficiency virus (HIV) infection (Bloom and Murray, 1992).

Influenza was a major cause of death in the nineteenth century. In the twentieth century its importance has declined, except that from time to time pandemics occur as the virus itself changes. The worst pandemic occurred in 1918, being particularly lethal in young adult males. More recent, less lethal, influenza epidemics in 1969–70 and 1989–90 were responsible for deaths in individuals mainly over the age of 85.

Whilst it is undoubtedly the case that the twentieth century might overall be considered a series of 'victories' over infectious disease, nevertheless there is at the end of the century concern about a 'recrudescence of infection' (Galbraith and McCormick, 1997). To date, many have only modest epidemi-ological significance: outbreaks of meningococcal disease and the importing of diseases such as malaria and cholera from increased international travel.

In terms of public alarm, the appearance and spread of acquired immune deficiency syndrome (AIDS) in Britain in the early 1980s was a major epidemi-ological development. However, whilst world-wide it is thought that over 20 million individuals are infected with the virus responsible for AIDS (HIV), to date the AIDS epidemic in Britain has not been extensive and it is projected that in the year 1999 about 2000 new cases can be expected to appear (Adler et al., 1997).

Cardiovascular diseases

If infectious diseases were the main group of causes of death in the nineteenth century, the circulatory diseases are the main cause of death at the end of the twentieth century, accounting for 45 per cent of all deaths, with coronary heart disease and stroke accounting for 25 and 11 per cent of all deaths respec-tively (Charlton, et al., 1997).

If trends are examined in more detail, it appears that, for men, rates of coronary heart disease began rising in the 1920s, peaked in the 1970s and then began markedly to decline. Women have throughout this period experienced lower absolute rates of heart disease but the trends over time have broadly followed those experienced by men. The pattern of rise and fall over the century, occurring in similar ways for men and women and different age groups, makes it resemble an epidemic.

Death from stroke has declined steadily throughout most of the century, for both men and women. Diagnostic and coding practices have been particularly unstable for this disease and make the interpretation of trends difficult. Nevertheless, it is very unlikely that the downward trends are an artefact. The greatest declines have been in the age-group 45–64; for example, in men the mortality rate for strokes was 991 per 1 000 000 in 1901, 511 in the middle of the century and 188 at the end of the century. Declines have accelerated since the 1970s. To a somewhat greater extent than is considered the case with heart disease, some of the improvement in stroke mortality may be due to improved survival after the occurrence of a stroke.

Cancer

The history of cancer is particularly problematic because of high levels of under-diagnosis as well as inconsistencies in diagnosis and recording. In 1911 (when more stable figures can be found) cancer was responsible for 7 per cent of all deaths; by the 1990s it was responsible for 26 per cent of deaths.

In terms of specific sites, lung cancer increased markedly over the twentieth century and only began to decline again for men in the 1970s. It also appears that cancer of the prostate amongst men has steadily risen over the century, as has ovarian cancer for women. At the end of the century, the most common specific causes of death amongst cancers are cancer of the lung, followed by cancer of the colon and rectum, female breast cancer and prostate cancer.

Some cancers have recently appeared to undergo significant increases. For example, the incidence and mortality rates for oesophageal cancer have increased, especially for men. The incidence of cancer of the prostate has increased, although it has been paralleled by improved survival rates after onset. Mortality from malignant melanoma has also increased.

Some other causes of death

Other diseases contribute far less to the overall pattern of deaths but reveal important developments. Amongst striking trends in this period is the fall in mortality due to diabetes. For young and middle-aged individuals death rates from this disease have fallen steadily since the 1920s and markedly since World War II. Clearly, the development of insulin treatments as well as better control of infections contributed substantially to the decline. Pregnancy and child-birth were responsible for over 3000 deaths per annum in the first decade of the twentieth century, but by the 1990s less than 50 women per annum die as a result of these events. There would appear to have been a substantial decline in deaths from suicide over the course of twentieth century (Table 3.5). Deaths from diseases of the digestive system such as cirrhosis of the liver and gastric and duodenal ulcers have declined considerably in significance over the century, although in recent years deaths from cirrhosis of the liver have increased in younger age groups. Asthma has attracted considerable attention because of increased hospital admissions in the latter part of the century. However, there is little overall pattern in mortality from the condition for the century as a whole, except that there is agreement on an epidemic of asthma mortality in the 1960s due to the adverse effects of a particular aerosol treatment used in that period.

Morbidity and use of health services

There are virtually no data comparable to mortality statistics that would permit analysis of time trends in sickness over the last 100 years. Whereas

**Table 3.5 Standardized mortality
ratios for suicide: England and Wales,
1901–90**

Year	SMR All ages, base years 1950–1952
1901–05	149
1911–15	132
1921–25	125
1931–35	150
1941–45	91
1951–55	105
1961–65	112
1971–75	75
1981–85	82
1990	72

Source: OPCS (1992).

death is the subject of compulsory registration, there is no equivalent recording of episodes of sickness, and in any case it is known that the majority of episodes of sickness are not taken to the health service: they are self-managed in what has been termed a 'clinical iceberg' of ill-health. In Britain a comprehensive system of primary care should mean that some estimate of morbidity levels is possible but the problems of accurately diagnosing sickness are legion. Therefore, only some very elementary evidence can be used to quantify trends in morbidity.

Grundy (1997) analyses sickness absence recorded for members of Friendly Societies during specific time-periods and provides evidence for improved levels of morbidity in the period 1921–23 compared with earlier periods in the late nineteenth century. However, she acknowledges that the differences observed are just as likely to be selection effects and differences of recording in the different time-periods.

A more accurate comparison of morbidity can be found in surveys of General Practice surgeries. Between two periods for which comparable data are available, 1981–82 and 1991–92, they noted an increase from 71 per cent to 78 per cent of the population consulting the General Practitioner (GP) (Fraser et al., 1997). This was paralleled by increases in the rates of consultation for the majority of categories of illness distinguished in the survey. For example, the prevalence of consultation of cancer increased by 20 per cent in men and 34 per cent in women. As Fraser and his colleagues comment, such trends are consistent with stable incidence of cancer combined with increased survival, and do not necessarily mean real increases in the occurrence of cancer. The two most recent series show continuities with trends for consulting rates from a simpler but broadly comparable survey for the 1950s and 1970s (Table 3.6).

Table 3.6 Patient consulting rates per 1000 population by sex for principal diseases, England and Wales, 1955–56 to 1991–92

International Classification of Diseases	Sex	1955–56	1971–72	1981–82	1991–92
Infectious and parasitic diseases	male	57.7	82.4	127.6	113.7
includes bacterial and viral diseases	female	52.7	82.4	105.8	165.0
	persons	55.0	82.4	117.2	139.9
Neoplasms	male	8.7	9.5	11.0	19.0
includes cancers and leukaemia	female	12.5	14.6	15.7	28.6
	persons	10.7	12.1	13.5	23.9
Endocrine, nutritional and metabolic diseases	male	37.5	16.1	19.8	30.5
includes diabetes	female	62.5	36.9	37.0	44.6
	persons	50.8	27.0	28.8	37.7
Diseases of blood and blood–forming organs	male	4.7	5.3	3.6	4.9
includes anaemias	female	22.9	18.4	11.5	14.3
	persons	14.3	12.1	7.8	9.7
Mental disorders	male	32.4	73.6	55.4	50.3
includes dementia and other psychoses	female	65.6	149.1	112.7	94.4
	persons	50.0	113.0	85.4	72.8
Diseases of nervous system and sense organs	male	115.5	109.8	131.3	153.8
includes meningitis and Alzheimer's disease	female	123.7	117.9	149.7	191.9
	persons	119.8	114.0	140.9	173.2
Diseases of the circulatory system	male	54.4	56.1	75.4	83.9
includes heart disease and strokes	female	80.9	75.5	93.8	102.0
	persons	68.4	66.2	85.0	93.1
Diseases of the respiratory system	male	257.7	264.3	256.3	272.2
includes pneumonia and bronchitis	female	270.0	264.4	281.8	340.4
	persons	264.2	264.4	269.6	307.0
Diseases of the digestive system	male	110.5	81.4	67.8	75.7
includes stomach ulcers and liver disease	female	103.9	82.4	75.8	97.1
	persons	107.0	81.9	72.0	86.6
Diseases of the genito-urinary system	male	18.1	23.0	28.7	35.9
includes nephritis (kidney inflammation)	female	83.8	125.0	138.9	187.6
	persons	52.9	76.2	86.4	113.3
Complications of pregnancy, child-birth	male	–	–	–	–
and the puerperium	female	16.9	20.9	15.7	21.1
	persons	–	–	–	–
Diseases of skin and subcutaneous tissue	male	107.0	103.5	106.1	127.1
	female	104.4	117.6	128.5	163.1
	persons	105.6	110.8	117.8	145.5
Diseases of the musculoskeletal system	male	75.4	81.8	115.0	129.5
and connective tissue	female	97.0	99.8	149.1	173.8
includes rheumatoid arthritis and osteoporosis	persons	86.8	91.2	132.8	152.1

Table 3.6 continued ...

International Classification of Diseases	Sex	1955–56	1971–72	1981–82	1991–92
Congenital malformations	male	2.4	3.3	3.2	5.4
	female	1.7	2.4	2.1	5.5
	persons	2.0	2.9	2.6	5.3
Certain conditions originating in	male	2.8	0.1	0.4	1.2
the perinatal period	female	2.3	0.2	0.2	1.3
	persons	2.6	0.1	0.3	1.3
Symptoms and ill–defined conditions	male	82.9	110.4	134.4	121.8
	female	105.3	138.2	182.4	179.1
	persons	94.8	124.9	159.5	151.0
Accidents	male	35.1	102.0	117.1	135.6
	female	69.7	81.2	110.2	142.3
	persons	53.4	91.1	113.5	139.0
Supplementary Classification	male	35.1	88.1	121.1	230.1
includes preventive medicine, family planning,	female	69.7	178.6	272.6	435.3
admin. procedures & misc. social and familial	persons	53.4	135.3	200.3	334.8
problems					

Sources: GRO (1958); Royal College of General Practitioners, OPCS and DoH (1974; 1986); McCormick et al. (1995).

They also observe dramatic increases in the numbers of individuals consulting doctors for asthma in the two time-periods, an increase of 114 per cent in men and 165 per cent in women. However, here too it is difficult to disentangle real changes in the incidence of the disease from improved detection rates arising from increased attention to the disease.

The one other major source of data on morbidity with comparable observations at different time-periods is the General Household Survey. This survey

Table 3.7 Trends in self–reported longstanding illness by age, Great Britain, 1972–95

Both sexes

age group	1972	1975	1979	1981	1983	1985	1989	1991	1993	1994	1995
0–4	4	7	7	10	10	10	12	12	13	13	13
5–15	8	10	12	15	15	16	18	16	19	20	19
16–44	13	16	20	21	23	22	24	23	26	24	23
45–64	30	34	38	41	44	43	43	41	45	42	41
65–74	48	52	51	55	61	56	58	58	60	56	55
75 and over	62	62	61	67	69	63	66	65	67	63	63
all ages	21	24	27	29	32	30	32	31	34	32	31

Source: ONS (1997b).

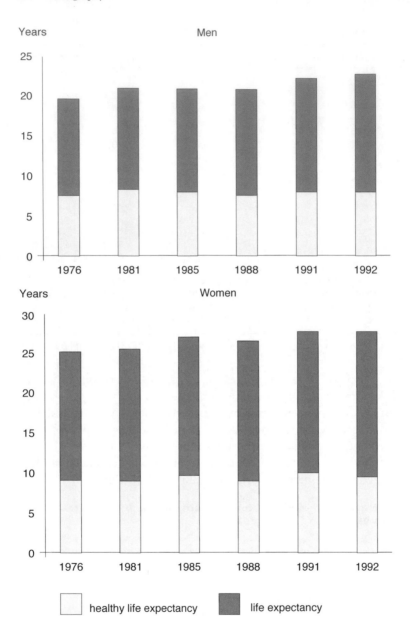

Figure 3.3 Life expectancy and healthy life expectancy at age 65, England and Wales, 1976–92

Source: Bone et al. (1996).

has, for most years since the early 1970s, asked a representative sample of adults in Britain several questions about acute and longstanding illness (Table 3.7). The survey shows no evidence of any improvement in morbidity over the period 1977–93, and indeed provides some evidence for poorer self-reported health in later surveys. However, whilst not vulnerable to the problems of sampling bias of General Practice statistics, it is not possible to determine the extent to which changes in self-reported health in the GHS reflect changing levels of expectations or tolerance levels rather than underlying morbidity.

The extra years of survival observed in the latter part of this century may not actually be associated with extra years of good health; for example, if more individuals survive health problems such as strokes and heart disease but live their remaining years with disability. This possibility has substantial consequences for planning health and social services as considerable extra demands result. To estimate the scale of such a possible trend, the concept of 'healthy life expectancy' has been developed, and calculations have been made of trends in life expectancy free of substantial health problems (Dunnell, 1997). Such estimates suggest that whilst, over the period 1976–92, gains were observed in overall life expectancy, they were not matched by gains in healthy life expectancy (Figure 3.3).

The assessment of the prevalence of mental health problems in the population is particularly problematic because of considerable problems of definition and measurement. However, a recent major government-sponsored survey was conducted to provide a benchmark estimate of the prevalence and nature of mental illness in Britain (Meltzer et al., 1995). It found 18 per cent of women and 12 per cent of men reporting significant neurotic symptoms such as fatigue, sleep problems and irritability. The higher rates for women than men exist at all ages, except that for 20–24-year-olds where the greater prevalence of mental illness amongst young men is partly accounted for by higher levels of drug and alcohol dependence. Evidence from trends in General Practice consultation rates have appeared to indicate an increase in major psychiatric illness. However, such evidence is very difficult to interpret and may be due instead to the continued policy of managing mental illness in the community rather than in hospital, that has prevailed for most of the last 40 years (discussed in Chapter 15).

Social patterning of health

In the nineteenth century statistical evidence was accumulating that mortality was unequally distributed. Farr used registration data to show that, for the 1880s, if mortality for all males was taken as 1000, then whilst male clergy and schoolmasters experienced death rates of 556 and 719 respectively, barmen and general labourers had death rates of 2205 and 2020 (Leete and Fox, 1977). Surveys by Charles Booth in London and Seebohm Rowntree later in the

century further confirmed the importance of social differences in mortality
(Rowntree, 1901; Oddy, 1970).

The first systematic attempt to analyse social patterns of mortality was
undertaken in 1911 by Dr Stevenson, the Registrar-General, responsible for
government registration of vital events – births, marriages and deaths. He
devised a classification of occupations that grouped together into five social
classes relatively homogeneous occupations according to the degree of skill
and social position involved. With this classification he was able to show that
in 1911 the infant mortality rate for children born to families in Social Class I,
upper and middle occupations, was 76, compared to 113 in Social Class III,
skilled occupations, and 153 in Social Class V, unskilled manual occupations.
In the same way, adult male deaths rose from Social Class I, through Social
Class III to Social Class V, with standardized mortality ratios of 88, 96 and 142
respectively. The Registrar-General's Classification of Occupations has regularly been criticized for its rather broad and unsophisticated distinctions
between occupation. It has undergone several modifications of format, not
least because of major changes in the nature of the British economy, patterns
of work skill and status (see Chapters 7 and 8). For example, clerks were classified as being in Social Class I in 1911, but by 1931 were classified as in Social
Class III, reflecting declines in skill and status. Despite such changes, the
scheme has provided a powerful window on to the social patterning of
mortality through most of the last 90 years.

**Table 3.8 Mortality by social class: standardized mortality ratios for men
aged 20–64 from all causes, England and Wales, 1910–12 to 1991–93**

Registrar-General's social classes	1910–12	1921–23	1930–32	1949–53	1959–63	1970–72	1979–83	1991–93
I	88	82	90	86	76	77	66	66
II	94	94	86	92	81	81	76	72
III (NM)[a]	96	95	101	101	100	99	94	100
III (M)[b]						106	106	117
IV	93	101	104	104	103	114	116	116
V	142	125	118	118	143	137	165	189

Sources: McPherson and Coleman (1988); Drever and Bunting (1997).

Notes: [a]NM = non-manual.
    [b]M = manual.

It has already been shown that mortality rates improved markedly in the twentieth century. However, it is apparent that inequalities in mortality between
males of different social classes have persisted throughout this period. Indeed,
it also appears that after the period 1949–53 the degree of inequality of experience between Social Class I and Social Class V became greater (Table 3.8). In

other words, for most of the second half of the century improvements in mortality were greater for individuals in Social Classes I and II than for individuals in Social Classes IV and V.

The resulting inequalities in life expectancy have existed for virtually all age-groups from infancy to old age. The poorer mortality rates of lower social

Table 3.9 Mortality rate ratios (RR) by social class, major causes of death, men and women aged 35–64, England and Wales

Cause of death Social class	Women			Men		
	1976–81	1981–85	1986–92	1976–81	1981–85	1986–92
Ischaemic heart disease						
I/II	0.45[a]	0.67[a]	0.50[a]	0.80[a]	0.69[a]	0.69[a]
III (NM)	0.66[a]	0.84[a]	0.66[a]	1.24[a]	0.99	0.70[a]
III (M)	1.00	1.00	1.00	1.00	1.00	1.00
IV/V	1.23[a]	1.13[a]	1.33[a]	1.18[a]	1.09[a]	1.15[a]
Manual v. non–manual	2.21[a]	1.49[a]	2.21[a]	1.18[a]	1.34[a]	1.59[a]
Cerebrovascular disease						
I/II	0.72[a]	0.61[a]	0.76[a]	1.10[a]	0.62[a]	0.88[a]
III (NM)	1.00	0.93[a]	1.22[a]	0.92[a]	1.03[a]	0.84[a]
III (M)	1.00	1.00	1.00	1.00	1.00	1.00
IV/V	1.19[a]	1.30[a]	1.89[a]	1.32[a]	1.31[a]	1.23[a]
Manual v. non–manual	1.39[a]	1.68[a]	1.88[a]	1.17[a]	1.59[a]	1.33[a]
Respiratory disease						
I/II	0.47[a]	0.49[a]	0.47[a]	0.30[a]	0.63[a]	0.35[a]
III (NM)	0.52[a]	0.43[a]	0.50[a]	1.28[a]	1.04[a]	0.57[a]
III (M)	1.00	1.00	1.00	1.00	1.00	1.00
IV/V	1.00	1.27[a]	1.23[a]	1.38[a]	1.57[a]	1.33[a]
Manual v. non–manual	2.03[a]	2.51[a]	2.41[a]	2.00[a]	1.80[a]	2.89[a]
Lung cancer						
I/II	0.84[a]	0.68[a]	0.47[a]	0.57[a]	0.58[a]	0.45[a]
III (NM)	0.96[a]	0.30[a]	0.50[a]	0.76[a]	0.93[a]	0.64[a]
III (M)	1.00	1.00	1.00	1.00	1.00	1.00
IV/V	1.82[a]	1.06[a]	1.35[a]	1.24[a]	1.13[a]	1.04[a]
Manual v. non–manual	1.75[a]	1.06[a]	2.60[a]	1.82[a]	1.55[a]	1.99[a]
Breast cancer						
I/II	0.85[a]	1.30[a]	1.14[a]			
III (NM)	1.23[a]	1.24[a]	1.06[a]			
III (M)	1.00	1.00	1.00			
IV/V	0.78[a]	0.88[a]	1.17[a]			
Manual v. non–manual	0.87[a]	0.72[a]	1.00			

Note: [a]Rate ratio differs significantly from 1.00.

Source: Hattersley (1997).

1974

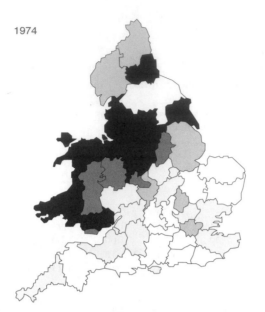

SMR in 1974

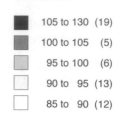

105 to 130 (19)
100 to 105   (5)
95 to 100   (6)
90 to 95 (13)
85 to 90 (12)

1995

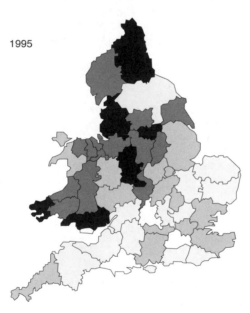

SMR in 1995

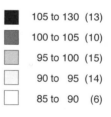

105 to 130 (13)
100 to 105 (10)
95 to 100 (15)
90 to 95 (14)
85 to 90   (6)

Figure 3.4 Regional differences in standardized mortality ratios (all causes of death), England and Wales, 1974 and 1995

Sources: OPCS (1976); ONS (1998).

classes have also been observed for most causes of death (Table 3.9). An exception was a period in the 1930s in which higher rates of heart disease prevailed in Social Class I. This poorer mortality rate continued until the 1950s and may partly be why heart disease is sometimes referred to as a 'disease of affluence'. However, from the 1960s the pattern of poorer heart disease mortality in Social Classes IV and V was established and persisted until the end of the century. In most recent years the poorer death rates in the lower social classes have been clear for all major causes of death except that for a period in the 1970s and early 1980s women from Social Classes I and II experienced significantly more breast cancer mortality. As has already been argued, measurement of morbidity is more problematic. However, evidence from surveys of self-reported morbidity have consistently shown poorer health being reported by lower Social Classes.

It is widely accepted that Social Class is a rather blunt measure and a number of other aspects of social position have been examined in relation to health. Powerful evidence has particularly accumulated from cohort studies where the time order of social position and onset of health problems can be measured to evaluate the possibility that poorer health results in poorer position rather than the reverse. Thus a study of Whitehall civil servants using a more precise measure of occupational grade found steeper gradients of health inequality than other studies, with three times higher rates of mortality in lowest occupational grades when followed up over time (Marmot et al., 1984).

Similarly, unemployment has been found to be an important risk factor for ill-health. A nationally representative sample of men unemployed in 1971 were found to have excess mortality rates (SMR 121) when monitored over the following ten years even after other social disadvantages were taken into account. A similar pattern of excess mortality was found when a group of unemployed men identified in 1981 was tracked (Moser, 1987).

The health of ethnic groups who migrated to Britain has not been well monitored and patterns are hard to summarize. Amongst clearly identified problems have been the elevated rates of hypertension and strokes of individuals of African and Caribbean origin, and higher mortality rates amongst babies of mothers from Pakistan (Whitehead, 1988).

In addition to social inequalities, there have been major and persistent differences in mortality by region (Figure 3.4). Roughly, this may be termed a 'north–south divide'. In 1970 the standardized mortality ratio of the North Yorkshire and Humberside region, after adjusting for its age and social class composition, was 113 compared with 90 for the south-east of England. These patterns have persisted into the 1990s. However, it is increasingly clear that even within local areas, whether of the north or south of England, extremes of health have been associated with levels of affluence (Townsend et al., 1988).

Use and availability of health services

At the beginning of the twentieth century, a minority with higher incomes could afford private fees for health care. Individuals otherwise hoped to obtain their health care by contributing to voluntary insurance schemes, such as those provided by the Friendly Societies and trade unions. The poor received minimal charitable care. In 1911 a National Health Insurance scheme was introduced whereby those working men below a certain income threshold received free access to GP services. The scheme excluded their dependants and did not extend free access to include hospital services. By 1939 40 per cent of employed males were covered by the scheme.

Thus access to primary care was uneven and access to hospital care limited by ability to pay or charitable care. The hospital service itself was fragmented and

Table 3.10 Health service personnel workforce: rates of staff per 1000 population, England and Wales, 1949–94

Year	Hospital: medical and dental	Nursing and midwifery	General Medical Practioners
1949	0.27	3.35	–
1959	0.36	4.46	0.50
1969	0.47	5.72	0.44
1979	0.79	7.74	0.50
1989	0.96	8.55	0.58
1996	1.15	6.82	0.59

Sources: DHSS (1972; 1982); Welsh Office (1980; 1990; 1997).

Table 3.11 Hospitals: beds and patient activity per 1000 population, 1949–94

	1949[a]	1959[a]	1969[a]	1979[b]	1989[b]	1994[b]
In-patients Average daily available beds	10.3	10.6	9.4	7.8	5.7	4.3
Out-patients attendances New patients	140	159	165	165.2	178	213
Accident and emergency New cases	89	121	165	197	234	245

Notes: [a]England and Wales.
　　　[b]England.

Sources: DHSS (1972; 1982); DoH (1996).

dramatically underfunded. In 1948 the National Health Service (NHS) was established, essentially making both primary and hospital care free at the point of use and supported by tax revenues to central government. Thus the first half of the century transformed levels of basic access. The second half of the century has seen the increasing use of an expanding public health care system by the British people. This increased availability of services is reflected in a significant increase in the numbers of GPs per capita in Britain, but a much larger increase in hospital medical and nursing staff, reflecting the dominant importance of hospital medicine since 1948 (Table 3.10). In the later decades of the century, use of private health insurance re-emerged as a significant source of health care – largely as a benefit of certain forms of employment – and has come to play a significant role especially in areas such as non-emergency surgery (for example, hip and knee replacement surgery) in the south of England.

Table 3.12 Percentage of patients consulting a GP by sex, England and Wales, 1955–56 to 1991–92

Sex	1955–56	1970–71	1981–82	1991–92
Persons	67	66	71	78
Male	63	62	65	70
Female	70	70	77	86

Sources: GRO (1958); Royal College of General Practitioners, OPCS and DoH (1974; 1986); McCormick et al. (1995).

There are few reliable figures regarding use of health care facilities prior to the NHS. However, the increased use of services, especially hospital out-patient and accident and emergency facilities, since the establishment of the NHS is clear (Table 3.11). The numbers of hospital beds declined because of shorter lengths of hospital stay for in-patients, increased substitution of alternatives to hospital admission and increased efficiencies in hospitals. In the period 1955–56, 67 per cent of individuals had consulted a GP in the course of a year. By 1991, 78 per cent of individuals consulted a GP in the course of a year (Table 3.12). If the evidence of General Practice consultation rates is examined in more detail it is clear that consulting rates have increased for almost every category of disease.

Explanations for health trends

Explanations for the dramatic changes in health that have been observed for Britain in the twentieth century are largely to be found in a range of social and economic changes that, as has already been mentioned, had begun in the previous century. For the first time in human history medical science also began to make a positive contribution to health, although, as is discussed below, the relative importance of this contribution compared to social factors is still in dispute.

Nutrition and standard of living

Despite improving living standards through much of the latter part of the nineteenth century, Charles Booth found that living standards for 32 per cent of the population at the beginning of the twentieth century were below his criterion for poverty (Oddy, 1970). Rowntree similarly defined 28 per cent of the population in York (Rowntree, 1901). Central to both studies was evidence of insufficient calorie intake to provide energy for activity and insufficient protein for general nutritional status. Almost certainly the single most important contribution to health in the first half of the twentieth century was the steady improvement in the diet of the population as a whole. Orr (1936) estimated that whereas in the period 1903–13 annual per capita consumption of fruit was 61 lb, by 1934 this had become 115 lb. Similarly, he estimated that annual consumption of vegetables other than potatoes rose from 60 lb to 98 lb over this period. Thus rising real incomes contributed to improved diet which in turn raised resistance to a wide range of serious infectious diseases as well as enhancing general health status.

Whilst private living standards steadily improved health status in the first half of the century, public interventions to improve diet also began to be important. Partly arising from evidence of the poor physical and nutritional status of recruits to the army – for example, 38 per cent of volunteers for the Boer War were deemed physically unfit – the need for state intervention was accepted. In 1906, legislation permitted schools to provide school meals and

Table 3.13 Consumption of foods per person per week: 1950–94, Great Britain, grams

Year	Fresh fruit	Fresh veg.	Sugar	Meat & meat products	Total fats	Butter	Lard
1950	408.6	824.8	287.2	846.3	329.2	129.3	55.6
1960	522.0	857.1	503.5	1017.6	339.4	161.0	58.4
1970	542.7	766.1	480.3	1120.8	338.8	169.8	62.7
1980	590.0	801.0	316.7	1139.5	318.1	114.8	51.3
1990	604.8	736.6	171.3	967.1	255.2	45.6	22.7
1991	610.4	719.9	166.7	962.0	248.4	43.7	25.2
1992	618.1	724.4	156.2	950.4	245.5	40.8	25.0
1993	616.7	717.0	151.1	955.8	229.9	40.0	22.4
1994	645.0	–	187.0	943.0	226.0	39.0	15.0

Source: Charlton and Quaife (1997).

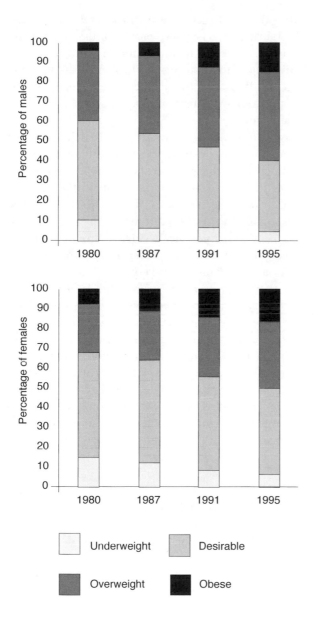

Figure 3.5 Trends in distribution of BMI in males and females: British population aged 16–64

Note: BMI is calculated as weight (kg)/height (m)^2.

Sources: Knight (1984); Gregory et al. (1990); Bennett et al. (1995); Prescott-Clarke and Primatesta (1997).

in the 1930s, a scheme to provide milk at school was introduced (see Chapter 15). At the same time, health departments began to provide milk, vitamin and iron supplements at reduced cost or free to families suffering proven malnutrition. In many respects, rationing of food during World War II paradoxically may have improved overall nutritional status, as steps were taken by the government to increase the nutritional content of foodstuffs and to increase equity in access to an adequate diet.

However, the very trends in nutritional status that had such beneficial effects on general fitness and resistance to infection increasingly had some adverse effects. Diet is an important contributory factor in cardiovascular disease, particularly because of the role of high saturated fats in the development of atheroma, the narrowing of arteries. Around the 1930s the consumption of such fats, especially in the form of butter and lard, began to increase markedly (Table 3.13). As epidemiological evidence linking saturated fats to atheroma became more widely known, food consumption patterns changed again in the 1970s. This rise and fall of fats very closely coincides with the epidemic of heart disease that occurred in the twentieth century.

In the latter part of the century concern has resurfaced about poor nutritional status. In part this concern focuses upon growing inequalities in health, of which diet is a contributory cause. In part there is concern about over-consumption of food, combined with inappropriate consumption of 'fast' and 'convenience' foods. These trends have combined with decreasing levels of physical activity in many sections of the population to produce a clear increase in obesity (usually measured by body mass index, a ratio of weight to height) in the course of the 1980s and 1990s (Figure 3.5). Obesity is an epidemiological risk factor in a wide range of diseases from heart disease and diabetes through to osteoarthritis.

Smoking

The role of smoking in ill-health is well established and very extensive. Doll and his colleagues (1997) use the most reliable epidemiological evidence available to demonstrate that it is a direct cause of lung cancer and deaths from chronic obstructive lung disease, but also has some causal connection with a wide range of other cancers and cardiovascular disease. Smoking may therefore be considered one of the most malignant influences on health in Britain in this century, for, whilst the behaviour was established in the nineteenth century, its rapid spread throughout the population happened in the twentieth century.

Tobacco smoking before the twentieth century usually occurred via pipes; in the twentieth century cigarettes were the main form of consumption. At the beginning of the century adult males consumed 0.5 kg of tobacco per annum

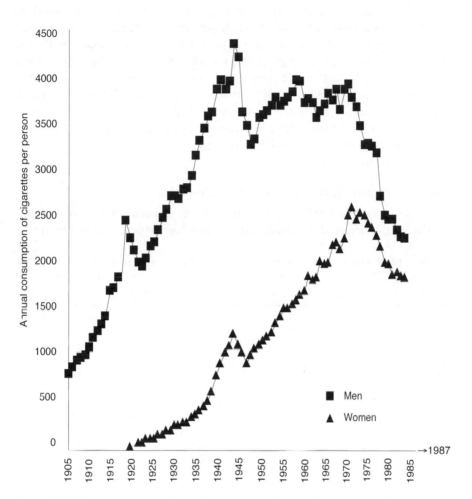

Figure 3.6 UK anual consumption of manufactured cigarettes per person by sex, 1905–87

Source: Wald and Nicolaides-Bouman (1991).

on average, via cigarettes. By the 1940s this rose dramatically to 4.1 kg (Figure 3.6). The widespread consumption of tobacco by women, almost exclusively via cigarettes, did not begin until the 1920s. By the late 1970s this had become on average 1.9 kg per annum. From that period consumption declined amongst women to reach 1.6 kg per annum by the late 1980s. An important change was the reduction in the average tar yield per cigarette which occurred through a change in consumer preferences and voluntary action by the tobacco industry in the 1960s.

Dissemination of knowledge regarding the ill-health effects of smoking resulted in tobacco consumption levels beginning to fall in men at some point in the late 1960s, and in women a few years later. The most marked effect of reductions in rates of smoking and the reduced tar yield was in the incidence of lung cancer. From its height, lung cancer declined in the last 30 years by 60 per cent in men aged 40–49 and by half in men aged 50–69, with a slightly lower proportional reduction in women (Doll et al., 1997). Similar improvements were observed from the 1960s onwards in deaths from bronchitis. The exact role of reduced smoking in the declining rates of heart disease is less clear but undoubtedly causally implicated.

Social patterning: the search for explanations

This chapter has outlined the social inequalities in health that have persisted and arguably increased in Britain. There have been several major attempts to

Table 3.14 Prevalence of cigarette smoking by sex and social class, 1974–94

Social class	Percentage smoking cigarettes				
Men	1974	1976	1978	1980	1982
I	29	25	25	21	20
II	46	38	37	35	29
III (NM)	45	40	38	35	30
III (M)	56	51	51	48	42
IV	56	43	53	49	47
V	61	58	60	57	49
Total non–manual	45	37	36	33	28
Total manual	56	52	51	49	44
Ratio of manual to non-manual	1.24	1.41	1.42	1.48	1.57
Ratio of social class V to I	2.10	2.32	2.40	2.71	2.45
Women	1974	1976	1978	1980	1982
I	25	28	23	21	21
II	38	35	33	33	29
III (NM)	38	36	33	34	30
III (M)	46	42	42	43	39
IV	43	41	41	39	36
V	43	38	41	41	41
Total non–manual	38	35	32	32	29
Total manual	45	41	41	41	38
Ratio of manual to non-manual	1.18	1.17	1.28	1.28	1.31
Ratio of social class V to I	1.72	1.36	1.78	1.95	1.95

Source: OPCS (1996).

find explanations and policies to reduce inequalities. In 1980 the Department of Health's Working Group on Inequalities in Health produced the most comprehensive assessment of evidence. It considered four possible classes of explanations. The first possibility was that inequalities were an artefact of health statistics. For example, it is possible that under-representation of Social Classes IV and V in the census would have the effect of exaggerating their death rates, as census data is the denominator in much of the evidence on inequalities. The likelihood of artefacts across a wide range of evidence was considered remote in the view of the Working Group. Moreover, cohort studies, showing clear social inequalities, were free of such problems of estimating the denominator.

The second explanation considered was 'social selection'; essentially, that poorer health resulted in downward occupational and social mobility. Whilst there is clear evidence of such patterns in the case of schizophrenia, the nature

1984	1986	1988	1990	1992	1994
17	18	16	16	14	16
29	28	26	24	23	20
30	28	25	25	25	24
40	40	39	36	34	33
45	43	40	39	39	38
49	43	43	48	42	40
28	26	24	23	22	21
43	40	40	38	36	35
1.54	1.54	1.67	1.65	1.64	1.67
2.88	2.39	2.69	3.00	3.00	2.50

1984	1986	1988	1990	1992	1994
15	19	17	16	13	12
29	27	26	23	21	20
28	27	27	27	27	23
37	36	35	32	31	29
37	35	37	36	35	32
36	33	39	36	35	34
27	26	25	25	23	21
37	36	36	34	33	31
1.37	1.38	1.44	1.36	1.43	1.48
2.40	1.74	2.29	2.25	2.69	2.83

and early age of onset of this disease make it atypical and overall social selection was not considered important.

More evidence could be found for what the Working Group considered 'cultural/behavioural' explanations. The role of smoking in health has already been documented. Rates of smoking have been consistently higher in the lower social classes in the second half of the twentieth century (Table 3.14). Similarly, the Group found evidence of lower rates of uptake of preventive health services such as immunization and antenatal care. However, it regarded the most important explanations to be 'materialist or structuralist ... emphasising the role of economic and associated socio-structural factors' (Townsend et al., 1988, p.106). In particular, it stressed the evidence of direct consequences of low income. Hence many of its policy recommendations were targeted at child poverty. However, none of its recommendations were implemented because of a change from a Labour to a Conservative government at the time the report was published.

At the end of the century a Labour government again set up an expert review on inequalities in health (Acheson, 1998). The report assembled substantial evidence demonstrating that health inequalities had widened in recent years. The conclusions and policy recommendations of the report were very similar to those of the Working Group. The report concluded that, in order to reduce health inequalities, priority should be given to the health of women of child-bearing age, expectant mothers and young children, and that further steps should be taken to reduce income inequalities and improve the living standards of poor households. It went further than the policies of the Working Group 18 years previously by arguing that all policies likely to have a direct or indirect effect on health should be evaluated in terms of

Table 3.15 Per capita expenditure on health care in selected countries and various mortality rates (1991–92)

Country	Per capita expenditure on health care (US$)	Life expectancy, males	Life expectancy, females	Infant mortality (deaths per 1000 live births)
US	3094	72.0	78.9	8.9
Canada	1949	73.8	80.4	6.8
Germany	1775	72.9	79.3	6.7
France	1745	73.0	81.1	7.8
Holland	1449	74.1	80.2	6.5
Sweden	1317	74.9	80.5	6.1
Denmark	1163	72.2	77.7	7.3
UK	1151	73.2	78.8	8.9

Source: Adapted from Fitzpatrick (1997).

their impact on health inequalities, and all such policies should be formulated to favour the less well-off and so contribute to reducing health inequalities. However, whilst radical in tone, this expression of a form of positive discrimination may prove too general in terms substantially to alter health policies.

The role of medicine

The most challenging question of all is to estimate the contribution of health services to the improvements in health documented in this chapter. One of the defining developments of the twentieth century has been the growth of scientific medicine. Yet for many of the improvements in health that have occurred in this century it is hard to demonstrate a central role for medicine. Thus McKeown (1979) provided evidence that most of the decline in mortality rates in the nineteenth and twentieth centuries occurred before the treatment of TB with streptomycin, from 1947, and shortly afterwards, BCG (bacillus of Calmette and Guerin) vaccinations. He attributes almost all improvements to the benefits of improved diet and consequent increased host resistance. He argues similarly against the importance of medical interventions in such diverse infectious diseases as pneumonia, whooping cough and measles.

The evidence of such analyses is often combined with comparative evidence from diverse Western industrial societies invariably showing no association between levels of per capita expenditure on health services and health status (Table 3.15). Cochrane (1971) wrote a highly influential critique of the NHS arguing that too few of the practices and interventions commonly provided by it have ever been shown to be effective by the most rigorous of methods. Against this general climate of therapeutic scepticism it is important to present some postulated successes of health services.

Undoubtedly the most spectacular medical contribution in the century has been the discovery and widescale use of antibiotics from World War II onwards. Despite the prior impact on infectious disease mortality from improvements in diet and hygiene, antibiotics have further improved death rates for many infections. In addition, immunization programmes have been successful in relation to diphtheria, poliomyelitis, tetanus and, more recently, measles, mumps and rubella begun in 1988.

Amongst non-infectious diseases, the introduction of insulin must be an important factor in the reduction of mortality from diabetes, especially after World War II when other general improvements occurred in the management of diabetes, such as more effective control of infections. More recently, drug treatments for hypertension have been developed that are considered effective in reducing cardiovascular and stroke mortality. Greater efforts have also been made in the last 20 years to detect high blood pressure in primary care. Developments in radiotherapy and chemotherapy have improved the outcomes of treatment and survival rates of certain cancers, such as cancer of the testis and Hodgkin's disease. Chemotherapy and bone marrow transplantation have increased survival rates for leukaemia at younger ages.

One of the most important developments in the field of surgery has been joint replacement to treat the severest forms of osteoarthritis and related conditions. Thus hip replacement surgery is successful in removing pain and disability for the vast majority of recipients, such that ten years later only 10 per cent require further surgery. In Britain, 50 000 patients a year benefit from this surgery. Knee replacement surgery is just as successful and rates of this form of surgery are catching up with those of hip surgery.

Conclusion

The last example of an outstanding achievement in twentieth-century medicine in the form of joint replacement surgery also raises a fundamental issue about how we evaluate the contribution of health services to health care. As was emphasized at the beginning of the chapter, we are almost entirely dependent on mortality data to inform our judgements about major trends in health in the last 100 years. By that criterion, joint replacement surgery would not have received a mention because it has no significant consequences for mortality. Instead, it has, for the last 30 years, transformed the lives of tens of thousands. We must, at the end of the century, judge the role of medicine against the criterion of what is increasingly referred to as 'health-related quality of life' as well as mortality. The majority of interventions, whether involving drugs, surgery or simply professional health care and support are primarily intended to benefit this much broader sense of health.

We therefore end where we began, with the WHO's expanded sense of health. The achievements of the twentieth century documented in this chapter have made it possible for us now to raise our expectations of health to encompass health-related quality of life; that is, our well-being in physical, psychological and social terms.

References

Acheson, D. (1998) *Independent Inquiry into Inequalities in Health*, The Stationery Office, London.

Adler, M., Phillips, A. and Johnson, A. (1997) 'Communicable diseases: sexually transmitted diseases, including AIDS', in Charlton, J. and Murphy, M. (eds) *The Health of Adult Britain 1841–1994*, vol. 2, The Stationery Office, London, pp.21–9.

Bennett, N., Dodd, T., Flatley, J., Freeth, S. and Bolling, K. (eds) (1995) *Health Survey for England 1993*, HMSO, London.

Bloom, B. and Murray, C. (1992) 'Tuberculosis: commentary on a resurgent killer', *Science*, 257, pp.1055–64.

Bone, M., Bebbington, A., Jagger, C., Morgan, K. and Nicholaas, G. (1996) *Health Expectancy and Its Uses*, HMSO, London.

Charlton, J. (1997) 'Trends in all-cause mortality: 1841–1994', in Charlton, J. and Murphy, M. (eds) *The Health of Adult Britain 1841–1994*, vol. 1, The Stationery Office, London, pp.17–29.

Charlton, J. and Murphy, M (1997) 'Trends in causes of mortality: 1841–1994 – an overview', in Charlton, J. and Murphy, M. (eds) *The Health of Adult Britain 1841–1994*, vol.1 , The Stationery Office, London, pp.30–57.

Charlton, J., Murphy, M., Khaw, K., Ebrahim, S. and Smith, G. D. (1997) 'Cardiovascular diseases', in Charlton, J. and Murphy, M. (eds) *The Health of Adult Britain 1841–1994*, vol. 2, The Stationery Office, London, pp.60–81.

Charlton, J. and Quaife, K. (1997) 'Trends in diet 1841–1993', in Charlton, J. and Murphy, M. (eds) *The Health of Adult Britain 1841–1994*, vol.1 pp.93–113, The Stationery Office, London.

Cochrane, A. (1971) *Effectiveness and Efficiency*, Nuffield Provincial Hospitals Trust, London.

Department of Health (DoH) (1996) *Health and Personal Social Services Statistics for England 1996*, The Stationery Office, London.

Department of Health (1998) *Health and Personal Social Services Statistics for England 1998*, The Stationery Office, London.

Department of Health and Social Security (DHSS) (1972) *Health and Personal Social Services Statistics for England and Wales 1972*, HMSO, London.

Department of Health and Social Security (1982) *Health and Personal Social Services Statistics for England 1982*, HMSO, London.

Doll, R., Darby, S. and Whitley, E. (1997) 'Trends in mortality from smoking-related diseases', in Charlton, J. and Murphy, M. (eds) *The Health of Adult Britain 1841–1994*, vol. 1, The Stationery Office, London, pp.128–55.

Drever, F. and Bunting, J. (1997) 'Patterns and trends in male mortality', in Drever, F. and Whitehead, M. (eds) *Health Inequalities*, The Stationery Office, London, pp.95–107.

Dunnell, K. (1997) 'Are we healthier?', in Charlton, J. and Murphy, M. (eds) *The Health of Adult Britain 1841–1994*, vol. 2, The Stationery Office, London, pp.173–81.

Fitzpatrick, R. (1997) 'Organizing and funding health care', in Scambler, G. (ed.) *Sociology as Applied to Medicine,* 4th edition, W. B. Saunders, London, pp.271–86.

Fraser, P., Fleming, D., Murphy, M., Charlton, J., Gill, L. and Goldacre, M. (1997) 'Morbidity statistics from health service utilisation', in Charlton, J. and Murphy, M. (eds) *The Health of Adult Britain 1841–1994*, vol. 1, The Stationery Office, London, pp.58–73.

Galbraith, S. and McCormick, A. (1997) 'Infection in England and Wales, 1838–1993', in Charlton, J. and Murphy, M. (eds) *The Health of Adult Britain 1841–1994*, vol. 2, The Stationery Office, London, pp.1–20.

General Register Office (GRO) (1958) *Morbidity Statistics from General Practice, 1955–56*, HMSO, London.

Gregory, J., Foster, K., Tyler, H. and Wiseman, M. (1990) *The Dietary and Nutritional Survey of British Adults*, HMSO, London.

Grundy, E. (1997) 'The health and health care of older adults in England and Wales, 1841–1994', in Charlton, J. and Murphy, M. (eds) *The Health of Adult Britain 1841–1994*, vol. 2, The Stationery Office, London, pp.182–203.

Hattersley, L. (1997) 'Expectation of life by social class', in Drever, F. and Whitehead, M. (eds) *Health Inequalities*, The Stationery Office, London, pp.73–82.

Knight, I. (1984) *The Heights and Weights of Adults in Great Britain*, HMSO, London.

Leete, R. and Fox, J. (1977) 'Registrar-General's classes: origins and uses', *Population Trends*, 8, pp.1–7.

McCormick, A., Fleming, D. and Charlton, J. (1995) *Morbidity Statistics from General Practice: Fourth National Study, 1991–92*, HMSO, London.

McKeown, T. (1979) *The Role of Medicine*, Blackwell, Oxford.

McPherson, K. and Coleman, D. (1988) 'Health', in Halsey, A. H. (ed.) *British Social Trends since 1900*, Macmillan, Basingstoke, pp.398–461.

Marmot, M., Shipley, M. and Rose, G. (1984) 'Inequalities in death – specific explanations of a general pattern?', *Lancet*, 2, pp.1003–6.

Meltzer, H., Gill, B., Petticrew, M. and Hinds, K. (1995) *OPCS Surveys of Psychiatric Morbidity in Great Britain, Report 1: The Prevalence of Psychiatric Morbidity Among Adults Living in Private Households*, HMSO, London.

Moser, K. (1987) 'Unemployment and mortality: a comparison of the 1971 and 1981 longitudinal study census samples', *British Medical Journal*, 294, pp.86–90.

Oddy, D. (1970) 'Working-Class Diets in Nineteenth-Century Britain', *Economic History Review*, 23, pp.314–22.

Office for National Statistics (ONS) (1997a) *Mortality Statistics, General, England and Wales, 1993, 1994 and 1995*, The Stationery Office, London.

Office for National Statistics (1997b) *Living in Britain: Results from the 1995 General Household Survey*, The Stationery Office, London.

Office for National Statistics (1998) *Key Population and Vital Statistics: Local and Health Authority Areas 1995*, The Stationery Office, London.

Office of Population Censuses and Surveys (OPCS) (1976) *Local Authority Vital Statistics*, HMSO, London.

Office of Population Censuses and Surveys (1992) *Mortality Statistics, Serial Tables 1841–1990*, HMSO, London.

Office of Population Censuses and Surveys (1996) *Living in Britain: Results from the 1994 General Household Survey*, HMSO, London.

Omran, A. (1971) 'The epidemiological transition: a theory of the epidemiology of population change'. *Milbank Memorial Fund Quarterly*, 49, pp.509–38.

Orr, J. (1936) *Food, Health and Income*, Macmillan, London.

Prescott-Clarke, P. and Primatesta, P. (eds) (1997) *Health Survey for England 1995*, The Stationery Office, London.

Registrar-General for Scotland (1997) *Annual Report 1996*, General Register Office for Scotland, Edinburgh.

Registrar-General for Northern Ireland (1996) *Annual Report 1995*, The Stationery Office, Belfast.

Rowntree, B. S. (1901) *Poverty: A Study of Town Life*, Macmillan, London.

Royal College of General Practitioners, Office of Population Censuses and Surveys and Department of Health (1974) *Morbidity Statistics from General Practice: Second National Study, 1970–71*, HMSO, London.

Royal College of General Practitioners, Office of Population Censuses and Surveys and Department of Health (1986) *Morbidity Statistics from General Practice: Third National Study, 1981–82*, HMSO, London.

Townsend, P., Davidson, N. and Whitehead, M. (1988) *Inequalities in Health*, Penguin, Harmondsworth.

Wald, N. and Nicolaides-Bouman, A. (1991) *UK Smoking Statistics*, Oxford University Press, Oxford.

Welsh Office (1980) *Health and Personal Social Service Statistics for Wales*, HMSO, Cardiff.

Welsh Office (1990) *Health and Personal Social Service Statistics for Wales*, Mid Wales Litho Ltd, New Inn, Pontypool.

Welsh Office (1997) *Health Statistics Wales 1997*, Mid Wales Litho Ltd, New Inn, Pontypool.

Whitehead, M. (1988) *The Health Divide*, Penguin, Harmondsworth.

Wilmoth, J. and Lundstrom, H. (1996) 'Extreme longevity in five countries', *European Journal of Population*, 12, pp.63–93.

Further reading

Charlton, J. and Murphy, M. (eds) (1997) *The Health of Adult Britain 1841–1984*, volumes 1 and 2, The Stationery Office, London.

4

Immigration and Ethnicity

Ceri Peach, Alisdair Rogers, Judith Chance and Patricia Daley

> Their sorrows must be our sorrows. In the most scrupulous regard ... for the Muslim sentiment as to their places of worship ... I write this [as a Hindu], because I love the English nation, and I wish to evoke in every Indian the loyalty of Englishmen.
>
> Mohandas K. Gandhi, *An Autobiography: The Story of my Experiments with Truth*, 1927–29.

This chapter is divided into three parts. First, we consider the background to immigration; second, the characteristics of the main minority groups will be outlined; third, the prospects for ethnic groups in British society will be discussed. The chapter deals specifically with Great Britain, although most of the legislation and some of the statistics cover the more inclusive unity of the United Kingdom. The chapter confines itself to questions of ethnicity produced by immigration during the twentieth century and the end of the nineteenth.

Part I

Background

Between 1901 and 1991, the population of the United Kingdom grew from 38 to 57 million. Of the 1991 population, 55 million lived in Great Britain itself; 47 million in England, 5 million in Scotland and just under 3 million in Wales. The 1991 census was the first in Britain to include a question on ethnicity, and the population appeared extremely homogeneous. The ethnic minority population, as defined by the census, accounted for 5.5 per cent of the British total while 94.5 per cent was white. Of the 55 million persons living in Britain, 52 million had been born in Europe and, of these, 51 million in the UK itself. Over a million more people had emigrated from the UK during the century than had immigrated: an estimated net migration loss of 1.3 million between 1901 and 1995 (Table 4.1).

Table 4.1 UK net annual migration balance, 1901–95

Years	Migration
1901–11	–820000
1911–21	–920000
1921–31	–670000
1931–51	220000
1951–61	120000
1961–71	–140000
1971–81	–270000
1981–91	430000
1991–95	740000
Total	–1310000

Source: Annual Abstract of Statistics 1997, ONS, 1997.

Yet this picture conceals a much more dynamic set of movements, a much more ethnically heterogeneous white population and a much faster rate of natural increase of the ethnic minority than the white population. Discounting the English, Scottish and Welsh, whose ethnicity is not the concern of this chapter, there is nevertheless a significant degree of diversity among the white population. Most important is the contribution of the Irish and the Jewish populations whose dimensions are rather opaque in census terms. However, there are also the 'invisible' survivors and descendants of European refugee populations from World War II, returning administrators and settlers from the colonies with their white but colonial-born families (340 000 whites born in the New Commonwealth) and settlers, students and transients from Australia (72 000) Canada (62 000) New Zealand (40 000), and South Africa (61 000). There are also the Italians and the Cypriots (Greek and Turkish) for whom we lack space for discussion. We also exclude other groups brought by the increasing flow of multinational employees and the free circulation of European Union (EU) citizens; just under half a million people (494 000) in Britain in 1991 had been born in the EU, excluding the United Kingdom and the Irish Republic, though this number includes a significant number of children born to British forces stationed in Germany.

The most striking change to occur to the population of Great Britain since the turn of the century has been the growth of its Third World ex-colonial population from negligible numbers at the end of World War II to the 1991 census, when the ethnic minority numbered three million and accounted for 5.5 per cent of the total population. As a very broad generalization, one could argue that, during the course of the nineteenth century, immigration into Britain was predominantly Irish, that at the end of the nineteenth and the beginning of the twentieth century it was predominantly Jewish, and that in the middle of the twentieth century it was predominantly West Indian and South Asian. This is not to ignore the fact that, as the former metropolitan and historical heart of an imperial power, peoples from all over the world have settled in Britain, nor that, as a continuing industrial, financial and intellectual global centre, new communities continue to develop. Nor is it to underestimate the importance of two world wars, post-colonial dislocations, wars and civil wars that have cast up new minorities on Britain's shores.

During the period 1900–95, in common with other Western European industrialized nations, Britain's immigration field expanded from local-international labour and refugee movements to a world-wide catchment area. The historical links are important, but in some ways it is too tempting to stress the linkage between the tiny ethnic minority communities of the pre-war period and the large post-war growth. These links will be referenced in this chapter, but it is more important to grasp that the growth of the minority populations has more in common with similar developments in Germany, France and the Benelux countries than with historical antecedents in Britain itself (Peach, 1997).

Part II

Irish migration

We lack precise data on the ethnic Irish in Britain, but there are over one million people living in households headed by a person born in Ireland. The Irish have been migrating to Britain in substantial numbers for at least 150 years, and now form the largest single ethnic minority group in the country, exceeding the Indian ethnic population, which in 1991 numbered 840 000.

Historical background

Migration between the two countries has, except during World War II, been free from restriction. The proximity, the low cost of passage, and the effective communication networks, both formal and informal, mean that migration flows have been very sensitive to economic changes in both countries. Irish migration to Britain has come in three main phases: (1) 1840–1918; (2) 1931–61 and (3) the 1980s onwards. The first period includes the Irish Potato Famine of 1845–50. During this period a million people, out of the then total population of eight million, perished. The tide of emigration established by the disaster halved the population of the island by the end of the century.

The famine coincided with the Industrial Revolution in Britain itself and a large part of the tide of emigrants was swept into the rapidly expanding industrial cities of Britain, where their abject conditions were graphically (if unsympathetically) described by Engels (1971) in the 1840s.

In the twentieth century, the peak period for emigration from Ireland was 1931–61, a time of great rural poverty, and relative lack of industrial investment in the South. Whereas the United States had been the most favoured destination, the introduction of immigration quotas there led to an increased flow to Britain. The value of the Southern Irish as a replacement labour force during World War II saw relaxation of the restrictions imposed in 1940, and even extended to direct recruitment of both men and women. In the case of Irish women the war opened up new areas of employment in Britain, with clerical and factory work replacing domestic service (Lennon, 1988). The huge demand for labour in the post-war period saw a massive influx: in the decade 1951–61 net emigration from Southern Ireland was 409 000. During this period emigration from the North was relatively unimportant because the heavy industries of the North, together with the textile industry, were generating sufficient domestic employment, and politically the area was enjoying relative quiet.

By the early 1970s the Southern Irish economy was booming, thanks in no small part to membership of the European Union (EU). The period saw, for the first time since 1840, an increase in population size and, even more surprisingly, net immigration into Ireland (MacLaughlin, 1994). The boom in Ireland was opening up new opportunities, while the British economy was already beginning to show signs of recession. Families, especially those who had bought houses in the south-east of Britain, were able to realize their asset and use the capital to establish businesses in the Republic of Ireland. In particular, expertise acquired in the building trade in Britain was valuable in the construction boom in Ireland, where EU funds were available for road building, housing programmes and commercial developments. The same period saw an increase in emigration from the North, reflecting both growing unemployment and the rapid escalation of violence from 1969.

By the mid-1980s Southern Ireland's bubble economy had burst, and emigration was rising. The 1986 Irish Census indicated that net emigration 1981–86 was 75 300 (CSO, 1986). Not all of these emigrants would have come to Britain: the absence of any monitoring of passenger flows between the two countries makes it impossible to tell how many came to Britain, but it is clear that Britain remained the single most common destination (MacLaughlin, 1994).

The 1980s saw a rise in Protestant emigration from the North of Ireland, but by 1991 there was net migration from Britain to Northern Ireland, amounting to a net gain of about 3000 (OPCS, 1993). Estimates for the first five years of the 1990s suggest continued population loss in Southern Ireland: in spite of an estimated birth rate of 14 per 1000 and an estimated death rate of only 9 per 1000, the projected population growth is –0.2 per cent (CSO, 1994).

Table 4.2 shows the numbers of Irish-born residents in Britain in the period 1901–91.

Table 4.2 Numbers of Irish–born (32 counties) in Great Britain, 1901–91

Date	Number
1901	631629
1911	550040
1921	523767
1931	505385
1951	716028
1961	950978
1971	952760
1981	850387
1991	836934

Sources: Chance (1996); Census Reports, 1901–91.

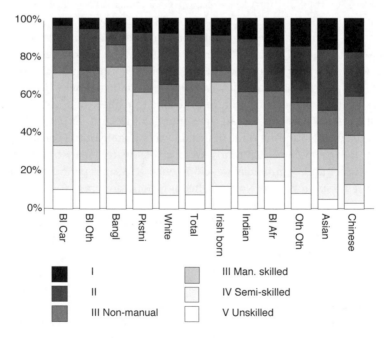

Figure 4.1 Ethnicity by socio-economic class, men 16+, Great Britain, 1991

Source: OPCS, 1993, Table 16.

Although retaining a distinct identity, the socio-economic differences between the Irish and the rest of the British population are the least of all of the groups which we consider in this chapter. Their family and household structures differ little from those of the white British population as a whole. They are spatially very mixed with the rest of the white British population, showing very low rates of segregation. They are highly intermarried with the white British population. Irish men have a slightly more blue-collar profile than the population as a whole (Figure 4.1), while Irish-born women are somewhat over-represented at both the top and bottom ends of the occupational ladder (Figure 4.2). Their housing tenure also reflects a more working-class pattern than the population as a whole, with a slightly higher proportion in local authority and other social housing than the national average.

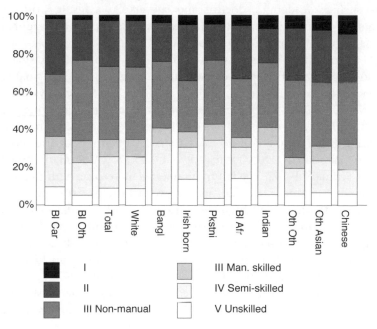

Figure 4.2 Ethnicity by socio-economic class, women 16+, Great Britain, 1991

Source: OPCS, 1993, Table 16.

The Jews

Jewish migration to Britain has had a very different history and trajectory from that of the Irish. There is an early and chequered history of Sephardic Jewish settlement, expulsion and readmission, but from the perspective of the twentieth century the major events were the refugee waves produced first by the Russian and Polish pogroms of the late nineteenth century and then by the Nazi persecutions of the 1930s.

Jews first arrived in the UK as merchants and financiers accompanying Norman settlers, although the community was subsequently expelled by Edward I in 1290. Thereafter, there were three main phases of Jewish settlement. Cromwell readmitted Sephardic Jews in 1664, and these families of merchants formed the basis of Anglo-Jewry. By 1875 there was a Jewish community of around 51 250 centred on London (Holmes, 1988). A second migration took place between 1881 and 1914 as Jews living in the Russian Pale of Settlement, principally from Poland, fled persecution. By 1911 there were 68 420 Russian Jews in London, the vast majority living in Stepney. The third phase occurred in the 1930s, when Jews living in Germany and German-controlled Europe sought refuge in the UK. Around 50 000 out of the 360 000–370 000 who fled from the Nazi terror before 1939 found their way to Britain. Many of these refugees were professionals such as academics, doctors and lawyers. As a result, Britain's Jewish community became the second or third largest in Europe and the fourth or fifth largest in the world at that time (Rubenstein, 1996).

Since 1939 the number of Jews arriving in Britain has been relatively small. Some 2000 so-called 'Baghdadi Jews' came from India after 1947 and smaller numbers migrated from North Africa and the Gulf States. Few Soviet Jews came to Britain in the 1980s. The population reached its numerical peak during the 1950s, probably numbering some 430 000 (Englander, 1993). Since then it has steadily declined, to an estimate of no more than 330 000 in 1985 and more recently to an estimated 290 000 in the late 1990s (Alderman, 1995; *Independent*, 17 February 1997). The fall in numbers is in keeping with the fate of Jewish communities throughout Europe. It owes a little to net emigration but more to low birth rates and high death rates; in 1988 deaths exceeded births by 954 (Alderman, 1992; Wasserstein, 1996). The number and proportion of synagogue marriages has gradually declined since the 1940s. Rates of out-marriage are estimated at between one-third and two-fifths, an increase from only 10 per cent in the 1940s (Rubenstein, 1996; Cohen, 1997).

Despite a decline in numbers, the Jewish community has made substantial social and economic advances. Although the core of Anglo-Jewry came from the merchant classes, most of the refugees from Poland were peasants and craftsmen. They met with frequent bouts of anti-Semitism, including violence in Bethnal Green (1903 and 1917) and Tredegar (1911), and accusations that they worked too hard and caused overcrowding. The British Union of Fascists targeted Jews in the East End during the 1930s. But close communities of Jewish refugees rapidly developed in urban areas separate from the more acculturated Anglo-Jewry, notably in the East End of London, Chapeltown in Leeds, Manchester, Glasgow, Birmingham and Liverpool. Often working in the garment, boot and furniture industries, hard work, frugality and entrepreneurial flair converted many operatives into employers. They also advanced in retailing. Jews were also active in the trade unions and labour movements at this time. The

German refugees often discovered that their qualifications did not count in Britain and met with considerable hardship in the early years of settlement.

A strong emphasis on education ensured social mobility for the second and subsequent generations. They are now statistically over-represented in sectors such as the medical profession, education, the judiciary, estate agency and accountancy (Waterman and Kosmin, 1986a). Most Jews are now in the middle class, with substantial representation in intellectual circles of academics, playwrights and authors. Rubenstein reports that between 10 and 15 per cent of Britain's wealthiest people are Jewish (Rubenstein, 1996).

British Jews have always been an urban population, with around two-thirds of them concentrated in London this century. With social mobility has come suburbanization. Since the 1930s many of the old communities have declined. Jews from the East End of London moved to boroughs further north, notably Hackney, Barnet, Brent, Harrow and Redbridge. Five London boroughs contain half the British Jewish population, and within these boroughs they remain spatially concentrated (Waterman and Kosmin, 1986b; Alderman, 1992). This has facilitated the maintenance of a dense network of organizations, including 356 synagogues throughout Britain in 1990 (Schmool and Cohen, 1991), kosher shops and restaurants, Jewish supplementary schools and welfare organizations such as Jewish Care which operates residential homes for the elderly. In 1985 it was estimated that there were still large Jewish communities in Manchester (30000), Leeds (14000) and Glasgow (11000), but in many smaller towns the population was in decline and synagogues were closing; for example, in Derby. Communities in South Wales and Northern Ireland have also declined (Englander, 1993; Wasserstein, 1996).

In the 1990s many commentators on the British Jewish community have expressed pessimistic views about its future as a religious body. Wasserstein describes a 'vanishing diaspora' of European Jews, as numbers decline, spiritual adherence to Judaism as a daily presence withers and Yiddish language-use declines (Wasserstein, 1996). Others, however, note a continuation of religious observance at home and relatively high rates of exposure to Jewish education among children (Rubenstein, 1996). In 1991 a third of Jewish children attended Jewish day schools and over half received some form of Jewish education. Such anxieties aside, Jews in Britain have never been as highly regarded by the rest of society as they are in the late twentieth century. Despite a rash of anti-Semitic attacks in the 1990s there has been no general increase in anti-Semitism in Britain to compare with some other European countries. As part of the Jewish diaspora British Jews have played their part in defending Israel, helping Soviet Jews and remembering the Holocaust, which provides a common set of causes overriding any internal divisions. Secular consensus exists alongside religious plurality, with disputes centring on issues such as the role of women in synagogues, homosexuality and the right of the Board of

Deputies to speak for all Jews on issues such as *shechita* (ritual slaughter) (Alderman, 1992) and plans to construct an *eruv* in Hendon between 1993 and 1997. (An *eruv* is an area demarcated by a boundary, such as a nylon thread, which is treated as an extension of the home. This allows actions such as carrying keys or pushing a wheelchair, which are not otherwise permitted outside the home, to be carried out by the orthodox on the Sabbath).

The Polish population

The non-Jewish Polish population in Britain is almost entirely a product of the twentieth century. Whereas Polish Jews began arriving in Britain from 1881 onwards, as late as 1931 there were less than 5000 Christian Poles in the whole of the UK. These were concentrated in three main areas – London, Lanarkshire and the Manchester region. Poles worked in the garment industry and the personal services sector in Whitechapel and Beckton. In Lanarkshire they were miners and labourers in the steel industry. In Cheshire, Poles were employed in the salt works (Zubrzycki, 1956).

The major period of growth for Britain's Polish population was World War II. After the partition of Poland by German and Soviet forces in 1939, the authorities formed a government in exile in London. Following the fall of France they were joined by over 27 000 members of the Polish armed forces who reformed in Britain. When the USSR joined the war in 1941 a further 100 000 or more Poles held captive by the Soviets were released to form the Polish Second Corps, who went on to fight in Palestine, North Africa and Italy. The Corps was repatriated to Britain at the end of the war and resettled by the Polish Refugee Corps in 60 temporary camps throughout Britain. Finally, immediately after the war, a further 21 000 political prisoners, 33 000 members of military families and 14 000 European Volunteer Workers were added to Britain's Polish population (Patterson, 1961). The workers were allocated to mines, textile factories and hospitals (Holmes, 1988).

As a result of these movements, the core of the Polish community in Britain was built around a government further exiled by the Yalta Conference and a military organization who had experienced suffering and hardship, and who had felt betrayed by the Allies. In 1945 the UK recognized the new government in communist Poland. Few communities begin life in a new country with such a complete social and political organization, including government and military officials, a religious hierarchy, political parties and a network of welfare and civic societies. The central institution of the Polish community has been the Federation of Poles in Great Britain, founded in 1947 and with 80 member organizations in 1998. (The Federation of Poles in Great Britain operates a website at www.zem.co.uk/polinuk/fed/fed.htm). From the 1960s onwards, the rate of naturalization among Poles rose as they came to terms with being an exiled community.

The number of Poles in Britain is difficult to estimate. There were perhaps 130 000–135 000 in 1960, falling to less than 100 000 in the early 1980s (Patterson, 1977). This figure includes ethnic Poles born in the UK. The 1981 census recorded 88 286 Polish-born individuals in England and Wales, falling to 70 115 in 1991. There were a further 5083 in Scotland. The main concentrations in 1991 were London (with over 20 000), and the main English metropolitan areas. The Federation of Poles in Great Britain estimates a community of perhaps 150 000, although no reliable figures are known. The community was initially heavily tilted towards the professions, with one in ten of the refugees having some higher education. It was also notably homogeneous in terms of age, with a high proportion of adults, and possessed an imbalanced sex ratio of 3 women to every 8 men. Whilst this stimulated significant out-marriage, natural demographic trends have gradually corrected the imbalance among British-born Poles. Many Poles suffered loss of status on arrival in the UK, but by the 1980s this had been partially overcome. Poles became well represented in the medical profession, judiciary and educational sector, and there has been a movement from unskilled jobs into self-employment and white-collar positions.

There is an active network of Polish community organizations, including veterans' societies, educational societies and the Polish Social and Cultural Association (PSOK) in London. There were also 117 Polish community centres, 82 Polish Catholic parishes and 67 Polish Saturday schools in 1998. They have campaigned for such things as Polish A levels, community health care and the maintenance of a Polish-language radio programme in the West Midlands. The *Polish Daily* newspaper has a circulation of 10 000. Since the collapse of communism and the emergence of Poland from the Soviet orbit, these organizations have become more active in campaigning and lobbying on issues concerning the Polish diaspora and Poland itself. These include the abolition of visas and Poland's requests to join both the North Atlantic Treaty Organization (NATO) and the EU. In 1993 the body of Poland's war-time leader, General Sikorski, was returned to his native land while more British Poles are travelling to Poland itself as tourists. In 1991 the last of the war-time resettlement camps, at Ilford Park in Devon, was closed and its remaining 96 residents were rehoused (*Independent*, 6 November 1991). The past decade therefore marked a turning point for the British Polish community. The war-time generation has dwindled, the UK-born have become integrated into society and, after 50 years, British Poles are now able to return freely to their homeland.

Post-1948 developments in immigration and ethnicity

World War II marked a watershed in British ethnic history. Before, nearly all immigration had been white; after, a significant part was non-European. The year 1948 is often cited as the beginning of the new era, because it was the year in which 417 Jamaican immigrants arrived in Britain on the *Empire Windrush*. Ironically, the *Empire Windrush* was on the return leg of a voyage in which she had taken British emigrants to Australia. However, although 1948 marked a new beginning, it was also a continuation of migrations which had begun during the war with the recruitment in the Caribbean of workers for munitions factories and with the volunteers for British armed forces, particularly the RAF (Glass, 1960, p.46; Patterson, 1963, p.38).

Non-European ethnic minorities have a long history in Britain, going back to Elizabethan times. From the eighteenth century until after World War II, there were small colonies of African, Asian and Arab seamen in British ports such as Cardiff, Liverpool, Tyneside and London (Little, 1947; Banton, 1955; Collins, 1957; Halliday, 1992). There were also individuals including doctors, politicians and potentates who made notable contributions to various aspects of British life. Numbers were small and the communities were geographically isolated.

After 1948, however, numbers grew rapidly, first through immigration and then through natural increase. In 1951, the combined Caribbean and South Asian population of Great Britain amounted to less than 80 000; by 1961 it had reached 500 000, or about 1 per cent of the population; by 1971 it was about 1 500 000, or roughly 3 per cent of the population; and by 1981 it was 2 200 000 or 4.1 per cent. The 1991 census figure puts the ethnic minority population at just over 3 000 000, or 5.5 per cent of the population. The overall percentage of the population formed by ethnic minorities is thus not high, but it is characterized by a high rate of growth.

The driving force for this dramatic demographic change can be understood from Figure 8.3 in Chapter 8, which traces the changes in unemployment throughout the century. After 1945, unemployment reached the lowest peacetime level ever and remained low from then until 1973. Immigration was concentrated into this period of time.

Net immigration from the Caribbean showed a high degree of sensitivity to fluctuations in the British labour market, and over the period 1955–74 maintained a high and significant inverse correlation with the British unemployment rate (Peach, 1991). Immigration from India and Pakistan showed a similar but more modest correlation (Robinson, 1986).

The oil crisis, precipitated by the Yom Kippur War in the Middle East, brought the period of demand for labour to a sudden end. Figure 4.2 demonstrates that the bulk of immigrants from the Caribbean and South Asia present in Britain in the late 1980s had arrived in the 1955–74 period. Net Caribbean immigration to Britain came to an end after 1974, but immigration from India, Pakistan and Bangladesh continued, albeit at a reduced rate. This was because while Caribbean immigration had been gender balanced from the beginning, the early movement from South Asia was predominantly male. Later migration was largely a process of family reunion or for marriage purposes.

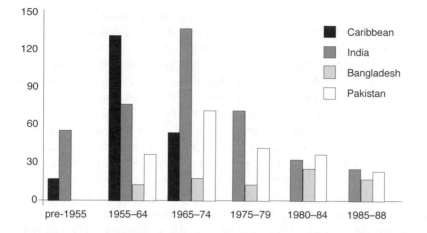

Figure 4.3 Date of arrival in Britain of those present from the Caribbean, India, Pakistan and Bangladesh in 1988

Source: *Labour Force Survey* 1990 and 1991, London, HMSO, 1992, Table 6.39, p.38.

Although the broad composition of the ethnic minority population is generally agreed, the precise details are much less clear. Race and ethnicity are highly contested issues in political and academic discourse and it was only in 1991 and after considerable difficulty (Sillitoe, 1978; 1987) that an ethnic question was included in the British census.

Essentially there has been a struggle between two schools of thought (Spencer, 1997). On the one hand, there is the belief that all British subjects are equal before the law. The classical Roman view of *Civis Romanus sum* was enacted into British law as late as 1948, when the British Citizenship Act confirmed citizenship of the United Kingdom and Colonies on all people who were citizens of British colonies, former colonies and the Dominions, whether or not they had citizenship of their newly independent countries. Thus about a quarter of the world's population was given citizenship of the UK and colonies (including all citizens of India and Pakistan) which carried the right of entry and settlement in the UK. On this basis, it was thought discriminatory even to count, let alone control, entry of people to the UK from any of the countries of the former empire or Commonwealth or colonies. The contrary view was that massive discrimination was practised against racial minorities in Britain and that until ethnic records were kept, it would not be possible to measure and eradicate such practices.

As a result, until the 1962 Commonwealth Immigrants Act was enforced, no official statistics were kept on entry or departure of citizens of the UK and Colonies, nor of citizens of the Commonwealth to the UK. The only official statistics that were kept dealt with entry and departure by ship, by country of departure and destination. In an era of air travel and in situations in which country of departure and that of citizenship may bear no relationship to each other, such statistics had obvious limitations. Unofficial statistics were kept by the Home Office, basically on the basis of race. The census, however, continued to perform a convoluted juggling act, using surrogate measures for the categories in which politicians, academics and the public were really interested. Country of birth was the main measure, but by 1971, parents' country of birth had been added to capture the statistics of the British-born generation. An ethnic question was almost included in the 1981 census, but the inner-city rioting in Bristol in 1980 and the widespread riots in 1981 led to its abandonment. However, this was at such a late stage in census planning that even the question on parental country of birth could not be included in its stead.

The result was that 'persons born in the New Commonwealth and Pakistan or to parents born in those countries' became the surrogate measure of non-European ethnic minority population in the UK. This had significant shortcomings (Peach and Winchester, 1974). White British children, born to administrators of the Raj in India, or to military forces in Egypt, Cyprus or elsewhere, were recorded as Indian-, Egyptian- or Cypriot- born. Indians born in East Africa were recorded as African-born, and so on.

The correlation of birthplace and ethnicity, already shaky (but disputed) in the 1960s, had broken down substantially by the 1970s, and by the 1991 census nearly half (47 per cent) of the ethnic minority population was British-born. When an ethnic question was included in the British census for the first time in 1991, it demonstrated that 20 per cent of those born in the New Commonwealth were white. Similarly, nearly two-thirds of those born in East Africa were of Indian rather than African ethnicity; just under 30 per cent of

Table 4.3 Relative concentration of ethnic minority population in selected metropolitan counties, Great Britain, 1991

	Total	White	Black Caribbean
Great Britain	54888844	51873794	499964
Greater London	6679699	5333580	290968
West Midlands metropolitan county	2551671	2178149	72183
Greater Manchester metropolitan county	2499441	2351239	17095
West Yorkshire metropolitan county	2013693	1849562	14795
Percentage ethnic group in named areas	25.04	22.58	79.01

Source: OPCS (1993), Table 6.

the Indians born outside the UK were born in East Africa rather than India, and 15 per cent of those born in India were white.

Although the census included an ethnic question for the first time in 1991, other official surveys such as the Labour Force Survey (LFS) and the General Housing Survey (GHS) had used such categories since 1979. However, these surveys included minority populations as part of a national sample, so numbers were small and thus the sampling error was large. Nevertheless, there is broad agreement between the figures generated by the LFS and the GHS and the census. Regrettably, however, categories such as 'Arab' and 'Mixed', which were used by the LFS, were not adopted by the census, so that interpretation of the 1991 results is not unproblematic.

Causes of post-war migration

The immigrants from the Caribbean and South Asia were drawn in by very specific sectors of demand in the labour market, which were, in turn, determined by economic and geographic changes in the British economy. Broadly, the post-war British economy created new openings for the indigenous population and created gaps at the bottom in the less attractive sectors with unsocial hours, poor pay and difficult working conditions. The railways, underground, buses, the postal service and hospital services all had poor pay and conditions and were short of labour. In manufacturing, the textile mills of Lancashire and Yorkshire and some of the metal industries of the Midlands were in a similar situation.

Added to this were changes in the geographical location of growth industries. White movement to these locations largely blocked the possibilities for ethnic minority entry. The larger urban centres ceased to expand for three

Black African	Black-Other	Indian	Pakistani	Bangladeshi	Chinese
212362	178401	840255	476555	162835	156938
163635	80613	347091	87816	85738	56579
4116	15716	141359	88268	18074	6107
5240	9202	29741	49370	11445	8323
2554	6552	34837	80540	5978	3852
82.66	62.83	65.82	64.21	74.45	47.70

main reasons. The first was that there were conscious policies to stop urban sprawl by the creation of 'green belts' – areas of land on which development is prohibited. Linked with this was the policy of creating new towns beyond the green belt and decanting workers and industries from the big cities to these locations. Added to this was the regional policy which encouraged the under-pinning of the existing distribution of labour by encouraging industry to move to areas of high unemployment rather than moving labour to areas where industry wished to expand.

The combined effects of these policies was to reverse the relationship between urban growth and urban hierarchy which had existed from the nine-teenth century until the middle of the twentieth. The large conurbations lost population and the fastest growth was in smaller centres. Critically, demand for labour grew in the large cities, which were increasingly unattractive to the white population. The ethnic minority population settled as a replacement population to fill these gaps in the large cities. In 1991, less than a quarter of the white population lived in Greater London, Greater Manchester, the West Midland Metropolitan County (Greater Birmingham) and the West Yorkshire Metropolitan County (Leeds–Bradford), while the ethnic minority population was two, three or four times more concentrated in these locations (Table 4.3).

Although this account of the ethnic minority populations as measured by the 1991 census has tended to represent them as labour migrants and their children, this is an oversimplification in several important respects. The African population was not motivated by labour search and a substantial part of the Indian ethnic migration was a refugee movement from East Africa. The Black-Other population is overwhelmingly British-born.

The Caribbean population

The 1991 census gave an ethnic population of 499 964 Black-Caribbeans living in Great Britain. The true number is probably somewhat larger because it omits the 58 106 who categorized themselves as Black British; there was under-enumeration, particularly of the young; and it is uncertain the extent to which children of mixed Caribbean/white unions were ascribed to the Black-Other rather than Black-Caribbean category (Ballard and Kalra, 1994; Owen, 1996). Almost the whole of Caribbean primary immigration took place between 1948 and 1973 and numbers have fluctuated at around the half million mark since the 1970s (Table 4.4).

However, while the total figure has been relatively stable, there has also been substantial growth of the second generation, partly offset by return migration of some of the first (Table 4.4). The Caribbean-born element of the population had decreased by about 40 000 between the censuses of 1971 and 1991. Rather little of this decrease in the Caribbean-born population is likely to have been caused by death (Balarajan and Bulusu, 1990, Table 9.8; Peach,

1991, p.12). Return migration for retirement or onward migration to North America seem probable as causes for the decrease. By 1971 a majority of the Caribbean ethnic population was British-born, and by 1991 that figure had increased to 54 per cent.

Table 4.4 Caribbean ethnic population of Great Britain, 1951–91

Year	Caribbean birthplace	UK-born children of WI-born (est.)	Best estimate Caribbean ethnic population
1951	17218	10000	28000
1961	173659	35000	209000
1966	269300	133000	402000
1971	304070	244000	548000
1981a	295179	250565	546000
1981b	268000	244000	519000
1984	242000	281000	529000
1986–88	233000	262000	495000
1991	264591	268337 to 326443	499964 to 558070 [a]

Note: [a]The official ethnic Black-Caribbean total is 499 964 (OPCS 1993, Table 5, p.403). Note that if those who designated themselves 'Black British' were included (58 106) (OPCS, 1993, vol. 2, Table A, p.831) the total would be 558 070.

Sources: 1951 and 1961, Censuses; 1966; Census (10 per cent count), Sample Census 1966, Great Britain, *Commonwealth Immigrant Tables*, Table 2, p.12; 1971, Census, Great Britain, Country of Birth Tables; 1981a, Census 1981, Great Britain, Country of Birth Tables; 1981b and 1984, Labour Force Survey; 1986–88, *Population Trends*, 1990, 60, pp.35–8; 1991, Census, Great Britain, *Ethnic Group and Country of Birth* (OPCS, 1993).

During the 1950s and early 1960s, net West Indian immigration tracked the demand for labour in Britain, with perhaps a three month lag (Peach, 1968, p.39; 1991) (Figure 4.4). The threat of legislation to curb immigration by British passport holders, who often had no citizenship other than that of the UK and Colonies, had the paradoxical effect of increasing immigration in a rush to beat the ban (Figure 4.1). However, it seems to have restricted the movement to Britain without drying up the supply of migrants. After 1962, net immigration to Britain decreased considerably, but liberalization of the US and Canadian immigration legislation led to renewed migration, particularly of skilled workers (Thomas-Hope, 1986; 1992; Byron, 1994).

The Caribbean population of Great Britain is young in comparison with the population as a whole, but not as youthful as more recently arrived groups such as the Pakistanis or Bangladeshis. The youthfulness shows up not so much in the younger age-groups as in those of retirement age, where in 1991 only 6 per cent of the Caribbean population is found, compared with 19 per cent of the total population. The age-structure of the Black-Caribbean population is hourglass-shaped. The peak of Caribbean migration to Britain was in

1961, 30 years before the 1991 census, and this is reflected in the upper segment of the hourglass of those aged 45 and over. Hardly any Caribbean-born persons are present aged 20 or under. The British-born children born of the first generation dominate the lower segment of the hourglass in the age 0–30 section.

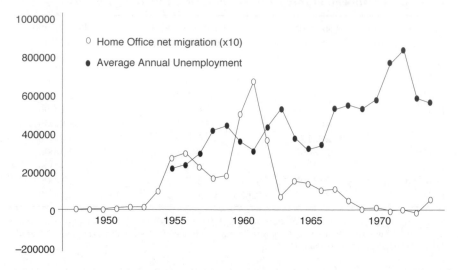

Figure 4.4 Net West Indian migration to Britain, 1948–74 against average annual unemployment

Source: Peach (1996b).

Gender

Unlike the South Asian ethnic groups, the Black-Caribbean population shows a slight preponderance of women: 239 484 men to 260 480 women. It is notable that the migration from the Caribbean was always balanced in gender terms and did not show the South Asian pattern of male advance migration with a marked lag before their womenfolk joined them (Table 4.5). This gender

Table 4.5 Gender balance for selected ethnic groups, Great Britain, 1991

Ethnic group	Men	Women	Male to Female ratio
Black-Caribbean	239484	260480	100 : 105
Indian	422891	417364	100 : 98
Pakistani	245572	230983	100 : 94
Bangladeshi	84944	77891	100 : 92
Chinese	77669	79269	100 : 102

Source: OPCS (1993) vol. 2, Table 7, pp.636–7.

imbalance is true both of those born inside and outside the UK. It partly reflects a degree of under-enumeration of young males. The 1991 census is known to have a 2.2 per cent overall under-enumeration (OPCS, 1993, pp.5–7), which is unevenly distributed across ethnicities, gender and location. The Black-Caribbean population is thought to have an overall under-count of 3 per cent, but this rises to 11 per cent for those aged 25–29 and to 16 per cent for young men in this age bracket. Under-counting for this group is thought to be higher still in Inner London.

Household size

Black-Caribbean household size is rather similar to that of the total population and in turn differs substantially from that of the South Asian groups. Household size tends to be small: while 29 per cent of the Indian households, 54 per cent of Pakistani and 61 per cent of Bangladeshi households are 5 persons or larger, only 11 per cent of the Caribbean and 8 per cent of total households are in this category (Table 4.6).

Table 4.6 Household size by birthplace group of household head, Great Britain, 1991 (%)

Household size (persons)	1	2	3	4	5	6	7+	Average size
Total households	27	34	16	16	5	2	1	2.47
Caribbean	27	27	20	15	7	3	1	2.60
Indian	14	20	15	22	15	8	6	3.58
Pakistani	8	11	11	15	16	17	21	4.82
Bangladeshi	5	7	10	15	15	17	29	5.36

Source: OPCS (1993) Table H, p.954.

Family structure

Although household size is similar to that of the white population, there are significant differences in family structure. In particular, the Caribbean pattern of female-headed households (and allied to this, single-female-headed households with dependent children) is much more common than in the white population or in the South Asian groups. The 1991 census (OPCS, 1993, vol. 2, Table 18, p.828) shows that 20 per cent of households headed by a Black-Caribbean were lone-parent families with dependent children. The corresponding figure for the white population was 5 per cent; for Indians, 4 per cent; for Pakistanis, 7 per cent; and for Bangladeshis, 8 per cent. If the calculation were to exclude households with no families, the prominence of single-parent families for the Black-Caribbean population would appear more prominent. Table 4.7 illustrates the contrasts between the white, Black-

Table 4.7: Ethnic group by household structure, Great Britain, 1991

	Total	White	Black-Carib	Black-Afr
Households with no family				
One-person household	26.3	26.6	27.7	25.1
Two or more-person household	3.3	3.2	4.2	11.7
Households with one family				
Married-couple family				
With no children	24.3	24.8	10.3	8.2
With dependent children	22.4	21.8	13.8	24.6
With non–dependent children	8.6	8.7	7.5	1.5
Cohabiting-couple family				
With no children	3.3	3.4	3.4	2.5
With dependent children	1.8	1.8	3.5	2.0
With non–dependent children	0.2	0.2	0.4	0.1
Lone-parent family				
With dependent children	5.2	5.0	20.2	20.6
With non–dependent children	3.7	3.7	7.4	2.6
Households with two or more families	0.9	0.8	1.6	1.1
Total Households	100.0	100.0	100.0	100.0

Source: OPCS (1993) vol. 2, Table 11, p.770.

Caribbean and Indian household types. Single-person households are common for both whites and Black-Caribbean, but the high proportion of lone parents with dependent children is prominent for the Black-Caribbean, but not for whites or Indians. Extended, or multi-family household, families are significant for the Indians, but not for the other two groups.

Ethnically mixed households

The Samples of Anonymized Records produced by the 1991 census indicate a significant proportion of black and white households. Of the households in which either the head or partner gave their ethnic group as Black-Caribbean, 37.2 per cent were headed by a female with no male present; 18.1 per cent were headed by a male with no female present. In 26.8 per cent of cases, both the head and partner were Black-Caribbean; in 10.1 per cent of cases there was a Black-Caribbean male with a white female partner, while the obverse case obtained only half as frequently (4.8 per cent of cases). There were very few cases of other ethnicities being partners in Black-Caribbean households, although, given the relative sizes of the different ethnic populations, this is to be expected. One of the consequences of this high proportion of mixed unions is that is that one-third of the Caribbean children living with both parents in

Black-Other	Indian	Pak	B'deshi	Chinese	Other Asian	Other-Other	Born in Ireland
26.5	9.5	7.6	6.2	21.1	17.8	26.4	30.0
5.9	2.7	2.9	4.3	9.1	6.8	6.9	4.9
8.3	12.7	7.3	4.7	13.7	12.9	12.9	21.0
19.0	49.7	58.3	63.6	38.6	42.7	29.3	17.3
2.8	8.1	4.1	2.4	4.9	4.8	4.3	10.5
5.1	0.8	0.5	0.3	1.8	1.7	3.8	3.0
4.3	0.5	0.5	0.4	0.5	0.9	1.9	1.3
0.1	0.0	0.1	0.0	0.1	0.1	0.1	0.3
24.1	4.5	7.2	8.3	5.3	7.3	10.6	5.2
3.1	2.6	1.9	0.8	2.5	2.7	2.8	5.6
0.8	8.9	9.6	9.0	2.5	2.4	1.1	1.0
100.0	100.0	100.0	100.0	100.0	100.0	100.0	100.0

the 4th Policy Studies Institute (PSI) survey had one white and one black parent (Modood et al., 1997, p.15).

Socio-economic status

There is a very high participation rate of the Black-Caribbean population in the labour force: 285 442 out of the 390 557 aged 16 and over were economically active (73 per cent). This high participation rate was true of both men (147 419 out of 184 147, or 80 per cent) and women (138 023 out of 206 410, or 67 per cent) but the lower female rate probably reflects the high proportion of female-headed households with dependent children.

Female unemployment in 1991 was 13.5 per cent compared with 6.3 per cent for white women. Black-Caribbean male unemployment was 23.8 per cent compared with 10.7 per cent for white men. For Black-Caribbean men aged 18–19, unemployment stood at an appalling 43.5 per cent and the unemployment rate in each age cohort was generally double that of the white male population. Thus, Black-Caribbeans fared worse than whites, Black Caribbean men fared worse than Black-Caribbean women and young Black-Caribbean men were in particularly vulnerable positions.

The occupational structure for Black-Caribbean men is skewed towards the manual categories: two-thirds of the men are in such occupations in comparison with only half of the white male working population (Figure 4.1). Similarly, the proportion in professional occupations is the least of any of the ethnic groups (2.6 per cent, compared with 7.1 per cent for white men)

Black-Caribbean female employment is much more similar to white female employment (Figure 4.2). Unlike the male pattern, it is skewed towards the non-manual side of the distribution. Two-thirds of Black-Caribbean females are in non-manual occupations. Thus while Black-Caribbean men are blue-collar workers, on the whole, Black-Caribbean females are white-collar. While the Black-Caribbean male occupation pattern differs significantly from that of whites, that of the females is much more similar.

Housing tenure

Caribbean housing tenure is distinguished from that of the whites, Indians and Pakistanis by its higher concentration in the public sector. Local authority housing accommodates 21.4 per cent of white households, but 35.7 per cent of Black-Caribbean households. Housing Associations accommodate a further 9.7 per cent of Black-Caribbean households compared with 3 per cent for

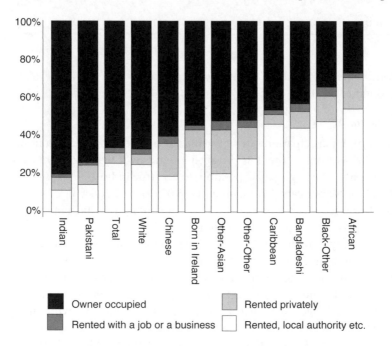

Figure 4.5 Housing tenure by ethnicity, Great Britain, 1991

Source: OPC, 1993, Table 11.

whites. However, it should be noted that nearly half Caribbean households own their own homes, even though this is less than the two-thirds of white households in this position. The proportion of Caribbean households in council housing is in line with expectations from their socio-economic class position, particularly for men, but less so for women (Peach and Byron 1993) and there is evidence of decrease in this category with the advent of the 'Right to Buy' legislation (Peach and Byron, 1994). The 1991 picture represents a major shift in the tenure pattern over the last 30 years. In the 1950s and early 1960s, private rentals dominated, but since that time, there has been a break-through into public housing, an increase in owner-occupation and the collapse of the private rental sector (see Figure 4.5).

Geographical distribution

The Black-Caribbean population of Great Britain is heavily concentrated into the English conurbations. Nearly 80 per cent of the total is found in four main metropolitan clusters: Greater London and the Metropolitan counties of the West Midlands (Birmingham), Greater Manchester and West Yorkshire. This compares with less than a quarter of the white population. Greater London alone accounts for 58 per cent of the Black-Caribbean population (Table 4.3). Within these metropolitan areas, the Caribbean population has an inner-city concentration, although it does not exhibit the ghetto scale of concentration of the North American cities.

Segregation levels

Black-Caribbean levels of segregation show some variability between the south-east and the Midlands, on the one hand, and northern towns, on the other. Greater London and Birmingham which contain over two-thirds of the Caribbean population have Indices of Dissimilarity (ID) of 49 and 54 respec-tively compared with the white population at enumeration district level (Table 4.8). The ID represents the percentage of the population which would have to shift from its area of residence in order to replicate the distribution of the population with which it is being compared. It has a range from 0 (no segre-gation) to 100 (total segregation). To put these values into perspective, the average ID for African-Americans in cities in the United States is about 80.

The level of segregation is not only moderate, but is decreasing. The London value of 49 represents a significant decrease in levels of concentration compared with earlier studies. Comparison for Greater London, at a variety of scales from 1961–91, shows a progressive decrease in the levels of segregation at all available scales – borough, ward and enumeration district (Peach, 1996b). Given that the initial levels of segregation were not high by US standards and that the trend in segregation is downwards, this suggests significant differences in terms of ethnic tolerance between Great Britain and the US.

**Table 4.8 Segregation levels of the white population against selected
ethnic minority populations in British cities, 1991 enumeration
district level**

	Caribbean	African	Black-Other	Indian	Pakistani
London	49	46	41	51	54
Birmingham	54	49	43	60	74
Sheffield	49	55	41	35	71
Leeds	69	51	57	45	64
Liverpool	54	61	53	43	51
Bradford	47	45	37	57	63
Bristol	59	50	43	38	64
Manchester	56	51	38	45	58
Kirklees	64	41	53	58	54
Coventry	28	34	30	41	67
Sandwell	43	36	30	47	61
Oldham	44	38	32	53	76
Wolverhampton	35	44	33	39	70
Leicester	38	44	32	58	56
Luton	24	19	16	25	65
Blackburn	36	49	42	62	61
Oxford	33	20	29	27	48
Pendle	53	48	46	37	62
Slough	26	30	20	35	50
Unweighted average Index of Dissimilarity[a]	45	43	38	45	62

Source: Special tabulations calculated from ESRC Small Area 1991 Census Data Centre at
Manchester University.

Coupled with this decrease in the IDs of the Caribbean born population, there
is evidence of progressive outward diffusion (Lee, 1973). It is clear that
substantial decreases have taken place in areas of inner concentration while
the major areas of increase are further away from the centre. Running a regression of absolute change in the Caribbean-born population against absolute
numbers of that population shows a very high inverse relationship: the higher
the numbers in 1981, the greater the decrease in 1991.

The highest proportion that Black-Caribbeans form of any ward in Great
Britain is 30.1 per cent in Roundwood in Brent (London). Of the top ten such
wards, nine are in London (Moss Side in Manchester is ranked 9). Even if the
Black-Other and Black African populations are added, the highest proportion
is still less than 50 per cent.

The picture which emerges from this analysis is of a population which has
matured from a first-generation immigrant population, which arrived between

B'deshi	Chinese	Other Asian	Other -Other	Irish-born	ID	IS	N[b]
65	30	34	29	26	8	35	5050537
80	37	57	44	22	14	53	641018
72	43	46	37	18	3	46	471511
82	40	43	41	28	4	47	455760
71	35	44	38	14	2	35	427811
75	34	57	37	16	9	54	380605
49	26	38	32	15	2	35	350013
67	32	49	37	23	7	40	333932
72	34	46	33	31	5	44	329184
68	21	40	21	11	5	30	245149
68	31	44	30	29	7	42	244423
79	20	46	29	15	6	59	194914
50	31	42	29	18	7	36	194177
81	29	46	36	13	16	52	188831
70	23	31	19	17	8	32	128253
57	22	51	51	18	9	54	113492
50	22	26	15	12	2	18	95036
83	47	47	40	16	6	54	75449
47	29	26	18	11	11	34	69710
68	31	43	32	19	7	42	525779

Notes: [a]The Index of Dissimilarity (ID) measures the percentage of the group which would have to change its area of enumeration in order to replicate the distribution of the rest of the population. The Index of Segregation (IS) is a variant of the ID. It shows the percentage of the group which would have to move to replicate the distribution of the total population, minus itself.
[b]N = Numbers.

1948 and 1974 and which now has a larger number of second than first generation. It is a group with a high concentration in London and Birmingham, within which traces of the original chain migration from different islands can still be seen. Levels of segregation are much lower than for African-Americans in the United States and for Pakistanis and Bangladeshis in this country. Surburbanization of the population is clearly evident in their London distribution.

There are also high levels of mixed Black-Caribbean and white households and evidence of the emergence of a Black British identity. It is both a hard-working and a disadvantaged population. Participation rates in the workforce are among the highest of all groups for both men and women. On the other hand, unemployment rates are unacceptably high, more than double the white average, and double this figure again for young men.

Housing tenure has shown a remarkable degree of change from the patterns of the 1960s. At that stage, the Caribbean population was largely concentrated in private rentals and almost entirely absent from public housing. Since then, there has been a substantial advance into both the private sector and into local authority and housing association property. Even in council housing, there has been significant evidence of purchase. The Caribbean population is much more concentrated into flats than houses. Even after one has controlled for the position of lone mothers with dependent children, who are exceptionally highly concentrated in the Caribbean population, the degree of flatted accommodation is high.

There is a conflict in the evidence on the integration of the Caribbean population in Britain. On the one hand there is the positive evidence of high participation in the labour force, a significant increase in home ownership and high levels of mixed unions and decreasing levels of segregation. On the other hand, levels of unemployment are significantly higher for the Caribbean population than for whites. The high proportion of single-female-headed households with dependent children represents stressful conditions and the history of police brutality, discrimination and indifference represented by such examples as the Stephen Lawrence case, point in the opposite direction. The Notting Hill and Nottingham anti-black riots of the late 1950s have been replaced by the 1981 Brixton riots by blacks.

One of the most telling summaries of the differences between the Caribbean and Asian settlements in Britain was that the Caribbeans faced an Irish future while the Asian future was Jewish. Apart from the ironic drawback that we have little firm information on the Jewish and Irish population in Britain, the implication of the statement is that the Black-Caribbean population is working class, waged labour, state educated and council housed, while the Asian population will become self-employed, owner occupiers and white-collar workers, with professional qualifications. There is some truth as well as counter-evidence for such an assertion for both groups. The Jewish future seems to be coming about for the Indian and to an extent the Pakistani population, although not for the Bangladeshis. However, in the case of the Black-Caribbean population, there seems to be a gender divide between the white-collared female socio-economic structure and the manual male structure. Certainly, the other model for Caribbean settlement that has haunted the literature, that of the African-American ghetto, has not come about.

The Indians, Pakistanis and Bangladeshis

These three groups, collectively referred to as the South Asians, account for nearly half of the three million ethnic minority population of Britain, as defined by the 1991 census. Indians, the largest group, numbered 840 255; Pakistanis numbered 476 555, and Bangladeshis, 162 835. The three groups share significant characteristics in terms of family and social organization, but differ from one another in their economic profiles. Their national labels also conceal important degrees of internal differentiation by place of origin, religion and language. All three groups remain socially distinct, but differ significantly from each other in their degree of economic success.

The key characteristic which the groups share is adherence to traditional family structures. Marriage is prevalent and nuclear or extended families are the norm. Marriage is overwhelmingly an intra-group affair (Table 4.9) and marriages are very often arranged (Modood et al., 1997). Married couples with dependent children account for between one-half and two-thirds of the South Asian households. This is three times the rate for white families in the case of the Bangladeshis and more than double in the case of the Indians (Table 4.7). Households with more than one family (our surrogate for extended families) account for about 10 per cent of all South Asian households. This is more than ten times the rate for white families. Cohabitation, lone-parent families with dependent children and single-person households, the forms that have become increasingly common in white and Caribbean household structures, are all uncommon for South Asians. Cohabiting couples without children account for only 0.3 per cent of Bangladeshi households, for example; this is one-tenth of the rate of white households (Table 4.7).

Economically the South Asian groups diverge considerably from one another. The Indian male socio-economic profile is fairly close to that of the population as a whole. In fact, the Indian male white-collar class in the 1991 census formed a larger proportion of the Indian population than it did for the population as a whole. However, this was offset by a higher than average representation of Indians among the semi-skilled and unskilled categories, so that while the overall profile was close to the average, in reality the Indian distribution was bipolar (Figure 4.1). However, it is clear that Indians have made one of the most successful adaptations to British economic life.

While the Indian group, particularly those from East Africa, appear to have made rapid socio-economic progress, the Pakistanis and, to a greater extent, the Bangladeshis had a much more blue-collar profile. Figure 4.1 shows that the majority of Pakistani and Bangladeshi male workers were in manual occupations and that they were under-represented among the white-collar group. Both Pakistanis and Bangladeshis suffered high rates of unemployment, double the national average in 1991. There was an exceptionally low rate of female participation in the formal labour force.

There are several factors involved in this divergence.

(1) All three groups did not start from the same base. Although there were many rural agricultural labourers in the migration, Indians, on the whole, started from a higher socio-economic base in their sending societies than Pakistanis and Bangladeshis. The Indian community contains a significant

number of academics and medical professionals, for example. Among those of rural origins, a significant proportion came from the relatively prosperous canal-fed irrigation areas of the Punjab, while many of the Pakistani Punjabis came from poorer rain-fed areas.

(2) The large majority of Indians are Sikhs and Hindus with fewer social inhibitions over the employment of women in the formal economy outside the home, than is the case with the largely Muslim Pakistani and Bangladeshi populations. Over half (55 per cent) of the Indian women aged 16 and over are in the formal labour force, a figure which is double that of the Pakistanis (27 per cent) and more than double the Bangladeshi rate of 22 per cent. There is therefore a higher proportion of dual income families than is the case for the other groups.

(3) A significant proportion of the Indian ethnic population (30 per cent) originated in East Africa. This was the group forced out from Kenya, Uganda and Tanzania by the Africanization policies of the post-colonial period and actually expelled from Uganda by Idi Amin during the late 1960s and early 1970s (Marret, 1989; Robinson, 1986, 1995). In East Africa, the Asians formed the middle class and the entrepreneurs. They were the traders, merchants, civil servants, bankers, academics, lawyers, doctors and dentists. A high proportion had been educated through the medium of English and were skilled at negotiating complex bureaucratic systems. Many had already embarked upon a strategy of intergenerational social mobility centring on education (Robinson, 1996). They brought their skills and to a certain extent their capital with them when they settled in Britain. They settled as family groups from the beginning and were not encumbered with the 'myth of return' to either East Africa or India. They saw their future in the West. Nevertheless, Robinson (1996) has shown through analysis of the Longitudinal Survey that there has also been considerable upward economic mobility by the Indian population.

Both Pakistanis and Bangladeshis have a large average household size (Table 4.6). The average in 1991 for Great Britain was 2.4; for Caribbean households it was 2.5, for Indians it was 3.8, for Pakistanis it was 4.8, and for Bangladeshis, 5.3. Coupled with large household size come very poor living conditions. This is particularly the case for the Bangladeshis. There is a high degree of crowding. Nearly a fifth (19 per cent) of Bangladeshi households lived at the highest density given by the census of over 1.5 persons per room. Less than 0.5 per cent of the total resident population lived at this density and only 8 per cent of Pakistani households existed at this density. Nearly a quarter of Bangladeshi households (24 per cent) lacked central heating (compared with the average of 19 per cent). Over 60 per cent of Bangladeshi households had no car compared with one-third of all households (OPCS, 1993, vol. 2, Table 11, p.770). Perhaps as a reflection of these living conditions, a striking proportion of Bangladeshis are permanently sick: 9 per cent of men aged 16 and over are in this position and 2 per cent of women. Nationally, 5 per cent of men and 3 per cent of women aged 16 and over are permanently sick (OPCS, 1993, vol. 2, Table 10).

The combination of manual occupations, high unemployment and crowded living conditions places Bangladeshis in particular in a highly disadvantageous position in British life (Eade et al., 1996). Islamic traditions are sometimes proposed to explain the situation, but it is likely that the rural background of many of the original migrants is a more important variable. The Ismaili Muslims from East Africa, for example, where they had an urban and educationally sophisticated background, do not share the characteristics of the Sylhetis of Tower Hamlets.

It is apparent that the migrations from India, Pakistan and Bangladesh affect only very geographically restricted parts of the Subcontinent. The migrants come overwhelmingly from the Punjab (both sides of the border between India and Pakistan) and the Gujarat with a relatively small contribution from Bengal and very little from the south of the Subcontinent. Among the non-East African Indians in the 1994 Policy Studies Institute survey, 62 per cent of respondents said that they spoke Punjabi, 20 per cent that they spoke Gujarati, 33 per cent that they spoke Hindi, 20 per cent that they spoke Urdu, and 2 per cent that they spoke Bengali (Modood et al., 1997, p.310). These figures sum to more than 100 per cent because many Indians are polyglot. Urdu is a national rather than a regional language and Hindi has both a national and a regional currency. Hindi and Urdu share a common oral base, but in their written forms, Urdu has a Persian script while Hindi has a Sanskrit form.

The reasons for this geographical selectivity are not clear, although once the migration has been set on course, the chain process has sustained and intensified the initial nodes. One possible variable is that most of the areas involved in the migration are those affected by the population movements of the 1947 Partition or by other forcible upheavals such as the Mangla Dam construction. This argument would seem to hold true for the Punjab where both Sikhs and Pakistanis were deeply affected. Against this argument is the fact that not all areas affected by Partition are involved in the movements. Bengal, in particular, was deeply affected by partition, but little involved in the early migrations. Similarly, the Muhajirs, refugees from India who fled to Pakistan at the time of Partition, seem relatively little affected by the movement to Britain. The operation of individuals, however, such as those who had served in the armed services (Shaw, 1988) or travel agents, is clearly important (Knights, 1996).

The migration from the rural areas was motivated by a wish to earn money, often for the purchase of land in the home village (Dahya, 1974). Thus, initially, the movement was largely of young men and there was a large gender imbalance. This imbalance is still visible in the Bangladeshi community where the migration was much later than for the Indians and Pakistanis (Peach, 1990). However, as the legislative noose restricting immigration was drawn much tighter in Britain, it proved more attractive to bring dependants to join workers in Britain than to return to the homeland. In a way, the ownership of property in Britain may be seen as a substitute for land purchase in the home village. Indians and Pakistanis have extraordinarily high levels of owner-occupation, though this is not yet the case for the more recently settled Bangladeshis. Gradually, the myth of return (Anwar, 1979) is diminishing, but one should not exaggerate the point.

One of the consequences for the different socio-economic positions of the Indian, Pakistani and Bangladeshi populations is their sharply different social geographies. This applies at the regional scale and within cities. The Bangladeshi population, the most disadvantaged of all of the ethnic minority groups, is concentrated in Inner London. A quarter of the entire Bangladeshi population of Britain in 1991 lived in the single London borough of Tower Hamlets. This was the borough with the highest degree of deprivation in the whole of London. Bangladeshis also showed the highest degree of segregation of any ethnic group in the country. In the 11 cities in which they numbered 1000 or more in 1991, the mean unweighted Index of Segregation (IS) score at ward level was 69. Bangladeshis were also highly segregated in these cities from all other ethnic minority populations.

Pakistanis differed from most other ethnic minority groups by having a lower concentration in London and a much more northern centre of gravity (Table 4.3). They were particularly prominent in the West Yorkshire and Lancashire textile towns (Bradford–Leeds, Manchester, Blackburn). Within these cities they were concentrated in Victorian terraced housing, often with poor amenities. Their segregation levels were lower than those of the Bangladeshis, but nevertheless quite high. The unweighted average for the 20 cities with 1000 or more Pakistanis in 1991 was 11 points lower than for the Bangladeshis at 58.

The Indian ethnic population had a more south-east and Midland concentration than the Pakistanis. Like the Bangladeshis, they had a high concentration in London, but unlike the Bangladeshis, they were decisively suburban rather than inner city with 80 per cent located in Outer rather than Inner London. Their suburban distribution was also reflected in much lower levels of segregation than either the Pakistanis or Bangladeshis. The unweighted ID for Indians in cities having 1000 or more in 1991 was 46. These tendencies for suburban locations were even more marked for the East African Indian population (Robinson, 1996).

In summary, we can argue that the South Asian groups are accommodating rather than assimilating to British life. In some ways the three groups could be thought of as representing three different stages of adjustment. The Indians are the longest established and most economically successful, followed by the Pakistanis, and the most recently arrived group, the Bangladeshis, occupy the most marginal position. Despite their blue-collar socio-economic profile,

Pakistanis have one of the highest rates of owner-occupation for their homes. They also display a significant rate of self-employment and entrepreneurial activity, for example, in running taxi firms and small shops. Bangladeshis represent something of a paradox. They are the youngest and most newly arrived group. It is not clear whether their high degree of representation in council and other forms of social housing represents a triumph over British bureaucracy and discriminatory practices or a failure to achieve the same level of property ownership as the Indians and Pakistanis. The PSI survey (Modood et al., 1997) showed a lesser degree of enthusiasm for house purchase among Bangladeshis than among other minority ethnic groups. While in some ways the Bangladeshi situation appears abject, in other ways it seems vibrant. A significant number of 'Indian' restaurants in Britain are owned and run by Bangladeshis (Eade et al., 1996).

What is interesting about the Indian model is that upward economic progress has not significantly loosened the social and family traditions which characterize all three groups. Upward economic movement has produced suburbanization, but not residential dispersal. The parallels might be with the Jewish movement from the East End of London at the beginning of the century to suburban Golders Green and Finchley by the middle of the century (Waterman and Kosmin, 1986b).

Black-Africans

The African presence in Britain goes back centuries but it is only recently that the size of the resident population has necessitated the introduction of the specific census category Black-African. From numbering about 10 000 in the 1940s, their numbers increased to 212 362 in the 1991 census. Most of the population came in different cohorts between the 1950s and 1970s. The first group to arrive were students sent by the British colonial authorities to learn the modern skills needed to take over the apparatus of the soon to be independent states. Independence led to a vast increase in their numbers as professional skills in medicine, engineering, law, and so on, were much in demand. British qualifications guaranteed prosperity for returning students and many went back home.

The educational origin of the Black-African population meant that for some time they were viewed as temporary migrants. Eventually wives and sometimes children accompanied the largely male student population signalling the development of a settled community. Unstable political conditions in late 1970s and 1980s Africa led to an influx of refugees from former British colonies such as Uganda, Somalia, Ghana, Kenya and Nigeria. They were a mixed group comprising ex-government ministers, writers, teachers, lawyers and some without formal education. While they numbered not more than 8500 between 1980 and 1991 they have helped to create a more diverse Black-African population. Nigerians and Ghanaians formed the largest group, constituting 22 and 15 per cent respectively (Daley, 1996).

Points of entry and migration goals tended to determine areas of settlement at the outset. Pre-World War II immigrants were mainly sailors and settled in ports such as Cardiff and Liverpool. As the population was essentially oriented around places of education, concentrations tended to be in the large cities with a range of educational institutions such as London, Leeds, Manchester and Birmingham. Discrimination in housing and employment opportunities meant that few could exercise choice in their residential location within large cities. They settled where landlords were known to rent to blacks or where Africans had bought houses and paid mortgages by renting to others, often in poor and overcrowded inner city conditions. This pattern persists into the 1990s. In the 1991 census, 80 per cent of the population lived in Greater London and of this group 66 per cent in Inner London. Nevertheless, there are signs that a process of suburbanization is beginning to occur.

While housing conditions have improved as many have shifted into council housing, discrimination in local authorities' housing allocation still acts to locate them in some of the least desirable inner-city estates in the London boroughs of Lewisham, Haringey, Newham and Southwark. Many continue to live in overcrowded conditions. In 1991, 16 per cent lived in households of five or more persons.

As recent migrants their demographic profile shows a population which is relatively youthful: 29 per cent were below the age of 16 and 64 per cent between the ages of 20 and 44, with fewer in retirement age than other ethnic groups. About 36 per cent of the population is now UK-born.

Lack of child care and the pursuance of academic qualifications by both husbands and wives led to the development of the practice of fostering out African children to white households (Goody and Groothues,1973). While there is virtually no database on the size of the fostered population, one can hypothesize that a significant proportion of children of Nigerian and Ghanaian parentage were privately fostered in the 1960s and 1970s. Even though attempts have been made to discourage this practice, it remains popular with Africans where both partners have independent ambitions which could be hindered by the demands of child care in a situation where extended family support is non-existent and child care expensive.

Because of their educational origins, Black-Africans were the most qualified ethnic group, with 26 per cent over the age of 18 possessing higher qualifications. This was not, however, reflected in levels and areas of employment. While 32 per cent of those employed were in professional occupations as managers and administrators, mainly within local government, Africans had some of the highest unemployment rates in Britain – 27 per cent of the economically active were unemployed compared to a national average of 10 per cent and a Greater London average of 7 per cent. Many can be found engaged in casual, part-time or peripatetic work, such as cleaners or night-watchmen, with most cherishing the hope of fulfilling their ambitions in a professional capacity. Consequently, many would be involved in multiple occupations or part-time study. Many Africans have found that qualifications gained in Africa are not recognized in Britain. Under-employment is therefore a key characteristic of the work experience of Africans in Britain and elsewhere (Amissah, 1996). This has implications for social progress and well-being (for example, they are the only census category where the expected pattern of social class and tenure does not hold true).

While a minority of young Africans have progressed rapidly in British society as television entertainers, magazine editors, journalists, doctors, and so on, the majority of the British-born youth seem fated to have the same social trajectories as the Black-Caribbean population. The 1991 Black-African unemployment rate of 27 per cent was the third highest rate in Great Britain behind the Bangladeshi and Pakistani rates. Unemployment is highest among the youth who tend to have lower levels of academic qualifications than their parents' generation. Settled communities facilitate the emergence of a distinct social and cultural life that may reflect regional or national origins: West African, Somali or Ugandan. There exist numerous regional, ethnic and national associations (Atampugre, 1992), many providing much needed social networks for child care, employment, credit, and so on. The most significant association is the growth of the religious population. In September 1998, the Hackney-based West African church, Kingsway, opened the largest religious building to be built in Britain for centuries. Other African churches with large congregations have proliferated in various parts of London. African entrepreneurs are also establishing community-based businesses such as hairdressing, as well as moving into mainstream activities. There is no doubt that the economic downturn on the continent of Africa has made reluctant settlers of many of the Black-African population. They are now a permanent feature of multi-cultural Britain.

The Chinese

The Chinese population is the smallest of the ethnic minority populations enumerated in the 1991 census. Like the Caribbean and South Asian groups, its current numbers are the result of post-war immigration, but like the South Asian groups rather than the Caribbeans, much of that immigration post-dates the 1962 controls. Although its image has been that of the restaurant and catering trade, the reality is that the Chinese population is enormously differentiated between the relatively poorly educated and unskilled Hong Kong population and the highly educated and professionalized classes from Southeast Asia and the People's Republic of China.

Despite more than 100 years' presence, there were fewer than 5000 Chinese in this country up to the end of World War II (Shang, 1984; Cheng, 1996). The first wave of Chinese migration to Britain started in the second half of the nineteenth century. The opening up of the China trade to British merchants after China's defeat in the Opium Wars increased the need for Chinese seamen. The British East India Company recruited cheap labourers from the villages in southern China to work on British ships. Some Chinese seamen jumped ship to work in better paid jobs in the British ports, and became the first Chinese settlers in this country.

Towards the end of the nineteenth century, Chinese communities in port cities, such as Liverpool, Cardiff and London, began to take shape. Provision stores and restaurants were opened to cater for Chinese seamen, dock workers and students who had come study in Britain (Shang, 1984). The early twentieth century saw the Chinese move away from the dockland occupations into laundries and the catering trade. Up until World War II, this migration, which consisted mainly of males, remained a trickle.

The second wave of migration brought into Britain the majority of today's Chinese population. The post-war British demand for ethnic cuisine coupled with deteriorating economic conditions in rural Hong Kong formed the major pull-push factors of this migration (Baxter, 1988). The second wave of immigration took place as early as the 1950s, but the large influx of the Chinese did not follow until the 1960s (Cheng, 1996).

The Chinese chain migration and concentration in catering were heavily affected by the Commonwealth Immigration Act in 1962. The Act required prospective immigrants of working age to hold an employment voucher for a specific job with a single named employer in Britain (Baxter, 1988). The Hong Kong Chinese had already moved into the catering trade and it proved an ideal channel for operating chain migration within this system (Cheng, 1996).

The Chinese population is relatively young and has the smallest proportion of any ethnic minority population of children born in the UK (28 per cent). The average age of Chinese in Britain in 1991 was 29, and was 9 years younger than an average white person. The mean age of the overseas born Chinese was 36, and that of a British-born Chinese, 13.

The Chinese population comes from a remarkably diverse set of sources. Nearly half (48 per cent) of those not born in the UK were born in Hong Kong; 17 per cent were born in the People's Republic of China, 14 per cent in Malaysia, 4 per cent in Singapore, and 8 per cent in Vietnam. Mauritius and the Caribbean supplied a further 12 per cent each. Migration to Britain from Southeast Asia for educational purposes has been a particularly important source of migrants. Since the 1980s, there has been a resurgence of immigration from mainland China. Various categories of students and scholars arrived in Britain, after mainland China was opened to the Western world. Many stayed on after completing their education. This group, which is small in number but rapidly growing, contains the most highly qualified Chinese migrants Britain ever received.

The Vietnamese Chinese came to Britain as political refugees. After the fall of Saigon in 1975, the Chinese in Vietnam were persecuted and many had to flee the country. Britain received 20 000 Vietnamese refugees as part of an international settlement effort (Jones, 1982). Because of a relatively non-selective system of admittance, few of the British Vietnamese possess transferable skills and their knowledge of English is poor. As a result, only a few are employed casually within the Chinese catering business, or consigned to other areas of menial work. Most of them remain unemployed due to lack of qualifications or deficiencies in governmental resettlement policies (Peach et al., 1988).

One of the consequences of movement to Britain from Malaysia, Singapore, the People's Republic of China and Taiwan for educational and training purposes has been that the Chinese have the highest socio-economic profile of any ethnic minority group in the country. The Chinese male percentage in Class I (Professional) is 17.6 – more than double the average of 6.8. They are under-represented in each of the manual classes compared with the average. They also have a lower than average rate of male unemployment. Chinese women also have the highest proportion of any group in the top professional class (over four times the average; Figure 4.2). They have a relatively low rate of unemployment compared with other ethnic minority populations, but rather higher than average for the population as a whole.

On the other hand, the public image of the Chinese has been that they are over-represented in the catering and related industries. Estimates of the Chinese working in catering have varied from about 90 per cent (Home Affairs Committee, 1985) to around 67 per cent (Cheng, 1994). The census, which covers the whole Chinese population in Britain, shows that about 55 per cent of the Chinese work in distribution. Within this group, the Chinese are markedly concentrated in a single industry: restaurants, snack bars, cafes and other eating places (Watson, 1977). Altogether, 41 per cent of the Chinese work in this single industry. Moreover, the industrial distribution varies with ethnic origins. For instance, we find that 58 per cent of the Hong Kong-born Chinese and 42 per cent of the Chinese born in other parts of the world work in this industry.

However, only 10 per cent of the Southeast Asian Chinese fall into this category. Outside distribution, the Chinese are also concentrated in other services and banking, which employ 20 per cent and 12 per cent of them respectively. The Chinese are known to have a lower unemployment rate than whites (Cheng, 1994). An explanation is that the family oriented catering business serves as a safety net, which creates jobs for its own members during hard times. It could also be the fact that a greater proportion of the Chinese have above A level qualifications. Therefore, they are more likely to be employed in the expanding service sector, which generally requires good skills from employees. On the other hand, whites with lower qualifications on average, may have a greater propensity to work in manufacturing industries, which suffered from more job losses in the 1980s. If this hypothesis is true, we would expect ethnic differences to disappear once education is held constant. However, if ethnic differences persist, the safety-net hypothesis would be true.

Gender

The Chinese have a balanced gender distribution (Table 4.5). Compared with the British-born whites, for whom there are 107 women for every 100 men, the Chinese have a higher proportion of males. But compared with South Asian groups, the Chinese have a much lower proportion of men.

However, the Chinese population is not a homogeneous one. We know from their migration history that nearly all voluntary migrants of Chinese origin came to Britain to improve their economic opportunities, but there was already marked difference in their economic status at the time of migration and hence different expectations. The Chinese from Hong Kong, for instance, consist primarily of economic immigrants in the traditional sense. But those from Southeast Asia are more likely to be second-time migrants, whose forebears left China a long time ago. These people, who were more economically prosperous than the former group, came to Britain for better education and greater career opportunities, which their first country of settlement could not provide.

There is substantial difference in sex distributions within the Chinese population. The Chinese from Hong Kong are the only group marked by an excess of men, 100 men for 99 women. The Chinese from Southeast Asia and other parts of the world have more female than male members. The highest disproportion is for those born in Malaysia and Singapore, for whom there are 161 women for every 100 men (Cheng, 1996). Chinese migration from Southeast Asia is clearly dominated by the migration of women. Many of these women had fairly good qualifications and came to work in the British health professions (Cheng, 1994).

Region

The regional distribution of the Chinese is characterized by the concentration in the south-east and wide dispersion in other parts of Britain. Altogether, 53 per cent of the Chinese live in the south-east compared with 30 per cent of whites. The percentage of the Chinese living in inner London is much higher than that of whites: 17 per cent compared with 3 per cent of whites. In all the other regions, the Chinese are under-represented compared with the white population. Even in the north-west, where the second largest concentration of the Chinese is found, the number living there as a proportion of the total Chinese population in Britain is still lower than the proportion of the white population, 10.5 per cent versus 11.3 per cent.

The regional distribution of the Chinese varies with the country (or place) of origin and is affected by employment patterns. The Hong Kong Chinese, who have the highest percentage of caterers, are the most widely dispersed across the country. Their level of concentration in the south-east, which is 46 per cent, is the lowest among all Chinese immigrants. The demand for ethnic cuisine, which started in the 1960s, encouraged the gradual diffusion of the Chinese into progressively smaller towns and even villages across the country (Cheng, 1996).

The Chinese from Southeast Asia have the highest level of concentration in the south-east. Altogether 66 per cent live in this region. This pattern might be explained by the fact that many people from this group are either professionals or have technical skills. Therefore, they are more likely to work in the south-east where such jobs are more readily available than in other parts of the country. The concentration in the south-east is also notable for the Chinese from other parts of the world. This group is mixed. Their pattern of settlement is due to a combination of the Vietnamese refugees who, in spite of the government's intention of dispersal, came to live in London (Peach et al., 1988), and the qualified Chinese from China who hold professional or skilled jobs. The north-west is the region with the second largest Chinese concentration. It attracts 11 per cent of the Hong Kong Chinese and 10 per cent of the Chinese from other parts of the world. However, only 4 per cent of the Southeast Asian Chinese are found in this region, a pattern reminding us again of the differences in employment patterns.

Household size and family structure

The average size for households with a head born in China or Hong Kong is 3.1 persons, slightly larger than the average household, which has 2.5 persons. It can be seen from Table 4.6 that while 61 per cent of all households have 2 or fewer people, only 54 per cent of the Chinese are in households of the same size. Similarly, only 8 per cent of all households contain 5 or more people, but 19 per cent of the Chinese live in such households. Two factors are likely to account for the relatively larger Chinese household. They have a higher percentage of multi-family households (2.5 per cent of households compared with an average of 0.9 per cent for the population as a whole) and a higher than average proportion of married couple households with dependent children (Table 4.7).

Presence of dependent children, too, contributes to the household size. While 53.2 per cent of whites live in families with dependent children, 71.3

per cent of the Chinese do so. This reflects the different age-structures between the Chinese and the host population noted earlier. The Chinese are, on average, younger than the host population. Therefore, they are more likely to have young children living in the households and are less likely to have grown up children who live elsewhere.

Housing tenure

The Chinese have a lower level of home ownership than the total population. Figure 4.7 shows that 64 per cent of the Chinese are home owners, as compared with 70 per cent of whites. The Chinese have a lower level of rented housing from the public sector than the white population. Of the Chinese, 15 per cent live in rented accommodation from the local authority versus 20 per cent of whites, although housing associations accommodate a similar proportion of 2 per cent of both the white and Chinese populations. The Chinese display a higher level of rental from the private sector than whites. Tenants of the private sector form 17 per cent of the Chinese, but only 8 per cent of whites. This reflects the fact that the Chinese have a higher proportion of students (Chan, 1994).

There is substantial diversity in housing tenure within the Chinese population itself. Among immigrants, the level of home ownership is the highest among those from Hong Kong (69 per cent) and it is the lowest among those from 'other parts of the world' (49 per cent). As most Hong Kong Chinese run their own business in catering, they may be more likely than other groups to accumulate wealth, which gives them greater housing security. The bulk of the Chinese from other parts of the world are either Vietnamese refugees, among whom the unemployment rate is high, or those from mainland China, for whom immigration is a new phenomenon. It is no surprise, therefore, that the level of rental from the public sector is the highest among this group. For instance, 31 per cent of the Chinese from other parts of the world are accommodated by either local authorities or housing associations (Cheng, 1996).

Educational levels

The Chinese as a whole are better educated than whites. Among the Chinese, 2.3 per cent have higher degrees. This compares with only 0.6 per cent of the white population. The proportion of the Chinese with first degrees and above is 10.7 per cent, and that of whites, 5.2 per cent. At the other end of the spectrum, a greater proportion of whites than Chinese are unqualified – 90 per cent versus 83 per cent.

There is substantial differentiation among the Chinese with regard to educational level (Cheng and Heath, 1993). Of all immigrant groups, the Chinese from Southeast Asia are the best qualified and those from Hong Kong the least qualified, with those from other parts of the world coming in between. Over 22 per cent of the Southeast Asian Chinese hold first degrees and above, compared with 11 per cent of the Hong Kong Chinese. At the other end of the spectrum, 85 per cent of the Hong Kong Chinese have qualifications below A level versus only 59 per cent of the Southeast Asian Chinese.

The British-born Chinese display the lowest level of qualification among all sub-groups of the Chinese. Only 4 per cent have attained first degrees and 94 per cent have qualifications lower than A level. This is the only Chinese sub-group that is less qualified than whites. However, the explanation seems to be that this group is fairly young and most may still be engaged in continuous full-time education. Controlling for this shows that British-born Chinese actually display some ethnic advantage over the white population in becoming qualified (Cheng, 1996).

Industry

There is considerable internal differentiation among the Chinese with regard to the risks of unemployment. At one end of the spectrum, we find the Hong Kong-born Chinese sheltered from unemployment by their family-orientated catering business, where jobs can be created for all members during hard times (Runnymede Trust, 1985). For instance, the odds of a white person being unemployed rather than employed are 1.4 times that of a Chinese person born in Hong Kong. It is 2.0 times when we compare men, and 1.3 times when we compare women. At the other end of the spectrum, the Chinese born in other parts of the world display greater risks of unemployment than whites. For instance, the odds of the Chinese born in other parts of the world being unemployed rather than employed are twice those of the whites. The size of ethnic difference is the same for men and women. Previous research informs us that the Chinese born in Vietnam came to Britain as refugees. They possessed poor language and technical skills, and were marked by high rates of unemployment (Jones, 1982). Although the Sample of Anonymised Records (SARs) does not allow us to distinguish the Vietnamese Chinese from the rest within the category of Chinese born in other parts of the world, it is likely that the high risks of unemployment are primarily characteristics of the Vietnamese Chinese (Cheng, 1996). (The SARs are small samples of individuals and households which the OPCS draws from the total census. They allow researchers to produce cross-tabulations by any census category and are therefore more flexible than published tables.)

Conclusion

The profile of the Chinese in Britain is one of a successful ethnic minority. It is small in size, young in age, balanced in gender and it is one of the latest arrivals on the British scene. The Chinese are well educated; the proportion of college-educated and above surpassing that of the white population. They have a lower unemployment rate and are disproportionately over-represented in professional and skilled occupations. In education and occupation, the Chinese have out-performed the whites and present a socio-economic profile reminiscent of the Chinese in the United States. Given that the Chinese have been successful in getting into the top occupational groups, it remains to be seen whether they are also successful in obtaining the most desirable jobs within the top occupational groups.

The Chinese are not a homogeneous group. Our analyses suggest the need to differentiate the Chinese into various sub-groups, which present different demographic and socio-economic profiles. The restaurateur image is true for only 40 per cent of the working Chinese population and is mainly character-istic of the Hong Kong-born Chinese. Immigration from Southeast Asia and more recently from mainland China is characterized by the selected migration of the well educated, who aspire to greater career opportunities. They appear at the top of the Chinese socio-economic profile, followed by the Hong Kong Chinese and Vietnamese refugees, who appear at the bottom.

Part III

The major non-European groups with which this chapter has been concerned all owe their current size to the post-war surge of immigration in response to acute shortages of labour. Most of these populations had existing finger-holds in Britain, but their post-war growth was of a completely different order even if the early settlement was of importance in facilitating the later flow. On the whole, accounts exaggerate the importance of pre-World War II antecedents. The latter were important in affecting the mix of peoples, not in creating the flow itself. Britain's post-war immigration was powered by the same dynamic that transformed the demography of post-war Germany, France and the Benelux countries. The post-war locations bear little resemblance to those of the pre-war period.

Yet, although Britain's post-war ethnic minorities were lumped together as 'coloured immigrants' at the beginning of this sequence of events in the 1950s, by the 1990s, race was no longer the defining characteristic of the groups. Differences in human capital between and within these groups have broken up the superimposed solidarity of race. The emphasis has changed from race to ethnicity, and for some groups, religiously defined ethnic identity.

The Chinese have emerged in the 1990s as the most successful of the new minorities. They have higher educational qualifications than other groups, including whites, and have a higher proportion in white-collar occupations, including the professional classes. They have lower rates of unemployment. Yet their popularly perceived image as restaurateurs, take-away food propri-etors and workers and waiters is also true. But it is more true of the Hong Kong

Chinese than those from the mainland, Malaysia, Taiwan or Singapore. There is not one Chinese population but many, and there is a major contrast between the profile of those from Hong Kong and the highly educated cohorts from the other countries mentioned. Interestingly, the sex ratio of the Hong Kong Chinese is male-dominated, while those from Southeast Asia have a female surplus. It seems to be among the latter group that the relatively high rate of Chinese out-marriage is most marked.

The Indian population also stands out as economically successful. It has a higher than average proportion of white-collar workers, particularly among the professional classes. It is educated, qualified, self-employed, property-owning and suburbanized to a considerable extent. However, like the Chinese population, it is not a single entity. There are differences of religion, caste and language within the group that came directly from the Subcontinent that the census cannot capture. Most importantly there are considerable economic differences between those who came directly from the Subcontinent and those who came from East Africa. The elites and the rural peasantries are very different.

The Pakistanis, by contrast, are less economically successful. They have a higher proportion of manual workers than average, and higher than average unemployment. Female participation in the formal labour force is low; family size is high. Yet Pakistanis have also shown entrepreneurial ability in the generation of small businesses – notably shops, but increasingly taxi operations (Ballard, 1996). They also have an extraordinarily high rate of owner-occupation, although admittedly in inner-city Victorian terraced property.

The Bangladeshis represent the most economically disadvantaged of all of the ethnic minorities that we have considered. They have the lowest proportion in non-manual occupations, the highest rates of unemployment, the largest families, the most crowded conditions, the least owner-occupation. They are also the most highly segregated of all ethnic minority groups. Yet they are also the most recently arrived group and show entrepreneurial skills in the rag trade and in restaurants. It is too soon to judge whether they are stuck at the bottom of the economic heap or whether they are on the move.

All three South Asian groups share characteristics of strong family structures. The anthropological literature is full of examples of the power of kinship and community (Dahya, 1974; Robinson, 1986; Shaw, 1988; Ballard, 1990). This is particularly striking in relation to the way in which individual economic action is targeted at family improvement. This is evident from the way in which early migration was aimed at improving the family status in sending villages (Dahya, 1974; Shaw, 1988). It is also evident in the high rates of owner-occupation of Indians and Pakistanis in Britain. It is evidenced in the high proportion of households which consist of married couples with children and the significant proportion of extended family households. The South

Asian households are notably ethnically homogeneous. Intermarriage is low: over 90 per cent of all Indian, Pakistani and Bangladeshi men are in unions with women from their own ethnic group (Table 4.9, panel 2); for the women of all three groups it is 95 per cent, and for Bangladeshi women the figure reaches almost 100 per cent (Table 4.9 panel 3). Economic advance has not led to a notable weakening of traditional values. The South Asian groups are accommodating rather than assimilating.

The Chinese share some of the South Asian social characteristics. Extended family households, although not numerous, are proportionately more impor-

Table 4.9 Inter–ethnic unions: all married and cohabiting men and women, resident population, Great Britain, 1991[ab]

Panel 1

Ethnic group of male partner	Ethnic group of female partner				
	White	Black-Carib.	Black-African	Black-Other	Indian
White	**126150**	102	41	63	71
Black-Carib.	225	**559**	8	10	4
Black-African	48	16	**208**	4	2
Black-Other	76	3	2	**62**	1
Indian	134	2	4	1	**1762**
Pakistani	42	0	0	1	6
Bangladeshi	7	0	2	0	4
Chinese	34	0	0	0	2
Other Asian	55	4	1	1	4
Other-Other	218	2	1	2	7
Total	126989	688	267	144	1863

Panel 2: Unions expressed as percentage of male's ethnic group

Ethnic group of male partner	Ethnic group of female partner				
	White	Black-Carib.	Black-African	Black-Other	Indian
White	**99.49**	0.08	0.03	0.05	0.06
Black-Carib.	**27.27**	**67.76**	0.97	1.21	0.48
Black-African	**17.08**	**5.69**	**74.02**	1.42	0.71
Black-Other	**51.70**	2.04	1.36	**42.18**	0.68
Indian	6.93	0.10	0.21	0.05	**91.06**
Pakistani	5.05	0.00	0.00	0.12	0.72
Bangladeshi	3.00	0.00	0.86	0.00	1.72
Chinese	**12.59**	0.00	0.00	0.00	0.74
Other Asian	**14.71**	1.07	0.27	0.27	1.07
Other-Other	**50.46**	0.46	0.23	0.46	1.62
Total	126989	688	267	144	1863

tant than for the white population (2.8 per cent versus 0.8 per cent) and family size is larger than average. However, there is a strikingly high rate of out-marriage, particularly for Chinese women with white men (nearly a quarter, Table 4.9, panel 3).

The Caribbean family structures are at the polar extreme from those of the South Asian groups. Marriage is far less widespread, cohabitation more prevalent and single-parent families, particularly with female heads of household, are common. These features have become more widespread among the white population, but in the Caribbean case owe much to family structures found in

Pakistani	Bangladeshi	Chinese	Other Asian	Other-Other	Total
10	0	79	148	139	126803
2	0	2	3	12	825
1	0	0	0	2	281
0	0	0	2	1	147
18	0	5	4	5	1935
775	0	0	4	3	831
1	**217**	0	0	2	233
0	0	**234**	0	0	270
4	1	2	**296**	6	374
4	0	2	5	**191**	432
815	218	324	462	361	132131

Pakistani	Bangladeshi	Chinese	Other Asian	Other-Other	Total
0.01	0.00	0.06	0.12	0.11	100
0.24	0.00	0.24	0.36	1.45	100
0.36	0.00	0.00	0.00	0.71	100
0.00	0.00	0.00	1.36	0.68	100
0.93	0.00	0.26	0.21	0.26	100
93.26	0.00	0.00	0.48	0.36	100
0.43	**93.13**	0.00	0.00	0.86	100
0.00	0.00	**86.67**	0.00	0.00	100
1.07	0.27	0.53	**79.14**	1.60	100
0.93	0.00	0.46	1.16	**44.21**	100
815	218	324	462	361	132131

Table 4.9 cont ...

Panel 3: Unions expressed as percentage of female's ethnic group

Ethnic group of male partner	Ethnic group of female partner				
	White	Black-Carib.	Black-African	Black-Other	Indian
White	**99.40**	**14.83**	**15.36**	**43.75**	3.81
Black-Carib	0.18	**81.25**	3.00	6.94	0.21
Black-African	0.04	2.33	**77.90**	2.78	0.11
Black-Other	0.06	0.44	0.75	**43.06**	0.05
Indian	0.11	0.29	1.50	0.69	**94.58**
Pakistani	0.03	0.00	0.00	0.69	0.32
Bangladeshi	0.01	0.00	0.75	0.00	0.21
Chinese	0.03	0.00	0.00	0.00	0.11
Other Asian	0.04	0.58	0.37	0.69	0.21
Other-Other	0.17	0.29	0.37	1.39	0.38
Total	100	100	100	100	100

Source: Based on Ann Berrington in Coleman and Salt (1996), Table 7.9.

the West Indies. There, matrifocal families are common and marriage for working-class people is often a middle-age institution which takes place after a family has been raised. The Caribbean structure is thus much more individuated, as compared with the Asian families. At the same time there is a great deal of intermarriage and inter-ethnic cohabitation. Table 4.9 shows that 27 per cent of families with a Caribbean male partner also had a white partner (panel 2) and 15 per cent of families with a Caribbean female partner had a white partner (panel 3). The Caribbean pattern was thus one of economic deprivation but social assimilation. This was borne out in a number of other ways. The levels of segregation were some of the lowest of any group. The group's representation in council and social housing was at about the level expected for its socio-economic characteristics.

In the 1950s, 1960s and 1970s ethnic minorities were seen in official eyes in terms of race. Legislation was framed to outlaw racial discrimination. The Race Relations Acts were passed in 1965 and 1968 and 1976. The Race Relations Board (1965) and the Community Relations Commission (1968) were created by the 1965 and 1968 Race Relations Acts. The 1976 Race Relations Act established the Commission for Racial Equality, charged with working towards eliminating racial discrimination, promoting racial equality and good race relations. By the 1980s and 1990s minorities were conceived of in a more differentiated way. Religion, particularly for Muslims, was becoming the defining criterion. All of these definitions, of course, continue to play a part in identity, but the ground has shifted over time. Among young people

Pakistani	Bangladeshi	Chinese	Other Asian	Other-Other	Total
1.23	0.00	**24.38**	**32.03**	**38.50**	126803
0.25	0.00	0.62	0.65	3.32	825
0.12	0.00	0.00	0.00	0.55	281
0.00	0.00	0.00	0.43	0.28	147
2.21	0.00	1.54	0.87	1.39	1935
95.09	0.00	0.00	0.87	0.83	831
0.12	**99.54**	0.00	0.00	0.55	233
0.00	0.00	**72.22**	0.00	0.00	270
0.49	0.46	0.62	**64.07**	1.66	374
0.49	0.00	0.62	1.08	**52.91**	432
100	100	100	100	100	132131

Notes: [a]Statistically high selections are highlighted in bold type.
[b]Berrington's original figures for total Caribbean in Panel 1 are 40 too high, both row and column.

born in Britain, a Black British and a British Asian identity has developed. Most notable, however, has been the growth in numbers of the children of mixed unions so that one-third of the children in families in which one partner was Caribbean and both parents were present are in this group. While legislation to outlaw discrimination has been passed, relations between the police and the ethnic minority communities – particularly the black groups – have continued to be poor. Events such as the 1981 urban riots (Peach, 1986) had police operations as the catalyst in several cases. This was most notably the case in 'Operation Swamp' in Brixton. Since then there has been a series of high-profile cases which have continued to blight police–ethnic minority relations, including that of Stephen Lawrence, an innocent black teenager murdered in a racist attack in London, in which the police were accused of mishandling the case and failing to investigate it professionally.

For Pakistanis, Bangladeshis and other Muslim minorities, the issues of friction have been of a different sort. Schools have proved a difficult arena. There have been issues of providing *halal* meat for school dinners. Gymnastics and swimming for girls have been condemned by some imams, and co-education itself has proved offensive to some. There has been a major and so far unsuccessful attempt to gain state aid for Muslim schools, in the same way that it has been provided for Roman Catholic, Church of England and Jewish schools. On the other side, the public burning of Salman Rushdie's *The Satanic Verses* in Bradford and the support for the Ayatollah Khomeini's *fatwah* on the author offended majority sensitivities.

Thus the picture at the end of the century is mixed. Britain has changed from a country which claimed a quarter of the world's population as its citizens in 1948 to one in which patriality, with its strong overtones of whiteness, has become the criterion of Britishness. The economic, entrepreneurial and intellectual contribution of the ethnic minorities is undoubted, but suspicions remain on all sides. The genesis of a Black British and British Asian identity among those raised in the country and the growth of a significant 'mixed' population offer signs of hope.

References

Alderman, G. (1992) *Modern British Jewry*, Clarendon Press, Oxford.

Alderman, G. (1995) 'The defence of *shechita*: Anglo-Jewry and the "human conditions" regulations of 1990', *New Community*, 21, pp.79–93.

Amissah, C. K. (1996) 'Sub-Saharan Africans in the US labor market: The Cost of Being Black', *National Journal of Sociology*, vol. 10 (1), pp.57–82.

Anwar, M. (1979) *The Myth of Return: Pakistanis in Britain*, Heinemann, London.

Atampugre, N. (1992) 'Migrants and development: a study of Ghanaian migrant associations in Britain', mimeo produced for the Panos Institute in London.

Balarajan, R. and Bulusu, L. (1990) 'Mortality among immigrants in England and Wales, 1973–1983', in Britton, M. (ed.) *Mortality and Geography*, OPCS Series DS no. 9, HMSO, London, pp.135–50.

Ballard, Roger (1990) 'Migration and kinship: the impact of marriage rules on Punjabi migration to Britain', in Clarke, C., Peach, C. and Vertovec, S. (eds) *South Asians Overseas*, Cambridge University Press, Cambridge.

Ballard, R. (1996) 'The Pakistanis', in Peach, Ceri (ed.) *The Ethnic Minority Populations of Great Britain*, vol. 2, *Ethnicity in the 1991Census*, HMSO, London.

Ballard, Roger and Kalra, Virinder Singh (1994) *The Ethnic Dimensions of the 1991 Census*, Manchester Census Group, University of Manchester, Manchester.

Banton, Michael (1955) *The Coloured Quarter*, Jonathan Cape, London.

Baxter, S. C. C. (1988) 'A Political Economy of Ethnic Chinese Catering Industry', unpublished PhD thesis, Aston University, Birmingham.

Byron, M. (1994) *Post-War Caribbean Migration to Britain: The Unfinished Cycle*, Avebury, Aldershot.

Central Statistical Office (CSO) (1986) *Preliminary Report on the 1986 Census*, Central Statistical Office, Dublin.

Central Statistical Office (1994) *Social Trends 24*, HMSO, London.

Chan, Yiu Man (1994) 'The Chinese in Greater Manchester: a demographic profile', *New Community*, 20, pp.655–9.

Chance, Judith (1996) 'The Irish: the invisible minority', in Peach, Ceri (ed.) *The Ethnic Minority Populations of Britain*, vol. 2, *Ethnicity in the 1991 Census*, HMSO, London.

Cheng, Y. (1994) *Education and Class: Chinese in Britain and the United States*, Avebury, Aldershot.

Cheng, Y. (1996) 'The Chinese', in Peach, Ceri (ed.) *The Ethnic Minority Populations of Britain*, vol. 2, *Ethnicity in the 1991 Census*, HMSO, London.

Cheng, Y. and Heath, A. (1993) 'Ethnic origins and class destinations', *Oxford Review of Education*, 19, pp.151–65.

Cohen, Robin (1997) *Global Diasporas*, UCL Press, London.

Coleman, D. A. and Salt, J. (1996) *The British Population: Patterns, Trends and Processes*, Oxford University Press, Oxford.

Collins, Sydney (1957) *Coloured Minorities in Britain*, Lutterworth Press, London.

Dahya, B. (1974) 'The nature of Pakistani ethnicity in industrial cities in Britain', in Cohen, A. (ed.) *Urban Ethnicity*, Tavistock, London.

Daley, Patricia (1996) 'Black-African: students who stayed', in Peach, Ceri (ed.) *The Ethnic Minority Populations of Britain*, vol. 2, *Ethnicity in the 1991 Census*, HMSO, London.

Eade, J., Vamplew, T. and Peach, C. (1996) 'Bangladeshis: the encapsulated community', in Peach, Ceri (ed.) *The Ethnic Minority Populations of Britain*, vol. 2, *Ethnicity in the 1991 Census*, HMSO, London.

Engels, F. (1971) *The Condition of the Working class in England* (translated and edited by Henderson, W. O. and Chaloner, W. H. from the original German first edition of 1845), Blackwell, Oxford.

Englander, D. (1993) 'Integrated but insecure: a portrait of Anglo-Jewry at the close of the twentieth century', in Parson, G. (ed.) *The Growth of Religious Diversity: Britain from 1945, Volume I*, Routledge, London.

Glass, Ruth (1960) *Newcomers: The West Indians in London*, Allen and Unwin, London.

Goody, E. N. and Groothues, C. Muir (1973) *Factors Relating to the Delegation of Parental Roles among West Africans in London*, SSRC, London.

Halliday, Fred (1992) *Arabs in Exile: Yemeni Migrants in Urban Britain*, I. B. Tauris, London.

Holmes, C. (1988) *John Bull's Island: Immigration and British Society 1871–1971*, Macmillan, Basingstoke.

Home Affairs Committee (HAC) (1985) *Chinese Community in Britain*, HMSO, London.

Jones, P. (1982) *Vietnamese Refugees: A Study of Their Reception and Resettlement in the UK*, Home Office Research and Planning Unit, London.

Knights, M. (1996) 'Bangladeshi immigrants in Italy: from geopolitics to micropolitics', *Transactions Institute of British Geographers*, New Series, 21 (1), pp.105–23.

Lee, T. R. (1973) *Race and Residence: The Concentration and Dispersal of Immigrants in London*, Clarendon Press, Oxford.

Lennon, M. et al. (1988) *Across the Water*, London, Virago.

Little, K. S. (1947) *Negroes in Britain*, Kegan Paul, Trench, Trubner and Co., London.

MacLaughlin, Jim (1994) *Ireland: The Emigrant Nursery and the World Economy*, Cork University Press, Cork.

Marret, V. (1989) *Immigrants settling in the City*, Leicester University Press, London.

Modood, T. et al. (1997) *Ethnic Minorities in Britain: Diversity and Disadvantage*, Policy Studies Institute, London.

Office of Population Censuses and Surveys (OPCS) (1993) *1991 Census: Ethnic Group and Country of Birth*, 2 volumes, HMSO, London.

Owen, D. (1996) 'The Black-Other', in Peach, Ceri (ed.) *The Ethnic Minority Populations of Britain*, Vol.2, *Ethnicity in the 1991 Census*, HMSO, London.

Patterson, S, (1961) 'The Polish exile community in Britain', *Polish Review*, 6.

Patterson, S. (1963) *Dark Strangers*, Tavistock, London.

Patterson, S. (1977) 'The Poles: an exile community in Britain', in Watson, J. L. (ed.) *Between Two Cultures*, Blackwell, Oxford.

Peach, Ceri (1968) *West Indian Migration to Britain: A Social Geography*, Oxford University Press, London.

Peach, Ceri (1986) 'A geographical perspective on the 1981 urban riots in England', *Ethnic and Racial Studies*, 9 (3), pp.386–94.

Peach, Ceri (1990) 'Estimating the growth of the Bangladeshi population of Great Britain', *New Community*, 16 (4), pp.481–91.

Peach, Ceri (1991) *The Caribbean in Europe: Contrasting Patterns of Migration and Settlement in Britain, France and the Netherlands*, Research Paper in Ethnic Relations 15, Centre for Research in Ethnic Relations, University of Warwick.

Peach, Ceri (ed.) (1996a) *The Ethnic Minority Populations of Great Britain*, vol. 2, HMSO, London.

Peach, Ceri (1996b) 'Does Britain have ghettos?', *Transactions of the Institute of British Geographers*, 22 (1), pp.216–35.

Peach, Ceri (1997) 'Postwar migration to Europe: reflux, influx, refuge,' *Social Science Quarterly*, 78 (2), pp.269–83.

Peach, Ceri and Byron, M. (1993) 'Caribbean tenants in council housing: "race", class and gender', *New Community*, 19 (3), pp.407–23.

Peach, Ceri and Byron, M. (1994) 'Council house sales, residualisation and Afro Caribbean tenants', *Journal of Social Policy*, 23 (3), pp.363–83.

Peach, G. C. K. and Winchester, S. W. C. (1974) 'Birthplace, ethnicity and the under-enumeration of West Indians, Indians and Pakistanis in the Censuses of 1966 and 1971', *New Community*, 3 (4), pp.386–93.

Peach, Ceri et al. (1988) 'Immigrants and ethnicity' in Halsey, A. H. (ed.) *British Social Trends Since 1900: A Guide to the Changing Social Structure of Britain*, Macmillan, Basingstoke.

Robinson, Vaughan (1986) *Migrants, Settlers and Transients*, Clarendon Press, Oxford.

Robinson, Vaughan (1995) 'The migration of East African Asians to the UK', in Chen, R. (ed.) *The Cambridge World Migration History*, Cambridge University Press, Cambridge.

Robinson, Vaughan, (1996) 'Indians: onwards and upwards', in Peach, Ceri (ed.)*The Ethnic Minority Populations of Britain*, vol. 2, *Ethnicity in the 1991 Census*, HMSO, London, Chapter 6.

Rubenstein, W. D. (1996) *A History of the Jews in the English-Speaking World: Great Britain*, Macmillan, Basingstoke.

Runnymede Trust (1985) 'The Chinese community in Britain: background paper', *Runnymede Trust Bulletin*, 178, pp.8–15.

Schmool, M. and Cohen, F. (1991) *British Synagogue Membership in 1990*, Community Research Unit, Board of Deputies of British Jews.

Shang, A. (1984) *The Chinese in Britain*, Batsford, London.

Shaw, Alison (1988) *A Pakistani Community in Britain*, Blackwell, Oxford.

Sillitoe, Ken (1978) 'Ethnic origins: the search for a question', *Population Trends*, 13.

Sillitoe, Ken (1987) 'Questions on race/ethnicity and related topics for the Census', *Population Trends*, 49, pp.5–11.

Spencer, I. R. G. (1997) *British Immigration Policy Since 1939: The Making of Multi-Racial Britain*, Routledge, London.

Thomas-Hope, Elizabeth (1986) 'Transients and settlers: Varieties of Caribbean migrants and the socio-economic implication of their return', *International Migration*, 24 (3), pp.559–71.

Thomas-Hope, Elizabeth (1992) *Explanation in Caribbean Migration*, Macmillan, London.

Wasserstein, B. (1996) *Vanishing Diaspora: The Jews in Europe Since 1945*, Hamish Hamilton, London.

Waterman, S. and Kosmin, B. (1986a) *British Jewry in the Eighties*, Board of Deputies of British Jews, London.

Waterman, S. and Kosmin, B. (1986b) 'The Jews of London', *Geographical Magazine*, LVIII.

Watson, J. L. (1977) 'The Chinese Hong Kong villagers in the British catering trade', in Watson, J. L. (ed.) *Between Two Cultures: Migrants and Minorities in Britain*, Blackwell, Oxford.

Zubrzycki, J. (1956) *Polish Immigrants in Britain*, Martinus Nijhoff, The Hague.

Part II
Social Reproduction

5
Schools

George Smith

> A national system of education involves, implicitly or explicitly, a definite theory as to the right ordering of national life. The establishment of educational unity presupposes general agreement as to national aims, and as to the best form of social organisation.
>
> Michael Sadler, 1902[1]

Michael Sadler, in his observations to the Board of Education in 1902, no doubt had in mind the fragmented state of schooling in England and Wales at the beginning of the century. But his proposition also serves as backdrop for this review of schooling in Britain from 1900 to 2000. While we could now, at the end of the century, claim a far more national system of education, it is still in many ways a composite of the different aims and theories of social organization and control that held sway at different periods. There may have been times of clear consensus about aims or support for radical proposals for the way ahead; for example, in the landmark legislation that set the major changes (for England and Wales – the 1902 Act, the 1944 Act and, arguably, the 1988 Education Reform Act). But our national tendency to reform and build on, rather than completely eradicate, what went before is very clearly seen in the variety of institutional forms found throughout the school system. This makes any coherent account of its development a formidable task. This task is further complicated by the existence of three, and now increasingly four, separate systems of education at school level (in Scotland, Northern Ireland, and England and Wales, but with Wales increasingly following – or rediscovering – its own direction since responsibility for schools was transferred to the Welsh Office in 1970).[2]

From one perspective the development of education in Britain over the twentieth century looks like a clear success story, with school-based education playing the major part. What was for most a relatively brief prelude to adult life at the beginning of the century had by its close extended not only upwards, but also downwards into the pre-school years, to cover a very substantial proportion of the first 20 years of life for almost all. By the end of the century more than 75 per cent of all aged 2–18 (or approximately 10 million pupils) were attending *schools* in the United Kingdom, and this does not include students in further or higher education. Explicit national targets for education are now in place to push these figures higher still in the next decades. In the early 1980s, for the first time, more than 50 per cent of adults (aged 16–69) claimed to have a qualification (OPCS, 1996). While some of these qualifications would not have been obtained in schools, and some not even in this country, much of the credit must be attributed to schools at least in part. By the end of the century the figure had risen steeply to 70 per cent. And in the final years of the century there were signs that education, if not schooling, was pushing down to include the 0–2-year-olds, as responsibility for the education and care of this age-group was formally transferred to the Department for Education and Employment (DfEE).

Yet the pattern is very far from a straightforward 'upward and onward' trend. Many of the issues that featured in policy debates at the start of the century (the organization, management and funding of education, attendance and access to schools, and the international competitiveness of the results) were recognizably back on the policy agenda at the century's conclusion. And if we have to place a high point in this development, the mid-1970s – when there were more than 11 million pupils in UK schools and the proportion of GDP spent on education reached its apogee – are as good a candidate as the end of the century. Since then, demography and fiscal policy have combined to push for more from the same, or even less expenditure. Significantly perhaps for schools, in the final decade of the century the majority of those in full-time education aged 16–18 years were, in England, to be found in the further education sector and no longer in school sixth forms.

A fuller account would have to give prominence to broader demographic and social changes. In the United States, James Coleman (1987) drew attention to the steep decline in the number of households containing children in school. On his estimation, the percentage of households *not* containing any children under 18 rose from about 25 per cent in 1870 to about 65 per cent by 1980. For Great Britain, data on households containing dependent children show a continuing fall. Thus in 1961 some 40 per cent contained dependent children. By 1991 this had fallen to 31 per cent, though the figure for Northern Ireland was higher at 41 per cent (ONS, 1998, Table 2.3). In some urban areas the figure was approximately one household in five.

Scope and coverage

This chapter concentrates on schools, including nursery schools, not on 'education' more widely defined. The further education (FE) sector is touched on only where it provides an increasingly significant part of post-compulsory full-time education (further and higher education are the focus of Chapter 6). In one sense, schools as institutions have increasingly monopolized the provision of formal education; very few parents have exercised their right to educate their children 'otherwise than at school'. Only a few children are excluded from school and not subsequently enrolled elsewhere. Yet in another sense, schools provide only one among an increasing number of educational inputs. As Heath and Clifford put it graphically in the title of their review of Rutter's *Fifteen Thousand Hours* (Rutter et al., 1979) – roughly the number of hours a pupil spends in secondary education – what about 'the seventy thousand hours that Rutter left out'? (Heath and Clifford, 1980): a reference to the hours *not* spent in school.

In this brief review it is not possible to follow the developments in all four home countries. The main focus, as with previous editions, is on England and Wales, but with some data from the other countries, particularly where there are significantly different trends. As England typically makes up more than 80 per cent of the school-age population of the United Kingdom, reporting the UK figures alone could conceal important differences – perhaps not a cultural, but certainly a numerical form of imperialism.

The data presented is organized into three main sections, broadly representing three overlapping questions that have run through debates on educational reform throughout the century – first, *access* to schools, to different levels and types of schooling; second, *resources* for schools; and third, *outcomes and results*. In all cases we can ask not just about the overall pattern, but how different groups have fared, though official statistics are not often very helpful here. Inevitably many areas are not covered. There is little on teachers, for example, or on the internal organization and curriculum within schools.

Sources of useful statistics

Education Statistics for the United Kingdom has been published annually since 1967 and covers the period since 1965. Since 1997 the title has become *Education and Training Statistics for the United Kingdom*. The four home countries each produce their own annual volumes of statistics. Those for England currently include volumes on 'Schools', 'Public Examinations – GCSE/GNVQ and GCE' and 'Teachers'. They have been published in various formats since 1961 covering England and Wales until 1980. Wales is now covered by its own series *Statistics of Education and Training in Wales*. For Scotland there is *Scottish Education Statistics: Annual Review*, and in Northern Ireland *Education in Northern Ireland*. For England and Scotland there are *Statistical Bulletins* published at intervals.

For the early part of the century, there are the *Statistics of Public Education in England and Wales*. There are also the annual reports, published separately for each year, initially by the Board of Education, later by the Ministry and subsequently Department. For Wales there is L. J. Williams' heroic *Digest of*

Welsh Historical Statistics. The second volume includes education up to 1976. Scottish data can be found in *Statistics of Public Education in Scotland*, published annually in parliamentary papers. B. R. Mitchell's *British Historical Statistics* (1988) has tables covering most of the period for the four countries separately.

For the social dimension it is possible to draw on some of the results from surveys conducted since the war – for example, on social mobility (Glass, 1954; Halsey et al., 1980), as well as data from the British Election Surveys from 1979 to 1997.[3] In both cases the method employed is to construct cohorts based on date of birth to estimate changes in educational experiences over time. Inevitably there are problems with this method; for older cohorts it cannot take account of differential mortality, emigration and immigration, and there may well be problems of selective recall. But it provides a perspective that cannot be constructed from other sources. The Youth Cohort Studies (Payne et al., 1996; Payne, 1998) provide data on the rapid changes in the post-compulsory period at the end of the century.

At international level, comparative data have been patchy and unreliable until the coming of the massive OECD INES (Indicators of Education Systems) project in the 1980s. Since then the publication *Education at a Glance* has become a near-annual series (OECD, 1992, 1993, 1995, 1997, 1998), its increasing size rather undermining its title and purpose. It includes data on resources, access and participation rates, and student achievement at school and tertiary levels.

Access and participation

Grant-aided and maintained schools and pupils

Official educational statistics for the period up to World War II do not provide a complete account of the educational system as a whole. They mainly cover schools for which the state made direct or indirect contribution: that is, following the 1902 Act, schools provided by the local education authorities, denominational schools now funded through the rates or secondary schools on the grants list. It is not until 1960 when the 1944 Education Act's requirement for independent schools to be registered was completed that we finally begin to have a complete statistical picture of the system. For the state sector it also makes sense to divide the tables at World War II. This is not just because education statistics were in abeyance during the war. The 1944 Education Act effectively completed the slow transition to a fully articulated primary and secondary system with a fixed point of transfer.

1901–38

By the start of the century the elementary schools in England and Wales were already enrolling approximately 90 per cent of the 5–11 age-group (using census-based estimates), rising to about 94 per cent by 1938. In fact, it was the younger age-group (under 7) which had slightly lower participation rates (87 per cent rising to 89 per cent over the same period). Table 5.1 shows the overall numbers enrolled, but attendance was always a major problem. The Board of Education Report for 1903 shows an attendance figure of 83 per cent in 1900/01, but this had improved to 89 per cent by 1938 (in 1997 primary school attendance averaged 94 per cent and secondary 91 per cent in England). Table 5.1 also shows by implication improvements in educational quality as the number of teachers increased and numbers of pupils remained steady or fell.

What is not shown is the increasing number of older children in the elementary schools. In 1901 approximately 15 per cent of elementary school pupils were aged over 11 years, and this had risen steadily to over 23 per cent

Table 5.1(a) Number of elementary pupils and teachers (000s), 1901–38: four home countries

	England	Wales	England & Wales	Scotland		Northern Ireland	
	Pupils	Pupils	Teachers	Pupils	Teachers	Pupils	Teachers
1901	5374	398	119.4	767	13.9	–	–
1911	5609	453	162.9	845	20.0	–	–
1921	5436[a]	466	167.9	707	17.9	198[a]	4.2[a]
1931	5136	436	171.8	657	19.5	204	5.4
1938	4742	356	169.8	617	19.6	192	5.3

Note: [a]1922.

Sources: Board of Education Statistics; Willlams (1985); Mitchell (1988); parliamentary papers.

Table 5.1(b) Number of pupils and teachers in grant-aided secondary schools, 1901–38: four home countries

	England	Wales	England & Wales	Scotland		Northern Ireland	
	Pupils	Pupils	Teachers	Pupils	Teachers	Pupils	Teachers
1901	108258[a]	7668	n/a	17687	937	–	–
1911	145609	14951	9540	20532	1147	–	–
1921	308958	27878	17668	154256[b]	5679[b]	n/a	n/a
1931	371302	40007	21694	154072	6571	12300	706
1938	424618	45385	25039	152781	6908	14100	790

Notes: [a]Combined total of day science and arts scholars.
[b]After 1918/19 pupils attending intermediate schools in Scotland were reclassified as secondary, as were pupils in preparatory departments of secondary schools, previously classified as primary.

Sources: Board of Education Statistics; Williams (1985); Mitchell (1988); parliamentary papers.

by 1938. While numbers of pupils in grant-aided secondary schools increased steeply, as Table 5.1 demonstrates, this expansion had not kept pace with the demand. Thus by 1938 there were more than 1.1 million pupils in elementary schools over the age of 11, approximately three times the number of the equivalent age in grant-aided secondary schools in England and Wales.

In grant-aided secondary schools the reverse was the case. Thus by 1938 some 16 per cent of pupils registered in these schools were under 12, reflecting the parallel nature of the elementary and secondary school systems. After the 1902 Act, grant-aided secondary schools included both the older grammar schools, now aided by the local education authority, and newly established county secondary schools. From 1907 the Free Place Regulations provided higher grants to fee paying secondary schools to admit free-place pupils who had spent at least two years at public elementary school. The number was set at 25 per cent of the previous year's entry. Candidates for free places had to pass 'an entrance test of attainment and proficiency', intended as a qualifying test but, as demand exceeded supply, increasingly used as a competitive examination. As Table 5.1 shows, numbers of pupils in secondary grant-aided schools had more than

Table 5.2: School, pupil (000s) and teacher (000s) numbers in maintained primary, secondary and all–age schools by home country, 1950–97[a]

Maintained primary and all-age schools

| | England | | | Wales | |
	Schools	Pupils	Teachers	Schools	Pupils
1950/51	20848	3729	122	2258	276
1960/61	21134	3866	133	2178	266
1970/71	21083	4720	175	1990	303
1980/81	21018	4020	181	1908	272
1990/91	19047	3782	176	1717	259
1996/97	18392	4113	184	1681	272

Maintained secondary schools

| | England | | | Wales | |
	Schools	Pupils	Teachers	Schools	Pupils
1950/51	4470	1617	78	377	116
1960/61	5445	2653	130	402	176
1970/71	4984	2953	165	311	190
1980/81	4654	3840	231	239	240
1990/91	3897	2853	184	230	185
1996/97	3569	3041	184	228	191

Note: [a]Numbers rounded to nearest thousand.

doubled in England and Wales by 1921, but then the rate of increase fell back in the 1920s and 1930s – a result of economic pressures rather than falling demand. The proportion of the intake with free places, however, continued to rise: to 49 per cent of the intake of grant-aided secondary schools in 1931 in England and Wales. Figures for Wales were consistently much higher, up to 70 per cent of the intake. Table 5.1 shows the effect in Scotland of the reclassification of pupils from intermediate schools and preparatory departments of secondary schools into the secondary category, in the wake of the 1918 Education (Scotland) Act. However, Scottish secondary school statistics continued to reflect the two tiers ('preparatory' and 'post-primary'). In England and Wales, any form of secondary education was a minority experience until after World War II. Floud (in Glass, 1954) reports that only 12 per cent of the adult population in 1949 had been through secondary schools.

1951–97

The 1944 Education Act effectively set the pattern for maintained primary and secondary schools in England and Wales for the rest of the century, by

Teachers	Schools	Scotland Pupils	Teachers	Schools	Northern Ireland Pupils	Teachers
11	2103	546	19	1665	194	6
11	2320	583	20	1550	192	6
12	2497	628	23	1229	218	8
13	2522	492	24	1056	199	8
12	2372	441	23	999	190	8
12	2313	440	22	920	179	9

Teachers	Schools	Scotland Pupils	Teachers	Schools	Northern Ireland Pupils	Teachers
4	909	233	14	120	41	2
9	771	288	18	228	97	4
11	510	314	20	205	96	5
14	444	408	28	205	119	8
12	424	294	24	239	141	10
12	403	317	24	238	153	11

Sources: *Statistics of Education*; Williams (1985); Mitchell (1988); *Education Statistics for the United Kingdom*.

completing the move to define the primary and secondary stages of education as part of an articulated system with a break at 11-plus – a development stemming back to the Hadow Report of 1926. But it did not settle the form of secondary education. The statistics in Tables 5.1 and 5.2 reflect the scale of the change, though there were still nearly a million pupils in 'all-age' schools in 1946 (a residue of the pre-war elementary school system) and these did not finally disappear until the 1970s.

What is striking about the overall numbers, shown in Figure 5.1, is the steep rise in numbers in secondary schools until 1980. This was driven by a mix of demography, increases in the school leaving-age (to 15 in 1947 and to 16 in 1972), and increasing staying-on rates above the compulsory level to the point where for a brief period there were nearly as many pupils in secondary schools as in the primary sector. The steep demographic decline in pupil numbers at both primary and secondary level from the late 1970s through the 1980s meant – for the first time in the post-war period – school closures and amalgamations as a result of 'falling rolls'. Only in the final decade of the century did numbers begin to rise again, though, as Table 5.2 shows, the number of schools has continued to decline.

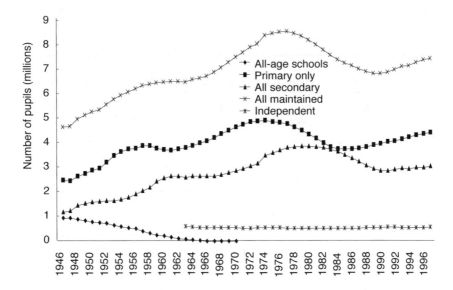

Figure 5.1 Primary, all-age, and secondary maintained school pupils, England only, 1946–97, and independent school pupils (all ages), 1963–97

Source: *Statistics of Education in England.*

Maintained and independent schools

Cohort studies (for example, Halsey et al., 1980, p.35) as well as national statistics suggest that throughout the century a remarkably uniform 5–8 per cent of the school aged population has been enrolled in private schooling. At various points in the century it might have been tempting to present the relationship between the maintained and private sectors as one where the relentless rise of the public sector would gradually extinguish the fee-paying sector, to a point where it would either wither away or be abolished *de jure*. A serious move in this direction could have been made in the late 1960s. The shift to comprehensive secondary education following Circular 10/65 in England and Wales underlined the anomalous position of the prestigious direct grant and 'public schools'. But the resulting Public Schools Commission's first report in 1968 sheered away from any radical proposals for abolition or takeover of the private sector, proposing instead a scheme of assisted places with fees paid by the state. A second report in 1970 adopted a tougher line with the direct grant schools. But it was not until 1975 that the direct grant schools were required either to enter the maintained sector or to become independent. About one-third opted for the state sector while the rest became independent.

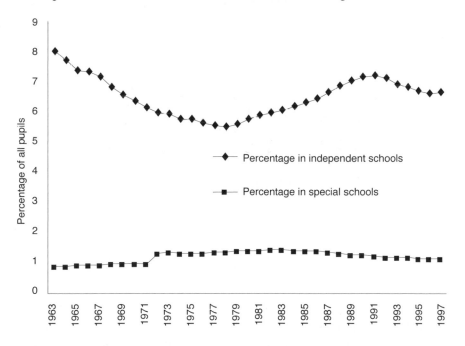

Figure 5.2 Percentage of all pupils in independent schools; Percentage of all pupils in special schools, England only, 1963–97

Source: *Statistics of Education in England.*

However, the private sector has always included a much wider range of schools than simply these high-prestige examples of 'public' schools maintained by endowment and governed by trust. Thus at the time of the Bryce Commission in 1895 there were estimated to be some 18 000 private schools with up to 750 000 pupils, and estimates for earlier periods were much higher (Glennerster and Wilson, 1970). In many cases these would have been small, private or 'proprietary' establishments providing for a few children. By the mid-1930s there were still estimated to be 10000 such schools covering about 300 000 pupils. By 1938 approximately 7 per cent of pupils in England and Wales were attending private schools.

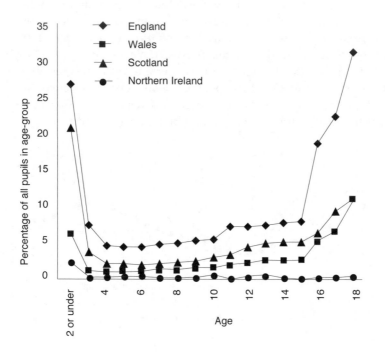

Figure 5.3 Percentage of age-group in school in non-maintained provision, 1996/97, four home countries

Source: *Education Statistics for the United Kingdom.*

In the post-war period the proportion in the private sector declined steadily until 1979, as Figure 5.2 (England only) demonstrates. However, the proportion then began to rise again. This is probably explained by a combination of demographic change (overall numbers in all schools were dropping at this point), and the introduction of the Assisted Places Scheme following the 1980 Education Act. In 1998, 8.5 per cent of pupils in independent schools[4] were being helped through the Assisted Places Scheme, although the scheme is being phased out at the end of the century.

While there may have been a slight reduction in private schools overall since the 1960s (from 7 per cent of pupils in all UK schools in 1965/66 to 6.2 per cent in 1996/97), the private sector has continued to flourish, with numbers particularly at the bottom and top of the age-range. In the 1998 annual survey conducted by the Independent Schools Information Service (ISIS), 1306 schools (including 243 belonging to the Headmasters' Conference – HMC) appeared, catering for 478 769 pupils aged up to 19. The strength of the non-maintained sector is demonstrated particularly in its proportion of higher-level qualifications. What we are seeing here is the impact of the large independent schools where staying on to age 18 is the norm.

The non-maintained sector covers a heterogeneous group of institutions. At one end of the age-range it includes an increasing amount of pre-school educational provision. As Figure 5.3 demonstrates, it varies very significantly by age. Thus it constitutes a large proportion of provision for children under three (particularly in England), covers typically 5 per cent or less of the primary age-range, rises slightly in early secondary, and then climbs steeply in the post-compulsory period. For 18-year-olds, it peaks at more than 30 per cent of this age group in schools in England, although only just over 10 per cent in Scotland and Wales, and an insignificant number in Northern Ireland.

Special schools and special educational needs

The development of special education over the century can conveniently be split into three separate but related strands. The first is an essentially expanding definition of 'educability', to include groups with disabilities that would have consigned them at earlier times to a category not considered educable. However, it was not finally until the Education (Handicapped Children) Act 1970, which transferred training centres for those with serious mental disabilities to the education service, that for the first time all children, whatever their disabilities, were defined as educable. The second strand was one of increasing distinctions of categories of children as in need of special educational provision. Thus, for example, 'maladjustment' was recognized between the two wars increasingly as needing special provision, but it was not until the 1944 Act and the regulation that followed in 1945 that it was specifically included as a category. By this time there were 11 separate categories of pupils identified (blind, partially sighted, deaf, partially deaf, delicate, diabetic, educationally sub-normal, epileptic, maladjusted, physically handicapped and those with speech defects). The third strand is that of integration into normal or 'mainstream' schooling. While the aim of integrating children with disabilities into the mainstream was not unknown in the earlier period, the emphasis was largely on separate provision. The increased emphasis on the rights of those with disabilities, as well as research on the effects of labelling and separate provision, paved the way for the Warnock Committee's report. This gave priority 'to a continuum of special educational need, rather than discrete categories of handicap', embracing 'children with significant learning difficulties and emotional or behavioural disorders as well as those with disabilities of mind or body' (Warnock, 1978, p.327). The result was a much broader definition of special educational needs, with up to one in six pupils at any time and up to one in five children at some time during their school career seen to be in need of some form of special assistance. The 1981 Act that followed introduced the category of special education needs (SEN); the various levels of diagnosis and support from a full statement of need to lower levels of additional assistance within school or class were set out in the 1994 Code of Practice following the 1993 Education Act.

The trends in numbers of pupils in special schools over the century reflect legislative change, which in turn reflects these changing definitions of educability and disability. The Board of Education statistics for 1900/01 record just over 8000 pupils in 182 grant-aided special schools for 'handicapped pupils' in England and Wales (this included hospital schools, as well as schools for blind, deaf, 'defective' and epileptic children). Ten years later the number of schools had nearly doubled and pupils nearly trebled. This was still less than 1 per cent of the total pupil population recorded in public and other elementary schools in England and Wales. By the late 1930s the number of schools had peaked at 611 and pupils at 51 422, but by 1950 numbers of both schools and pupils had dropped back, if only temporarily.

In the post-war period the proportion of pupils educated in special schools rose, particularly after the 1970 Act which transferred to mainstream education those in training centres, and peaked in the mid-1980s. Since then – possibly in response to Warnock-influenced moves to greater integration – special schools and pupils have declined as a proportion of the school age population. As Figure 5.2 shows, pupils in special schools have fluctuated since the early 1960s from just below to just above 1 per cent of all pupils in English schools; the 1996/97 figure for Wales and Scotland is less than 1 per cent.

In 1996/97 the proportion of all pupils in England with a statement of special educational needs was 2.9 per cent. Approximately 60 per cent of these were in mainstream primary and secondary schools. In addition, a further 17 per cent of primary-age pupils and 14.5 per cent of secondary-age pupils were defined as in special educational need but without a statement. In special schools 94 per cent of pupils had statements of special educational needs, although this amounted to only 37 per cent of all pupils with statements. Thus the numbers of pupils with statements of special educational needs are well on the way to the Warnock estimates of between one in five and one in six of all pupils. However, changing definitions make these statistics hard to interpret, with greater integration of pupils with special needs into mainstream schools and the broader definition of educational needs employed. This nets up to 20 per cent of the pupil population.

Table 5.3 Grant-aided special schools for 'handicapped pupils', 1900–50: England and Wales

Year	Schools	Pupils[a]
1900/01	182	8153
1910/11	336	22791
1920/21	500	36459
1930/31	607	48934
1937/38	611	51422
1950	601	47119

Note: [a]Day and boarding pupils; boarding includes hospital schools.

Source: *Education in 1950*, Historical Tables, England and Wales.

Table 5.4 Numbers of special schools and pupils in special schools: 1965–97: England only

Year	Special schools[a]	Pupils (full- and part-time)	Percentage of all pupils
1965	847	71915	1.0
1970	951	84304	1.0
1975	1529	127809	1.4
1980	1597	129724	1.5
1985	1529	116273	1.5
1990	1398	99295	1.3
1995	1291	98390	1.2
1997	1239	98249	1.2

Note: [a]Includes maintained and non-maintained special schools

Source: *Statistics of Education in England*, 1997, DfEE.

Pupils in special schools and in the private sector complete the overall picture of the school-age population. Since the 1960s official statistics have covered the full UK school population. Table 5.5 sets out the trends in overall numbers in schools in the UK since 1965.

Schooling for the under-fives

The story of pre-school provision during this century is one of decline and rise. At the beginning of the century, large numbers of very young children were attending elementary schools – in 1900–01, this was the case for 43.2 per cent of the three to four age-group (approximately 618 000 children under five) in

Table 5.5 Number (000s) and percentage of pupils by school type, 1965/66–96/97, UK

Type	1965/66		1970/71		1975/76	
	N	%	N	%	N	%
Nursery	31	0.3	35	0.3	47	0.4
Primary	5152	56.8	5883	57.8	5940	53.0
Secondary	3165	34.9	3555	34.9	4448	39.7
Non–maintained	632	7.0	606	5.9	615	5.5
Special	88	1.0	103	1.0	150	1.3
All schools	9068	100.0	10182	100.0	11200	100.0

Source: *Education Statistics for the United Kingdom.*

England and Wales. However, conditions rapidly came to be seen as unsuitable for this age-group: ten years later, the proportion in school had fallen to 22.7 per cent (some 350 600 children under five), and continued to fall (with a slight exception at the end of the 1930s) to the 1950s. But by the 1960s, the number of pre-school children in education was beginning to expand. Figures for the UK show a steady rise from 14.4 per cent of children aged three and four in school in 1965/66 to 52.7 per cent in 1991/92 – more than half of the age-group overall, although for four-year-olds this rose to over seven in ten children. By 1997, the rate for England had risen to 56 per cent.

Table 5.6 Proportion of under-fives in grant-aided schools, 1900–50: England and Wales

Year	Percentage of Population aged three[a] and under five
1900/01	43.2
1910/11	22.7
1920/21	15.3
1930/31	13.4
1937/38	15.9
1950	12.3

Note: [a]Includes pupils under 3 years.

Source: *Education in 1950*: Historical Tables: England and Wales.

Much of the increase in participation since the mid-1960s, however, has been in part-time pupils. Between 1965–66 and 1991–92, children under five attending school part-time in the UK increased from 4 per cent to 50 per cent of the total (from 11 000 to 409 000 children), while children attending full-time fell from 95 per cent to 49 per cent of the total (an increase from 258 000

| 1980/81 | | 1985/86 | | 1990/91 | | 1996/97 | |
N	%	N	%	N	%	N	%
56	0.5	57	0.6	60	0.7	83	0.8
5087	48.3	4521	48.2	4,812	53.1	5380	54.3
4606	43.8	4080	43.5	3473	38.3	3709	37.4
629	6.0	597	6.4	604	6.7	610	6.2
147	1.4	130	1.4	113	1.2	116	1.2
10525	100.0	9385	100.0	9062	100.0	9905	100.0

to 408 000). This represents a steep increase in the numbers in part-time nursery and reception classes in primary schools, which by the late 1990s catered for more than half the children under five in maintained schools. The slight rise in nursery schools overall in the UK over the last decade, despite their decline in England and Wales, is explained by the increasing number in Northern Ireland and especially in Scotland.

Table 5.7 All pupils (full-time and part-time) aged two to four[a] attending all types of school, 1965/66–91/92: UK and component countries

Year	UK (000s)	UK percentage[b]	England	Wales	Scotland	N. Ireland
1965/66	269	14.4	237.9	11.2	9.2	10.7
1975/76	576	34.4	473.4	48.5	31.5	22.6
1985/86	671	46.8	546.9	49.6	51.0[c]	23.5
1991/92	817	52.7	682.2	54.5	56.2	24.6

Notes: [a]Excludes 'rising fives' – that is, pupils aged four at 31 August who became five years of age by 1 January.
[b]As a percentage of all children aged three and four. The numbers of two-year-olds are about 5 per cent of the total.
[c]1984/85 data for Scotland.

Source: *Education Statistics for the UK*, 1993, Table 16.

Table 5.8 Numbers of nursery schools, 1985/86–96/97: UK and home countries

Country	1985/86	1990/91	1994/95	1995/96	1996/97
UK	1262	1364	1477	1486	1538
England	560	566	551	547	544
Wales	59	54	52	52	52
Scotland	559	659	783	796	851
N. Ireland	84	85	91	91	91

Source: *Education and Training Statistics for the UK, 1997*, Table 2.1, DfEE, 1998.

Staying on at school

The school leaving-age was raised to 12 years in 1899 without exemptions, and school boards were given permissive powers to raise the school leaving age to 14 in 1900. However a system of partial or total exemptions for pupils who proved by examination to have reached a specified level meant that leaving before 14 was widespread until 1922, when age 14 was fixed without exemption. Board of Education figures for elementary school leavers in England and Wales in 1921 show more than a quarter of elementary school leavers were aged under 14 years. Even by 1938, data from the same source suggest that only about 12 per cent of leavers from grant-aided schools were aged 16 or over. Data from social mobility studies (Halsey et al., 1980) indicate higher levels of staying on in cohorts attending schools before World War II. Their data include those who would have attended private schools. The official statistics, by recording leaving age at fixed points in the school year and not on actual leaving day, may have produced rather lower estimates. The leaving age was raised again in 1947 to 15 and in 1972 to 16 years.

Table 5.9 shows the trends in the population above compulsory school leaving-age staying on in grant-aided and maintained schools. This excludes pupils in private schools. The estimates are based on the relevant census, or predicted estimates for non-census years.

Table 5.9 Percentage of population above compulsory school leaving-age in grant-aided schools, England and Wales: 1900–38

Year	Percentage aged 14 and under 18
1900–01	2.1
1910–11	4.0
1920–21	9.8
1930–31	14.6
1937–38	14.9

Source: *Education in 1950*, Historical Tables, England and Wales.

Table 5.10 carries this picture forward and shows the impact of raising the school leaving-age. The comparison with the powerful and selective direct-grant grammar schools over the same period is instructive. Even in 1946/47 they were retaining more than 80 per cent of their leavers to age 16 or above, as Table 5.11 shows.

From the mid-1960s we have data for all schools (maintained and independent) in the United Kingdom showing the proportions in schools at different ages. The data are presented in Table 5.12. There was a major change in 1980/81 in the way age was calculated, which very substantially affects the apparent trends.

Table 5.10 Age at leaving full-time school: maintained secondary schools,[a] England and Wales: 1946–71

Year	13	14	15	Age 16	17	18+	All
1946/47	9.8	57.4	11.2	13.3	4.6	3.7	100
1950/51	–	14.8	66.3	12.2	3.1	3.5	100
1955/56	–	14.3	62.6	13.9	4.1	5.2	100
1960/61	–	–	72.7	15.7	5.1	6.5	100
1965/66	–	–	58.9	23.0	7.0	11.1	100
1970/71	–	–	49.1	28.3	8.4	14.2	100

Note: [a]Excludes direct-grant grammar schools.

Source: *Statistics of Education for England and Wales*, 1971, Historical Tables.

Table 5.11 Percentage of leavers aged 16+ in direct grant schools and all secondary maintained schools, England and Wales: 1946–71

Year	Percentage of all secondary maintained leavers 16+	Percentage of direct grant leavers 16+
1946/47	21.7	80.1
1950/51	18.8	87.5
1955/56	23.1	92.3
1960/61	27.3	94.2
1965/66	41.1	96.2
1970/71	50.9	95.9

Source: *Statistics of Education for England and Wales*, School Leavers, 1971, Historical Tables.

Table 5.12 Percentage of age-group in school, 1965–1997: all UK schools

Year	15	Age[a] 16	17	18+
1965/66	61.0	27.7	14.8	5.1
1970/71	70.6	35.6	20.3	7.0
1975/76	99.5	50.6	20.7	6.8
1980/81	97.7	29.0	17.8	2.3
1985/86	97.3	32.1	18.8	3.0
1990/91	99.5	40.6	25.5	3.8
1996/97	97.0	38.4	28.2	2.9

Note: [a]Until 1975/76, age was measured as at 31 December. From 1980/81, it was measured at 31 August or the beginning of the school year.

Source: *Education Statistics for the United Kingdom*, 1993, 1997.

Part of the reason for the apparently slow development of schooling post-16 in the most recent period was the growth in the proportion entering further education colleges, increasingly on a full-time basis. And also, as Table 5.13 indicates, there were growing proportions already in full-time higher education at age 18. This table (for England only) illustrates the distribution of those in education and training by main type in 1996/97.

Table 5.13 Percentage[a] of age-group in different forms of post-16 education, 1996/97 (England only)

| Type | Age | | | |
	16	17	18	16–18
Full-time school	33.9	26.2	3.1	20.8
Full-time further education	36.4	31.3	15.1	28.0
Part-time further education	7.1	8.3	8.3	7.9
Higher education	–	0.5	20.5	6.6
All education and training	86.4	78.7	59.7	75.4
Not in any education or training	13.6	21.3	40.3	24.6

Note: [a]Percentages do not total 100 as only the main types of education and training have been included in the table.

Source: *Education and Training Statistics for the United Kingdom*, 1997.

Denominational schools

The very rapid growth of local board elementary schools in England and Wales in the last quarter of the nineteenth century meant that by 1901 they had reached near parity of provision with voluntary schools (predominantly Church of England). In the early 1880s board schools were still enrolling less than a third of total recorded numbers at elementary level. But by 1901, of the 4.9 million pupils recorded in elementary schools, some 48 per cent were in board schools, while of those in voluntary elementary schools, some 76 per cent were in Church of England (National Society) schools, with Catholic schools providing for 11 per cent. The decline in the voluntary schools continued, matched by the rise of board and, after 1902, council schools. By 1938, more than two-thirds of elementary pupils were in council schools. Among voluntary schools, while just under three-quarters of the pupils were in Church of England schools, there was a steady rise in the relative proportion in Catholic schools, to just under a quarter, and a decline in the 'other' category (Methodist, Jewish and non-denominational voluntary schools).

In the post-war period, the change at primary level was more gradual. There was a slight increase in the county (local education authority – LEA) schools, providing for just under seven in ten pupils in 1950 to just over seven in ten in 1990. The Catholic contribution to the voluntary sector rose over the same period from just over a quarter to just over a third. In the last two decades the slight increase in the proportion in voluntary schools may have been a result of the sharp decline in overall pupil numbers and the possibility that voluntary schools were more likely to survive closure or reorganization.

At secondary level in the post-war period, county (LEA) schools dominated provision in the maintained sector, providing for almost nine in ten secondary school pupils in 1960 but falling back slightly to just over eight in ten in 1990. In 1950, Church of England schools provided for just under three in ten of the pupils in the voluntary sector while Catholic schools provided for just over one in five. But from 1960 onwards Catholic schools increased from over a third of pupils in voluntary secondary schools in 1960 to over half by 1981.

The arrangement for voluntary schools following the 1944 Act was either to adopt voluntary-aided status (where they were required to raise part of the maintenance costs) or to become voluntarily controlled (where they received full costs). Catholic schools, almost without exception, have aided status, whereas about six in ten Church of England primary schools and approximately half of secondary schools are controlled. Thus Catholic schools followed a route of retaining a higher degree of independence, whereas Church of England schools moved to a higher level of accommodation with the fully maintained system.

While the settlements of 1902 (which brought eight in ten of the voluntary schools into state funding) and 1944 may have produced a relatively stable and consensual set of relations with the state in the post-World War II period, there are signs at the end of the century of a revival of controversy over denominational schools in England. Debate centres on the claims of other faiths for equal treatment; state funding has been sought and granted to a limited number of Islamic and other faith schools. At the same time renewed attention has been given to the contribution that voluntary schools can make to their community, particularly Catholic schools through the strength of their local support network.

Selective and non-selective secondary education

For the first half of the century, secondary education in England and Wales was almost without exception selective, either by fees or tests of aptitude or ability. The post-World War II pattern of maintained secondary schools, in effect, systematized the pattern of secondary education evolving in the pre-war period; that is, for different types of schools to meet different kinds of aptitude and ability: grammar schools for the academically able, technical schools for those with more applied skills, and finally modern schools for those with more concrete practical interests. The Norwood Committee in 1943 spelled out these distinctions most explicitly for what it termed 'the main features of a new secondary education which will cover the whole child population of the country ...' (Norwood, 1943), though it was building on earlier reports, notably the Spens Committee Report of 1938 and Hadow Report of 1931. In all cases the plea was for parity of prestige or esteem between the different types.

In practice the evidence has been consistently clear that educational selection has a strong social dimension. Both the 1949 social mobility study (Glass, 1954) and the 1972 study (Halsey et al., 1980) show the close link between social background, as measured by father's occupation, and attendance at a selective secondary school. There may be some argument whether there are any trends in the data (Heath and Clifford, 1996), but the consistent patterns are shown in Table 5.14.

Table 5.14 Percentage in each birth cohort attending selective secondary schools, 1972 (males only)

Father's class	Date of birth			
	1910–19	1920–29	1930–39	1940–49
Higher service	69	77	86	74
Lower service	57	70	77	62
Routine non-manual	34	54	51	47
Petty bourgeoisie	35	41	49	41
Foremen	22	34	38	33
Skilled working	19	25	30	21
Semi and unskilled	15	23	27	23
All	26	35	40	35
N	1802	1969	1880	2231

Sources: Heath and Clifford (1996), Oxford Social Mobility Study data.

The movement for a common form of secondary schooling was given impetus by the evidence of research on these links between social background and educational selection, by the anomalies from one area to another in the proportion of selective places available and by doubts about the reliability and fairness of the methods of selection (the '11+' tests). By the time that Circular 10/65 (in 1965) set out six options for 'going comprehensive' there were already significant numbers of pupils in comprehensives in England and particularly in Wales, as Table 5.15 shows.

Table 5.15 shows that Wales and Scotland moved more or less in step towards 100 per cent comprehensive secondary education. England, however, effectively reached a plateau at 85 per cent, though the inclusion of middle schools (deemed secondary) would push this above 90 per cent. Northern Ireland retained a selective system, with voluntary grammar schools, formerly in the independent sector, added to the public sector after 1989.

Table 5.15 Percentage of public sector secondary school pupils by school type, 1960/61–96/97

	1960/61	1965/66	1970/71	1975/76	1980/81	1985/86	1990/91	1996/97
England								
Middle	0.0	0.0	1.9	6.0	7.0	6.6	5.6	5.1
Secondary modern	60.5	55.1	38.0	15.5	6.0	4.2	3.5	2.7
Grammar	23.9	25.0	18.4	7.7	3.4	3.0	3.8	4.2
Technical	3.6	2.8	1.3	0.4	0.3	0.1	0.1	0.2
Comprehensive	4.6	9.9	34.4	68.8	82.5	85.4	86.1	86.7
Other[a]	7.4	7.2	6.0	1.6	0.8	0.7	0.9	1.1
Wales								
Secondary modern	52.6	39.3	22.3	6.8	1.8	0.6	0.0	0.0
Grammar	35.0	29.5	15.4	4.3	1.3	0.5	0.0	0.0
Comprehensive	10.8	28.3	58.5	88.5	96.6	98.5	99.2	99.1
Other	1.5	2.9	3.7	0.4	0.3	0.3	0.8	0.9
Scotland								
Selective			28.3	1.1	0.1	0.0	0.0	0.0
Comprehensive			58.7	87.6	96.0	100.0	100.0	100.0
Part selective			13.0	11.3	3.8	0.0	0.0	0.0
Northern Ireland								
Secondary intermediate			87.7	89.3	88.6	88.2	61.4	59.6
Grammar[b]			11.8	10.7	11.4	11.8	38.6	40.4
Technical			0.5	0.0	0.0	0.0	0.0	0.0

Notes: [a]Includes bilateral and multilateral schools.
[b]Includes voluntary grammar schools from 1989, formerly allocated to independent sector.

Sources: *Statistics of Education; Education Statistics for the United Kingdom.*

Grant-maintained schools

The 1988 Education Reform Act for England and Wales introduced the possibility of schools 'opting out' of local authority control. This was extended by the 1993 Education Act. This policy had substantial impact in England, but relatively little in Wales and subsequently Scotland. Within England the policy was also very patchy in its impact. Schools in some areas moved in large numbers to opt out. In other areas almost all schools remained with the local authority. The impact was substantially greater at secondary than at primary level. A major motivation for opting out was both the increased access to funding, and the possibility of shifting the ethos of the school, sometimes formally, to a more selective entry.

By 1997 there were 664 grant-maintained secondary schools in Great Britain, and just 488 primary schools. Almost all of these were in England, where they catered for about 3 per cent of primary-age pupils and 19.8 per cent of secondary-age pupils. Almost all these opt-outs occurred between 1990/91 and 1994/95. Part of the stated policy objective was towards greater 'choice and diversity', the title of the 1992 White Paper (Secretaries of State for England and Wales, 1992). Legislation at the end of the century aimed to bring these schools under greater local control, but greater diversity continued to be a major objective of secondary school policy. There is no doubt that many of the schools 'opting out' represented the more powerful and self-sufficient institutions, in some cases moving to increase the selective nature of their intake. Within the policy context of a developing 'quasi-market' in education following the 1988 Education Reform Act, they were able to take advantage of the increased emphasis on parental choice and devolved school budgets. These formula-based budgets were directly linked to pupil numbers under the local management of schools (LMS) initiative in the 1988 Act.

Expenditure and resources for schools

Educational expenditure

In their pioneering account of educational expenditure in the United Kingdom since 1920, Vaizey and Sheehan (1968) identify four distinct phases. They argue that in the first phase, between the wars, while overall expenditure rose only marginally there was an improvement in quality, as prices, teacher salaries and overall pupil numbers all fell. The second phase was the immediate post-war period when reconstruction in every sense was the main concern. The third phase began in the mid-1950s with a surge in pupil numbers at both primary and secondary level. There was a corresponding increase in the proportion of total resources going to education. The fourth phase they identify as one when economic growth was no longer adequate to sustain continued expansion and there were other competing priorities for government expenditure. This they place in the late 1960s.

They were perhaps a little premature. Net current expenditure continued to rise as did education's share of the national budget until the mid-1970s, driven in part by the increasing numbers of pupils. But since the mid-1970s the commitment of national resources, as measured by the proportion of GDP, has not again reached these levels. The sharp fall after the mid-1970s in the numbers of primary school pupils and the drop in numbers at secondary level in the 1980s initially cushioned the impact of these overall reductions. As a result it was possible for governments in the 1980s to point to overall steep increases in resources *per pupil* at all levels of the school system, even when price inflation was taken into account. This was much less dramatic if educational cost inflation (for example, teachers' salaries) was taken into account. However, the lobby for increased educational spending as an end in itself was significantly weaker after 1975, perhaps undermined by the pessimistic but fashionable view at the time that schools made little or no difference. There was growing emphasis instead on the content and quality of education, measured not by inputs and resources, but by outcomes such as examination results.

By the 1990s, however, overall numbers began to rise again, and education returned to the centre of the policy agenda with a flurry of new legislation, and increased demands on schools and teachers in the wake of the 1988 Education Reform Act. While overall resources began to rise again in the final decade of the century, they did not keep pace with rising numbers, particularly at secondary level. Part of the central thrust of the post-1988 educational changes was to link resources more tightly to the school level, by devolving budgets to individual schools, part of the strategy of developing a responsive educational 'market'. These budgets were in turn primarily driven by pupil numbers. Thus, in principle, resources can be more easily related to results and achievement at the school level. One consequence of this narrowing of education's purpose was a reduction in resources going to some of the social and welfare support services for schools, for example, school meals.

Table 5.16 Public expenditure on education – spending by local authorities, 1900–38: source and proportion of expenditure, England and Wales only

Year	Expenditure on education by LEAs at current prices (£m)	Percentage met from local rates	Percentage met by govt grant	Percentage of rates spent on education
1900–01	16.2	43.6	56.4	14.2
1910–11	27.5	51.5	48.5	21.8
1920–21	70.5	43.9	56.1	20.4
1930–31	82.3	46.8	53.2	25.7
1937–38	92.4	50.5	49.5	26.3

Source: *Education in 1950*, Historical Tables, England and Wales.

Table 5.17 Net current and capital educational expenditure in the UK at current and 1997 prices, 1920–55, as a percentage of national income

Year	Net expenditure at current prices (£m)	Net expenditure at 1997 prices[a] (£m)	Percentage of net national income
1920	66.0	1444.7	1.2
1930	100.3	3456.3	2.4
1940	124.6	3718.1	2.4
1950	314.7	5938.4	3.1
1955	488.1	7033.5	3.3

Note: [a]Calculated using standard formulae supplied for this volume (Appendix 1).

Source: Calculated from Vaizey and Sheehan (1968).

Data on public expenditure on education prior to the 1920s suggests an increase over the first decade of the century as numbers of pupils increased, and numbers of teachers also rose. This apparently remained steady over the second decade, and rose again in the 1920s. Table 5.16 shows the pattern of expenditure by local education authorities and its source.

Table 5.18 Net current and capital educational and related public expenditure on education in the UK at current and 1997 prices, 1960/61–95/96, as a percentage of GDP

Year	Net expenditure[a] at current prices (£m)	Net expenditure at 1997 prices (£m)	Percentage of GDP	Schools[b] expenditure at 1997 prices (£m)	Percentage of GDP
1960/61	947	11904	4.3	n/a	n/a
1965/66	1644	17295	4.6	n/a	n/a
1970/71	2740	22813	5.2	12148	2.8
1975/76	7009	30741	6.3	18035	3.8
1980/81	12941	29609	5.4	17183	3.2
1985/86	17288	28439	4.8	16310	2.8
1990/91	26728	32688	4.8	19053	2.8
1995/96	35429	37165	5.1	22027	2.9

Notes: [a]Excludes loan charges.
[b]Expenditure on nursery, primary, secondary and special schools: excludes related education expenditure.

Source: *Education Statistics for the United Kingdom.*

Table 5.16, drawn from Vaizey and Sheehan (1968), overlaps with the previous table, but uses a broader definition of educational expenditure, and includes capital expenditure, which grew steeply in the post-war period. Table 5.17 also shows the increasing proportions of national income devoted to education. Table 5.18 continues the account, now drawing on data from the finance tables in the UK Education Statistics. It also extracts data on specifically school-related expenditure, with typically less than 3 per cent of GDP spent on this category. The mid-1970s are the exception, when expenditure as a proportion of GDP – and pupil numbers – reached a peak.

Table 5.19, for England only, presents data on unit (per pupil) costs over the period since 1979/80, standardized to 1997 prices. While there was a steep increase over the final two decades of the century, particularly on pupils in special schools, if we take account of general cost inflation then per capita pupil expenditure on secondary schools has fallen since 1990/91. If educational cost inflation is taken into account a rather different profile emerges. Figure 5.4 shows this profile for England and Wales over a similar period. This takes into account teacher salaries and other items that have tended to run ahead of general inflation. Figure 5.4 shows a steep rise in the early part of the 1980s turning into a fall

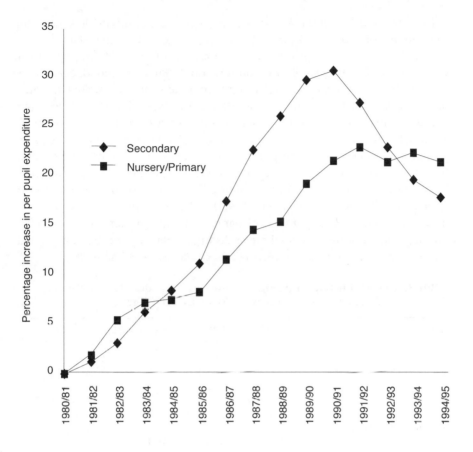

Figure 5.4 Per pupil increase in expenditure by local authorities; primary and secondary education cost index, England and Wales, 1980/81–94/95

Source: CIPFA Education Statistics: Actuals.

Table 5.19 Unit costs for primary, secondary and special school pupils at 1997 prices: England – maintained schools only, 1979/80–96/97 (£ per pupil p.a.)

	1979/80	1983/84	1987/88	1990/91	1994/95	1996/97[a]
Nursery/Primary	1140	1330	1530	1640	1760	1730
Secondary	1615	1850	2310	2470	2400	2330
Special	5095	6170	7990	9560	9570	9630

Note: [a]Provisional data for 1996/97.

Source: DfEE, *Statistical Bulletins: 13/93, 5/97* and *7/98.*

in the 1990s, particularly at secondary level. On these grounds it is less surprising that funding of schooling returned to the centre of debate in the 1990s.

Finally, Table 5.20 shows the distribution of expenditure by sector, excluding as far as possible expenditure not related to school-age pupils, though the administration category must include some non-school responsibility. It shows the growing importance of expenditure on secondary education after the war, and the increased proportion spent on school meals. Table 5.21, by contrast, shows that from the 1970s there was an increase in the proportion going to the nursery and primary stages – in large part the result of increased expenditure on the under-fives. Expenditure on under-fives increased from 3 per cent of the current educational expenditure by LEAs in England in 1979/80 to 8 per cent by 1996/97. Additionally there was a growing move to reduce the historical imbalance between primary and secondary funding. Expenditure on school meals declined sharply over the same period. (For figures on the numbers receiving school meals, see Chapter 15.)

Table 5.20 Distribution of public expenditure on educational services: England and Wales, selected years, 1920–65 (percentage)

Service	1920	1930/32	1938	1950	1965
Primary	63.8	64.7	61.5	41.2	35.8
Secondary	22.3	20.1	21.4	30.3	40.9
Special	2.5	2.7	3.2	1.6	2.5
Meals	1.5	1.5	2.2	16.7	12.7
School health	2.0	3.2	3.9	3.9	2.3
Admin. and inspection	7.9	7.7	7.9	6.3	5.7
	100	100	100	100	100

Source: Vaizey and Sheehan (1968), Appendix B.

Table 5.21 Distribution of educational expenditure by main school-related sectors: UK, 1970/71–95/96 (percentage)

	1970/71	1974/75	1980/81	1984/85	1990/91	1995/96
Nursery/primary	36.4	35.5	34.4	33.1	37.1	42.1
Secondary	42.2	43.5	44.5	45.2	41.4	40.7
Special	3.4	4.2	5.3	5.7	6.3	6.6
Admin.	5.4	5.4	5.9	6.3	7.4	4.6
Health	1.8	0.1	0.2	0.3	0.9	1.4
Meals	7.2	7.9	5.4	4.7	2.8	0.6
Youth	1.7	1.7	1.9	2.2	2.0	1.8
Transport/misc.	2.0	1.8	2.4	2.5	2.1	2.3
Total	100	100	100	100	100	100

Source: *Education Statistics for the United Kingdom.*

Resources

The major cost of schooling is the labour of teachers. In 1996/97 the costs of teachers made up 66 per cent of pre-primary and primary maintained schools costs in England and 71 per cent at secondary level (books and equipment added another 4 per cent, and premises 12 per cent). The rest was spent on non-teaching staff (14 per cent at primary level, 8 per cent at secondary). One of the major difficulties in making any substantial cost savings in educational budgets is that class sizes are themselves treated as important measures of quality.

Pupil–teacher ratios (PTRs) have been used with reasonable consistency throughout the century as an easily calculable, though indirect, measure of educational quality. Crudely, they represent the number of pupils per teacher (using full-time equivalence). Though there may be better ways of measuring the level and quality of resources – for example, directly by class sizes, or the more sophisticated 'class contact ratios' (that is, the proportion of the time any teacher is engaged in teaching), or even adult–child ratios (that take account of non-teaching staff) – these all have their own difficulties. For example, pupils may not necessarily be taught in fixed classes but in groups of varying sizes. It may be difficult to establish what non-teaching staff actually do. So PTRs still provide a useful benchmark.

Table 5.22 covers the period before World War II in England and Wales. Figures fall sharply for elementary schools from 48 pupils per teacher in 1901 (compare the primary PTR in India for 1996 of 52.4) to 30 in 1938. The very different world of grant-aided secondary schools is shown by the fact that the earliest PTR of 16 in 1910/11 was not reached again until the 1990s (though there may be doubts about the strict comparability of data over this timescale). Table 5.23 takes up the story in the post-war period. PTRs continued to decline until 1990 or so and then began to rise. The primary rate fell rather more steeply, perhaps some evidence of the greater importance attached to primary education following the Plowden and Gittins Committee reports in the 1960s. The separate figures for Scotland are instructive. The decline in PTRs has been steeper since 1970 and by the end of the century staffing levels in Scotland were significantly better than for England and Wales.

Table 5.22 Pupil teacher ratios in grant-aided schools: England and Wales, 1900–38

Year	Elementary	Grant-aided secondary	All grant-aided
1900/01	48.3	–	48.3
1910/11	37.2	16.0	36.0
1920/21	35.2	19.3	33.6
1930/31	32.4	19.3	30.9
1937/38	30.0	19.5	28.6

Source: *Education in 1950*, Historical Data.

Table 5.23 Pupil–teacher ratios in maintained and assisted schools: England and Wales, 1946/47–96/97; Scotland, 1971–96/97

Year	England and Wales		Scotland	
	Primary	Secondary	Primary	Secondary
1946–47	29.4	20.8		
1951	29.5	20.5		
1961	28.0	20.3		
1971	26.1	17.9	27.9	16.1
1980–81	22.5	16.6	20.3	14.4
1990–91	22.0	15.3	19.5	12.2
1996–97	23.4[a]	16.7[a]	19.6	13.2

Note: [a]England only for 1996/97.

Sources: *Statistics of Education*, 1972, Historical Data; *Education Statistics for the UK.*

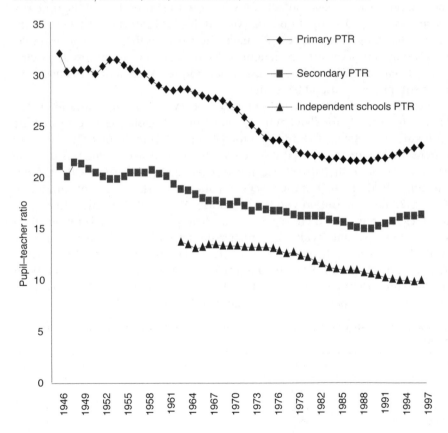

Figure 5.5 Primary, secondary and independent school pupil–teacher ratios, 1946–96/97, England only

Source: *Statistics of Education in England.*

Figure 5.5 shows the trend in PTRs for England only for maintained primary and secondary schools since the war, and also for the independent sector (all ages) since 1964. What is striking about the patterns revealed by Tables 5.22 and 5.23 is the continuing rapid decline in pupil–teacher ratios effectively until the late 1980s. Falling rolls helped the rate to continue declining even as resources were being squeezed. Since the late 1980s, Figure 5.5 shows an increase in PTRs in state schools in England, but a continuing slight fall in the private sector. The difference in staffing levels between the maintained and non-maintained sectors was both very substantial and apparently widening.

Qualifications and destinations

By the early 1920s qualifications were reorganized into two standard external examinations, the School Certificate (normally taken at 16) and the specialized sixth form Higher School Certificate (taken two years later), recognized by the coordinating Secondary School Examination Council for England and Wales. In 1951 the external examination system was again reorganized into the General Certificate of Education (GCE) with three levels, Ordinary (O) at 16, and Advanced (A) and Scholarship (S) two years or so later. The lower-level Certificate of Secondary Education (CSE) was introduced in the mid-1960s, and in 1988 O level and CSE were combined into the General Certificate of Secondary Education (GCSE). The National Curriculum Assessment, following the 1988 Education Reform Act, introduced formal assessment at ages 7, 11 and 14 to add to the existing examinations at 16 and 18. Finally, in the last decade of the century there were moves to embrace the full range of vocational and academic qualifications into a single framework of different 'levels'. A series of national targets was established for the proportion of young people that should reach these levels by the year 2000 and beyond. Thus by age 19–21, 85 per cent were to reach Level 2 (that is, five or more GCSEs at grade C or better, or an equivalent vocational qualification); 60 per cent of 21–23-year-olds were to reach Level 3 (that is, two A levels or equivalent vocational qualifications). However these new vocational qualifications and structures had made limited impact on schools by the end of the century.

There are several ways of reporting qualifications obtained. First, we can look at the stock of qualifications in the adult population, using national survey data. This allows some historical reconstruction using birth cohorts. Second, we can look at flows through the system. Since 1960/61 information on qualifications nationally has been based on school leaver data and subsequently on surveys of school leavers. These are data on school leavers of any age. From 1991/92 data from England made use of the school performance or 'league tables', based on a complete census of examinations taken and the relevant age-group population as the denominator. Finally, it is possible to use cohort studies to pick up the pattern of experience over time by the same individuals.

Stock of qualifications in the adult population

By breaking adult population surveys into birth cohorts it is possible to provide some trend data over a substantial part of the century. We cannot know from these data whether the qualifications were earned at school, at college, or possibly from the workplace, or indeed whether they were acquired in this country.

Figure 5.6, drawn from questions about highest qualification obtained in surveys of the adult population at the time of the British general elections, shows the rapid increase in the overall stock of qualifications. In the period from 1979 to 1997, the level of qualifications in the adult population rose sharply and the numbers without any qualifications fell steeply from 57 per cent of the population in 1979 to about one-third in 1997. Those with A levels or better rose from 17 per cent to 36 per cent over the same period.

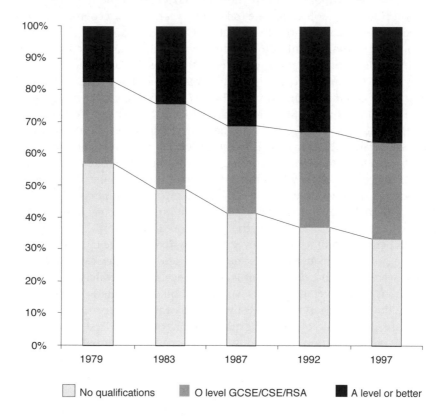

Figure 5.6 Stock of qualifications in the adult population, 1979–97

Source: British General Election Studies, 1979–97.

The position is even more dramatic if these samples of the adult population are used to construct groups born at different periods in the century. This, of course, leaves out those who have died or emigrated, but includes those educated elsewhere but living in the UK at the time.

If we ignore the oldest age cohort (those born before 1900), and note that members of the youngest cohort (those born after 1970) would not all have fully completed their educational career by the time of the surveys, Tables 5.24(a) and 5.24(b) show the pattern of qualifications for males and females separately.

Table 5.24(a) Highest level of qualifications in adulthood by date of birth: males

Qualifications	1900–09	1910–19	1920–29	1930–39	1940–49	1950–59	1960–69	1970–79
None	71.4	61.0	57.0	45.2	35.9	24.5	13.4	7.8
Other: RSA, CSE etc.	14.3	14.9	12.5	11.6	8.7	8.9	13.9	15.0
O level or equivalent	4.0	6.5	8.5	13.7	18.3	20.2	28.6	26.6
A level or similar	2.4	2.4	3.3	5.9	9.5	14.9	19.9	33.8
Prof. qual.	5.6	12.0	13.0	14.3	17.9	18.7	13.1	9.2
Degree	2.4	3.3	5.8	9.3	9.7	12.8	11.2	7.5

Source: British Election Surveys, 1979–97.

Table 5.24(b) Highest level of qualifications in adulthood by date of birth: females

Qualifications	1900–09	1910–19	1920–29	1930–39	1940–49	1950–59	1960–69	1970–79
None	84.6	77.4	69.8	59.6	46.2	32.3	14.8	9.1
Other: RSA, CSE etc.	4.0	4.3	5.4	6.4	11.0	11.5	13.8	10.4
O level or equivalent	3.4	7.0	10.4	13.9	19.6	23.5	34.4	34.2
A level or similar	0.8	2.2	2.8	3.1	4.7	9.1	17.1	30.9
Prof. qual.	6.1	7.5	9.2	12.7	13.0	12.9	11.8	9.1
Degree	1.1	1.6	2.4	4.4	5.4	10.7	8.1	6.2

Source: British Election Surveys, 1979–97.

These tables show the clear pattern of increasing qualification. The proportion with no qualifications fell sharply – down to just 7.8 per cent of the 1970–79 birth cohort for males, and 9.1 per cent for females. At the higher end the number with A levels or equivalent qualifications rose from less than 3 per cent for the earliest male cohort to 20 per cent for the 1960–69 birth cohort and 34 per cent of the 1970–79 cohort. For females the shift was even more dramatic, from less than 1 per cent gaining A level equivalents for the cohort born in the first decade of the century to 17 per cent in 1960–69 and 31 per cent for the 1970–79 birth cohort.

Qualifications obtained at school

Part of the reason for the increased stock of qualifications in the adult population seen in Figure 5.6 is the sharp increases in qualifications achieved in the school system in the last quarter of the century, particularly the last 15 years. The pace of change here raises the obvious question of whether standards were allowed to fall over this period. The pattern of change is seen graphically (Figure 5.7) in the figures for Scotland where data for school leavers over the period 1974/75–96/97 show a dramatic decline in the proportions with no Standard Grade Scottish Certificate of Education (SCE – roughly equivalent to GCSE) from approximately 35 per cent of leavers in 1974/75 to 6.5 per cent in 1996/97. At the other end of the spectrum, proportions with three or more Higher Grade SCEs (roughly equivalent to two or more A levels) increased from just over 17 per cent of leavers in 1974/75 to 30 per cent by 1996/97. These higher-level qualifications show clearly the diverging pattern of performance by males and females over this period, from near parity in 1974/75 to a gap approaching 10 per cent between males and females.

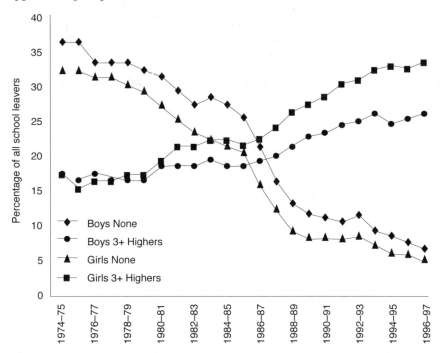

Figure 5.7 Scottish school leavers with no SCE qualifications and those with three or more Higher SCE by gender, 1974/75–96/97

Source: *Scottish Education Statistics, Annual Review 3*, 1998.

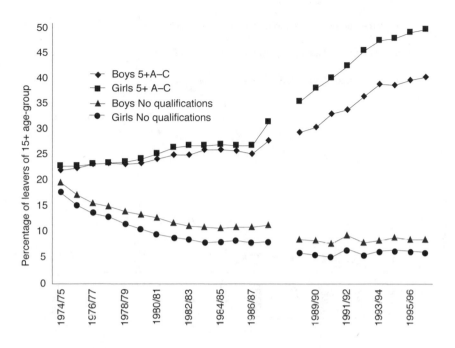

Figure 5.8 O level/CSE/GCSE Results: those with five or more A–C and those with no graded results, by gender: all schools, England only, 1974/75–96/97

Source: *Statistics of Education*: Public examinations GCSE/GNVQ and GCE in England, 1997.

Figure 5.8 (for England only) over the same period shows a similar but less dramatic decline in those with no qualifications and an equivalent rise in those with five or more Grades A–C (at O level, CSE Grade 1 and GCSE). The same pattern of diverging results by gender is clearly seen.

Data based on school leavers show that the proportions gaining A levels rose strongly over the decade 1961–71 to just under 16 per cent of the estimated 17-year-old age-group. However, the rise in the next decade was marginal, with 9 per cent gaining three or more passes, and 16 per cent gaining one or more (Table 5.26). Figure 5.9 shows the steep rise in the proportion with three or more A levels over the final decade or so. It includes the contribution of the FE sector. The kinks in the school and FE lines after 1991/92 reflect the shift of sixth form colleges from the school to the FE sector following the 1992 Further and Higher Education Act. More than a third of the 17-year-old population was estimated to have at least one A level in 1996/97. In terms of gender there is the same pattern seen at GCSE, with girls moving ahead of boys in the proportions with three or more A levels. In 1997, 54 per cent of A level candidates were female; 46 per cent were male. And 23 per cent of females obtained three or more A levels, compared with 19 per cent of males as a percentage of

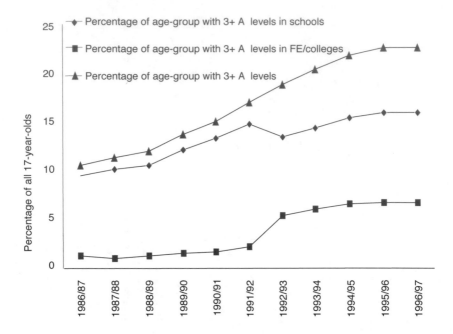

Figure 5.9 Percentage of 17-year-olds with three or more A levels by type of institution, 1986/87–96/97, England only

Source: *Statistics of Education*: Public examinations in England, 1997.

the estimated 17-year-olds in England. Until the 1980s, boys had significantly outperformed girls at this level. There are, of course, other important differences in subject choices and entry policies (see Arnot et al., 1998).

Table 5.25 School leavers with at least five O levels/GCSEs (A–C) by type of secondary school and qualification: England and Wales

	Grammar/Selective	Secondary modern/ other secondary	Comprehensive/ other maintained
1961/62	56.0	0.7	10.3
(%)	(15.2)	(66.0)	(13.0)
1970/71	64.6	1.9	14.9
(%)	(15.2)	(37.1)	(40.9)
1980/81	75.0	10.6	20.9
(%)	(3.0)	(7.4)	(83.6)
1990/91[a]	88.1	18.9	31.6
(%)	(2.5)	(4.5)	(83.5)
1996/97[b]	94.1	29.0	41.8
(%)	(3.5)	(3.5)	(83.0)

Notes: [a]Statistics for 1990/91 are for England only and cover pupils aged 16 years, not leavers.
[b]Statistics for 1996/97 are for England only and cover pupils aged 15 years, not leavers.

Qualifications by type of secondary school

So far the figures presented have been for all schools, and for A level include the contribution of the FE sector. However, we can also fairly ask, particularly during the period of selective secondary education, for the relative success rate by different types of schooling. For the pre-war period, the bulk of the population attended elementary schools and thus their education was largely terminated before they reached the stage of external qualification at the age of 16. The data for 1961/62 in Table 5.25 show that the secondary modern schools which then catered for the majority of maintained secondary pupils continued this tradition in terms of the proportion gaining five or more O levels. Less than 1 per cent of leavers from these schools reached this level. Yet already more than half of leavers from grammar schools were reaching this level and even more in the direct grant and independent school sector. As Table 5.25 shows, the grammar schools and other selective institutions continued to push upwards with up to 94 per cent of the relevant age-group reaching the five or more higher-grade GCSE criteria in grammar schools in 1996/97. Comprehensive schools, increasingly educating the bulk of the age-group, improved steadily. Some 42 per cent of their leavers had achieved this standard in 1996/97. However, as O level and GCSE increasingly became the entry ticket to the next stage of education rather than a terminal point, the story is taken up by Table 5.26 which shows the same pattern for A levels. Here the gap is still very wide, with leavers from selective schools steeply increasing in the proportions of leavers gaining one or more A levels. More than half the pupils in the grammar schools and independent sector were achieving three or more A levels by 1991, compared to about 11 per cent of leavers from comprehensive schools.

All maintained		Direct grant		Independent		All	
						%	000s
10.5		67.0		59.0		14.0	
	(94.2)		(2.0)		(3.9)	(100)	726.46
18.1		76.6		66.6		21.6	
	(93.3)		(2.5)		(4.2)	(100)	613.42
21.8		–		76.1		25.1	
	(94.0)				(6.0)	(100)	733.96
32.7		–		80.1		36.8	
	(91.6)				(8.4)	(100)	555.20
42.2		–		80.4		45.1	
	(92.3)				(7.7)	(100)	586.77

Sources: *Statistics of Education*, School Leavers; *Statistics of Education*, Public Examinations in England; *Statistical Bulletin*.

Table 5.26 School leavers with one or more A level by type of secondary school by qualification, England and Wales: percentage within school type

	Grammar at least		Secondary modern at least		Comprehensive at least	
	1	3+	1	3+	1	3+
1961[a]	33.1	26.8	0.1	–	4.3	2.8
1971	50.0	26.8	0.7	0.1	11.8	4.9
1981[b]	56.5	35.0	3.2	1.3	12.8	6.6
1991[b]	77.1	54.8	4.7	1.5	19.6	10.8

Notes: [a]2+ A levels.
[b]England only.

However, the non-selective sector contained increasing numbers of pupils at this level, and the transfer of sixth form colleges to the FE sector in 1992 influences this pattern significantly. If we include the increasing numbers of pupils taking A levels at FE colleges, then the independent sector recedes in importance. In 1996/97 some 41 per cent of all 17-year-old students with three or more A levels were from comprehensive schools; some 11 per cent from maintained selective schools, and 20 per cent from the independent sector – but sixth form colleges made up a further 18 per cent, and FE colleges 9 per cent.

Destinations on leaving school

From 1910, information on destinations of those leaving school was collected in official statistics, initially from grant-aided secondary schools, and subsequently for elementary schools as well. This data series continued after World War II. At the start the categories include three different forms of further and higher education (university, teacher training and further education); the other category – 'employment' – is clearly residual, including those who stayed at home or for whom no information was recorded. By the 1930s, typically 5–6 per cent of leavers from grant-aided schools were recorded with university as their destination; and another 18 per cent were entering teacher training or further education. Only 1 per cent of leavers from elementary schools were recorded in anything other than the residual 'employment' category. Table 5.27 reproduces these data for the post-war period, distinguishing between maintained secondary schools and the direct grant and subsequently independent sector.

Even if we allow for substantial misreporting of destinations, the contrasts are striking. Already by 1951 more than a third of leavers from direct grant schools were entering various forms of higher or further education. Only 6 per cent of pupils from maintained schools were reaching these destinations. By 1981 only a third of the leavers from independent schools were recorded with destinations other than HE or FE, compared with 76 per cent of leavers from maintained schools.

All maintained at least		Direct grant at least		Independent at least		All at least	
1	3+	1	3+	1	3+	1	3+
6.0	4.7	48.3	42.2	35.7	28.9	8.0	6.4
13.7	6.5	67.1	43.4	54.0	28.6	16.7	8.4
13.5	7.1	–	–	63.0	45.3	16.5	9.4
18.8	10.4	–	–	72.7	57.2	25.6	16.0

Source: *Statistics of Education*, School Leavers.

Table 5.27 Destination on leaving school, England and Wales, 1950/51–80/81: percentage by school type

Year	Type of school	'Employment'/ unknown	University	Teacher training	Further education	All 000s N
1950/51	Maintained secondary	93.8	1.7	1.1	3.4	476.4
	Direct grant	64.5	14.7	6.7	14.2	10.7
1960/61	Maintained secondary	88.7	2.6	1.8	6.8	571.2
	Direct grant	49.3	25.5	8.2	17.0	13.8
1970/71	Maintained secondary	81.1	4.6	3.0	11.2	572.0
	Direct grant	35.1	34.3	9.5	21.1	15.4
1980/81[a]	Maintained secondary	75.5	6.3	0.4	17.8	689.9
	Independent	34.3	35.3	0.6	29.8	44.1

Note: [a]1980/81 for England only.

Source: *Statistics of Education*, School Leavers, 1971, Historical Tables.

Table 5.28 Economic and educational activity of 16-year-olds: percentage of age-group in education and employment, England only, 1979/80–90/91

Percentage in:	1979/80	1983/84	1986/87	1989/90	1990/91
Full-time education	41	45	45	53	59
Of which: School	28	30	29	35	40
FE	14	15	16	18	18
Youth training schemes	5	24	26	22	14
Other (including work)	54	31	29	25	28

Source: *Statistical Bulletins: Educational and Economic Activity of Young People Aged 16–18*.

From the 1980s onwards there was a steady and, by the end of the decade, steep increase in the overall numbers staying on in full-time education beyond the minimum age, as Table 5.28 shows.

Data from different waves or sweeps of the Youth Cohort Study (YCS) complete the picture. Table 5.29, drawn from the YCS cohorts, shows the virtual disappearance of a job market for minimum-age school leavers and the increasing dominance of the educational system. However, an increasing proportion of this is in further education rather than schools.

Table 5.29 Activity after the end of compulsory schooling, 1989–96 (age 16–17)

	YCS4 1989	YCS5 1991	YCS6 1992	YCS7 1994	YCS8 1996
Full-time education	48	58	66	72	72
Full-time job	23	16	11	8	7
Govt.-supported training	24	16	15	12	12
No full-time activity	5	10	8	8	10
Total	100	100	100	100	100

Source: Payne (1998).

We have now come almost full circle. At the start of the century only a small minority of school leavers continued with education in any form; the majority were recorded as entering the labour market, or their status was unknown. By its close, only 7 per cent were recorded as entering full-time work and a further 10 per cent had no recorded full-time activity. More than 70 per cent continued in some form of full-time education.

The impact of social class

The persistent link between social class as measured by father's occupation, and opportunity as measured, for example, by access to selective or independent schooling, has already been recorded. In this section, the strong association between types of secondary schooling and differences in qualifications and destinations has been charted. But as we move to a position where the majority of the population will have attended some form of comprehensive schooling, then the key question may no longer be that of access, but rather of outcome. Does social background now have less impact on outcomes such as qualification or destination? Has educational reform and expansion, particularly the spread of comprehensive secondary education, led to a reduction in educational inequality?

The 'Schools' chapter in the previous edition of *British Social Trends* (Halsey, 1988) drew extensively on the experience of male cohorts drawn from the Oxford Social Mobility Study in 1972 (Halsey et al., 1980). Its focus is particularly on staying-on rates and access to higher levels of the educational system. It points to the way that some forms of educational expansion were associated with reductions in inequality. Thus, in terms of staying on until 16 or later, the gap apparently narrowed between boys from the 'service' class (higher non-manual occupations) and the working class. However, this was not the case for staying on until 18 or later, or in terms of attendance at university. But overall Halsey et al. concluded that 'in the context of the whole structure of opportunity beyond school ... then it appears that expansion has brought a slow and steady diminution of class inequality' (Halsey et al., 1988, p.265).

Since then it has been possible to build up a longer timespan of data, including data on those passing through comprehensive schools. To take the overall expansion of the system into account and assess the relative chances of different social groups over time, analysts have increasingly used the 'odds-ratio'; that is, for example, the odds that one group has of getting A levels, compared with the odds of another. It is then possible to compare these ratios over time in different birth cohorts. To take account of the multiple comparisons, loglinear modelling is used. This tests whether there are changes in the relative position, taking account of overall changes in opportunity.

Using these methods on more recent cohort data drawn from the British Election Surveys, Heath and Clifford (1996) come to a rather more pessimistic set of conclusions. Testing for success in terms of O level or equivalent qualifications in their birth cohorts from the 1930s to the 1960s, they first point to the high levels of expansion – particularly marked among the working-class groups who start from a low base and therefore make more absolute progress. However, in testing for changes in the relative chances over time, they conclude that the '"constant relative chances" model gives an excellent fit to this data' (Heath and Clifford, 1996, p.222) – that is, there have been no significant reductions in inequality on this measure of educational outcome. Using slightly different data sets but also focusing on educational qualifications, Marshall et al. (1997) come to a similar set of pessimistic conclusions of a 'generally unchanging relationship between class origins and educational achievement' over their birth cohorts which extend from those born before 1920 to the 1960s.

Data from the British Election Surveys from 1979 to 1997 illustrate some of the patterns over time in the relationship between social origin and educational qualifications. First, these data underline the very steep gradient in qualification level by birth cohort. Thus someone born in the 1960s was 28 times as likely to have acquired an A level or equivalent (compared to no qualifications) than someone born in the first decade of the century; and the odds ratio is nearly as high for lower level qualifications (more than 25 times as likely to have a low-level qualification than none). Second, there are steep gradients in terms of qualification by social origin. Thus someone whose father was in the highest social ('service') class is approximately 14 times as likely to have A levels (compared with no qualification) than someone from a semi-skilled or unskilled manual background. Yet these ratios have largely remained stable across cohorts, indicating that while the overall level of qualifications has increased dramatically, particularly in the final 20 years of the century, the relative chances of people from different social backgrounds of acquiring these qualifications have remained surprisingly constant. Figure 5.10 illustrates some of these apparent trends, using selected social groups and qualifications. The closely parallel trends observed for the two social groups selected suggests a relatively unchanging relationship, despite the substantial expansion in qualifications at all levels.

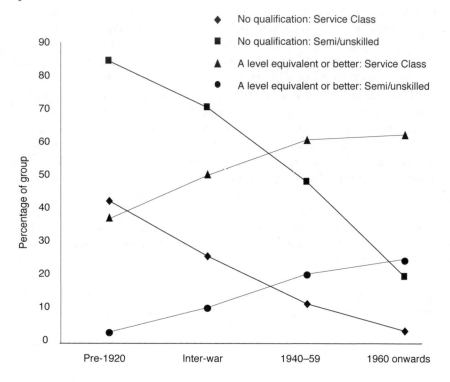

Figure 5.10 Educational performance by father's occupation: birth cohorts since 1900

Source: British General Election Studies, 1979–97.

Epilogue

At the start of the century, Michael Sadler set out some of the conditions required to develop 'a national system of education'. Looking back at the developments over the century, he might, if invited to reflect on progress, have been impressed by the moves to a far more national system for the majority of pupils. But he might have been surprised that it was not until the 1960s that it became routinely possible to describe statistically the overall pattern of schooling, including the very resilient independent sector. He might also have observed, particularly in England, the residual pieces of earlier systems that had never been completely overwritten by later developments. And he might speculate on whether, with the latest emphasis on greater diversity and parental choice, we were not beginning to move away from a national system of education, at least as this would have been understood at the height of confidence in central state direction. Finally, he would surely find it striking in the extreme that despite the massive expansion in all aspects of education, and the quite dramatic increases in staying-on rates and qualifications in the last two decades of the century, the relative chances of children from different social backgrounds were still apparently as unequal as they had been at the start of the century.

Acknowledgements

I am very grateful for the help of a number of people in compiling the material for this chapter: particularly Ben Roberts, Derek Kilmer, Lucinda Platt and Helen McColm. Numerous statisticians in the DfEE, Scottish Office, Welsh Office and DENI have been exceedingly helpful in providing data or fielding queries. My colleagues, Michael Noble and Teresa Smith, have helped with particular sections. Any errors or misinterpretations are my responsibility.

Notes

1. Quoted in Dalglish (1996).
2. For recent developments in Wales, see Jones (1997).
3. I am very grateful to Anthony Heath of Nuffield College, Oxford, who supplied data from the British General Election database and provided some of the analyses that follow.
4. Data from the Independent Schools Information Service (ISIS) 1998 Annual Survey. Not all independent schools are members of ISIS.

References

Arnot, M., Gray, J., James, M. and Rudduck, J., with Duveen, G. (1998) *Recent Research on Gender and Educational Performance*, OFSTED Reviews of Research, The Stationery Office, London.

Coleman, J. (1987) 'Families and schools', *Educational Researcher*, August–September 1987, pp.32–8.

Dalglish, N. (1996) *Education and Policy-making in England and Wales: The Crucible Years, 1895–1911*, The Woburn Press, London.

Glass, D. V. (ed.) (1954) *Social Mobility in Britain*, Routledge and Kegan Paul, London.

Glennerster, H. and Wilson, G. (1970) *Paying for Private Schools*, Allen Lane, London.

Halsey, A. H. (1988) 'Schools', in Halsey, A. H. (ed.) *British Social Trends Since 1900*, Macmillan, Basingstoke.

Halsey, A. H., Heath, A. F. and Ridge, J. M. (1980) *Origins and Destinations: Family, Class, and Education in Modern Britain*, Clarendon Press, Oxford.

Heath, A. and Clifford, P. (1980) 'The seventy thousand hours that Rutter left out', *Oxford Review of Education*, 6 (1).

Heath, A. and Clifford, P. (1996) 'Class inequalities and educational reform in twentieth-century Britain', in Lee, D. J. and Turner, B. S. (eds) *Conflicts about Class – Debating Inequality in Late Industrialism: A Selection Of Readings*, Longman, London.

Jones, G. E. (1997) *The Education of a Nation*, University of Wales, Cardiff.

Marshall, G., Swift, A. and Roberts, S. (1997) *Against the Odds? Social Class and Social Justice in Industrial Societies*, Clarendon Press, Oxford.

Mitchell, B. R. (1988) *British Historical Statistics*, Cambridge University Press, Cambridge.

Norwood, C. (1943) *Curriculum and Examinations in Secondary Schools: Report of the Committee of the Secondary Schools Examinations Council*, HMSO, London.

Office for Population Censuses and Surveys (OPCS) (1996) *Living in Britain: Results from the 1994 General Household Survey*, The Stationery Office, London.

Office for National Statistics (ONS) (1998) *Social Trends 28*, The Stationery Office, London.

Organization for Economic Co-operation and Development (OECD) (various years) *Education at a Glance: OECD Indicators*, 1992, 1993, 1995, 1997, 1998, OECD, Paris.

Payne, J. (1998) *Routes at Sixteen: Trends and Choices in the Nineties: An Analysis of Data from the England and Wales Youth Cohort Study*, Policy Studies Institute, London.

Payne, J. with Cheng, Y. and Witherspoon, S. (1996) *Education and Training for 16–18-year-olds: Individual Paths and National Trends*, Policy Studies Institute, London.

Rutter, M. et al. (1979) *Fifteen Thousand Hours: Secondary Schools and their Effects on Children*, Open Books, London.

Secretaries of State for England and Wales (1992) *Choice and Diversity: A New Framework for Schools*, Cm 2021, HMSO, London.

Vaizey, J. and Sheehan, J. (1968) *Resources for Education: An Economic Study of Education in the United Kingdom 1920–1965*, George Allen and Unwin, London.

Warnock Report (1978) *Special Educational Needs: Report of the Committee of Enquiry into the Education of Handicapped Children and Young People*, HMSO, London.

Williams, L. J. (1985) *Digest of Welsh Historical Statistics*, Welsh Office, Cardiff.

6
Further and Higher Education

A. H. Halsey

Oxford is widowed.
Lord Jenkins on the death of Sir Isaiah Berlin, 1998

Even the New Universities are ancient. You might think, listening to Eric James, that the University of York had medieval origins but an undistinguished run of Vice Chancellors until he himself was appointed.
A. H. Halsey, 1968

Introduction

Looking back over the twentieth century it becomes clear that two views of education, especially education beyond the fundaments of literacy and numeracy, have been in contention. One has been progressive, populist, Protestant, seeking emancipation from traditional pieties and folklore, encouraging liberty and equality, pursuing the spread of Enlightenment ideas in religion, science, politics and society, celebrating the advancement of control over human health, wealth and welfare. The other has been traditionalist, seeking refuge against revolution and the collapse of social solidarity in established elitism, fearing the dissemination of modernization in political, religious and sexual affairs, exuding pessimism about educability, emphasizing limits to the popular 'pool of ability'.

This chapter, then, is the story of the triumph; slow, perhaps still contested and overdue, of the one over the other. Thus the British universities (Halsey and Trow, 1970; Halsey, 1995) entered the twentieth century as a restricted and elite group of institutions. In England, Oxford and Cambridge stood at the apex, the University of London had emerged as a federation of heterogeneous colleges in the capital, and university charters were being granted to colleges in the major provincial cities. Scotland, meanwhile, had four well-established universities.

The system as a whole mustered less than 25 000 students out of a population of 40 million. But later, especially after World War II, there was more substantial growth from this tiny base. The number of students rose from 25 000 before World War I to over 40 times as many at the present time, so that in 1999 there were well over a million university students on full-time or part-time courses.

In other words, the twentieth century has been the first in which further and higher education have become recognized as a democratic right of citizenship. Expansion has accordingly been the reformist watchword, and tertiary systems have gradually moved from a highly restricted binary organization along mainly class and sex lines (the university versus the technical college or 'night school') towards the American conception of a universal and co-educational system covering both universities and community colleges. Many words and phrases have come into use to describe this widening aspiration. Secondary, post-secondary, further (FE), higher (HE), adult, continuing, recurrent and *l'education permanente* are among them. They all reflect an evolving set of arrangements and opportunities for life-long learning as perhaps the key goal of the twenty-first century; they all set problems of definition and comparability over time and between countries.

The evolution of a national system of further and higher education goes back to royal patronage of Oxford and Cambridge in the Middle Ages. When England and Scotland united in 1707 the Crown took over the Scottish government's financial grants and Parliament paid them from 1832. Later in the nineteenth century state money began to flow towards the Welsh universities and colleges and still later to other British institutions of higher education.

The phrase 'further education' may be used in a general sense to cover all non-advanced education after the period of compulsory schooling. But more commonly it excludes those staying on at secondary school and those studying higher education at universities, polytechnics and some other colleges. FE students are now included (as a separate category) in the university statistics of the Higher Education Statistics Agency (HESA). In 1996/97 there were 177 higher education institutions in the United Kingdom. On 1 December 1996 almost 1.8 million students attended these universities and colleges: but 2.3 per cent of them (40 902) were classified as studying further rather than higher education (HESA, 1998). In short, a residual ambiguity survived the twentieth century.

In 1910 in England and Wales there were 26 000 full-time students in further education, 68 000 on part-time day courses and 558 000 night school students – a total of 652 000. By mid-century the total had risen to two million and by the end of the century to over four million despite the invasion from and expansion of higher education. At the beginning of the century full-time students in higher education amounted to barely more than 1 per cent of the relevant age-group. While the universities, and indeed the whole system of education in the United Kingdom, were dominated for better and for worse by Oxford and Cambridge, the mass was confined to elementary schooling. At the end of the century a mass provision of tertiary education was in view. Full-time students in higher education had risen to nearly a third of the relevant age-group. In addition there were at least half a million part-timers. Adult or continuing or third-age education was also flourishing.

Putting the whole picture together, by the late 1990s there were about five million students in tertiary education. The Prime Minister, Tony Blair, promised at the 1997 Labour Party conference that 'We will lift the cap on student numbers and set a target for an extra 500 000 people in higher and further education by 2002.' The story, in short, is of expansion in both sectors together with a growing invasion after the Robbins Report (Robbins, 1963) of further by higher education.

Our purpose in this chapter is to fill in some of the significant detail, including the acceleration of growth in the last decade of the century, the changing balance of the curriculum, the social composition of students, the shift of resources, and the multiplication of colleges and universities from a handful to nearly 200 institutions of higher education scattered widely throughout the country. The story, if only for statistical convenience, falls into three main phases:

1 Restricted growth, 1900–63
2 The binary phase, 1964–92
3 Mass tertiary education, 1992–2000

Restricted growth, 1900–63

In 1963, and looking back over the preceding 60 years, the Robbins Committee defined higher education for their purposes as follows:

> In the main we have concentrated on the universities (whose charters empower them to grant degrees) in Great Britain and those colleges, within the purview of the Ministry of Education and the Scottish Education Department, that provide courses for the education and training of teachers or systematic courses of further education beyond the advanced level of the General Certificate of Education (in Scotland, beyond the higher grade of the Scottish Certificate of Education) or beyond the Ordinary National Certificate or its equivalent. (Robbins, 1963, Chapter 1, para. 6)

The definition is further elucidated by a consideration of further education which covered, 'in addition to the colleges of advanced technology, the advanced work undertaken at a great number of technical and commercial

colleges and schools of art, but it excludes the initial stage of much professional and other education provided in such colleges' (Robbins, 1963, para. 7).

The trends in further education for the whole century are presented in Table
6.1. Up to 1970 they are limited to England and Wales. From 1970 the
numbers for Scotland and Northern Ireland are added to form a picture of the
United Kingdom, and from 1990/91 they are restricted to England. Thus the
figures are not strictly comparable over time. But within the limits indicated

**Table 6.1 Further education: course enrolments in maintained, assisted
and grant–aided establishments, 1910/11–96/97 (000s)[a]**

	Full-time and sandwich				Adult	Total full-
		Initial			education	time and
	All	teacher training	Part-time	Evening	centre	part-time
	students	(included in	day	only		
		previous column)				
England and Wales						
1910/11	26	13	68	558		652
1920/21	30	12	90	754		874
1930/31	26	13	76	930		1032
1937/38	30	10	89	1203		1322
1949/50	75	21	284	761	1263	2383
1951	71	25	298	550	993	1912
1960	151	34	488	713	877	2229
1965	259	73	680	796	1253	2988
United Kingdom						
1970	382	111	749	736	1422	3289
1975	486	99	743	802	1982	4013
1980	509	30	733	635	1645	3512
England only						
1990/91	721	35	946	852	1352	3871
1993/94						
(excluding SFC[b])	1048	49	980	851	1401	4280
1993/94						
(including SFC[b])	1148	49	987	862	1401	4398
1996/97						3816

Notes: [a]The main breaks in the comparability of the figures are shown by lines across the table. The
figures for the years 1951–60 have been adjusted to take account of the change of basis of collection in 1961 (a fuller explanatory note appears on p.21 of *Statistics of Education*, 1961, Part 2).
Agricultural institutes are included from 1958 onwards. The Cranfield Institute of Technology
(formerly the College of Aeronautics, Cranfield) is included from 1961 onwards. The colleges of
advanced technology are excluded from 1965 onwards when they obtained university status.
[b]Sixth form colleges were transferred to the FE sector in 1993/94 when the figures are accordingly
presented with and without the sixth form college students.

Source: *Statistics of Education 1980*, Pt 2, Table F1. For 1990/91 to 1996/97 statistics were provided
by DfEE.

in the table the trend has been one of vigorous expansion right through the century: despite transfers to higher education there was at least a fourfold increase from the beginning of the century to the end.

The pattern of higher education in 1962 as described by Robbins, and using his definitions, may be summarized as follows. At the turn of the century nearly all full-time higher education was provided by universities: the courses then given in teacher training colleges and colleges of education involved only two years of study and the standard of instruction was correspondingly restricted. The training colleges had grown substantially in the years before the Robbins Committee, both because of rising standards of entry and, in England and Wales, because of the introduction of three-year courses in 1960. The stature of some colleges engaged in further education had also grown dramatically in the 1950s. While the number of university students had slightly more than doubled since before the war, the number in training colleges and colleges of education had increased just over fourfold. But even more striking had been the marked increase in the number of full-time students in advanced courses in further education. This group had been negligible at the beginning of the century but by 1962 constituted a fifth of all full-time students in higher education (Table 6.2). Most part-time higher education was provided in institutions of further education. In 1962/63 there were 54000 advanced students attending these institutions for at least one day a week (compared with 29000 in 1954/55): most of them were released by their employers for the purpose. Another 54000 advanced students attended only in the evening. In the universities the number of part-time students was 9000 (over two-thirds of them at post-graduate level) compared with 6000 before the war. Students in training colleges and colleges of education were almost always full-time.

Table 6.2 Higher education students, full-time, Great Britain, 1900/01–62/63

Year	University	Teacher training	Further education advanced courses	All full-time higher education[b]
1900/01	20000	5000	–	25000
1924/25	42000	16000	3000[a]	61000
1938/39	50000	13000	6000[a]	69000
1954/55	82000	28000	12000	122000
1962/63	118000	55000[c]	43000	216000

Notes: [a]Figures for further education in 1924/25 and 1938/39 are approximate.
[b]The table does not include full-time advanced students in the colleges of music and other colleges mentioned in paragraph 8 of chapter 1 of *Higher Education*.
[c]Part of the large increase in teacher training between 1954/55 and 1962/63 was due to the lengthening of the training college course in England and Wales.

Source: *Higher Education*, Table 3, p.15.

Table 6.3 Percentage of age-group entering full-time higher education, Great Britain, 1900–62[a]

Year	University	Teacher training	Further education	All full-time higher education
1900	0.8	0.4	–	1.2
1924	1.5	1.0	0.2	2.7
1938	1.7	0.7	0.3	2.7
1954	3.2	2.0	0.6	5.8
1955	3.4	2.0	0.7	6.1
1956	3.5	2.1	0.8	6.4
1957	3.9	2.2	0.9	7.0
1958	4.1	2.4	1.2	7.7
1959	4.2	2.8	1.3	8.3
1960	4.1	2.7	1.5	8.3
1961	4.1	2.5	1.7	8.3
1962	4.0	2.5	2.0	8.5

Note: [a]For 1970–97 see Figure 6.1

Source: *Higher Education*, Table 4, p.16.

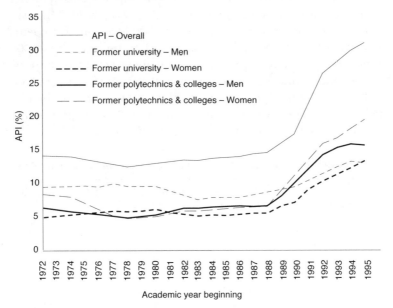

Figure 6.1 Higher education age participation index (API), GB Institutions, 1972–95[a]

Note: [a]The API is the number of young (under 21) home domiciled initial entrants to full-time courses of HE in FE or HE institutions across GB expressed as a percentage of the averaged 18–19-year-old GB population. Initial entrants are those entering a course of full-time higher education for the first time. Figures for 1994/95 and 1995/96 are provisional.

Source: DfEE.

Robbins also presented the growth of higher education to 1962 in terms of percentages of the age-group. For those entering full-time higher education courses they are given in Table 6.3, and for 1970–97 in Figure 6.1. The growth of full-time higher education is shown to be sevenfold from 1900 to 1962. Yet by standards officially accepted for the twenty-first century the growth has to be described as restricted. By 1997 the Dearing Committee (Dearing, 1997) was forecasting that more than half of today's school leavers will experience higher education at some time in their lives.

The binary phase, 1964–92

The Robbins Report heralded accelerated growth in higher education. In 1962 there were 31 British universities, 10 colleges of advanced technology (first designated in 1956 with origins in the Mechanics' Institutes of the nineteenth century), 150 teacher training colleges and upwards of 600 technical colleges and other institutions of further education in which about 33 000 students were enrolled on courses of higher education standard. Robbins set targets for 1973 of 219 000 university students, 122 000 teacher-trainees in (renamed) colleges of education, and 51 000 in technical colleges on advanced courses. These targets were reached by 1970 and surpassed by over 40 000 in the case of the technical colleges. Between 1963 and 1970/71 the total student population in full-time higher education doubled to 457 000. In this period the colleges of advanced technology were given university charters, seven new universities were founded in England and one in Scotland, where, in addition, two others were formed from leading technical institutions. The colleges of education doubled their student places, but many were subsequently drawn into the university or polytechnic sectors with their students reading for Bachelor of Education degrees.

In 1964 the Secretary of State for Education and Science, C. A. R. Crosland, announced a 'binary policy' for higher education – a division between the autonomous 44 universities and a 'public sector' led by 30 polytechnics. The number of full-time advanced students in the polytechnics or 'public sector' institutions grew considerably – to 215 000 in 1970/71 and further to 532 000 in 1997/98. Putting together all full-time higher education students in universities and public sector institutions from the UK and abroad the numbers rose from 457 000 in 1970/71 to 1 131 000 in 1997/98 (Table 6.4). In addition, by 1997/98 there were 506 600 part-time higher education students in the universities and the public sector institutions (Table 6.5). As percentages of the relevant age-group, new entrants to full-time higher education are shown in Table 6.6 and Figure 6.1 for the period 1970 to 1997/98. In the early 1900s only one young person in eighteen went from school to full-time higher education. By the late 1990s the figure for the UK was one in three and as much as 45 per cent in Scotland and Northern Ireland.

Table 6.4 Higher education – full-time students: by origin, sex and age, 1970/71–97/98, UK (000s)

Students	Males UK 1970/71	UK 1980/81	GB 1990/91	GB 1995/96
Full time students by origin[a]				
From the UK Universities				
– undergraduate	128.3	145.1	142.4	182.0
– post-graduate	23.9	20.7	21.6	30.7
Public sector higher education	102.0	111.9	172.6	252.2
Total full-time UK students	254.2	277.7	336.6	464.9
From abroad	20.0	40.7	48.6	77.8
Total full-time students	274.2	318.4	385.2	542.7
Full-time students by age[b]				
18 or under	28.7	50.3 }	198.7	69.1
19–20	99.0	117.8 }		180.9
21–24	104.6	95.6	115.5	173.0
25 or over	42.0	54.5	71.0	119.6

Notes: [a]Origin is of fee-paying students except for European Community students domiciled outside the UK who from 1980/81 are charged home rates but are included with students from abroad
[b]In 1980 measurement by age changed from 31 December to 31 August.

Table 6.5 Higher education – part-time students: by type of establishment, sex and age, UK, 1970/71–97/98 (000s)

	Males UK 1970/71	UK 1980/81	GB 1990/91
Part-time students by establishment			
Universities	18.1	22.6	28.8
Open University	14.3	37.6	49.3
Public sector higher education	n/a	n/a	159.4
Part-time day course	69.8	110.5	n/a
Evening-only course	39.8	35.1	n/a
Total part-time students	142.0	205.8	237.5
Part–time students by age			
18 or under	n/a	11.8	34.7
19–20	n/a	33.9	
21–24	n/a	48.3	44.5
25 or over	n/a	111.7	158.4

Source: Social Trends, no. 16, Table 3.1. Figures from 1990/91 from DfEE and HESA.

GB 1997/98	Females UK 1970/71	UK 1980/81	GB 1990/91	GB 1995/96	GB 1997/98
186.6	57.0	96.2	116.7	173.2	192.8
29.0	8.0	11.3	15.5	25.3	26.4
242.3	113.1	96.4	171.3	276.8	290.0
457.9	178.2	203.9	303.5	475.3	509.2
87.6	4.4	12.6	29.2	61.3	76.1
545.5	182.6	216.5	332.7	536.6	585.3
77.8	30.4	41.6 }	186.2	74.1	88.3
186.2	82.3	89.7 }		189.3	206.2
166.9	44.5	53.5	90.7	158.5	165.0
114.7	25.3	31.5	61.3	114.8	125.9

Sources: *Social Trends*, no. 16, Table 3.12. Figures from 1990/91 from Dearing Report and DfEE.

GB 1997/98	Females UK 1970/71	UK 1980/81	GB 1990/91	GB 1997/98
91.9	5.7	10.7	23.2	113.7
62.2	5.3	30.1	45.6	61.2
102.7	n/a	n/a	111.2	137.7
n/a	6.7	30.8	n/a	n/a
9.7	5.0	15.2	n/a	13.3
256.8	22.7	86.8	180.0	312.6
1.4	n/a	3.2	13.9	1.1
5.6	n/a	7.5		4.4
24.3	n/a	16.0	28.2	26.5
225.4	n/a	60.1	137.9	280.7

Table 6.6 Higher education – home students entering full-time and sandwich courses for the first time: by age, 1970/71–97/98, Great Britain (000s)

Students	1970/71	1975/76	1980/81	1983/84	1990/91	1997/98
New Students (000s)						
Aged under 21	102.6	107.4	124.0	135.9	172.7	263.7
Aged 21 and over	27.3	31.4	66.3	69.4	101.8	214.0
Total	129.9	138.8	190.3	205.3	274.5	477.8
New Students aged 21 or over as a % of all new students	21.0	22.6	34.9	33.8	37.1	44.8
New Students aged under 21 as a % of the average of 18- and 19-year-old populations	13.7	13.6	12.7	13.3	19.0	33.0

Source: *Social Trends*, no. 16, Table 3.14. Figures from 1980/81 from HESA and DfEE.

It is possible to compare the Robbins plan with the actual experience in the period 1962–80. The comparison of programme and performance is taken from the work of John Carswell (1985). In Tables 6.7–10 the first line of each table gives the 1962 position as stated in the Robbins Report. All the figures refer to full-time students at degree level (or equivalent) and above, and include full-time students at advanced level in further education. Overseas students, who formed between 9 and 12 per cent of the whole student body at different times during the period, are included. Since part-time students are not included the tables do not show the contribution of the Open University. The figures are for Great Britain, and do not include Northern Ireland.

Table 6.7 gives the overall picture divided by 'sectors'. The colleges of advanced technology appear in the 'university sector' figures for 1962, though they did not join the UGC Grant List until afterwards. The 'public sector' institutions include polytechnics, other further education institutions offering advanced courses, colleges of education in England, Scotland and Wales, central institutions in Scotland, and the two specialized higher educational institutions still financed by the Department of Education and Science – the Royal College of Art and the Cranfield Institute.

The table shows that overall performance came within 6 per cent of programme, and at mid-term considerably exceeded it but, as between the 'sectors', the programme was not achieved in the way the Robbins Report proposed. The last line of the table does not indicate a failure on the part of the University Grants Committee (UGC) institutions to achieve the Robbins objective, but reflects the subsequent decision to develop further education on a much larger scale than the Robbins Report had proposed, with a consequent redistribution of both numbers and resources.

Table 6.7 Development of the 'sectors', 1962–80, Great Britain (000s, full-time students)

Students	UGC[a] institutions[b]	'Public Sector' institutions[c]	Total
(1) Actual 1962	130	86	216
(2) Addition for 1967 proposed by Robbins Committee	67	45	112
(3) Total (1) + (2)	197	131	328
(4) Actual 1967	200	179	379
(5) Further addition proposed by Robbins Committee for 1980	149	81	230
(6) Robbins proposal; for 1980 (3) + (5)	346	212	558
(7) Actual 1980[d]	301	223	524
(8) Difference between programme and performance	–45	+11	–34

Notes: [a]UGC = University Grants Committee.
[b]All the entries in the first column include the colleges of advanced technology, though they did not in fact become universities until 1964.
[c]The entries in the second column bring together further education to advanced level in England and Wales and the equivalent in Scotland, and teacher training in Great Britain as a whole. Lines 2, 6 and 7 should be read with the important reservations that (i) the Robbins Report greatly overstated the need for teacher training, and (ii) further education expanded far more quickly than the Robbins Committee had proposed. While these departures in opposite directions almost cancel each other out, the components of the figures 212 in line 6 and 223 in line 7 are very different.
[d]Line 7 includes advanced courses.

Source: Carswell (1985) Appendix 1.

Table 6.8 contrasts the proposed and actual expansion of student numbers in science/technology and in 'other subjects' taken as a whole. The shorthand 'science/technology' is taken as including mathematics, physics, chemistry, biology and all forms of engineering and computer studies, but excludes medicine, dentistry and veterinary studies. The table shows that the numbers fell short by about 25 per cent in science/technology over the 20-year period, and that, despite the cutback in teacher training, 'other subjects' exceeded the objective by about 17 per cent in compensation. These 'other subjects' include business studies, economics and medicine as well as the humanities, and it should be noted that, because of the length of the medical course, medical students bulk larger *in any given year* in relation to 'opportunity' at one end or graduate output at the other, than most other groups.

Table 6.9 shows the intended and actual distribution of places between the sexes, so far as the former can be estimated from the Report. Broadly speaking, over the 19-year period, the number of women students trebled, and that of men doubled, so that women rose from just over 30 per cent of the student body to more than 40 per cent. This growth, however, was mainly in non-science subjects, as is shown in Table 6.10 which contrasts the growth in

Table 6.8 Science/technology contrasted with all other subjects, 1962–80, Great Britain (000s, full-time students)

		UGC institutions	
Students		Science/ technology	Other subjects
(1)	Actual	59	71
(2)	Addition to 1980 proposed by Robbins Committee[a]	136	80
(3)	Robbins proposal for 1980 ((1) + (2))[a]	195	151
(4)	Actual 1980[b]	112	188
(5)	Difference between programme and performance[c]	−83	+37

Notes: [a]Lines 2 and 3 have been estimated on the basis that the Robbins Committee intended that about two-thirds of the additional places which they proposed in universities and further education should go to science/technology; and that in teacher training colleges the balance of subjects should remain unchanged.
[b]Line 4 includes advanced courses.

Table 6.9 Male and female students at degree and advanced level, all students and all types of institution, 1962–80, Great Britain (000s, full-time students)

Students		Women	Men	Total
(1)	Actual 1962	68	148	216
(2)	Addition to 1980 proposed by Robbins Committee[a]	185	157	342
(3)	Robbins proposal for 1980 ((1) + (2))	253	305	558
(4)	Actual 1980[b]	214	310	524
(5)	Difference between programme and performance	−39	+ 5	−34

Notes: [a]The additional places in line 2 have been estimated on the bases that the additions assigned by Robbins to the universities and further education were to be equally divided between the sexes, but that two-thirds of the extra places assigned to teacher training would be filled by women. Although the rundown of teacher training was largely compensated by the development of further education institutions, the difference between lines 3 and 4 for women students should be read with this in mind.
[b]Line 4 includes advanced courses.

Source: Carswell (1985).

science/technology numbers as between the sexes. It shows that the expansion came very near the objective in respect of men (though here students from overseas played an important part), so that almost the whole of the shortfall in science/technology shown in Table 6.9 is attributable to the absence of the women students who had been hoped for. The number of women students in science/technology did indeed more than double over the period, but the base in 1962 was so low that this made little difference. The prognostications required it to expand by more than eight times.

'Public sector' institutions		Totals all institutions		Grand total all institutions all subjects
Science/ technology	Other subjects	Science/ technology	Other subjects	
36	60	85	131	216
38	88	174	168	342
64	148	259	299	558
64	160	176	348	524
nil	+12	−83	+49	−34

ᶜLine 5 should be read bearing in mind that the Robbins 'target' for further education, which envisaged successive transfers of further education institutions to the 'university sector', was almost at once superseded by the 'binarist' policy of developing the 'public sector' separately.

Source: Carswell (1985).

Table 6.10 Science/technology at degree of advanced level, distribution between male and female students, all types of institution, 1962–80, Great Britain (000s, full-time students)

Students	Women	Men	Total
(1) Actual 1962	12	73	85
(2) Addition to 1980 estimated by reference to Robbins Committee	87	87	174
(3) Estimated target for 1980 on basis of Robbins Report ((1) + (2))	99	160	259
(4) Actual 1980	28	148	176
(5) Difference between programme and performance	−71	−12	−83

Source: Carswell (1985).

Mass tertiary education, 1992–2000

The Robbins Report (1963) confirmed the fact of expansion in the 1950s and heralded further expansion in the 1960s and 1970s. What, then, of the 1980s and 1990s? The number of students has certainly increased since Robbins; but the more interesting questions are: what kinds of students, in what kind of institutions, and what proportions of their contemporaries in the population at large did they represent?

From 1963 to 2000 expansion continued in such a way as to obliterate Robbins as a numerical landmark. Absolute numbers of students in the higher education system as a whole rose every year. In 1962 the total number of full-

Table 6.11 Expansion of higher education by type of establishment, sex and mode of attendance, 1970/71–95/96, UK

	Universities[a]					Polytechnics and colleges – the '1992 Universities'		
	1970/71	1989/90	1995/96	1970/71–89/90 rise (%)	1989/90–95/96 rise (%)	1970/71	1989/90	1995/96
	(000s)	(000s)	(000s)			(000s)	(000s)	(000s)
Full-time								
Men	167	200	499	20	150	107	170	94
Women	68	151	465	122	308	114	169	124
Part-time								
Men	18	31	158	72	510	110	159	85
Women	6	23	185	283	804	12	103	82

Notes: [a]From 1993/94 figures include former polytechnics and HE Colleges which became universities as a result of the Further and Higher Education Act 1992.

time students was 216 000. By 1989/90, including home and overseas students, part-timers in universities, the Open University, the polytechnics and other colleges offering advanced courses, it was 1 095 000. (Table 6.11). By 1995/96 it was 1.8 million.

Apparently, therefore, Britain has had an accelerating record of successful development of its investment in higher education through fluctuating economic fortunes. In fact, the story is less simple and more interesting. Less simple because the numbers have risen at varying rates. More interesting because the definition has widened from the original concept with which Robbins began. The stereotyped view of higher education as a three-year residential system of high-quality learning for young men has been overturned. The definition moved gradually, and continues to move, towards an American concept of higher education as all post-compulsory or post-secondary schooling, including the Open University founded in the 1960s and the University for Industry founded by the government at the end of the century.

The statistics cited begin with full-time or sandwich-course students and end with all full-time and part-time students in a wide range of colleges in addition to those in the pre-1992 universities. The White Paper (*Higher Education: A New Framework*, Cmnd 1541, May 1991) described the higher education system in the UK as one in which the polytechnics and colleges (including Scottish central institutions) took 53 per cent of the student total, with the Open University taking 4 per cent and the universities 42 per cent. Underlying this description lies the commitment to mass provision of post-compulsory opportunities towards which educational reformers were slowly moving from the end of the nineteenth century.

Open University

1970/71– 89/90 rise (%)	1989/90– 95/96 rise (%)	1970/71 (000s)	1989/90 (000s)	1995/96 (000s)	1970/71– 89/90 rise (%)	1989/90– 95/96 rise (%)
59	−45	–	–	–	–	–
48	−27	–	–	–	–	–
−45	−47	14	47	65	236	138
758	−20	5	42	62	740	148

Source: *Education Statistics for the United Kingdom.*

From Robbins to Dearing, that is, from 1962 to 1996, the number of university students continued to rise. However, the annual rate of increase was by no means steady. It averaged 12 per cent between 1962/63 and 1972/73, during which time the former Colleges of Advanced Technology were incorporated and the new greenfield universities of the 1960s opened their gates. These were direct consequences of the Robbins surge. But advance slowed down in 1972/73 and turned to retreat after 1981 when severe funding cuts were imposed by the government. There was absolute numerical decline in the universities from 1982 to 1985 when economic slump gave way to boom, from which point growth accelerated each year to 1996 with a dramatic leap, at least nominally, in 1992 when polytechnics were allowed to become universities. Thus the expansion rates of the late 1960s and early 1970s were recaptured in the closing years of the century.

Diversification

At this point we are in a position to see the evolving institutional and opportunity pattern of developments since Robbins. The general pattern of expansion is disaggregated in Table 6.11 for the period from 1970 to 1996. Total enrolment rose but the composition of the student body crucially shifted. The traditional pattern of higher education – the full-time male undergraduate in a university – was the one that rose most slowly. For example, the proportion of full-time male undergraduates in universities in 1995/96 was 150 per cent higher than in 1989/90. The comparable figure for women was 308 per cent. The alternative forms expanded more rapidly; for example, the number of part-time female students at polytechnics or colleges of higher education (which became 'the 1992 universities') rose by 758 per cent between 1970 and 1990 and Open University female undergraduates went up by 740 per cent in the same two decades (Table 6.11).

Specialization and the changing balance of studies

University studies in the twentieth century have widened dramatically in scope, and the balance between the faculties has also shifted. Widening the scope of studies has meant that university students and their teachers have specialized increasingly in their academic interests, the latter choosing between research and teaching, and between undergraduate and graduate supervision. One crude but dramatic illustration of the widening range of specialisms may be derived from the official statistics in the branches of study pursued by advanced students. In 1928, 123 subjects were distinguished; a quarter of a century later there were 382. In the meantime, economics had been divided into economics, industrial economics, econometrics and economic history, amongst others; the number of branches of engineering had risen from 7 to 22, and such subjects as Ethiopic studies, fruit nutrition, immunology, personnel management, medical jurisprudence and space

Table 6.12(a) Full-time students by type of faculty, 1919–82, Great Britain (%)

	1919–29[a]		1929/30	
	Men	Women	Men	Women
Arts (including theology, fine art, music, economics[d] and education)	23.8	54.6	44.8	74.7
Social Studies (including social, administrative and business studies)	–	–	–	–
Pure Science	19.4	15.2	17.1	15.0
Medicine (including health and dentistry)	33.4	28.6	23.3	8.8
Technology (including engineering, applied chemistry, etc.)	21.3	0.5	12.5	0.5
Agriculture (including forestry, horticulture and veterinary science)	2.0	1.1	2.2	0.9
Total	100.0	100.0	100.0	100.0
	24768	9183	32682	12921

Notes: [a]Excluding Oxford and Cambridge.
[b]Birmingham figures include two-year teacher training figures.
[c]Figures for United Kingdom. 1971/72 refers to entrants, not all students.
[d]Economics was included in arts until 1960 and after that in social studies.

science had appeared. In the second half of the century and especially with the sudden expansion of the term 'university' in 1992, the spread of vocationally orientated studies has proceeded apace. Business, computing, accounting and media studies now loom large; nursing and studies allied to medicine have been added.

Students in universities

The relative numerical importance of different faculties also changed substantially from 1920 to 1991 (Table 6.12(a) and (b)). Pure science has been the most popular faculty for men since 1960, followed by technology and social studies while in 1920 medicine was the largest faculty followed by the arts and then technology. For women the pattern is different: the arts faculties (now subdivided into languages, humanities and creative arts as well as 'buried' under multi-disciplinary studies) have by far the largest number of students, followed by social studies and then pure science; and it was arts subjects that were also most popular among women in 1920, with medicine coming next but attracting only half as many. Even with the addition of nursing and other health-related studies the position for women remains much the same in the 1990s.

1938/39		1950/51		1960/61		1971/72[c]		1981/82[c]	
Men	Women	Men	Women	Men	Women	Men	Women	Men	Women
38.7	64.7	37.2[b]	63.0[b]	25.4	52.7	15.3	40.8	14.6	37.3
–	–	–	–	11.5	9.4	21.0	22.6	22.5	25.1
15.2	15.9	21.1	17.0	25.5	21.7	28.5	22.1	26.0	19.4
30.3	17.3	21.1	16.6	14.5	13.6	9.7	10.8	10.5	12.0
13.6	0.8	15.8	1.1	19.5	1.3	23.9	2.6	24.2	4.3
2.3	1.3	4.9	2.4	3.6	1.3	1.5	1.1	2.1	1.9
100.0	100.0	100.0	100.0	100.0	100.0	100.0	100.0	100.0	100.0
38368	11634	65831	19483	81330	26369	45438	21903	152497	100874

Sources: *Returns from Universities and University Colleges, Statistics of Education*, vol. 6, Table 101981–2; *University Statistics*, vol. 1, Table 1.

Table 6.12(b) Full-time students by type of faculty, 1981/82 and 1990/91, Great Britain

1981/82	Male Number	%	Female Number	%
Education	5642	3.1	7060	6.1
Medicine, dentistry, health	18292	9.9	13314	11.5
Engineering and technology	39885	21.6	3329	2.9
Agriculture, forestry, vet. science	4080	2.2	2184	1.9
Biology, physical science	47969	26.0	21699	18.8
Admin., business, social studies	41309	22.3	28770	24.9
Architecture, other prof./				
vocational studies	3707	2.0	1935	1.7
Language, literature, area studies	11855	6.4	23722	20.6
Arts, other than language	12089	6.5	13354	11.6
	184828	100.0	115369	100.0

1990/91	Male Number	%	Female Number	%
Medicine, dentistry	13661	6.8	11760	7.7
Studies allied to medicine	3589	1.8	6654	4.3
Biological sciences	11287	5.7	13459	8.8
Veterinary, agriculture, related				
sciences	3404	1.7	2692	1.8
Physical sciences	21747	10.9	8128	5.3
Mathematical sciences	17016	8.5	5626	3.7
Engineering, technology	37504	18.8	5587	3.7
Architecture, related sciences	3982	2.0	1646	1.1
Social studies	27128	13.6	24147	15.8
Business, financial studies	11104	5.6	6679	4.4
Librarianship, information science	588	0.3	788	0.5
Languages, related studies	11093	5.6	24593	16.1
Humanities	11106	5.6	9784	6.4
Creative arts	1987	1.0	2935	1.9
Education	4244	2.1	8442	5.5
Multi-disciplinary studies	20114	10.1	20100	13.1
	199554	100.0	153020	100.0

Source: University Statistical Record now held by DfEE.

University students may live at home or in halls of residence or in lodgings; Table 6.13 shows the extent of the move away from living at home. The number and proportion in halls of residence or colleges have increased very substantially since 1920 and the home-based student has been effectively replaced. How far this trend will continue in the twenty-first century, given the introduction of student contributions to tuition as well as loans for maintenance, remains to be seen. The official publication of student term-time residence statistics ceased in 1980. The trend had reflected the 'postalization' of student maintenance grants from Robbins. However, the addition of polytechnics to the university list in 1992 may have reduced the proportion of students in halls of residence.

Table 6.13 Term-time residence of full-time university students[a], 1920–80, Great Britain (%)

Year	In colleges or halls of residence			In lodgings			At home		
	Men	Women	Total	Men	Women	Total	Men	Women	Total
1920/21	4.2	27.9	10.2	43.0	22.4	37.5	52.8	49.7	52.0
1929/30	20.6	35.9	24.9	39.4	16.5	32.9	40.0	47.6	42.1
1938/39	21.4	37.3	25.1	37.5	19.2	33.2	41.1	43.5	41.7
1950/51	20.0	38.9	24.3	42.3	28.4	39.1	37.7	32.7	36.6
1960/61	23.5	39.3	27.4	54.3	39.7	50.7	22.2	21.0	21.9
1971/72	37.9	41.4	39.7	43.1	40.2	41.7	16.7	15.9	16.3
1979/80	46.4	46.4	46.4	35.8	34.1	35.0	14.1	15.0	14.6

Note: [a]Excluding Oxford and Cambridge students

Sources: UGC, *Returns from Universities and University Colleges*, 1971–2 and 1979–80; *Statistics of Education*, vol. 6.

Demographic and educational trends

Demographic and educational factors underlie the trend of higher education numbers. The total number of 18-year-olds in the UK peaked at over a million in 1965, fell to 800000 in 1973, rose again to nearly a million in 1981 and then fell to nearly the 1973 level in 1990. These wide, even wild, oscillations were, however, evened out by the rising productivity of the secondary schools. The percentage of the age-group in England with two or more A levels in GCE rose from under 8 per cent in 1962/63 to approaching three times that proportion by the late 1980s (20.0 per cent of boys and 22.2 per cent of girls in 1988/89).

For full-time students in higher education as a whole there was a transformation in the age participation rate (APR). Before World War II it was less than 3 per cent. Just before Robbins in 1962/63 it was 7.2 per cent. It rose steadily until 1972/73 but then fell (to 12.7 per cent in 1977/78) and did not climb back to the 1973 level again until 1984 when it rose to 15.2 per cent and further to 20.3 per cent in 1990. According to calculations by the Department for Education and Employment (DfEE), the age participation index (API) (virtually the same as APR; that is, the number of home initial entrants to full-time higher education as a proportion of the 18–19-year-old population) was 13.7 in 1984 and reached 19.3 in 1990. The index was projected to increase to 32.1 in 2000

(Appendix 2 of Cmnd 1541). The declared intention of continuing expansion to include more than ten times the post-war proportion of young people by the end of the century had in fact been achieved by 1995 (Figure 6.1).

Quality

But did more mean worse? For the universities we can check Robbins' confidence that student quality had not declined (and need not fall, on the Committee's expansion plans) from the records of the A level qualifications of accepted home candidates over the period from 1971. Standards were distinctly higher in 1991 than they were in 1971 (Table 6.14). They rose markedly between 1976 and 1984 and then fell back slightly. It cannot, of course, be maintained that the merit or the aptitude of candidates is exactly represented by A level results. However, in the terms of the argument before and after Robbins there is no better practical calculus. The 'pool of ability' had yet to be exhausted. On the standards that obtained when Robbins reported there remained ample scope for expansion of universities. Whether that scope was ample enough to meet the sudden explosion of 1992, when polytechnics and the other colleges were allowed to call themselves universities, is thrown into serious doubt by the drop in high-flying A level scores after 1991 (Table 6.14).

Table 6.14 British university entrants: A level scores of home candidates accepted through UCCA, 1971–99 (% with various scores)[a]

Scores	3–6	9–12	13–15	Total
1971[b]	28.0	46.7	25.3	43561
1976[b]	29.8	43.9	26.2	51561
1981[b]	24.2	45.7	30.0	57861
1984	15.7	52.3	37.9	54891
1988	16.6	48.5	34.9	61225
Scores	6–15	16–25	26–30	Total
1989	12.5	54.2	33.3	70219
1990	17.0	51.4	31.6	80251
1991	17.9	51.0	31.1	84661
1996	32.0	44.0	24.0	157680
1997	31.7	44.3	24.0	175837

Note: [a] Up to 1988, A level scores were calculated by giving 5 points to an A, 4 to a B and so on. From 1989, 10 points were awarded for an A, 8 to a B and so on.
[b] In 1971, 1976 and 1981 UCCA give sample data. From 1984 onwards whole population data are used.

Sources: 1971–88 UCCA *Statistical Supplements* – Table G1; 1989–91 UCCA *Statistical Supplements* – Table 2C; 1996 and 1997 UCAS *Annual Report* – Table F1.1.

For the higher education system as a whole the picture is in any case less clear. Part-time students and older entrants with 'non-traditional' qualifications have to be taken into account along with higher-degree candidates and students from overseas. The most direct and simple measure of degree seeking potential for the nation is the profile of qualifications of successive school leavers. The quality of the young, as judged by examination performance at the end of secondary schooling, had been rising gently since before the period of expansion ushered in by the Robbins Report. Moreover, using the more stringent criterion of a very high score in three A level subjects (AAA, AAB, AAC or ABB) the proportion of high-flyers among university entrants rose from 25.3 per cent in 1971 to 35.7 per cent in 1984, but fell back to 24.0 per cent in 1996 (Table 6.14).

However, all in all the Dearing Committee in 1997 concluded that there was no basis for the view that entry via A level to higher education had become significantly easier. Nevertheless, it must be noted that in 1997, soon after Dearing reported, the pass rate at A level rose again for the 16th year in succession, though the proportion of passes of A at A level had levelled off. Ministers and the leaders of teacher unions congratulated both students and teachers. Critics deplored the declining standards of examiners. The general line of development is clear. At the time of Robbins, the academic world was looking cautiously towards modest expansion and envisaging a system of higher education not fundamentally different from the previous one of highly restricted access. Public discussion, supported by a growing conviction among industrialists and politicians that a much more highly educated younger generation was needed to ensure the wealth of the nation, took a more expansionist view. The experience of larger numbers in the post-Robbins decade encouraged more and more university teachers to believe that larger proportions of each new generation were capable of receiving what they had to offer.

Table 6.15 Description by academic staff of academic ability of students entering and graduating from universities and polytechnics in 1989 compared with a decade earlier (% of responding academic staff)

	On entry		On graduation	
	University	Polytechnic	University	Polytechnic
Lot worse	4	8	1	2
Little worse	23	30	15	16
About the same	40	26	48	32
Little better	23	25	25	32
Lot better	10	11	11	18

Source: Halsey (1995) Appendix 1.

The bulk of the expansion in the binary phase took place in the polytechnics and colleges. A 1989 survey contains judgements of student quality at graduation as well as admission. It suggests that quality on entry had been maintained in universities and had been allowed to fall only slightly in polytechnics (now renamed universities) and that universities and polytechnics saw themselves as capable of giving considerable added value to the ability of the students they admitted (Table 6.15).

As to the internal characteristics of the universities, it must be noted that staff–student ratios deteriorated over the post-Robbins period. The ratio is defined in terms of full-time students and full-time staff who are wholly financed from university funds. The measure is a crude one, but it unequivocally describes a decline, from a ratio of 1 to 8 in 1971/72 to 1 to 11.6 in 1990/91 (Halsey, 1995, p.99, Table 4.5). And, without doubt, the further expansion of the 1990s combined with reduced state expenditure per student has resulted in further deterioration.

If we look at international comparisons, British universities before 1992 emerge as historically uniquely privileged from the point of view of intensive contact between teachers and learners, not only because of the ratio, which is typically 17 or 18 in comparable foreign institutions, but also because of residential arrangements, student maintenance and an entrenched culture of devotion to tutorial and pastoral relationships. The consequence is that drop-out rates were low and graduate output compared better with other countries than undergraduate input.

Furthermore, modern teaching techniques, especially capital-intensive methods of the kind used in the Open University, allow internal differentiation of staff–student contact, adapted to the type of course or subject and the stage of education or training of particular students.

At the end of the century the question of teaching quality must therefore remain open. All we can say is that some departure from the traditional ideal, and some retreat from the universities' defence of the unit of resource, has been a feature of post-Robbins expansion.

Gender and social class

The expansion of opportunity for women may be regarded as a further exemplification of the same general pattern. The proportion of all students who were women was less than a quarter before World War II, began to rise significantly after the mid-1960s, and became 51.8 per cent by 1986, a proportion maintained in the 1990s. Oxford and Cambridge traditionally had an especially small proportion of women but by 1980/81 they held 30 per cent of the places. As is clear from Table 6.4, the growth in full-time university undergraduate places has accommodated more women both absolutely and relatively. However, the evidence of differential relative expansion is also there. Women have gained on men but their advance has been disproportionately in the newer forms of higher education. All part-time categories have risen faster for women than for men over recent decades. It can be calculated from Table 6.11 that between 1970/71 and 1983/84 the number of women in full-time higher education rose by 34.8 per cent compared with 22.0 per cent for men. But the expansion of opportunities for women in higher education has been markedly in part-time studies where the percentage growth over the same period was 354.6 for women and 47.9 for men.

For social classes the general tendency towards relative inequality of educational attainment persists. General Household Survey data show that, measured in relative terms, the proportions of those entering higher education from manual working families have scarcely shifted by comparison with those from the professional and managerial classes. For degree holders in 1974 whose fathers were professionals or managers, the ratio was 2.75; that is, they were graduating at nearly three times the rate that would obtain if degree-holding were randomly distributed. At the other extreme the children of semi-skilled and unskilled workers had a ratio of 0.28 and the children of skilled manual workers 0.52. By 1985 these ratios had moved to 2.05, 0.36 and 0.50, respectively. The numbers of entrants to higher education from manual social origins had risen absolutely but not relatively to their numbers in the population. This is cold comfort for those who seek the 'classless society'. Moreover, the movement from grants towards loans inaugurated in 1989 and the logic of education as a 'positional good', might well produce greater class inequality in British higher education in the future.

Trends in the relation between class and origin and university entrance are set out in Table 6.16. The figures in the table reflect the fact that the universities

Table 6.16 Attendance at university by birth cohort, 1913–22 to 1943–53, Great Britain (%)

Father's social class[a]	1913–22	1923–32	1933–42	1943–53
I. II (Service)	7.2	15.9	23.7	26.4
	208[b]	*258*	*233*	*214*
III. IV. V. (Intermediate)	1.9	4.0	4.1	8.0
	75	*120*	*58*	*95*
VI. VII. VIII. (Working)	0.9	12.2	2.3	3.1
	0	*0*	*0*	*0*
All	1.8	3.4	5.4	8.5
No.	(1846)	(1879)	(1856)	(2246)

Notes: [a]For details of this class schema see Halsey et al. (1980).
[b]Figures in italics give log distances.

Source: Halsey et al. (1980) Table 10.8.

expanded throughout the century. It appears that the university expansion kept pace with the growth of the service or professional and managerial classes and that 'Robbinsian expansion' was an effective response to the post-war baby boom. The familiar picture also emerges, as with educational expansion generally, that though the fastest *rates* of growth almost always accrue to the working class, the greatest absolute increments of opportunity go to the upper-middle class.

The general pattern which has emerged from sociological research on education is that the origins of the modern education system can be described as a minimal education for the majority, with further opportunity for the minority. For a minority within that minority the golden road to high opportunity was provided by selected secondary education and by the universities. Educational expansion has developed the system in two main ways – by raising the output of children qualified to go beyond secondary education, and by differentiating the opportunities available to those, whether qualified or not, who stayed past the minimum school leaving age. All forms of post-secondary education have been selective in the sense of not being universal. And there has been a correlation between class origin and selective educational destination.

Trends in class access to part-time further education and to post-secondary education as a whole are shown in Table 6.17. For part-time education class access has slowly changed with expansion from the familiar positive correlation of class and opportunity to an *inverse* relation for those born after World War II.

Table 6.17 Percentage attending part-time further education, and any form of post-school education, by social class and birth cohort, 1913–22 to 1943–52, Great Britain

Percentage attending part-time further education

Father's social class[a]	1913–22	1923–32	1933–42	1943–52
I. II (Service)	50.0	46.2	59.3	45.1
III. IV. V. (Intermediate)	40.3	41.7	55.1	57.2
VI. VII. VIII. (Working)	29.9	36.9	46.4	50.8

Percentage attending any form of post-school education

Father's social class[a]	1913–22		1923–32		1933–42		1943–52	
I. II (Service)	60.6	*65*[b]	64.6	*50*	77.1	*44*	73.9	*30*
III. IV. V. (Intermediate)	43.5	*32*	48.0	*21*	60.4	*19*	67.4	*21*
VI. VII. VIII. (Working)	31.5	*0*	38.9	*0*	49.9	*0*	54.6	*0*

Notes: [a]For details of this class schema, see Halsey et al. (1980).
[b]Figures in italics give log distances.

Source: Halsey et al. (1980).

Thus in the earlier decades it was not usefully seen as an alternative route for the working class so much as an extension of class-biased educational opportunity. For the last cohort, born during and after the war, the alternative route description is more accurate. For the whole structure of educational opportunity beyond school it appears that expansion has brought a slow and steady diminution of class inequality. This trend is shown by the log distances in the table: that between the service class and the working class fell from 65 to 30 as between those born in 1913–22 and those born in 1943–52.

Why, then, did this expansion continue and even become the first priority of all political parties? The answers are not complete. Both economic fortunes and political pressure moved in the late 1980s. A restructuring of the economy with movement towards integration with continental Europe had educational consequences. The quest for competitive advantage impelled renewed educational expansion. International comparisons also stimulated reorganization of training arrangements and reinforced pressure towards inclusion of vocational education in schooling. From different standpoints and with different assumptions, all political parties began to share the view that a mass system of tertiary education was inevitable for twenty-first-century Britain.

University finance

The growth of reliance on the state for financial support expresses itself dramatically in Table 6.18(a) which shows the income of universities from 1920–97 distributed by its source.

The redefinition of higher education, after Robbins and before Dearing, dwarfed all previous experience. Second, an increasing proportion of university income was provided by the state. By 1983/84 the income from fees, endowments, donations and subscriptions had fallen to 14.3 per cent compared with 46.9 per cent in 1920/21. After the creation of the University Grants Committee (UGC) the total income of the universities on the grant list rose from just over £3 million in 1920/21 to nearly £2000 million in 1983/84. State expenditure per student then fell during the 1980s and, as may be seen from Figure 6.2, continued to do so into the 1990s.

By 1997 there were 177 institutions of higher education in the UK, of which 115 are given the title of Universities (which include the federal universities of London and Wales). Robbins had reported 31. Expansion, to repeat, has been rapid in the later decades of the century, and many further education colleges also offer higher education as well as private establishments such as the University of Buckingham and the churches with their 19 colleges and nearly 60 000 students.

Dearing reported that in 1995/96 total expenditure by higher education institutions was over £10 billion, representing 1.4 per cent of GDP. From 1976

Table 6.18(a) Sources of university income, 1920–93/94 (sources as % of total income)

Year	Total income of universities	Parliamentary grants	Grants from local authorities
United Kingdom	£ m		
1920/21	3.0	33.6	9.3
1923/24	3.6	33.5	12.0
1928/29	5.2	35.9	10.1
1933/34	5.6	35.1	9.2
1938/39	6.7	35.8	9.0
1946/47	13.0	52.7	5.6
1949/50	22.0	63.9	4.6
1953/54	31.1	70.5	3.6
1955/56	38.9	72.7	3.1
1961/62	74.1	76.5	2.1
1964/65	124.2	79.9	1.4
1967/68	216.2	72.9[b]	0.9
Great Britain[c]			
1969/70	258.9	73.2	0.7
1979/80	1266.6	63.1	not shown
1983/84	1982.8	61.8	separately
1990/91	4258.4	38.4	
1993/94	5676.6	32.6	

Notes: [a]Includes payment for research contracts from 1955/56.
[b]The amount of parliamentary grant shows an apparent drop in 1967/68 because, for that year only, grants from the Exchequer are distinguished in the statistics. Grants and payments for research from other government departments are included in 'other sources'. Previously, all parliamentary grants had been grouped together.
[c]From 1969/70 the figures are for Great Britain only. Parliamentary grants are Exchequer grants and grants from government departments. (Payments for research included in 'other'.) From 1969 the total is net income; that is, exclusive of repayment of Selective Employment Tax.

Table 6.18(b) Sources of university income, 1996/97, Great Britain

	Total income	Funding council grants	Academic fees/ support grants
	£ million	%	%
New universities	3051	45.3	29.8
Old universities	6953	34.0	20.7

Source: DfEE and HESA's Financial Record.

Fees	Endowments	Donations and subscriptions	Other sources[a]
%			
33.0	11.2	2.7	10.2
33.6	11.6	2.5	4.8
27.8	13.9	2.4	9.9
32.8	13.7	2.4	6.8
29.8	15.4	2.6	7.4
23.2	9.3	2.2	7.0
17.7	5.7	1.7	6.4
12.0	4.3	1.6	8.0
10.8	3.8	0.9	8.7
9.0	2.7	0.9	8.9
8.1	1.9	0.6	8.1
7.4		1.7	17.1[b]
7.3		1.7	16.0
15.9		0.9	20.1
13.1		1.2	23.9
20.7		3.6	37.3
23.6		4.1	39.6

Sources: 1920–68: UGC Returns; 1967/68: *Statistics of Education*, 1968, vol. 6, p.xviii; 1969/70: *Statistics of Education*, 1970, vol. 6, p.xviii; 1979/80: *Statistics of Education*, 1980, vol. 3, Table 2; 1983/84: *University Statistics*, 1983–4, vol. 3, Table 2; 1990–94: DfEE.

Research grants	Other services rendered	Other general income	Endowment/ interest
%	%	%	%
3.7	9.3	10.7	1.2
21.5	5.6	15.1	3.1

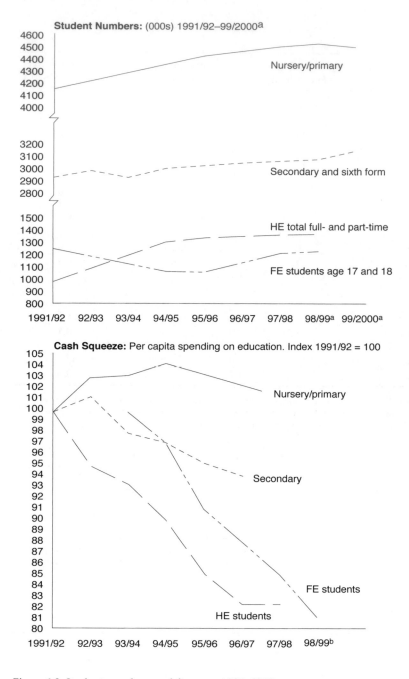

Figure 6.2 Student numbers and finance, 1991–2000

Notes: [a]Estimated   Source: DfEE (THES, 29 May 1998).
[b]Planned.

to 1996 public expenditure on higher education grew by about 45 per cent. At the same time the growth of student numbers which we have described, the demands of research, and the determination of governments in the 1980s and 1990s to restrain state spending, have resulted in a decline of funding per student from the mid-1970s (about a 50 per cent fall from 1976–97) (Figure 6.2). The government's drive towards increasing reliance on tuition fees will give more freedom to market forces. The government is also encouraging universities and colleges to seek funds from private sources, particularly from industry and commerce, benefactors and alumni as well as from students. The different sources of financial support between pre- and post-1992 universities are shown in Table 6.18(b) in figures for 1996/97. Essentially the difference is that the old universities earn a great deal more in research grants.

Britain in international perspective

An expansionist race in education is, at the end of the twentieth century, world-wide. We therefore end with a glimpse of Britain's international position. The British track record in the race is increasingly focused on tertiary education. We summarize the British track record in the mid-1990s in Table 6.19 and Figure 6.3. The UK, it appears from OECD statistics, is among the leaders in the race (which is in general led by the OECD member states).

Table 6.19 Educational indicators, 1994, UK and other industrialized countries

	UK	US	France	Germany	OECD countries mean
		Mean			
Educational expenditure per student in equivalent US dollars at tertiary level	7600	15510	6090	8381	7740
Ratio of students to teaching staff	14.0[b]	14.4	19.0	m[a]	14.4
Net entry rate to university level	43	52	33	27	31
Tertiary attainment (25–64-year-olds)	21.5	33.2	18.6	22.6	21.9
Unemployment rate of university graduates (25–64-year-olds)	3.5	2.5	7.0	4.7	4.0

Notes: [a]m = missing
[b]UK figure refers to pre-1992 universities only.

Source: OECD (1997) pp.10–11.

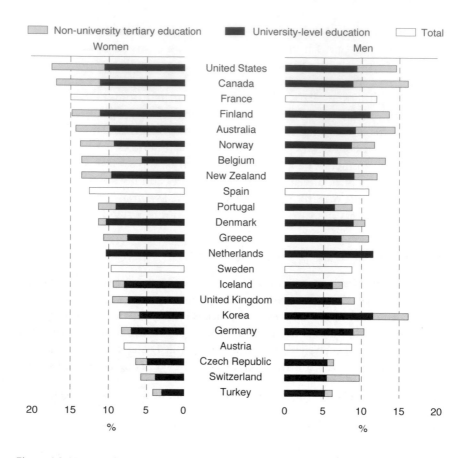

Figure 6.3 Net enrolment in tertiary education for persons aged 17–34 by tertiary level and gender (1995)[a]

Note: [a]Countries are ranked in descending order of the total net enrolment rate for women.

Source: OECD (1997).

We also note the position of the UK with respect to the intake of foreign students (Figure 6.4). Again Britain emerges as a major receiver (that is, the UK has education as a major export industry). For example, the proportion of full-time students from EC countries increased from 18 per cent in 1988/89 to 31 per cent in 1992/93.

Conclusion

The picture at the end of the century was a mixture of buoyancy and depression. Numbers had never been greater and they dwarfed those of the early years of the century. Of the 1.75 million students at British universities in

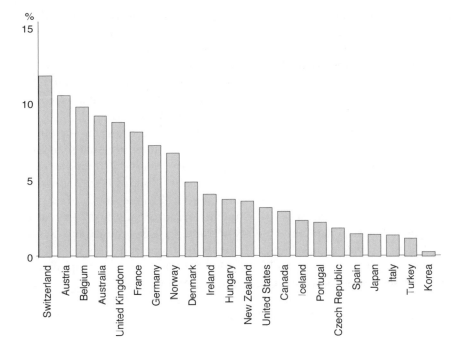

Figure 6.4 Percentage of tertiary students enrolled who are not citizens of the country of study (1995)[a]

Note: [a]Countries are ranked in descending order of the percentage of foreign students enrolled.

Source: OECD (1997).

1996/97, two-thirds were in full-time or sandwich programmes, eight out of ten were undergraduates and just over half were full-time first degree students. Women made up over half (52.5 per cent) of the HE population and overseas students made up 11.3 per cent of the total student body. As many as 35 per cent of the full-time post-graduates were foreign.

Statistical sources

Statistics on further education throughout the century have remained shrouded in the obscurities of local government. As Dearing says: 'consistent data on all (as distinct from full-time) students are not available for the full period from the early 1960s to the present' (Dearing, 1997, Chapter 3).

The figures in Table 6.1 cover all courses in public sector and assisted establishments of further education. The main source is *Statistics of Education*, Part 2, from 1961. Before that it was the Ministry of Education's Annual Report,

Part 2, for England and Wales. Separate figures were provided for Scotland and for Northern Ireland. Summary statistics for the United Kingdom are given in *Statistics of Education*, published by the Stationery Office.

With the foundation of the University Grants Committee (an offshoot of the Treasury) in 1919, statistics began seriously. The UGC's *Returns from Universities and University Colleges* became annual. University statistics were published in a more conventional form from 1966 in *Statistics of Education*, vol. VI.

In 1993 the Higher Education Statistics Agency (HESA) became the official body for collecting quantitative data on higher education in response to a call in the 1991 White Paper, *Higher Education in a New Framework*, for more coherence in higher education statistics. It covers publicly funded higher education in the UK and receives subscriptions from all the 182 universities and colleges: the annual publications cover staff, students, resources and first destinations of graduands. HESA and the Universities and Colleges Admissions Service (UCAS) also provide comprehensive coverage on the World Wide Web.

Other useful sources are the Department for Education and Employment, the Scottish Office, the Welsh Office and the Northern Ireland Office, all of which publish statistical bulletins. UCAS publishes statistics on applications and admissions. The Office for National Statistics (ONS) (until 1996 the Central Statistical Office) has published its annual *Social Trends* since 1970 which contains a section on further and higher education.

Two official landmarks in British higher education may be added. They define higher education as courses which are higher than the Advanced Level of the General Certificate of Education, the Higher Grade of the Scottish Certificate of Education, or the BTEC or SCOTVEC National Certificate/ Diploma. Further education covers all other forms of post-secondary schooling. Of the two governmental inquiries, the first is the Robbins Report of 1963 (Cmnd 2154) with its five appendices, and the second, the Dearing Report of 1997. The first set new standards of 'political arithmetic' with its six appendices giving a comprehensive description of British higher education in 1962. However, it ignored the concurrent Anderson Committee (1960) on student grants. The second tackled the urgent problem of higher education finance, proposing student contributions to both tuition and maintenance. It describes the dramatic expansion confirmed by the 1992 Act but is less impressive as political arithmetic.

Three private sources may be remarked. First is John Carswell (1985) *Government and the Universities in Britain*, which analyses Robbins' plans in relation to outcomes from 1962 to 1980. Second is A. H. Halsey (second edition 1995*), Decline of Donnish Dominion*, which uses surveys in 1964, 1976, and 1989 for an account of British higher education in the twentieth century, and especially for what we have termed the Binary Phase. Third is the report of the National Committee on Education, *Learning to Succeed* (1993).

Finally, for international comparisons, the OECD in Paris began an annual publication in 1992, *Education at a Glance*; the figures begin in 1988.

Acknowledgement

I am much indebted to Michael Davidson, Peter Roberts and John Cuthbert for checking my figures from official sources from 1981 at the DfEE.

References

Carswell, J. (1985) *Government and the Universities in Britain*, Cambridge University Press, Cambridge.

Dearing, R. (1997) National Committee of Inquiry into Higher Education Report, *Higher Education in the Learning Society*, HMSO, London.

Halsey, A. H. (1995) *The Decline of Donnish Dominion*, 2nd Edition, Oxford University Press, Oxford.

Halsey, A. H., Heath, A. F. and Ridge, J. (1980) *Origins and Destinations*, Clarendon Press, Oxford.

Halsey, A. H. and Trow, M. (1970) *The British Academics*, Faber, London

Higher Education Statistics Agency (HESA) (1998) *Students in Higher Education Institutions, 1996/97*, HESA, Cheltenham.

National Committee on Education (1993) *Learning to Succeed*, Heinemann, London.

Organization for Economic Co-operation and Development (OECD) (1997) *Education at a Glance*, OECD, Paris.

Robbins, L. (1963) *Higher Education, Report and Appendices*, Cmnd 2154, HMSO, London.

Further reading

(In addition to the items listed in the References)

Annan, Noel (1990) *Our Age: Portrait of a Generation*, Weidenfeld and Nicolson, London

Clark, B. R. (1983) *The Academic Life: Small Worlds, Different Worlds*, New Jersey.

Harrison, B. (ed.) (1992) *History of the University of Oxford*, vol. 8, Oxford University Press, Oxford.

Kerr, C. (1963) *The Uses of the University*, Harvard University Press, Cambridge, Mass.

Moberley, W. (1949) *The Crisis in the University*, SCM Press, London.

Perkin, H. (1969) *Key Profession: The History of the Association of University Teachers*, Routledge and Kegan Paul, London.

Rothblatt, S. (ed.) (1992) *The OECD, the Master Plan and the California Dream*, Berkeley, CA.

Scott, P. (1983) *The Crisis of the University*, Croom Helm, London

Truscot, B. (1945) *Redbrick University*, Faber and Faber, London

Venables, P. (1978) *Higher Education Developments: The Technological Universities 1956–1976*, Faber, London.

7

Social Mobility

Anthony Heath and Clive Payne

You are all brothers, fellow-citizens, but when God made you he mixed gold in the nature of those who are fitted to be rulers – and that is why they are held in the highest esteem. He put silver in those who were to be their assistants, and iron and bronze in the farmers and workers. Children will usually have the same nature as their parents, but since you all come from the same stock there will sometimes be 'golden' parents with a 'silver' child, 'silver' parents with a 'gold' child, and so on. God's first and most important commandment to the rulers, therefore, is that they must scrutinize the mixture of metals in their children's characters. If one of their own children has iron or bronze in its make-up, they must harden themselves and assign him to his appropriate level among farming or working people.

Plato, Republic, 415a

> When I was a lad I served a term
> As office boy to an Attorney's firm
> I cleaned the windows and I swept the floor
> And I polished up the handle of the big front door
> I polished up that handle so carefullee
> That now I am the Ruler of the Queen's Navee!
>
> W. S. Gilbert, HMS Pinafore, 1879

This chapter is concerned with the intergenerational mobility of men and women. That is to say, we investigate how far, and in what way, the social positions of adults have changed from those of their parents. Studies of this kind enable us to chart the trends in the 'openness' of society. For example, do children largely follow in their father's footsteps, or do people move freely up and down the social ladder? An open society in which people's positions do not depend upon ascribed social characteristics such as their social origin is

254

often thought to be both more efficient – better use being made of the available talent in society – and more in accordance with social justice. While the arguments about the relationship between social mobility, economic efficiency and social justice are by no means uncontroversial (see, for example, Marshall et al., 1997), there is none the less considerable interest in documenting trends in the openness of society.

Following established practice in sociology (for example, Glass and Hall, 1954), we will focus on the social class positions of men and women in Britain, and we shall compare these positions with those of their fathers. While it would be wrong to equate social class with the broader concept of social position, social class is none the less a powerful index of people's social advantages and disadvantages, their likely income and material conditions, their security and prospects, their health and their life-styles (see Reid, 1998). It is probably the most useful single index of social position. This will give us a picture of the overall mobility experience of the population as a whole. There is a separate tradition of research which has focused more narrowly on recruitment to elite positions, such as Parliament and to higher levels of the civil service, business, church and military. However, it is beyond the scope of this chapter to explore patterns of elite recruitment (Heath, 1981, gives a summary of previous research in this field).

Again, following conventional practice, we shall compare people's social positions with those of their fathers. Sociologists have in the past regarded the family as the unit of class stratification and have taken the father's position to be the best guide to the social class of the household as a whole. With the growing number of female-headed households in Britain and of dual-career families in which husbands and wives have full-time occupations, this is becoming a more controversial assumption, and at some stage in the future sociologists will need to take more account of mothers' social class positions. However, in a chapter concerned with historical trends, it is sensible to follow the conventional procedure (Sorensen, 1994 gives a comprehensive review of this debate).

There were some small-scale studies of mobility at the beginning of the century, focusing on the recruitment to particular occupations (Chapman and Marquis, 1912; Chapman and Abbott, 1913; Ginsberg, 1929). These showed considerable openness, but one could not generalize their findings to the society as a whole. The first major nationally representative study was that of Glass and his associates – the 1949 mobility survey. This provided a picture of mobility trends over the first half of the century (Glass, 1954; Kelsall and Mitchell, 1959). It portrayed a society with considerable inequality in mobility chances, and with especially high rates of social closure at the apex of the class structure:

the general picture so far is of a rather stable social structure, and one in which social status has tended to operate within, so to speak, a closed circuit. Social origins have conditioned educational level, and both have conditioned achieved social status. Marriage has also to a considerable extent taken place within the same closed circuit. (Glass, 1954, p.21)

The data also suggested that there had been some net downward mobility (although there were some problems here since the 1949 study compared respondents' current occupations with their fathers' last main occupation).[1]

Glass and his associates expected mobility to increase in the second half of the century, due to increasing equality of opportunity. They were writing shortly after the 1944 Education Act, which had provided for free secondary education for all, abolishing the fees that some students had previously had to pay in pre-war grammar schools. It was widely hoped at the time that greater equality of opportunity for educational success and hence occupational advancement would follow.

The third quarter of the century has been described by the work of Goldthorpe and his associates, based on a 1972 survey of men's mobility in England and Wales (Goldthorpe et al., 1980; Goldthorpe and Payne, 1986; Heath, 1981). (There were also parallel studies in Scotland and Ireland: see Payne et al., 1976; Hout, 1989.) The 1972 study told a very different story from the 1949 survey. By 1972 there was increasing 'room at the top' and a considerable surplus of upward over downward mobility. The driving force behind this change was the expansion of professional and managerial occupations and decline of manual occupations (see Chapter 8). Hence mobility rates, especially upward mobility, increased substantially in the post-war period.

However, Goldthorpe also suggested that fluidity, or relative mobility rates, had not changed very much. That is to say, the observed changes in the overall rates of class mobility were primarily due to changes in the distributions of fathers and sons in the class structure, not to equalization of the terms on which people from different origins competed. In this sense, although chances of upward mobility had increased for everyone, the relative competitive chances of people from different social origins had not greatly changed. Thus Glass's hopes for increased equality of opportunity and openness in society had not been fulfilled. (For a more detailed examination of Glass's thesis, using the 1972 data but focusing on education, see Halsey et al., 1980; Kerckhoff and Trott, 1993.)

This has been one of the most controversial conclusions in mobility research. Many theorists had expected that the logic of industrialism would lead to greater openness or fluidity in society. And some empirical research (especially Ganzeboom et al., 1989) had claimed to find that social fluidity had indeed increased over time.

We shall explore this issue of trends in fluidity, or relative mobility rates, later in this chapter, using recent data which enable us to bring the trends almost up to the end of the century, to 1997. First, however, we shall focus on the trends in absolute mobility.

Data and methods

To explore British experience of social mobility during the twentieth century we use the cumulated files for the 1964–97 British Election Surveys (BES).[2] These are nationally-representative sample surveys of the British electorate, excluding Northern Ireland, conducted after each of the ten elections from 1964 to 1997 (Breen and Whelan, 1999, give an up-to-date account of trends in mobility in Northern Ireland and in the Republic of Ireland). The BES is the longest-running academic survey series in Britain. Unlike the 1972 study used by Goldthorpe, these surveys cover both men and women. They have been conducted and coded in closely comparable ways and hence it is reasonable to pool them.[3] The British Election Surveys do not, of course, reach as far back as the 1949 survey, but unfortunately the coding procedures of the 1949 survey have not been preserved and it has proved impossible to establish comparability between the 1949 survey and subsequent research (Macdonald and Ridge, 1972; Ridge, 1974; Hope, 1981). It is not therefore possible to add the 1949 survey to the cumulated BES files.

In order to chart trends over the whole century we use cohort analysis; that is, we use the older respondents in our surveys to tell us what mobility was like earlier in the century. Since, in all the election surveys, retired people reported their last main occupation, we actually have a few respondents from the 1964 and 1966 surveys who entered the labour market at the beginning of the century. We use the same pattern of ten-year birth cohorts as did Glass, and thus distinguish the following birth cohorts:

1 people born before 1900 and entering the labour market early in the century
2 people born 1900–09, entering the labour market around the time of World War I with their careers spanning the Depression
3 people born 1910–19, entering the labour market during the Depression and having their careers interrupted by World War II
4 people born 1920–29, entering the labour market around World War II, but their careers benefiting from the 'long boom' of the post-war period
5 people born 1930–39, entering the labour market after World War II and again benefiting from the 'long boom'
6 people born 1940–49, benefiting from the free secondary education of the 1944 Education Act and entering the labour market around the 1960s
7 people born 1950–59, our youngest cohort, whose careers cover the last third of the century.

There are some well known problems with cohort analysis. First, there is the problem of differential mortality and migration. For example, survivors from the 1920–29 birth cohort interviewed in, say, 1997 may not be representative of the original cohort born before the war. Some of the original birth cohort may have emigrated, and others may have died. To deal with this problem we have compared our results drawn from later surveys with those for the same birth cohort drawn from earlier surveys.[4]

The second main problem is that mobility is a lifetime process: young people tend to enter the labour market in lower positions and subsequently get promoted. So there is the risk that, when we compare birth cohorts, we are comparing people at different stages of their careers and intergenerational processes will thus become confused with intragenerational ones. To deal with this problem we consider only people who have reached 'occupational maturity' at the time of the survey. Following Goldthorpe et al. (1980), we assume that there is relatively little career mobility after the age of 35 and that most people over this age will have reached 'occupational maturity'.[5] Glass, in his work on the 1949 survey, made a more conservative cut-off at the age of 50, but our checks suggest that the trends are much the same whether we use the younger or the older cut-off. By using the younger cut-off we can of course increase our sample size and explore mobility experiences of more recent birth cohorts.

We cannot claim that our solutions to these problems are perfect, and so all conclusions – especially those about the oldest and youngest birth cohorts – must be treated with caution. On the other hand, the problems of alternative methods are probably even greater, and the fact that we can compare results from several different surveys means that our results are likely to be more robust than those of any previous investigators.

The class schema

To measure the class positions of respondents and their fathers we use a modified version of the class schema devised by Goldthorpe and his associates. Goldthorpe distinguished seven classes, but we have combined two of these – the foremen/technician and skilled manual classes (Goldthorpe's classes V and VI). We do this because there are relatively few women in either of these classes and the numbers become too small for effective analysis. We thus use the following class schema (retaining Goldthorpe's numbering):[6]

I   Higher salariat (professionals, managers and administrators in large enterprises)

II   Lower salariat (semi-professionals, managers and administrators in small enterprises)

III Routine white-collar workers

IV   Petty bourgeoisie (farmers, small employers and self-employed workers)

V/VI Higher working class (manual foremen, technicians and skilled manual workers)

VII   Lower working class (semi-skilled and unskilled manual workers, including agricultural workers).

Broadly speaking, this class schema distinguishes three main groupings: first, the salariat (sub-divided into higher and lower levels of Classes I and II), largely consisting of salaried employees with relatively secure employment, some promotion prospects and various staff benefits such as pension and sick pay schemes; second, the petty bourgeoisie (Class IV), consisting of independents who are directly exposed to market forces and are not cushioned by the presence of the bureaucratic employers of the salariat; and third, the rank-and-file manual workers of the working class (again sub-divided into higher and lower levels of Classes VI and VII) with relatively higher risks of unemployment, poorer promotion prospects and fewer fringe benefits. Goldthorpe argues that the routine white-collar workers (Class III) can be thought of as marginal to the salariat, sharing some of its characteristics but with lower pay and privileges, while the foremen/technician class (Class V) can be thought of as marginal to the working class.

An important point to note about this class schema is that it is not a completely hierarchical one. Unlike the scale used by Glass (the Hall-Jones scale), it is not intended to be a hierarchical measure of social status where occupations can be ranked on a single dimension of 'social standing'. In particular, in Goldthorpe's schema, Classes III, IV, V and VI cannot be ranked in any straightforward way relative to each other. Classes V and VI, for example, may have higher take-home pay than classes III and IV, but their promotion prospects will be inferior to those of Class III and their opportunities for acquiring wealth and assets inferior to those of Class IV. These classes have different employment relations from each other, and their members have distinct mobility experiences, but we should not attempt to rank them relative to each other.

This means that, when we want to talk about upward or downward mobility in a vertical sense we ought to exclude movement between Classes III, IV and V/VI. The movements between these classes can better be thought of as horizontal rather than vertical movements.

Table 7.1 charts the changing distribution of our male respondents in each birth cohort.[7] The overall picture is a familiar one from studies of the labour market: there is a gradual expansion of the salariat, rising from 18 per cent of the oldest, pre-1900, birth cohort to 42 per cent of the younger, 1950–59 cohort. The expansion was relatively gradual over the three oldest birth cohorts but then accelerated among the cohorts that benefited from the long boom of the post-war period. If there has been an expansion of the salariat, then there must be compensating contractions elsewhere, and as we can see it is the working class (Classes V–VII) that has taken the brunt: in our oldest birth cohort 62 per cent of the respondents held working-class positions, but by the time of the youngest cohort only 38 per cent did so.

Table 7.1 Class profiles of men aged 35 and over at the time of the survey (column percentages)

	Pre-1900	1900–09	1910–19	1920–29	1930–39	1940–49	1950–59
I	7.0	10.1	11.6	16.1	17.1	21.6	23.2
II	11.0	9.2	11.2	13.1	15.0	16.3	19.1
III	7.9	8.3	9.1	6.9	5.8	4.3	4.5
IV	12.2	10.3	8.7	8.9	13.3	15.0	15.3
V/VI	31.9	30.3	30.8	31.9	25.6	22.6	22.0
VII	30.0	31.7	28.7	23.1	23.2	20.2	15.8
N	417	941	1393	1840	1617	1095	565

Sample: Men aged 35 and over at the time of the survey and on the GB electoral registers. Retired or economically inactive men are assigned to classes on the basis of their last occupation. Economically inactive men (other than retired) are excluded.

One question that can be raised about this picture is whether the classes have really remained comparable over time (Crompton, 1980; Goldthorpe et al., 1980). To some extent, as the classes have changed in size, so they have also changed in character. Certainly, the salariat of the youngest birth cohort contains occupations such as computer programming that simply did not exist among the earlier birth cohorts. Other occupations, such as the public sector professionals, will have seen their privileges decline relative to other salaried employees. However, it is likely that much of the change will have taken place within the broad classes that we have distinguished: while the situation of particular occupations will have changed for the better or worse, the salariat as a whole is still broadly characterized by lower rates of unemployment and more favourable terms and conditions than the working class.

Table 7.2 shows the changing class distribution of women.[8] Again the overall picture is a familiar one: women are concentrated in the lower white-collar work of Class III and are under-represented (relative to men) in the higher salariat and in the higher levels of the working class. However, although the overall distribution is very different, the trends are much the same as for men: women's employment in the salariat has been expanding while that in the working class has been contracting. The one notable divergence between the two tables is that women's employment in Class III has also been expanding while men's has been contracting. This indicates that there has been a major 'feminization' of Class III and the argument that classes do not retain the same character over time may well apply to Class III more than it does to any other class.

Table 7.2 Class profiles of women aged 35 and over at the time of the survey (column percentages)

	Pre-1900	1900–09	1910–19	1920–29	1930–39	1940–49	1950–59
I	1.6	2.5	2.3	3.7	4.3	6.7	9.4
II	11.4	13.8	13.5	12.2	16.2	19.3	27.2
III	23.9	27.6	30.9	34.5	37.0	36.3	34.7
IV	11.4	5.3	5.1	3.0	4.5	6.6	5.8
V/VI	14.7	10.4	10.8	9.3	7.4	6.3	4.1
VII	37.0	40.3	37.4	37.3	30.6	24.7	18.9
N	184	513	868	1311	1121	911	428

Sample: Women aged 35 and over at the time of the survey, and on the GB electoral registers. Women who have never had a job or who describe themselves as 'looking after the home' are excluded. Women who describe themselves as 'retired' are assigned to classes on the basis of their last occupation.

Table 7.3 Class profiles of respondents' fathers

	Pre-1900	1900–09	1910–19	1920–29	1930–39	1940–49	1950–59
I	4.1	4.4	5.2	5.2	6.3	9.1	10.8
II	8.2	6.7	6.8	7.5	6.4	8.6	10.5
III	3.9	4.3	4.8	5.5	5.8	6.2	5.8
IV	17.8	16.1	16.3	14.9	14.5	13.0	15.6
V/VI	34.9	36.1	35.1	35.2	37.8	36.8	32.6
VII	31.1	32.3	31.8	31.7	29.1	26.4	24.7
N	562	1357	2074	2882	2502	1821	902

Sample: Both men and women respondents, men as in the note to Table 7.1 and women as in the note to Table 7.2.

Table 7.3 then shows the changing distribution of the respondents' fathers.[9] Although the fathers and respondents are by definition a generation apart, we cannot neatly allocate fathers to birth cohorts, since of course father's age at the time of the child's birth will vary both between respondents and over time. However, the broad outlines of Table 7.3 are quite similar to that of the earlier cohorts in Table 7.1. We see the same predominance of fathers in the working class that we saw among our older birth cohorts of respondents, and we see a gradual expansion of the salariat over time. But we do not see, and should not expect to see, in the fathers' generation the more rapid expansion associated with the 'long boom' of the post-war period.

Men's outflow mobility

In the study of social mobility it is helpful to distinguish between outflow and inflow mobility. In the case of outflow mobility, we examine the class destinations of respondents from different social origins, and we calculate the row percentages. Table 7.4 gives an example of an outflow table. Analysis of outflow mobility is useful for exploring the question how similar are the chances of people from different origins. For example, how equal are the chances of people from salariat and working-class origins of gaining access to the privileged ranks of the salariat?

In contrast, the analysis of inflow mobility is concerned with the social composition of the different classes, and is based on column percentages. Table 7.10 gives an example of an inflow table. Inflow analysis thus tells us where the current occupants of a particular class came from. Is a class homogeneous in its composition, or does it include people from a wide variety of social origins? These questions about the social composition of the classes may have implications for the extent of 'class formation' and the potential for collective class action (Goldthorpe et al., 1980, Chapter 9; De Graaf et al., 1994).

We begin with outflow mobility and then turn in the next section to inflow mobility. Before looking at the trends over time, however, it is useful to look at the picture for the cumulated sample as a whole. The overall table for men is given in Table 7.4.

Table 7.4 Men's outflow mobility (row percentages)

| Father's class | Son's class | | | | | | |
	I	II	III	IV	V/VI	VII	N
I	46	23	5	11	8	6	447
II	30	29	10	10	12	9	535
III	27	21	12	9	19	13	381
IV	15	13	7	29	20	17	1103
V/VI	12	12	7	8	38	23	2626
VII	9	9	5	7	32	38	2204
All	16	14	7	11	28	24	7296

Sample: See note to Table 7.1.

The main diagonal running from the top-left to bottom-right of Table 7.4 shows the proportions from each origin class who were intergenerationally stable: that is, who followed in their father's footsteps. Respondents who lie in the cells above and below the diagonal can be thought of as intergenerationally mobile. Looking down the diagonal, we see the highest chance of following in father's footsteps is at the apex of the class structure, where 46 per cent of sons from Class I origins themselves had moved into Class I positions at the time they were interviewed. The percentage then falls sharply as we move down the diagonal, reaching a low of 12 per cent among men from Class III origins. The percentage then rises again to 29 per cent in the petty bourgeoisie, 38 per cent in the upper working class and 38 per cent again in the lower working class. The general character of this picture is the same as that which Glass had found 50 years ago: 'the highest rigidity is found in the professional and high administrative cadres, and the least in the ... routine-non-manual category. The latter category is, in fact, a kind of valley, the rigidity increasing on each side' (Glass, 1954, p.19).[10]

Looking down the first column, we see that men from Class I backgrounds had far superior chances of reaching Class I themselves than did men from lower working-class backgrounds: 9 per cent of men from lower working-class origins compared with 46 per cent from higher salariat origins. Similarly, looking down the last column, men from Class I backgrounds had better chances of avoiding demotion to the lower working class.

Short-range mobility is also more common than long-range movement. Thus it was more common for men from Class I origins to move the short step down to Class II than it was for them to move all the way down to the working class. Similarly, men from Class VII origins were much more likely to move the short distance to the upper working class than they were to achieve long-range mobility to the salariat. Again, this parallels Glass's findings from the 1949 study.

On the other hand, unlike the findings from 1949, there has clearly been a surplus of upward over downward mobility. The percentages below the diagonal are generally rather larger than those above the diagonal.

How has this overall picture changed over time? In Table 7.5 we show, for each of our birth cohorts, the proportions of intergenerationally stable men from each class origin; that is, the proportions lying on the main diagonal. For example, the cell in the top-right corner, for the 1950–59 birth cohort, shows that 68 per cent of men in this cohort from Class I origins themselves were in Class I positions at the time they were interviewed. The next cell down shows that 40 per cent of men in this cohort from Class II backgrounds were themselves in Class II when they were interviewed, and so on. In the bottom two rows of the table we combine the upper and lower salariat and the upper and lower working class respectively. This enables us to see how many men from the salariat or from the working class as a whole followed in their father's footsteps.

Some of the percentages in Table 7.5 are based on rather small numbers of respondents, and so there will be considerable sampling variation. Nevertheless, there are some clear trends. First, the proportion of sons from Class I and II backgrounds who have been able to achieve the same positions as their fathers has tended to increase over time. In the oldest birth cohort, 51 per cent of sons from salariat backgrounds secured positions in Class I or II themselves, while by the youngest birth cohort this figure had risen to 73 per cent. Second, there has been a comparable decline in stability in the working class. In the oldest birth cohort, 76 per cent of men from working-class origins were intergenerationally stable, but this figure had fallen to 50 per cent by the time of the youngest cohort. Third, and contrastingly, intergenerational stability in the petty bourgeoisie has been pretty well unchanged over the whole period, oscillating around 35 per cent. These trends can be checked against the data of the 1949 and 1972 studies; the figures for the corresponding cohorts in the different studies are comfortingly close, except for Glass's youngest cohort who had not at that time reached occupational maturity (Glass, 1954, p.186).

Table 7.5 Trends in intergenerational stability (percentage remaining in the same class as their father): men

	Pre-1900	1900–09	1910–19	1920–29	1930–39	1940–49	1950–59
Class I	–	36	39	48	47	44	68
	(14)	(36)	(72)	(87)	(100)	(90)	(48)
Class II	19	22	33	28	38	22	40
	(31)	(55)	(92)	(124)	(88)	(93)	(51)
Class III	–	21	21	15	6	7	1
	(15)	(38)	(58)	(86)	(85)	(65)	(34)
Class IV	34	32	25	28	31	28	31
	(74)	(136)	(208)	(248)	(239)	(124)	(75)
Class V/VI	49	38	41	40	34	31	35
	(144)	(319)	(445)	(622)	(536)	(385)	(175)
Class VII	53	47	46	34	35	28	33
	(119)	(303)	(417)	(536)	(437)	(263)	(129)
Salariat (I + II)	51	49	61	69	67	62	73
Working class (V/VI + VII)	76	75	73	67	60	53	50

Sample: See note to Table 7.1. Figures in brackets give the numbers for the origin class.

From these tables we can calculate some summary indices of mobility. Thus the first row of Table 7.6 shows the overall proportion in each birth cohort as a whole who remained in the same class as their fathers. The figure falls fairly steadily from 43 per cent in the oldest cohort to 28 per cent in the penultimate cohort. There is then a rise in the final, youngest cohort. The decline in the percentage who were intergenerationally stable should not surprise us. While, as Table 7.5 showed, the increasing mobility out of the working class was matched by increasing stability in the salariat, the working class was, for much of our period, considerably larger than the salariat. Hence the overall figure of stability tended to decline, reflecting the numerical predominance of men mobile out of the working class. In the youngest cohort, in contrast, the salariat has actually grown somewhat larger than the working class; hence the increase in overall stability.

Table 7.6 Summary indexes of mobility: men

	Pre-1900	1900–09	1910–19	1920–29	1930–39	1940–49	1950–59
Percentage stable	43	39	38	35	34	28	35
Upwardly mobile	27	29	30	39	38	42	42
Downwardly mobile	20	21	20	17	18	19	13
Horizontal movements	10	11	12	9	10	11	10
N	397	890	1303	1778	1572	1074	533

Sample: See note to Table 7.1.

Table 7.6 also shows the trends in upward and downward mobility. Recall that we must treat movements between Classes III, IV and V/VI as horizontal rather than vertical. Upward mobility therefore excludes these horizontal movements but includes all movements out of Class VII, all movements into Class I and all movements from below into Class II. As we can see, there has been a substantial net surplus of upward over downward mobility throughout our period, the surplus in fact tending to rise and reaching a maximum in our youngest birth cohort of 29 points.

This pattern is largely driven by the changes in the class structure which we described earlier. As we argued in the introduction, there has been increasing 'room at the top' and hence an increase in upward mobility is arithmetically inevitable.

Women's outflow mobility

The picture for women is rather different from that for the men. Comparing Table 7.7 with Table 7.4, we can see that fewer women than men followed in their father's footsteps into the higher salariat, into the petty bourgeoisie or into skilled manual work. Instead, there is a lot of movement from all classes alike into the lower white-collar work of Class III. These patterns largely reflect the differing class distributions of men and women: since there are so many more women than men in Class III, it is hardly surprising that there is more mobility into it. However, after taking account of the differences in their class distributions, there are still some significant differences in women's mobility patterns from those of men. In particular, women show a weaker tendency to inherit positions in the petty bourgeoisie; they are also less likely to follow in their fathers' footsteps into either the upper or the lower working classes.[11]

Table 7.8 shows the trends over time in women's intergenerational stability. Although, as we have just seen, the absolute levels are very different from men's, the trends are more similar. Thus there has been a trend towards greater stability for women from salariat origins, the percentage stable rising from 33 per cent in the oldest cohort to 50 per cent in the youngest, although this is a somewhat less powerful trend than that for men. There is also a trend towards reduced stability for women from working-class origins, the percentage stable falling from 68 per cent to 30 per cent. This is a rather more dramatic trend for women than for men.

Table 7.7 Women's outflow mobility (row percentages)

Father's class	I	II	Daughter's class III	IV	V/VI	VII	N
I	14	32	35	9	3	7	314
II	6	32	41	5	4	13	373
III	9	23	42	5	4	17	271
IV	5	17	34	10	7	28	722
V/VI	3	13	35	4	10	35	1712
VII	2	10	29	3	11	46	1413
All	4	16	34	5	9	33	4804

Sample: See note to Table 7.2.

Table 7.8 Trends in intergenerational stability (percentage remaining in the same class as their father): women

	Pre-1900	1900	1910	1920	1930	1940	1950–59
Class I	–	8	10	15	15	15	14
	(9)	(24)	(36)	(61)	(58)	(76)	(50)
Class II	–	27	32	33	36	28	34
	(15)	(37)	(49)	(93)	(73)	(63)	(43)
Class III	–	50	42	35	49	40	24
	(7)	(20)	(43)	(73)	(61)	(48)	(19)
Class IV	19	12	14	6	10	7	10
	(26)	(82)	(130)	(183)	(124)	(112)	(66)
Class V/VI	17	16	11	13	7	8	4
	(52)	(171)	(283)	(392)	(409)	(285)	(119)
Class VII	46	58	47	53	41	37	30
	(56)	(136)	(242)	(377)	(291)	(217)	(94)
Salariat (I + II)	33	40	37	40	42	43	50
Working class (V/VI + VII)	68	64	56	57	44	41	30

Sample: See note to Table 7.2.

Turning to the summary indexes for women's outflow mobility (Table 7.9), we see that the trends are roughly similar to the men's, although the levels are different. Thus there is in all birth cohorts more downward mobility and less upward mobility for women than for men; but over time there has been a marked increase in upward mobility, just as there has been for men, and a modest decline in downwards mobility. Thus for women upwards mobility has increased by 12 percentage points compared with a 15-point rise for men over this period. Women's downward mobility has declined by 3 percentage points, compared with a decline of 7 points for men.

Table 7.9 Summary indexes of mobility: women

	Pre-1900	1900–09	1910–19	1920–29	1930–39	1940–49	1950–59
Percentage stable	31	29	26	28	22	20	17
Upwardly mobile	24	22	27	23	29	32	36
Downwardly mobile	30	32	30	28	27	26	27
Horizontal movements	15	17	18	21	22	22	20
N	219	602	1000	1403	1164	886	298

Sample: See note to Table 7.2.

Horizontal movements, between Classes III, IV and V/VI, have, however, increased somewhat more for women, and so the net result is a slightly larger decline in immobility. In the case of women, immobility has fallen by 14 points, from 31 per cent to 17 per cent; whereas for men the decline was 8 points, from 43 per cent in the oldest birth cohort to 35 per cent in the youngest.

Again, it is very important to emphasize that these changes have been very largely driven by the changing class distributions over time of the women and of their fathers. There has been less room at the top for women, and so their gains in upward mobility have been less dramatic than men's. But there has been much more room in the middle for women as routine non-manual work has become feminized.

Inflow mobility

We now turn to the analysis of inflow mobility. As we explained earlier, inflow mobility tells us about the composition of social classes and tells us how diverse a class's members are in their social origins. It thus addresses questions about the extent of class formation, the assumption being that a class which is homogeneous in its composition will exhibit a more distinct sub-culture of its own.

In the analysis of inflow mobility we follow a rather different strategy from that of outflow mobility. If we are interested in how homogeneous a class is, then the issue of occupational maturity is no longer so relevant. The fact that a class may have a lot of young people in it at an early stage of their careers still tells us something about the composition of that class.

Nor is birth cohort analysis quite so relevant to the analysis of trends over time in class composition: members of several different birth cohorts may all be members of a class at the same moment in historical time. We therefore look at each survey separately rather than conducting a pooled analysis of birth cohorts.

Finally, there is no substantive reason to distinguish men from women, unless we believe that men and women form different class sub-cultures (in fact, the separate inflow tables for men and women are very similar). We therefore pool both men and women. However, it could also be argued that, from the point of view of class formation, it may be better to treat the family as the unit of stratification and to assign husbands and wives to the same class position. How this should be done is a contentious matter (see Sorensen, 1994), but it is unlikely that alternative methods will produce greatly differing pictures of the trends over time.

We begin, as with the analysis of outflow mobility, by looking at the pattern for the sample as a whole in Table 7.10 and we then turn to the trends over time in Table 7.11.

Table 7.10 Inflow mobility (column percentages)

Father's class	Respondent's class						
	I	II	III	IV	V/VI	VII	All
I	20.7	13.4	8.6	7.7	3.0	2.3	7.7
II	15.7	16.8	11.0	6.5	4.4	3.6	8.7
III	8.5	7.8	7.4	4.3	3.4	3.2	5.4
IV	13.4	14.0	13.5	36.2	9.9	11.5	14.1
V/VI	26.7	29.9	35.1	25.8	46.3	36.2	35.3
VII	14.9	18.1	24.6	19.5	33.1	43.1	28.8
N	1885	2589	3388	1367	3673	4589	17490

Sample: Economically active or retired men and women on the GB electoral registers. Retired or economically inactive respondents are assigned to classes on the basis of their last occupation. Those looking after the home are excluded. Respondents are aged 21 and over in 1964; 18 and over in later surveys.

Table 7.10 shows how many members of each class are what might be termed 'second generation'; that is, how many originated in the same class that they currently occupy. This shows a remarkable contrast with the outflow tables: for example, very few members of the salariat are 'second generation'. Most are newcomers who have been upwardly mobile, with a particularly large number of newcomers from the working class. The routine white-collar class (Class III) then shows a particularly diverse composition, the social origins of its members closely matching the origins of the sample as a whole (as shown in the final column of the table).

In contrast, the petty bourgeoisie (Class IV) shows a relatively high proportion of second-generation members, as do the upper and lower working classes. Indeed, if we combine Classes V, VI and VII, we find that around 80 per cent are second-generation members; this contrasts with around 30 per cent for the salariat. The key conclusion, then, is that the salariat is much more diverse in its origins than the working class. This is a very different story from the one Glass told, when he claimed that 'the general picture so far is of a rather stable social structure, and one in which social status has tended to operate within, so to speak, a closed circuit'.

Is this because British society has changed since the 1949 survey? We attempt to answer this question in Table 7.11 which charts inflow mobility from a selection of the British Election Surveys.

Table 7.11 Percentage of second-generation members of each class: men and women

	1949	1964	1970	1979	1987	1997
Class I		13	21	22	22	24
		(76)	(84)	(164)	(320)	(307)
Class II		16	18	12	16	18
		(135)	(164)	(185)	(441)	(335)
Class III		7	4	9	7	3
		(181)	(207)	(227)	(573)	(359)
Class IV		47	44	36	29	30
		(71)	(91)	(110)	(210)	(181)
Class V/VI		43	41	47	49	44
		(284)	(325)	(344)	(475)	(315)
Class VII		51	56	41	39	44
		(358)	(391)	(372)	(625)	(369)
Salariat	51	29	27	30	34	37
	(664)					
Working class	77	79	82	79	78	75
	(2807)					

Sample: As in note to Table 7.10. Figures in brackets give the base numbers.

Table 7.11 shows remarkable consistency in the inflow figures from 1964 to 1997. The percentage of second-generation members in the salariat has remained around 30 per cent, while that in the working class has remained around 80 per cent. The one notable change is the decline in the proportion of second-generation members in the petty bourgeoisie.

As we argued earlier, the classification of social status used by Glass and Hall is not comparable with that used in the later surveys. However, we can make a rough approximation,[12] and this suggests that, in 1949, the salariat had a much higher proportion of second-generation members (although still not as high as the working class). This must be treated with caution, but it makes reasonably good sense: in 1949 the salariat had not yet started to expand. It was the continued expansion in the later post-war period that required the salariat to recruit so many people from below, but before the expansion began it is likely that social status did indeed tend to operate within a more closed social circuit.

Relative mobility rates

The trends which we have observed so far have been largely influenced by the changes in the class distributions of the respondents and their fathers. In particular, increasing room at the top has meant that there could simultaneously be improved chances of people from privileged backgrounds remaining in the salariat and also improved chances of people from less privileged backgrounds gaining access to the salariat.

However, it is also interesting to ask whether the changes in the distributions are the whole story or whether there has been an increase in interchange between the classes over and above that which would have been expected from the changing distributions. An earlier generation of sociologists divided total mobility into 'forced' or 'structural' mobility and 'exchange' or 'pure' mobility. The structural mobility was that amount which was required by the changing distributions; thus if there was increasing room at the top, some upward mobility was inevitable. Exchange mobility covered all the rest of the movement up and down; by definition the upward component of exchange mobility would be balanced by an equal downward movement.

It is now customary to think of this exchange mobility as the underlying fluidity in the mobility process, and it is measured by odds ratios. Odds ratios are not directly affected by the changes in the class distributions of the respondents and their fathers, and thus are a convenient way of measuring fluidity. They can be thought of as measuring the relative risks (or odds) of people from two different origins reaching a given destination and of avoiding another destination.

In a mobility table, there are many possible odds ratios that can be calculated. For simplicity we shall focus on what are termed the symmetrical odds ratios. Thus in Table 7.4, 46 per cent of men from Class I origins stayed in Class I, while 6 per cent were downwardly mobile into Class VII; this can be expressed as odds of 7.7:1 (since 46/6 = 7.7). However, only 9 per cent of men from Class VII origins reached Class I, while 38 per cent stayed in Class VII, giving odds of 1:4.2 (since 38/9 = 4.2). The ratio of these two odds is 32.3:1.

An odds ratio of 1 would indicate that the two classes concerned had equal competitive chances of reaching one destination and avoiding the other. The odds ratios would all be 1:1 in a society where social origins were unrelated to class destinations. The larger the odds ratio, the more unequal the competition, and the ratio of 32:1 suggests that the competition is extremely unequal.

Table 7.12 Symmetrical odds ratios: men

	Pre-1900	1900–09	1910–19	1920–29	1930–39	1940–49	1950–59
Salariat:working class	16.0	10.0	19.0	14.0	10.3	5.6	7.7
Salariat:petty bourgeoisie	5.5	7.0	6.7	9.4	6.8	4.1	7.3
Petty bourgeoisie: working class	9.5	11.0	9.6	8.2	5.8	3.2	4.9

Sample: As in note to Table 7.1.

Table 7.12 illustrates the trends by focusing on three symmetrical odds ratios: that between men from salariat (Classes I and II combined) and working-class origins (Classes V, VI and VII) to reach the salariat and avoid working-class destinations; that between men from salariat and petty-bourgeois origins to reach the salariat and avoid the petty bourgeoisie themselves; and that between people from petty-bourgeois and working-class origins to reach the petty bourgeoisie and avoid the working class.

As we can see, the most unequal competition is that between men from salariat and working-class origins, where the odds ratios have been around 10:1. The competition between men from salariat and petty-bourgeois origins is rather more equal in general, with odds ratios around 6:1, while that between men from petty-bourgeois and working-class origins is of broadly similar magnitude.

However, there does seem to be some suggestion that the odds ratios have declined somewhat over the period. In particular, the working class seems to have improved its competitive situation *vis-à-vis* the other two classes. Thus the salariat:working class odds ratio falls below 10:1 in the youngest two cohorts, while the petty bourgeoisie:working class odds ratio falls below 5:1. In both cases, the two youngest cohorts exhibit the smallest odds ratios in the series.

Table 7.13 Symmetrical odds ratios: women

	Pre-1900	1900–09	1910–19	1920–29	1930–39	1940–49	1950–59
Salariat:working	–	17.2	15.2	13.4	7.3	10.6	5.8
Salariat: routine non-manual	–	2.1	1.0	1.5	1.7	1.3	0.6
Routine non-manual: working	–	6.5	4.5	1.9	3.3	2.7	3.2

Sample: As in note to Table 7.2. The figures for the oldest cohort have very large confidence intervals and are therefore not shown.

In the case of women we focus not on the petty bourgeoisie, of which few women are members, but on the routine non-manual class. As we can see from Table 7.13, the salariat:working class odds ratio is broadly comparable to that for the men, although the downwards trend is less apparent. The odds ratio for the salariat:routine non-manual contrast, however, becomes close to unity, while the working-class:routine non-manual ratio is also quite low.

Odds ratios, like other statistical measures based on sample surveys, are subject to sampling error, and the odds ratios reviewed in Tables 7.12 and 7.13 are only a small selection of all the possible ratios that we could calculate. Fortunately, we can conduct a general statistical test of whether the complete set of odds ratios has remained constant across birth cohorts by using loglinear models. The results are reported in Table 7.14.

Table 7.14 Loglinear models of trends in social fluidity

	Men			Women		
	Chi^2	df	p	Chi^2	df	p
F,R,C[a]	2050.1	235	.000	1078.6	235	.000
+FC,RC[a]	1642.4	175	.000	742.6	175	.000
+FR[a]	217.8	150	.000	175.9	150	.055
Unidiff[b]	192.0	144	.0002	167.2	144	.09

Note: [a]F = father's class; R = respondent's class; C = cohort.
[b]Uniform difference model. See text for explanation.

Sample: As in notes to Tables 7.1 and 7.2. For technical reasons concerned with model fitting, 0.01 has been added to all empty cells.

We fit a sequence of models (for a more detailed discussion of fitting trends to multi-way tables see Payne et al., 1994). The first model postulates that the three variables of father's class (F), respondent's class (R) and cohort (C) are independent of each other. This model gives a very poor fit to the data. The second model postulates that the class distributions of both respondents and their fathers have changed across birth cohorts, but that father's class and respondent's class are independent of each other. This model gives a somewhat better fit but is still a long way short of accounting for the observed patterns.

The third model then postulates that there is, in addition, an association between father's and respondent's class but that this association (as measured by the full set of odds ratios) has remained constant across birth cohorts. This is the key model for testing whether fluidity has remained constant over time and we can describe it as a 'constant fluidity model'. The model makes a dramatic improvement in fit compared with the second model, but in the case of men it still falls somewhat short of an acceptable fit to the data.

The story told by Table 7.14, then, is that we should reject the hypothesis that, in the case of men, the odds ratios have remained constant across the birth cohorts. The discrepancy between the predictions of the model and the observed mobility patterns is greater than could be expected by chance. In the case of women, however, the hypothesis cannot be confidently rejected since the discrepancies between the model and the observed data could have occurred by chance (at the conventional 0.05 level). In other words, there seems to have been some change in men's fluidity, but possibly not in the case of women.

Our third model provides a global test of the hypothesis that social fluidity has been constant across birth cohorts; it does not tell us what form the changes have taken. However, we can gain some more insight into the pattern of the changes in fluidity if we fit the 'uniform difference' model. This is a log-multiplicative model that was developed independently by Xie (1992), van der Heijden and Jansen (1992) and by Erikson and Goldthorpe (1992). The model starts from the assumption that there is a general pattern to the association between father's class and respondent's class (as defined by the odds ratios) which persists over time even though the overall strength of the association may vary from survey to survey. The model imposes the constraint that all the odds ratios either uniformly increase or uniformly decrease as we move between surveys, and it estimates a 'uniform difference' parameter for each survey (essentially, these parameters are multipliers which operate on the full set of odds ratios). These parameters can be thought of as measuring the extent to which the association between father's class and respondent's class strengthened or weakened in each survey.

Table 7.14 shows that, in the case of men, the uniform difference model gives a significant improvement in fit over the 'constant social fluidity' model. Figures 7.1 and 7.2 plot the uniform difference parameters (together with the 95 per cent confidence intervals) for men and women respectively over our seven birth cohorts. We set the first cohort to 1, and the subsequent parameters show the changes in fluidity relative to the first cohort. In the case of men we can see a fairly clear downward trend over time, albeit one that is reversed among the final birth cohort. All the estimates are less than 1, indicating that the association between father's and son's class is weaker in the younger birth cohorts; that is, the odds ratios tend to become smaller (since they are being multiplied by a parameter that is less than 1). A weakened association is of course another way of saying that fluidity has increased.

In the case of women, there are also hints of a downward trend although the changes are smaller and, as we noted earlier, we cannot strictly reject the hypothesis that women's fluidity has remained constant over time.

The result for men is at some variance with the conclusions reached by Goldthorpe et al. (1980) and Goldthorpe and Payne (1986) who had found that fluidity had remained constant across birth cohorts in Britain. Goldthorpe's work was based on a 1972 survey of men (later updated by the

Figure 7.1 Parameter estimates from the uniform difference model: men

Note: The broken lines indicate the 95% confidence level.

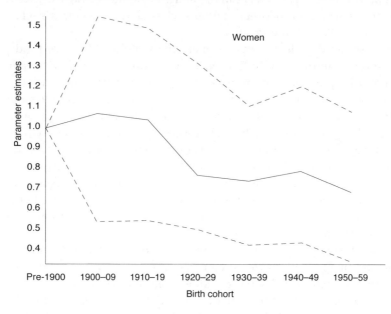

Figure 7.2 Parameter estimates from the uniform difference model: women

Note: The broken lines indicate the 95% confidence level.

1983 BES) and did not cover either our two earliest cohorts or the most recent one.[13] The discrepancy between his results and ours, therefore, may simply reflect the different time periods covered. It is possible that, over the longer time-period available to us, there has been a real, albeit small, increase in the openness of British society that was not visible over the shorter time-period covered by Goldthorpe's work.

However, we should also recognize that there might be methodological explanations for the apparent trend. In particular, the data on the earliest birth cohorts come from reports given by the oldest respondents and they may be subject to some systematic errors. While cohort analysis is the only practical way to investigate trends in mobility over the twentieth century, its limitations must be borne in mind.

Acknowledgements

The British Election Surveys have been made available by the Data Archive at the University of Essex. We are grateful to them and to the original investigators, who include David Butler and Donald Stokes, Ivor Crewe, Bo Sarlvik and David Robertson, and Anthony Heath, Roger Jowell, John Curtice and Pippa Norris (1983–97). The BES has been funded by a number of bodies, and we would especially like to thank the ESRC and the Gatsby Charitable Trust. Kenneth Macdonald and John Ridge wrote this chapter for the second edition of *British Social Trends* in 1988. We are much indebted to them and have built on their work using new data.

Notes

1   In the 1949 survey respondents were asked about their own *current* occupation but about the *last main* occupation of their fathers. For younger respondents, then, the occupational data refer to an earlier stage of their occupational careers from that of their fathers. Given the general tendency of men (although less so of women) to move upwards in the course of their careers, this procedure is likely to underestimate the eventual amount of upward mobility that will take place among the respondents.

2   Most of the surveys used the electoral register as the sampling frame and then drew clustered random samples from this frame. In some cases alternative frames have been used, such as the Post Office address files in the case of the 1997 survey, but with the use of appropriate filters it is possible to establish electorate samples throughout. The electorate will not be identical to the adult population: there will be some residents who fail to register and others who are not eligible. The 1992 and 1997 surveys over-sampled in Scotland in order to permit more detailed investigation of Scottish voting behaviour, and these two surveys have been weighted so as to make them representative of Great Britain as a whole. The total (weighted) sample size is 25 573. After age and birth cohort selections this falls to 17 595 (8311 men and 9283 women).

3   The great strength of the election surveys, for our present purpose, is that they have all carried out a detailed coding of both respondents' and fathers' occupations, using the official government classifications of occupations. These classifications have been revised for each new census, and this will have introduced some element of incomparability over the series. However, the checks that we have been able to carry out suggest that, at least when occupations are aggregated into social classes, the errors are of an acceptable level.

4   For example, in the case of men in cohorts 3, 4 and 5 it is possible to check our results against those obtained by the 1972 survey.

5   Goldthorpe used the notion of 'occupational maturity' in his analysis of men's mobility. The concept may have less relevance for women's mobility, since many married women leave the labour market, or work part-time, when their children are young and then return to paid employment, but at much the same level as before, in their mid-thirties. In the absence of any better alternative we use the same cut-off for the women as for men.

6   We do, however, depart from Goldthorpe's nomenclature. First, we use the term 'salariat' rather than his term 'service class' to refer to Classes I and II. Second, we broaden the term 'working class' to include Class V along with Classes VI and VII. Goldthorpe terms Class V one of the intermediate classes, but our own preference is to group it with the other manual classes (with whom we believe it has more in common).

7   Men who have never had a job, or who gave inadequate occupational data, are excluded. There were 148 men in total who have therefore been excluded.

8   The earlier British Election Surveys did not ask for the previous occupation of married women who described themselves as housewives, and accordingly we have excluded such women throughout. This makes good substantive sense too as any previous occupation may have come from the beginning of the woman's career. However, in the case of surveys which ascertained the previous occupations of women who described themselves as 'retired', we have treated such women in the same way as men and have included their previous occupation. These occupations will have been their last main occupation before retirement.

9   Throughout the surveys respondents were asked to give the details of the occupation that their father had had when the respondent was growing up. This is preferable to the practice followed by Glass in the 1949 survey of asking about the father's last main occupation. We combine both men and women since there is no statistically significant difference in the class distributions of the fathers of the men and women in our selected sample.

10   In this quotation Glass is summarizing his findings from an analysis which used the index of association, rather than the simple percentages on the diagonal which we have used. While there are some well known problems with the index of association (Billewicz, 1955), Glass's remarks as quoted actually apply quite well to the simple percentages reported by Glass and Hall.

11   These conclusions are based on a loglinear analysis which controls for the marginal distributions. The model which postulates that the association between father's and respondent's class is the same for women as it is for men is on the borderline of statistical significance: Chi square = 38.0 for 25 degrees of freedom, p = .046. However, inspecting the residuals for this model we see that there are highly significant residuals for the diagonal cells representing class inheritance of petty-bourgeois positions (–3.21 for women), of upper working-class positions (–2.49) and of lower working-class positions (–3.24).

12 The figures for 1949 in Table 7.11 include both men and women and are based on figures presented in Glass and Hall (1954) and Kelsall and Mitchell (1959).
13 The 1972 study covered men aged 20–64 and it is thus possible to track cohorts born from 1908 to 1952. However, the younger men would not have reached occupational maturity by 1972 and therefore Goldthorpe's cohorts effectively overlap only with our middle three cohorts.

References

Billewicz, W. Z. (1955) 'Some remarks on the measurement of social mobility', *Population Studies*, 9, pp.96–100.

Breen, Richard and Whelan, Christopher T. (1999) 'Social mobility in Ireland: a comparative analysis', in Heath, A. F., Breen, R. and Whelan, C. (eds) *Ireland North and South: Perspectives from Social Science*, Proceedings of the British Academy, London.

Chapman, S. J. and Abbott, W. (1913) 'The tendency of children to enter their father's trades', *Journal of the Royal Statistical Society*, 76, pp.599–604.

Chapman, S. J. and Marquis, F. J. (1912) 'The recruiting of the employing classes from the ranks of the wage earners in the cotton industry', *Journal of the Royal Statistical Society*, 75, pp.293–306.

Crompton, R. (1980) 'Class mobility in modern Britain', *Sociology*, 14, pp.117–19.

De Graaf, N. D., Nieuwbeerta, P. and Heath, A. F. (1994) 'Class mobility and political preferences: individual and contextual effects', *American Journal of Sociology*, 100, pp.997–1027.

Erikson, R. and Goldthorpe, J. H. (1992) *The Constant Flux: A Study of Class Mobility in Industrial Societies*, Clarendon Press, Oxford.

Ganzeboom, H. B. G., Luijkx, R. and Treiman, D. J. (1989) 'Intergenerational class mobility in comparative perspective', *Research in Social Stratification and Mobility*, 8, pp.3–79.

Ginsberg, H. (1929) 'Interchange between social classes', *Economic Journal*, vol.49, pp.554–65.

*Glass, D. V. (1954) 'Introduction', in Glass, D. V. (ed.) *Social Mobility in Britain*, Routledge & Kegan Paul, London.

Glass, D. V. and Hall, J. R. (1954) 'Social mobility in Great Britain: a study of inter-generation changes in status', in Glass, D. V. (ed.) *Social Mobility in Britain*, Routledge & Kegan Paul, London.

*Goldthorpe, J. H. with Llewellyn, C. and Payne, C. (1980) *Social Mobility and Class Structure in Modern Britain*, Clarendon Press, Oxford.

Goldthorpe, J. H. (1980) 'Reply to Crompton', *Sociology*, 14, pp.121–3.

Goldthorpe, J. H. and Payne, C. (1986) 'Trends in intergenerational class mobility in England and Wales 1972–1983', *Sociology*, 20, pp.1–24.

Halsey, A. H., Heath, A. F. and Ridge, J. M. (1980) *Origins and Destinations*, Clarendon Press, Oxford.

*Heath, A. F. (1981) *Social Mobility*, Fontana, Glasgow.

Hope, K. (1981) 'Trends in the openness of British society in the present century', *Research in Social Stratification and Mobility*, 1, pp.127–70.

Hout, M. (1989) *Following in Father's Footsteps: Social Mobility in Ireland*, Harvard University Press, Cambridge, Mass.

Kelsall, R. K. and Mitchell, S. (1959) 'Married women and employment in England and Wales', *Population Studies*, 13, pp.19–33.

Kerckhoff, A. C. and Trott, J. M. (1993) 'Educational attainment in a changing educational system: the case of England and Wales', in Shavit, Y. and Blossfeld, H-P. (eds) *Persistent Inequality: Changing Educational Attainment in Thirteen Countries*, Westview Press, Boulder, Colorado.

Macdonald, K. I. and Ridge, J. M. (1972) 'Social mobility', in Halsey, A. H. (ed.) *Trends in British Society since 1900*, Macmillan, Basingstoke.

Marshall, G., Swift, A. and Roberts, S. (1997) *Against the Odds? Social Class and Social Justice in Industrial Societies*, Clarendon Press, Oxford.

Payne, C., Payne J. and Heath, A. F. (1994) 'Modelling trends in multi-way tables', in Dale, A. and Davies, R. B. (eds) *Analyzing Social and Political Change: A Casebook of Methods*, Sage, London, pp.41–74.

Payne, G., Ford, G. and Robertson, C. (1976) 'Changes in occupational mobility in Scotland', *Scottish Journal of Sociology*, 1, pp.57–79.

Reid, Ivan (1998) *Class in Britain*, Polity Press, Cambridge.

Ridge, J. M. (ed.) (1974) *Mobility in Britain Reconsidered*, Clarendon Press, Oxford.

Sorensen, Annemette (1994) 'Women, family and class', *Annual Review of Sociology*, 20, pp.27–47.

van der Heijden, P. G. M. and Jansen, W. (1992) 'A class of models for the simultaneous analysis of square contingency tables', in Fahrmeir, L. et al. (eds) *Advances in GLIM and Statistical Modelling*, Springer, Berlin, pp.125–30.

Xie, Y. (1992) 'The log-mulitplicative layer effect model for analysing mobility tables', *American Sociological Review*, 57, pp.380–95.

Further reading (In addition to asterisked items in the References)

Hayes, B. C. and Miller, R. L. (1993) 'The silenced voice: female social mobility patterns with particular reference to the British Isles', *British Journal of Sociology*, 44, pp.653–72.

Hout, M. (1983) *Mobility Tables*, Sage, Beverly Hills, California.

Jonsson, J. O. and Mills, C. (1993) 'Social mobility in the 1970s and 1980s: a study of men and women in England and Sweden', *European Sociological Review*, 9, pp.229–47.

Miles, Andrew G. (1999) *Social Mobility in Nineteenth and Early Twentieth-Century England*, Macmillan, Basingstoke.

Payne, G., Jones, G. and Abbott, P. (1990) *The Social Mobility of Women*, Falmer Press, Basingstoke.

Part III
Economy

8
The Labour Force

Duncan Gallie

Steady application to work is the healthiest training for every individual, so it is the best discipline of a state. Honourable industry travels the same road with duty; and Providence has closely linked both with happiness.

Smiles, *Self-help*, 1859

The worker becomes poorer the richer is his production ... The depreciation of the human world progresses in direct proportion to the increase in the value of the world of things.

Marx, *Economical and Philosophical Manuscripts*, 1844

The twentieth century has witnessed a far-reaching transformation of the nature of work and of the skills of the workforce. In particular, it has seen the emergence of an economy dominated by the service industries, with work tasks increasingly involving work with people rather than on objects. At the same time, technical change and the growing complexity of work processes have been associated with a marked increase in the level of skill in the overall workforce. These changes in the forms of work have been accompanied by a dramatic shift in the gender composition of the workforce. In this chapter, we examine the basic pattern of such developments and also explore how they are linked to changes in the conditions of employment – in particular in work safety, representation, and job security. (Trends in pay and pay differentials are dealt with in Chapter 10.)

Industrial change and types of work

A central source of change in the nature of work has been the shift in the sectoral composition of employment. While the general trends can be established for earlier periods, more detailed analysis of changes in the industrial structure is only possible from 1921. Even after that, changes in classification between censuses and the inherent difficulties of allocating employment to specific industries, given an increasingly complex economic structure, mean that trend figures should be seen as approximate. For the inter-war period there was variation in whether those out of work were included or excluded from the tables (they were included in 1921 and excluded in 1931 and 1951). Even for the post-war period, obtaining a consistent series of figures for employment in different industries is far from straightforward. The Standard Industrial Classification (SIC) was heavily recast in 1968. There was a further adjustment of the industry categories for the 1980 Classification, which has required substantial reallocation of particular industrial categories to maintain consistency.

Very broadly the pattern of industrial development in Britain can be divided into two phases, separated around the mid-point of the century. The major developments in the first half of the century were the expansion and diversification of manufacturing industries and the sharp decline of coal mining and domestic services. Unlike most other European societies, the reduction of employment in agriculture had been very largely carried through in Britain in the nineteenth century. Whereas in 1871 agriculture still employed an estimated 14.6 per cent of the working population of England and Wales, by 1911 this had declined to 7.6 per cent (Ashworth, 1972). The decline of agricultural employment in the first half of the twentieth century was much more gradual, falling to approximately 6 per cent by 1931 and to 5 per cent in 1951. By the mid-century, less than a million people (916000) were still employed in agriculture. In contrast, manufacturing had seen a marked expansion of its workforce (Table 8.1). Whereas in 1921, 6821000 of the occupied population in Great Britain were in manufacture, by 1951 this had risen to 8337000 (an increase from 35 per cent to 38 per cent of the workforce). This general expansion reflected very different patterns in particular manufacturing industries. Between 1931 and 1951 employment in chemicals expanded by 115 per cent and in the metal industries by 104 per cent. In contrast, textiles and clothing (the dominant manufacturing industries at the beginning of the century, employing some 40 per cent of the manufacturing workforce (Routh, 1987, p.22)) saw a sharp decline. Outside manufacturing, the other two industries that saw a major reduction in employment were coal mining and personal services. In 1921, over a million people (1333000) were employed in coal mining, whereas by 1951 the number had fallen by over a third (679000). Just as notable was the decline of personal services, in particular as a result of the collapse of domestic service. In 1921, 11.6 per cent of the occupied population was in personal services, by 1951 only 7.6 per cent.

After the mid-century the pattern of economic development changed fundamentally. Instead of an expansion of manufacturing, the decades after 1951 saw a sharp contraction (Table 8.2). The number of employees in manufacturing fell by 43 per cent between 1966 and 1991. By the end of 1991, only

21 per cent of the total workforce in employment in Britain was in manufacturing. It can be seen that the reduction in manufacturing employment was very widespread, affecting in a similar way each of the broad categories of manufacturing: metal/manufacture and chemicals, mechanical engineering and other manufacturing. This was also a period that saw an intensification of the long-term trend over the century of declining employment in the extractive industries, partly accounting for the particularly sharp reduction in the 'energy and water' industry.

Table 8.1 Industrial Change, Great Britain, 1921–51[a]

	1921		1931		1951		Change 1951 as % of 1921
	000s	%	000s	%	000s	%	
Extractive	2782	14.4	2227	12.0	1967	8.9	71
Manufacturing	6821	35.3	5959	32.1	8337	37.7	122
Building and contracting	794	4.1	926	5.0	1388	6.3	175
Commerce and finance	2565	13.3	3099	16.7	3109	14.0	121
Transport/communications	1570	8.1	1508	8.1	1704	7.7	109
Personal services	2246	11.6	2445	13.2	1686	7.6	75
Public administration	690	3.6	777	4.2	946	4.3	137
Defence	317	1.6	245	1.3	759	3.4	239
Professional services	841	4.4	918	4.9	1524	6.9	181
Gas, water and electricity	179	0.9	225	1.2	357	1.6	199
Entertainment and sport	133	0.7	163	0.9	216	1.0	162
Miscellaneous	389	2.0	58	0.3	141	0.6	36
Total	19328	100	18550	100	22135	100	115

Note: [a]The table is based on Table 32 in Marsh (1958). It has been expanded to include Scotland, and the full tables were used for 1951 rather than the 1 per cent tables which were used by Marsh. Some distortion caused by changes in classification has been removed. In particular, Post Office workers have been classified with Transport and Communications throughout (in 1921 and 1931 the censuses classified them with Public Administration), and education workers (both central and local) have been classified with Professional Services throughout (in 1921 and 1931 the censuses classified them with Public Administration). In 1921 the census covered those aged 12 and over, in 1931 those 14 and over, and in 1951 those aged 15 and over. In 1921, the unemployed are included in the figures (Marsh, 1958, p.104) but in 1931 and 1951 they are excluded. This helps to explain the dip in the figures for 1931.

Sources: Census of England and Wales 1921, industry tables, Tables 1,2 and 4; Census of Scotland 1921, volume III, Table 12; Census of England and Wales 1931, industry tables, Table 1; Census of Scotland 1931, volume III, Table 15; Census of England and Wales 1951, industry tables, Table 1; Census of Scotland 1951, volume IV, Table 12.

In contrast, the post-war decades saw a rapid growth of employment in the service industries. By 1966 just under half of all employment (49.8 per cent) was in services and by 1971 this was the case for a majority of employees (52 per cent). By 1991, more than two-thirds (67 per cent) of all people in employment were in the service industries. In part, this reflected the expansion of the role of the Welfare State with substantial increases in education and in medical services (as well as in central and local government). Employment in education rose by 33 per cent between 1966 and 1991 and in medical services by 60 per cent. But there was also a rapid development of both business and leisure services. Indeed, financial and business services saw the greatest increase of all over this period, followed by recreational services. In both cases, the workforce doubled over the period.

Table 8.2 Industrial change, Great Britain, 1966–91

	1966	1971	1981	1991	1991 as % of 1966
	000s	000s	000s	000s	
Agriculture	753	635	515	456	61
Energy and water	968	764	709	448	46
Metal manufacture/chemicals	1478	1407	941	655	44
Mechanical engineering	3725	3669	2839	2148	58
Other manufacture	3258	3049	2413	2025	62
Construction	1880	1669	1606	1731	92
Distribution, hotels and catering	4396	4206	4405	4808	109
Transport and communications	1614	1564	1496	1492	92
Financial industries	1193	1348	1796	2821	236
Public administration	1400	1572	1638	1567	112
Education	1094	1370	1434	1459	133
Medical services	900	988	1247	1439	160
Recreational services	268	260	438	540	201
Other services	1173	1056	1245	1659	141
All industries	24169	23733	22916	23452	
All manufacturing	8460	8125	6194	4828	57
All services	12039	12362	13699	15784	131

Sources: Data derived from the 10% sample of the censuses for Great Britain: 1966; 1971; 1981; 1991. There was a major revision of the Standard Industrial Classification in 1968. The 1971 census, however, provides a reclassification of the 1966 industry data into the 1971 categories, so it is possible to begin the new series from 1966. The earlier censuses have been aligned on the industry categories used for the 1991 census, with an additional sub-division by the author of the service industries. Figures for all industries include a small proportion of unclassifiables.

These general trends between 1951 and 1991 continued in the final decade of the century. This can be seen from data from the annual Labour Force Surveys (Table 8.3). The sample numbers are smaller and the industry categorization is different, so the two sets of figures cannot be compared directly. However, exactly the same trends emerge. The spectacular decline of the energy, water and mining industries continued and there was also a further sharp fall in agricultural employment. While manufacturing was less affected than in the 1980s, its workforce continued to reduce. In contrast, there was growth of employment in all of the service industries, in particular in finance and business and in the welfare services.

Table 8.3 Industrial change, 1991–97, Great Britain

Industries	1991	1994	1997	1997 as a % of 1991
	000s	000s	000s	
Agriculture, fishing	532	502	459	86.3
Energy, water, mining	457	341	279	61.1
Manufacturing	5270	4784	4873	92.5
Construction	2020	1820	1806	89.4
Distribution, hotels, restaurants	5205	5032	5267	101.2
Transport, communications	1579	1566	1676	106.1
Banking, finance, insurance	3432	3429	3767	109.8
Public admin., education, health	5600	6019	6263	111.8
Other services	1477	1461	1536	104.0
Total services	17294	17508	18509	107.0

Source: *Labour Force Survey*, Historical Supplement, 1997. Spring surveys.

Overall there was an extensive process of industrial restructuring, in which the typical types of work in society changed in a fundamental way. The distinctiveness of the service industries compared with manufacturing or the extractive industries emerges very clearly from national survey data (Gallie et al., 1998). Only 22 per cent of those employed in the extractive industries mentioned that dealing with people constituted at least half their working time and in none of the manufacturing industries was the proportion higher than 30 per cent. In contrast, this type of work was given by 52.6 per cent of those in banking, finance and insurance, by 59 per cent of those in national or local government and by over 80 per cent of those in the welfare and in the leisure industries. The only industry predominantly involving dealing with people that declined over the century was 'personal services'. Overall, the shift in sectoral composition has had major implications for the types of work tasks that people are engaged in and hence for the types of skills required.

How did Britain compare with other European countries, as the century drew to a close? It is clear from comparative data (Eurostat, 1997, pp.90–1) that the United Kingdom was by no means exceptional in terms of the shift to a service-based economy. The proportion working in non-service industries was very close to the European average, with only Italy and Germany standing out as having substantially higher proportions employed in this sector. The overall proportion employed in services was somewhat higher in the UK than the EU average, but very close to countries such as Belgium, Denmark, Finland, France and Sweden. The Netherlands and Luxembourg had an even higher proportion working in the service sector. The countries which had a smaller service sector were mainly those that still had a large proportion of the workforce employed in agriculture. The growth of the service sector represented then a development that was very general across the advanced European economies.

Occupations and skill

With the changing structure of industry, there was a transformation of the occupational structure of the British workforce. To begin with, there was a marked diversification of occupations reflecting an increasingly specialized division of labour. This is reflected in the increase in the number of job titles listed in the official classifications for coding the censuses. In 1851 about 7000 separate occupations were identified, in 1881 this had risen to 12000, and in 1980 the classification contained 23000 entries. While this in part resulted from modifications in procedure, it primarily came about through the concern to capture the emergence of new occupations created by the rapid industrial change over the period.

However, the process of diversification of occupations over the century makes it inherently difficult to trace the pattern of occupational change for specific occupations. To map the broad trends it is necessary to focus on a higher level of aggregation – namely that of occupational classes (see also Chapter 7). Quite new occupations may emerge but they may be broadly equivalent to a range of former occupations in terms of the general level of skill or training they require. The most rigorous attempt to date to achieve a picture of the longer term trends is by Guy Routh (1981; 1987). Routh elaborated a set of classes by combining the principles underlying the allocation of occupations to the Registrar-General's classes with information about employment status, that is to say whether people were employers or employees and whether they were responsible for supervising the work of others. A subsequent modification of the Routh classes was made by George Bain (1970), primarily to isolate a separate category of salesmen and shop assistants. An updated version of this Routh/Bain class schema forms the basis for the subsequent discussion. It distinguishes seven principal classes: a higher and lower group of professionals, managerial and administrative employees, employers and proprietors (excluding those in the professions) clerical workers, salesmen and shopkeepers, foremen and inspectors and finally a class of manual workers. A variant of the schema sub-divides the manual working class into three categories: skilled, semi-skilled and unskilled.

The problems of constructing a consistent series across censuses are acute. Not until 1921 was a reasonably clear distinction made between an industrial and an occupational classification. The data for 1911 are put together from very diverse sources: census information, industry reports, and Board of Trade earnings and hours reports. There were changes over time in the allocation of categories (for instance, draughtsmen were placed with clerks in the 1911 census, but were given separate status in 1921). Hence the comparisons must be treated as very approximate. In the 1931 and 1961 census, a distinction was no longer drawn between 'employers and proprietors' and 'managers and administrators', so the relevant proportions have to be inferred from the adjacent censuses. Each census produced some modification of procedures that is likely to affect strict comparability, although there was a particular major alteration of the classification of occupations between 1951 and 1961 which makes it very difficult to form a consistent picture of the evolution of the different subcategories of the manual working class for the century as a whole. But while considerable caution must be taken in placing weight on particular percentage changes, the general pattern of change at the level of broad occupational classes is so clear that it is unlikely to be merely an artefact of procedural variations.

In the first half of the century the most striking development was the growth of the class of clerical employees (Table 8.4). Between 1911 and 1951, the numbers of people in clerical work rose nearly threefold from 832 000 to 2 341 000. The period also saw a substantial increase of the overall occupied population – from 18 347 000 in 1911 to 22 514 000. But, even allowing for that, the share of clerical workers in overall employment greatly increased. Whereas in 1911, they represented 4.5 per cent of the working population, by 1951 the figure was 10.4 per cent. The increase was particularly marked for women. The period saw a profound change in the gender composition of clerical employment, moving from a situation in which it was predominantly male to one in which women were in a majority. As late as 1931 men still constituted 56 per cent of clerical workers, but by 1951 their share had fallen to 41 per cent (Routh, 1987, p.32).

There was also a significant expansion of professional work, especially of the lower professions. The share of employment of the lower professions rose from 3.1 per cent to 4.7 per cent, while that of the higher professions rose from 1.0 to 1.9 per cent. In the lower professions, the growth was particularly marked among nursing and other subordinate medical jobs. Among the higher professions, there was a striking increase in the numbers of accountants, engineers and scientists. There was also, especially in the period between 1921 and 1951, a marked increase in the proportion of managers and administrators (from 3.6 per cent to 5.5 per cent), partly reflecting the growing functions of the state in the aftermath of the world wars.

However, despite the rising importance of the clerical and professional classes, the occupational structure of the first half of the century was still dominated by manual work. In 1911 three-quarters of all jobs were manual jobs and in 1951 they still represented nearly two-thirds of all jobs (64.2 per cent). Indeed, in absolute terms the numbers of manual workers increased over the period from 13 685 000 to 14 448 000. The numbers of skilled and semi-skilled workers remained very much the same and there was an increase in the

Table 8.4 Occupational class in Great Britain, 1911–91 (000s)

	1911	1921	1931	1951	1971	1981	1991
Higher professions	184	195	240	434	824	988	1314
Lower professions	560	680	728	1059	1946	2736	3435
Employers and proprietors	1232	1318	1409	1118	1056	904	806
Managers and administrators	629	704	770	1246	1706	2305	3729
Clerical workers	832	1256	1404	2341	3479	3761	3800
Foremen, supervisors	236	279	323	590	968	1032	944
Sales	989	980	1376	1278	1364	1370	1394
Total manual workers	13685	13921	14779	14448	13680	12309	9322
Total in employment	18347	19333	21029	22514	25021	25406	24746
Skilled manual	5608	5573	5619	5616	5410	4470	3566
Semi-skilled manual	6310	5608	6045	6123	5145	5133	4354
Unskilled manual	1767	2740	3115	2709	3125	2706	1402

Percentage of workforce	1911	1921	1931	1951	1971	1981	1991
Higher professions	1.0	1.0	1.1	1.9	3.3	3.9	5.3
Lower professions	3.1	3.5	3.5	4.7	7.8	10.8	13.9
Employers and proprietors	6.7	6.8	6.7	5.0	4.2	3.6	3.3
Managers and administrators	3.4	3.6	3.7	5.5	6.8	9.1	15.1
Clerical workers	4.5	6.5	6.7	10.4	13.9	14.8	15.4
Foremen, supervisors	1.3	1.4	1.5	2.6	3.9	4.1	3.8
Sales	5.4	5.1	6.5	5.7	5.5	5.4	5.6
Manual workers	74.6	72.0	70.3	64.2	54.7	48.4	37.7
Skilled manual	30.6	28.8	26.7	24.9	21.6	17.6	14.4
Semi-skilled manual	34.4	29.0	28.8	27.2	20.6	20.2	17.6
Unskilled manual	9.6	14.2	14.8	12.0	12.5	10.7	5.7

Source: The principal source of data is Routh (1981; 1987). The version adopted here includes the modification of the Routh class schema by Bain (1970), designed to separate out sales workers. The data have been updated from the census to include 1991.

number of unskilled manual workers. The persisting dominance of manual work was consistent with the central importance of manufacturing in the economic structure through the first half of the century.

The second half of the century, however, saw a marked change in the trends of occupational development. Even though the total number employed continued to grow, there was a sharp decline in the number of manual workers. Indeed, by 1991, there were some five million fewer manual workers than there had been in 1951. This affected all categories of manual worker, although the drop was particularly marked among the unskilled. The overall share of manual jobs plummeted from two-thirds of employment to only 38 per cent. In contrast, there was a continued, albeit slower growth of clerical work, and a spectacular expansion of both higher and lower professional work. There was also a very marked increase in the number of managers. Between 1951 and 1991, the numbers both in professional and in managerial jobs tripled.

Overall, then, the century saw a fundamental shift in the relative importance of different occupational classes. Between 1911 and 1991, manual work declined from three-quarters to a minority of all jobs. Professional and managerial jobs on the other hand increased from 7.5 per cent to 33 per cent of all jobs. In short, there was a change from an occupational structure heavily dominated by manual work to one where there was a fairly even division between three broad categories: professional/managerial work, intermediary occupations and manual work.

It is clear that this shift in the occupational structure was closely linked to the changing structure of industry. The service sector industries which had provided most of the expansion in jobs in the second half of the century – in particular the welfare services – had much higher proportions of professional employees than the manufacturing industries which had seen their workforces decline. Data from the 1991 census show that in education and medical services, nearly two-thirds of employees (65 per cent) were in either professional or managerial/technical occupations, and in the finance industries nearly half (46 per cent). In contrast, in metal manufacturing and engineering industries, the proportion was just over a quarter (27 per cent) and in other manufacturing even lower (20 per cent). The decline of manual employment and the rise of professional employment were then integrally linked to the sectoral shifts in the economy.

The Routh/Bain occupational classes were intended to differentiate employees in terms of the learning time (in general education and vocationally specific training) required to be able to carry out tasks (Routh, 1987, pp.25–6). The shift in the occupational structure over the century could be viewed then as reflecting a far-reaching process of upskilling of the British workforce. However, it might be argued that this fails to take into account the possibility that the growth of 'higher' classes may have been accompanied by the deskilling of work *within* these classes. An overall estimate requires information about skill trends within classes, which for most of the century is only available on a fragmentary basis for particular occupations at highly specific points of time.

However, for the 1980s and 1990s, there is some more widely representative evidence from surveys. These asked people whether the skills required in their jobs had increased, decreased or stayed the same over the previous five years. As can be seen in Table 8.5, in both 1986 and 1992, a majority of employees had experienced an increase in their skills. Moreover, this was true for all occupational classes other than that of semi-skilled and unskilled workers.

It is clear that those in professional and managerial occupations had been particularly likely to experience a skill increase. Overall, only 9 per cent of employees in either time-period felt that there had been a decrease in the skill level of their jobs. Furthermore, if the two periods are compared, there was an acceleration over time in the process of upskilling. Whereas in 1986, 52 per cent of employees reported that the skill requirements of their jobs had increased over the previous five years, by 1992 this was the case for 63 per cent. This upward shift is evident for all occupational classes. In short, the available evidence does not support the view that extensive deskilling was occurring within classes. Rather the increase in skill levels reflected by the rapid growth of the professional/managerial classes after World War II was accompanied by a major process of upskilling within classes. With the exception of non-skilled workers, the overall picture then is one of a substantial rise in skill levels across the greater part of the workforce.

Table 8.5 Skill change by occupational class, Great Britain, 1986–92

| | *Percentages experiencing an increase in skill* | |
	1986	*1992*
Professional/managerial	67	74
Lower non-manual	55	70
Technician/supervisory	56	73
Skilled manual	50	64
Semi & unskilled manual	33	45
All employees	52	63

Source: Gallie et al. (1998). For the 1980s the data are from the Social Change and Economic Life Initiative surveys and for the 1990s from the Employment in Britain survey.[1] The 1980s surveys were part of a comparative study of local labour markets. However, extensive comparisons with national data suggest that the combined sample provides a very faithful portrait of the national workforce at the time. The 1990s data come from a fully representative national sample. The occupational class schema is that developed by Erikson and Goldthorpe (1992).

But while the changing structure of industry is one of the major factors that accounts for the general tendency of skills to rise, this has been accentuated by the very rapid and widespread technological change that swept British industry from the early 1980s. The advent of micro-processors provided an opportunity for automating work processes and restructuring work not only in manufacturing but also in the service industries. Survey evidence indicates just how fast the pace of change was over this period. In 1986, only 39 per cent of employees were working with computerized or automated equipment. However, by 1992 the figure had risen to over half the workforce (56 per cent).[2] Those whose work involved the use of new technologies in 1992 were very much more likely to report that the skill requirements of their jobs had increased (Gallie et al., 1998, pp.48–9).

The sexual division of employment

This far-reaching transformation of the industrial and skill structure of the working population was accompanied by a major change in the sex composition of the workforce. Whereas at the beginning of the century women were much less likely to be economically active than men and formed only a minority of those in work, as the century progressed their participation rates increased sharply and so did their share of employment. At the same time, there was a progressive widening of the types of jobs to which they had access. Whereas at the beginning of the century women were crowded into a very restricted set of industries and occupations, by its end they were much more widely dispersed across the range of different types and levels of jobs in the economy. There remained, however, substantial sex segregation in types of work, and considerable differences with respect to the nature of employment contracts. This raises the issue of whether much higher levels of representation implied that women were becoming fully integrated into the workforce or whether they were better seen as some type of secondary workforce.

It can be seen in Table 8.6 that, while the overall level of participation remained very similar from the beginning to the end of the century, this concealed an important change in the relative participation rates of men and women. The figures are adjusted to take account of the most obvious source of change in participation rates, namely changes in the mandatory school leaving age.

Men's participation rates have consistently declined through each decade, from 94 per cent in 1911 to 71 per cent in 1998. In contrast, there has been a strong trend for women's participation in the labour force to rise. In 1911, just over a third of women (35 per cent) were in the workforce; by 1998 this was the case for over half (54 per cent). Whereas at the beginning of the century there was a 58 percentage-point difference in the participation rates of men and women, by the end the difference had been reduced to one of only 18 percentage points. The overall effect of the decline of men's participation and the increase in women's has been a remarkable stability of the overall participation rate across the century.

The increase in women's participation in the labour market largely reflected changes in the activity of married women. In Table 8.7, it can be seen that participation rates for single women have been consistently high over the century. In 1911, 69 per cent of all single women over compulsory school age were economically active, whereas by 1991 this was the case for 64 per cent. In contrast, there has been a striking growth in the participation rates of married women. The 10 percentage-point jump over the period 1931 to 1951 is likely to reflect the impact of the war in legitimating a role for women in employment. Facilitated by the collapse of the marriage bar, the trend moved steadily upwards. Whereas in 1951 less than a quarter of married women were in the workforce, by 1991 this was the

case for half of all married women. The change was particularly marked for
married women aged between 35 and 54. For instance, of those aged 35 to 44,
only 10 per cent were economically active in 1911, whereas the proportion had
risen to nearly three-quarters (72 per cent) by 1991.

Table 8.6 Labour force participation rates, Great Britain, 1911–98

	Males	Females	All	Women as percentage of labour force
1911	93.5	35.3	63.0	29.3
1921	91.8	33.1	60.6	29.0
1931	90.5	34.2	60.7	29.8
1951	87.6	32.7	58.6	29.5
1961	86.3	37.5	62.8	31.3
1966	84.1	42.2	64.6	34.3
1971	81.5	42.6	61.1	36.5
1981	77.8	45.5	61.0	38.9
1991	73.3	49.9	61.0	42.7
1998	71.3	53.8	62.3	44.3

Source: Data for the series 1911–91 are from the censuses for Great Britain. Those for 1998 are from
the *Labour Force Survey, Quarterly Supplement* no. 2, August 1998, p.13 (Spring, UK, not adjusted, based
on all aged 16+).

**Table 8.7 Female participation rates by marital status and age, Great
Britain, 1911–91**

Marital status	Year	Age 14/15/16–24	25–34	35–44	45–54	55+	All ages 14/15/16+
Single	1911	73.1	73.6	65.6	58.5	34.5	69.3
	1921	70.7	76.2	67.6	59.7	36.6	68.1
	1931	75.7	80.4	72.4	63.9	36.4	71.6
	1951	84.6	86.9	81.0	74.8	29.7	73.1
	1961	77.6	89.5	84.9	81.6	32.1	69.6
	1971	65.6	85.8	85.0	82.4	24.4	59.7
	1981	66.7	85.7	81.9	81.4	16.4	60.8
	1991	66.4	80.0	78.8	73.2	11.7	63.7
Married	1911	12.0	9.9	9.9	9.9	7.2	9.6
	1921	12.7	9.4	8.9	8.4	6.3	8.7
	1931	18.5	13.2	10.2	8.5	5.3	10.0
	1951	36.6	24.4	25.7	23.7	8.4	21.7
	1961	41.8	29.5	36.4	35.3	14.0	29.4
	1971	45.3	38.4	54.2	56.8	24.0	42.0
	1981	53.7	48.4	63.8	64.3	22.6	47.2
	1991	61.7	62.3	72.3	70.3	21.2	53.1

Source: Censuses for Great Britain.

By the final decade of the century Britain had a female participation rate that was relatively high by European standards (Eurostat, 1997). It was well above the average rate for the EU, which was 45.3 per cent. It lay between the exceptionally high rates characteristic of the 'northern' European countries – Denmark, Finland, and Sweden, and those of the 'central European' countries, such as France and Germany. It was far above the rates of female participation to be found in the southern European countries and in Ireland.

The increase in female participation was reflected in women's increased share of jobs. The figures in Table 8.8 show that between 1931 and 1951, there was only a very slight rise in women's share of employment, although it must be remembered that this conceals the massive if temporary entry of women into jobs during World War II. But from mid-century the rise in women's share was rapid and continuous. Whereas in 1951 less than a third of jobs were held by women (30.8 per cent), by 1997 it was nearly half (46.2 per cent).

Table 8.8 Sex composition of employment, Great Britain, 1931–98

	All	Men	Women	Percentage Women
1931	21029	14761	6264	29.8
1951	22514	15584	6930	30.8
1971	25021	15884	9138	36.5
1981	25406	15527	9879	38.9
1991	24746	14057	10689	43.2
1998	26448	14177	12271	46.4

Source: Figures for 1931–91 are from the censuses (1921 has been omitted because the published tables include the unemployed). Figures for 1998 (June, seasonally adjusted) are from the *Labour Market Trends, Historical Supplement*, December 1998.

How far did this increase in women's involvement in the labour market lead to a decline in sex differences in types of employment? As can be seen in Table 8.9, at the beginning of the century there was a very high level of sex segregation in the labour market, with men and women working in very different types of occupation. In 1901, nearly half of male workers (47 per cent) were in occupations in which only men worked and 89 per cent were in occupations where at least 70 per cent of workers were male. For women, the extreme forms of segregation were less marked, with only 11 per cent working in totally female occupations. But the great majority of women were still working in female-dominated occupations: 71 per cent of women were in occupations where 70 per cent or more of workers were women.

However, over the century there was a steady decline in the extent to which both men and women worked in occupations in which there were predominantly people of their own sex. The proportion of men in all male occupations had halved by the mid-century and by the closing decade had become altogether insignificant. Moreover all of the other categories of highly segregated male work had also declined. For instance, the proportion of men in jobs that were 70 per cent or more male had fallen from 89 per cent to 68 per cent. A broadly similar picture of change over the century can be found for women. Although women were less likely than men to be working in predominantly female jobs at the beginning of the century, there was still a clear tendency for segregation to decline. By the 1960s, the category of those in 100 per cent female occupations had disappeared altogether, and the proportion in occupations with at least 90 per cent women had halved between 1901 and 1991. Taking the 70 per cent+ threshold as the indicator of gender segregation, the proportion of women in female jobs fell from 71 per cent to 63 per cent. But, whereas the decline of segregation was relatively consistent across the century for men, this is rather less clear for women. There was some evidence of a rise in the proportion of women in such jobs in the 1980s and 1990s. It was then primarily employment in the very heavily female occupations (100 per cent or 90 per cent+) that had declined; women were still as likely as in the early part of the century to be working predominantly with other women.

Table 8.9 Occupational segregation, Great Britain, 1901–91

	% of men working in occupations with:						% of women working in occupations with:					
	100 %	90 %+	80 %+	70 %+	60 %+	50 %+	100 %	90 %+	80 %+	70 %+	60 %+	50 %+
	Men workers						Women workers					
1901	47	74	83	89	92	95	11	52	54	71	74	82
1911	44	70	76	86	90	93	3	45	50	64	68	78
1921	29	70	76	83	86	92	0.1	40	48	56	61	72
1931	35	69	75	84	90	94	0.1	41	52	62	69	73
1951	20	61	73	82	85	92	0.3	31	39	50	64	68
1961	22	62	73	77	84	85	0	21	32	53	56	79
1971	14	53	69	77	84	87	0	25	44	51	75	77
1981	2	50	67	72	79	81	0	25	38	63	70	78
1991	0	38	58	68	77	83	0	23	37	63	70	76

Source: Figures for 1901–71 are from Hakim (1979), p.24. These have been updated using the 1981 and 1991 censuses for Great Britain.

Another indicator of whether there had been a tendency towards sex integration in employment is women's changing share of specific occupational classes. As Hakim (1979) has argued, an adequate measure of change in women's representation has to take account of their level of participation in the workforce at different historical periods. Table 8.10 indicates the extent to which women had above or below the share of an occupational class that could be expected on the basis of their proportion of the workforce. At the beginning of the century, they were heavily under-represented among employers and proprietors, managers and administrators and clerks. But the highest under-representation of all was among higher professionals and foremen. In contrast, they had a share of manual work that was equal to their weight in the overall workforce. The two occupational classes where women were over-represented were the lower professions and sales occupations. In the course of the century, there were only two occupational classes for which the gender pattern changed fundamentally. By 1991, women had come to have a lower share of manual work than would be expected. In contrast, they vastly increased their share of clerical work. They moved from a position of under-representation in clerical occupations at the beginning of the century to one where, by the mid-century, they had twice their expected share of such jobs. Clerical work had become effectively feminized and this pattern remained relatively unchanged through the second half of the century, despite some sign of the beginnings of a reversal of the trend in the 1980s. Finally, a significant change in women's position in the more recent period was a marked increase in their representation in the higher professions, although such occupations still remained predominantly male.

Table 8.10 Under- and over-representation of women in major occupational groups in relation to the female proportion of the total workforce, Great Britain, 1911–91

Occupational groups	1911	1921	1931	1951	1961	1971	1981	1991
Higher professionals	0.20	0.17	0.25	0.27	0.30	0.27	0.27	0.43
Lower professionals and technicians	2.13	2.01	1.97	1.74	1.57	1.43	1.46	1.47
Employers and managers	0.64	0.69	0.66	0.65	0.63	0.68	0.65	0.58
Managers and administrators	0.67	0.58	0.44	0.49	0.48	0.59	0.51	0.71
Clerical workers	0.72	1.51	1.54	1.95	2.01	2.00	1.96	1.89
Foremen and inspectors	0.14	0.22	0.29	0.44	0.32	0.36	0.59	0.63
Salesmen and shop assistants	1.19	1.48	1.25	1.68	1.69	1.64	1.58	1.54
Manual workers	1.03	0.95	0.97	0.85	0.8	0.81	0.75	0.68

Source: Figures for 1901–71 are from Hakim (1979), p.28. These have been updated using data on women's distribution in the Routh classes (see source Table 8.4) calculated from the 1981 and 1991 censuses for Great Britain.

The re-fragmentation of employment statuses

The feminization of the workforce was a trend that characterized the century as a whole. However, with respect to the last quarter of the century, a number of commentators have pointed to another major change in the structure of employment: the decline of the traditional full-time employment contract and its replacement by a variety of non-standard contracts. This development has often been seen as linked to a growing divergence between a core workforce of relatively privileged full-time employees and a secondary workforce of those with sub-standard terms of employment. Those on non-standard contracts are thought to constitute a 'flexible workforce', which could be easily disposed of to help employers cope with the increased volatility of product market conditions in an increasingly competitive and global economic environment. The three groups that are seen as constituting this secondary or flexible workforce are part-time employees, the self-employed and temporary employees.

The growth of part-time employment

Numerically, the most important source of the growth of non-standard contracts has been part-time work. Consistent data however have only been available for all women employees since 1971. Prior to this there are figures for female employees in manufacturing industry and figures from the census which are based on self-reported part-time work without a clear definition in terms of hours worked. The longest consistent series of data (from 1971) comes from employer surveys, which use a definition of part-time work as 30 hours or less. These provide estimates of the total number of part-time jobs, not the number of individuals working part-time in their main job. A person holding two jobs would be counted twice in the figures. In practice, the difference is a limited one. In the spring of 1994, there were 5.9 million part-time jobs, while there were 5.4 million working part-time in their main job. The figures for part-time jobs presented here include both employees and self-employed but exclude people on work-related government training programmes. Although these trainees are sometimes included with part-time work in official statistics, there are insufficient data before 1983 and their part-time status is simply assumed in the statistics.

The growth of female part-time jobs is certainly one of the most striking changes in the labour market in the second half of the century. The early data must be regarded as very approximate. It appears that at the mid-century only a very small proportion (about 11 per cent) of women's jobs were part-time (Table 8.11). However, the importance of part-time work grew rapidly over the next two decades and by 1971 it represented approximately a third of female employment. The overall number of part-time jobs nearly doubled from 2 757 000 in 1971 to 5 168 590 in 1998. The proportion of female employees who were working part-time rose from 34 per cent in 1971 to 46 per cent in 1998. Taking the absolute figures, the number of full-time jobs held by women actually fell between 1971 and 1997. The whole of the very substantial increase in women's jobs over the last three decades can be accounted for by the growth of part-time work.

**Table 8.11 Part-timers as a percentage of
female employees, Great Britain, 1950–98**

	Manufacturing	All female employees
1950	11.8	n/a
1951	12.2	11.0
1961	13.7	25.0
1965	15.9	n/a
1971	18.7	33.5
1975	22.6	39.6
1981	22.6	41.5
1985	20.5	42.8
1991	20.5	44.9
1995	19.1	45.6
1998	19.3	45.6

Sources: 1951 and 1961 all female employees from Census of the
Population (self-reported part-time without hours qualification);
Department of Employment Gazette, November 1973, p.1089;
Employment Gazette, Historical Supplement, October 1994; *Labour
Market Trends*, March 1996 (updated 1992 onwards); *Labour
Market Trends*, October 1997; *Labour Market Trends, Historical
Supplement*, no. 5, 1997; *Labour Market Trends, Historical
Supplement*, December 1998 (adjusted June figures).

An examination of the industry distribution of part-time work in the 1998
Labour Force Survey shows that its growth has had far more to do with the
expansion of the service sector than with developments in manufacturing
industry (where it has been in decline since the mid-1970s). The greatest
concentrations of female part-time workers were in 'distribution, hotels and
restaurants', which accounted for nearly a third (31 per cent) of all women
working part-time and in 'public administration, education and health', which
accounted for 39 per cent. Indeed, taking the services as a whole, 92 per cent
of female part-time workers were working in service industries. In contrast, the
proportion in manufacturing was very small indeed (6 per cent). At least in
part, the close relationship between the service sector and part-time employment reflects the fact that part-time work is a way in which employers can
meet the need for service provision outside standard working hours – for
instance, in the evenings and at weekends.

The importance of part-time work in women's employment has raised the
issue of whether, despite the sharp rise in their labour market participation,
women's commitment to employment is very different from that of men.
Given that they retained primary responsibility for the home and for child-
rearing, it was conceivable that employment was regarded less as something
centrally important in its own right than as a secondary activity needed to

boost the family income. There are no trend data for any length of time about such family and work values. However, we do have comparable survey data for the 1980s and 1990s. It is notable that while there was a very clear difference by sex in longer-term commitment to employment in the 1980s, this had almost entirely disappeared in the 1990s (Table 8.12). Even among female part-timers there had been a striking rise in commitment to employment, leaving only a small difference by contract status.

Table 8.12 Non-financial employment commitment, Great Britain, 1981–92[a]

% committed	1981[bc]	1986[d]	1992[c]
Men	69	67	68
Women	60	62	67
Women full-time	65	63	69
Women part-time	54	59	64

Notes: [a]The survey question was: 'If you were to get enough money to live as comfortably as you would like for the rest of your life, would you continue to work, not necessarily in your present job, or would you stop working?'
[b]The figures for 1981 are derived from Warr (1982). The overall figures for women have been weighted to provide the correct proportions of full-time and part-time workers for that year.
[c]The 1981 and 1992 studies were representative national surveys.
[d]The 1986 data are from a comparative survey of local labour markets the sample of which has been shown to be very close to the national picture for that year.

Sources: 1981: SAPU Survey of Non-Financial Employment Commitment; 1986: Social Change and Economic Life Initiative; 1992: Employment in Britain Survey.

Self-employment

Although the overall numbers were less considerable, the growth of self-employment was also a notable feature of the closing decades of the century. The common assumption had been that as societies reached an advanced stage of industrialization, self-employment would become an increasingly anachronistic feature of the employment structure. The economies of scale and the research capacity of larger firms would eventually doom the small producer to extinction. It was all the more striking then that in the 1980s, far from disappearing, self-employment expanded apace (Table 8.13). In 1979, it accounted for only 7 per cent of employment; by 1989, however, its share had nearly doubled at 13 per cent. While men were much more likely to be self-employed than women, the same general trend can be found for both sexes. In the 1990s, the growth of self-employment appeared to have reached a plateau and there was little further expansion.

Table 8.13 The growth of self-employment, percentages, Great Britain, 1979–98

	All	Men	Women
1979	7.3	9.8	3.3
1981	9.2	12.4	4.6
1983	9.9	12.9	5.6
1985	11.3	14.6	6.6
1987	12.1	15.9	7.0
1989	13.1	17.6	7.1
1991	12.8	17.4	6.9
1993	12.5	16.9	7.0
1995	12.9	17.6	7.0
1998	12.1	16.1	7.2

Sources: *Labour Force Survey Historical Supplement*, 1997; *Labour Force Survey Quarterly Bulletin*, 3, November 1998.

There have been sharply contrasting interpretations of this sudden rise of self-employment. For some, it represented a rediscovery of the entrepreneurial spirit, encouraged by a Conservative government committed to a return to Victorian values. For others, it was a further example of the polarization of the labour market into a core of well-protected employees and a periphery of flexible workers. Employers in manufacturing, it has been suggested, were off-loading the risks arising from more competitive and volatile product markets by making greater use of workers for whom they had no long-term responsibility and who could be dispensed with quickly and with little cost.

As can be seen in Figure 8.1, the growth of self-employment between 1978 and 1997 was quite widespread across industry. There was certainly no sign that it was particularly linked to developments in manufacturing. Rather, the most rapid growth took place in quite diverse industrial settings. It was very marked in construction, where the concentration of self-employed has always been exceptionally high. There was a striking expansion in business services, which suggests a move to self-employment among people with specialized and highly marketable skills. There was a considerable increase in health-related jobs that may have been linked to the increased popularity during this period of alternative forms of medicine. Overall, the complex forces driving the growth of self-employment are difficult to assimilate to any sweeping interpretation in terms either of ideological change or of new employer labour force strategies.

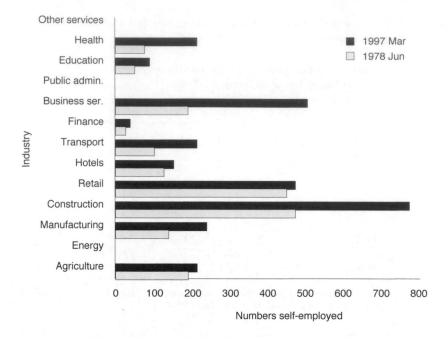

Figure 8.1 Growth of self-employment by industry, Great Britain, 1978–97

Source: *Labour Market Trends, Historical Supplement*, no.5, 1997.

Temporary work

The third category of non-standard work is that of people in temporary work either in casual jobs or on short-term contracts. Again there is clearly evidence of an expansion of such employees (Table 8.14). In 1984, they represented 5.3 per cent of the workforce, whereas by 1998 this had increased to 7.1 per cent. A higher proportion of women employees have been temporary workers, but it is notable that in the 1990s the sex differential diminished, reflecting a particularly sharp rise in the proportion of men who had temporary contracts.

Table 8.14 Temporary work, United Kingdom, 1984–98 (as % of employees)

	1984	1987	1989	1991	1993	1995	1997	1998
Men	3.8	3.9	3.7	3.9	4.9	6.2	6.5	6.0
Women	7.2	7.6	7.4	7.0	5.8	7.9	8.4	8.3
All employees	5.3	5.6	5.4	5.3	5.8	7.0	7.4	7.1

Sources: Figures for 1984–93 (UK) from Beatson (1995) p.10. Data are from the Spring LFS; figures for 1995 (GB) are from *LFS Quarterly Bulletin*, no.22, December 1997; figures for 1997 and 1998 (UK) are from *Labour Force Survey, Quarterly Supplement*, no. 2, August 1998. Figures are not seasonally adjusted.

The industry and occupational distributions of temporary workers however again fit poorly with the argument that their growth is mainly a result of the labour strategies of employers in manufacturing industry seeking greater flexibility in an increasingly competitive environment. To begin with, the industries that were most likely to make use of temporary workers were not the manufacturing industries, but rather public administration, the welfare industries and other services (such as the leisure and personal service industries). Further, the assumption that temporary workers were secondary workers in the sense of being relatively poorly qualified is clearly incorrect. The occupational group where their expansion was most marked in the 1990s was that of the higher professions (ONS, 1997). Moreover, the occupational profile of temporary workers in the mid-1990s shows that a significant proportion were highly skilled people who would have been relatively well-placed in the labour market.

Finally, it should be noted that there was a degree of mobility between different types of contract status, which undermines the view that temporary work generally tends to trap people into a distinctive sector of highly insecure work. Longitudinal data from the British Household Panel Study, comparing the types of jobs that the same people occupied in 1991 and one year later, show that only just over a third of those on fixed-term contracts were in either fixed-term contract or casual jobs the following year (CSO, 1996). In contrast, 45 per cent of male, and 50 per cent of female, temporary workers in 1991 had moved into permanent jobs.

Non-standard contracts in the European perspective

In the 1980s and 1990s Britain was depicted frequently as the European country which had moved most strongly towards greater labour market flexibility. Did this imply that, by the final decade of the century, it was distinctive in terms of the proportion of its workforce that was employed on non-standard contracts? The available comparative figures (Eurostat, 1997) cover the UK rather than Britain, although the figures are very similar indeed. It is clear that the pattern of employment, whether one takes Britain or the UK, was in several respects distinctive in European perspective.

It was one of the countries that had a very high proportion of women working part-time. Indeed, the proportion in the UK was the highest of all after the Netherlands. Sweden was the only other country with a broadly similar figure. On the other hand, the proportion of temporary workers in the UK was well *below* the European average (6.9 per cent compared with 11.7 per cent). Only Belgium and Luxembourg had a lower proportion of employees on such contracts. The introduction of temporary contracts had been taken furthest in Spain, where it affected a third of all employees. Finally, in comparative perspective, the size of the self-employed sector in the UK was far from exceptional. It was somewhat below the European average (12.6 per cent compared with 15.0 per cent) and close to the level to be found in countries such as France, the Netherlands and Sweden. Thus, it is difficult to characterize Britain (or the UK) in any overall sense as having made particularly extensive use of non-standard contracts in its search for labour market flexibility. While there was a high level of part-time work, temporary contracts were relatively rare and the proportion self-employed was below the EU average.

The quality of employment

Given the major shifts in the century both in the industrial and occupational structure, is there any evidence that there has been a change in the quality of working life? We are far from having the type of data over time that would be necessary to assess this rigorously, but it is possible to examine a few central aspects of the quality of employment. In particular, there are some reasonable trend data on safety at work, on the length of working hours and on employee representation.

Safety at work

By any criteria, the issue of safety at work must be judged one of the most fundamental aspects of the quality of working life. Information is collected on industrial accidents under three main headings: fatal accidents, non-fatal major accidents and injuries causing absence from work for over three days. The latter two series provide substantial problems of comparability over time. The definition of what constituted a major injury was substantially widened after 1986, when RIDDOR (the Reporting of Injuries, Diseases and Dangerous Occurrences Regulations, 1985) came into effect. There are missing years in the data about injuries leading to absences over three days, when the information was not collected, and it is suspected that there are serious problems of under-reporting, possibly in the region of 50 per cent (*Employment Gazette*, Occasional Supplement, no. 2, September 1991, p.6). It seems likely that data on major and minor injuries are particularly inadequate for the self-employed. For these reasons, there are grounds for focusing above all on the trends with respect to the number of people killed at work, since this data is both comprehensive and consistent across time.

There are very substantial fluctuations year by year in the number of fatal accidents, reflecting the impact of particular disasters. To provide a clearer view of the longer-term trends, the figures have been converted into the yearly average by decade (Table 8.15). It is immediately clear that the major trend over the century has been one of a substantial decline in the number of people killed as a result of industrial accidents. Indeed, the yearly average is now less than a quarter of the figure in the first two decades of the century. This decline has been progressive since the 1920s. Even if part of the change for the 1920s may be due to a change in the coverage of the statistics, which from 1922 excluded the Republic of Ireland, the strength of the long-term trend suggests that more fundamental factors were at work affecting the physical safety of work.

Table 8.15 Average number of persons killed per year in industrial accidents, United Kingdom, 1900–97

Year	All deaths	Coal mining & shipping as % of all	Aviation as % of all	Deaths excl. shipping, mining & aviation
1900–09	4341	26.7	33.4	2893
1910–19	4566	30.3	27.1	3327
1920–29[c]	3062	34.1	21.6	2400
1930–39	2501	35.2	16.8	2080
1940–49	2425	27.6	12.7	2118
1950–59	1564	25.5	12.2	1373
1960–68	1140	18.5	10.4	1021
1971–79[b]	758	7.7	14.6	647
1980–89/90[a]				605
1990/91–96/97				471

Note: [a]The yearly figures changed in the mid-1980s from a calendar year basis to a year starting 1 April.
[b]The data series from 1971 includes agriculture.
[c]The Republic of Ireland was excluded from the data from 1922.

Source: Figures from 1900–68 are derived from the *British Labour Statistics, Historical Abstract*. Later figures are drawn from: *Health and Safety Statistics UK* and *Employment Gazette*, September 1992, Occasional Supplement, no. 3; Health and Safety Commission: *Health and Safety Statistics* 1994/95, 1995/96 and 1996/97.

One of these underlying factors has been the changing industrial structure of employment. At the beginning of the century, fatal accidents were very heavily concentrated in two industries. In the first decade of the century, a third of all fatal accidents were attributable to the shipping industry and just over a quarter (27 per cent) to the coal mining industry. Already by the 1950s, shipping accidents had fallen to only 12 per cent of all accidents. The average yearly number of fatalities in the coal industry has also been declining since the second decade of the century, although its share of all fatal accidents rose in the inter-war years and still represented a quarter of all deaths in the 1950s. From the 1960s, however, deaths in the coal industry declined sharply both in absolute terms and as a share of all fatal accidents.

It is also clear that the shift to a service-based economy in the second half of the century involved the development of much safer work environments.

This is evident from an examination of the incidence, for each 100 000 people employed, of fatal accidents by industry. Taking the data by broad industrial sector for the 1980s and the first half of the 1990s, the rate of deaths through industrial accidents is consistently high in agriculture and above all in construction (Table 8.16). The energy industries show a highly fluctuating pattern, reflecting the continued prevalence of major collective disasters. For instance, the very high death rate for 1988–89 was due to the Piper Alpha catastrophe in the offshore oil industry. Relative to construction, agriculture and energy, the work environment in manufacturing was clearly very much safer, with average rates that were only a fifth of those in construction and a quarter of those in agriculture. But it was above all in the service sector that there was a consistently low rate of work-related deaths – just over a third of that in manufacturing.

Table 8.16 Average annual incidence rates of fatal injuries for employees per 100 000 people by industrial sector, Great Britain, 1981–96/97

Year	Agriculture	Energy	Manufacturing	Construction	Services
1981–90/91[a]	8.0	11.1	2.1	10.0	0.7
1991/92–96/97[b]	6.5	6.5	1.4	8.0	0.5

Notes: [a]Figures for 1981–90/91 relate to the SIC 80 industry classification.
[b]The figures for 1991/92–96/97 relate to the SIC 92 industry classification. The figures for 1996/97 are provisional.

Sources: *Employment Gazette,* September 1992, Occasional Supplement, no. 3; Health and Safety Commission: *Health and Safety Statistics* 1994/95, 1995/96 and 1996/97.

It could be argued that there were, however, other forms of work-related illness that became more prevalent with the changing structure of the economy and accompanying changes in the organization of work. In particular, it has been suggested that contemporary patterns of work are much more intensive and are more likely to be a source of work stress. This may be accentuated in the service-based economy, since the work is much more likely to involve working with people and, arguably, this is inherently more stressful than working on objects. There is accumulating evidence that the conditions that produce work stress can have severe longer-term consequences for people's health.

There are no reliable time series data on levels of stress. There is, however, an indication of the change in people's experiences in the late 1980s and early 1990s from a national survey which asked people whether the stress in their job had increased, decreased or stayed much the same in the previous five years. Over half of employees (54 per cent) reported that the stress in their job had increased (Table 8.17). While there is some sign that work pressures may have generally intensified, the occupational and industrial pattern is certainly consistent with the view that high levels of stress may be especially associated with the types of work that have been expanding in the last quarter of a century. It was above all those in professional work who reported that their stress levels had increased. Indeed, this was felt by two-thirds of professionals (68 per cent) compared with less than half of non-skilled manual workers (41 per cent). With respect to industry, the proportion reporting increased stress was particularly high in the energy and coal mining sectors (which also had a high and volatile incidence of fatal injuries), but it was also above average in many of the expanding service industries – finance, education, medical services, and welfare. In contrast, employees in manufacturing and especially in agriculture were substantially less likely to report rising levels of stress.

Table 8.17 Change in stress in work over previous five years, Great Britain, 1992 (employees only)[a] percentages

| | Compared with five years ago, stress has: | | | Total |
	increased	no change	decreased	
Professional/managerial	67.5	23.4	9.1	100
Lower non-manual	55.0	32.5	12.4	100
Technicians/supervisors	66.4	27.4	6.2	100
Skilled manual	43.4	44.5	12.1	100
Non-skilled manual	41.0	43.3	15.7	100
All employees	54.1	34.0	12.0	100

Note: [a]Sample size = 3178.

Source: Data are from the Employment in Britain Survey carried out in 1992 (see Gallie et al., 1998).

Working hours

The length of working hours is a more controversial indicator of the quality of employment. Jobs may be poor because they offer too few hours, or people may work long hours because they find their work especially interesting. None the less, there is a clear association between the length of working hours and the strain that people experience in their work, and there can be little doubt that in most jobs very long working hours are likely to produce levels of physical or mental exhaustion that can only be regarded as detrimental to the individual's well-being.

In practice, our measures of working hours are far from satisfactory. The longest consistent series is based on employer records and relates only to the hours of manual workers, a category of the workforce that was rapidly diminishing in the second half of the century. A wider series became available with the New Earnings Survey, but this too was far from comprehensive. It omitted a substantial proportion of part-time workers and the self-employed, both categories that have been expanding considerably in the last quarter of the century. The most reliable source of information for the workforce as a whole – the Labour Force Survey (LFS) – only provides reasonably consistent data from 1979. It collects two types of information on hours – the number of hours actually worked and the number of hours usually worked. Both measures have their problems: average actual hours (which include paid overtime and both paid and unpaid overtime from 1983) are sensitive to holiday breaks and periods of illness, whereas 'usual' hours tend to exclude overtime. Both measures suffer from the high level of proxy information in the LFS, which is thought to lead to an overestimation of hours worked (*Employment Gazette*, May 1995).

Table 8.18 Actual weekly hours of manual workers in manufacturing, 1900–97

	All	Men	Women
1900[a]	54.0	n/a	n/a
1910[a]	54.0	n/a	n/a
1924[b]	45.8	n/a	n/a
1935[b]	47.8	n/a	n/a
1938[b]	46.5	n/a	n/a
1945[b]	47.5	49.6	43.2
1951[b]	46.3	47.9	41.6
1955[b]	47.0	48.9	41.7
1961[b]	45.7	47.7	39.8
1965[b]	45.3	47.3	38.9
1971[b]	43.2	44.7	37.7
1975[b]	42.2	43.6	37.0
1981[b]	42.1	43.0	37.5
1985[c]	43.7	44.5	39.5
1991[c]	43.6	44.4	39.8
1995[c]	44.3	45.2	40.3
1997[c]	44.2	45.1	40.2

Notes: [a]Figures cover 'operatives' in manufacturing.
[b]Figures are for full-time manual workers in industries covered by the regular earnings inquiries.
[c]Figures are for full-time manual employees on adult rates.

Sources: The figures for actual weekly hours for 1900–10 are tentative and are supplied by the London and Cambridge Economic Service, 'The British Economy, Key Statistics 1900–1966' (n.d.); those for 1924–76 are from the *British Labour Historical Abstract* and the *British Labour Yearbook 1976*; those for 1981 are from Bain and Price (1988); and those from 1985 are from the *New Earnings Survey*.

The long-term trend data for manual workers in manufacturing suggest that the greater part of the century witnessed a steady decrease in average working hours, moving from 54 hours a week in 1900 to 42 hours a week in 1975 (Table 8.18). The data for the beginning of the century are very tentative, so it is the decline in hours between the mid-1950s and the mid-1970s that is particularly noteworthy. This contrasts sharply with the pattern in the following two decades, in which the hours of manual workers began to rise again.

Taking the series for the wider workforce, which runs only from 1979–98, the overall picture is one of remarkable stability in hours worked through the 1980s and 1990s (Table 8.19). There is some sign of cyclical variation, with hours declining during the years of high unemployment in the early 1980s and early 1990s, and there may be some slight indication of a renewed tendency for work hours to go down in the most recent years. But, given that this has been a period of expansion of part-time employment, the notable feature is just how little average working hours changed. If full-time and part-time employees are considered separately, there is no sign of a decrease in the working hours of full-time employees between the end of the 1970s and the late 1990s; there has been some reduction among part-time employees, but, even for these, average hours have been very stable since the early 1980s.

Table 8.19 Actual average hours of work, Great Britain, 1979–98

	All main job	All main + second job	All full-time employees: main job	All part-time employees: main job
1979	35.6	35.8	38.5	17.4
1981	32.0	32.1	34.7	15.0
1982	33.7	33.9	36.8	15.8
1983	34.6	34.8	37.8	16.0
1984	33.4	33.7	36.9	15.1
1985	34.1	34.4	37.7	15.5
1986	34.1	34.4	37.9	15.6
1987	33.8	34.1	37.7	15.2
1988	34.5	34.9	38.7	15.4
1989	34.4	34.7	38.4	15.3
1990	34.0	34.4	37.9	15.4
1991	34.0	34.4	38.1	15.2
1992	33.0	33.3	37.4	15.0
1993	33.2	33.6	38.0	15.2
1994	33.3	33.8	38.2	15.5
1995		34.1	38.5	15.6
1996		33.9	38.6	15.5
1997		33.5	38.1	15.5
1998		33.4	38.2	15.5

Sources: For 1979–84 and for 'all main job', *Employment Gazette*, May 1995; for other 1985–97, *Labour Force Survey, Historical Supplement*, 1997, Tables 18a and 17b. Figures are for spring, non-adjusted. For 1998 (UK), *LFS Quarterly Supplement*, no. 2, August 1998.

Finally, in the last decade of the century the working hours of male employees in Britain were relatively high compared to the European average. The available data (Eurostat, 1997) compare countries in terms of average hours *usually* worked rather than the actual hours worked, so the figures are not directly comparable with those used above to assess trends within Britain. The series uses figures for the UK rather than Britain, although these are very similar. It is clear that men in the UK worked the longest hours of men in any country in Europe. Only the southern European countries of Portugal and Greece approached the UK figures. Men in the UK worked approximately four and a half hours a week longer than those in Germany and France, five and half hours longer than those in Sweden and as much as seven hours longer than those in Denmark and the Netherlands. The situation for women was more complex. Women in full-time work also had the longest working hours for women in Europe. However, given that a high proportion of women in the UK worked part-time, the overall hours worked by women were a little lower than the European average (30.6 compared with 32.8). Working time in UK is then highly polarized, and to a considerable extent this reflects a major difference in the working hours of men and women. While men have the longest hours in Europe, women are employed for less than the average working week.

Trade union membership

A third aspect of the quality of employment is the extent to which people can participate in decision-making in their organizations. While there are a range of different forms of participation, in Britain the most prevalent has been that of representation through trade unions. The collective organization of workers was the prerequisite for the joint regulation of terms of employment through collective bargaining. The trends in trade union membership can be taken then as an important indicator of such collective voice.

The only series that provides a picture of trends over the century is that based on returns by the trade unions themselves to the Certification Officer for Trade Unions and Employers' Associations. The coverage of these figures is extensive throughout the period, embracing all organizations which have the objective of negotiating with employers in order to regulate the wages and working conditions of their members. They can include staff associations so long as these are concerned with collective bargaining. The major potential deficiency of the series is its dependence on the records of trade unions which may lack the organizational resources to keep these in a rigorous or up-to-date way.

There are a number of different ways of estimating trade union density (or the proportion of potential membership) depending on the population that is taken to represent the relevant base. This can range from, at the broadest, the whole workforce, including those in self-employment to, at the narrowest, those people who are in work as employees. The current estimates take an intermediary base – trade union density figures are calculated as a proportion of the 'employee workforce'. They include both employees and the unemployed but exclude the self-employed and those in the armed forces.

Since 1989, there has existed an alternative, survey-based, source of figures on union membership from the Labour Force Surveys. This shows consistently lower levels of membership than the administrative figures, partly because the Certification Officers' data include members who are not in employment (for instance the unemployed) and people whose usual residence is not in the United Kingdom. The trends revealed by the two data series for the period in which they can be compared are, however, very similar (see ONS, 1996b, p.53).

The history of trade union membership across the century has been a turbulent one (Figure 8.2). There was a strong upsurge of membership in the militant years immediately prior to 1914. But this was dwarfed by the huge increase in membership in the immediate post-war period, driven by the rise in social aspirations resulting from the human costs and collective endeavour of World War I. At the peak in 1920, union density reached nearly half of the potential membership. However, in the following decade, in the wake of unsuccessful strikes and the onset of much higher levels of unemployment, membership collapsed heavily, reaching its nadir in 1933 when union density was only 22.6 per cent. In absolute terms, membership nearly halved, falling from 8 348 000 in 1920 to 4 392 000 in 1933. The recovery of trade unions in the second half of the 1930s was slow; it was not until the mid-century, in 1948, that union density had returned to the level of 1920.

The second half of the century divides into three distinct phases. Between 1947 and 1969 union density remained very stable. In fact union membership was expanding, but only to the extent of keeping up with an ever-larger workforce. The 1970s, however, saw a sharp increase in union density, with the level rising from 45 per cent in 1969 to a peak of 54 per cent in 1979. This was the high point of union membership strength during the century, with 13 289 000 members. With the economic crisis of the early 1980s and the introduction by the Conservative governments of a major legislative programme to curb union influence, membership levels once more began a precipitous decline. By 1995, union density was down to 33 per cent, a figure lower than at any time since the end of the inter-war years, while absolute membership had fallen to as low as 8 089 000.

The end-of-century decline in trade union strength was accompanied by an important shift in the composition of trade union membership. Throughout the century union density was very much higher among men than among women. The difference was particularly great between the late 1940s and the mid-1960s. But especially since the 1970s there has been a significant convergence between the union density levels for men and women. The unions have lost members among both sexes, but the decline has been much greater among men. Whereas in 1948, women's union density rate was only 43 per cent of that of men, by 1995 it had risen to 79 per cent. Interestingly, the decline of trade unionism has seen the emergence of a much more equal sex distribution of membership.

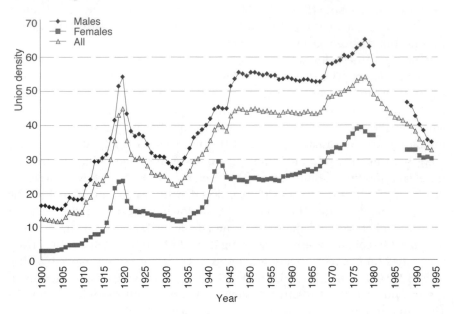

Figure 8.2 Trade union density, UK, 1900–95

Sources: For 1900–74, data are drawn from Bain and Price (1980), Table 2.1. For 1975–82, the membership series is derived from the trade union membership statistics published annually by the Department of Employment; and the potential membership series is compiled from the annual Census of Employment with the addition of the unemployed as estimated by the Department of Employment. The membership series from 1983–95 is from *Labour Market Trends*, February 1997, p.39 and potential membership (excluding self-employed and armed forces, including unemployed) is from *Labour Market Trends, HS,* 1997, Table 1.1. Data on male/female membership from *Employment Gazette*, May 1995, p.207; *Labour Market Trends*, February 1997, p.40.

A second change in the closing three decades of the century was in the occupational composition of trade union members. The great increase in the 1970s was in good part an expansion of trade unionism among white-collar workers. Figures for Great Britain show that between 1971 and 1979, while manual worker membership increased by 602 300, white-collar membership rose by 1 379 000 (Waddington and Whitston, 1995, p.160). This largely reflected the rapidly changing occupational structure. During the decline of membership after 1980, it was above all membership among manual workers that fell, reflecting the collapse of many of the heavily manual traditional manufacturing industries such as steel, coal, textiles and vehicles in which the unions had had a particularly powerful presence. As can be seen in Table 8.20, this trend continued in the 1990s. Between 1991 and 1996, there was a sharp decline in union density among craft workers, plant and machine operatives and the non-skilled. In contrast, there was very little change in union strength among professionals, associate professional and technical workers, or even among clerical workers. The result of this shift was that by the mid-decade union density was higher among professionals and associate professionals than it was among the manual working class which had dominated trade union membership for the greater part of the century.

Table 8.20 Occupational class and trade union density, 1991–96, percentages

Occupational group	Spring 1991	Spring 1996
Managers/administrators	25	20
Professional	52	52
Assoc. Prof. & technical	50	47
Clerical and secretarial	31	27
Craft and related	46	36
Personal & protective	32	28
Sales	15	11
Plant and machine operatives	50	41
Other (non-skilled)	36	26

Sources: *Employment Gazette*, May 1995, p.193; *Labour Market Trends*, June 1997, p.235. Data drawn from Labour Force Surveys.

Where did this sharp decline in membership leave Britain relative to other countries? Trade union membership figures are very difficult to compare cross-nationally, since there are wide variations both in reporting practices and in the notion of what is required for somebody to be counted as a member. But the most careful attempt to date to provide comparative figures for a number of European countries (Visser, 1994) suggests that Britain was still middle-ranking in the strength of its trade unions. For the period 1986–91, the average trade union density in Britain was 41 per cent. By far the highest levels of membership were to be found in the Nordic countries: in Denmark the figure reached 75 per cent and in Sweden 84 per cent. In contrast, membership in France had fallen to only 10 per cent and in the Netherlands to 25 per cent.

Unemployment

The most central issue of public preoccupation with respect to employment trends has unquestionably been that of unemployment. A corollary of this is that unemployment statistics have been unusually controversial. Quite apart from the normal problems of consistency of measurement, it has been suspected that governments may at times have deliberately manipulated unemployment statistics in order to provide a more favourable image of the outcomes of their policies.

There are in practice two main types of measure of unemployment. The first is based on administrative sources, using data either about the number of people registered as seeking work or the number receiving benefit. The second is based on survey data, relying either on people's self-report of their status or their answers to a number of questions about their current employment status and whether or not they are seeking and available for work. The first of these sources gives by far the longest continuous series of data; indeed, it can be tracked back as far as 1881. In contrast, survey-based measures have only been available since the early 1970s and a consistent series only from 1984. Since the administrative series is based upon a complete count, it also does not suffer from problems of sampling error. But it has been subject to frequent changes in administrative procedures, and it is the source that is most vulnerable to deliberate government intervention.

Despite its apparent continuity, the published administrative series in fact is composed of the juxtaposition of six quite separate series. Before 1912, the figures are drawn from the records of a number of trade unions which paid unemployment benefits, most particularly trade unions representing skilled workers. Even by 1912, these covered only 1.4 million members, at a time when membership was 3.4 million. After 1912 and up to 1948, the basis of unemployment figures changed from trade union records to statistics collected with respect to a number of different National Insurance systems. Unemployment rates represent the number of insured unemployed as a percentage of the total number of insured people. Successive National Insurance Acts steadily increased the coverage of National Insurance, thereby altering the base on which unemployment figures were calculated. The first National Insurance Act of 1911 covered some 2.25 million manual workers in a range of industries that were thought to be particularly insecure (building, construction of works, ship-building, mechanical engineering, ironfounding, construction of vehicles and sawmilling). The coverage was extended in 1916, bringing in a further 1.25 million workers, and more notably in 1920, when an additional 8 million workers were brought within the scope of the National Insurance Act.

From 1920 to 1948 there is a reasonably consistent series. From this date the figures cover most manual workers and a substantial proportion of non-manual workers. However their coverage remained far from complete since they excluded agricultural workers, domestic servants, civil servants, nurses, teachers, most railway employees and all other non-manual workers earning more than £250 a year. It is likely that the population that was covered was disproportionately vulnerable to unemployment, leading to an overestimation of the level of unemployment. An alternative series of unemployment estimates has been constructed by Charles Feinstein to make allowance for these potential biases.

It is only for the second half of the century that we have figures based on the full workforce. The National Insurance Act which came into operation in 1948 covered all male and female employees aged 15 or over. This led to a radical revision of the basis of the statistics with the creation of the 'registrant' count, showing the number of people who had registered as unemployed at the Ministry of Labour's Employment Exchanges (later known as job centres). Unemployment rates were now calculated with respect to the overall number of employees in employment. Eligibility depended on people being 'available' and 'capable of work', but it was not directly tied to receipt of or entitlement to benefit. This remained the basis for figures right up to 1982, when it was replaced by what is termed the 'claimant' count, that is to say the number of people claiming unemployment benefit at Unemployment Benefit Offices. Since this excluded unemployed people who were not eligible for benefit, it brought about, by definitional fiat, an immediate reduction in the level of unemployment of around 3.7 per cent.

The claimant count has remained the basis of unemployment figures until the present period. This apparent consistency, however, must be seen in the light of a large number of technical changes in the rules governing eligibility for unemployment benefit that have affected the precise account. The Unemployment [Benefit] Unit has suggested that there were some 31 changes with a significant effect between 1979 and 1996; while the government's statistical office (Office for National Statistics – ONS) considers that there were nine significant discontinuities (ONS, 1996a). This was prior to the alterations introduced by the major revision of the benefit system with the introduction of the Jobseeker's Allowance (see also Chapter 16), which are also likely to have had a substantial impact on the count.

Given the weaknesses in the continuity of the series, the comparative figures over time must be regarded with some caution. None the less, the differences between historical periods are so substantial, and fit sufficiently well with other evidence, that we can have some confidence in the broad pattern that emerges from the trend data (Figures 8.3 and 8.4). Unemployment rates fluctuated sharply in the first decade of the century. They rose very sharply immediately after World War I when governments failed to anticipate the problems of the reintegration of the members of the armed forces, and then settled down to what was still a relatively high level by the standards of the first decade of the century. With the Depression at the end of the decade, the number of people unemployed doubled from 1 276 000 in 1929 to 2 813 000 by 1932. Although the level declined sharply in the remaining years of the 1930s, it was not until 1937 that it had returned to a level that was comparable with the 1920s.

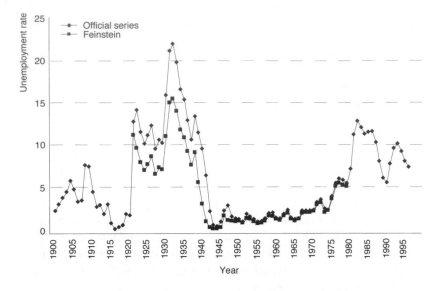

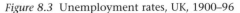

Figure 8.3 Unemployment rates, UK, 1900–96

Sources: *British Labour Statistics, Historical Abstract*, Tables 160, 161, 165, 166, 167; 'Unemployment Statistics from 1881 to the present day', *Labour Market Trends*, January 1996; *Labour Market Trends*, November 1997; Feinstein, C. (1972) *National Income, Expenditure and Output of the United Kingdom 1855–1965*, Cambridge University Press, Cambridge, Table 57.

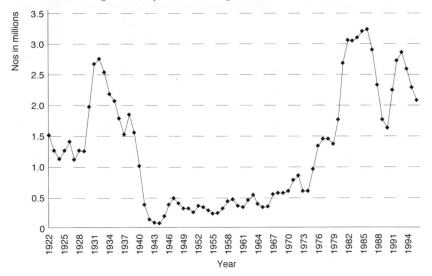

Figure 8.4 Numbers unemployed, UK, 1900–96

Sources: *British Labour Statistics, Historical Abstract*, Tables 160, 161, 165, 166, 167; 'Unemployment Statistics from 1881 to the present day', *Labour Market Trends*, January 1996; *Labour Market Trends*, November 1997.

The post-war period divides into two quite distinct phases. The years between 1945 and 1974 saw levels of peace-time unemployment that were unprecedentedly low for the century, with an unemployment rate lower than 2 per cent until 1962 and lower than 3 per cent until 1971. Then from the time of the 'oil crisis' of the early 1970s, the unemployment rate rose, accelerating sharply with the two recessions of the early 1980s and early 1990s. Finally, in the mid-1990s, there was a relatively sharp decline in the unemployment rate, which returned to a level close to that at the end of the 1970s.

There has been some speculation as to whether the unemployment crises of the final two decades of the century reached proportions similar to those of the Great Depression in the early 1930s. Given the very different ways in which the statistics have been estimated for different periods, any conclusion is bound to be tentative. On the basis of the available data it would seem that the unemployment rate in this period did not reach the level of the worst years of the 1930s, peaking at 13 per cent in 1982 compared to an estimated rate of 15.6 per cent in 1932. However, the absolute number of people unemployed was greater in the 1980s than at the height of the economic crisis of the inter-war years, with 3 292 900 unemployed in 1986 compared with 2 813 100 in 1932. This difference in pattern between the rate and the absolute level of unemployment must be seen in the context of the expansion over the century in the size of the active population, affecting the base upon which unemployment rates are calculated.

What does the arrival of alternative survey-based series of unemployment statistics from the early 1980s tell us about the nature and reliability of the 'official' count? To begin with, it should be noted that the broad picture of change in the level of unemployment provided by the administrative and the survey-based (or International Labour Organization – ILO) measures is very similar. The difference lies in the precise level of unemployment recorded and in the composition of unemployment. Taking the period 1987–96, the ILO measure gave a somewhat higher number of people unemployed, although the amount of the difference varied substantially depending on the particular year. There is some sign that the gap was greater in the years of economic recovery after the recession of the early 1980s and reduced when recession returned in the early 1990s. At the point of greatest divergence, in 1990, the ILO measure gave an unemployment rate of 6.7 per cent, while the administrative count gave a rate of 5.8 per cent.

One source of difference between the measures is likely to lie in the type of people covered. The ILO measure defines the unemployed as people who are without work, available for work and actively seeking work, whether or not they are eligible for social security benefits. As a result, it provides substantially higher estimates of the number of women unemployed, since women (particularly when returning to the labour market after bringing up children) are less likely to be eligible for benefit. It is notable, however, that even on the basis of the ILO measure, which is better at recording female unemployment, the consistent pattern that emerges is that men in Britain are considerably more likely to experience unemployment than women (Table 8.21). In this respect, unemployment patterns in Britain differ sharply from those in most other EU countries.

Table 8.21 Unemployment rates, United Kingdom, 1984–97

Year	Men	ILO survey-based count Women	All	All Administrative count
1984	11.8	11.5	11.7	11.5
1985	11.4	10.7	11.1	11.7
1986	11.5	10.6	11.1	11.8
1987	11.0	10.2	10.7	10.5
1988	8.9	8.4	8.6	8.3
1989	7.2	6.9	7.1	6.3
1990	6.9	6.5	6.7	5.8
1991	9.1	7.2	8.3	8.0
1992	11.4	7.3	9.6	9.8
1993	12.3	7.6	10.3	10.3
1994	11.3	7.3	9.6	9.4
1995	10.0	6.8	8.6	8.3
1996	9.6	6.3	8.1	7.6
1997	8.1	5.8	7.1	
1998	6.3	5.5	6.9	

Sources: Labour Force Surveys (Spring). Unadjusted figures from *LFS Historical Supplement*, 1997, pp.9; 55; *Labour Force Survey, Quarterly Supplement*, no. 3, November 1998.

Is there any evidence that the return of higher unemployment led to a shift in the class composition of the unemployed? It is clear from historical accounts that, in the inter-war period, the burden of unemployment fell primarily on the manual working class. A number of surveys have shown that this was also true for the better part of the post-war period (Gallie et al., 1993; White, 1991). But there has been some suggestion that, with the emergence of new technologies since the 1980s, the traditionally secure non-manual occupations may have been becoming increasingly vulnerable, leading to less marked class inequalities in unemployment.

Table 8.22 Unemployment rates relative to managers, 1991–97, percentages

	Profs	Assistant profs	Clerical service	Craft	Personal	Sales	Operatives	Other (non-skilled)
1991	63.6	115.2	148.5	263.6	184.8	206.1	293.9	306.1
1992	58.7	108.7	145.7	282.6	169.6	169.6	287.0	302.2
1995	69.2	102.6	148.7	256.4	187.2	215.4	276.9	328.2
1997	59.4	93.8	146.9	225.0	181.3	196.9	268.8	340.6

Source: Labour Force Surveys.

While the time-period of data for assessing such change is relatively limited, it is possible to compare the occupational background of unemployed people from 1991–97. For each year, the unemployment rate of a given occupational class has been calculated as a proportion of that of managers (Table 8.22). It can be seen that the rank order of occupations in terms of vulnerability to unemployment remained unchanged. Professionals were the least likely of all to be unemployed, followed by associate professionals who had similar unemployment rates to managers. Personal service and sales workers had a considerably higher risk of unemployment. But by far the most vulnerable groups were the craft, operative and non-skilled workers. Although the class hierarchy in job security remained, there were some shifts over time in relative vulnerability. In particular, there was some decline in the relative rates of craft workers and operatives. This did not, however, indicate a general decrease in class differentials, for the relative rate of the non-skilled increased sharply over the period. While more skilled manual workers may have improved their position, that of the non-skilled deteriorated even further.

Table 8.23 Unemployment in Europe, 1985–97 (% of labour force)

	Average 1985–95	1996	1997
Austria	5.1	6.3	6.2
Belgium	11.1	12.8	12.7
Denmark	9.7	8.6	7.6
Finland	9.2	16.3	14.5
France	10.4	12.3	12.4
Germany	7.8	10.3	11.4
Greece	8.2	10.3	10.4
Ireland	15.2	11.9	10.2
Italy	10.0	12.1	12.3
Luxembourg	1.8	3.3	3.6
Netherlands	7.1	6.7	5.6
Norway	4.3	4.9	4.1
Portugal	6.2	7.3	6.7
Spain	19.5	22.2	20.8
Sweden	4.0	8.1	8.0
United Kingdom	9.1	8.0	6.9
EU average	9.9	11.4	11.2

Source: OECD (1998), p.5.

Finally, for the limited period in which good comparative data are available, how did Britain's unemployment record compare with that of other European countries? The OECD provides an adjusted comparative series (see Table 8.23), which includes data for the UK. Given that the level of unemployment fluctuates so considerably over the business cycle, it is particularly instructive to look at the average figures for the ten-year period 1985–95. It can be seen that in longer-term perspective, the UK's level of unemployment has been very close indeed to the European average (9.1 per cent compared with 9.9 per cent). It has had much higher levels of unemployment than countries such as Austria, Norway and Sweden, but lower unemployment than countries such as Belgium, France, and Italy, and much lower than Ireland and especially Spain. In the mid-1990s, the position of the UK improved substantially compared to the European average, reflecting its earlier move into a phase of economic growth after the recession of the early 1990s. If the UK's pattern has been distinctive it has been less in terms of its average level of unemployment, taken over the longer-term, than in the abruptness with which it has moved between periods of very sharp recession and periods of particularly rapid growth.

Conclusion

In the course of the century the nature of work changed fundamentally. In the early decades of the century, the core industries had been manufacturing industries and work primarily involved the production of objects. By the end of the century the core industries were service industries and work primarily involved dealing with people. This transformation was accompanied by a major shift in the structure of occupations. Whereas in the first decade of the century, manual workers constituted three-quarters of the workforce, by the close of the century, they represented only just over a third. In their place, the intervening decades had seen a massive increase first of the clerical workforce and then of professional and managerial occupations. These changes involved a substantial upskilling of the workforce, a process that was accelerated in the final two decades of the century by the rapid spread of new computer technologies.

The rise of the service industries was paralleled by a marked change in the position of women in employment. In the first half of the century, only 30 per cent of the workforce were women; but from the mid-century the proportion rose continuously, reaching 44 per cent in 1997. This largely reflected the growing tendency for married women, especially those in the child-rearing years, to remain economically active. It was more questionable, however, how far women became fully integrated into the employment structure. While the extremes of gender segregation certainly declined, it remained the case that at the end of the century the majority of women still worked in female-dominated occupations. Similarly, although women's share of higher professional occupations showed a very marked increase in the final decades of the century, the majority of such jobs were still held by men. But if there was still far to go in terms of women having an equal share of the most skilled and best rewarded occupations, it is clear that by the end of the century their commitment to employment had become every bit as strong as men's. There had been a revolution in the centrality of employment in women's lives that was unlikely to be reversed rapidly.

The later decades of the century also witnessed the growing importance of new types of employment – in particular, part-time work, temporary work contracts and self-employment. Given the dearth of truly comparable data for the early part of the century, it is difficult to assess just how far-reaching a change this was in longer-term historical perspective. But it was clearly an important change from the type of employment pattern that characterized the mid-century. It seems unlikely that it can be accounted for solely in terms of the desire of employers to create an insecure peripheral workforce to help meet the uncertainties of an increasingly competitive and global market. In part the new patterns of work corresponded to the more complex hour schedules required for the provision of services; in part they reflected the new opportunities available to highly skilled people to work outside traditional employment structures in a period of rapid technical change. Types of employment became more diversified, but this did not lead to any simple polarization between a core and a peripheral workforce.

How far were the changes in the nature of work over the century accompanied by an improvement in the quality of employment conditions? In one respect there was clearly outstanding progress. There was a dramatic fall over the century in the number of people who were killed at work. While in good part this reflected the decline of employment in exceptionally dangerous industries such as shipping and coal mining, it is also clear that there was a more general improvement in physical safety at work. However, against this, there is also evidence that the changing patterns of work may have increased certain types of health problem. In particular, the greater complexity and the more intensive pace of work, may well have increased the psychological stress of work. Certainly, greater work demands were not offset by any progressive reduction in working hours. While average working hours did decline from the first half of the century, this trend largely ceased in precisely the period when technological change accelerated in the 1980s. Nor did the century see any sustained trend towards greater citizenship at work, with employees gaining greater control over the decisions that affected their lives. After the major expansion of trade union membership in the immediate post-war decades, there was a very sharp decline in union strength during the 1980s and 1990s. Finally, despite the 30 post-war years of relatively full-employment, it was clear by the end of the century that the scourge of unemployment remained as threatening as ever, especially for manual workers. The last two decades of the century saw the return of mass unemployment on a scale that bore comparison with the deepest crisis of the inter-war years, in absolute if not relative terms.

Acknowlededgments

The chapter builds upon its predecessor: authored by George Bain and Robert Price (1988). I am very much indebted to Jo Webb for her help in updating many of the statistics in the chapter and to Justine Gallie for assistance with data preparation for the tables.

Notes

1   For a description of the Social Change and Economic Life Initiative surveys, see Gallie et al. (1993); for the Employment in Britain surveys, Gallie et al. (1998).
2   The figures for 1986 are taken from the Social Change and Economic Life Initiative surveys; for 1992, from the Employment in Britain survey.

References

Ashworth, W. (1972) *An Economic History of England 1870–1939*, Methuen, London.

Bain, G. S. (1970) *The Growth of White-Collar Unionism*, Clarendon Press, Oxford.

Bain, G. S. and Price, R. (1980) *Profiles of Union Growth: A Comparative Statistical Portrait of Eight Countries*, Blackwell, Oxford.

Bain, G. S. and Price, R. (1988) 'The labour force', in Halsey, A. H. (ed.) *British Social Trends since 1900*, Macmillan, Basingstoke.

Beatson, M. (1995) *Labour Market Flexibility*, Employment Department, Research Series, no. 48, London.

Central Statistical Office (CSO) (1996) *Social Trends 26*, HMSO, London.

Erikson, R. and Goldthorpe, J. H. (1992) *The Constant Flux. A Study of Class Mobility in Industrial Societies*, Oxford University Press, Oxford.

Eurostat (1997) *Labour Force Survey. Results 1996*. Office for Official Publications of the European Communities, Luxembourg.

Gallie, D., Marsh, C. and Vogler, C. (1993) *Social Change and the Experience of Unemployment*, Oxford University Press, Oxford.

Gallie, D., White, M., Cheng, Y. and Tomlinson, M. (1998) *Restructuring the Employment Relationship*, Clarendon Press, Oxford.

Hakim, C. (1979) *Occupational Segregation,* Department of Employment Research Paper no. 9, London.

Marsh, D. C. (1958) *The Changing Social Structure of England and Wales 1871–1951*, Routledge and Kegan Paul, London.

Office for National Statistics (ONS) (1996a) *Labour Market Trends*, January.

Office for National Statistics (1996b) *Labour Market Trends*, February.

Office for National Statistics (1997) *Labour Market Trends*, September.

Office for National Statistics (1998a) *Labour Force Survey, Historical Supplement 1997*, ONS, London.

Office for National Statistics (1998b) *Labour Market Trends, Historical Supplement, No. 5* ONS, London.

Organization for Economic Co-operation and Development (OECD) (1998) *Employment Outlook 1998*, OECD, Paris.

Routh, G. (1981) *Occupation and Pay in Great Britain*, Cambridge University Press, Cambridge.

Routh, G. (1987) *Occupations of the People of Great Britain*, Macmillan, Basingstoke.

Visser, J. (1994) 'European trade unions: the transition years', in Hyman, R. and Ferner, A. (eds) *New Frontiers in European Industrial Relations*, Blackwell, Oxford.

Waddington, J. and Whitston, C. (1995) 'Trade unions: growth, structure and policy', in Edwards, P. (ed.) *Industrial Relations: Theory and Practice in Britain*, Blackwell, Oxford.

Warr, P. B. (1982) 'A national study of non-financial employment commitment', *Journal of Occupational Psychology*, 55, pp.297–312.

White, M. (1991) *Against Unemployment*, Policy Studies Institute, London.

Further Reading

Changes in occupations and skills

The seminal contributions on trends in the occupational structure are:

Routh, G. (1981) *Occupation and Pay in Great Britain*, Cambridge University Press, Cambridge.

Routh, G. (1987) *Occupations of the People of Great Britain*, Macmillan, Basingstoke.

For an examination, using a variety of research techniques, of developments in skill and the way they are related to technological change:

Penn, R., Rose, M. and Rubery J. (eds) (1994) *Skill and Occupational Change*, Oxford University Press, Oxford.

For an assessment of the broader implications of skill change between the 1980s and 1990s for the nature of work and for conditions of employment:

Gallie, D., White, M., Cheng, Y. and Tomlinson, M. (1998) *Restructuring the Employment Relationship*, Clarendon Press, Oxford.

Women's employment and gender segregation

The path-breaking study was:

Martin, M. and Roberts, C. (1984) *Women and Employment: A Lifetime Perspective*, HMSO, London.

Catherine Hakim has made a number of influential contributions to the analysis of gender segregation; *inter alia*:

Hakim, C. (1979) *Occupational Segregation*, Department of Employment Research Paper no. 9, London.

Hakim, C. (1998) *Social Change and Innovation in the Labour Market*, Oxford University Press, Oxford.

For an interesting analysis deploying a range of research methodologies:

Scott, A. (1994) *Gender Segregation and Social Change*, Oxford University Press, Oxford.

A wider perspective on the changing characteristics of women's work in Europe is given in:

Rubery, J., Smith, M., Fagan, C. and Grimshaw, D. (1998) *Women and European Employment*, Routledge, London.

Non-standard contracts and flexible labour

For a still-interesting theoretical discussion of why employers may be looking for greater flexibility in employment practices:

Berger, S. and Piore, M. (1980) *Dualism and Discontinuity in Industrial Societies,* Cambridge University Press, Cambridge.

The study which, perhaps because of its conciseness, most influenced the British debate:

Atkinson, J. (1984) 'Manpower strategies for flexible organizations', *Personnel Management*, August, pp.28–31.

For a sophisticated approach, both theoretically and empirically, to the issues of flexibility:

Rubery, J. and Wilkinson, F. (eds.) (1994) *Employer Strategy and the Labour Market*, Oxford University Press, Oxford.

An unusually rigorous study of the employment conditions associated with part-time work in Britain and their longer-term career implications is:

Tam, M. (1997) *Part-time work: A Bridge or a Trap*, Avebury, Aldershot.

For an interesting discussion, comparing Britain and France, of the way strategies for flexibility can vary between societies:

O'Reilly, J. (1994) *Banking on Flexibility*, Avebury, Aldershot.

The most comprehensive study of the characteristics of people on non-standard contracts in Britain:

Dex S. and McCulloch, A. (1997) *Flexible Employment*, Macmillan, Basingstoke.

Trade unionism

The authoritative account of the growth of British trade unionism in the early part of the century is:

Clegg, H. A., Fox, A. and Thompson, A. F. (1964) *A History of British Trade Unions since 1889*, volume 1, 1889–1910, Clarendon Press, Oxford.

For a well informed analysis of the state of play in the more recent period:

Edwards, P. K. (1995) *Industrial Relations. Theory and Practice in Britain*, Blackwell, Oxford.

And for an analysis of the causes of trade union decline towards the end of the century:

Gallie, D., Penn, R. and Rose, M. (eds) (1994) *Trade Unionism in Recession*, Oxford University Press, Oxford.
Milward, N. (1994) *The New Industrial Relations*, Policy Studies Institute, London.

Unemployment

A good guide to the minefield of British unemployment statistics remains:

Garsfield, W. R. (1980) *The Measurement of Unemployment in Great Britain 1850–1979. Methods and Sources,* Blackwell, Oxford.

The classic study on the socially constructed nature of unemployment figures is:

Salais, R., Baverez, N. and Reynaud, B. (1986) *L'invention du chômage*, Presses universitaires de France, Paris.

On the context and nature of the re-emergence of mass unemployment in the 1980s:

McLaughlin, E. (ed.) (1992) *Understanding Unemployment*, Routledge, London.
White, M. (1991) *Against Unemployment*, Policy Studies Institute, London.

For the impact of unemployment on people's lives:

Gallie, D., Marsh, C. and Vogler, C. (1994) *Social Change and the Experience of Unemployment*, Oxford University Press, Oxford.

9

The Economic Environment

Andrew Dilnot and Carl Emmerson

> Be fruitful, …. and replenish the earth, and subdue it
>
> Genesis 1.28

> increased productivity is the one characteristic achievement of the age, as religion was of the Middle Ages or art of classical Athens … the century … has seen the greatest increase in productivity since the fall of the Roman Empire …
>
> R. H. Tawney, *The Acquisitive Society*, 1921

A great deal of the change that has occurred during the twentieth century has been due to greater affluence, which itself was a result of the impact of technological advances on economic growth. Whilst economic success is far from being the perfect indicator of a country's, or indeed an individual's, well-being, it is likely at least to indicate the potential for greater choice. Continued economic growth, especially since the end of World War II, and a substantially larger role played by government, have led to many changes. These include the introduction and expansion of the social security system, the National Health Service and greater access to education. Changes described in other chapters such as health, housing and family structure are all likely to have been affected by higher levels of income. This chapter shows how both level and composition of incomes have changed over the century. It also details how the allocation of this income has changed between different types of private and public consumption and investment.

Guide to the statistics used

Where possible, series are shown from 1900 to 1995. All information relates to the United Kingdom, which in the years until 1920 includes Southern Ireland, something which should be considered when making comparisons between years before and after this date.[1] For the years 1900 to 1965 the main source used is Feinstein (1976). For years beyond 1965, statistics come from the Central Statistical Office publication *United Kingdom National Accounts: The Blue Book* (in more recent years produced by the Office for National Statistics).

In addition, data on long-term trends in government expenditure and revenue are from the October 1987 edition of *Economic Trends*, with more recent years coming from *Stability and Investment for the Long Term: Economic and Fiscal Strategy Report 1998* (HM Treasury, 1998)

Finally, a table presenting a comparison of Gross Domestic Product (GDP) per capita amongst the 25 OECD countries is from a House of Commons Library publication (1998), *GDP per capita in OECD Countries: The UK's Relative Position*.

Graphs are used to show changes in composition of income and expenditure over time. These show, for example, interesting trends in the composition of both private and public spending as incomes grew. Generally, tables are used to present the statistics in five-yearly intervals in constant 1997 price levels.[2] Whilst this makes comparisons over time easier, over longer periods they can only be interpreted with caution. Using a general price deflator will ignore relative changes in prices, making it difficult to see whether, for example, a reduction in 'real' spending on an item actually reflects a reduction in the quantity consumed. In addition, changes in the quality of products, and indeed the introduction of new ones, will be more significant over longer time-periods. Notes for individual figures are contained within the main text, whilst those relating to tables are given in the relevant footnote.

How big is the UK economy?

We begin by looking at the level of GDP, after adjusting for price changes over the century, in Figure 9.1. This shows the logarithm of GDP at factor cost in 1997 prices. The logarithm is used so that comparisons in growth of GDP between different periods are more easily made. A constant slope would imply constant percentage growth in GDP. The most striking feature, and the most important, is the very substantial growth in GDP which has persisted throughout the period. As can be seen in Table 9.1, which provides the data behind Figures 9.1 and 9.2, over the century as a whole the real level of GDP will have increased sevenfold.

The average annual rate of growth is very slightly less than 2 per cent, although there have been significant fluctuations. Over the first quarter of the century, growth averaged less than 1 per cent p.a., rising to 2.2 per cent p.a. in the second quarter, 2.9 per cent in the third, and 2 per cent in the last.

The scale of these increases is hard to grasp; since the end of World War II, GDP has more than trebled in real terms, while over a lifetime of 75 years, GDP has typically risen by a factor of around four and a half. It is this dynamic of

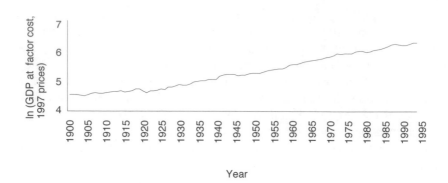

Figure 9.1 GDP at factor cost, 1900–95 (logarithmic scale)

Sources: Feinstein (1976) for the years to 1965; CSO (various years) thereafter.

Table 9.1 GDP at factor cost, by income, 1900–95 in 1997 prices (£ billion)

Year	Employment	Self-employment	Private companies	Public corporations
1900	54.558	19.386	13.805	0
1905	54.187	18.399	13.532	0
1910	58.364	18.697	14.833	0
1915	68.697	a	38.411	0
1920	75.499	16.461	13.594	0
1925	74.699	20.134	14.452	0
1930	85.633	21.227	14.163	0
1935	99.076	23.996	19.609	0.305
1940	114.675	23.603	33.093	2.298
1945	139.216	25.389	31.914	2.813
1950	143.921	26.210	40.118	3.699
1955	162.026	23.935	41.587	4.539
1960	191.825	25.351	47.298	6.818
1965	225.547	26.766	51.237	10.577
1970	259.701	35.241	50.839	12.300
1975	315.689	42.103	53.852	14.260
1980	324.617	42.740	65.641	14.864
1985	327.769	50.623	85.158	12.091
1990	391.877	73.301	82.063	4.747
1995	399.435	71.543	96.216	4.898

Note: [a]For the years 1914–19 separate figures were unavailable for self-employment and private company income, and similarly for public corporations and other government bodies between 1939 and 1945. Figure 9.2 makes the assumption of a constant change in the relative proportions between these years.

increased income that has driven and made possible many of the enormous social changes Britain has seen during the century, and the massive increase in average material standards of living. Table 9.2 shows that this growth in GDP has been greater than the increase in population over the century. Despite the population growing by 50 per cent between 1900 and 1995, GDP per capita by the end of the period was over four times larger.

An important issue is what does this increase in average income actually mean for the 'well-being' of the population? The answer will depend on what is actually meant by 'well-being'. Certainly individuals today can, on average, afford to consume much larger quantities of goods, services and leisure than those living at the start of the century. Of course, average incomes may not be as good a measure of well-being as is first imagined. First, there are problems of measurement, discussed in Chapter 1, since GDP only records economic transactions. Second, an individual's 'well-being' may be in part influenced by his or her income relative to that of the population as a whole. (Changes in

Other government bodies	Rent	Total domestic income	Stock appreciation	GDP at factor cost
0.480	12.544	100.774	0	100.774
0.772	13.472	100.361	0	100.361
0.966	13.582	106.443	0	106.443
1.148	11.435	119.691	−8.830	110.861
0.438	4.903	110.895	4.378	115.273
1.297	8.955	119.536	4.292	123.829
1.861	12.475	135.359	7.340	142.699
2.289	15.756	161.031	−0.992	160.039
[a]	14.472	188.141	−14.920	173.221
[a]	9.574	208.907	−1.182	207.725
2.623	10.171	226.742	−12.266	214.476
1.614	11.398	245.100	−2.824	242.275
2.264	15.737	289.293	−1.708	287.585
1.020	19.464	334.611	−3.763	330.848
1.522	26.767	386.368	−9.019	377.349
0.585	34.305	460.794	−25.446	435.348
0.424	38.542	486.827	−15.057	471.770
0.440	41.134	517.214	−4.559	512.655
0.015	53.782	605.786	−7.658	598.129
0.648	71.334	644.073	−5.181	638.892

Sources: Feinstein (1976) for the years to 1965; CSO (various years) thereafter.

Table 9.2 Aggregate and per capita GDP at factor cost, by income, 1900–95 in 1997 prices (£ billion)

Year	GDP at factor cost	Population (millions)	GDP per capita (£)
1900	100.774	41.155	2449
1905	100.361	42.981	2335
1910	106.443	44.916	2370
1915	110.861	46.340	2392
1920	115.273	43.718	2637
1925	123.829	45.059	2748
1930	142.699	45.866	3111
1935	160.039	46.868	3415
1940	173.221	48.226	3592
1945	207.725	49.182	4224
1950	214.476	50.565	4242
1955	242.275	50.947	4755
1960	287.585	52.352	5493
1965	330.848	54.350	6087
1970	377.349	55.632	6783
1975	435.348	56.226	7743
1980	471.770	56.330	8375
1985	512.655	56.685	9044
1990	598.129	57.561	10391
1995	638.892	58.606	10901

Sources: Feinstein (1976) for the years to 1965; CSO (various years) thereafter. Population for the years are, from 1965 onwards, mid-year estimates from CSO (1996).

the distribution of income and wealth over the century are discussed in Chapter 10.) Third, other factors in addition to absolute and relative income, such as job satisfaction and security, are also likely to affect an individual's 'well-being'. Hence changes in incomes should be considered alongside those described in the other chapters in this book, on subjects as diverse as health, crime, the labour force and social mobility.[3]

Composition of national income and expenditure

Figure 9.2 shows how the component parts of national income have changed over the century. This is from the same data as presented in real terms in Table 9.1, but with other government bodies being included as public corporations. In addition, a constant change in the relative percentage coming from self-employment and private companies is assumed for the years 1914–19 since separate data are unavailable.

The share of employment grew slowly from 54 per cent at the start of the century to 68 per cent around the mid-1960s, mirroring a decline in the contribution of self-employment. Since then, the process has been reversed, with a

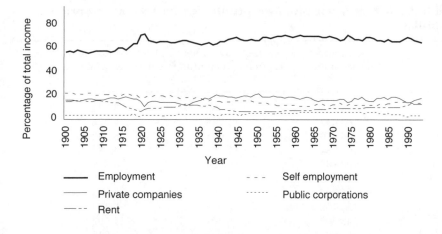

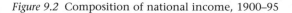

Figure 9.2 Composition of national income, 1900–95

Sources: Feinstein (1976) for data up to 1965; CSO (various years) thereafter.

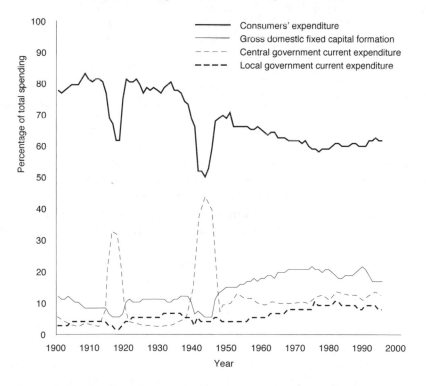

Figure 9.3 Composition of national expenditure, 1900–95

Sources: Feinstein (1976) for data up to 1965; CSO (various years) thereafter.

Table 9.3 GDP at factor cost, by expenditure,[a] 1900–95 in 1997 prices (£ billion)

Year	Consumers' expenditure	Central government current expenditure	Local government current expenditure
1900	98.253	7.382	3.541
1905	103.032	4.748	4.926
1910	106.670	5.001	5.342
1915	105.254	41.457	4.680
1920	109.888	6.064	4.619
1925	119.753	5.744	6.979
1930	135.497	6.203	9.063
1935	150.120	7.973	10.453
1940	143.202	76.301	11.787
1945	151.083	88.839	10.212
1950	178.529	28.135	10.775
1955	188.915	33.489	12.191
1960	214.924	36.230	16.432
1965	244.022	40.692	22.227
1970	272.969	46.589	30.235
1975	302.304	64.779	44.233
1980	326.457	73.114	44.649
1985	362.113	78.823	46.497
1990	434.061	87.565	53.490
1995	472.740	102.173	55.821

Note: [a]GDP at factor cost by expenditure will differ from GDP at factor cost by income in Table 9.1 due to measurement error.

slight decline in employment income and growth in self-employment income. Gross trading profits of private companies have fluctuated markedly with the economic cycle, falling in the early 1980s and early 1990s for example, but are otherwise relatively stable. Profits from public corporations rose after the post-war nationalization programme and then fell away during the 1980s as most were sold back into the private sector.

Figure 9.3 decomposes national expenditure. Between 1900 and the early 1970s there was a steady decline in the share of total expenditure which went to private consumption, with sharp falls occurring during the two world wars. Since the early 1970s, the share of consumers' expenditure has risen slightly as the share of gross domestic fixed capital formation (broadly speaking, investment) and of local government spending have fallen by more than enough to offset the continued rise in central government spending. Before the 1970s the century saw a steady rise in the share of local and central spending, and a rapid rise in gross domestic capital formation in the third quarter of the century, driven by large-scale public investment, which has subsequently fallen back rapidly.

Gross domestic fixed capital formation	Gross domestic product at factor cost	Gross national product at factor cost
11.914	109.356	115.599
10.505	113.180	120.481
7.729	117.581	127.242
5.740	129.404	136.688
10.551	122.847	128.232
12.970	130.159	137.323
14.990	145.697	153.106
17.396	160.192	167.097
15.517	200.465	205.240
8.274	205.053	206.945
32.079	215.911	223.383
40.766	242.088	244.595
52.118	285.371	288.294
67.299	327.829	332.825
82.756	375.777	380.843
96.950	445.815	449.921
97.918	475.422	474.991
101.095	512.657	516.478
134.364	598.129	599.714
111.392	638.259	648.376

Sources: Feinstein (1976) for the years to 1965; CSO (various years) thereafter.

Table 9.3 shows each component of GDP by expenditure in real terms. Both GDP and GNP at factor cost are given. The difference between these is that GDP represents income generated *domestically*, whilst GNP represents income generated by *nationals*, and hence includes net property income from abroad. (For a more thorough explanation of national accounts, see the introductory chapter in a recent edition of the government publication, *United Kingdom National Accounts: The Blue Book* (CSO, various years).)

Public finances

Figure 9.4 illustrates the development of the state during the twentieth century. The dramatic peaks in the size of state activity occur during the century's two world wars, running from 1914–18 and 1939–45, although the peaks extend a little either side of both wars reflecting the process of preparation and demobilization. Less noticeable 'war effects' can be seen at the very beginning of the century, arising from the Boer War of 1899–1902 and again during the

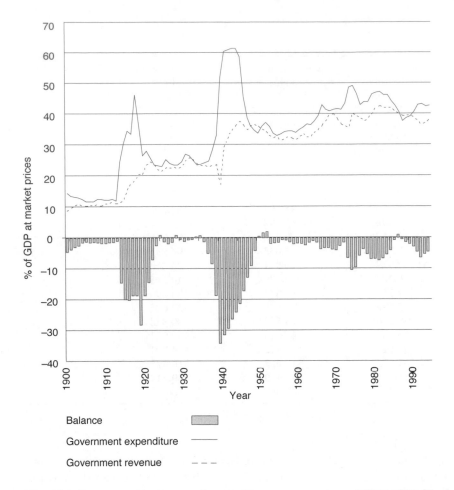

Balance

Government expenditure

Government revenue

Figure 9.4 Government revenue and expenditure as a percentage of GDP, 1900–95

Sources: Feinstein (1976) for data up to 1965; CSO (various years) thereafter.

Korean War in 1951–52. The Gulf War in late 1990/early 1991 had relatively little to do with the rise in public spending as a share of GDP seen at that time, which largely reflected a domestic economic recession.

While tax revenue also tended to be increased during war-time, it is clear from Figure 9.4 that much of the additional spending was financed by borrowing. This had the effect of spreading the burden of financing each of the two main wars across future generations.

The scale of taxation and public spending had been rising for several decades before the beginning of the century, as the state took on growing responsibilities, although still quite small by modern standards, in education, public health and welfare. In the early decades of the century, epitomized by the introduction of old-age pensions in 1908 and the so-called 'People's Budget' of 1911 which introduced higher rates of income tax on those with very high incomes, the role of government activity in tax-financed redistribution grew. The effect of war seems to have been to 'ratchet-up' expectations of government, both reflecting a sense of the competence of government to achieve its objectives, and the increased sense of community which flowed from war-time experience.

In the inter-war years there was a steady expansion of social security provision, and of educational and health care activity. And we should not neglect the effect of increased longevity on the numbers of people living into retirement and so receiving payments from the state. In the aftermath of World War II the whole range of 'Welfare State' activity was reformed, with the Beveridge report forming the basis of the new social security system, the Butler White Paper forming the basis of education, and the founding of the National Health Service in 1948.

Figure 9.5 shows a more detailed breakdown of the composition of current public spending over the century (real terms data are shown in Table 9.4). General government spending on goods and services, such as health care, education, personal social services, roads, defence, and law and order, dominated massively at the beginning of the period, and continued to do so until the end of World War I, when the very large debt built up during the war began to be paid off, leading to a dramatic jump in the burden of debt service payments, and a corresponding fall in the share of total spending devoted to goods and services. At the same time, the steady increase in the number of elderly, growing unemployment and a developing social security system, led to a growth in the share of transfer payments. The 1939–45 war, and preparation for it, saw large

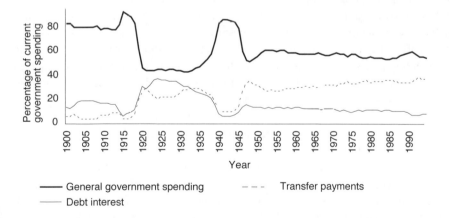

Figure 9.5 Composition of current government expenditure, 1900–95

Sources: Feinstein (1976) for data up to 1965; CSO (various years) thereafter.

Table 9.4 Total current government expenditure, by source, 1900–95 in 1997 prices (£ billion)

Year	Current expenditure		Subsidies and grants
	Central government	Local authorities	
1900	7.382	3.541	0.660
1905	4.748	4.926	0.415
1910	5.001	5.342	0.909
1915	41.457	4.680	1.280
1920	6.064	4.619	6.129
1925	5.744	6.979	4.601
1930	6.203	9.063	4.755
1935	7.973	10.453	7.821
1940	76.301	11.787	8.236
1945	88.839	10.212	15.862
1950	28.135	10.775	16.851
1955	33.489	12.191	13.243
1960	36.230	16.432	15.724
1965	40.692	22.227	18.050
1970	46.189	30.235	22.772
1975	62.378	44.233	36.457
1980	70.654	44.649	43.871
1985	78.823	46.497	54.808
1990	87.565	53.490	48.582
1995	102.173	55.821	73.348

Sources: Feinstein (1976) for the years to 1965; CSO (various years) thereafter.

increases in spending on goods and services, especially defence-related, a large fall in transfer payments as almost all available labour was called into use, and a temporary decline in debt interest payments. Debt service payments did rise again after the war, but to a much lower level than after World War I. Since the late 1940s debt servicing has become steadily less significant as unanticipated inflation has eroded the value of outstanding debt, and Britain has experienced a long period without borrowing on the scale associated with wars.

Transfer payments have grown steadily since the early 1950s reflecting a wide range of forces. First, government policy in the period from the end of the war until 1980 was to increase the level of social security benefits in line with earnings increases in the economy. This meant substantial real increases in social security benefit levels. Second, the number of elderly people grew rapidly in the decades after the war, raising the cost of pension provision. Third, unemployment rose in the 1970s to levels far higher than had been seen since the 1930s, and although it fell in the 1980s, it rose again in the early 1990s, remaining well above the levels seen in the quarter-century after the war. Fourth, we have seen an enormous growth in the numbers of people on

National Insurance benefits	Debt interest	Total
0	1.921	13.505
0	2.374	12.464
0	2.273	13.526
0.397	3.223	51.037
0.328	7.508	24.648
2.007	10.746	30.077
4.480	12.199	36.700
4.197	10.568	41.011
3.133	8.922	108.379
2.459	11.773	129.145
7.322	10.397	73.480
8.848	11.110	78.880
12.549	12.966	93.901
18.868	14.340	114.177
23.052	17.213	139.460
29.387	19.021	191.476
33.931	25.652	218.757
38.437	29.281	247.845
38.349	23.351	251.338
43.594	27.271	302.207

long-term sickness and disability benefits, who now account for one-quarter of all social security spending. Fifth, the number of lone parents has risen dramatically. In 1996, 21 per cent of families with dependent children were headed by a lone parent, nearly three times the proportion in 1961 (ONS, 1998). Finally, deliberate policy changes, such as the shift from direct subsidy of council house rents to support through means-tested Housing Benefits have moved spending from other departments into the social security budget. (For more details on social security arrangements, see Chapter 16.)

Looking back to Figure 9.4, it is clear that the middle of the 1970s marked a peak in the share of public spending in national income, and thus the end of a growth in the scale of government which had continued for a century. In the mid-1970s, the economy was stagnating, inflation was high, unemployment rising, public sector borrowing unprecedentedly high for a period of peace, and the era of growing government came to an end.

Since then, while Britain has seen cyclical fluctuations in the scale of government, the trend has been towards stability or decline, with public spending dipping once more below 40 per cent. For the foreseeable future, it seems unlikely that any of the major political parties in the UK will seek to return to a trend of substantial growth in government.

Given the stability in the overall size of government, the data in Table 9.5 seem somewhat surprising. The table shows real levels of spending in the three main areas of the Welfare State since the early 1950s. Education spending grew by 35 per cent in real terms from 1980–95, roughly keeping pace with the economy, but health grew by 58 per cent and social security by 81 per cent, much more quickly than the economy. This can be seen even more clearly in Figure 9.6, which shows the share of these three 'Welfare State' items in total government spending, rising from just over 30 per cent in 1953 to 60 per cent by 1995.

Table 9.5 Government spending on education, health, personal social services and social security, 1953–95 in 1997 prices (£ billion)

Year	Education	Health and personal social services	Social security	Total
1953	7.098	8.523	13.690	29.311
1955	7.882	8.920	14.309	31.111
1960	11.587	11.625	18.823	42.036
1965	16.849	14.669	25.597	57.115
1970	21.522	19.006	33.329	73.857
1975	30.539	28.553	41.043	100.135
1980	30.067	27.407	59.939	117.414
1985	28.776	29.785	77.000	135.561
1990	33.378	34.680	78.597	146.655
1995	40.515	43.170	108.325	192.009

Source: CSO (various years).

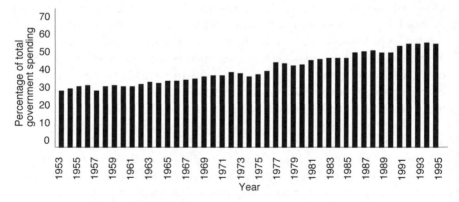

Figure 9.6 Percentage of total government spending[a] on education, health, social services and social security, 1953–95

Note: [a]Government spending includes both capital and current spending.

Source: CSO (various years).

Governments in the last quarter of the century paid for continued rapid growth in Welfare State spending not by raising taxes as they had in the earlier part of the century, but by cutting spending elsewhere within government.

Figure 9.7 shows the composition of gross domestic fixed capital formation (broadly speaking, investment), whilst Table 9.6 gives the figures in real terms. (No values are available from 1937 to 1948.) This is one area where recent cuts in public spending have been especially marked. Since 1975 the level of public sector capital formation has dropped radically, not only in real terms as shown in Table 9.6, but as a share of GDP. Some of the decline in total public sector gross domestic fixed capital formation (GDFCF) has followed privatization of public corporations, but the decline in local authority GDFCF is especially marked. This reduction in GDFCF has been the single largest source of funds for increasing Welfare State spending, although the halving of defence spending as a share of national income since the mid-1980s has also been important.[4]

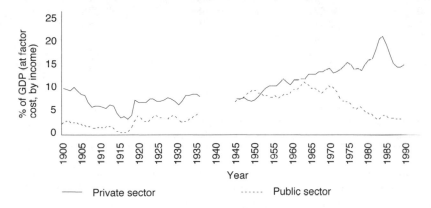
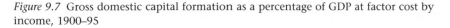

Figure 9.7 Gross domestic capital formation as a percentage of GDP at factor cost by income, 1900–95

Sources: Feinstein (1976) for data up to 1965; CSO (various years) thereafter.

Figure 9.8 decomposes government revenue, with Table 9.7 showing the underlying data in real terms. The most dramatic change in the composition of revenue has been the decline in local taxes, from almost one-third of total revenue in 1900 to less than 3.5 per cent in the 1990s. A range of forces account for this decline. First, the scale of government has grown, with new taxes such as National Insurance Contributions being introduced and then growing. Second, there has been a steady growth of central government expenditure, which has outstripped that of local government, seen clearly in the dips in local taxation as a share of the total after each world war. Third, the main local taxes for most of the period, domestic and non-domestic rates, were not

Table 9.6 Gross domestic fixed capital formation, 1900–95ᵃ in 1997 prices (£ billion), by sector

Year	Private Sector	Public Corporations	Central Government
1900	9.843	0	0.090
1905	8.546	0	0.119
1910	6.365	0	0.114
1915	4.989	0	0.088
1920	8.296	0	0.285
1925	9.202	0	0.525
1930	10.441	0.207	0.517
1935	13.009	0.267	0.534
1940	n/a	n/a	n/a
1945	n/a	n/a	n/a
1950	16.606	5.435	2.378
1955	21.658	8.228	2.767
1960	31.271	9.968	3.238
1965	37.556	13.745	3.168
1970	47.745	14.246	5.015
1975	55.861	18.067	5.812
1980	68.515	16.087	4.149
1985	79.778	9.875	5.205
1990	112.364	6.189	8.012
1995	92.887	5.342	5.964

Note: ᵃDue to rounding, the total gross domestic fixed capital formation figure stated here may differ slightly from the total given in Table 9.2. No breakdown is available for the years 1939–47.

naturally buoyant, requiring highly visible increases to maintain revenue. Fourth, reform of the local tax system in the late 1980s and early 1990s replaced locally variable business rates with a national tax, halving the level of local taxation. Finally, the ill-fated Community Charge, or, as it was more commonly known, the Poll Tax, was so unpopular and caused such political and administrative chaos that a shift in revenue from local domestic taxes to the national consumption tax, VAT (Value Added Tax), occurred in 1991. Britain now has a local government system with local revenue accounting for less than one-fifth of the total.

While local taxes have declined in significance, National Insurance Contributions have grown dramatically. In the years until 1960, National Insurance Contributions were flat-rate amounts, regardless of the earnings of the employee. In 1961, the lump sum contributions were supplemented by an earnings-related contribution, which applied up to a specified earnings range (around 1–1.5 times average male earnings). In 1975, the lump sum contribution was abolished for employees and their employers, with a move to entirely earnings-related contributions, although still with a ceiling of between 1 and 1.5 times average earnings, beyond which no further contributions were due.

Local Authorities	Total Public Sector	Total
1.981	2.071	11.914
1.840	1.959	10.505
1.250	1.364	7.729
0.662	0.751	5.740
1.970	2.255	10.551
3.242	3.767	12.970
3.825	4.549	14.990
3.586	4.387	17.396
n/a	n/a	19.176
n/a	n/a	20.170
7.661	15.473	32.079
8.113	19.108	40.766
7.641	20.847	52.118
12.830	29.743	67.299
15.751	35.012	82.756
17.210	41.089	96.950
9.167	29.403	97.918
6.237	21.317	101.095
7.799	22.000	134.364
7.199	18.505	111.392

Sources: Feinstein (1976) for the years to 1965; CSO (various years) thereafter.

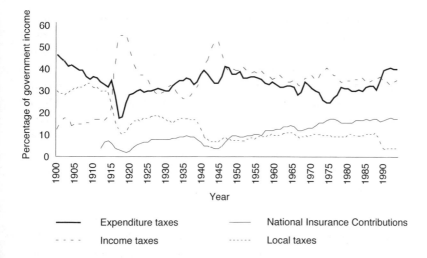

Figure 9.8 Composition of current government income, 1900–95

Sources: Feinstein (1976) for data up to 1965; CSO (various years) thereafter.

Table 9.7 Total government revenue, by source, 1900–95 in 1997 prices (£ billion)

Year	Income taxes	Expenditure taxes	NI contributions	Local taxes	Other	Total
1900	1.200	4.682	0	3.001	1.320	10.203
1905	1.840	5.104	0	3.917	1.959	12.820
1910	2.273	5.001	0	4.319	2.273	13.867
1915	3.620	5.563	0.927	3.885	2.384	16.380
1920	13.331	7.311	0.613	3.502	1.554	26.312
1925	10.623	8.924	2.007	5.188	3.829	30.571
1930	10.441	10.614	2.791	5.962	6.375	36.183
1935	10.835	14.230	3.739	7.058	5.570	41.431
1940	18.710	20.112	3.581	6.804	4.864	54.070
1945	45.743	28.510	3.239	5.839	3.948	87.279
1950	34.174	32.607	8.303	6.359	6.038	87.481
1955	33.417	31.371	8.560	6.845	7.536	87.728
1960	34.471	33.143	11.549	9.753	10.639	99.556
1965	42.764	40.033	17.912	13.054	12.990	126.752
1970	62.798	56.015	22.568	15.530	17.468	174.378
1975	77.238	46.357	31.562	18.335	20.810	194.302
1980	73.041	66.470	32.840	19.463	24.274	216.088
1985	85.911	71.643	40.310	22.707	24.244	244.815
1990	96.017	91.388	43.037	17.184	18.664	266.289
1995	95.840	109.340	46.773	9.663	17.212	278.829

Sources: Feinstein (1976) for the years to 1965; CSO (various years) thereafter.

In 1985, the Conservative government abolished the ceiling on contributions from employers, and reduced the contribution rate for those on the lowest earnings. Further changes in 1989 and 1999 have reduced the burden of the contributions at low earnings still further.

At the same time as the regressivity of the National Insurance system was reduced, the overall amount raised was increased, not least in the 1980s and 1990s as the Conservative government sought to finance reductions in income tax rates. Much of the reduction in income tax rates was financed by increases elsewhere, such as VAT (for example, 1979), other excise duties (for example, 1981), increases in National Insurance Contribution rates (from 6.5 per cent for employees in 1979 to 10 per cent by the early 1990s), or reductions in the value of income tax allowances (for example, 1981, 1993).

At the beginning of the period taxes on spending were more important than any other form of taxation, while income taxes were of little significance. Both world wars saw large increases in the role of income taxes, which were only partially reversed in peace-time. The contribution of taxes on spending, which grew slowly in the second quarter of the century and declined in the third, has grown again in the fourth quarter. The introduction of VAT in 1973 was followed by increases in both the VAT rate and the coverage of the tax, offsetting reductions in many excise duties. In the 1990s, the growth of VAT has been supplemented by substantial rises in excise duties on tobacco (reflecting concerns about health) and petrol (reflecting environmental objectives).

Composition of consumer spending

We began the chapter by emphasizing how much national income had grown over the century. We stressed, when discussing public finances and public spending, that there has been a shift towards higher shares of national income being spent on areas such as health, education, and income in retirement. In Figure 9.9 and Table 9.8 we examine the development of consumer spending over the period. Table 9.8 shows that in total, consumer spending rose a little less than fivefold, more slowly than national income, reflecting the growth of government consumption over the century.

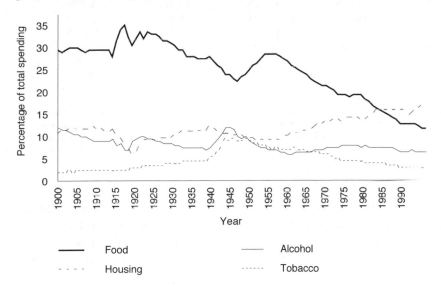

Figure 9.9 Composition of consumers' expenditure, 1900–95

Sources: Feinstein (1976) for data up to 1965; CSO (various years) thereafter.

Perhaps the most striking illustration of increased affluence, especially in the post-war period, has been the declining share of spending on household food, which accounted for one-third of consumer spending in the 1920s, compared with little more than 10 per cent now. At the other extreme, vehicle running costs have risen very rapidly, and housing, too, has increased its share. Spending on alcohol and tobacco was especially high during and after World

Table 9.8 Selected items of consumers' expenditure, 1900–95 in 1997 prices (£ billion)[a]

Year	Household food	Alcohol	Tobacco	Housing
1900	27.849	11.224	1.621	10.023
1905	29.794	10.208	1.840	11.514
1910	30.347	9.263	2.103	11.991
1915	31.965	7.903	2.163	10.022
1920	33.864	9.851	2.627	5.954
1925	38.322	10.437	3.582	10.036
1930	40.077	10.372	4.824	12.923
1935	40.210	10.415	5.837	15.870
1940	37.121	11.280	7.758	15.756
1945	33.049	16.666	13.286	14.562
1950	44.741	13.851	14.454	15.870
1955	52.092	11.989	12.681	16.168
1960	53.826	12.068	14.421	20.999
1965	54.266	15.041	15.180	27.064
1970	54.137	19.550	14.620	34.408
1975	55.128	22.344	12.606	40.260
1980	55.731	23.454	11.358	44.599
1985	51.044	26.059	11.665	54.277
1990	52.229	26.677	10.803	60.345
1995	51.634	27.857	12.319	76.727

Note: [a]Changing levels of consumption over time should be considered with care. For example it is not true that less is being spent on food now than in the mid-1970s. What has happened is that more is being spent on restaurant food, rather than on food which is prepared and consumed at home.

Sources: Feinstein (1976) for the years to 1965; CSO (various years) thereafter.

War II, not least because of very high levels of taxation on both commodities. When considering the quantities of each product being consumed it is important to consider the impact of relative price effects. For example, in recent years the price of tobacco has increased faster than the general price level. This means that whilst spending in real terms on tobacco in recent years has remained approximately constant, less tobacco is actually being consumed.

International trade

Figure 9.10 and Table 9.9 show how trade in goods and services has developed over the century. One important point to note is that the scale of trade relative to total economic activity is very close now to its level at the beginning of the century, and was only persistently lower during the 1930s and 1940s. The low levels of trade in the 1930s and 1940s reflected the global Depression of the early 1930s, and then the build-up to and experience of World War II.

Fuel & light	Clothing	Public travel & communications	Vehicle running costs	Total
4.502	9.183	3.841	0.960	98.253
3.739	9.318	4.273	0.890	103.032
3.808	10.116	4.660	0.909	106.670
3.664	8.521	4.150	0.883	105.254
3.809	17.403	4.378	0.919	109.888
4.879	13.340	6.083	1.297	119.753
5.583	14.404	6.754	2.033	135.497
6.257	14.802	7.058	2.785	150.120
6.624	14.950	5.491	1.373	143.202
6.123	12.647	7.636	0.969	151.083
6.718	20.059	7.982	2.095	178.529
7.608	18.690	7.911	3.516	188.915
9.500	20.835	8.994	5.705	214.924
11.555	21.887	9.992	9.865	244.022
12.708	23.401	11.416	14.748	272.969
13.306	23.994	13.799	18.819	302.304
14.972	23.261	17.310	22.717	326.457
17.582	24.828	19.088	27.709	362.113
15.300	26.074	22.568	31.407	434.061
15.979	27.272	25.296	34.930	472.740

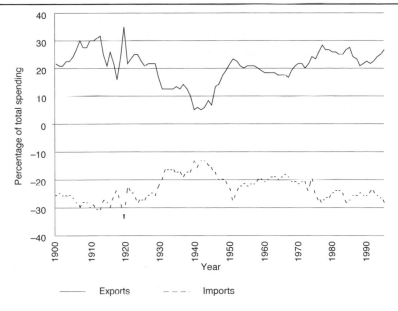

Figure 9.10 Imports and exports, as a proportion of total expenditure, 1900–95

Sources: Feinstein (1976) for data up to 1965; CSO (various years) thereafter.

Table 9.9 Levels of exports and imports of both goods and services, 1900–95 in 1997 prices (£ billion)

Year	Export of goods	Export of services	Total exports
1900	21.367	6.662	28.029
1905	24.274	7.478	31.752
1910	30.461	8.809	39.270
1915	22.075	11.038	33.113
1920	36.425	10.157	46.582
1925	29.120	6.639	35.759
1930	23.088	7.374	30.463
1935	20.639	5.684	26.324
1940	11.936	5.968	17.904
1945	10.638	8.274	18.912
1950	42.665	13.851	56.516
1955	44.282	15.909	60.191
1960	47.210	17.925	65.135
1965	50.780	18.220	68.999
1970	69.088	28.747	97.835
1975	88.424	35.388	123.812
1980	111.083	36.440	147.523
1985	129.855	40.043	169.898
1990	127.046	39.277	166.323
1995	161.030	47.833	208.863

Sources: Feinstein (1976) for the years to 1965; CSO (various years) thereafter.

It is still true that the great bulk of both imports and exports are goods, not services; there has been very little growth in the share of services in exports through the century.

The rest of the world

Table 9.10 shows the GDP per capita of the OECD countries in a range of years, relative to that of the UK. In 1974, Australia, for example, had a GDP per capita 14 per cent above that of the UK; by 1995 the Australian figure was 9 per cent higher than that in the UK.

For the OECD as a whole there has been little change relative to the UK over this period, with average GDP per capita in the OECD ranging from 11 per cent above the UK in 1974 and 1979, to only 6 per cent above in 1989 at the peak of the late 1980s boom in the UK, and as much as 12 per cent above in 1984 when the UK was still recovering from the early 1980s recession. The UK's position in the 'League Table' of countries has stayed very stable at 17, 18, or 19 out of 25.

Import of goods	Import of services	Total imports	Balance
29.110	3.001	32.111	−4.081
31.277	2.374	33.651	−1.899
35.917	2.898	38.815	0.455
37.086	5.740	42.826	−9.713
39.665	4.903	44.568	2.014
37.303	4.601	41.904	−6.145
32.840	5.066	37.906	−7.443
27.621	4.731	32.351	−6.028
29.840	16.412	46.252	−28.348
16.548	23.640	40.188	−21.276
43.627	14.417	58.044	−1.528
48.792	15.779	64.571	−4.381
52.346	17.912	70.258	−5.123
53.671	19.070	72.741	−3.742
69.207	25.169	94.376	3.460
103.426	29.327	132.753	−8.941
107.886	27.834	135.720	11.804
135.424	29.391	164.815	5.083
150.538	34.670	185.208	−18.885
173.321	41.341	214.662	−5.799

Table 9.10 GDP per capita relative to the UK amongst OECD countries, 1974–95 (UK = 100).

Country	1974	1979	1984	1989	1994	1995
Australia	114	112	115	107	109	109
Austria	107	111	115	108	117	115
Belgium	114	112	115	109	121	118
Canada	125	130	132	125	119	118
Denmark	114	114	119	110	120	120
Finland	101	99	109	109	96	100
France	122	122	121	114	113	111
Germany[a]	104	108	111	105	116	115
Greece	63	68	67	62	68	68
Iceland	107	118	123	116	114	122
Ireland	63	67	70	70	92	96
Italy	102	106	110	107	109	109
Japan	98	104	113	114	124	123
Luxembourg	141	129	136	151	177	175
Mexico	43	45	44	35	46	41
Netherlands	116	113	111	104	110	111
New Zealand	116	100	107	91	96	95

continued

Table 9.10 *(cont...)*

Country	1974	1979	1984	1989	1994	1995
Norway	104	115	126	116	129	127
Portugal	60	58	57	60	71	70
Spain	82	76	76	77	81	80
Sweden	124	118	123	114	103	105
Switzerland	168	148	151	139	142	140
Turkey	31	31	32	29	31	32
United Kingdom	100	100	100	100	100	100
United States	160	160	159	149	151	150
OECD average	111	111	112	106	110	109

Note: [a]Germany refers to an estimate of the whole of Germany throughout the period. Table calculated using GDP converted to US$ using current purchasing power parities.

Source: House of Commons Library (1998).

Notes

1   Although Southern Ireland became independent in 1922 it is excluded from statistics for 1920–22 in order to make comparisons of years between World War I and World War II easier.
2   Figures in current (that is, nominal) prices for every year are available from the authors on request. For details of the price indices used, see Appendix 1.
3   The United Nations' annual *Human Development Index Report* provides other potential indicators of a country's economic 'well-being', such as life expectancy and adult literacy rate. Jackson and Marks (1994) use a range of indicators including environmental factors to calculate an index of 'well-being' which can be compared to GNP. The impact of income on an individual's 'happiness' compared to other factors such as job satisfaction is discussed, amongst others, by Oswald (1997).
4   Most defence spending is counted as current rather than capital spending, although this will change shortly with the introduction of the 1995 European System of Accounts (ESA95).

References

Central Statistical Office (CSO) (various years), *United Kingdom National Accounts: The Blue Book*, HMSO, London.

Central Statistical Office (1996) *Annual Abstract of Statistics 1996*, HMSO, London.

Feinstein, C. H. (1976), *Statistical Tables of National Income, Expenditure and Output of the UK, 1855–1965*, Macmillan, Basingstoke.

HM Treasury (1998) *Stability and Investment for the Long Term: Economic and Fiscal Strategy Report 1998*, HM Treasury, London.

House of Commons Library (1998), *GDP per capita in OECD Countries: The UK's Relative Position*, House of Commons Library Research Paper 98/64, London.

Jackson, Tim and Marks, Nic (1994), *Measuring Sustainable Economic Welfare – A Pilot Index: 1950–1990*, Stockholm Environment Institute, Stockholm.

Office for National Statistics (1998) *Social Trends 28*, The Stationery Office, London.

Oswald, Andrew (1997) 'Happiness and economic performance', *The Economic Journal*, 107, pp.1815–31.

United Nations (various years) *Human Development Report*, Oxford University Press, Oxford.

Further reading

Central Statistical Office (various years) *Public Finance Trends*, HMSO, London.

Crafts, N. F. R. and Woodward, N. (1991) *The British Economy since 1945*, Clarendon Press, Oxford.

HM Treasury (1998) *Modern Public Services for Britain, Investing in Reform; Comprehensive Spending Review*, The Stationery Office, London.

White, G. and Chapman, H. (1987) 'Long term trends in public expenditure', *Economic Trends*, October pp.124–7.

10
Distribution of Income and Wealth

A. B. Atkinson

Riches are needless, then, both for themselves,
And for thy reason why they should be sought –
To gain a sceptre, oftest better missed
> Milton, *Paradise Regained* (Jesus' reply to Satan), 1671

Introduction: reviewing a century

This chapter reviews the distribution of income and wealth in Britain over the twentieth century. Material circumstances – earnings, savings, taxes and benefits – are only part of the human story of the century, as Milton reminds us. It is not enough to know how much people earn or what is their family income. There are other dimensions. The typical manual worker in 1900 worked longer hours than today, in less pleasant and more dangerous conditions; he would have left school earlier than his great-great-grandchildren today; if he or his family fell sick there was nothing comparable to modern medicine. Money income – on which attention is focused in this chapter – is an imperfect indicator of the quality of life. At the same time, it is an important ingredient. Over the century, national output of goods and services has risen markedly, and the implications of this growth depend crucially on how rising prosperity has been shared.

A century is a long span of years, and to do justice to the distributional record requires a historian's skills, which I do not possess, and a perspective which will only become possible with the passage of time. The more modest aim of this chapter is to assemble the available statistical information. This evidence has serious limitations. Statistics collected at different dates are often not comparable and hence do not allow conclusions to be drawn about changes over time. Every effort is made here, as in other chapters, to warn the reader where data sources are not consistent, since this problem is not always recognized in the literature, series often being joined regardless of cautionary footnotes, creating the impression that more can be deduced than is safe. There are in fact major gaps in what we can say. Of the eight graphs that contain time-series information, only four begin before World War II.

Consistency is the first theme of the chapter. The second is the relation between statistical data and real-life experiences. On looking at charts or tables, it is easy to lose sight of the fact that they are based on actual people, so I illustrate the figures with reference to individual circumstances, beginning with the survey of York by Seebohm Rowntree in 1899 and Violet Butler's account of Oxford in 1912. What was meant by a particular standard of living in 1900? What were the low-paid jobs, and what are they now? Who were, and are, the wealthy?

In comparing earnings or incomes at different dates during the century, a crucial issue is the adjustment to be made for rising prices and standard of living. What does a shop porter's wage of 17s (£0.85)[1] a week before World War I mean in 1999? What was the 26s (£1.30) a week paid in Unemployment Insurance to a couple in 1936 worth in today's prices? The Central Statistical Office (CSO; now Office for National Statistics – ONS) has published in *Retail Prices 1914–1990* (1991) cost-of-living indices covering this period, which we can link forwards with the all items retail price index. On this basis, £1.30 in 1936 had the purchasing power of some £37 in 1997. The use of these indices is, however, open to debate, since there are good reasons for believing that the official price index understated inflation during World War II. Using an alternative price indicator for the period 1938–48 (from Feinstein, 1972, Table 65) indicates that the Unemployment Insurance Benefit of 1936 had the purchasing power of £48 in 1997, bringing it closer to that actually paid (£78 a week). As this illustrates, statistics are open to debate, and we have to make choices. In this chapter, I use the Feinstein index (see Appendix 1).

A century of rising incomes

Material living standards in Britain as a whole have risen substantially over the century, as has been shown in Chapter 9. Most of the growth in national income took place after 1920, and in the subsequent 75 years the average growth rate of per capita disposable personal income was 1.75 per cent per year in real terms, or a rise by a factor of 3.7.[2] The magnitude of this increase should be emphasized. It would require a very considerable worsening of the distribution for this not to translate into an all-round improvement. Suppose, hypothetically, that the share of the bottom fifth in total income had halved over the period. The bottom 20 per cent would still be nearly twice as well off today in purchasing power as their counterparts at the start of the century.

The rise in living standards is evident from qualitative evidence about lifestyles. To make the link between statistics and people, I have drawn in Table 10.1 on the work of Rowntree: first the 1899 survey of York (Rowntree, 1901), and, second, the report of the Joseph Rowntree Foundation 'Inquiry into Income and Wealth' (Hills, 1995). The upper part of Table 10.1 summarizes three biographies of families in Rowntree's study of York in 1899. They are drawn from his Class D, which is the top working-class category. Average total earnings for families in this class were 41s 9¹/4d, or in 1997 prices some £125 a week. The living standard is most obvious from the housing conditions, which, even for this relatively comfortably-off group, were crowded (in family 29, four adults and five children live in 5 rooms) or had poor amenities (family 46 shared a water tap).

Table 10.1 Family biographies from 1899 and 1990/91

Class 'D' in 1899 (broadly,
40th to 70th percentile)

Family 2	*Family 29*	*Family 46*
Couple aged 70. Own house, 5 rooms. Home clean and comfortable. Man worked from age 7 to age 70. Had large family, one son now clergyman.	Couple, man works as joiner. Tenant, 5 rooms. Son (18) stonemason; son (16) apprentice joiner; and 5 children school-age or under. House clean and comfortable.	Couple aged 41, man works as sawyer. Tenant, 5 rooms, shares one water tap with 8 other houses. Son (18) apprentice sawyer; son (15) apprentice moulder; daughter day-domestic; and 4 children school-age or under.

Middle fifth in 1990/91
(amounts at April 1993
prices)

Family 21	*Family 23*	*Family 29*
Single male pensioner aged 71. Owns house. Receives state and occupational pension. Net income £119 week.	Couple aged 36 and 41, with 2 sons (14 and 11) and daughter (3). Buying house on mortgage. Man self-employed; woman, employee. Receive child benefit. Total net income £333 week.	Couple aged 44 and 45. Council tenants. He works full-time; she works part-time. Total net income £246 week.

Sources: 1899 from Rowntree (1922), Chapter III; 1990/91 from Hills (1995), volume 2, *UK Income Parade.*

The lower part of Table 10.1 shows three biographies of families constructed from the Family Expenditure Survey for 1990/91 by the Rowntree Inquiry (they are fictional but are based on statistical data). The families are drawn from the middle fifth of the 1990 income distribution (40th to 60th percentiles). Little reference is made to housing quality; plumbed bathrooms and kitchens being taken for granted by the great majority of today's population. These biographies illustrate some of the social and economic changes which have taken place over the century. Owner-occupation is now widespread. It is much rarer for young adults to live at home with their parents or as lodgers. People live independently to a much greater degree than in 1900, with many more single-person households. Family size has fallen. Married women are typically in paid work. There are state and occupational pensions. These changes are important both substantively and because they may influence the interpretation of the statistics. As Titmuss (1962) warned, changing forms of remuneration, of fiscal policies, of family composition, all affect the significance of the recorded income distribution.

Economic forces and personal incomes

National income per head has risen, but the step from the national income accounts of Chapter 9 to household incomes is not a straightforward one. We cannot read directly from one to the other. Figure 10.1 shows the main elements of GNP and of household income, with their magnitudes in 1996. Two elements are broadly the same: employment income and self-employment income are received directly by individuals (although people would not regard as part of their income the contributions paid by employers for social security and other schemes, and these have been deducted in moving from GNP to household income).

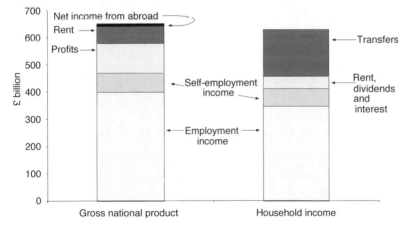

Figure 10.1 Gross national product and household income,[a] 1996

Note: [a]Income in kind in the household sector has been added to employment income.
Source: CSO, *United Kingdom National Accounts*, 1997 edition, Tables 1.4 and 4.9.

Profit income, on the other hand, is received by companies or by public corpo-rations or by government. Where it is received by shareholder-owned companies, then it ultimately accrues to individuals, but household income records only the dividends and interest paid currently, not that part of profit retained within companies for reinvestment. Part of the profit is paid abroad; conversely, property income is received from abroad. Rent is paid to individuals or accrues to companies or the public sector. A large part of dividend, interest income and rent goes to pension funds and other financial intermediaries. Again these ultimately benefit individuals, but the payments which appear in household income are in the form of occupational pensions and other benefits (shown as 'Transfers' in Figure 10.1). When we come to look at the distribution among individuals, the statistics only record the amounts actually received, so that a sizeable amount of total income remains unallocated. Conversely, state transfers form a major element of household income which has no counterpart in gross national product, and are substantial, amounting in total to the same as income from self-employment plus rent, dividends and interest.

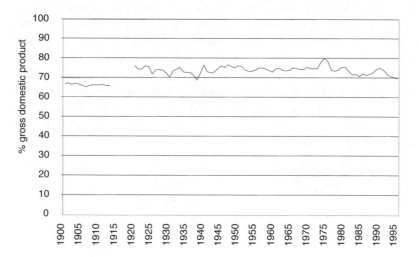

Figure 10.2 Share of employment income[a][b] in gross domestic product, 1900–95

Notes: [a]Share of employment income is income from employment expressed as a proportion of gross domestic product (income-based) at factor cost after allowing for stock appreciation minus income from self-employment (before allowing for stock appreciation).
[b]Income from self-employment is not shown separately for 1914–19, so that these years are missing; figures prior to 1920 include Southern Ireland.

Sources: Prior to 1950, from Feinstein (1972), Table 1 (column 1 divided by (column 9 – column 2)); 1950–59 from CSO, *National Income and Expenditure 1972*, Table 1 (row 13 divided by (row 22 – row 21 – row 14); 1960–74 from CSO, *National Income and Expenditure 1982*, Table 1.2 (income from employment divided by (gross domestic product (income-based) – income from self-employment)); 1975–96 from CSO, *United Kingdom National Accounts*, 1997 edition, Table 1.4 (DJAO – (CAOM – GIXQ – CFAN)).

Earnings from employment are the single largest source of income. Changes over the century in the share of employment income are shown in Figure 10.2. Part of self-employment income also represents reward to labour, and the figure has been calculated on the assumption that it is split in the same way as the rest of national output.[3] (There is a break in continuity in 1920, since the earlier figures include Southern Ireland.) At first sight, Figure 10.2 suggests a remarkable degree of distributional stability. The share of employment income has varied between 70 and 80 per cent since 1920. However, this is quite a wide range. When viewed in terms of the share of non-employment income, it means that this share has varied between 20 and 30 per cent. Within the period we can detect periods of increase and decrease. The share of employment income cycled around a downward tendency in the inter-war period, was higher after World War II, and, after a rise in the mid-1970s, fell again. The macro-economic distribution of income is not an unchanging constant.

Earnings differentials: the end of stability?

Information about earnings can be obtained from household surveys, such as the regular Family Expenditure Survey (FES), used, for example, by Gosling et al. (1994) to measure the trends over time in the distribution of earnings. The main source since 1968 has, however, been the employer-based survey of earnings, the New Earnings Survey (NES), which provides a rich source of information about individual earnings (although, unlike the FES, it does not allow information to be combined for different members of the same household). The NES is based on a sample defined in the same way each year (all workers whose National Insurance number ends in 14). It has a significant element of non-response, but has the advantage of a large sample size: the 1997 figures, for example, are based on some 110 000 returns.

Figure 10.3 shows the changes in earnings dispersion over the period 1968–97. The figures relate to all full-time workers, male and female, and include both those paid at adult rates and those on other rates, thus avoiding the discontinuity in the published figures in 1983 (when the definition was changed from 'adult' to 'those paid on adult rates'). Dispersion is represented in terms of the bottom decile (10th percentile) and top decile (90th percentile) expressed as a percentage of the median. The ratio of these two (top decile over bottom decile) is typically referred to as the 'decile ratio'.

Conventional wisdom is that the distribution of earnings in Britain was stable for the first 75 years of this century and then in the Thatcher years began to show widening dispersion. In fact, Figure 10.3 suggests that over the 1970s the bottom decile was rising relative to the median, and the top decile falling. These changes may have been associated with high rates of inflation or with government measures, such as income policies which included at one

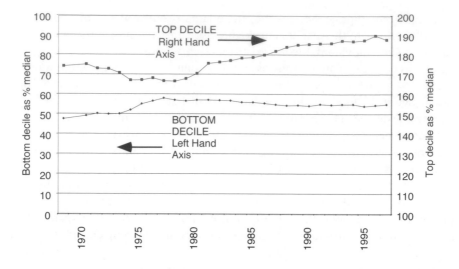

Figure 10.3 Earnings dispersion, 1968–97[a]

Note: [a]Earnings of all workers, male and female, working full-time whose pay was not affected by absence.

Sources: Prior to 1983, from Atkinson and Micklewright (1992), Table BE1; 1983–86 from New Earnings Survey, 1993, Table A17; from 1987 from New Earnings Survey, 1997, Table A30.2.

time a restriction of increases to £6 a week (see references in Atkinson, 1997). From the late 1970s the distribution began to widen steadily. The bottom decile fell as a percentage of the median, losing some but not all of the ground gained in the 1970s. The deterioration in the position of the bottom decile appears to have stopped in the 1990s. More marked, and continuing in the 1990s, is the rise in the top decile, which increased from 167 per cent of the median to 187 per cent in the 15 years after the election of Mrs Thatcher. Overall, the decile ratio increased from 2.87 in 1977 to 3.41, 20 years later.

Within the overall distribution there have been changes. The Equal Pay Act was passed in 1970, requiring full compliance in equal pay for men and women by 1975, and the Sex Discrimination Act was also introduced in 1975. The median earnings of adult women working full-time rose from 54 per cent of the male median in 1970 to 66 per cent in 1983 (Atkinson and Micklewright, 1992, Table BE3), and continued subsequently, median earnings for those paid on adult rates rising from 67 per cent in 1983 to 75 per cent in 1997 (New Earnings Survey, 1993, Table 15; 1997, Table A36). However, the picture is more complicated than these headline figures suggest. Over the 1980s, the dispersion of earnings was widening, so that the earnings of the bottom decile of women in fact ceased to gain on those of the median male – see Figure 10.4. The top decile of women continued to move ahead, so that they rose from the male median (in 1980) to a third higher (in 1997). These

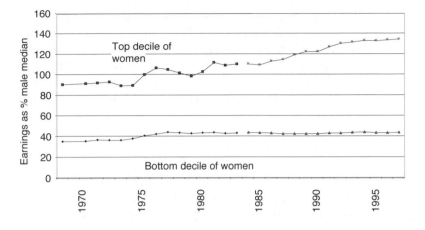

Figure 10.4 Earnings of women relative to male median, 1968–97[a]

Note [a]Earnings of workers paid on adult rates (adult workers prior to 1983) working full-time whose pay was not affected by absence.

Sources: Prior to 1991, from Atkinson and Micklewright (1992), Table BE3; from 1991, from New Earnings Survey, 1997, Tables A28.1 and A28.2.

figures relate to full-time workers. Harkness et al. (1995) using data from the General Household Survey show that the gains for part-time women workers have been much less, so that the wife in Family 29 in Table 10.1 may not have enjoyed the same rise relative to her male counterpart.

Returning to the overall distribution, we have seen that the period post-1968 cannot be characterized as one of stability. What of the earlier part of the century? There is no evidence comparable with the New Earnings Survey, but the Board of Trade in 1906[4] and Ministry of Labour in 1938 and 1960 undertook earnings surveys. For full-time male manual workers, in the sectors covered, the lowest decile was 66.5 per cent of the median in 1906, 67.7 per cent in 1938, and 70.6 per cent in 1960, according to the figures of A. R. Thatcher, who comments that, 'in a period when the level of adult male manual earnings increased [tenfold], it appears that their dispersion ... changed very little' (Thatcher, 1968, p.163), although he goes on to add that: 'This appears to conflict with the widely held view that there has been a narrowing of the differentials between skilled and unskilled workers.'

Moreover, the figures for the top decile show more volatility: 156.8 per cent of the median in 1906, 139.9 per cent in 1938, and 145.2 per cent in 1960. So that, between 1906 and 1938 there appears to have been a significant narrowing, although less than the change which took place in the opposite direction in the shorter period of the 1980s.

There are several reasons why we should be cautious in drawing conclusions about stability. First, considering a few years can be misleading. For instance, looking only at 1970 and 1981 one might conclude from Figure 10.3 that the top decile had not changed relative to the median, missing the fall and then rise in the 1970s. Second, the sources are not comparable. The pre-1968 surveys did not provide complete coverage of manual workers: the 1938 inquiry did not cover agriculture, coalmining, dock labour, shipping, distributive trades, catering trades, entertainment industries, commerce and banking, and domestic service (Ainsworth, 1949, p.35). Male manual workers are only part of the labour force and, as is shown in Chapter 8, they have declined to not much more than a third of the total.

The pattern of earnings by occupational group has been studied by Routh (1980), whose estimates for men are summarized in Figure 10.5. In 1913–14, higher professionals (including the self-employed) earned on average 3.5 times the overall male average, by 1978 this had fallen to 1.7 times. Skilled manual workers' wages were 13 per cent higher than the average in 1913–14, but by 1978 had fallen to 91 per cent of the average. The overall average has been increased by the substantial shift from lower-paid to higher-paid occupational groups, but the inter-group ratio of higher professional average earnings relative to those of unskilled workers has fallen from 5.2 in 1913–14 to 2.4 in 1978, and of skilled workers to unskilled workers from 1.68 times in 1913–14 to 1.28 in 1978. Evidence for the last part of the period shown is drawn from the New Earnings Survey. Using the same source, Elliott and Murphy conclude that 'the period 1970–1982 has witnessed a general reduction in skill differentials' (1990, p.89).

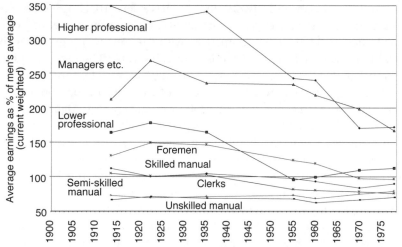

Figure 10.5 Average earnings of occupational groups: men, 1913/14–78

Source: Routh (1980), Table 2.29.

Who are in these groups? The mean for all male workers in 1913–14 was around £1.80, or 36s (Routh, 1980, p.120). According to C. Violet Butler, writing about social conditions in Oxford in 1912 (Butler, 1912), 30s was then the minimum-time standard wage for printers, who were the largest group of skilled trades in the town, and a 'prosperous' carpenter could make around 36s at the busiest time, as could plumbers. The counterparts of these people in York were in Rowntree's top working-class category. Journeyman bakers earned between 20s and 26s; and overall, in Oxford in 1912, men's weekly wages ran between 17s and 40s, with the lower figure being received by carters, milkmen and shop porters. Around the same date, Maud Pember Reeves and members of the Fabian Women's Group reported that in Lambeth 'some of the more enviable and settled inhabitants' had wages ranging from 18s to 30s a week. As recorded in *Round About a Pound a Week*, these people, with between 50 and 80 per cent of the male average,

> generally are somebody's labourer, mate, or handyman ... they may be fish-fryers, tailors' pressers, feather-cleaners' assistants, railway-carriage washers, employees of dust contractors, carmen for Borough Council contractors, or packers of various descriptions. (Reeves, 1913, pp.2–3)

Moving up the scale, and drawing on literary rather than factual evidence, Freddy Eynsford Hill in *Pygmalion* (1912) regarded a clerkship on 30s a week as below his dignity, Lupin Pooter in *The Diary of a Nobody* (1892) started a new job at £200 a year, and the chef in Arnold Bennett's *Grand Babylon Hotel* (1902) had a salary of £2000 a year raised by the new owner to £3000 (or around £180 000 in 1997 prices).

In April 1997, the mean earnings of men working full-time paid on adult rates were £408.70 a week (New Earnings Survey, 1997, Table A28). Groups with average earnings close to this amount included sales representatives, computer engineers and printers (New Earnings Survey, 1997, Table A13). Male carpenters and joiners on average earned £294.30; bakers earned £273.10; farm workers, £249.10; and hospital porters, £198.50 (that is, less than half the mean). Those in non-manual occupations earning above the average included secondary teachers averaging £489.90; chartered accountants, £565.30; and personnel managers, £668.60.

Changes in occupational differentials are only part of the story, and may be consistent with stable or increasing overall dispersion. Dispersion within the non-manual group is greater than that within the manual group, and a narrowing differential between the groups could have been offset by the rising importance of non-manual employment, as well as, in recent years, widening intra-group dispersion. It should be stressed that there is very considerable dispersion *within* occupations. The 1997 decile ratio for carpenters, for example, is 2.07; that is, the top tenth of carpenters earn at least twice more a week than the bottom tenth. The decile ratio for chartered and certified accountants is 2.16; that for engineers and technologists, 2.40. Even if we were to turn ourselves into a nation solely of engineers and technologists, we would have no less earnings dispersion than the whole of Czechoslovakia prior to 1990 (Atkinson and Micklewright, 1992, Table CSE1).

Spreading popular wealth?

Capital income is the smaller part of total national income (see Figure 10.1), but it is more unequally distributed than earned income. Rather surprisingly, it is also the case that information is more readily available, since estimates have been made of the shares in total wealth owned by the richest 1 per cent, 5 per cent and 10 per cent for much of the whole century. These estimates are obtained from the data on estates left at death which are collected by the Inland Revenue as part of the operation of Inheritance Tax/Capital Transfer Tax, or previously Estate Duty. By applying age and sex-related multipliers (to

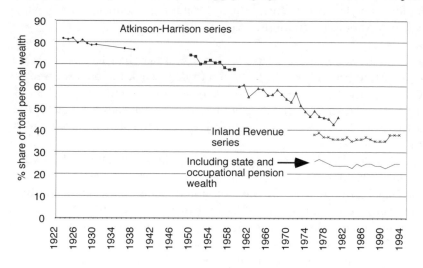

Figure 10.6 Share of top 5 per cent in total personal wealth, 1923–94[a]

Note: [a]Share of top 5 per cent of adult population in total personal wealth.

Sources: 1923–72 from Atkinson and Harrison (1978), Table 6.5 (note that there are breaks in the series between 1938 and 1950 and 1959 and 1960, and that the estimates before 1950 relate to England and Wales, those after relate to Great Britain). These estimates are continued to 1982 from Atkinson et al. 1989, Table 1. The estimates from 1976 shown with crosses are produced on a different basis by the Inland Revenue, as is the series including state and occupational pension rights. These series relate to the United Kingdom. (*Inland Revenue Statistics 1972*, Tables 11.5 and 11.7 (latest valuation), and 1997, Tables 13.5 and 13.7 (latest valuation)).

allow for differential mortality by age and sex), we obtain the estimates shown in Figure 10.6 of the share in total personal wealth of the top 5 per cent of adults. This is not a continuous series, as is indicated by the breaks in the lines.

Overall, even taking account of the breaks in the series, it is evident that the share of the top wealth group has fallen over the century, particularly in the period 1950–80. A major factor has been the spread of 'popular wealth'. As described by Tawney (1931, p.81), the majority of people before World War I were 'almost propertyless'. Of the eight working-class weekly budgets in Oxford in 1909 itemized by Butler (1912), only one refers to putting money by for clothing, one to paying off debts, and one to a parish savings card. Few at that time were owner-occupiers, and only a small minority had deposits in savings banks. In 1900, there were only 585 000 share accounts in building societies (Boléat, 1982, Table 1.1), compared with over 30 million accounts in the 1990s (*Annual Abstract of Statistics*, 1996, Table 17.17). In 1900 there were 1.6 million depositors in Trustee Savings Banks (Horne, 1947, Appendix II), or considerably fewer than 10 per cent of the adult population. The households in York in 1899 described by Rowntree had little in the way of consumer durables.

By the 1930s, as is shown in Chapter 14, more people owned their own houses. Personal savings were also more widespread, although Figure 10.6 shows that wealth was still heavily concentrated. In 1938, newspapers made a great deal of the fact that 'working-class savings' had reached £3 billion, or £300 per family, equivalent to £11 000 in 1997 prices. The composition of this sum was examined by Hilton in his book *Rich Man, Poor Man* (1944), where he shows how misleading averages can be. There were 11 million people with accounts in the Post Office Savings Bank, but in 70 per cent of the cases in 1934 the balance was less than £25, the average being £4.05. Holdings were heavily skewed towards small amounts.

As may be seen from Figure 10.6, when, at the 1963 Royal Variety Show, John Lennon asked people in the cheaper seats to clap and the rest to 'rattle your jewellery', there had already been a substantial decline in the share of the top wealth groups, and this continued for the next 20 years. By the 1990s, two-thirds of householders had become owner-occupiers, and a quarter owned their houses outright (*Social Trends*, 1998, Table 10.6). Personal savings have continued to grow, and many people have significant wealth in the form of personal possessions, even if we net off the hire purchase and credit card debt. Of course, the relative price of personal property, notably consumer durables, has fallen. In 1922 William Morris cut the price of a four-seater Cowley car from £525 (equivalent to around £15 750 in 1997 prices) to £341 (Adeney, 1993, p.76). Personal computers are a contemporary example.

A sizeable part of personal wealth now takes the form of prospective pensions, and an innovation in official statistics has been the extension of the wealth estimates to include the value of state and occupational pension rights. In 1993 these represented some £1600 billion, or not far short of total marketable wealth of £1863 billion (*Inland Revenue Statistics 1997*, Table 13.4). The impact of including pension wealth on the share of the top 5 per cent is shown in Figure 10.6. The share of the bottom 50 per cent rises from 7 per cent of marketable wealth to 17 per cent of total wealth when the estimated value of pension rights is included (*Inland Revenue Statistics 1997*, Tables 13.5 and 13.7). It is interesting to note how the value of state pension rights has been scaled down following the move in the Social Security Act 1980 to price rather than earnings indexation, and the reduction in the value of the State Earnings Related Pension following the Social Security Act 1986 (Stewart, 1991, pp.103–4).

What is perhaps surprising in Figure 10.6 is that the downward trend in wealth concentration so evident up to 1980 then became less marked; after 1980 the shares of the top wealth groups scarcely changed, despite the avowed intention of the Conservative governments to encourage popular capitalism. One explanation is that privatization and the sales of council houses have been slow to have effect. According to Good, writing in 1990,

> the sale of houses ... can, as yet, have had only a small effect on the distri-bution of wealth ... Although large discounts were available, most houses were subject to mortgage ... There has been an increase of about 6 million shareholders [but] most shareholders have only a small holding ... and the new share owners will not necessarily be concentrated among the least wealthy. (1990, pp.145–6)

Working in the opposite direction has been the substantial rise in share prices. Atkinson and Harrison (1978) found a strong positive association between the level of share prices and the share of top wealth groups.

Who indeed are the wealthy? In his pioneering study of inheritance, Josiah Wedgwood (1939) listed those leaving estates over £200000 in 1924/25 (this date being virtually the beginning of the series in Figure 10.6), based on the *The Times* list of wills. Top of his list was Sir Everard Hambro, former Director of the Bank of England, who left the equivalent in 1997 prices of £72 million; followed by Sir Edward Hulton, newspaper proprietor, with a similar sum; and the 3rd Baron Masham, chief shareholder in Manningham Mills and owning about 24000 acres, together with 'some first-class pictures – Gainsborough, Sir Joshua Reynolds, Romney, etc.' leaving nearly £50 million (*Who Was Who, 1916–1928*). Rubinstein (1981 and 1986) listed large estates left at death in the post-World War II period (up to 1979). The largest was that of Sir John Ellerman, of the shipping line, who left £52 million in 1973, or some £350 million in 1997 prices. In the early 1980s, large estates included £28 million left by Sir Charles Clore, the financier; and £18 million left by the 6th Earl of

Bradford (Rubinstein, 1986, p.153). *The Times* list of wills in the 6 months February–July 1998 contained relatively few estates in excess of the £6 million corresponding to Wedgwood's 1924/25 cut-off. It included Mr R. W. Diggens, company director, with a net estate of £77 million; Mr C. Sanders, with £22 million; and the 9th Earl of Dartmouth, with £8 million.

Fall and rise of overall inequality?

We have discussed individual earnings and the wealth which generates capital income in the form of rent, dividends, and interest, or indirectly in the form of pensions, payments from life assurance, etc.[5] To these forms of income we have to add transfers paid by the state, and deduct the amounts paid in income tax and National Insurance Contributions, in order to arrive at *disposable income*, which is the subject of this section. Taxes and transfers are examined in greater detail in the next section.

Earnings and wealth have been considered in *individual* terms, but in assessing economic circumstances we have to look at the income of the *family* or *household* as a unit. In the case of Family 29 (of the 1990/91 survey) in Table 10.1, since both adults are working they appeared separately in the New Earnings Survey (although the wife was not in fact in the figures cited earlier since she works part-time). We now add together their joint earnings, so that the resulting distribution of family income depends on who is married to whom. We have to resort to other sources of information, since the New Earnings Survey and the estate returns do not 'marry' up people. The main sources are the income tax returns and household surveys, such as the Family Expenditure Survey (FES). The official estimates of income inequality made up to the mid-1980s, the *Blue Book* estimates,[6] shown in Figure 10.7, were based on the Survey of Personal Incomes (SPI) drawn from the income tax records of a sample of taxpayers, carried out originally at five-year intervals,[7] but now annually (see *Inland Revenue Statistics 1997*, p.30). The SPI was supplemented by information from other sources, particularly about non-taxpayers, in order to arrive at the *Blue Book* estimates (see Ramprakash, 1975). The information available in the tax records is now less than in the past, and the *Blue Book* series has not been published for years later than 1984/85. Official distributional statistics now rely largely on the FES, which is the basis for the other series shown in Figure 10.7.[8] The FES has several limitations which must qualify conclusions drawn with respect to the distribution of income. It is undoubtedly the case that certain forms of income, such as from self-employment and capital income, are understated in the survey. The survey covers only the household population. None the less, it is a very fruitful source of information, and public access to these data has greatly enriched the analysis of income distribution.

Combining the incomes of those living together means that we have to address two important questions. What should be the unit of analysis? How should we allow for different-sized families or households? Most current statistical analysis of income inequality takes the household as the unit: that is, the incomes are added of all those living in a particular household. This differs from the unit used when assessing entitlement for social security benefits, which takes account of other members of the household but is essentially based on the nuclear family, including only dependent children. Non-dependent children, or others living in the same household, are treated as separate units. The *Blue Book* estimates use the income tax unit, which is close to the nuclear family, and this is the basis for the Microsimulation Unit series. The more recent official estimates, the *Households Below Average Income* (HBAI) series produced by the Department of Social Security (DSS) are, as the name indicates, based on the household. The same practice is applied in the Institute for Fiscal Studies (IFS) series, produced by Goodman and Webb (1994), which is constructed in a similar way to the HBAI estimates. It is open to debate whether grown-up children, or elderly parents, living at home, can be assumed to be have exactly the same level of living as the core family, which is the assumption underlying choice of the household as the unit of analysis. On the other hand, even if we adopt the family unit, this leaves unaddressed the distribution between family members.

Differences in family or household size could be ignored. This was the practice adopted in the *Blue Book* series, the same total income received by single people and couples being regarded as equivalent. The other estimates in Figure 10.7 apply an 'adult equivalence scale', which divides total income by a scale based on household size and composition. For Family 23 in Table 10.1, for example, the scale applied in the HBAI estimates is 2.8 compared to 1 for a single person, so that their total net income of £333 a week, divided by 2.8, is equivalent to £119 a week for a single person, which puts them in the same position as the single pensioner in Family 21. (Although one could argue that the elderly have greater needs than younger single people.) The Microsimulation Unit estimates apply the equivalence scale implicit in the Supplementary Benefit scale.

The distribution of disposable income is depicted in Figure 10.7 in the form of the Gini coefficient, which is a summary measure ranging from 0 if all incomes are equal to 100 per cent if all income is concentrated in the hands of one single person. One interpretation is in terms of drawing two families at random from the population and asking what difference you would expect to find between them. A Gini coefficient of 30 per cent implies that the expected difference is 60 per cent of the mean (that is, twice the Gini coefficient). A better known interpretation is in terms of the Lorenz curve, which shows on the horizontal axis the population lined up in order of income, and on the vertical axis the cumulative share in total income of the bottom *x* per cent of the population. Where incomes are unequal, this curve lies below the 45° line (the bottom *x* per cent have less than *x* per cent of total income until we reach 100 per cent). The Gini coefficient is the ratio of the area between the Lorenz curve and the 45° line to the maximum such area.

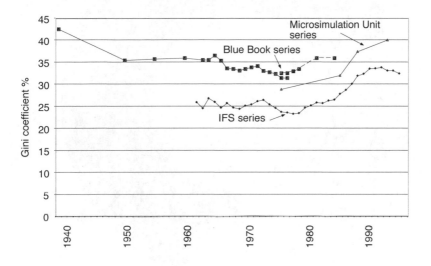

Figure 10.7 Overall income inequality, 1938–95/96[a]

Note: [a]There is a break in the Blue Book series in 1975/76 (overlapping years).

Sources: 1938 from Royal Commission on the Distribution of Income and Wealth (1979), Table 2.4; 1949–1984/85 from Atkinson and Micklewright (1992), Table BI1; IFS series 1961–91 from Goodman and Webb (1994), p.A2 and further figures supplied by IFS; Microsimulation Unit series supplied by Holly Sutherland.

This interpretation of the Gini coefficient makes clear that a single statistic cannot capture the complete distributional story. A stable Gini coefficient may correspond to no change in the Lorenz curve or to the combination of an inward shift at one point and an outward shift elsewhere. While useful, the Gini is not a complete substitute for looking at the whole distribution. In order to emphasize this, I show in the 'double doughnut' diagram (Figure 10.8) the shares in total disposable income (outer ring) in 1991 of four income groups, compared with their population shares (inner ring), the data being those underlying the IFS series in Figure 10.7. The bottom 40 per cent have about half their proportionate share in total income; the middle 40 per cent, from the 40th to the 80th percentile, broadly hold their own; and the next-to-top 10 per cent and top 10 per cent have more than their proportionate shares (a quarter in the case of the top 10 per cent).

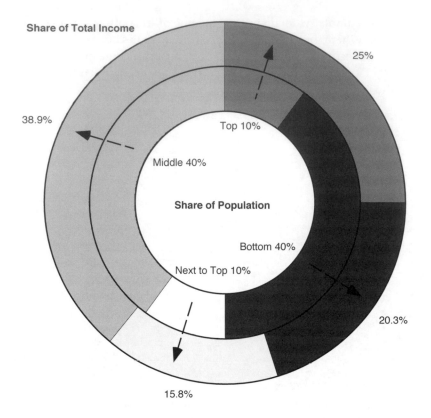

Figure 10.8 Shares in total income in UK, 1991

Source: Goodman and Webb (1994), Figure 2.3.

The estimates of income distribution in Figure 10.7 have many shortcomings. Although some of the criticisms made by Titmuss (1962) have been addressed in more recent research, a number of serious problems remain. As elsewhere in this chapter, I am considering only a snapshot picture, taking no account of the variation of incomes over people's lifetimes. Income retained by the corporate sector, and that not paid out by institutions such as pension funds, is not allocated in the distribution (no adequate allowance is made for capital gains). Various fringe benefits are not included. The figures refer to money incomes without regard to the fact that prices may rise at different rates for different income groups.

Bearing in mind the reservations, what conclusions can be drawn from Figure 10.7? The single estimate from before World War II suggests that inequality was then considerably greater; the Gini coefficient was 8 percentage points higher than in the 1950s. Some commentators have argued that much of the levelling of pre-tax income could be attributed to the omission of undistributed profits (Brittain, 1960), but extensive analysis of different adjustments left Lydall concluding in 1959 that, 'the trend in income distribution over the past two decades has been much more strongly egalitarian than in any previous period of our history' (1959, p.33).

Behind the fall in the Gini coefficient lay a large decline in the share of the top 1 per cent (from 12.1 per cent to 6.4 per cent), but a much smaller change in the share of the next 9 per cent (from 22.3 per cent to 20.7 per cent – Royal Commission on the Distribution of Income, 1979, Table 2.4). As noted by Paish (1957), the levelling concerned primarily the top incomes. This pattern continued, and Seers (1956) observed that the Lorenz curves for 1949 and 1954 crossed: there was no shift in the distribution between the top 30 per cent and the bottom 70 per cent. Between 1954 and 1964 the estimated share of the bottom 40 per cent fell from 18.0 per cent to 17.2 per cent in 1964 (Atkinson and Micklewright, 1992, Table BI2). From 1964–76/77, the bottom groups did gain, but the decline at the top was limited to the top 10 per cent whose total income was reduced from 25.9 per cent to 22.4 per cent (Atkinson and Micklewright, 1992, Table BI2). It was a limited form of redistribution. On the other hand, when inequality rose after 1977, both the next-to-top 10 per cent and the top 10 per cent gained (Goodman and Webb, 1994, p.A3).

The changes after 1977 were large. Between 1977 and 1990, according to the IFS estimates, the Gini coefficient increased by 10 percentage points, and the sharp rise is paralleled in the other series. The post-1979 period in fact consisted of distinct phases. Up to 1985 a major cause of the widening inequality was the decline in the proportion of families with incomes from work (see Atkinson, 1993), resulting from the rise in unemployment, ageing of the population and decline in labour force participation, together with the increased earnings dispersion evidenced in Figure 10.3. From 1985–90 income inequality increased more sharply, reflecting the reduced redistributional contribution of the government budget, discussed below, together with continued increases in earnings dispersion. After 1990 inequality fell slightly. These forces affected not only the overall degree of inequality, but also the shape of the distribution. Cowell et al. (1996) have argued that the distribution of income moved over the 1980s from having a single peak to having a second peak in the middle income ranges. They explain this in terms of a shift to more dispersion among working households, combined with a rise in the proportion of households receiving Income Support (a heavily concentrated distribution).

What about the years before 1938 for which there is no evidence comparable with that in Figure 10.7? The period prior to World War I has been much debated by economic historians as part of the larger question as to whether income inequality first rose and then fell during the British Industrial Revolution (for two different views, see Williamson, 1985, and Feinstein, 1988). The impact of the 1905 Liberal government and World War I is less controversial. According to contemporary commentators, there was significant equalization.

Writing in 1922, Seebohm Rowntree compared the situation before and after World War I: 'It cannot be denied that the war greatly raised the standard of living among the workers, especially the low-paid workers' (1922, p.xv).

A more extensive, quantitative, account is provided by Sir Arthur Bowley in his study *Some Economic Consequences of the Great War* (1930). He notes that there were 4100 people with disposable income of at least £10000 a year in 1914, compared with only 1300 people with the equivalent income in 1925 (£18000).[9] He attributes this to 'the combined effect of the rise of prices, of income-tax, super-tax, and death duties, and the stationariness of income from land' (1930, p.139).

He notes the narrowing of skill differentials, as shown in Figure 10.5, and the contribution made by unemployment insurance, noting: 'the general improvement in the economic position of the poorer of the manual labourers' (1930, pp.161–2). He concludes that: 'The general result of the whole system of taxation, wage-adjustments, and social expenditure has been a very marked redistribution of the National Income' (1930, p.160).

If this assessment of the first quarter-century is correct, then the twentieth century began with an epoch of equalization and ended with a major reversal. (Although the sharp-eyed reader will note that the equalization began five years into the century and that my statistics end five years before the millennium.)

How does this leave Britain compared with other industrialized countries? International comparisons of income inequality are fraught with difficulty, but the scope for such comparisons has increased in recent years with the development of sets of micro-data for this purpose, notably the Luxembourg Income Study (LIS). Complete comparability can never be attained, and statistics for different countries will always need to be interpreted in the light of differing social and economic circumstances, but the LIS data used in Figure 10.9 represent a major advance. The graph shows the Gini coefficient in the United Kingdom in 1995[10] compared with those in other European countries, and the United States, at about the same date. Lower inequality is to be found in Scandinavia and the Benelux countries, with the UK having the highest recorded inequality apart from the United States.

Rise and fall of the redistributive state?

The only social security system to which the York families in Rowntree's study of 1899 had access was the Poor Law. On 1 January 1901, 492 people were in York Workhouse and 1049 received outdoor relief, making, with those in asylums, 2.1 per cent of the population, a figure close to the average for England and Wales (Rowntree, 1922, pp.424–5). In 1908, the Liberal govern-

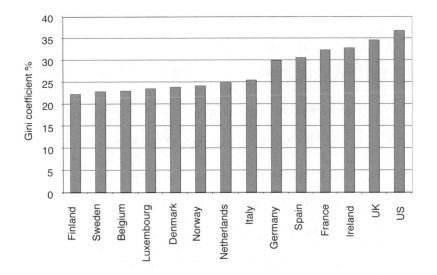

Figure 10.9 United Kingdom income inequality relative to Europe (and US), 1995[a]

Note: [a]Figures relate to 1987 (Ireland), 1989 (France), 1990 (Spain), 1991 (Finland, Netherlands, Italy), 1992 (Belgium, Denmark, Sweden), 1994 (Germany, Luxembourg, US), 1995 (Norway, UK). The estimates relate to household disposable income per equivalent adult using an equivalence scale of the square root of household size and using individual weights.

Source: Gottschalk and Smeeding (forthcoming), Figure 2.

ment introduced old-age pensions, and in 1911 there was the National Insurance Act. The state had begun to play a much greater role in cash transfers. On the financing side, the budget of 1909 introduced 'supertax'.

The measures just described undoubtedly had a redistributive effect in terms of the distribution of income. Whether other forms of public spending, such as that on goods and services, and other increases in taxation, have had progressive distributional consequences is more open to debate. The precise redistributive impact of the increased size of the state budget has long been the subject of interest by economists, from the calculations of W. S. Jevons in 1869, through Lord Samuel's address (1919) on 'The Taxation of the Various Classes of the People', to the study of redistribution by Barna (1945), and, in the post-war period, the *Economic Trends* series produced regularly since 1961 by the ONS. These studies are based on a specific set of assumptions about the reaction of firms and households: for instance, the *Economic Trends* figures assume that indirect taxes are fully reflected in consumer prices. They are also limited in their coverage: the *Economic Trends* studies do not cover all taxes; omitting, for example, Corporation Tax; nor all of public spending; excluding, for example, defence. Despite these qualifications, the estimates represent a valuable first step in understanding the impact of the government budget.

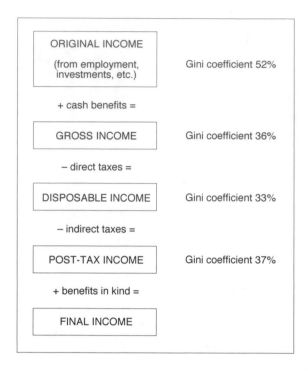

Figure 10.10 Stages of redistribution, 1995/96

Source: OCS, *Economic Trends*, March 1997, p.26 and Table C.

The *Economic Trends* studies are built up from calculations for each household which follow the lines set out in Figure 10.10. Households have incomes from market sources, referred to as 'original' income, although it should be stressed that this is not necessarily the income that they would have in the absence of the government budget. If there were no state old-age pension, then more people would stay on at work, and their original income would be higher. Arithmetically, we add cash benefits and subtract direct taxes to arrive at disposable income, analysed in the previous section. If we further subtract indirect taxes, this gives post-tax income. Finally, the official estimates add benefits from government spending on health, education and housing, and transport subsidies to give final income. Figure 10.10 shows at each stage the value of the Gini coefficient in 1995/96. The addition of cash benefits to original income reduces recorded inequality substantially, but direct taxes have only a modest effect. The reduction in the Gini coefficient associated with direct taxation is more than offset by the indirect taxes.

The development over time of original and post-tax, or final, income since 1961 is shown in Figure 10.11. Since the ONS has been improving the methodology of these calculations, and it has not been possible to reproduce earlier estimates on the same basis, there is not a fully consistent series. Figure 10.11 shows two long runs of data, from 1961–86 and from 1977–90, but there are several breaks in the 1990s which are sufficiently important to affect conclusions drawn about the Major years. Some idea of the effect of changes in method can be deduced where there are overlapping years: the inclusion of company car benefit in 1990 caused the post-tax Gini coefficient to rise by half a percentage point (CSO, *Economic Trends*, January 1993, p.159).

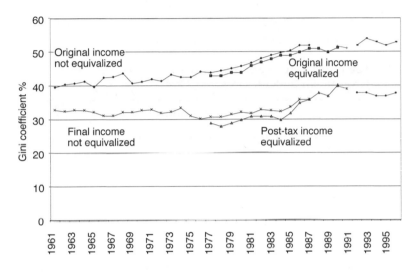

Figure 10.11 Economic Trends studies of redistribution, 1961–96/97[a][b]

Notes: [a]First series (from 1961) distribution (not equivalized) among households of original income and final income.
[b]Second series (from 1977) distribution among households of equivalized original income and post-tax income. There are breaks in the series in 1990, 1992 and 1996/97 (although a figure is given for this year on the previous basis).

Sources: First series: 1961–75 from Royal Commission on the Distribution of Income and Wealth (1977), pp.247 and 251; 1976– from CSO, *Economic Trends*, January 1982, p.105 (for 1976), December 1982, p.112 (for 1977–81), November 1983, p.87 (for 1982), December 1984, p.95 (for 1983), July 1986, p.103 (for 1984), July 1987, p.103 (for 1985), and May 1990 (for 1986, 1987). Second series: CSO, *Economic Trends*, April 1998, p.58 (for 1977, 1979, 1981, 1983, 1985, 1987, 1989, 1991, 1993/94–96/97), December 1994, p.65 (for 1978, 1980, 1982, 1984, 1986, 1988, 1992), and January 1993, p.159 (for 1990).

Inequality of original income has varied cyclically, but the predominant impression from Figure 10.11 is of a long-run steady rise in the Gini coefficient for original income since the mid-1960s. In the 20 years from 1965 to 1984, the coefficient increased from 40 per cent to 50 per cent. Even more striking is the fact that the coefficient for final income showed scarcely any rise over this period. The redistributive impact of cash transfers and taxation increased by enough to offset the more unequal market incomes.

After 1984, the story is quite different. Inequality in original income continued to rise, but between 1984 and 1990 the Gini coefficient for post-tax income increased much more sharply. Measured in terms of the difference between the two coefficients, the redistributive contribution of transfers and taxes fell from 19 percentage points (the difference between the two Gini coefficients in 1984) to 11 percentage points: see Table 10.2. The reduction in redistributive impact was attributable to a smaller impact of cash transfers (minus 5 percentage points), less progressive direct taxes (minus 1 percentage point) and more regressive indirect taxes (minus 2 percentage points).

Table 10.2 Gini coefficient and impact of government budget, 1984 and 1990

	Gini coefficient	
	1984	1990
Original income	49	51
Gross income	31	38
Disposable income	28	36
Post-tax income	30	40

Sources: CSO, *Economic Trends*, January 1993, Table Q; and January 1994, p.122.

The interpretation of these calculations raises a number of major issues, such as the incidence of taxation, the separation of life-cycle from other redistribution, and the valuation of public spending on goods and services. But, taken at face value, the *Economic Trends* estimates suggest that the state budget has ceased to offset the rising inequality of market incomes, and that the rise in inequality from 1984–90 was attributable to the reduced redistributive ambitions of the government.[11]

Has poverty persisted?

The last decades of the nineteenth century saw growing concern about poverty in Britain, notably on account of the surveys of London carried out by Charles Booth, which had considerable impact: 'Recent revelations as to the misery of the abject poor have profoundly touched the heart of the nation' (*Illustrated London News*; quoted by Fraser, 1984, p.132). The survey by Seebohm Rowntree in 1899 of all working-class households in York was stimulated by a desire to see 'how far the general conclusions arrived at by Mr Booth in respect of the metropolis would be found applicable to smaller urban populations' (1922, p.xvii), but he went further in seeking to estimate the income of all individual households in the survey and to compare these with a poverty line intended to capture the 'minimum necessaries for the maintenance of merely physical efficiency', based on rent, a minimum diet and an allowance for clothing, light, and fuel. For a couple with three children, the 'primary' poverty line, including rent of 4s a week, was 21s 8d, or £65 a week in 1997 prices (Rowntree, 1922, p.143). Rowntree emphasized the severity of the standard he was applying:

> the diet is even less generous than that allowed to able-bodied paupers in the York Workhouse, and ... no allowance is made for any expenditure other than that absolutely required. (1922, p.167)

He spelled out what the latter meant:

> A family living upon the scale ... must never spend a penny on railway fares or omnibus. ... They must never purchase a halfpenny newspaper ... they must write no letters ... They must never contribute anything to their church or chapel ... The children must have no pocket money. (1922, p.167)

Applying this severe criterion, Rowntree found that 9.9 per cent of the total non-institutional population of York were in primary poverty and that a further 3.2 per cent were within 2s of the line (Rowntree, 1922, p.144). The most important 'immediate' cause of poverty (52 per cent of those living in families below the primary poverty line) was that the chief wage-earner was 'in regular work, but at wages insufficient to maintain a moderate family (i.e. not more than four children) in a state of physical efficiency' (1922, p.153).

The subsequent 'Five Towns' surveys carried out by Bowley and Burnett-Hurst (1915) developed Rowntree's approach by the introduction of sampling (every twentieth house or building being selected, rather than a complete census). They applied both Rowntree's poverty standard and their own modified 'New Standard', and concluded that: 'It can hardly be too emphatically stated that of all the causes of primary poverty ... low wages are by far the most important' (Bowley and Burnett-Hurst, 1915, p.42).

The Five Towns study was repeated by Bowley and Hogg in 1923–24 in an attempt to answer the question posed in their title *Has Poverty Diminished?* (1925). The findings were summarized by Bowley as follows:

> in 1913 in a considerable number of cases the wages of unskilled labour were below [the standard] for a family including three children, while in 1924 wages under [the equivalent level] were extremely rare for a full week's

work for an able-bodied man … in families where a man is normally at work, the proportion in poverty in 1924 was only one-fifth of the proportion in 1913. (1930, pp.162–4)

However, he goes on to qualify this conclusion by saying that, 'two-thirds of the improvement due to wages was lost … owing to unemployment' (1930, p.164); but even allowing for this, 'the proportion in poverty in 1924 was little more than half that in 1913' (Bowley and Hogg, 1925, p.16), although the reduction did not apply to Stanley, in the coal fields of Durham.

The 1930s saw a variety of local studies of poverty, including the New Survey of London Life and Labour, the Social Survey of Merseyside, surveys of Bristol and Southampton, and Rowntree's second survey of York in 1936 (Rowntree, 1941). These studies were cited by Beveridge as the basis for the 'diagnosis of want' which underlay his plan for social security: 'The plan … starts from facts, from the condition of the people as revealed by social surveys between the two wars' (1942, p.8).

It was the same method which was used to assess the impact of the post-war Welfare State. In 1950, Rowntree carried out his third survey of York. He found a 'remarkable decrease in poverty between 1936 and 1950' (Rowntree and Lavers, 1951, p 32). This finding was seized upon by contemporary commentators. According to *The Times* at the time, there had been a 'remarkable improvement – no less than the virtual abolition of the sheerest want' (quoted in Coates and Silburn, 1970, p 14).

As we now know, the euphoria was misplaced. The Beveridge plan was not implemented with respect to the level of National Insurance benefits, thus undermining his central principle that the national minimum should be provided by social insurance, with social assistance playing a residual and diminishing role. Dependence on means-testing remained. The Attlee government did not accept Beveridge's proposal of unlimited duration for Unemployment Benefit (with condition of attendance at work or training centre after six months). The success claimed for the post-war Welfare State was in fact questioned by Townsend (Political and Economic Planning, 1952). Rowntree's own 1950 survey could have been used to show that there was sizeable non-take-up of National Assistance and that many people were living below this level (re-analysis of the Rowntree schedules by Atkinson et al., 1981).

It was not in fact until the early 1960s that poverty in Britain was rediscovered by the British public. The early studies by Townsend (1962) and Wedderburn (1962) were followed by Abel-Smith and Townsend's *The Poor and the Poorest* (1965). This study broke new ground in two respects. It used secondary analysis of already existing survey material (the FES), hence providing national coverage, and it applied as a poverty criterion the level of eligibility for National Assistance. They were asking how far the government was providing an effective safety net at the level set by Parliament.

The Poor and the Poorest revealed that about two million people (3.8 per cent of the population) were in fact living below the National Assistance scale. For about a quarter of the poor, the problem was inadequate earnings and family allowances – exposing the existence of the 'working poor'. For nearly half the poor, the problem was that of inadequate social insurance benefits coupled with unwillingness to apply for National Assistance. The existence of these problems was confirmed in official inquiries into *Financial and other circumstances of Retirement Pensioners* (Ministry of Pensions and National Insurance, 1966) and *Circumstances of Families* (Ministry of Social Security, 1967). These investigations in turn were followed by the Townsend survey of poverty (Townsend,

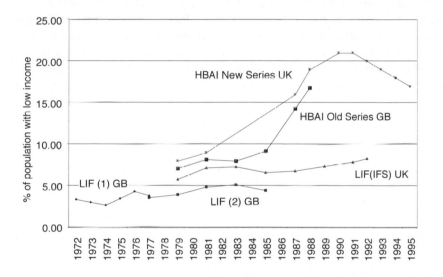

Figure 10.12 Low-income families[a] and households below half average income[b], 1972–94/95

Notes: [a]*Low-Income Families* (LIF) series relates to persons living in benefit units below the level of income of eligibility for Income Support/Supplementary Benefit and not in receipt of this benefit. Estimates for 1972–76 (LIF (1)) end-year estimates; estimates for 1977–85 (LIF (2)) annual averages. [b]*Households Below Average Income* (HBAI) series shows proportion of population living in households with equivalent disposable income (before housing costs) below half the mean. New series adopts changes in methodology and relates to UK.

Sources: LIF: absolute figures 1972–79 from Atkinson (1983), Table 10.2; other years from DHSS, *Low Income Families*. These cover Great Britain. Estimates for 1979–92 marked LIF(IFS) produced by IFS; these cover the UK (House of Commons Social Security Committee 1992 and 1995). HBAI: DSS, *Households Below Average Income*, 1992, 1993, 1994, 1995, 1996, and 1997 (years of publication), Table F1. The estimates are based on the Family Expenditure Survey (information for the most recent years is also available from the Family Resources Survey) and include the self-employed.

1979), which was important first as a purpose-designed national survey of poverty and second in its attempt to develop a new deprivation standard.

The application of the administrative standard to secondary analysis of the FES data was taken up in the official *Low-Income Families* (LIF) series shown in Figure 10.12, later continued by the IFS. These demonstrate that a small, but significant, proportion of the population – around 3 per cent – were living in families with incomes below the Supplementary Benefit (SB) (later Income Support) scale and not receiving SB. These families were either not claiming the SB to which they were entitled or were not eligible (for example, because they were in full-time work).

Viewed as a performance target, the SB standard makes sense, but as a measure of low income it has the disadvantage that the recorded extent of poverty is increased if benefits are made more generous, and vice versa. This point is addressed by Piachaud (1988) who compares the results with those obtained by adopting a relative poverty standard which is fixed proportionately with per capita disposable income. This alternative series shows a distinct dip in the mid-1970s, and he comments that, 'the policy of substantially increasing social security benefits for pensioners, as occurred in 1974, did have a clear impact on the extent of poverty' (Piachaud, 1988, p.349). (The dip is visible, but to a lesser extent, in the LIF series in Figure 10.12.)

A relative income approach has been adopted in the *Households Below Average Income* (HBAI) series which replaced the LIF statistics. This series records the equivalent disposable income of individuals according to the position, relative to the mean, of the household in which they live.[12] In European analyses of low incomes, it has become conventional to take a cut-off of 50 per cent of the mean; although essentially arbitrary, it is easily described in public debate. The HBAI series in Figure 10.12 relates to this threshold. It shows that there has been a sharp rise in the proportion below 50 per cent of the mean: from 8 per cent of the population in 1979 to around 20 per cent. The rise took place after 1985 and the divergence between the HBAI and the LIF (IFS) series illustrates dramatically the difference between the two approaches to measuring low income.

There are problems with all of the studies of low income reviewed here. They typically ignore those sleeping rough or in institutions. They may tell us little about the duration of poverty. Use of national surveys does not fully reveal the local dimension of poverty. Moreover, it is clearly difficult to compare findings at different dates. The poverty studied by Rowntree in 1899 was obviously different from that recorded in the official low-income statistics of the 1970s. How far the rise in the poverty standard can be measured by applying price indices has been the subject of controversy.[13] Comparison with per capita disposable income provides a benchmark, but the structure as well as the level of the scale changed over time.

In view of these complications, no attempt is made here to summarize the changes over the century. Simply I note that, despite the improvements which were apparently associated with the two world wars, we are ending the century just as we began, with a widespread concern about poverty.

Nor is this concern limited to Britain. The European Commission has taken an active role in the development of measures of poverty in Europe. Its statistics have been based on the half average income criterion described above, this being the concrete implementation of the definition adopted by the Council of Ministers of 'persons whose resources (material, cultural and social) are so limited as to exclude them from the minimum acceptable way of life in the Member State in which they live' (Council Decision, 19 December 1984).

Application of the European Community standard for the 1980s showed that 50 million people in the then 12 members of the Community were living in poverty, or 15 per cent of the total population.

Solid basis for the 50 million figure is provided by the study carried out by Hagenaars et al. (1994) using data for the late 1980s from national household surveys. Their results are reproduced in Figure 10.13, showing the proportion of the population in each member state below 50 per cent of the mean income for the country in which they live. As with overall income inequality, lower

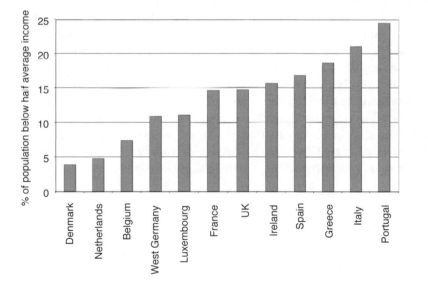

Figure 10.13 Low incomes in the UK compared with the European Community, 1988[a]

Note: [a]Figures relate to 1988, except Denmark, Ireland and Luxembourg (1987) and France and Portugal (1989).

Source: Hagenaars et al. (1994), Table 3.2.

figures are to be found in Denmark and the Benelux countries, now joined by West Germany with a below-average percentage with low incomes. The UK at that time (1988) was around the European average.

Concluding reflections

What can be learned about the future prospects for the distribution of income from this review of the twentieth century? The main lesson that I draw is that it is unwise to look for broad trends or critical watersheds. The advent of the Thatcher government might be seen as such a turning point, but the two decades post-1979 themselves consisted of distinct phases: widening inequality arising from earnings and an increased proportion of families without work up to the mid-1980s, followed by a more rapid rise in inequality associated with a reduction in redistribution. Underlying the distribution of income are many forces, and what we observe is their resultant. It is not therefore surprising that at times one force dominates but that at a later date another force takes us in a different direction. Understanding these mechanisms requires more space than possible here, but it seems safe to conclude that some at least of the forces are subject to the influence of our elected representatives. To that extent, the distribution of income in the twenty-first century is in our own hands.

It is therefore of great importance that public debate should be informed about the empirical features of the distribution of income and wealth. Empirical evidence has played a significant role in the past. Statistical investigations of taxable capacity influenced political discussion of progressive taxation 100 years ago. Writing 50 years ago, Mark Abrams stated that, 'the social survey in the hands of Booth, Rowntree and Bowley provided the State with an analysis of poverty which possibly saved Britain from violence and revolution and set her on the road to economic democracy' (1951, pp.142–3).

The publication on Christmas Eve of *The Poor and the Poorest* (Abel-Smith and Townsend, 1965) reawakened concern in post-war Britain about the persistence of poverty. Statistical evidence can be very powerful.

Acknowledgements

I am most grateful to Jo Webb for her help with this chapter. In particular, I have made extensive use in the section on poverty of material contained in a paper she has prepared on 'Poverty surveys 1900–2000'. I thank Chris Giles of IFS for supplying more recent income distribution data, and Essie Linton for very helpful research assistance. Janet Mandeville has kindly supplied me with literary evidence on earnings to supplement more conventional sources. More generally, I have drawn heavily on work that I have done over the years jointly with Alan Harrison, John Micklewright and Holly Sutherland.

Helpful comments were made at a seminar at Nuffield College in the Summer of 1997. I am grateful to Andrea Brandolini for useful discussions during his visit to Nuffield in 1998, and to Chelly Halsey, Holly Sutherland and Jo Webb for their most helpful comments on the July 1998 draft.

Finally, I thank Chelly Halsey for being a source of inspiration and encouragement, and for suggesting the opening quotation.

Notes

1   There were 20 shillings (s) in a pre-decimal pound, 12 pennies (d) in each shilling, and 4 farthings in a penny. Decimal currency was introduced in February 1971.

2   This is based on personal disposable income per capita given by Feinstein (1972, Table 17), extended from 1966 to 1996 using *National Income and Expenditure* (CSO, 1997). I have also extended the series back to 1900–13 making use of other tables in Feinstein (1972) and the assumption that net payments from the corporate sector to the personal sector were the same proportion of gross trading profit as in the period 1922–29. Details can be obtained from the author.

3   As explained in the figure's notes, the calculation is slightly asymmetric in that, to generate a consistent series over time, stock appreciation is not allowed for in the self-employment element.

4   There had been a Wage Census in 1886, used in Thatcher's (1968) table and by others, such as Gosling et al. (1994), Table 1, but, according to Bowley:

> though it purports to show the distribution of wages of individuals, it was often assumed that operatives doing the same kind of work were paid at the same rate, or more exactly that the variation of wages from the average in each occupation in the district observed was insignificant. (1937, p.41)

According to the Department of Employment, in the 1888 survey:

> Employers were asked to state the numbers of wage-earners in each category (men, women, etc.), in each separate occupation, in each establishment, and to give average rates of wages which were paid to each such group ... In many cases the groups, which were mostly very small, were further sub-divided to show the numbers on each separate wage rate. (DoE, 1971, p.92)

They go on to say that:

> Although the wages of an individual might differ slightly from the average of his group, the groups were so numerous, small and homogeneous that the variation from the true numbers thus arising cannot be material. (1971, p.92)

Despite this assertion, it seems clear that the 1886 survey was conducted on a different basis from that in 1906, where 'the main consideration was to ascertain the actual earnings of each individual' (DoE, 1971, p.94).

5   I have not considered explicitly the role of self-employment income, the importance of which has varied over the century. On the distribution of income among the self-employed, see Meager et al. (1996) and Parker (1997).

6. So called since they were first published in the National Income *Blue Book* (for example, CSO, *National Income and Expenditure 1958*, Table 31).
7. The timing is complicated. The figure for '1938' in the *Blue Book* series is based on the 1937–38 Survey of Personal Incomes (CSO, *National Income and Expenditure 1958*, p.74), but according to Stark (1978, p.48) most of the income related to 1936–37. This survey is used by Barna (1945), who refers to it as '1937'.
8. The data relate to the United Kingdom. No adjustment is made for regional differences in price levels across the country; on this, see Johnston et al. (1996).
9. Expressed as a proportion of per capita disposable income, this threshold is equivalent to some £2 million in 1996, whereas the 1995/96 SPI shows 12 000 people with after tax incomes above £200 000 (this is the top range identified).
10. The data used are similar to those in Figure 10.7, but there are differences in method, including the equivalence scale and the adjustments for differential non-response.
11. For a detailed comparison of the tax and benefit policy in 1978/79 with that in 1996/77, see Redmond et al. (1998).
12. For a summary of qualitative information about life on a low income, see Kempson (1996); for an imaginative approach by the media, see the Channel 4 Commission on Poverty (Townsend, 1996).
13. See, for example, the account by Hennock (1991) of Bowley's attempt to arrive at a standard for the New Survey of London Life and Labour comparable with the original data of Booth.

References

Abel-Smith, B. and Townsend, P. (1965) *The Poor and the Poorest*, G. Bell and Sons, London.

Abrams, M. (1951) *Social Surveys and Social Action*, Heinemann, London.

Adeney, M. (1993) *Nuffield: A Biography*, Robert Hale, London.

Ainsworth, R. B. (1949) 'Earnings and working hours of manual wage-earners in the United Kingdom in October, 1938', *Journal of the Royal Statistical Society*, 112, Series A, pp.35–65 (including discussion).

Atkinson, A. B. (1983) *The Economics of Inequality*, second edition, Clarendon Press, Oxford.

Atkinson, A. B. (1993) 'What is happening to the distribution of income in the UK?', *Proceedings of the British Academy*, 82, pp.317–51.

*Atkinson, A. B. (1996) *Incomes and the Welfare State*, Cambridge University Press, Cambridge.

Atkinson, A. B. (1997) 'Bringing income distribution in from the cold', *Economic Journal*, 107, pp.297–321.

*Atkinson, A. B. (1998) *Poverty in Europe*, Basil Blackwell, Oxford.

Atkinson, A. B., Gordon, J. P. F. and Harrison, A. J. (1989) 'Trends in the shares of top wealth-holders in Britain, 1923–1981', *Oxford Bulletin of Economics and Statistics*, 51, pp.315–31.

Atkinson, A. B. and Harrison, A. J. (1978) *Distribution of Personal Wealth in Britain*, Cambridge University Press, Cambridge.

Atkinson, A. B., Maynard, A. K. and Trinder, C. G. (1981) 'National Assistance and low incomes in 1950', *Social Policy and Administration*, 15, pp.19–31.

Atkinson, A. B. and Micklewright, J. (1992) *Economic Transformation in Eastern Europe and the Distribution of Income*, Cambridge University Press, Cambridge.

Barna, T. (1945) *Redistribution of Incomes Through Public Finance in 1937*, Clarendon Press, Oxford.

Beveridge, Sir William (1942) *Social Insurance and Allied Services*, HMSO, London.

Boléat, M. (1982) *The Building Society Industry*, Allen and Unwin, London.

Bowley, A. L. (1930) *Some Economic Consequences of the Great War*, Butterworth, London.

Bowley, A. L. (1937) *Wages and Income in the United Kingdom since 1860*, Cambridge University Press, Cambridge.

Bowley, A. L. and Burnett-Hurst, A. R. (1915) *Livelihood and Poverty*, Bell, London.

Bowley, A. L. and Hogg, M. H. (1925) *Has Poverty Diminished?*, King, London.

Brittain, J. A. (1960) 'Some neglected features of Britain's income levelling', *American Economic Review*, 50, pp.593–603.

Butler, C. V. (1912) *Social Conditions in Oxford*, Sidgwick and Jackson, London.

Central Statistical Office (CSO) (1991) *Retail Prices 1914–1990*, HMSO, London.

Central Statistical Office (various years) *National Income and Expenditure*, HMSO, London.

Central Statistical Office (various years) *United Kingdom National Accounts*, HMSO, London.

*Central Statistical Office (various issues) 'The effects of taxes and benefits on household income', *Economic Trends*, HMSO, London.

Coates, K. and Silburn, R. (1970) *Poverty: the Forgotten Englishmen*, Penguin, London.

Cowell, F. A., Jenkins, S. P. and Litchfield, J. A. (1996) 'The changing shape of the UK income distribution; kernel density estimates', in Hills, J. (ed.) *New Inequalities*, Cambridge University Press, Cambridge.

Department of Employment (DoE) (1971) *British Labour Statistics Historical Abstract 1886–1968*, HMSO, London.

Department of Health and Social Security (DHSS) (various years) *Low Income Families*, Government Statistical Service, London.

*Department of Social Security (DSS) (various years) *Households Below Average Income*, HMSO, London.

Elliott, R. F. and Murphy, P. D. (1990) 'Manual Skill Differentials', in Gregory, M. and Thomson, A. W. J. (eds) *A Portrait of Pay, 1970–1982*, Clarendon Press, Oxford.

Feinstein, C. H. (1972) *Statistical Tables of National Income, Expenditure and Output of the UK 1855–1965*, Cambridge University Press, Cambridge.

Feinstein, C. H. (1988) 'The rise and fall of the Williamson Curve', *Journal of Economic History*, 48, pp.699–729.

Fraser, D. (1984) *The Evolution of the British Welfare State*, Macmillan, London.

Good, F. J. (1990) 'Estimates of the distribution of personal wealth', *Economic Trends*, 444, pp.137–57.

*Goodman, A. and Webb, S. (1994) *For Richer, For Poorer*, Commentary no. 42, Institute for Fiscal Studies, London.

Gosling, A., Machin, S. and Meghir, C. (1994) 'What has happened to men's wages since the mid-1960s?', *Fiscal Studies*, 15 (4), pp.63–87.

Gottschalk, P. and Smeeding, T. M. (forthcoming) 'Empirical evidence on income inequality in industrialized countries', in Atkinson, A. B. and Bourguignon, F. (eds) *Handbook of Income Distribution*, North Holland, Amsterdam.

Hagenaars, A., de Vos, K. and Zaidi, A. (1994) *Poverty Statistics in the late 1980s*, Eurostat, Luxembourg.

Harkness, S., Machin, S. and Waldfogel, J. (1995) 'Evaluating the Pin Money Hypothesis', Welfare State Programme Discussion Paper 108, London School of Economics, London.

Hennock, E P (1991) 'Concepts of poverty in the British social surveys from Charles Booth to Arthur Bowley', in Bulmer, M., Bales, K. and Sklar, K. K. (eds) *The Social Survey in Historical Perspective 1880–1940*, Cambridge University Press, Cambridge.

*Hills, J. (1995) *Income and Wealth*, Joseph Rowntree Foundation, York

*Hills, J. (ed.) (1996) *New Inequalities*, Cambridge University Press, Cambridge.

*Hills, J. (1998) *Income and Wealth: The Latest Evidence*, Joseph Rowntree Foundation, York.

Hilton, J. (1944) *Rich Man, Poor Man*, Allen and Unwin, London.

Horne, H. (1947) *A History of Savings Banks*, Oxford University Press, Oxford.

House of Commons Social Security Committee (1992) *Low Income Statistics: Low Income Families 1979–89*, Session 1992–93, Second Report, HMSO, London.

House of Commons Social Security Committee (1995) *Low Income Statistics: Low Income Families 1989–92*, Session 1994–95, First Report, HMSO, London.

*Inland Revenue (various years) *Inland Revenue Statistics*, HMSO, London.

Johnston, R., McKinney, M. and Stark, T. (1996) 'Regional price level variations and real household incomes in the United Kingdom, 1979/80–1993', *Regional Studies*, 30, pp.567–78.

Kempson, E. (1996) *Life on a Low Income*, Joseph Rowntree Foundation, York.

Lydall, H. F. (1959) 'The long-term trend in the size distribution of income', *Journal of the Royal Statistical Society*, 122, pp.1–37.

Meager, N., Court, G. and Moralee, J. (1996) 'Self-employment and the distribution of income', in Hills, J. (ed.) *New Inequalities*, Cambridge University Press, Cambridge.

Ministry of Pensions and National Insurance (1966) *Financial and Other Circumstances of Retirement Pensioners*, HMSO, London.

Ministry of Social Security (1967) *Circumstances of Families*, HMSO, London.

Paish, F. W. (1957) 'The real incidence of personal taxation', *Lloyds Bank Review*, 43, pp.1–16.

Parker, S. C. (1997) 'The distribution of self-employment income in the United Kingdom, 1976–1991', *Economic Journal*, 107, pp.455–66.

Piachaud, D. (1988) 'Poverty in Britain 1899 to 1983', *Journal of Social Policy*, 17, pp.335–49.

Political and Economic Planning (Townsend, P.) (1952) 'Poverty: Ten years after Beveridge', *Planning*, 344.

Ramprakash, D. (1975) 'Distribution of income statistics for the United Kingdom, 1972/73: sources and methods', *Economic Trends*, 262, pp.78–96.

*Redmond, G., Sutherland, H. and Wilson, M. (1998) *The Arithmetic of Tax and Social Security Reform*, Cambridge University Press, Cambridge.

Reeves, M. P. (1913) *Round About a Pound a Week*, G. Bell and Sons, London.

*Routh, G. (1980) *Occupation and Pay in Great Britain 1906–79*, second edition (previous edition covered period up to 1960), Macmillan, London.

Rowntree, B. S. (1922) *Poverty: A Study of Town Life, new edition*, Longman, London (second edition of Rowntree, 1901).

Rowntree, B. S. (1941) *Poverty and Progress*, Longman, Green and Co., London.

Rowntree, B. S. and Lavers, G. R. (1951) *Poverty and the Welfare State*, Longman, London.

Royal Commission on the Distribution of Income and Wealth (1977) *Report no. 5, Third Report on the Standing Reference*, Cmnd. 6999, HMSO, London.

Royal Commission on the Distribution of Income and Wealth (1979) *Report no. 7, Fourth Report on the Standing Reference*, Cmnd.7595, HMSO, London.

Rubinstein, W. D. (1981) *Men of Property*, Croom Helm, London.

*Rubinstein, W. D. (1986) *Wealth and Inequality in Britain*, Faber and Faber, London.

Samuel, Lord (1919) 'The taxation of the various classes of the people', *Journal of the Royal Statistical Society*, 82, pp.143–82.

Seers, D. (1956) 'Has the distribution of income become more unequal?', *Bulletin of the Oxford University Institute of Statistics*, 18, pp.73–86.

Stark, T. (1978) 'Personal Incomes', in Maunder, W. F. (ed.) *Reviews of United Kingdom Statistical Sources*, vol. 6, Pergamon, Oxford.

Stewart, I. (1991) 'Estimates of the distribution of personal wealth II', *Economic Trends*, 457, pp.99–110.

Tawney, R. H. (1931) *Equality*, Allen and Unwin, London.

Thatcher, A. R. (1968) 'The distribution of earnings of employees in Great Britain', *Journal of the Royal Statistical Society*, 131, pp.133–80.

Titmuss, R. M. (1962) *Income Distribution and Social Change*, Allen and Unwin, London.

Townsend, P. B. (1962) 'The meaning of poverty', *British Journal of Sociology*, 13.

*Townsend, P. B. (1979) *Poverty in the United Kingdom*, Allen Lane, London.

Townsend, P. B. (chair) (1996) *Report of the Channel 4 Commission on Poverty*, Channel 4, London.

Wedderburn, D. (1962) 'Poverty in Britain today – the evidence', *The Sociological Review*, 10.

Wedgwood, J. (1939) *The Economics of Inheritance*, Penguin Books, London (new edition).

Williamson, J. G. (1985) *Did British Capitalism Breed Inequality?*, Allen and Unwin, Boston, Mass.

Further reading

(In addition to the asterisked items in the References)

The chapter has concentrated on the distribution of economic advantage (earnings, income and wealth); for references to the related, but distinct, literature on social stratification, see:

Marshall, G. (1997) *Repositioning Class*, Sage Publications, London.

The ethical principles underlying choice of variables on which to focus ('equality of what?') are set out in:

Sen, A. (1992) *Inequality Reexamined*, Clarendon Press, Oxford.

A great deal of material is published in the official studies of the distribution of income and redistribution, such as those of the DSS, the CSO and Inland Revenue (see References).

Part IV
Politics

11
Electors and Elected

David Butler

> Democracy is the worst form of government except all those other forms that have been tried.
>
> Winston Churchill, House of Commons, 11 November 1947

Introduction

This chapter covers some of the most readily defined or quantifiable aspects of the political process in Britain – the legal and social composition of the electorate, the votes recorded at parliamentary elections and the social and party composition of the House of Commons and the Cabinet. It is important to stress that quantifiable statements about political institutions are far from representing the whole truth about them.

All sorts of considerations that are relevant to balanced discussion of the evolution or the efficacy of the central instruments of British government are left untouched in this chapter, simply because they cannot be reduced to tables or other irrefutable statements of fact. The Notes on Sources at the end of the chapter do, however, include some general evaluative and analytical writing.

Electorate

Parliamentary franchise

In 1900 there were 6 731 000 names on the parliamentary electoral roll (approximately 58 per cent of the male population over 21). In 1997 the number was 43 700 000 (almost equal to the total population over 18). In 1900 only men were entitled to vote and the franchise qualifications, under the Representation of the People Acts of 1867 and 1885, and the Registration Act of 1885, limited the number, mainly by requiring 12 months' residence and occupancy of premises worth £10 a year; on the other hand some people could vote in more than one constituency, through having business premises or university qualifications or a second residence. By the Representation of the People Act of 1918, the qualifications were simplified and the vote was extended to almost all women over 30; by the Representation of the People Act of 1928, women were placed on a virtually equal footing with men. By 1931 the electorate was equal to 94 per cent of the adult population although, since there were 137 000 university electors (0.5 per cent of the total) and 365 000 business electors (1.4 per cent), and since there were some inaccuracies in the register, the proportion of the adult population able to vote cannot have exceeded 90 per cent. The Representation of the People Act of 1945 – and special war-time factors – greatly curtailed the business qualification and there were only 49 000 business electors entitled to vote in 1945; on the other hand, graduates on the lists for the 12 university constituencies now numbered 217 000.

Under the Representation of the People Acts of 1948 and 1949, all plural voting was abolished. The 1950 register was equivalent to 99 per cent of the adult population although a 1950 study by the Government Social Survey suggested that about 4 per cent of the names were there in error (Gray and Corlett, 1950); a 1967 study found a similar rate of inaccuracy (Gray and Gee, 1967); a 1982 study found that errors had risen to 6.5 per cent and redundant names to 10.4 per cent (Todd and Butcher, 1982); and a 1992 study found 7.1 per cent omissions and 7.9 per cent redundant names (Smith, 1991; 1993).

Under the Representation of the People Act of 1969, the voting age was lowered to 18 – although it was estimated that less than 70 per cent of the population between 18 and 21 were inscribed in the first register which came into force on 15 February 1970. The 1982 and 1992 Office of Population Censuses and Surveys (OPCS) studies showed that omissions varied by area; only 50 per cent of young blacks in city centres were on the register.

Local government franchise

From 1889 to 1945 the local government franchise was confined to householders or occupiers of business premises, and from 1918 onwards, their wives (until 1928, only if over 30). By the Representation of the People Act of 1945, the parliamentary and local government franchises were assimilated. The business vote, although eliminated for parliamentary purposes in 1948, continued for local government purposes until the Representation of the People Act of 1969 when, except for the City of London, it was abolished (Keith-Lucas, 1953).

Electoral administration

From 1900–18 electoral arrangements were governed primarily by the Representation of the People Act, 1867, as modified by the Ballot Act, 1872; the Corrupt Practices Act, 1883; the Franchise Act, 1884; the Registration Act, 1885; and the Redistribution of Seats Act, 1885. The Representation of the People Act, 1918; the Equal Franchise Act, 1928; the Representation of the People Act, 1948 (consolidated in 1949); the Representation of the People Act,

1969; and the Representation of the People Act, 1985, constitute the only major legislation in the twentieth century.

Redistribution

The Redistribution of Seats Act, 1885, left the House of Commons with 670 members. While removing the worst anomalies, it specifically rejected the principle that constituencies should be approximately equal in size. This principle was, however, substantially accepted in the Representation of the People Act, 1918, on the recommendation of the Speaker's Conference of 1917, although Ireland was allowed to retain a disproportionate number of seats. The 1918 Act increased the size of the House of Commons to 707, but this fell to 615 in 1922 on the creation of the Irish Free State. Population movements produced substantial anomalies in representation and the Redistribution of Seats Act, 1944, authorized the immediate sub-division of constituencies with more than 100 000 electors, which led to 25 new seats being created at the 1945 election and raised the number of MPs to 640. It also provided for the establishment of Permanent Boundary Commissioners to report every three to seven years.

The Boundary Commissioners' first recommendations were enacted in the Representation of the People Act, 1948 (with the controversial addition by the government of 17 extra seats as well as the abolition of the 12 university seats), and the 1950 Parliament had 625 members. The next reports of the Boundary Commissioners, given effect by resolutions of the House in December 1954 and January 1955, increased the number of constituencies to 630. The controversy caused by these changes led to the Redistribution of Seats Act, 1958, which modified the rules governing the Boundary Commissioners' decisions and asked them to report only every 10–15 years. The Boundary Commissioners started their revision in 1965; when their recommendations came before Parliament in 1969, the Labour government insisted upon their rejection. The Conservative government gave effect to them in October 1970. As a result the House of Commons had 635 members from 1974–83. The next redistribution, started in 1976, was only completed, after some litigation, just in time for the 1983 election. It increased the House from 635 to 650 members. That rose to 651 in 1992 (when an extra seat was created at Milton Keynes) and to 659 following the general redistribution in 1997. In 1994 the Redistribution of Seats Act changed the timescale to 8–12 years.

Election results

General election statistics

It is impossible to present election statistics in any finally authoritative way. British statutes make no acknowledgement of the existence of political parties, and in most general elections the precise allegiance of at least a few of the candidates has been in doubt. This, far more than arithmetic error, explains the discrepancies between the figures provided in various works of reference. Such discrepancies, however, are seldom on a serious scale (except, perhaps, for 1918). Election figures suffer much more from being inherently confusing than from being inaccurately reported. The complications that arise from unopposed returns, from plural voting, from two-member seats, and, above all, from variations in the number of candidates put up by each party are the really serious hazards in psephological interpretation. In the figures which follow an attempt is made to allow for these factors by a column which shows the average vote won by each opposed candidate (with the vote in two-member seats halved, and with university seats excluded). This still gives a distorted picture, especially when, as in 1900 or 1931, there were many unopposed candidates or when, as in 1929, 1931, or 1950, there was a sharp change in the number of Liberals standing; in 1918 the situation was so complicated that any such statistics are omitted, as they are likely to confuse more than to clarify; for other elections they should be regarded as corrective supplements to the cruder percentages in the previous column rather than as substitutes for them. The turnout percentages are modified to allow for the distorting effect of the two-member seats which existed up to 1950. To simplify classification, some arbitrary decisions have been made. Before 1918 candidates have been classified as Conservative, Liberal, or Irish Nationalist, even if their designation had a prefix such as Tariff Reform or Independent, but only officially sponsored candidates are classed as Labour. From 1918 onwards candidates not officially recognized by their party have been classified with 'Others' (except that in 1935 Independent Liberals are placed with Liberals). Liberal Unionists have been listed as Conservatives throughout. Liberal National, National Labour, and National candidates are listed with Conservatives except in 1931. From 1974 onwards all Northern Ireland candidates are classed as 'Other', and votes for the few Conservative candidates are left in that category.

Table 11.1 General election results, 1900–97

	Total votes	MPs elected	Candidates	Unopposed returns	% Share of total vote	Vote per opposed candidate
1900: 25 Sep–24 Oct						
Conservative	1797444	402	579	163	51.1	52.5
Liberal	1568141	184	406	22	44.6	48.2
Labour	63304	2	15	–	1.8	26.6
Irish Nat.	90076	82	100	58	2.5	80.0
Others	544	–	2	–	0.0	2.2
Elec. 6730935	3519509	670	1102	243	100.0	–
Turnout 74.6%						

Table 11.1 (*cont...*)

	Total votes	MPs elected	Candidates	Unopposed returns	% Share of total vote	Vote per opposed candidate
1906: 12 Jan–7 Feb						
Conservative	2451454	157	574	13	43.6	44.1
Liberal	2757883	400	539	27	49.0	52.6
Labour	329748	30	51	–	5.9	39.9
Irish Nat.	35031	83	87	74	0.6	63.1
Others	52387	–	22	–	0.9	18.8
Elec. 7264608	5626503	670	1273	114	100.0	–
Turnout 82.6%						
1910: 14 Jan–9 Feb						
Conservative	3127887	273	600	19	46.9	47.5
Liberal	2880581	275	516	1	43.2	49.2
Labour	505657	40	78	–	7.6	38.4
Irish Nat.	124586	82	104	55	1.9	77.7
Others	28693	–	17	–	0.4	15.4
Elec. 7694741	6667404	670	1315	75	100.0	–
Turnout 86.6%						
1910: 2–19 Dec						
Conservative	2420566	272	550	72	46.3	47.9
Liberal	2295888	272	467	35	43.9	49.5
Labour	371772	42	56	3	7.1	42.8
Irish Nat.	131375	84	106	53	2.5	81.9
Others	8768	–	11	–	0.2	9.1
Elec. 7709981	5228369	670	1190	163	100.0	–
Turnout 81.1%						
1918: 14 Dec *(The results were declared on 28 Dec 1918)*						
Coalition						
Unionist	3504198	335	374	42	32.6	
Coalition Lib.	1455640	133	158	27	13.5	
Coalition Lab.	161521	10	18	–	1.5	
(Coalition)	(5121359)	(478)	(550)	(69)	(47.6)	
Conservative	370375	23	37	–	3.4	
Irish Unionist	292722	25	38	–	2.7	
Liberal	298808	28	253	–	12.1	
Labour	2385472	63	388	12	22.2	
Irish Nat.	238477	7	60	1	2.2	
Sinn Fein	486,867	73	102	25	4.5	
Others	572503	10	197	–	5.3	
Elec. 21392322	10766583	707	1625	107	100.0	
Turnout 58.9%						

continued

Table 11.1 (*cont...*)

	Total votes	MPs elected	Candidates	Unopposed returns	% Share of total vote	Vote per opposed candidate
1922: 15 Nov						
Conservative	5500382	345	483	42	38.2	48.6
National Lib.	1673240	62	162	5	11.6	39.3
Liberal	2516287	54	328	5	17.5	30.9
Labour	4241383	142	411	4	29.5	40.0
Others	62340	12	59	1	3.2	28.3
Elec. 21127663	14393632	615	1443	57	100.0	–
Turnout 71.3%						
1923: 6 Dec						
Conservative	5538824	258	540	35	38.1	42.6
Liberal	4311147	159	453	11	29.6	37.8
Labour	4438508	191	422	3	30.5	41.0
Others	260042	7	31	1	1.8	27.6
Elec. 21281232	14548521	615	1446	50	100.0	–
Turnout 70.8%						
1924: 29 Oct						
Conservative	8039598	419	552	16	48.3	51.9
Liberal	2928747	40	340	6	17.6	30.9
Labour	5489077	151	512	9	33.0	38.2
Communist	55346	1	8	–	0.3	25.0
Others	126511	4	16	1	0.8	29.1
Elec. 21731320	16639279	615	1428	32	100.0	–
Turnout 76.6%						
1929: 30 May						
Conservative	8656473	260	590	4	38.2	39.4
Liberal	5308510	59	513	–	23.4	27.7
Labour	8389512	288	571	–	37.1	39.3
Communist	50614	–	25	–	0.3	5.3
Others	243266	8	31	3	1.0	21.2
Elec. 28850870	22648375	615	1730	7	100.0	–
Turnout 76.1%						
1931: 27 Oct						
Conservative	11978745	473	523	56	55.2 }	–
Nat. Labour	341370	13	20	–	1.6 }	62.9
Liberal Nat.	809302	35	41	–	3.7 }	–
Liberal	1403102	33	112	5	6.5 }	28.8
(Nat. Govt)	(14532519)	(554)	(696)	(61)	(67.0)	–
Ind.Liberal	106106	4	7	–	0.5	35.8
Labour	6649630	52	515	6	30.6	33.0

Table 11.1 (*cont...*)

	Total votes	MPs elected	Candidates	Unopposed returns	% Share of total vote	Vote per opposed candidate
1931: 27 Oct (*cont...*)						
Communist	74824	–	26	–	0.3	7.5
New Party	36377	–	24	–	0.2	3.9
Others	256917	5	24	–	1.2	21.9
Elec. 29960071	21656373	615	1292	67	100.0	–
Turnout 76.3%						
1935: 14 Nov						
Conservative	11810158	432	585	26	53.7	54.8
Liberal	1422116	20	161	–	6.4	23.9
Labour	8325491	154	552	13	37.9	40.3
Ind. Lab. Party	139577	4	17	–	0.7	22.2
Communist	27117	1	2	–	0.1	38.0
Others	272595	4	31	1	1.2	21.3
Elec. 31379050	21997054	615	1348	40	100.0	–
Turnout 71.2%						
1945: 5 Jul (*The results were declared on 26 July 1945*)						
Conservative	9988306	213	624	1	39.8	40.1
Liberal	2248226	12	306	–	9.0	18.6
Labour	11995152	393	604	2	47.8	50.4
Communist	102780	2	21	–	0.4	12.7
Common Wealth	110634	1	23	–	0.4	12.6
Others	640880	19	104	–	2.0	15.4
Elec. 33240391	25085978	640	1682	3	100.0	–
Turnout 72.7%						
1950: 23 Feb						
Conservative	12502567	298	620	2	43.5	43.7
Liberal	2621548	9	475	–	9.1	11.8
Labour	13266592	315	617	–	46.1	45.7
Communist	91746	–	100	–	0.3	2.0
Others	290218	3	56	–	1.0	12.6
Elec. 33269770	28772671	625	1868	2	100.0	–
Turnout 84.0%						
1951: 25 Oct						
Conservative	13717538	321	617	4	48.0	48.6
Liberal	730556	6	109	–	2.5	14.7
Labour	13948605	295	617	–	48.8	49.2
Communist	21640	–	10	–	0.1	4.4
Others	177329	3	23	–	0.6	16.8
Elec. 34645573	28595668	625	1376	4	100.0	–
Turnout 82.5%						

continued

Table 11.1 (*cont...*)

	Total votes	MPs elected	Candidates	Unopposed returns	% Share of total vote	Vote per opposed candidate
1955: 26 May						
Conservative	13286569	344	623	–	49.7	50.2
Liberal	722405	6	110	–	2.7	15.1
Labour	12404970	277	620	–	46.4	47.3
Communist	33144	–	17	–	0.1	4.2
Others	313410	3	39	–	1.1	20.8
Elec. 34858263	26760498	630	1409	–	100.0	–
Turnout 76.7%						
1959: 8 Oct						
Conservative	13749830	365	625	–	49.4	49.6
Liberal	1638571	6	216	–	5.9	16.9
Labour	12215538	258	621	–	43.8	44.5
Communist	30897	–	18	–	0.1	4.1
Plaid Cymru	77571	–	20	–	0.3	9.0
SNP[a]	21738	–	5	–	0.1	11.4
Others	12464	1	31	–	0.4	11.0
Elec. 35397080	27859241	630	1536	–	100.0	–
Turnout 78.8%						
1964: 15 Oct						
Conservative	12001396	304	630	–	43.4	43.4
Liberal	3092878	9	365	–	11.2	18.5
Labour	12205814	317	628	–	44.1	44.1
Communist	45932	–	36	–	0.2	3.4
Plaid Cymru	69507	–	23	–	0.3	8.4
SNP[a]	64044	–	15	–	0.2	10.7
Others	168422	–	60	–	0.6	6.4
Elec. 35892572	27655374	630	1757	–	100.0	–
Turnout 77.1%						
1966: 31 Mar						
Conservative	11418433	253	629	–	41.9	41.8
Liberal	2327533	12	311	–	8.5	16.1
Labour	13064951	363	621	–	47.9	48.7
Communist	62112	–	57	–	0.1	3.0
Plaid Cymru	61071	–	20	–	0.2	8.7
SNP[a]	128474	–	20	–	0.5	14.1
Others	201302	2	49	–	0.6	8.6
Elec. 35964684	27263606	630	1707	–	100.0	–
Turnout 75.8%						

Table 11.1 (*cont...*)

	Total votes	MPs elected	Candidates	Unopposed returns	% Share of total vote	Vote per opposed candidate
1970: 18 Jun						
Conservative	13145123	330	628	–	46.4	46.5
Liberal	2117035	6	332	–	7.5	13.5
Labour	12179341	287	624	–	43.0	43.5
Communist	37970	–	58	–	0.1	1.1
Plaid Cymru	175016	–	36	–	0.6	11.5
SNP[a]	306802	1	65	–	1.1	12.2
Others	383511	6	94	–	1.4	9.1
Elec. 39342013	28344798	630	1837	–	100.0	–
Turnout 72.0%						
1974: 28 Feb						
Conservative	11868906	297	623	–	37.9	38.8
Liberal	6063470	14	517	–	19.3	23.6
Labour	11639243	301	623	–	37.1	38.0
Communist	32741	–	44	–	0.1	1.7
Plaid Cymru	171364	2	36	–	0.6	10.7
SNP[a]	632032	7	70	–	2.0	21.9
National Front	76865	–	54	–	0.3	3.2
Others (GB)	131059	2	120	–	0.4	2.2
Others (NI)[b]	717986	12	48	–	2.3	25.0
Elec. 39798899	31333226	635	2135	–	100.0	–
Turnout 78.7%						
1974: 10 Oct						
Conservative	10464817	277	623	–	35.8	36.7
Liberal	5346754	13	619	–	18.3	18.9
Labour	11457079	319	623	–	39.2	40.2
Communist	17426	–	29	–	0.1	1.5
Plaid Cymru	166321	3	36	–	0.6	10.8
SNP[a]	839617	11	71	–	2.9	30.4
National Front	113843	–	90	–	0.4	2.9
Others (GB)	81227	–	8	–	0.3	1.5
Others (NI)[b]	702094	12	43	–	2.4	27.9
Elec. 40072971	29189178	635	2252	–	100.0	–
Turnout 72.8%						
1979: 3 May						
Conservative	13697690	339	622	–	43.9	44.9
Liberal	4313811	11	577	–	13.8	14.9
Labour	11532148	269	623	–	36.9	37.8
Communist	15938	–	38	–	0.1	0.9
Plaid Cymru	132544	2	36	–	0.4	8.1
SNP[a]	504259	2	71	–	1.6	17.3

continued

Table 11.1 (*cont...*)

	Total votes	MPs elected	Candidates	Unopposed returns	% Share of total vote	Vote per opposed candidate
1979: 3 May (*cont...*)						
National Front	190747	–	303	–	0.6	1.6
Ecology	38116	–	53	–	0.1	2.0
Workers Rev. P.	13535	–	60	–	0.1	0.5
Others (GB)	85338	–	129	–	0.3	1.3
Others (NI)[b]	695889	12	64	–	2.2	18.8
Elec. 41093264	31220010	635	2576	–	100.0	–
Turnout 76.0%						
1983: 9 Jun						
Conservative	13012315	397	633	–	42.4	43.5
Liberal	4210115	17	322	–	13.7	27.7
Social Democrat	3570834	6	311	–	11.6	24.3
(Alliance)	(7780949)	(23)	(633)	–	(25.4)	(26.0)
Labour	8456934	209	633	–	27.6	28.3
Communist	11606	–	35	–	0.04	0.8
Plaid Cymru	125309	2	36	–	0.4	7.8
SNP[a]	331975	2	72	–	1.1	11.8
National Front	27065	–	60	–	0.1	1.0
Others (GB)	193383	–	282	–	0.6	1.4
Others (NI)[b]	64925	17	95	–	3.1	17.9
Elec. 42197344	42197344	650	2579	–	100.0	–
Turnout 72.7%						
1987: 11 Jun						
Conservative	13763066	376	633	–	42.3	43.4
Liberal	4173450	17	327	–	25.5	12.8
Social Democrat	3168183	5	306	–	9.7	20.6
(Alliance)	(7341290)	(22)	(633)	–	(22.5)	(23.2)
Labour	10029778	229	633	–	30.8	31.2
Plaid Cymru	123599	3	38	–	0.3	7.3
SNP[a]	416473	3	71	–	1.3	14.0
Others (GB)	151519	–	241	–	0.5	1.2
Others (NI)[b]	730152	17	77	–	2.2	22.1
Elec. 43181321	32529568	650	2325	–	100.0	–
Turnout 75.3%						
1992: 8 Apr						
Conservative	14048283	336	634	–	41.9	42.3
Liberal Democrat	5999384	20	632	–	17.8	18.3
Labour	11559735	271	634	–	34.4	35.2
Plaid Cymru	154439	4	38	–	0.5	8.8
SNP[a]	629552	3	72	–	1.9	21.5
Others (GB)	436207	–	838	–	1.0	1.3

Table 11.1 (*cont...*)

	Total votes	MPs elected	Candidates	Unopposed returns	% Share of total vote	Vote per opposed candidate
1992: 8 Apr (*cont...*)						
Others (NI)[b]	740485	17	100	–	2.2	17.2
Elec. 43249721	33612693	651	2325	–	100.0	–
Turnout 77.7%						
1997: 1 May						
Conservative	9600940	165	640	–	30.7	31.0
Liberal Democrat	5243440	46	639	–	16.8	17.3
Labour	13517911	419	639	–	43.2	44.5
Plaid Cymru	161030	4	40	–	0.5	12.4
SNP[a]	622260	6	72	–	2.0	22.1
Referendum	811827	–	547	–	2.6	3.1
Others (GB)	549874	1	1139	–	1.7	1.0
Others (NI)[b]	790778	18	117	–	2.5	15.3
Elec. 43784559	31287702	659	3724	–	100.0	–
Turnout 71.5%						

Note: [a]Scottish National Party.

[b]From 1974 no candidates in Northern Ireland are included in the major party totals.

Source: Butler and Butler (2000, forthcoming).

Table 11.2(a) General election results by region, 1900–45[a]

	1900	1906	Jan 1910	Dec 1910		1918[f]	1922	1923	1924	1929	1931	1935	1945
County of London													
Con.	51	19	3	30	*Coal.*	43	29	39	24	53	39	12
Lib.	8	38	25	26		53	9	11	3	2	4	1	–
Lab.	–	2	1	3	*Op.*	9	22	19	36	5	22	48
Other	–	–	–	–		9	1	–	–	–	–	–	–
Rest of Southern England[b]													
Con.	123	45	107	103	*Coal.*	130	89	150	111	156	147	88
Lib.	32	107	46	49		149	23	48	5	18	4	3	3
Lab.	–	3	2	2	*Op.*	9	27	10	35	5	15	91
Other	–	–	–	–		16	3	1	–	1	–	3	3
Midlands[c]													
Con.	60	27	49	50	*Coal.*	53	45	64	35	80	67	24
Lib.	27	59	31	30		67	17	17	2	5	3	1	–
Lab.	1	2	8	8	*Op.*	17	25	21	47	4	19	64
Other	–	–	–	–		16	–	–	–	–	–	–	2

continued

Table 11.2(a) (*cont...*)

	1900	1906	Jan 1910	Dec 1910	1918[f]	1922	1923	1924	1929	1931	1935	1945
North of England[d]												
Con.	98	31	45	50	*Coal.* 82	57	101	51	146	106		43
Lib.	55	102	86	82	121	27	48	9	10	9	5	2
Lab.	–	20	22	21	*Op.* 60	64	59	108	15	60		128
Other	1	1	1	1	50	2	2	2	2	1	–	–
Wales												
Con.	6	–	2	3	*Coal.* 6	4	9	1	11	11		4
Lib.	27	33	27	26	20	10	12	10	9	8	6	6
Lab.	1	1	5	5	*Op.* 18	19	16	25	16	18		25
Other	–	–	–	–	15	1	–	–	–	–	–	–
Scotland												
Con.	36	10	9	9	*Coal.* 13	14	36	20	57	43		29
Lib.	34	58	59	58	54	27	22	8	13	7	3	–
Lab.	–	2	2	3	*Op.* 29	34	26	37	7	20		37
Other	–	–	–	–	17	2	12	1	1	–	5	5
(Northern) Ireland[e]												
Con.	19	16	19	17	*Coal.* 10	10	12	10	10	10		9
Lib.	1	3	1	1	–	–	–	–	–	–	–	–
Lab.	–	–	–	–	*Op.* –	–	–	–	–	–		–
Other	81	82	81	83	101	2	2	–	2	2	2	3
University												
Con.	9	9	9	9	*Coal.* 8	9	8	8	8	9		4
Lib.	–	–	–	–	13	3	2	3	2	2	1	1
Lab.	–	–	–	–	*Op.* –	–	–	–	–	–		–
Other-	–	–	–	2	1	1	1	1	2	2	2	7
Totals												
Con.	402	157	273	272	*Coal.* 345	258	419	260	521	432		213
Lib.	184	400	275	272	478	116	159	40	59	37	20	12
Lab.	2	30	40	42	*Op.* 142	191	151	288	52	154		393
Other	82	83	82	84	229	12	7	5	8	5	9	22
Total	670	670	670	670	707	615	615	615	615	615	615	640

Notes: [a] The vertical lines indicate redistributions of seats.
[b] Southern England includes the rest of England, except for the County of London (the old LCC area), but from 1974 the seats in the outer areas of the Greater London Council are classed with the County of London and not with the rest of Southern England.
[c] Midlands includes Hereford, Worcestershire, Warwickshire, Northamptonshire, Lincolnshire, Nottinghamshire, Leicestershire, Staffordshire, Salop and Derbyshire.
[d] North of England includes Cheshire, Lancashire, Yorkshire, and all counties to their north.
[e] In 1918 all Coalition and all non-Coalition candidates are listed together. In fact a substantial number of the 48 Conservatives who were elected without the Coupon worked with the government.
[f] Read down this column.

Source: Butler and Butler (2000, forthcoming).

Table 11.2(b) General election results by region, 1950–97[a]

	1950	1951	1955	1959	1964	1966	1970	Feb 1974	Oct 1974	1979	1983	1987	1992	1997
London GLC														
Con.	12	14	15	18	10	6	9	42	41	50	56	58	48	11
Lib.	–	–	–	–	–	–	–	–	–	–	2	3	1	6
Lab.	31	29	27	24	32	36	33	50	51	42	26	23	35	58
Other	–	–	–	–	–	–	–	–	–	–	–	–	–	–
Rest of Southern England[b]														
Con.	144	153	163	171	156	134	169	136	128	146	168	170	161	95
Lib.	1	–	–	1	3	4	2	5	5	3	5	3	6	22
Lab.	54	46	42	34	46	67	34	21	29	13	3	3	10	48
Other	–	–	1	–	–	1	1	–	–	–	–	–	–	–
Midlands[c]														
Con.	35	35	39	49	42	35	51	43	40	57	70	67	57	28
Lib.	–	–	–	–	–	–	–	–	–	–	–	–	–	1
Lab.	59	59	57	47	54	61	45	54	58	41	30	33	43	74
Other	–	–	–	–	–	–	–	1	–	–	–	–	–	–
North of England[d]														
Con.	61	69	75	77	53	44	63	47	44	53	68	63	53	13
Lib.	–	2	2	2	–	2		4	3	4	6	4	3	5
Lab.	107	99	90	88	114	121	104	112	117	107	89	96	107	139
Other	–	–	–	–	–	–	–	1	–	–	–	–	–	1
Wales														
Con.	4	6	6	7	6	3	7	8	8	11	14	8	6	–
Lib.	5	3	3	2	2	1	1	2	2	1	2	3	1	2
Lab.	27	27	27	27	28	32	27	24	23	22	20	24	27	34
Other	–	–	–	–	–	1	1	3	2	22	2	3	4	4
Scotland														
Con.	32	35	36	31	24	20	23	21	16	22	21	10	11	–
Lib.	2	1	1	1	4	5	3	3	3	3	8	9	9	10
Lab.	37	35	34	38	43	46	44	40	41	44	41	50	49	56
Other	–	–	–	1	–	–	1	7	11	2	2	3	3	6
Northern Ireland														
Con.	10	9	10	12	12	11	8	–	–		–	–	–	–
Lib.	–	–	–	–	–	–	–	–	–	–	–	–	–	–
Lab.	–	–	–	–	–	–	–	–	–	–	–	–	–	–
Other	2	3	2	–	–	1	4	12	12	12	17	17	17	18

continued

Table 11.2(b) (*cont...*)

	1950	1951	1955	1959	1964	1966	1970	Feb 1974	Oct 1974	1979	1983	1987	1992	1997
Total														
Con.	298	321	344	365	304	253	330	297	277	339	397	376	336	165
Lib.	9	6	6	6	9	12	6	14	13	11	23	22	18	46
Lab.	315	295	277	258	317	363	287	301	319	269	209	229	271	419
Other	3	3	3	1	–	2	7	23	26	16	21	23	24	29
Total	625	625	630	630	630	630	630	635	635	635	650	650	651	659

Notes: [a] The vertical lines indicate redistributions of seats.
[b] Southern England includes the rest of England, except for the County of London (the old LCC area), but from 1974 the seats in the outer areas of the Greater London Council are classed with the County of London and not with the rest of Southern England.
[c] Midlands includes Hereford, Worcestershire, Warwickshire, Northamptonshire, Lincolnshire, Nottinghamshire, Leicestershire, Staffordshire, Salop and Derbyshire.
[d] North of England includes Cheshire, Lancashire, Yorkshire, and all counties to their north.

Source: Butler and Butler (2000, forthcoming).

Table 11.3 By-elections[a]

	Total by-el.[b]	Change	Conservative +	Conservative -	Liberal +	Liberal -	Labour +	Labour -	Other +	Other -	No. per year	% with change
1900–05	113	30	2	26	20	4	3	–	5	–	22	27
1906–09	101	20	12	–	–	18	5	–	3	2	25	20
1910	20	–	–	–	–	–	–	–	–	–	20	–
1911–18	245	31	16	4	4	16	2	4	10	8	31	13
1918–22	108	27	4	13	52	11	14	1	4	2	27	25
1922–23	16	6	1	4	3	1	2	–	–	1	16	38
1923–24	10	3	2	1	–	1	1	1	–	–	10	30
1924–29	63	20	1	16	6	3	13	1	–	–	14	32
1929–31	36	7	4	1	–	1	2	4	1	1	15	19
1931–35	62	10	–	9	–	1	10	–	–	–	5	16
1935–45	219	30	–	29	–	–	13	1	17	–	23	14
1945–50	52	3	3	–	–	–	–	–	–	3	11	6
1950–51	16	–	–	–	–	–	–	–	–	–	10	–
1951–55	48	1	1	–	–	–	–	1	–	–	13	2
1955–59	52	6	1	4	1	1	4	–	–	1	12	12
1959–64	62	9	2	7	1	–	6	2	–	–	15	14
1964–66	13	2	1	1	1	–	–	1	–	–	9	15
1966–70	38	16	12	1	1	–	–	–	15	3	9	42
1970–74	30	9	–	5	5	–	2	3	2	1	9	30
1974	1	–	–	–	–	–	–	–	–	–	1	–
1974–79	30	7	6	–	1	–	–	7	–	–	6	23
1979–83	20	7	1	4	4	–	1	1	1	2	5	35

Table 11.3 (*cont...*)

	Total by-el.[b]	Change	Conservative +	Conservative -	Liberal +	Liberal -	Labour +	Labour -	Other +	Other -	No. per year	% with change
1983–87	31	6	–	4	4	–	1	1	1	1	8	19
1987–92	23	8	–	7	3	–	4	1	1	–	4	35
1992–97	17	8	–	8	4	–	3	–	1	–	3	47

Notes: [a] Up to 1918, and to a lesser extent to 1926, the number of by-elections is inflated by the necessity for Ministers to stand for re-election on appointment. In 53 such cases the returns were unopposed.
[b] 15 of the 31 by-elections were in N. Ireland. In mainland Great Britain there were 16 by-elections – an annual incidence of 4 with a turnover rate of 31%.

Source: Butler and Butler (2000, forthcoming).

Referendums

The only referendum at the national level took place on 5 June 1975 when, on a 64.5 per cent turnout, the United Kingdom voted 64.5 per cent 'Yes' and 35.5 per cent 'No' to stay within the European Community (Butler and Kitzinger, 1976).

Table 11.4(a) Referendum on EEC membership, 5 June 1975

'Do you think that the United Kingdom should stay in the European Community (the Common Market)?'

	Total electorate	Total votes	Turnout	'Yes'[b] %	Highest 'Yes' %	Lowest 'Yes' %
England	33339959	21722222	64.6	68.7	76.3	62.9
Wales	2015766	1345545	66.7	64.8	74.3	56.9
Scotland	3698462	2286676	61.7	58.4	72.3	29.5
N. Ireland[a]	1032490	498751		47.4	52.1	
United Kingdom[c]	40086677	29453194	64.5	67.2	76.3	29.5

Notes: [a] The votes were counted on a county basis except Northern Ireland which was treated as a single unit.
[b] In 66 of the 68 counties there was a 'Yes' majority (Shetland voted 56.3% 'No' and Western Isles 70.5% 'No').
[c] The electorate figures are for the civilian electorate only. The 370 000 service votes are included only in the total votes and the 'Yes' percentages.

Source: Butler and Kitzinger (1976).

On 1 March 1979 referendums were held in Scotland and Wales on measures for devolution. In Scotland 32.9 per cent of the electorate voted in favour and 30.8 per cent voted against; 36.5 per cent did not vote. Since the Scotland Act required the support of '40 per cent of the electorate', the 'Yes' was insufficient. In Wales the vote was 11.9 per cent 'Yes' and 46.9 per cent 'No' with 41.1 per cent not voting.

On 11 September 1997, on a 60.2 per cent turnout, Scotland voted 74.3 per cent 'Yes' to a Scottish Parliament and 63.5 per cent 'Yes' to its having taxing powers. On 18 September, Wales, on a 50.1 per cent turnout, voted 50.3 per cent for a Welsh Assembly.

On 6 May 1999 the new Scottish Parliament was chosen. Each elector had two votes. 73 members were chosen directly, first-past-the-post, from the existing Westminster constituencies; 56 were elected on top-up lists from the eight Euro-constituencies.

Table 11.4(b) Elections to the Scottish Parliament, 6 May 1999

	Con.	Lab.	Lib D	SNP	Other
Top-up seats	18	3	5	28	2
Direct seats	–	53	12	7	1
Total seats	18	56	17	35	3
Top-up vote	15.4%	33.7%	12.4%	27.3%	11.2%
Direct vote	15.6%	38.8%	14.2%	28.7%	2.7%

Turnout 57%

On 6 May 1999 the new Welsh Assembly was chosen. Each elector had two votes. 40 members were chosen directly, first-past-the-post, from the existing Westminster constituencies; 20 were elected on top-up lists from the eight Euro-constituencies.

Table 11.4(c) Elections to the Welsh Assembly, 6 May 1999

	Con.	Lab.	Lib D	PC	Other
Top-up seats	8	1	3	8	–
Direct seats	1	27	3	9	–
Total seats	9	28	6	17	3
Top-up vote	16.5%	35.4%	12.5%	30.3%	5.1%
Direct vote	15.8%	37.6%	15.5%	28.4%	2.7%

Turnout 46%

On 7 May 1998, electors in the Greater London Council Area, on a 34 per cent turnout, voted 72.2 per cent in favour of a Mayor and Council for the Area.

On 8 March 1973, on a 58.1 per cent turnout, Northern Ireland voted 98.9 per cent 'Yes' for the Province to stay part of the United Kingdom. On 22 May 1998, on an 81.0 per cent turnout, Northern Ireland voted 71.1 per cent 'Yes' to endorse the Good Friday Agreement on the future government of the Province.

Table 11.5 Direct elections to the European Parliament

1979: 7 June

	%	% votes					% seats				
	Turnout	Con.	Lab.	Lib.	Nat.	Oth.	Con.	Lab.	Lib.	Nat.	Oth.
England	31.3	53.4	32.6	13.2	–	0.8	54	12	–	–	–
Wales	34.4	36.6	41.5	9.6	11.7	0.6	1	3	–	–	–
Scotland	33.7	33.7	33.0	13.9	19.4	–	5	2	–	1	–
GB	32.1	50.6	33.1	13.1	2.5	0.7	60	17	–	1	–
N. Ireland	55.7	–	–	0.2	–	99.8	–	–	–	–	3
UK	32.7	48.4	31.6	12.6	2.5	4.9	60	17	–	1	3

Electorate 41152763; Votes cast 13446083

Source: Butler and Marquand (1979).

1984: 7 June

	%	% votes					% seats				
	Turnout	Con.	Lab.	Lib.	Nat.	Oth.	Con.	Lab.	Lib.	Nat.	Oth.
England	31.6	43.1	35.0	20.4	–	1.5	42	24	–	–	–
Wales	39.7	25.4	44.5	17.4	12.2	0.5	1	3	–	–	–
Scotland	33.0	25.7	40.7	15.6	17.8	0.2	2	5	–	1	–
GB	31.8	40.8	36.5	19.5	2.5	0.8	45	32	–	1	–
N. Ireland	63.5	–	–	–	–	100.0	–	–	–	–	3
UK	32.6	39.9	36.0	19.1	2.4	5.6	45	32	–	1	3

Electorate 42493274; Votes cast 13998274

Source: Butler and Jowett (1985).

1989: 15 June

	%	% votes					% seats				
	Turnout	Con.	Lab.	Lib.	Nat.	Oth.[a]	Con.	Lab.	Lib.	Nat.	Oth.
England	35.8	37.2	29.2	6.6	–	16.9	32	34	–	–	–
Wales	41.1	23.1	49.7	3.2	12.2	13.0	–	4	–	–	–
Scotland	40.8	20.5	40.8	4.4	26.9	7.3	–	7	–	1	–
GB	35.9	34.7	40.1	6.4	–	19.0	32	45	–	1	–
N. Ireland	48.4	–	–	–	–	100.0	–	–	–	–	3
UK	36.8	33.5	38.7	6.2	3.2	2.8	32	45	–	1	3

Electorate 43180720; Votes cast 15893408

Note: [a] The Green Party won 14.9% of the Great Britain vote.

Source: Adonis (1989).

continued

Table 11.5 (*cont...*)

1994: 9 June

	%	% votes					% seats				
	Turnout	Con.	Lab.	Lib.	Nat.	Oth.	Con.	Lab.	Lib.	Nat.	Oth.
England	35.5	30.5	43.5	18.4	–	7.6	18	51	2	–	–
Wales	43.1	14.6	55.9	8.7	17.1	3.7	–	5	–	–	–
Scotland	38.2	14.5	42.5	7.2	32.6	1.6	–	8	–	2	–
GB	36.2	27.9	44.2	16.7	4.3	6.9	18	64	2	2	–
N. Ireland	48.7	–	–	–	–	100.0	–	–	–	–	3
UK	36.8	26.9	42.6	16.1	4.1	10.2	18	64	2	2	3
Electorate 43037821; Votes cast 15847417											

Source: Butler and Westlake (1995).

In 1999 the electoral system was changed to a list system of proportional representation (European Elections Act, 1998).

1999: 10 June

	%	% votes					% seats				
	Turnout	Con.	Lab.	Lib.	Nat.	Oth.	Con.	Lab	Lib	Nat	UKIP[a] Green
England	22.6	38.6	27.7	13.3	–	20.4	33	24	9	–	3 2
Wales	28.1	22.8	31.9	8.2	29.6	7.6	1	2	–	2	– –
Scotland	24.7	19.8	28.7	9.8	27.2	14.5	2	3	1	2	– –
GB	23.1	35.8	28.0	12.7	4.5	19.0	36	29	10	4	3 2
N Ireland	57.8	–	–	–	–	100.0	–	–	–	3	– –
UK	24.0	33.5	26.2	11.8	4.2	24.2	36	29	10	7	3 –
Electorate: 44499329; Votes cast 10689843											

Note: [a]United Kingdom Independence Party.

Source: European Parliament web site: http://www.europarl.eu.int/uk/index.html

Social bases of party support

Since the advent of opinion polls a large amount of data about the background of voters have become available. Table 11.6 offers three illustrations of the social composition of party support. The 1964 findings offer a broad picture, which had only changed a little during the first 20 years that such data were available. The MORI (Market and Opinion Research International) findings of 1983 and 1997 show different pictures.

Table 11.6(a) Party support by sex, age and social class, 1964

	All	Sex % Men	Women	Age % 21–24	25–34	35–54	55+	Class % ABC1	C2	DE	% Union	% Non-Union
All	100	48	52					39	39	31		
Con.	43	38	46	40	40	41	48	65	34	31	28	48
Lab.	45	52	42	49	48	46	41	20	54	59	62	38
Lib.	11	8	12	11	11	12	12	13	11	9	9	12
Other	1	2	1	1	1	1	1	1	1	1	1	1

Source: National Opinion Poll (NOP) (1964); 12000 in combined sample.

Table 11.6(b) Party support by sex, age and social class, 1987

	All	Sex % Men	Women	Age % 21–24	25–34	35–54	55+	Class % ABC1	C2	DE	% Union	% Non-Union
All	100	48	52	14	19	33	34	43	27	30	23	77
Con.	43	38	46	40	40	41	48	65	34	31	28	48
Lab.	32	32	32	40	33	29	31	18	36	48	42	29
Allia.	23	23	23	21	25	24	21	26	22	22	26	22
Other	2	2	2	2	3	2	2	2	2	2	2	2

Source: MORI (1987); 23396 in combined sample.

Table 11.6(c) Party support by sex, age and social class, 1996

	All	Sex % Men	Women	Age % 21–24	25–34	35–54	55+	Class % ABC1	C2	DE	% Union	% Non-Union
All	100	48	52	14	19	33	34	43	27	30	23	77
Con.	29	28	30	23	26	27	34	37	25	18	19	31
Lab.	53	55	52	59	56	54	49	43	59	65	63	51
Lib.	13	12	14	11	12	14	12	15	10	10	13	13
Other	5	5	4	7	6	5	5	4	6	7	5	5

Source: MORI.

Background of Members of Parliament

There are considerable difficulties in drawing up tables about the backgrounds of MPs. Some are very reticent about themselves and a few are actively misleading. The classification of education and occupation leaves many borderline ambiguities. These problems are discussed at various points in the main sources on the subject (see Notes on Sources).

Age

The average age of members has been very constant. At the beginning of every Parliament from 1918–97 it has lain between $48^1/_2$ and 52. Except in 1997 the average age of Labour members has always been slightly higher than the rest.

Interests and occupations

Table 11.7(a) Interests represented by MPs, 1900–10 (%)

	1900	1906	Jan. 1910
Conservatives			
Landowners	20	17	26
Commerce/industry	52	64	53
Legal/professional	18	11	12
Others	10	8	9
Total	100	100	100
Liberals			
Landowners	9	8	7
Commerce/industry	58	65	66
Legal/professional	29	23	23
Others	4	4	4
Total	100	100	100

Source: Thomas (1958), adapted by Guttsman (1963).

Table 11.7(b) Main occupations of MPs, 1918–51 (%)

	Conservative				Labour			
	1918–35[a]	1945	1950	1951	1918–35[a]	1945	1950	1951
Professional	52	61	62	58	24	49	47	46
Business	32	33	31	33	4	10	10	9
Unoccupied	12	3	5	6	–	–	–	–
Workers	4	3	3	5	72	41	43	45
Total	100	100	100	100	100	100	100	100

Note: [a] Average.

Source: Guttsman (1963).

Table 11.7(c) Main occupations of MPs, 1951–97 (%)

	51	55	59	64	66	70	Feb 74	Oct 74	79	83	87	92	97
Conservative													
Professional	41	46	46	48	46	45	44	46	45	45	42	39	37
Business	37	30	30	26	29	30	32	33	34	36	37	38	39
Miscellaneous	22	24	23	25	23	24	23	20	20	19	20	22	23
Workers	–	–	1	1	1	1	1	1	1	1	1	1	1

Table 11.7(c) (*cont...*)

	51	55	59	64	66	70	Feb 74	Oct 74	79	83	87	92	97
Labour													
Professional	35	36	38	41	43	48	46	49	43	42	40	42	45
Business	9	12	10	11	9	10	9	8	7	9	10	8	9
Miscellaneous	19	17	17	16	18	16	15	15	14	16	21	28	33
Workers	37	35	35	32	30	26	30	28	36	33	29	22	13

Source: Nuffield Election Studies.

Education

The educational background of Conservative and Labour Members of Parliament is shown in Table 11.8.

Table 11.8 Education of Conservative and Labour MPs, 1906–97 (%)

	Conservative		Labour	
	'Public school'	University educated	'Public school'	University educated
1906	67	57	0	0
Jan 1910	74	58	0	0
Dec 1910	76	59	0	0
1918	81	49	3	5
1922	78	48	9	15
1923	79	50	8	14
1924	78	53	7	14
1929	79	54	12	19
1931	77	55	8	17
1935	81	57	10	19
1945	85	58	23	32
1950	85	62	22	41
1951	75	65	23	41
1955	76	64	22	40
1959	72	60	18	39
1964	75	63	18	46
1966	80	67	18	51
1970	74	64	17	53
Feb 1974	74	68	17	56
Oct 1974	75	69	18	57
1979	77	73	17	57
1983	70	71	14	53
1987	68	70	14	56
1992	62	73	14	61
1997	66	81	16	66

Source: Nuffield Election Studies.

Sex

Table 11.9 Women candidates and MPs, 1918–97

	Conservative		Labour		Liberals		Others		Total	
	Cands	MPs	Cands	MPs	Cands	MPs	Cands	MPs	Cands	MPs
1918	1	–	4	–	4	–	8	1	17	1
1922	5	1	10	–	16	1	2	–	33	2
1923	7	3	14	3	12	2	1	–	34	8
1924	12	3	22	1	6	–	1	–	41	4
1929	10	3	30	9	25	1	4	1	69	14
1931	16	13	36	–	6	1	4	1	62	15
1935	19	6	35	1	11	1	1	1	67	9
1945	14	1	45	21	20	1	8	1	87	24
1950	28	6	42	14	45	1	11	–	126	21
1951	29	6	39	11	11	–	–	–	74	17
1955	32	10	43	14	12	–	2	–	89	24
1959	28	12	36	13	16	–	1	–	81	25
1964	24	11	33	18	25	–	8	–	90	29
1966	21	7	30	19	20	–	9	–	80	26
1970	26	15	29	10	23	–	21	1	99	26
Feb 1974	33	9	40	13	40	–	30	1	143	23
Oct 1974	30	7	50	18	49	–	32	2	161	27
1979	31	8	52	11	51	–	76	–	210	19
1983	40	13	78	10	115	–	87	–	280	23
1987	46	17	92	21	106	2	85	1	329	41
1992	59	20	138	37	144	2	227	1	568	60
1997	66	13	156	102	139	2	311	2	672	120

Sources: Craig (1989); Rallings and Thrasher (forthcoming).

The Cabinet

Table 11.10 shows the social and educational background of the Cabinet formed by each new Prime Minister on coming to office (except that Asquith's is not given for 1908 but for 1 August 1914; new war-time governments are omitted in 1915, 1916 and 1940; so is Baldwin's in 1923; MacDonald's National government is given for its termination in 1935, not its inception in 1913; and Thatcher's government is reassessed as it existed on 30 September 1986).

Schools are classified as public schools if they are members of the Headmasters' Conference. The Oxbridge column includes three Oxford men to every Cambridge one; there is not much difference between parties in this, although Mr Wilson's 1964 Cabinet was the only one in this century to contain no Cambridge men.

Table 11.10 Social and educational composition of British Cabinets, 1895–1997

			No.	Class[a]			Education			
				Aristo-crat[b]	Middle	Working[c]	Pub. Sch.	Eton	Univ.	Oxbridge
Aug	1895	Con.	Salisbury	19	8	11	–	16	7	15	14
Jul	1902	Con.	Balfour	19	9	10	–	16	9	14	13
Dec	1905	Lib.	C–Bannerman	19	7	11	1	11	3	14	12
Jul	1914	Lib.	Asquith	19	6	12	1	11	3	15	13
Jan	1919	Coal.	Ll. George	21	3	17	1	12	2	13	8
Nov	1922	Con.	Bonar Law	16	8	8	–	14	8	13	13
Jan	1924	Lab.	MacDonald	19	3	5	11	8	–	6	6
Nov	1924	Con.	Baldwin	21	9	12	–	21	7	16	16
Jan	1929	Lab.	MacDonald	18	2	4	12	5	–	6	3
Aug	1931	Nat.	MacDonald	20	8	10	2	13	6	11	10
Jun	1935	Con.	Baldwin	22	9	11	2	14	9	11	10
May	1937	Con.	Chamberlain	21	8	13	–	17	8	16	13
May	1945	Con.	Churchill	16	6	9	1	14	7	11	9
Aug	1945	Lab.	Attlee	20	–	8	12	5	2	10	5
Oct	1951	Con.	Churchill	16	5	11	–	14	7	11	9
Apr	1955	Con.	Eden	18	5	13	–	18	10	16	14
Jan	1957	Con.	Macmillan	18	4	14	–	17	8	16	15
Oct	1963	Con.	Home	24	5	19	–	21	11	17	17
Oct	1964	Lab.	Wilson	23	1	14	8	8	1	13	11
Jun	1970	Con.	Heath	18	4	14	–	15	4	15	15
Mar	1974	Lab.	Wilson	21	1	16	4	7	–	16	11
Apr	1976	Lab.	Callaghan	22	1	13	7	7	–	15	10
May	1979	Con.	Thatcher	22	3	19	–	20	6	18	17
Nov	1990	Con.	Major	22	3	17	2	14	2	20	17
May	1997	Lab.	Blair	22	–	15	7	8	–	21	3

Notes: [a] The class composition of governments is largely based upon the table on p.78 of Guttsman (1963).
[b] Aristocrats are those who had among their grandparents the holder of a hereditary title.
[c] Working class are those whose fathers appear to have had a manual occupation while they were growing up.

Sources: Guttsman (1963); Butler and Butler (2000, forthcoming).

Table 11.11 Women Cabinet Ministers, 1929–98

1929–31	Margaret Bondfield	1992–97	Gillian Shephard
1945–47	Ellen Wilkinson	1997–	Margaret Beckett
1953–54	Florence Horsburgh	1997–	Ann Taylor
1964–70 & 1974–76	Barbara Castle	1997–	Mo Mowlam
1968–69	Judith Hart	1997–98	Harriet Harman
1970–74 & 1979–90	Margaret Thatcher	1997–	Clare Short
1982–83	Lady Young	1998–	Lady Jay
1992–97	Virginia Bottomley		

Source: Butler and Butler (2000, forthcoming).

Table 11.12 Composition of the House of Lords, 1901–90 (including minors)

Year	Duke[a]	Marq.	Earl	Vt.	Baron	Life Peer[b]	Law Lord[c]	Scot[d]	Irish[d]	Bishops	Total
1901	26	22	123	32	314	–	4	16	28	26	591
1910	25	23	124	42	334	–	4	16	28	26	622
1920	26	29	130	64	393	–	6	16	27	26	716
1930	24	26	134	73	428	–	7	16	18	26	753
1939	24	28	139	84	456	–	7	16	13	26	785
1950	23	30	137	95	503	–	11	16	6	26	847
1960	25	30	132	111	531	31	8	16	1	26	908
1970	29	30	163	110	530	163	11	–	–	26	1057
1980	28	29	157	105	477	330	19	–	–	26	1171
1990	27	27	156	102	471	358	19	–	–	26	1186

Notes: [a] Including peers of the Blood Royal.
[b] Created by the Life Peerages Act, 1958.
[c] Life peers under the Appellate Jurisdiction Acts.
[d] Scottish and Irish peers sitting by virtue of UK title are listed under the latter. In 1963 all Scottish peers became entitled to sit and are listed under their senior title.

Source: Butler and Butler (2000, forthcoming).

Notes on Sources

Sources on franchise qualifications

- Butler, D. (1962) *The Electoral System in Britain since 1918*, Clarendon Press, Oxford.
- Keith-Lucas, B. (1953) *The English Local Government Franchise*, Blackwell, Oxford.
- Parker's *Election Agent and Returning Officer*, Knight, London (successive editions).
- Representation of the People Acts of 1883, 1918, 1928, 1945, 1948, 1949, 1969 and 1985.

A convenient summary of franchise qualifications at any given time is to be found in *Whitaker's Almanack* or (up to 1939) in *The Constitutional Year Book*.

Sources on electoral administration

- The reports of the Speaker's Conferences on Electoral Reform of 1917, 1943–44 and 1965–68, and the Ullswater Conference of 1930 (see Cd 8463/1917; Cmd 3636/1930; Cmd 6534/1944; and Cmd 6543/1944, Cmnd 2917 and 2932/1966; Cmnd 3202 and 3275/1967 and Cmnd 3550/1968.
- The Report of the Home Affairs Committee, HC 32/1982/3.
- The reports of the Boundary Commissioners (Cmd 7260, 7274, 7270, 7231 of 1947, Cmd 9311–14 of 1954. Cmnd 4084, 4085, 4086, and 4087 of 1969, and Cmnd 8753 of 1982 and Cmnd 8797, 9172, and 9176 of 1983. See also the judgment of Lord Justice Oliver in *R. v. Boundary Commission ex parte* Foot and others for a lucid exposition of the status of Boundary Commissions (All England Law Reports 1099 (1983)).
- Butler, D. (1955) 'The Redistribution of Seats', *Public Administration*, Summer, 125, 47.

- Morris, H. L. (1921) *Parliamentary Franchise Reform in England from 1885 to 1918*, Columbia University, New York.
- Leonard, R. L. (1996) *Elections in Britain Today: a Guide for Voters and Students*, 3rd edition, Macmillan, Basingstoke.
- Rossiter, D., Johnston, R. J. and Pattie, Charles (1999) *The Boundary Commissions: Redrawing the UK's Map of Parliamentary Constituencies*, Manchester University Press, Manchester.

Sources on election results

- *The Times House of Commons* (published after every election since 1880 except for 1906, 1922, 1923 and 1924).
- *The Constitutional Year Book* (published annually 1885–1939. Until 1919 it gave every result since 1885; after 1919 it only gave post-1918 results, and after 1931 only results since 1923 or 1924).
- Butler, D. and Butler, G. (2000, forthcoming) *British Political Facts 1900–2000*, Macmillan, Basingstoke, gives national totals and other electoral data.
- Craig, F. (1987) *British Parliamentary Election Results*, Parliamentary Research Services, Dartmouth (separate volumes for 1885–1918, 1918–49, 1950–70). These volumes record all constituency results with percentages. They constitute the most authoritative and convenient source of electoral data.
- Craig, F. (1989) *British Electoral Facts 1832–1987*, Parliamentary Research Services, Dartmouth, gives national totals and much else. A new edition of this book, by Colin Rallings and Michael Thrasher will be forthcoming shortly.
- Kinnear, M. (1968) *The British Voter 1885–1966*, Batsford, London, gives maps of each election.
- A detailed analysis of the results of each election is contained in Appendices to each of the Nuffield studies *The British General Election of 19...* , published after each contest since 1945 (Oxford University Press, 1947; Macmillan, 1950 onwards).
- A valuable source on pre-1914 election statistics is Pelling, H. (1967) *Social Geography of British Elections 1885–1910*, Macmillan, London.
- Local election statistics since 1973 are usefully summarized in Rallings, C. and Thrasher, M. (1997) *Local Elections in Britain*, Routledge, London. They have also published annual volumes giving results in detail every year since 1985.

Sources on voting behaviour

On a national scale, the Gallup Poll have published their findings in a monthly Bulletin since 1960. NOP have done the same since 1963; so have MORI since 1978. The ESRC (Economic and Social Research Council) Data Archive at the University of Essex has an exhaustive collection of poll data. Other sources on voting behaviour include:

- Alford, R. R. (1964) *Party and Society*, John Murray, London.
- Blondel, J. (1963) *Voters, Parties and Leaders*, Penguin, Harmondsworth.
- Bonham, J. (1954) *The Middle Class Vote*, Faber, London.
- Leonard, R. L. (1968) *Elections in Britain Today: a Guide for Voters and Students*, 3rd edition, Macmillan, Basingstoke.
- Pulzer, P. G. J. (1967) *Political Representation and Elections*, Allen and Unwin, London.
- Rose, R. (1965) *Politics in England*, Faber, London.
- Worcester, R. (1991) *British Public Opinion since 1945*, Blackwell, Oxford.

Local studies of voting conducted in the 1950s include:

- Benney, M., Pear, R. H. and Gray, A. P. (1956) *How People Vote*, Routledge & Kegan Paul, London.
- Milne, R. S. and Mackenzie, H. C. (1955) *Straight Fight*, Hansard Society, London
- Milne, R. S. and Mackenzie, H. C. (1958) *Marginal Seat*, Hansard Society, London

Special treatments of working-class voting, using specially collected survey material:

- Goldthorpe, J., Lockwood, D., Bechhofer F. and Platt, J. (1968) *The Affluent Worker*, vol. II, *Political Attitudes*, Cambridge University Press, Cambridge.
- McKenzie, R. T. and Silver, A. (1968) *Angels in Marble*, Heinemann, London.
- Nordlinger, E. A. (1962) *The Working Class Tories*, MacGibbon & Kee, London.

Comprehensive academic studies of voting behaviour, involving nation-wide sample surveys:

- Butler, D. and Stokes, D. (1974) *Political Change in Britain*, second edition, Macmillan, London.
- Franklin, M. (1984) *The Decline of Class Voting in Britain*, Clarendon, Oxford.
- Heath, A., Jowell, R. and Curtice, J. (1985) *How Britain Votes*, Pergamon, Oxford.
- Heath, A., Jowell, R. and Curtice, J .(1991) *Understanding Political Change,* Pergamon, Oxford.
- Heath, A., Jowell, R. and Curtice, J. (1994) *Labour's Last Chance*, Dartmouth, Aldershot.
- Miller, W. et al. (1990) *How Voters Change*, Clarendon, Oxford.
- Rose, R. and McAllister, I. (1986) *Voters begin to Choose*, Sage, London.
- Sarlvik, B. and Crewe, I. (1983) *Partisan Dealignment in Britain*, Cambridge University Press, Cambridge.

A large amount of material on voting behaviour is available in the 'Political Communications' volumes published after each general election since 1979.

- Crewe, I. and Harrop, M. (1986) *Political Communications: The General Election Campaign of 1983*, Cambridge University Press, Cambridge.
- Crewe, I. and Harrop, M. (1989) *Political Communications*: *The General Election Campaign of 1987*, Cambridge University Press, Cambridge.
- Crewe, I. and Gosschalk, B. (1995) *Political Communications*: *The General Election Campaign of 1992*, Cambridge University Press, Cambridge.
- Crewe, I., Gosschalk, B. and Bartle, J. (1998) *Political Communications: Why Labour Won the General Election of 1997*, Frank Cass, London.
- Worcester, R. and Harrop, M. (1982) *Political Communications: The General Election Campaign of 1979*, Allen and Unwin, London.

See also the *British Parties and Elections Year Book/Review*, published annually since 1991.

Sources on the background of MPs

- Guttsman, W. L. (1963) *The British Political Elite*, MacGibbon and Kee, London.
- Ross, J. F. S. (1944) *Parliamentary Representation*, second edition, Eyre and Spottiswoode, London.

- Ross, J. F. S. (1955) *Elections and Electors*, Eyre and Spottiswoode, London.
- Thomas, J. A. (1939) *The House of Commons 1832–1901*, University of Wales, Cardiff.
- Thomas, J. A. (1958) *The House of Commons 1900–1911*, University of Wales, Cardiff.

- Each of the Nuffield Studies covering each election since 1945.

References

Adonis, A. (1989) 'Great Britain', *Electoral Studies*, 3, pp.262–9.

Butler, D. and Butler, G. (2000, forthcoming) *British Political Facts 1900–2000*, Macmillan, Basingstoke.

Butler, D. and Kitzinger, U. (1976) *The 1975 Referendum*, Macmillan, London.

Butler, D. and Marquand, D. (1979) *European Elections and British Politics*, Longman, London.

Butler, D. and Jowett, P. (1985) *Party Strategies in Britain*, Macmillan, London.

Butler, D. and Westlake, M. (1995) *British Politics and European Elections 1994*, Macmillan, Basingstoke.

Craig, F. (1989) *British Electoral Facts 1832–1987*, Parliamentary Research Services, Dartmouth.

Gray, P. and Corlett, T. (1950) *The Electoral Register as a Sampling Frame*, Central Office of Information, London.

Gray, P. and Gee, F. A. (1967) *Electoral Registration for Parliamentary Elections*, HMSO, London.

Guttsman, W. L. (1963) *The British Political Elite*, MacGibbon and Kee, London.

Keith-Lucas, B. (1953) *The English Local Government Franchise*, Blackwell, Oxford.

Rallings, C. and Thrasher, M. (forthcoming) *British Electoral Facts*.

Smith, Stephen (1991) *Electoral Registration in 1991*, HMSO, London.

Smith, Stephen (1993) *The Electoral Register*, HMSO, London.

Thomas, J. A. (1958) *The House of Commons 1900–1911*, University of Wales, Cardiff.

Todd, T. and Butcher, P. (1982) *Electoral Registration 1981*, OPCS, London.

12

Towns, Urban Change and Local Government

Bruce Wood and Jackie Carter

> God made the country, and man made the town.
> William Cowper (1731–1800), *Table Talk*

Introduction

The link between patterns of residence, urbanization in particular, and the organization of local government was central to the Victorian creation of a universal system of democratic local authorities. The recognition of the town as deserving of its own status and local authority (which can be traced back much further, to the grant of a charter and of parliamentary representation) led to the borough reforms of 1835, and later the 'public health movement' saw the creation of separate urban and rural sanitary districts. The twin Local Government Acts of 1888 and 1894 consolidated the earlier legislation and designed a tripartite hierarchy: towns were to be governed by a county borough, a municipal borough or an urban district council.

This link between urbanization and local government lasted without serious challenge until 1974 and continued in some areas until the end of the twentieth century. It was based on the principle that a town consisted of and was defined by its built-up area. As towns grew, suburbs spilled across town boundaries into areas classified as 'rural'. Pressure from towns for an extension of their official limits led to controversy about claims for boundary extensions. The first section of this chapter focuses on the growth of towns using the traditional definition of a town as being a continuously built-up area recognized as an urban administrative unit of local government.

This traditional definition alone is no longer satisfactory. It reflects the social circumstances of Victorian England. At the end of the nineteenth century, personal mobility, certainly at a daily level, was extremely limited. Workers lived close to the factories, mills and offices in which they were employed. Shopping was a local activity and journeys of any distance were rare for the vast majority. Only a handful of the very affluent had the time, the money or the means of transportation to be regularly mobile. The traditional definition of a town thus broadly matched the general pattern of life.

The twentieth century has been marked by ramifying social, technical and economic changes which brought the traditional spatial concept of the town into question. The growing interdependence of town and country, through the development of suburbs and of personal mobility, challenged the local government system, while the decline of many inner urban economies questioned the viability of some of the biggest cities and led to new public policies designed to tackle urban deprivation. The second section of this chapter traces some of these socio-geographic changes and includes trends in populations at the regional level because towards the end of the century government increasingly began to see the importance of region-wide approaches to the resolution of what had previously been viewed as 'urban' problems.

In the third section changes to the structure of local government will be examined to see how they related to the demographic and socio-economic developments outlined in the first two sections. The traditional definition of a town as the basis for the local government system came under increasing pressure, and a series of reforms in the final three decades of the century recognized the significance of socio-economic change.

The data do not always permit full and flawless exposition of these trends in British society. Inevitably the data on the traditional town are more robust than that on socio-economic changes simply because such changes are only recognized retrospectively (the 1901 census could hardly be expected to collect data on journeys to work in an era before the advent of cars and buses, for example!). The first general problem of information is thus insuperable; it is the absence of desirable information to fully illustrate the pace of some changes in a century-long time-series.

A second general problem links the three sections of this chapter. It concerns the spatial basis of many statistics. Most census and other official data are collected for whole local government areas, and this has two related but also conflicting drawbacks for the student of trends: geographical continuity and socio-economic accuracy.

First, this use of local government areas means a loss of continuity because these areas have been subject to change. For most of the century boundary extensions led to a town's geographical size varying from census to census. This provides us with useful information about the physical growth of towns. However, it also makes time-series difficult to construct accurately and trends must be analysed with extreme caution. This leads directly to a second drawback. Boundary changes to towns only rarely matched the exact pattern of urban development. They tended both to take place some years or even decades after the physical changes had occurred, and to be minimal in scale due to political opposition to them from the 'losing' areas.

These drawbacks affect both the 'bricks-and-mortar' measurements of urbanization trends and the socio-economic data about 'towns'. They mean that most of the official information about urban size underestimates the significance of towns, and that mobility across boundaries is exaggerated because parts of some towns were misleadingly classified as rural. A long moratorium on boundary changes through the middle decades of the century exacerbated these problems. This was finally recognized at the time of the 1981 census, when an alternative 'bricks-and-mortar' definition of urbanization was utilized. In any event the radical reforms of local government in the 1970s and 1990s had major significance for trend data because the traditional concept of the 'urban' unit of local government was replaced in many parts of Britain by a socio-geographic principle under which many towns were joined with their hinterlands into new 'unitary councils'.[1]

The traditional 'town'

Urban area

On the briefest of visual inspections it is clear that almost all towns have spread outwards during this century. Suburbanization has meant that towns, as measured by a 'bricks-and-mortar' definition, are more significant and more important than they were in 1900. Indeed, in the very populous areas known as 'conurbations', or more officially as 'metropolitan areas', a number of originally separate towns have completely coalesced to form one continuous large urban area.

Such trends are best illustrated in the decennial census reports. From 1901–81 the figures reflected whole local government areas (the 1981 data used here were based on 1971 boundaries and did not use the new 1974 areas of local government). By 1981, however, the weaknesses of the use of traditional local government boundaries for the measure of urbanization were becoming increasingly apparent. The 1981 census *Preliminary Report for Towns* used the term 'town' in the broad sense, to include places designated as cities, boroughs and urban districts. In that report urban areas were defined in the same way as in previous censuses, using pre-1974 boundaries of boroughs and urban districts with the addition of New Towns. But in a separate report a new, longer-term measure was unveiled. This defined towns and cities to take into account the growth of towns beyond administrative boundaries. The 1981 special report deployed a new definition of 'urban area' based on land use which is 'irreversibly urban in character' (*Key Statistics for Urban Areas*, 1981), and which extended for 20 hectares or more and contained at least 1000 residents. The new urban areas also had to contain at least four census enumeration districts though a few exceptions were allowed. In addition, urban areas less than 200 metres apart could be joined to form a continuous area (this followed recommendations from the United Nations and other European census offices). Although the new definition was drawn up in 1981, for some reason the actual number of hectares of the new urban areas was not published as part of that census and so was not available until data for the 1991 census (which used the same new definition for urban areas) were released. Thus the 1991 urban area in Table 12.1 bears no relationship to local government status and is not comparable with the earlier figures in the table. The apparent 48 per cent decrease in the extent of urban area between 1981 and 1991 is no more than a reflection of the new methodology. Later, in Tables 12.2 and 12.3, population data for both the traditional and the new definition are given for 1981 to allow for easy comparison of the impact of the new definition.

Table 12.1 Urban areas, 1901–91, England and Wales[a]

Year	Urban area (hectares)
1901	1517194
1911	1625132
1931	1823119
1951	2134325
1961	2154454
1981	2222721
1991 (new definition)	1148822

Note: [a] England and Wales total area = 15 119 990 hectares. Figures prior to 1991 converted from acres to hectares.

Sources: 1901–1961, *Census Preliminary Reports*; 1981 census, *Preliminary Reports for Towns*; 1991 Census, *Key Statistics for Urban and Rural Areas*.

From 1901–81 there was a steady rise in urbanization, if anything underestimated in Table 12.1 because of the political difficulty for towns in obtaining boundary extensions (especially during the 1940s and 1950s when central government operated a moratorium on the grounds that wholesale reforms were under consideration). Nevertheless, the urban area increased by some 45 per cent to account in 1981 for more than one-seventh of England and Wales, though this area was sharply reduced when the more robust new definition rigorously excluded from the definition 'urban' many low-density areas which had traditionally been within some 'town' boundaries: the Lakes Urban District Council, for example, covered an area the size of Birmingham; large tracts of the East Anglia fens had similarly obtained urban status during the Victorian era.

Urban population

Towns may have only covered one-seventh of England and Wales (or only 8 per cent using the new 1991 definition), but in terms of population they are, of course, very dominant. Table 12.2 shows that at every twentieth-century census more than three-quarters of the population were living in local government 'towns'. That these towns by no means encompassed all areas which might be thought of as urban is strikingly shown by the new definition of an urban area, discussed above: it might have halved the terrain defined as urban but it found more than six million additional town-dwellers and close to 90 per cent of the population became defined as living in urban areas despite that tighter geographical definition. Clearly a range of alternative criteria, all defensible, can be utilized to distinguish town from country: there is no single 'correct' way to categorize urban and rural living patterns.

Table 12.2 Urban population, 1901–91, England and Wales

Year	Total population (000s)	Urban population (000s)	Urban %
1901	32528	25058	77.0
1911	36070	26163	78.1
1931	39952	31952	80.0
1951	43758	35336	80.8
1961	46105	36872	80.0
1981	49011	37691	76.9
1981 (new)	49155	44111	89.7
1991 (new)	49890	44744	89.7

Sources: 1901–81, *Census Preliminary Reports*; 1981 census, *Key Statistics for Urban Areas*; 1991 census, *Key Statistics for Urban and Rural Areas*.

The story of steady overall urban growth masks huge variety. Though most towns have grown in both area and population, some have not. In particular, the inner core of many of the largest cities underwent dramatic population decline, so much so that in the last third of the century successive governments introduced public policies designed to combat 'urban deprivation' – a topic for later exploration.

The size of towns

Inevitably, boundary changes make it very difficult to present fully comparable data on the numbers of towns falling in different size ranges at intervals since 1900. Table 12.3 highlights this and must be interpreted with great care. Two very obvious problems stand out in the first column alone: 150 towns did not disappear between 1931–61, nor did 900 suddenly appear in the 1960s and 1970s!

Table 12.3 Towns by population size, 1901–91, England and Wales

Year	Total number of 'towns'	Under 10000	10000 to 50000	50000 to 200000	200000 to 1 million	Over 1 million
1901	1122	686	361	61	13	1
1931	1120	591	416	94	17	2
1961	965	333	450	162	18	2
1981	864	250	451	145	17	1
1981 (new)	1852	1372	357	93	26	4
1991 (new)	1859	1382	354	92	27	4

Sources: 1901–81, *Census Preliminary Reports*; 1981 census, *Key Statistics for Urban Areas*; 1991 census, *Key Statistics for Urban and Rural Areas*.

The mid-century apparent reduction of 150 towns reflects the work of the County Councils who in the 1930s were given the task of reviewing district and borough council boundaries. In the final section of this chapter we will see that as a result of these reviews some 42 towns did lose their urban status: the other 100 or so merged with neighbouring towns. The apparent dramatic rise to about 1850 towns in the 1970s is no more than a further consequence of the new 1981 census definition of 'urban' discussed earlier, the figure for towns no longer bearing any relation to the local government status of an area.

Despite these problems of trend comparability, Tables 12.3 and 12.4 (which gives the proportions living in different sizes of town) do reveal some notable points about urbanization. The great growth in the middle-sized towns (50 000–200 000 population) stands out across the first two-thirds of the century. By 1961 close to 40 per cent of the total urban population lived in such towns, almost a doubling of the 1901 proportion. In contrast the larger cities were of declining importance: their numbers rose from 14 to 20 but their share of the urban population dipped from 36 per cent to 29 per cent.

Table 12.4 Proportion of urban population living in towns of various sizes, 1901–91, England and Wales

Year	Under 10000	10000 to 50000	50000 to 200000	200000 to 1 million	Over 1 million
1901	12.4	29.7	21.6	18.2	18.1
1931	8.5	28.1	27.3	19.2	16.9
1961	4.7	28.9	37.9	16.9	11.7
1991 (new)	11.5	16.5	18.9	22.6	30.6

Sources: *Census Reports* 1901, 1931, 1961; 1991 census, *Key Statistics for Urban and Rural Areas*

The new 1981/91 definition of 'urban', ignoring local government boundaries, in effect questions the validity of the earlier data. Now we see that as many as 53 per cent of the urban population lived in the bigger towns, the number of which rose after 1961 from 20 to 31. The use of continuous built-up area in the new definition indicates just how many Britons were living in a very small part of the country. Many of the former middle-sized towns (down in number from 162 to 92) have now been merged for census purposes with adjacent urban areas and the demographic picture of urban Britain is one of conurbation dominance rather than of the importance of the free-standing town.

The conurbation

'Conurbations' were first recognized by census officials in 1951, when a special report listed the six in Table 12.5 but drew their boundaries extremely tightly, even by the traditional 'bricks-and-mortar' definition. All six had experienced rapid growth in the latter part of the nineteenth century and continuing but slower population expansion until 1961, apart from Greater London where decline began in the 1950s. This slower growth meant that their share of total urban population fell from 54 per cent in 1901 to 46 per cent (and would have already fallen by 1901 had the census had full data for 1871). The data in Table 12.5 are not precisely comparable across the decades but the impact of some boundary changes to local authority areas was, declared the 1951 special census report, 'comparatively small'.

Table 12.5 The population of conurbations, 1871–1961, England and Wales

Area	Population (000s)				
	1871	1901	1931	1951	1961
Greater London	3889.5	6586.3	8215.7	8348.0	8182.6
SELNEC[a]	1385.9	2116.8	2426.9	2422.7	2427.9
West Midlands	968.9	1482.8	1933.0	2237.1	2346.6
West Yorkshire	1064.3	1523.8	1655.4	1692.7	1703.7
Merseyside	690.2	1030.2	1346.7	1382.4	1384.2
Tyneside	346.1	677.9	827.1	835.5	855.3
Conurbation totals	8344.9	13417.8	16404.8	16918.4	16900.2
Conurbation % of urban totals	–	54	51	48	46
Conurbation % of England and Wales totals	37	41	41	39	37

Note: [a] SELNEC = south-east Lancashire and north-east Cheshire (the Manchester-based conurbation).

Sources: Census 1951 and 1961.

The reforms of local government in the 1960s in Greater London and in the 1970s in the rest of England included recognition of, and the establishment of new 'metropolitan' authorities in, seven conurbations, South Yorkshire (based on Sheffield) being the addition. The new boundaries, although (Greater London apart) they were defined somewhat less conservatively than by 1951 census authors, were still tightly drawn along 'bricks-and-mortar' lines.

Table 12.6 The population of conurbations, 1961–2001, England and Wales

Area	Population (000s)				
	1961	1971	1981	1991	2001
Greater London	7992.4	7452.3	6696.0	6679.7	7169.8
Greater Manchester	2719.9	2729.0	2594.8	2499.4	2614.2
West Midlands	2731.9	2793.3	2644.6	2551.7	2616.8
West Yorkshire	2005.4	2067.7	2037.5	2013.7	2141.3
Merseyside	1718.2	1656.5	1513.1	1403.6	1427.3
Tyne and Wear	1243.8	1211.7	1143.2	1095.1	1133.4
South Yorkshire	1303.3	1322.5	1301.8	1262.6	1307.8
Conurbation totals	19714.9	19233.0	17931.0	17505.8	18410.6
Conurbation % of England and Wales totals	42.8	39.5	36.6	35.1	34.9

Sources: *Census Preliminary Reports*; 1991 census, *Key Statistics for Urban and Rural Areas*; 2001 figures for England: Office for National Statistics, personal communication (1993-based projections); 2001 figures for Wales: Welsh Office, personal communication (1996-based projections).

Table 12.6 gives population figures for the newly recognized conurbations and reveals that all seven of them experienced decline after 1971. From 1961–91 Greater London lost about 1.3 million or 16 per cent of its population, a proportion more than matched by Merseyside (18 per cent). The fastest rate of absolute decline was in the 1971–81 decade. From 1981–91 decline slowed, and in 1991–2001 several conurbations were apparently experiencing population gain although a problem of under-reporting experienced during the 1991 census (largely due to public concern about the Community Charge, or 'Poll Tax', then in place) means that 1991 census population figures are marginally lower than they should have been. The relative decline in importance of the conurbation continues, however. Though a little over one-third of the population of England and Wales continued to live in the conurbations in 1991–2001, this proportion was now lower than at any previous time in the twentieth century. Much of the explanation for this lies in the very rapid falls in population in the inner cities.

Planned urbanization: 'New Towns'

Most British towns developed naturally through their location and changing economic patterns. A few, however, were artificially created for specific reasons. The earliest planned new settlements date from the nineteenth century when Robert Owen, Titus Salt and George Cadbury built New Lanark (1816), Saltaire (1853) and Bourneville (1879) respectively to improve the living conditions of their workforces. Later, Ebenezer Howard paved the way for a wider public policy initiative with his 'Garden City Movement' and in the inter-war period both the London County Council (at Becontree) and Manchester City Council (at Wythenshawe) built large estates outside their boundaries to help alleviate the then overcrowding being experienced in their inner areas.

The post-war Labour government took this approach forward on a much larger scale. Its New Towns Act 1946 followed the recommendations of the Reith Committee's report and set up a series of ministerially appointed development corporations to plan and build a series of New Towns using extensive powers of land purchase but leaving the local governments to provide schools and other personal services. The policy aim was to disperse both people and jobs from the inner parts of those conurbations which were under severe spatial pressure at that time – notably Greater London and Tyneside.

Table 12.7 Area and population of the New Towns, England and Wales

New Town	Area (hectares)	Population				
		Original	1961	1971	1981	1991
1. London Ring designated 1946–49	17183	98540	335694	460259	513360	533787
2. Others designated 1947–50	5444	27960	92611	131105	139376	148831
Totals for original New Towns	22627	126500	428305	591364	652736	682618
3. Second wave, designated 1961–64	17566	–	151466	205060	321137	350965
4. Third wave, designated 1968–70	45603	–	582209	635795	761774	867120
Totals for second and third-wave New Towns	63168	–	733675	840855	1082911	1218085
Totals all New Towns	85796	126500	1161980	1432219	1735647	1900703

Sources: 1981 census, *New Towns*, Part 1, Table 3 (Area converted to hectares); 1991 census, *Key Statistics for Urban and Rural Areas*, Table 1.

There were three waves of New Towns, as Table 12.7 shows. From 1946–50, 12 were designated, of which 8 were to relieve London. Five more followed in 1961–64 and the final 6 began in 1968–74. The table illustrates the New Town population explosion in the 1950s as the original 12 were largely completed: they grew by about 300000 in that decade alone, and by about half that number again in the 1960s. In all, about half a million people moved, which was close to the original target. In the 1970s a further quarter of a million moved to the second- and third-wave New Towns, but the original plans for several of them were scaled down during the 1980s both as part of public spending restraint and because by then priority was being given to public policies designed to combat urban deprivation and inner-city decline. We earlier noted the extent of population decline in inner cities and the New Towns programme, which had been created precisely to move people out of such areas, had had its day.

The New Towns supplemented but did not replace local government initiatives (such as Becontree and Wythenshawe, referred to earlier) to deal with what widely became known as 'overspill' policies. Under the Town Development Act 1952 the 'exporting' local authorities received extra powers to assist 'importing' small towns in the planning of physical development and the provision of public services to their new residents, without any need to set up separate appointed development corporations. Some 66 formal agreements were negotiated, half by the Greater London Council and its predecessors. Others included 15 by Birmingham, and 4 each by Liverpool, Wolverhampton, Bristol and Manchester-Salford. Together these covered the building of about 160 000 houses for half a million people. Thus no fewer than 1.25 million city-dwellers were relocated to planned 'overspill' schemes of one type or another in the post-war decades, and many jobs were provided for them, ironically contributing to what was later designated the 'inner-city' problem of 'urban deprivation'.

Because most of this planned urbanization involved city residents moving to new urban areas, there was little impact on the total size of the urban population, given in Table 12.2 above. There was, however, a major impact on the total urban area. The New Towns alone accounted for almost all of the 88000 increase in urban hectares between 1951 and 1981, shown in Table 12.1.

The socio-economic 'town'

The Victorian local government structure was based on a clear distinction between town and country, an accurate reflection of prevailing socio-economic conditions in the era before mass public and private mechanized transport. Interestingly, that distinction held firm in many parts of the country as the basis of local government organization right through the twentieth century, despite rapidly changing social and economic conditions. Hence the first definition of the 'traditional' town, using municipal boundaries, had the appearance of continuing validity. In this section alternative approaches to urbanization, increasingly recognized as the century unfolded, are explored: they centre around the notion of a town area based on socio-economic criteria rather than on 'bricks-and-mortar' alone.

The urban–rural socio-economic distinction became increasingly less sharp as the twentieth century advanced. In Table 12.2 the proportion of the population living in the traditionally defined towns changed very little between 1901–81, ranging from 77 to 81 per cent at different times in the 80 years, yet most observers saw Britain as becoming increasingly 'urbanized'. When official statisticians introduced new criteria the result was an increase from 76.9 to 89.7 per cent in the urban share of the total population. This dispute about just what constitutes 'urban' and 'rural' is more than a semantic one between statisticians: it lay at the heart of much of the political debate about possible reforms to the structure of local government.

Agriculture

One indisputable fact is that the numbers working in agricultural and forestry jobs – the most traditional of rural occupations – fell dramatically, (as shown in Chapter 8): from 9 per cent in 1901 to 2 per cent in 1991. As a time-series the data are somewhat imperfect, but the fourfold or more decline seems broadly accurate. The definition of 'labourer' lacked rigour in the 1901 census, with some farm workers missed from the data as a result, and in 1911 and 1921 new and improved classifications consequently recorded an apparent absolute rise in the numbers in agricultural employment. Later data probably slightly underestimate agriculture-related employment by missing the rises in both agricultural engineers (farming technology was revolutionized during the century with the invention of tractors and other machinery), and in self-employed contractors for tasks such as harvesting. The data also cover fishing, but this too has been in decline and its numbers have always been a small part of the totals. But these are minor points: the very considerable decline in agricultural employment is not in dispute.

Even in the very rural areas, agriculture is now a minority occupation. Under the 'new' 1981 census definition of urban only 10.3 per cent of the population are now classified as living in rural locations, and fewer than one in seven of the economically active are in agricultural jobs. In the most agricultural of areas, such as deepest Powys (in mid-Wales), the proportion is no more than 30 per cent. Today, in contrast to 1901, 'rural' signifies habitation at low densities rather than a particular way of life centred on farming.

Transport

If any single factor has caused this change, it is the staggering growth in personal mobility resulting from the invention and spread of mechanized transportation. The motor car, in particular, has broken down the barriers between town and country which had led to the creation of separate local authorities under the Victorian local government system. (Chapter 13 contains statistics on vehicle licences and shows the dramatic growth in car ownership and the decline of public transport.)

Journey to work

To examine the precise consequences of this for the socio-economic definition of urbanization a set of time-series tables charting changes in lifestyles (work; shopping; entertainment; leisure) is needed. Because the mobility revolution grew apace and was, in particular, a post-World War II phenomenon, this type of material is almost completely unavailable for the early part of the century. The exception, an important one because it covers a daily activity, is journey-to-work data, first collected as part of the 1921 census, but only included in census questions on an irregular basis thereafter in the period up to the 1974 reforms to the local government system.

Robust trend data across the century are thus unavailable, but Tables 12.8 and 12.9 provide two valuable snapshots of the growth of both commuting and non-work travel covering the period 1921–95. The first, specially constructed for the Royal Commission reviewing the structure of local government in 1966–69 (the Redcliffe-Maud Commission), indicates the change and large increase in journeys to work which involved citizens resident in 'rural' areas who travelled to jobs in traditionally defined 'towns'. In 1921 some 14 per cent of rural inhabitants made such a journey; by 1966 the figure was over 37 per cent. In 1921 a mere 61 of 663 rural districts had 30 per cent or more of residents working in towns: by 1966 well over half (250 of 472) of the rural districts fell into this category and 86, or almost one in five of all rural districts, had *a majority* of their economically active residents travelling to urban-based employment.

Table 12.8 Rural to urban workplace movements, 1921 and 1966, England and Wales

Year	Population economically active: total for all rural districts	Of these, working in urban areas		Total no. of RDCs[a]	No. with proportions travelling into urban areas of			
		(No.)	(%)		0–10%	10–30%	30–50%	Over 50%
1921	3045900	425200	14.0	963	663	239	52	9
1966	4315700	1600300	37.1	472	42	180	164	86

Note: [a] RDCs = Rural District Councils.

Sources: Royal Commission on Local Government in England 1966–69 (1969), Table 6, Appendix 2, vol. 3. Figures for Welsh rural districts added from 1921 and 1966 census, *Workplace Tables*.

The trend of increased journeying across urban boundaries, clear as it is, might have been even more marked had the 1921 and 1966 figures been fully comparable. The 1921 census, delayed until mid-June for administrative reasons, overestimated the amount of travel to work: it took place when summer holidays were under way and it recorded data by where respondents happened to be that day rather than their usual place of residence (used in 1966). In over 50 rural districts with holidaymakers a population inflation of at least 3 per cent was estimated in the Census Report. Many of these additional people came from industrial towns having their annual 'wakes week' holidays and they were thus (mis)recorded as travelling from rural to urban areas to work.

Two additional complications in the data include a very high (15 per cent) non-response rate to this question in 1921, and the use of different levels of sampling based on movements of 25 or more people to any town in 1921, but 50 or more in 1966. The data analysis attempts to overcome the former by excluding all non-respondents, but the latter does mean that the extent of 1966 travelling should be slightly higher, or 1921 slightly lower, to be strictly comparable. To sum up, the increase from 14 to 37 per cent travelling to work in towns should probably be viewed as more than a trebling of the rate of job-related mobility.

The trend has almost certainly continued though the more recent snapshot is not totally comparable with the first one. In Table 12.9 survey data for 1975–95 show that increased use of the car is coupled with longer journeys to work (50 per cent longer in just two decades). The table also charts the increase in mobility for all activities, including shopping and leisure, with a rise from 451 to 578 journeys a year being made, an increase of over 25 per cent, in 20 years. There are no separate reliable nation-wide data on how many of these journeys involve rural to urban travel (or urban to rural, especially in the case of leisure) but the assumption must be that the general rate of increase in mobility is broadly applicable.

Table 12.9 Commuting and non-work journeys, Great Britain, 1975–95

	1975/76	1985/86	1981/91	1993/95
Proportion of commuter journeys by car (%)	51.8	59.0	66.0	68.9
Average distance of all commuter journeys (miles)	5.2	6.1	7.2	7.8
Average number of journeys per adult per year for non-work purposes	451	515	587	578

Source: Department of Transport (1996), Tables 4.1 and 4.3.

Regional population change

Equally lacking are reliable trend data across the century on regional populations. Because the key governmental institutions in Britain have been the central state and local authorities, the importance attached to the region, administratively and politically, has been inconsistent and variable. There is a long history of forms of regional administration, especially in Wales and Scotland. But in England that history incorporated the use of different regional boundaries by different central government departments or ministries with a (failed) attempt to standardize in the 1940s and a more successful move to coordination in the 1990s. Consequently, time-series data are rarely comparable and can be based on very different sets of regional boundaries: to give just one example, historically, Carlisle and the Lake District have sometimes been placed in the north-west and sometimes in the north.

Population change for the 1961–91 period, based on a continuous set of regional boundaries and on population estimates rather than on direct census outcomes, is shown in Table 12.10. The south-east has been divided to separate off Greater London where a decline of more than 16 per cent took place. Scotland, the north and the north-west of England also suffered absolute population decline between 1961 and 1991 while the south-east (outside London), south-west and East Anglia all expanded rapidly.

Table 12.10 Regional population change in Britain, 1961–91

Region[a]	1961 population (000s)	1971 population (000s)	1981 population (000s)	1991 population (000s)	1961–91 change (%)
North	3113	3152	3118	3092	–0.67
Yorks. & Humberside	4677	4902	4918	4983	6.54
East Midlands	3330	3652	3853	4035	4.74
East Anglia	1489	1688	1895	2082	21.17
Greater London	7977	7529	6806	6890	–13.63
South-east	8094	9596	10205	10747	32.78
South-west	3712	4112	4381	4718	27.10
West Midlands	4762	5146	5186	5266	10.58
North-west	6407	6634	6460	6396	–0.17
England	43460	46018	46226	46382	6.32
Wales	2644	2731	2790	2811	7.59
Scotland	5179	5228	5130	4962	–4.19

Note: [a] Regional populations are official estimates; country data are from *Census Reports*.

Sources: Central Statistical Office (CSO), *Abstract of Regional Statistics, no. 5* (1969); CSO (1985), Table 2.1; CSO (1986), Table 2.1; Department of the Environment (1996), Table 4.1; 1991 census, *Report for GB (Part 1)*.

The same boundaries are further used in Table 12.11 to explore in more detail, for the 1981–91 decade, the relative importance of natural change (births and deaths) and of migration in explaining these inter-regional differences in England. A very high rate of in-migration to both East Anglia and the south-west (a region popular as a place to settle on retirement) was experienced, while the three northernmost regions all had net outflows of migrants and simultaneously low rates of increase from natural change. The West Midlands also experienced out-migration.

Table 12.11 Components of regional population change in England, 1981–91

Region	1991 population (000s)	1981–91 change (%)	Natural change (%)	Net migration and other changes (%)
North	3092	–0.82	0.58	–1.41
Yorks. & Humberside	4983	1.31	1.32	–0.01
East Midlands	4035	4.74	1.98	2.76
East Anglia	2082	9.88	1.54	8.34
South-east	17637	3.68	2.65	1.03
South-west	4718	7.68	–0.14	7.82
West Midlands	5266	1.52	2.67	–1.15
North-west	6396	–0.98	1.36	–2.33

Source: Department of the Environment (1996), Table 4.1.

Increased personal mobility coupled with the European Union's significant use of regional policy in its allocation of grants-in-aid for large-scale projects designed to ameliorate regional poverty and decline, have led to an enhanced interest in the regional level as a basis for a range of public policies in recent decades. Talk of a 'north–south divide' has become commonplace and the population changes alone offer it some credence. The separate (and relatively small) historic town unit of local government has become somewhat less significant as a result. Ironically, a very different geographical focus – on the decline of the inner city – has also brought into question the role of the town unit: not because it is too small, but because it is too large!

The inner city and urban deprivation

So far we have revealed a clear pattern of change. Urban growth in the twentieth century was largely on the edges of cities, in adjacent rural areas, and in planned 'overspill' schemes. Mass personal mobility reduced the significance of traditionally drawn town boundaries. And population change differed from region to region, with northern Britain experiencing decline and the south (outside London) growth. These trends have been variously defined as both 'suburbanization' and as 'counter-urbanization' (the former relating to continuous outward sprawl from towns; the latter to deconcentration away from large towns towards more rural areas). They came about partly through social engineering to reduce inner-city congestion and partly through market forces as the middle classes sought houses close to green fields. In Table 12.6 one result was revealed: the seven English conurbations experienced an absolute loss of population between 1961–91 of more than 2.2 million, or over 11 per cent.

But these losses were not conurbation-wide. Typically, they were far greater in the older, often Victorian, neighbourhoods which lay closest to the city centres. Thus the City of Salford had a 1901 population of 221 000, but by 1981 this was down to under 100 000; and the population of inner London (the former London County Council area) fell from 4.5 million to 2.4 million in the same period. As a consequence, in Britain, as in many other developed countries experiencing these same trends, governments sought to design policies to combat what became styled as 'the inner-city problem'.

Population decline in itself need not be a 'problem': indeed, planned overspill policies were deliberately designed to ease congestion. But their significance was outweighed by the market-led moves of the better-off to relocate in suburbs or villages, or not to locate in inner areas when moving to a new region. The result was that inner cities, typically covering only part of a 'town', became areas of acute and multiple social and economic deprivation. A battery of policies to alleviate their worst problems began in the late 1960s and has continued apace ever since.

Table 12.12 Government indicators of urban deprivation, 1981 and 1991

DoE81		DoE91[a]	
Indicator	How measured	Indicator	How measured
Unemployed	Economically active residents unemployed	Unemployment	Unemployed persons
Pensioners	Households with single persons over 60/65	Poor children	Households with no earner or one parent in part-time employment
Overcrowding	Households living at > 1 person per room	Overcrowding	Households with > 1 person per room
Lack amenities	Households lack exclusive use of bath and inside WC	Lack amenities	Households lack or share bath/shower and/or WC, or in non-permanent housing
Single parents	Single-parent households (dependent children aged 0–15)	No car	Households without access to car
Ethnicity	Residents in households where head of household born in the New Commonwealth or Pakistan	Flat children	Children living in flats, not self-contained, or non-permanent housing

Note: [a] The DoE91 index was calculated for three levels; enumeration district (ED), electoral ward, and district as a whole. The indicators given here are those used at ED level. At ward and district level further indicators were added to these six.

Source: Lee (1995), Table 3.9.

The rapidity of policy change has been so great that robust trend data are not easily assembled. This difficulty is illustrated in Table 12.12 which compares the main criteria used by government in 1981 and in 1991 as a basis for recognition of a deprived area. Note that only one criterion of 'overcrowding' remained unchanged, and that three of the six 1981 criteria had been completely abandoned by 1991 and replaced by entirely new ones. The remaining two 1981 criteria were also modified, and measured slightly differently in 1991.

The Urban Programme, launched in 1968, has gone through a considerable number of major reincarnations in its 30 year history. Examples of major initiatives have successively included Partnership Areas, Programme Authorities, Designated Districts, Priority Estates Project, Urban Development Corporations, Enterprise Zones, Urban Priority Areas, City Challenge, and (from 1994) the Single Regeneration Budget which incorporated as many as 20 previously separate urban policy initiatives following criticism in 1991 from the Audit Commission that the government's support programme for urban regeneration was a 'patchwork quilt ... only loosely sewn together'. Amid all this change, some of which bypassed local authorities through the creation of new special-purpose agencies (or quangos (quasi non-governmental organizations)), the important point is that most of these multiple policy initiatives focused not on whole local authority areas but on quite small geographical sub-sets of them: the traditional town unit became increasingly less relevant as the determinant of what was 'urban'. Thus, for example, the 500 poorest areas in Britain under the 1991 criteria in Table 12.12 include no fewer than 258 in Greater London, which had only 33 local authorities. Boroughs like Tower Hamlets and Newham contained ten or more such areas within a single local authority of no more than 200 000 population. And Scotland, with only 32 local authorities in all, many of them very rural, contained 112 of the 500 poorest urban areas.

Local government reform and urbanization

The traditional town unit as the basis of a universal system of elected local government which separated 'urban' areas from 'rural' was a Victorian concept. The Local Government Acts of 1888 and 1894 consolidated earlier action. The larger towns were designated as County Boroughs, or autonomous all-purpose authorities (today such bodies are styled 'unitary'). County Council areas were divided up into Municipal Boroughs and Urban Districts for each town, and Rural Districts covering non-urbanized villages. The official 'bricks-and-mortar' definition of urbanization above was based on this constitutional status until the 1981 census used new criteria based on population density.

The relative advantages of one-tier and two-tier local government systems became a matter of debate from the moment the 1888 legislators differentiated between County and non-County (or Municipal) Boroughs, with the former 'all-purpose' and the latter sharing service provision with County Councils. The 1969 Redcliffe-Maud Report (Royal Commission on Local Government in England 1966–69, 1969) favoured the former approach, by now styled 'unitary', on grounds of both democracy (a single tier is easier to understand than a confusing two-tier system with a complex division of powers) and efficiency (coordination of services is more likely when all are provided by the same authority), but the 1970–74 Heath government rejected this and installed a two-tier County and District system across Britain in 1974. A decade or so later the Thatcher government moved to abolish the Greater London and Metropolitan County Councils primarily for ideological reasons but they used the practical argument that this would 'streamline the cities' because the remaining councils would become unitary and therefore more democratic and more efficient. From 1992 the Major government used the same arguments in announcing a policy of reform outside the conurbations.

In the event not everywhere became unitary in the 1990s. In Scotland and Wales the government made its own detailed proposals in 1993 White Papers, implemented by law with few changes a year later. But in England the decisions to set up yet another Local Government Commission, to require it to consult locally in each area of the country, and not to limit its remit to recommending only unitary authorities, backfired. Local vested interests were mobilized by county and district councils facing likely abolition and a mixed and often seemingly inconsistent bag of proposals – retention of two tiers in some places; a pattern of unitary councils elsewhere – resulted. Ministers approved some of the proposals; rejected or amended some others; referred those for 21 districts back to the Commission after appointing some new members; and lost a Court of Appeal hearing which deemed that in the case of Berkshire the Secretary of State had exceeded his legal powers. The eventual outcome of all these moves was a uniform system of unitary councils in Scotland and Wales, but the continued existence of both local government systems in England, as Table 12.13 reveals.

Table 12.13 Local authorities in Britain, 1998

Unitary	London	– 32 London Boroughs plus City of London Corporation
	English Conurbations	– 36 Metropolitan Boroughs
	England elsewhere	– 46 Unitary Councils
	Wales	– 22 Unitary Councils
	Scotland	– 32 Unitary Councils
Two-tier	England	– 34 County Councils
		– 238 District Councils

Source: *Municipal Year Book*, 1998.

The scale of change in the 1990s was greater than Table 12.13 may suggest in that more than 20 of the 34 English counties which survived despite government policy did not survive intact. Only 13 retained their two-tier structure in its entirety: in the others, parts of the former county area became unitary authorities. And Rutland, England's smallest county until its abolition in the 1960s, was reincarnated three decades later as its smallest unitary council!

Britain and Europe

With over 89 per cent of its population classified as living in urban areas, the United Kingdom is the second most urbanized nation in Western Europe: only Belgium has a higher ratio of urbanization, according to United Nations demographers, though Holland is not far behind the UK. The data in Table 12.14, which exclude very tiny states like Luxembourg, indicate that of the more populous European Union member states only Germany has a rate of urbanization anywhere near to that of the UK, and the 4 per cent gap between the two countries represents something like three million fewer town-dwellers there. Note that the 89.1 per cent figure for the UK is a little lower than the 89.7 per cent given earlier in Table 12.2 because the latter ratio was for England and Wales only, whereas in Table 12.14 'United Kingdom' relates to the whole of the UK, including Scotland and Northern Ireland where urbanization is slightly lower.

Table 12.14 Urbanization and local government in Europe

Country	Population 1990 (000s)	% Urban	Average population of basic local authorities
France	56718	72.7	1500
Belgium	9951	96.5	16740
Denmark	5140	84.8	18500
Germany	79365	85.3	7240
Greece	10238	62.6	1600
Holland	14952	88.7	17860
Ireland	3503	56.9	41910
Italy	57023	66.7	6800
Portugal	9868	33.5	34180
Spain	39272	75.4	4700
Sweden	8559	83 1	30000
UK	57411	89.1	N. Ireland 60480
			Wales 75870
			Scotland 91620
			England 127000

Sources: United Nations (1995); Batley and Stoker (1991), Table 2.2.

What is striking is the range of urbanization across Western Europe, usually considered to be a highly urbanized continent. Though Italy and Greece are often thought to be amongst the more rural, in Portugal only one in three citizens live in towns and in Ireland just over one in two. The overall range, from 33 to 96 per cent, indicates that Western Europe is a continent of far more demographic contrasts than is commonly thought.

But even more striking is the contrast between Britain's approach to local government, outlined above, and that of almost every other European country. The story of local government reform in the UK has been one of a belief in the cost-effectiveness of size. This has resulted in an emphasis on structures and geographical boundaries based more on the socio-economic town as a unit for local government than on representative democracy at the level of very localized grass-roots communities. As a consequence, when it comes to the average population size of the 'basic' service-providing unit of elected local government, the UK is a marked outlier, and very dramatically so.

The data in Table 12.14 speak for themselves: only Ireland has a local government system remotely close to Britain's, as measured by average population size. England's local authorities, in particular, are on average three times the size of Ireland's, seventeen times larger than those found in Germany, and eighty times that of France. Though it is the case that, particularly in rural areas, there is a system of more local 'parish' councils (sometimes styled 'town' or 'burgh') in Britain, these are responsible for far too few services to qualify as 'basic authorities'. In any event, parish councils do not exist at all in the larger towns which, in Table 12.4, were seen to dominate the UK's very high overall urbanization ratio.

Conclusions

The twentieth century was one of enormous demographic change. *Urbanization* continued, albeit at much slower rate than in the nineteenth-century era of the Industrial Revolution, and the proportion living in towns crept up from 77 to 80 per cent in the period 1901–31. In those same decades, personal mobility, using public and private transport, grew and *suburbanization* around the edges of the larger towns was witnessed on a large scale. At about that time the population of many of the larger cities peaked, and by the 1960s there was official recognition that *deurbanization*, partly fuelled by government policies like the New Towns initiative, was creating social and economic problems in the older urban areas. A series of explicit experimental inner-city policy initiatives followed. By the 1990s these policies were focusing on economic restructuring, but a common by-product of schemes to revive the fortunes of city centres was the construction of some residential accommodation, usually colonized by the middle classes, and often through the conversion of old commercial premises such as warehouses: in effect a modest amount of *reurbanization* occurred. The final change, *counter-urbanization*, is best measured regionally. In the south west, the outer south east, and in East Anglia there were enormous population increases in the 1961–91 period, largely due to migration from Greater London (with a consequent rise in long-distance commuting to work), but also often reflecting preferences about relocating on retirement.

The extent of these changes has been far-reaching. Not long before the century started a leading political analyst and observer of the day claimed that the local government reforms of 1888 and 1894 could not 'ignore the manifold and increasing differences between urban and rural districts', and the structure which resulted duly differentiated between the two. That structure survived through most of the twentieth century, and continues to survive in some places. But the story of urban change in the 1900–2000 era was one of a breaking down of the barriers between urban and rural due to social and economic develop-ments. Symbolic of this was the decision, finally taken as part of the 1981 census analysis, to construct a new definition of 'urban' because the longstanding link with the administrative areas used as a basis of town status could no longer be justified. The politics of local government reform had throughout the century centred on the often successful attempts of allegedly 'rural' (though increasingly urbanized) areas to resist incorporation into their adjacent cities. One measure of the success of the advocates of 'rural' status was that the new census's official definition of 'urban', based on land-use rather than administrative status, immediately increased the proportion of the British population deemed to be living in towns from 77 to almost 90 per cent.

The final tranche of local government reforms, in the mid-1990s, retained the Victorian concept of the 'bricks-and-mortar' town only in the cases of the largest conurbations and a handful of free-standing big cities. Elsewhere the new unitary authorities, along with those counties that have survived, embrace boundaries relating physically, if sometimes only approximately, more to the twentieth-century socio-economic town, based on patterns of social mobility and life-style. In a sense these new local authorities reflect today's patterns of urbanization just as much as did the Victorian local govern-ment reforms in their day. Quite simply, times have changed.

Short note on sources

The decennial *Census Reports* offer the most comprehensive trend data available on populations. Special reports on urban areas appeared in 1951, 1981 and 1991: their details are cited in sources to the appropriate tables.

Official population estimates have been used on occasion to provide further insights into population trends, notably into the relative importance of natural and of migration changes.

Information on the numbers, sizes and other features of every local authority is published annually in the *Municipal Year Book*.

Note

1   Some small 'towns' have retained separate town councils which do not exercise any major local government powers but which are akin to the (rural) parish councils created in 1894. For the purposes of this chapter these 'towns' are deemed to have lost their traditional status as significant local authorities (urban districts or non-county boroughs).

References

Batley, R. and Stoker, G. (1991) *Local Government in Europe: Trends and Developments*, Macmillan, Basingstoke.

Central Statistical Office (CSO) (1985) *Regional Trends 20*, HMSO, London.

Central Statistical Office (1986) *Regional Trends 21*, HMSO, London.

*Department of the Environment (1996) *Urban Research Report – Urban Trends in England: Latest Evidence from the 1991 Census*, HMSO, London.

Department of Transport (1996) *National Travel Survey 1993/5*, HMSO, London.

Lee, P. (1995) *Area Measures of Deprivation*, University of Birmingham Centre for Urban and Regional Studies, Birmingham.

Royal Commission on Local Government in England 1966–69 (1969) *Report, Cmnd 4040* (The Redcliffe-Maud Report), HMSO, London.

United Nations (1995) *World Urbanization Prospects: The 1994 Revision*, UN Population Division, New York.

Further reading

(In addition to the starred item in the References)

Bibby, P. and Shepherd, J. (1997) 'Projecting rates of urbanisation in England, 1991–2016', *Town Planning Review*, 68 (1), pp. 93–124.

Johnston, R. J. and Pattie, C. J. (1996) 'Local government in local governance: the 1994–5 restructuring of local government in England', *International Journal of Urban and Regional Research*, 20 (4), pp. 671–96.

Leach, R. (1997) 'Incrementalism and rationalism in local government reorganisation 1957–1996', *Public Policy and Administration*, 12 (3), pp. 59–72.

Lipman, V. D. (1949) *Local Government Areas 1834–1945*, Blackwell, Oxford.

Local Government Commission for England (1995) *Renewing Local Government in the English Shires: A Report on the 1992–5 Structural Review*, HMSO, London.

Local Government Commission For England (1995) *The 1995 Review of 21 Districts in England: Overview Report*, HMSO, London.

Policy Studies Institute (1992) *Urban Trends 1*, PSI, London.

Wood, B. (1976) *The Process of Local Government Reform 1966–74*, Allen & Unwin, London.

Part V
Policy

13
Transport and Communications

Amanda Root

I have always thought that the substitution of the internal combustion engine for the horse marked a very gloomy milestone in the progress of mankind.

Winston Churchill, 1954

Introduction

Transport facilities and various ways of sharing information were, until the early part of the twentieth century, collectively known as 'communications'. This meaning has largely disappeared: transport refers to the physical movement of people and goods; communications to the imparting of information and ideas, via print, telecommunications and the Internet. Yet still, in some cases, transport and communications share a common role; that of creating, either directly or indirectly, shared social 'space', formed by spatial and interpersonal relations. In other words, they facilitate a 'public' (that is, shared and participatory), culture. In other cases this does not happen. Transport modes such as cars allow access to a huge range of social events but also diminish public space in communities, through crashes, noise and other forms of pollution (Whitelegg, 1993, p.99). Mass communications, such as the cinema and the television, can also be said to be designed for particular kinds of personalized consumption. Many types of travel and communications constitute 'individuating' forces; that is, personal needs are met but social life is increasingly rendered 'private', in the sense of privileged and separate (Halsey, 1996, p.198).

The development of transport and communications in the twentieth century can be seen as an explosion (Table 13.1); vast increases in mobility, new uses of physical space, interacting with, and creating, social trends. Essentially 'private' modes (for example, cars, computer codes), have been pitted against more inclusive, mutual and collective 'public' forms (speech,

Table 13.1 Main motorized modes of travel: passenger mileage, Great Britain, 1900–97

	Cars, vans, taxis	Rail	million miles Bus and coach	Trams (electric and cable)	Air
1900	83ᵃ	23493	8	1484	0
1910	524	22366	38	4441	0
1920	2629	22900	69ᵇ	5177	0
1928	19246	21300	2200	5944	0
1938	40507	18993	45444ᶜ	4299	0
1948	41495	21140	61175ᵈ	2325	0
1958	70218	25477	49712	504	621
1968	173371	20506	39770	15	1243
1975	205684	22370	37284	15	1243
1980	241103	21749	32313	11	1864
1988	333070	25477	28584	11	3107
1997	384647	25477	26720	29	4226

Notes: ᵃFigures refer to 1904. Gallons of fuel consumed were not available for 1900, so average mileage per vehicle for 1910 was calculated and multiplied by numbers of vehicles licensed in 1904.
ᵇBased on vehicle mileage figures for 1918/19 (Munby, 1978, p.356).
ᶜBased on vehicle mileage figures for 1937 (Munby, 1978, p.356).
ᵈBased on vehicle mileage figures for 1949 (Munby, 1978, p.358).

Source notes: Walking, cycling and horse-drawn vehicles are omitted as there is insufficient data to estimate mileage. Journeys on ships, canal boats, trolley buses, the London Underground and other less common motorized forms of transport such as gas-powered or electric vehicles have also been omitted. Data are not always at regular intervals as sources do not allow uniformity.

For 1910–48, car miles have been estimated by using figures for motor fuel tax to find gallons of fuel sold (British Road Federation, 1938, p.23). Figures for passenger miles were divided by fuel in the period 1952–97 and linear best-fit trend was used to estimate earlier less efficient fuel use (DETR, 1998a, p.58). Gallons of fuel used were then multiplied by miles per gallon. Fuel used for freight transportation from 1900–51 is included in these figures as it would be difficult to accurately separate goods from travel mileage.

Rail figures before 1920 were estimated using linear best-fit trend on the set from 1920–39 from Munby (1978) p.104. Munby's figures exclude London Transport from 1933. Rail figures from 1920–48 are from Munby (1978), pp.104–5. After 1984, figures are from DETR (1998a), p.180.

Tram vehicle mileage 1900–70 is from Munby (1978), pp.352–4; later vehicle miles projected on basis of ratio of mileage changes to number of tram vehicles (DETR, 1998d, p.43). Seating capacity is derived from figures given in Munby (1978), pp.343–5 for 1924–37; that is, an average seating capacity divided by numbers of vehicles. Capacity of 25 per cent (that is, 15 passengers) was assumed. 1997 figures include mileage from the South Yorkshire Supertram, opened in 1994.

Figures for bus and coach vehicle miles for 1918–70 were taken from Munby (1978), pp.356–8. The higher of Munby's estimates were used. Estimated passenger numbers were obtained by dividing passenger miles by vehicle miles from 1952–70, (Munby, 1978, pp.356–8; DETR, 1998a, p.180). Twenty-five passengers per bus or coach was the average in the early 1950s and as the trend was for occupancy levels to increase, this figure was used for the earlier years as a conservative estimate of numbers. Figures for 1900 and 1910 assume that vehicle mileage stays the same per vehicle as 1920, they were estimated by finding the proportion of licensed vehicles and using that as the basis for mileage figures.

Air travel statistics are taken from DETR (1998d), p.41.

walking, carts and horses). It is not a story of the inevitability of progress from one form to another, but rather a set of exchanges that have been made between different ways of constituting individuality, which involves issues beyond the scope of this chapter. These patterns are also complex and non-linear inasmuch as transport and communication modes, such as the car or the television, can both create new social connections and also have profoundly anti-social effects.

The (partial) conquest of space and time: an outline of technological and social changes, 1900–2000

An abundance of speed, 1900–14

In the first decades of the century innovation and invention in communications were sufficiently fast and abundant that their effects have been referred to as the 'Edwardian shock of speed' (Liniado, 1996, p.7). For instance, in 1899 Marconi broadcast radio messages from England to France, and in 1901 he broadcast the first transatlantic radio signal from Poldhu in Cornwall to Newfoundland, Canada. The advent of the wireless telegraph, bicycle, car, X-ray, cinema, aeroplane and telephone transformed perceptions of personal and national identity, history, space, distance, community and the future (Kern, 1983, p.1).

The availability of train travel for working people had been improved from the 1860s when Parliament had allowed some railway companies to extend their lines but on requirement that they provided 'workmen's' trains with cheap fares, available to travellers of both genders, often 1d for each journey. These trains often ran only before 7 a.m. and after 6 p.m. but they provided indispensable commuter transport for low-paid manual workers. Prior to 1914, the London Underground offered the 'twopenny' Tube fare and several new lines were built, extending mobility for the poor.

In some areas, the horse-drawn hackney, the motor bus, tram and, to a lesser extent, the trolley bus provided a cheaper and more popular alternative to the train (Table 13.2). But until just after World War I the British railway system enjoyed supremacy as the principal form of passenger transport: there were 2064 million rail journeys in 1919 (Table 13.3). Part of the reason was that by 1920 Britain possessed a complete and comprehensive rail network of just less than 20 000 miles, a feat of Victorian engineering still unsurpassed.

By about 1900, the early experimental period in motor vehicle construction was ending. Most early lorries were steam-powered and these behemoths lasted until the 1940s, but petrol gave the advantage of immediate starting and immediate stopping. When wage-rates were important instant starting became a critical factor: no starting at 4 a.m. to get the boiler fired up for a wheels-turning departure at 6 a.m.

Table 13.2 Public transport vehicles, Great Britain, 1900–96/97

| | | Hackney vehicles[a] | | |
	Horse-drawn	Taxis[b]	Buses and coaches[c]	Trolley buses[d]
1900	n/a	n/a		n/a	n/a
1903	127410	–	5000	
1911	101965[f]		33199	6
1920	72000		74608	77
1930	6045[g]	48483	52122	526
1940	–		81300	n/a
1950	–	58845	73080	4086
1960	–	14543	74475	2409
1970	–	25200	73774	72
1980	–	38970	69200	n
1989/90	–	51000[i]	72500[j]	n
1996/97	–	64000	75900	

Notes: – = not applicable; n/a = not available; n = negligible (less than half the final
digit shown).
[a]Data for hackney vehicles up to 1945 should be treated with caution.
[b]Taxi column excludes private hire cars. Taxi surveys are infrequent so the series contains some
estimates.
[c]Including trolleybuses.
[d]Trolley buses are electrically powered by overhead wires but run on-street.

Source: DETR (1998d), Tables 3.2a and 3.2b.

**Table 13.3 Rail: length of national rail route at year end, and passenger
travel on National Rail and London Underground, Great Britain, 1900–97/98[a]**

	Length of National Rail route Total route (miles)	Electrified route (miles)	Open to passenger traffic (miles)
1900	18507	n/a	n/a
1919	20146	821	n/a
1928	20236	1181	n/a
1938	19935	2099	n/a
1948	19632	904	n/a
1958	18849	1008	14678
1968	12478	1977	9471
1978	11124	2309	8946
1989/90	10307	2825	8897
1997/98	10350	3210	9336

Note: [a]From 1994/95 route length is for Railtrack; from 1995/96 passenger traffic is for National Rail
and former British Rail Operating Companies.

| Trams | | Rail passenger carriages | | |
Electric, steam and cable	Horse-drawn	Light rail or metros/[e] Minor rail systems/ Glasgow Underground	London Underground	National rail network
6361	35987	58	1705	45537
9040	14058	58	1947	48265
12182	1526	54	2465	50882
13787	79	50	2272	52187
13321	–	50	2659	50834
6900	–	50	n/a	42811
4084[h]	–	50	3998	42218
440	–	50	4150	40091
92	–	257	4423	18678
75	–	420	4353	17042
79	–	134	3908	12514
81	–	752	3912	10600

[e]Light rail and metros comprise various light rail systems, supertrams and metros, such as the Glasgow Underground, Nexus (Tyne and Wear, from 1980), Docklands Light Railway (1988/89), Manchester Metrolink (1992/93) and Sheffield Supertram (1993/94). Minor rail systems comprise preserved, restored tourist railways open to fare-paying passengers.
[f]Horse-drawn cab data for 1911 refers to number of drivers. Last horse-drawn cabs were licensed in 1943.
[g]Figures for 1931.
[h]From 1950, this category consists of electric and cable trams only.
[i]Estimate
[j]New categorization of public transport vehicles.

| National Rail | | London Underground | |
Passenger journeys (million)	Passenger miles (billion)	Passenger journeys (million)	Passenger miles (billion)
n/a	n/a	n/a	n/a
2064	n/a	n/a	n/a
1250	n/a	n/a	n/a
1237	19.01	492	n/a
1024	21.25	720	3.85
1090	22.12	692	3.29
831	17.83	655	2.92
724	18.64	568	2.80
758	20.69	765	3.73
846	21.25	832	4.04

Sources: DETR (1997b), p.165; DETR (1998a), pp.118–20, p.187.

Table 13.4 Private and goods road vehicles in use, Great Britain, 1904–97[a]

Year	Private cars	Other private and light goods vehicles	Goods vehicles[b]
1904	8465	–	4000
1910	53169	–	30000
1920	186801	–	101000
1930	1056214	–	348441
1940	1423200	–	443900
1950	1979000	439000	439000
1960	4900000	894000	493000
1970	9971000	1421000	545000[h]
1980	14660000	1641000	507000
1990	19742000	2247000	482000
1997	21681000	2317000	414000

Notes: [a]From 1978 onwards figures are not strictly comparable, as they were prepared on a different basis. In 1982 vehicle types were given new taxation categories and previous years' figures have been revised on the basis of these new taxation categories.
   These figures do not include vehicles that were in use but not licensed. A July 1978 survey estimated that there were about one million cars and a similar or larger proportion of motor cycles and goods vehicles in this category.
[b]Combined categories of 'light goods vehicles' and 'heavy goods vehicles' until 1950, when separate figures are available for goods vehicles (over 3500 kg or 7700 lb. gross vehicle weight) and light goods vehicles – vans, private buses and coaches, and so on – which are under 3500 kg gross weight.
[c]Between 1937 and 1977 the figures include riders of mopeds and scooters but exclude sidecar passengers.
[d]Crown and exempt vehicles include agricultural tractors, tricycles, pedestrian controlled vehicles and showmen's haulage. From 1951 they include special machines, vehicles with special concessionary licences, and special and other vehicles.

The 1903 Motor Car Act gave legal recognition to 'motor cars' as distinct from 'light locomotives'. This Act established the motor car's independence and started its rapid growth as a mode of transport, an increase encouraged by successive transport policies and road lobbyists (Hamer, 1987; Castle, 1993, p.369). The number of private cars and goods vehicles rose from 12 465 in 1904 to 83 196 in 1910 (119 438 including motorcycles), increases of 567 per cent and 858 per cent, respectively (Table 13.4). The 1903 Act also introduced a speed limit of 20 miles per hour (mph), although many vehicles then being manufactured were capable of exceeding this limit and frequently ignored this restriction (Bagwell, 1974, p.217). The Mercedes 'Sixty', manufactured in 1903, could reach speeds of up to 80 mph (Liniado, 1996, p.11).

World War I, 1914–18

World War I created the need for communications, movements of troops and supplies on an unprecedented scale. In 1914 alone, 120 000 people were transported to France. Once World War I was declared, the government assumed control of the railways and about a third of the canal system on behalf of the

Motor cycles[c]	Bicycles	Crown and exempt vehicles[d]	Horse-drawn vehicles	All vehicles
–	–	–	–	12465
36242	–	–	–	119411
287739	440770	19099[e]	237342[f]	1035409
724319	508241	43566	53015	2680781
278300	1987000	98300	9274[g]	2085300
751738	3528000	367859	–	7504597
1861247	2278000	505714	–	10931961
1141400	1605000	574300	–	15257700
1372000	1696000	893000	–	20769000
833000	2250000	1253000	–	26807000
626000	2500000[i]	1857000	–	29395000

[e]1921 figure.
[f]1922 figure.
[g]1938 figure.
[h]Since 1970, Post Office vehicles have been licensed as goods vehicles.
[i]1996 figure.

Source notes: British Road Federation (1962, pp.2–5) for pre-1950 data and DETR (1998a), p.184, for 1950–97. Bicycle figures are for production. Figures for 1920 and 1930 from Board of Trade (1940). Figures are not available for 1940, instead are for 1935: from *Annual Abstract of Statistics*, no. 85, 1937–47; 1950 figures are from the *Annual Abstract of Statistics 1953*; 1960 and 1970 figures are from *Annual Abstract of Statistics 1971*; figures for 1980 are from *Annual Abstract of Statistics 1982*. 1990 and 1996 Bicycle Association (1997, p.3); these figures are for sales. Horse-drawn vehicles data are from Board of Trade (1926, p.178; 1940, pp.328–9).

war effort. In return for taking over the railways, the Railway Companies were guaranteed their approximate net revenues of 1913. This was a good deal from the point of view of shareholders and management since the last year of peace had been an exceptionally busy and profitable one (Bagwell, 1974, p.237).

Volunteering and enlistment depleted the civilian transport systems, including the canal network. About half of the canal staff, about 30 000 men, had enlisted by 1917, creating serious personnel shortages. Between 1914 and 1916 much of the former canal traffic was diverted to railways and most of the canal traffic lost in the early months of World War I was never regained (Bagwell, 1974, p.239).

World War I demonstrated the potentialities of the internal combustion engine, as the British Army used over 100 000 motor vehicles in France, many of them requisitioned civilian vehicles. Many men returned from World War I as experienced drivers, and continued this work afterwards. The bus regulation of the 1930s can be attributed to the need to control the resultant over-supply of vehicles which sometimes gave rise to predatory behaviour such as races to pick up passengers (Mackie and Preston, 1996).

Communications and road expansion, 1920–38

The first suburbs were really the products of the railway age, telephones and the new road infrastructure. Telegrams reached a peak of 101 million in 1920. The train allowed the managerial class to live in suburbs, often 20 or more miles from their work, hence Betjeman's 'metroland' of the 1920s and 1930s. Initially the moves were primarily by the middle class as their working hours were shorter and they could afford train fares out of their salaries. New forms of communication allowed people to span these and other distances. Trunk (inland long-distance) telephone calls doubled between 1910 and 1920 (Table 13.5), whilst postcards sent dropped by about a third (Table 13.6). Trunk telephone calls doubled again between 1920 and 1930, and local calls grew by about 50 per cent. Relatively orderly patterns of railway and road investment and subsequent town and country planning, prevented the sort of urban sprawl that developed in the US, but did not prevent the post-World War II domination of city centres by cars (Plowden, 1972, p.39).

Table 13.5 Telephone calls, UK, 1900–97/98

	Telephone calls made (millions)		No. of telephone
	Trunk[a]	Local[a]	stations[b] (000s)
1900	8	n/a	2
1910	27	n/a	98
1920	54	848	888
1930	118	1205	1896
1940	117	2098	3339
1950	235	2940	5171
1960	387	3900	7790
1970	1352	8270	13844
1980	3257	16600	26807
1984	3936	18750	29336
Call minutes (millions)[c]			
	National	Local	all calls
1992/93	28737	64236	98321
1997/98	43576	93158	154813

Notes: [a]Inland calls only.
[b]A station, since 1921, is a telephone directly or indirectly connected with the public exchange system. Previous private network instruments were wholly excluded.
[c]Data on the numbers of telephone calls were no longer publicly available after 1984. Subsequent data start with 1992/93 and are based on call minutes via fixed operators (Public Switch Trunk Network services). Local and national calls include only simple voice calls. All calls includes all private operators (primarily British Telecom, Kingston, Mercury and Cable), local, national and international calls, number translation services (including revenues from the called party), premium rate, directory enquiries, operator calls, the speaking clock and public payphones.

Sources: Mitchell (1988), p.566ff; Office of Telecommunications (1998), p.19; Office of Telecommunications (1999), p.13; ONS (1991), p.213; ONS (1998c), p.244.

Table 13.6 Post Office mail traffic, UK, 1900–97

	Postcards	Lettersª	(millions) Newspapers, packets, etc.	Parcels	Telegrams sent within the UK
1900	401	2247	866	75	90
1910	868	2947	1173	118	87
1920ᵇ	581	3832	1317	145	101
1930	420ª	3700	2280ª	161	71
1940	–	7460	–	193	63
1950	–	8350	–	243	52
1960	–	10200	–	235	35
1970	–	11400	–	208	29
1980	–	10210	–	180	16ᶜ
1990	–	15293	–	197ᵈ	–
1997	–	18101	–	n/a	–

Notes: ªFrom 1940 onwards, letters category includes postcards, newspapers, packets etc.
ᵇSubsequently excluding Southern Ireland.
ᶜTelegrams are included in letters, postcards, packets, and so on, from 1990.
ᵈFigures for 1988.
Sources: Mitchell (1988), p.563ff.; ONS (1998c), p.244.

Perhaps because of mass manufacturing techniques introduced by companies such as Raleigh, and subsequently relatively cheaper machines, bicycle ownership almost quadrupled between 1930 and 1940 (Table 13.4) and cycles were not only used for travel to work but also for holidays (tandems were popular). Many middle-class women had begun to use cycles in the 1890s, but in the 1930s looser clothing enabled more working-class women to ride bikes. High fashion in London parks hid the explosion of female mobility on bicycles: visiting friends, carrying goods to market in the country, taking factory and office workers to the cities. Bicycles, as in any Third World country today, initiated a revolution in transport, as they were cheap, easy to repair and allowed the poorest person to keep up with city traffic speeds and to carry heavy loads (Turner and Spencer, 1996).

The national road building programme was also started at this time and nearly 8500 miles of Class 1 and 2 roads were built (Table 13.7). Between 1920 and 1930, car registrations quintupled (Table 13.4). In 1914 motorists were a very privileged group: only 1 person in every 232 in Great Britain owned a car. By 1922, there was 1 motor vehicle to every 78 persons and car ownership had become much more commonplace amongst middle- and upper-class men. By 1938, 1 person in 15 was a car owner but, due to the recession, the high cost of vehicles relative to the average weekly wage, and the limited extent of hire purchase sales, car ownership was still largely confined to men in the middle classes.

Table 13.7 Public road lengths, Great Britain, 1909–97 (miles)

	Trunk[ab]	Class 1 or principal[a]	Class 2 or B[c]	Class 3 or C[c]
1909	–	n/a	n/a	–
1923	–	23230	14740	–
1933	–	26586	16645	–
1943	4459	23181	17730	–
1953	8255	19552	17701	48695
1960	8439	19739	17607	48915
1970	8987	20248	66667[e]	n/a
1980	9289	21244	17493	50169
1990	9735	21889	18541	50157
1997	9643	22295	18868	51518

Notes: n/a = not available; – = not applicable.
[a]Trunk and principal roads include built-up and non built-up roads.
[b]Trunk roads comprise a national network of through routes for which the Secretary of State for Transport in England, and the Secretaries of State for Scotland and Wales are the highway authorities. Non-trunk roads are roads for which local highway authorities (regional and island councils in Scotland) are responsible.

World War II, 1939–45

Massive movements of troops, supplies and civilians took place during World War II, some, like the D-Day landings in France, bigger than all previous war operations. In addition to the other vicissitudes of warfare, World War II gave rise to new aspirations, broader experiences and increased mobility, giving many people, primarily young men, their first extensive exposure to other national cultures (Dahl, 1993; Halsey, 1996; Clarke, 1997). There was also an involvement of the civilian population on a previously unprecedented scale, due to the development of aerial bombing, necessitating large-scale evacuations from cities within the UK.

In 1938 organizational structures were put in place to cope with transport needs in the event of the outbreak of World War II. A Railway Executive Committee was established which was given powers to administer the main line railways, the London Passenger Transport Board, some other less important railways and docks once a war broke out. Rail productivity was increased under this regime: railway freight traffic rose by nearly 50 per cent and passenger traffic rose by 68 per cent between 1938 and 1944 (Bagwell, 1974, p.298). New controls over buses and lorries as well as petrol rationing were introduced. Campaigns to reduce travel used posters that asked, 'Is your journey really necessary?'

The motorway, jet and television era, 1946–2000

The efficiency of war-time public transport contributed to a post-war belief in the virtues of nationalization. This belief paved the way for the Transport Act

Unclassified[d]	All	of which motorways		
		Trunk	Principal	Total
n/a	175471	–	–	–
139358	177328	–	–	–
134124	177355	–	–	–
n/a	n/a	–	–	–
92067	186270	–	–	–
99490	194190	95	–	95
104490	200392	635	22	657
112852	211047	1519	69	1588
122160	222482	1860	48	1908
127511	229835	2020	28	2048

[c]Non-principal roads are sub-divided into B and C classes.
[d]Unclassified roads are local distributor and access roads.
[e]Includes C roads.

Sources: DETR (1997b), p.169; DETR (1998a), p.82.

1947, which has been described as the Attlee government's 'biggest venture into nationalization' (*The Economist*, 1946, p.898). This Act vested ownership of all railways, steamships, canals and some road haulage and road passenger businesses with a body called the British Transport Commission. Further nationalization followed: a fully state-owned road haulage company was declared 'broadly complete' in 1951. Two airlines, namely British European Airways and British South American Airways, started operations as state-owned enterprises in 1946.

Reversal of the nationalization policies began in 1953, with the denationalization of some road haulage activities, and was broadly completed with the Railways Act 1993, which denationalized the railways. Buses (outside London) were deregulated and privatized by the 1985 Transport Act, which dissolved the state-run National Bus Company. These changes were accompanied by substantial fare increases and a big drop in passenger miles (Figure 13.1), but an increase in bus miles, partly caused by the replacement of double-deckers by large single-deckers. British Rail was privatized into 25 train operating companies (TOCs), an infrastructure operator (Railtrack) and rolling stock leasing companies by the 1993 Railways Act. The TOCs were given 7–15-year franchises, won on the basis of operating specified services with diminishing subsidies. Full competition on the track may be introduced in 2002. Immediate effects included a 60 per cent increase in the number of passenger complaints, a drop in punctuality and a growth in ticket types (and increased use of telesales), arguably to escape fare price regulation. By 1997, patronage was up by 12 per cent, but mainly due to strong performance of the economy.

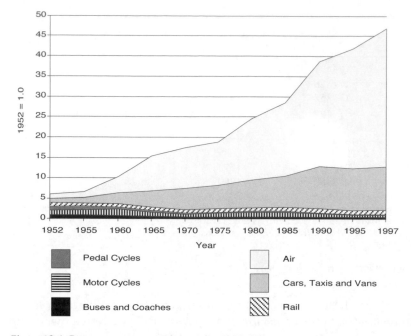

Figure 13.1 Passenger transport by mode, 1952–97

Source: DETR (1998a) p.180.

	1952	1955	1960	1965	1970	1975	1980	1985	1990	1995	1997
Buses and Coaches	1	0.99	0.86	0.73	0.65	0.65	0.57	0.53	0.50	0.48	0.47
Motor Cycles	1	1.14	1.57	1.00	0.57	0.86	1.14	1.14	0.86	0.57	0.57
Pedal Cycles	1	0.78	0.52	0.30	0.17	0.17	0.22	0.26	0.22	0.17	0.17
Rail	1	1.00	1.05	0.92	0.95	0.95	0.92	0.95	1.03	0.95	1.08
Cars, Taxis and Vans	1	1.43	2.40	3.98	5.12	5.71	6.69	7.60	10.14	10.28	10.67
Air	1	1.50	4.00	8.50	10.00	10.52	15.00	18.00	26.00	29.50	34.00

Other major reorganization of the railways had been introduced in 1963 when over 5000 miles (about a quarter) of railway line were abandoned and 2363 stations (about a third) were closed under proposals put forward by Dr Richard (later Lord) Beeching, the Chairman of the British Railways Board. These cuts were justified on the grounds that the branch railways to be closed – primarily branch rural lines and stations receiving coal – were economically unviable (Beeching, 1963, pp.46–8). Unsurprisingly, the closures promoted car use (Hillman and Whalley, 1980, p.88).

In the early 1950s only 14 per cent of all households had cars. They remained a luxury until the 1960s, when mass production and the resulting lower prices made buying, selling, (and often maintaining and upgrading) cars an option, for the first time, for the majority of households. By 1996, 70 per cent of all households owned cars, but nearly a third (30 per cent) did not (Table 13.8). This is a relatively large group, but the households without a car tend to be smaller than the car-owning ones. Access to cars is probably diminishing for those in non-car-owning households: car-drivers gave seven times more lifts to people from non-car-owning households in the late 1970s than they did in the mid-1990s (Root et al., 1996, p. 18). The proportion of households owning one car (45 per cent) has not changed since 1969. The growth has been in the number with two or more cars, and by the mid-1990s a quarter of all households had access to more than one car.

Table 13.8 Household car ownership, Great Britain, 1951–96

Households with:	1951	1960	(%) 1970	1980	1990	1996
No cars	86	71	48	41	33	30
One car	13	27	45	44	44	45
Two cars	1	2	6	13	19	21
Three or more cars	–	–	2	2	4	4

Source: DETR (1998c), p.61.

The costs of public transport are highly visible and, relatively, have risen more quickly than those of motoring. As Table 13.9 shows, motoring costs have stayed approximately level in real terms over the past 15 years, while public transport fares have risen. The fall in the cost of cars relative to income has been a fundamental driving force behind the growth in car ownership. Cars were cheaper to run and more fuel efficient in 1996 than 30 years earlier. Car

Table 13.9 Passenger transport price indices[a], UK, 1975–95/96 (constant prices: 1995 = 100)

	Motoring costs	Rail fares	Local bus fares	Taxi fares in London	Taxi fares ex. London	Other travel costs
1975	107.6	61.3	66.1	73.7	77.2	147.6
1980	107.0	76.2	78.9	74.5	81.2	140.8
1985/86	101.7	80.4	81.7	90.8	91.2	105.7
1990/91	93.3	86.3	88.9	97.6	–	98.5
1995/96	99.7	100.4	100.5	100.4	100.1	99.3
Percentage change: 10 years since 1975	–6	65	56	39	32	–32

Note: [a]Prices have been adjusted for general inflation using the retail price index.

Source: DETR (1999).

prices dropped by 25 per cent since 1964. The cost of fuel was about the same (it was 20 per cent higher after the oil crises of the 1970s) but at the end of the century cars were more fuel-efficient and cheaper to run, and average incomes had grown by about 2 per cent a year in real terms. This meant that the proportion of an average household's gross income required to own and operate a car fell by 40 per cent between 1964 and 1996 (Glaister and Graham, 1996).

Travel is, on average, the third most expensive item in the household budget, after housing (Table 13.10). An average household spent £54.71 per week on transport costs in 1997/98. This is not, of course, the whole story: most motorists spend a great deal more than would be necessary if they bought

Table 13.10 Spending on transport and communications as a percentage of total household expenditure, UK,[a] 1953/54–97/98

	1953/54	1960	1970	1980	1990	1997/98
Transport and vehicles[b]	7.0	12.2	13.7	14.6	16.2	16
Leisure goods and services[c]	n/a	n/a	n/a	n/a	13.3	17
Housing	8.8	9.3	12.6	15.0[d]	18.0[d]	16
Food and non-alcoholic drinks	33.3	30.5	25.7	22.7	18.1	17
Fuel and power[e]	5.2	5.9	6.3	5.6	4.5	4

Average weekly household expenditure on fares and other travel costs (£)

				40.02	54.70

Of which average weekly household expenditure on motoring (£)

				33.83	46.60

Average weekly household expenditure (£)

12.01	16.51	28.57	110.60	247.16	328.80

Average weekly household expenditure per person (£)

3.77	5.43	9.70	40.75	99.86	136.60

Notes: [a]All figures refer to the UK, except for the 1990 figures for expenditure on fares and other travel costs, average weekly expenditure on motoring and average weekly household expenditure, which relate to Great Britain.
[b]Includes 'motoring expenditure' and 'fares and other travel costs'.
[c]Purchase and repair of TV, video, computers and audio equipment, TV and cable TV licences, holiday and cinema costs, etc.
[d]Indicates a point where discontinuity occurs in the time-series.
[e]Gas, electricity and other fuels.

Sources: 1953/54 figures are taken from the *Report of Enquiry into Household Expenditure 1953/54*, quoted in ONS (1979), p.40; ONS (1996), p.102; DETR (1997b), p.19; ONS (1998b), pp.15 and 17.

a car that would efficiently get them from A to B. Cars are affordable luxuries that encourage greater mobility, spontaneity and comfort than most other forms of transport (ESRC Transport Studies Unit, 1995, pp.26–8). Cars confer status, personal space, power, and so on, and, in fantasy at least, they create and satisfy new types and levels of individuality, without the needs of others impinging (in practice, others do interfere, via speed limits, traffic jams, and so on). Cars are not just utilitarian conveniences, but, particularly for men, they are objects of lust, envy, greed, love, excitement, fantasy and possessiveness (Marsh and Collett, 1986). Women have different, perhaps more practical and pragmatic attachments to their cars (Greer, 1998, p.14). Complex relationships with cars, the status and the mobility they provide have been signified by everything from national obsessions with car advertising, young people's preferences for driving over voting (Solomon, 1998, p.7) to high expenditure on customized number plates, fashionable 'people carriers' and extravagant company car fleets.

Road transport increased tenfold from the early 1950s, to over 205 billion vehicle miles in 1990. The number of cars has risen from approximately 2.5 million in 1951 to a projected 25 million in 2000. Cars now comprise nearly 90 per cent of licensed road vehicles (Table 13.4). Road space is more scarce for UK drivers than those of the rest of the European Union (EU), as there are approximately 11 miles of road per 1000 cars in the UK, compared to an EU average of about 15 miles (Department of the Environment, Transport and the Regions (DETR), 1997a, p.14). The UK average daily vehicle flow of about 2000 vehicles per mile of road is also higher than France (1000) and Germany (1500) (DETR, 1997a, p.14) Unsurprisingly, UK roads are amongst the most congested in Europe, with 11 per cent of the roads outside urban areas being classified as 'congested' for four or more hours per day (*Local Transport Today*, 1996, p.3).

Goods traffic carried by road grew until it equalled that of railways in 1955 and has continued to increase since then (Table 13.11). Freight has been transferred from other modes to the roads in this period and it has also increased in absolute terms. The proportion of freight traffic carried by rail has declined from 21 per cent in 1955 to 6 per cent in 1990. The total volume of freight has increased by over 60 per cent since 1955 and the proportion carried by road has increased from 75 per cent to some 81 per cent. The proportion of freight moved by water (on canals and on the sea at the coast) has increased slightly, when measured by weight carried, from 5.9 per cent of all goods in 1972 to 6.4 per cent in 1996. The growth of transportation through pipelines has been huge, largely because of the extraction of North Sea oil and gas, after the energy crisis of the 1970s. Freight transport continues to grow: energy use for freight is projected to exceed that for passenger travel on a world-wide basis in the year 2020 (World Energy Council, 1995).

Table 13.11 Goods lifted and volume, Great Britain, 1953–97

	1953	1960	1970	1980	1990	1997	Index 1953 = 1.0
Goods lifted (million tonnes)							
Road	889	1211	1610	1395	1749	1740	2.0
Rail	294	252	209	154	140	105	0.4
Water	52	54	57	137	152	143	2.8
Pipeline	2	4	39	83	121	148	74.0
All modes	1237	1521	1915	1769	2162	2136	1.7
Goods moved (billion tonne miles)							
Road	20	30	53	58	85	98	4.9
Rail	23	19	16	11	10	11	0.5
Water	12	12	14	34	35	30	2.5
Pipeline	0.12	0.19	2	6	7	7	58.3
All modes	55	62	85	109	136	145	2.6

Source: DETR (1998a), p.182.

World War II gave an impetus for the development of technologies to support cheaper and more comfortable air flights. Aeroplanes began to compete with the costs of railways and passenger ships. Air flights had previously been the province of the brave or intrepid who had travelled with great discomfort to previously unfamiliar parts of the world. The arrival of popular and affordable air fares, and the development of the package holiday changed this, and rendered even the most distant parts of the world more physically accessible.

The last third of the century has seen a revolution in telecommunications that has both made simultaneous global communications a possibility and also new telematics applications for the control of transport. Many claims have been made that new information technologies will limit the need for travel, but these have not been upheld. Rather, the reverse appears to be the case as travel demand continues to increase in parallel with communication growth (Adams, 1996, p.17).

There are unresolved arguments as to whether the 'Information Age' has reduced or increased diversity and exclusivity, impoverished or enriched lives (Brown, 1998, p.132; Cairncross, 1998, p.240). The growth of what may be called exclusive and individuating forms of transport and communications, of which the Internet is a small part, over common or shared forms, is a visible trend. Yet caution in the interpretation of data is needed. Some transport and communications technologies are in their infancy, so predicting their impact is like trying to forecast the effects of mass car ownership in 1908 when the first Ford model T cars were made.

Satellite communications, linked to innovations in computer technologies, have made possible a variety of 'intelligent transport systems'. These include 'real time' bus stop or platform information about public transport arrival times, seen on the London Underground, dashboard guides for drivers to help them avoid congestion as well as a host of other functions, usually aimed at increasing traffic or aircraft volumes or flows by technological means.

In the 1990s the power and speed of computer chips was doubling every 18 months and the cost halving (Elkington and Hailes, 1998, p.214). Across the world, four quadrillion chips were made *each month* in the 1990s. (In total more than 500000 for each man, woman and child on the planet). The use of the Internet is doubling every half-year in the UK. The Internet is a vast international computer network that evolved in the 1960s in the US, out of the defence sector. Computers were linked so that the network would still survive even if parts of it were obliterated. The World Wide Web is a series of linked pages, which is accessed by using the Internet or 'Net'.

The Internet's biggest role is as a medium for business transactions and for every US$1 spent or invested in the 'real' economy, an estimated US$30–50 are floating in financial cyberspace (Brown, 1998, p.115). Most 'bandwidth', that is, transmission, use is for business information (status of stocks, location of personnel, flow of parts, sales, intelligence, and so on) rather than news, entertainment or private communication (gossip and chatter). Many firms now use satellites to transfer data on reservoir levels, sickness rates, and so on. The Internet is altering the shape of competition and commerce by the speed and the lack of transparency of the transactions that it carries.

Sustainability (environmental and equity issues)

There have been huge gains from the development of transport and communications, but there have also been major costs. Transport is responsible for a range of social and environmental damage. It is the fastest growing and largest end-user of energy and, hence, the single biggest source of climate change emissions (DETR, 1998a, p.59; Peake, 1994).

Environmental impacts

Although the process of climate change is complex and the full effects cannot be predicted, there is broad international expert agreement that anthropogenic change is taking place. For example, the Intergovernmental Panel on Climate Change (IPCC), a panel of 1500 distinguished scientists, noted a 'discernable human impact on the climate' in 1996 (IPCC, 1996). Nine out of the ten hottest years on record have occurred since 1983, with 1997 the warmest year yet observed (DETR, 1998b, p.12). Global average surface temperatures have increased by 0.3 to 0.6 °C since the late nineteenth century (National Aeronautics and Space Administration (NASA), 1998, DETR, 1998b, p.12). There has been an observed rise of between 10 cm and 25 cm in sea levels over the same period and this may be related to the rise in temperature. Many experts think that as a result of climate change the UK could experience more violent storms and the loss of the warming sea-borne Gulf Stream. Climate change in the UK could also cause reduced visibility, ozone smogs, and more overcast dull weather as well as reductions in rainfall and a lessening of seasonal differences (IPCC, 1996).

Climate change is primarily caused by carbon dioxide, which, together with other less important 'greenhouse gases' acts like an insulator. Transport is responsible for about a third of the total carbon dioxide produced (DETR, 1998a, p.63).

Transport also pollutes in other ways. In 1995 it was responsible for producing about two-thirds of nitrogen oxides in the UK, a contributor to acid rain. Transport emissions also include approximately three-quarters of annual carbon monoxide which can cause stress, asthma, headaches and fertility problems, the same proportion of lead which impairs mental development and 40 per cent of hydrocarbons (also known as volatile organic compounds). Exhaust fumes also produce just over half of the UK's particulates (the black smoke particularly associated with diesel engines), which damage respiratory and circulatory systems, and benzene, which is carcinogenic. There is no sanctuary inside cars: a recent study found that pollution in cars could be three times higher than ambient air outside (Environmental Transport Association, 1997, p.27). The EU requirement for all new cars to have catalytic converters from 1993 has only had an impact on some emissions, as they do not work properly until a car is fully warm; three-quarters of journeys are under five miles, and so will not allow them to function properly.

Transport infrastructure is a considerable absorber of resources: each mile of motorway takes nearly 10 hectares of land and damages ecology, ecosystems and the landscape. For example it is estimated that 47 500 badgers, 3000–5000 owls and 20 per cent of breeding amphibians are killed annually on the roads (Stokes et al., 1992, p.7). An estimated 14 000 hectares of land in Britain were used for highways and road transport between 1985 and 1990. Road building can also reduce water quality, increase flood hazard and cause river systems to be modified.

In addition, the visual and aesthetic impact of roads is enormous. This involves changes in the physical appearance of the landscape, as well as the effects of lighting, noise and vibration. These effects have been modelled by the Council for the Protection of Rural England (CPRE), to show the reduction of what they call 'tranquil areas' (areas unaffected by traffic noise or road lighting) in England over the last quarter of the century (Figure 13.2). Other data show that in 1995/6 nearly half a million (482 300) people were exposed to an average of 16 hours a day of continuous sound levels equivalent to 57 decibels, because they were living near to one of five English airports (Heathrow, Gatwick, Stansted, Manchester and Birmingham) (DETR, 1998a, p.65).

EARLY 1960s

EARLY 1990s

tranquil areas ENGLAND MAP

W   E
SW   SE
S

KEY

Tranquil areas

Semi-tranquil areas

Vulnerable

Less vulnerable

N

CPRE
COUNCIL FOR THE PROTECTION
OF RURAL ENGLAND

COUNTRYSIDE
COMMISSION

KMS   0   50

Source: CPRE/Countryside Commission.

Equity

There is inadequate measurement of the equity implications of transport and communications. There is no consistent measurement of the effects of race and racism, gender, age, social status or much information that is national and longitudinal on travel for people with disabilities. What is available is summarized below.

Social cohesion/dislocation

Mass ownership of cars has increased mobility and enriched lives. But the wish to limit car access has also won support from a variety of quarters. In 1970, Anthony Crosland, a government Minister, pointed out that many who opposed the growth of car use did so in order to preserve their class privilege:

> My working-class constituents ... want cars, and the freedom they give on weekends and holidays. And they want package tour holidays to Majorca, even if this means more noise of night flights and eating fish and chips on previously secluded beaches ... They [the affluent middle classes] want to kick the ladder down behind them. (Crosland, 1970)

In contrast to the positive image of car travel, the image of buses and their passengers is usually negative. Mrs Thatcher asserted, 'if a man finds himself a passenger on a bus having attained the age of 26, he can account himself a failure in life' (Thatcher, quoted in *The Observer*, 1998).

Habits of walking and cycling for short journeys have largely been lost, as has their perceived image as safe and acceptable forms of transport (Children's Play Council, n.d., p.2). In 1993–95, 71 per cent of journeys were of less than five miles – a distance that could be relatively easily walked or cycled – but 52 per cent of these trips were undertaken by car. Over a third of journeys less than two miles were travelled by car. Over one in four people from social classes C and DE said they were 'very worried' about car crime (Home Office, 1995). The figure was slightly less than one in five for those from social class AB, who tend to live in areas less affected by car crime and are, presumably, better able to withstand the losses caused by it.

Social class/income/regions

Access, on foot or by vehicle, not only also contributes to 'public space' but can also raise and lower investment levels, provide and remove employment, alter congestion levels, and change property values, sometimes blighting areas. Walking was used for effective protest in the 1930s. Mass 'trespasses' were organised by the Ramblers' Association to secure access to common land and the Jarrow Hunger Marchers walked to London to protest against unemployment in this period. There is a paradox of less easy access being created in the years after

World War II as local amenities, hospitals, supermarkets, industrial estates, and so on, moved to out-of-town or centralized locations on the assumption that everybody can drive cars. Superstores, the majority of which are located in out-of-town sites, are usually difficult to get to on foot or by public transport.

There are financial penalties to non-car-ownership. One study found that the price of food was up to 60 per cent higher in corner shops, which car-less households may rely on more since many supermarkets are located outside towns and so are difficult to reach without private transport (Piachaud and Webb, 1996). Not having a car in rural areas can also limit the number of locations that are visited. In one study of 'accessible' (that is, non-remote) rural areas, those in households without a car visited only a third of the destinations of those with cars (Root et al., 1996). Many rural people make sacrifices to afford cars: twice the percentage of people in the poorest rural households own cars compared to their urban counterparts (Stokes, 1995, p.39).

Gender

Do women move about and travel as much as men? Everyday use of outdoor space at the end of the century suggests not. Male dominance – from the boys

Table 13.12 Journeys and distance travelled by sex, and modes by sex, Great Britain, 1985/86 to 1994–96[a]

	Journeys: all modes per person per year		Distance travelled per person per year (miles)	
	Men	Women	Men	Women
1985–86	849	640	7368	4411
1989–91	927	734	8784	5462
1994–96	882	743	9002	5713
1994–96				
Walk	56	52	92	78
Bicycle	19	7	64	16
Car driver	617	342	6571	2247
Car passenger	95	222	1109	2277
Motorcycle	8	1	69	9
Other private	7	6	123	129
Bus in London	10	15	36	55
Other local bus	36	64	168	276
Non-local bus	1	2	75	132
LT Underground	8	7	67	60
Surface rail	14	11	486	348
Taxi/minicab	9	12	42	42
Other public	1	1	101	45

Notes: [a]This table excludes journeys under one mile; comparable data for journeys in earlier decades by mode and distance by sex is not available.

Source: DETR (1997c), p.24.

playing football in the school playground, to the paths or streets where unaccompanied women dare not venture – is part of daily life, and has been, largely unchanged, throughout history (French, 1985, p.65ff).

Women travel less far than men, in all modes apart from buses and 'other private' (Table 13.12). Even allowing for the fact that the statistics are distorted by a few men travelling a great deal, often in company cars, it would appear that the limitations of women's mobility are quite strongly correlated with child care, caring for the elderly and domestic responsibilities. Statistics for 1994–96 show that until the age of 20, women typically travel almost identical distances to men, but that between the ages of 26 and 59, the prime years of caring responsibilities, women's travel drops to just over half of men's, a pattern that was the same 20 years earlier (DETR, 1997c, p.31).

In the 1980s and 1990s women have taken up driving more rapidly than men, a factor that can be partly attributed to the poor quality of public transport. There was a 90 per cent increase in the proportion of women with driving licences between the mid-1970s and mid-1990s, but only a 17 per cent increase in the proportion of licence-holding men. In 1975/76 almost twice as high a proportion of men could drive as women, but by 1993–95 the difference had lessened to 50 per cent (Table 13.13).

Table 13.13 Full car driving-licence holders, Great Britain, 1975/76 to 1993–95

Private motoring: full car driving-licence holders
Percentage of individuals

	Male			Female			All adults		
	1975/76	1985/86	1993–95	1975/76	1985/86	1993–95	1975/76	1985/86	1993–95
17–20	35	37	50	20	29	42	28	33	46
21–29	77	73	82	43	54	68	60	63	74
30–39	85	86	90	49	62	74	67	74	81
40–49	83	87	89	37	56	72	60	71	80
50–59	75	81	88	25	41	59	50	60	73
60–69	59	72	82	15	24	39	36	47	60
70 or over	33	51	61	4	11	19	15	27	35
All adults	69	74	81	29	41	55	48	57	67
Estimated number of licence holders (million)	13.3	15.1	17.4	6.0	9.1	12.7	19.3	24.3	30.1

Source: DETR (1997b), p.55.

As Table 13.13 shows, the difference between men and women in the holding of a driving licence decreases amongst the younger age groups. Younger women are closest to men (there is an 8 per cent gap in the 17–20 age-group in 1993–95). This growing equality in licence holding will mean increasing numbers of older drivers, which, as the population ages, will cause an unprecedented increase in elderly drivers in the twenty-first century.

In 1994–96, women travelled shorter distances and made fewer journeys than men, and, when they did travel, they travelled more by less individuated means (buses, car passengers) (Table 13.12). In 1975/76 women drove about a fifth of the miles driven by men; in 1994–96 the gap had closed somewhat, with women driving about two-fifths of the miles covered by men (DETR, 1997c, p.31).

Women have somewhat different reasons for travelling than men (DETR, 1997c, p.32). In 1994–96 women made 28 per cent fewer commuter journeys and 68 per cent fewer trips during their work than men. Evidence in Chapter 18 shows that at the end of the twentieth century women were still taking a greater share of household responsibilities, and, linked to this, they were making 65 per cent more 'escort education' journeys (taking children to school) and approximately 30 per cent more shopping trips. The same pattern appears across the previous ten years. Unfortunately, category changes make longer comparisons impossible.

'Stranger danger' fears appear to be re-emerging, compared to the middle years of this century. In the late 1980s, using a variety of sources, it was found that between 50 and 70 per cent of women were frightened of going out after dark in cities (Atkins, 1990). In the mid-1990s one in eight women surveyed said that they felt so unsafe on public transport that they avoided using it (Home Office, 1995). Of the women interviewed 11 per cent never ventured out after dark. Nevertheless, despite the difficulties of travel, it would appear that women were, in general, less confined to their homes at the end than earlier in the century, albeit largely because of car ownership (Gavron, 1968; Hamilton et al., 1991, p.163). There is an irony in the fact that fewer men worry about attack, but they are more likely to suffer from it. According to the British Crime Survey (Home Office, 1995), nine out of ten attacks by male strangers were carried out against men.

Age

In 1995 up to one in five cars at peak hours was doing the school run, four times as high a proportion as 20 years before. For journeys to school by 5–15-year-olds between 1975 and 1995, car travel increased from 12 per cent to 26 per cent, and walking fell from 61 per cent to 53 per cent. There was an 80 per cent fall in the number of 10-year-olds allowed to go to school unaccompanied between 1971 and 1990 (Hillman et al., 1990, p.131).

Evidence shows that traffic accidents are class-related. Children from low-income families are five times more likely to be killed or injured on the roads compared to those from affluent areas. The UK has the second worst child pedestrian casualty rate in Europe (second only to Portugal) (Sustrans, 1998), although it had the lowest proportion of deaths through traffic accidents amongst industrialized countries (Evans, 1991, p.3). This paradox can partly be explained by the fact that in many of the poorer housing areas, children still often play on the street. Also, many areas of poor-quality housing are concentrated in urban centres where traffic density is high. In more affluent areas there tend to be more alternative play spaces, less traffic and more adult supervision (preventing play in dangerous places) (Whitelegg, 1997, p.140).

In the 1990s fewer under-fives were killed on roads but more teenagers died, perhaps because many adolescents' acquisition of 'road sense' has not been developed due to the childhood protection afforded to them from lifts in cars (Davis, 1992, pp.30–1). It has also been argued that the 1990s generation has not acquired as many independent social skills as the young had in previous decades because of the more continual adult supervision they have been given. Children were found to be three times more likely to be warned about 'stranger danger' than about traffic danger in a 1998 study (Royal Society for the Prevention of Accidents, 1998).

Accidents and other damage to health

Use of the motor car has led to virtually unprecedented rates of death. About 24 000 deaths annually are hastened by poor air quality, mainly attributable to emissions (Department of Health, 1998). In particular, the elderly and children are most at risk. In the 1990s one in seven children had asthma, and as many as one in three in cities. This condition is exacerbated by vehicle emissions (Edwards et al., 1994, pp.223–7; Weiland et al., 1994, pp.243–7). Increasingly,

Table 13.14 Road accidents and casualties, Great Britain, 1926–96

	Accidents (000s)	Pedestrians killed	Pedal cyclists killed	Motor cyclists killed	All other road users killed	All deaths	All injured (000s)
1926[a]	124	2774	644	1175	736	4886	134
1936	199	3068	1498	1187	808	6561	228
1946	n/a	2489	833	772	968	5062	157
1956	216	2270	650	1250	1197	5367	263
1966	292	3153	514	1134	3184	7985	384
1976	259	2335	300	990	2945	6570	333
1986	248	1841	271	762	2508	5382	316
1997	240	973	183	509	1934	3599	324

Note: [a]Pedestrians, pedal and motor cyclists and other road death figures are for 1927.

Sources: DETR (1998a), p.186.

car-based travel also contributes to lack of exercise – half the British population is overweight (see Chapter 3). Sedentary life-styles double the risk of heart disease.

Since their peak in the 1960s, fatalities have fallen substantially, but injuries have fallen at a slower rate (Table 13.14). One possible explanation is that because of the diminishing number of pedestrians and cyclists, there are fewer in the categories most vulnerable to death as opposed to injury (Davis, 1992, p.156).

The Information Superhighway?

Implicit in many cyberspace communications such as the Magna Carta of the Information Age (Progress and Freedom Foundation, 1998) are notions of the transcendence of environmental and social constraints. The Net, with its technocratic world-view and the 'search engines' which pre-sort and select in ways defined by manufacturers and not users, is not a replacement for older, more genuinely public and participatory media.

The Copyright, Designs and Patents Act 1988 defined intellectual property rights and is one factor limiting the democratic and participatory use of the Internet. As multinational companies are allowed to copyright vast swathes of information, exclusionary private realms are extended. Much data that are

Table 13.15 Journey purpose as percentage of all journeys,[a] Great Britain, 1965 to 1994–96

	(%)			
	1965	1975/76	1985/86	1994–96
To/from work	35.7	25.7	21.7	18.6
In course of work	3.6	4.3	3.9	4.4
Education	7.0	7.3	5.7	5.0
Escort (for education and other purposes)	4.6	5.5	10.0	12.0
Shopping	12.7	16.6	18.1	19.7
Personal business	7.2	8.9	8.6	9.4
Sport[b]	1.6	2.6	2.3	2.7
Entertainment/public activity/eating and drinking/visiting friends not at private home[c]	7.4	6.5	9.2	8.0
Visiting friends at private home/social trip[c]	14.3	16.8	15.0	14.3
Holiday, day trips, pleasure trips and other	5.9	5.8	5.5	5.7

Notes: [a]Numbers may not add up to 100 because of rounding. Data for 1965 and 1975/76 exclude walks under one mile; figures for 1985/86 and 1994–96 exclude all journeys under one mile.
[b]Prior to 1985/86, this category included both journeys to participate in sport and journeys to watch sport. From 1985/86 onwards, only journeys to participate in sport were included in the sport category, while journeys to watch sport were included in the entertainment category.
[c]Changes in the definition of these categories after 1975/76 make comparisons over time unreliable.

Sources: Adapted from Department of Transport (1979), p.13; and DETR (1997c), p.14.

commercially valuable – such as genetic information or 'genome' data – will not be publicly available. The growth of private networks is already advanced – most big multinationals have 'Intranets' not open to non-employees. It is possible that communications are returning to the eighteenth century when great commercial concerns, like the East India Company, held a quasi-monopoly of information (Brown, 1998, p.187).

The shared public spaces and communities created partly by transport and communications allow mutuality and exchange, as part of a common, accessible culture (Table 13.15). In contrast, some forms of communication, such as broadcasts or some types of computer software, consist of one-way, non-participatory flows of information or actions. (The audience or user does react to what is transmitted, but is disempowered by the content.) In these cases, communications are meeting needs but they are also changing the ways in which individuality is constituted and mass-producing or standardizing subjectivity. They are offering new opportunities to some but are also, at a global level, decreasing mutuality and increasing the extent to which experience and expectations are privatized, moulded and homogenized (Adams, 1996, p.10).

Responses to change

Environmental concern has increased: for instance, the percentage of people who say that 'exhaust fumes from traffic in towns and cities' are a 'very serious problem' rose to 63 per cent in 1995, up from 50 per cent in 1994. Those identifying congestion as a 'very serious problem' on motorways nearly doubled (from 22 per cent in 1993 to 42 per cent in 1995) (Taylor, 1997, p. 117). This is perhaps unsurprising when it is remembered that between 1980 and 1990 there was a 50 per cent increase in traffic volume, but only a 5 per cent increase in the length of the road network.

The frustration of road users has become an issue for research. In a survey in 1996, 64 per cent of the population admitted to 'road rage' (shouting, swearing or attacking other drivers) (ONS, 1998a, p.206).

Table 13.16 Activity at civil aerodromes, Great Britain, 1950–97

	Aircraft movements	Passengers (000s)	Cargo tonnes
1950	195	2133	31
1960	402	10075	279
1970	607	31606	580
1980	954	57823	744
1990	1420	102418	1193
1997	1764	146823	1956

Source: DETR (1998a), p.190.

The 1990s also saw several well publicized protests against road building. 'Swampy', erstwhile leader of the protesters, became a national anti-hero. Road protests marked the end of middle-class support for roads, traffic-friendly planning and supermarket car parks. Meanwhile, the same middle classes were taking more and more air flights (mainly for holidays) and travelling further (Tables 13.16; 13.17).

Table 13.17 Increases in personal travel, Great Britain, 1965 to 1994–96

	Travel distance per person per week (miles)	Number of journeys per person per week	Average journey length (miles)	Hours travelled per person per year	Cars per household
1965	70.1	11.2	n/a	n/a	0.46
1972/73	82.0	11.4	4.7	353	0.63
1975/76	85.9	12.4	5.0	330	0.68
1978/79	92.6	14.1	5.2	376	0.73
1985/86	99.5	13.2	5.9	337	0.84
1994–96	126.3	20.3	6.2	358	1.01

Sources: DETR (1976; 1983; 1997c; 1998c, p.4) and Potter (1997).

Conclusions

Both transport and communications are subject to the same tendencies, that of growth extending processes of individuation. There has been a proliferation of various forms of mobility and communications but at the expense of creating an increasingly atomistic, individualistic society in which the maintenance of public goods, such as a participatory public life, air quality or safe streets, are neglected.

By the end of the century, public concern was growing over the environmental harm and social dislocation caused by current travel growth, which contribute to the acceleration of the growth of vast global markets. But there were no indications that new forms of communication cut travel – the opposite is probably the case, since as communication networks extend, desire to meet grows too.

Because of the problems of congestion and environmental damage caused by travel, greater mobility both damages as well as enhances quality of life. It has damaged local sociability, as time spent in a car or plane cannot be used in participating in geographically close-knit communities, but it has also opened up for many a freedom to choose their friends, relatively unconstrained by distance.

Demands for more mobility and extended communications have created new social trends, opportunities and pleasures, but innovation in these areas has also, in complex ways, been responsible for causing environmental damage and reducing quality of life in ways that we have not sought. In other words, transport and communications are the servants of the people, but they are also our masters.

Sources and definitions

There is a reasonable amount of information about journeys in the last third of the century. One major source is the *National Travel Survey* (NTS) (DETR, 1997c) which is a household survey covering travel by residents in Great Britain. From 1965–86 it was produced periodically, with the last ad hoc survey in 1985. From mid-1988 the NTS became a continuous survey, with three years' data providing a representative sample for the whole of Great Britain. It is conducted by the Office for National Statistics (ONS) on behalf of the Department of the Environment, Transport and the Regions (DETR).

Another useful source is *Transport Statistics Great Britain* (DETR, 1997b) which is an annual compendium of statistics relating to all modes of transport and including a short historical series, compiled by the DETR with input from the Scottish Office Education and Industry Department, the Welsh Office and other government departments. The DETR started to publish *Transport Trends* (DETR, 1998c) annually from 1998, which offers further detail about transport patterns, modal shifts and short articles on key features of transport planning or behaviour, with some records starting from as early as the middle of the century.

Earlier measurement of transport and communications is usually mode specific and less comprehensive. The British Roads Federation has published an annual report *Basic Road Statistics* from 1938 to the present. This includes figures on licensed vehicles, motor taxation and road expenditure. Receipts and fares for railways annually up to 1938, with the exception of 1914–18, are found in *Railway Returns – Returns of the Capital, Traffic, Receipts and Working Expenditure etc. of the Railway Companies of Great Britain*. These were published as command papers until 1920, and afterwards by the Ministry of Transport. Information on all the main modes of transport can be found in the *Statistical Abstract for the UK* published by the Board of Trade and replaced by the *Annual Abstract of Statistics* after World War II. Another useful text is *Inland Transport Statistics Great Britain 1900–1970* by D. L. Munby, Volume 1, which includes detailed and extensive bibliographical and other information about railways, public road passenger transport and London's transport (Munby, 1978). Due to Munby's untimely death, further volumes were not published.

Information about use of postal services, telegraphs and telephones has been collected in the *Statistical Abstract for the UK 1924–1938* (Board of Trade, 1940) and information on the earlier years of this century is found in earlier annual *The Statesman's Yearbooks*. B. R. Mitchell makes some interesting international comparisons from 1920–60 in *European Historical Statistics* (1981).

These sources do not meet current needs. Shortcomings include the absence of systematic records on the number of passenger miles or journeys until World War II. Some types of journey have also been omitted. There are no systematically collected data on journeys of less than one mile before 1990, which means that most walking and cycling journeys have not been recorded for more than the last ten years. Consequently there is only a very limited amount of ad hoc information on these short journeys for the majority of the century. Information about gender and transport is very limited and data on race and travel by those of impaired mobility are almost entirely absent. Little data were provided on the energy consumption by transport until the late 1970s and information on air pollution has only been given in depth since the early 1990s.

Acknowledgements

Many people have contributed to this chapter. Amongst those whom I wish to thank are A. H. Halsey, Jo Webb, John Preston (Director of the Transport Studies Unit, University of Oxford), my partner, Martin Stott, Alastair Hanton, Laurie Michaelis and Juliet Solomon.

References

Adams, J. (1996) 'Can technology save us?', *World Transport Policy and Practice*, 2 (3), MCB University Press, Bradford.
Atkins, S. (1990) 'Personal security as a transport issue: a state of the art review', *Transport Reviews*, 10 (2).
* Bagwell, P. (1974) *The Transport Revolution from 1770*, Batsford, London.
Beeching, R. (1963) *The Reshaping of British Railways*, HMSO, London.
Bicycle Association (1997) *Britain by Cycle '97*, Bicycle Association, Coventry.
Board of Trade (1926) *Statistical Abstract for the UK 1910–1924*, HMSO, London.
Board of Trade (1940) *Statistical Abstract for the UK 1924–1938*, HMSO, London.
British Road Federation (1962) *Basic Road Statistics*, British Road Federation, London.
* Brown, D. (1998) *Cybertrends: Chaos, Power and Accountability in the Information Age*, Penguin, London.
Cairncross, F. (1998) *The Death of Distance: How the Communications Revolution will Change Our Lives*, Orion Business Books, London.
Castle, B. (1993) *Fighting All The Way*, Pan Books, London.
Children's Play Council (n.d.) *Home Zones: Reclaiming Residential Streets*, Children's Play Council, London.
Churchill, W. (1954) *Churchill Reader, A Self-Portrait*, Eyre and Spottiswoode, London.
Clarke, P. (1997) *Hope and Glory: Britain 1900–1990*, Penguin, London.
Crosland, A. (1970) 'A social democratic Britain', *Fabian Tract 404*, London.
Dahl, R. (1993) *Boy and Going Solo*, Puffin Books, London.

Davis, R. (1992) *Death on the Streets: Cars and the Mythology of Road Safety*, Leading Edge Press, Hawes, North Yorkshire.

Department of the Environment, Transport and the Regions (DETR) (1997a) *Developing an Integrated Transport Policy, Factual Background*, DETR, London.

Department of the Environment, Transport and the Regions (1997b) *Transport Statistics Great Britain 1997*, The Stationery Office, London.

Department of the Environment, Transport and the Regions (1976, 1983, 1997c) *National Travel Survey*, The Stationery Office, London.

Department of the Environment, Transport and the Regions (1998a) *Transport Statistics Great Britain 1998*, The Stationery Office, London.

Department of the Environment, Transport and the Regions (1998b) *The Environment in Your Pocket 1998*, Government Statistical Service, London.

Department of the Environment, Transport and the Regions (1998c) *Transport Trends*, The Stationery Office, London.

Department of the Environment, Transport and the Regions (1998d) *Busdata 1998*, The Stationery Office, London.

Department of the Environment, Transport and the Regions (1999) *Focus on Public Transport*, The Stationery Office, London.

Department of Health (1998) *Quantification of the Effects of Air Pollution on Health in the United Kingdom*, The Stationery Office, London.

Department of Transport (1979) *National Travel Survey: 1975/6 Report*, HMSO, London.

Economic and Social Research Council (ESRC) Transport Studies Unit, University of Oxford (1995) *Car Dependence: A Report for the RAC Foundation for Motoring and the Environment*, RAC Foundation for Motoring and the Environment, London.

Edwards, J., Walters, S. and Griffiths, R. (1994) 'Hospital admissions for asthma in pre-school children: relationship to major roads in Birmingham, United Kingdom', *Archives of Environmental Health*, 49 (4).

* Elkington, J. and Hailes, J. (1998) *Manual 2000: Life Choices for the Future You Want*, Hodder and Stoughton, London.

Environmental Transport Association (1997) *Road User Exposure to Air Pollution*, Environmental Transport Association, Weybridge.

Evans, L. (1991) *Traffic Safety and the Driver*, Van Nostrand Reinhold, New York.

French, M. (1985) *Beyond Power: Women, Men and Morals*, Jonathan Cape, London.

Gavron, H. (1968) *The Captive Wife: Conflicts of Housebound Mothers*, Penguin, Harmondsworth.

Glaister, S. and Graham, D. (1996) *Who Spends What on Motoring in the UK?*, Automobile Association, London.

Greer, G. (1998) 'Playmate of the weak', *Guardian*, 2 March.

Halsey, A. H. (1996) *No Discouragement: An Autobiography*, Macmillan, Basingstoke.

Hamer, M. (1987) *Wheels Within Wheels*, Routledge and Kegan Paul, London.

Hamilton, K., Jenkins, L. and Gregory, A. (1991) *Women and Transport: Bus Deregulation in West Yorkshire*, University of Bradford, Bradford.

Hillman, M., Adams, J. and Whitelegg, J. (1990) *One False Move*, Policy Studies Institute, London.

Hillman, M. and Whalley, A. (1980) *The Social Consequences of Rail Closures*, Policy Studies Institute no. 587, London.

Home Office (1995) *Anxiety About Crime: Findings from the British Crime Survey 1994*, Home Office, London.

Intergovernmental Panel on Climate Change (IPCC) (1996) *Climate Change 1995: Second Assessment Report* (3 volumes), Cambridge University Press, Cambridge.

Kern, S. (1983) *The Culture of Time and Space 1880–1918*, Weidenfeld and Nicolson, London.

Liniado, M. (1996) *Car Culture and Countryside Change*, The National Trust, Cirencester.

Local Transport Today, (1996) 'UK roads amongst the most congested in Europe, says study', 10 October.

Mackie, P. and Preston, J. (1996) *The Local Bus Market: A Case Study of Regulatory Change*, Avebury, Aldershot.

Marsh, P. and Collett, P. (1986), *Driving Passion: The Psychology of the Car*, Jonathan Cape, London.

Mitchell, B. R. (1981) *European Historical Statistics*, Macmillan, London.

Mitchell, B. R. (1988) *British Historical Statistics*, Cambridge University Press, Cambridge.

Munby, D. (1978) *Inland Transport Statistics Great Britain 1900–1970, Volume 1, Railways, Public Road Passenger Transport, London's Transport*, Clarendon Press, Oxford.

National Aeronautics and Space Administration (NASA) (1998) Web page: http://www.giss.nasa.gov/data/gistemp/seas.GLB.gif

Office for National Statistics (ONS) (1979) *Family Expenditure Survey 1978*, HMSO, London.

Office for National Statistics (1991) *Annual Abstract of Statistics 1991*, HMSO, London.

Office for National Statistics (1996) *Family Spending: A Report on the 1995/96 Family Expenditure Survey*, The Stationery Office, London.

Office for National Statistics (1998a) *Social Trends 1998*, The Stationery Office, London.

Office for National Statistics (1998b) *Family Spending: A Report on the 1997–98 Family Expenditure Survey*, HMSO, London.

Office for National Statistics (1998c) *Annual Abstract of Statistics*, HMSO, London.

Office of Telecommunications (OFTEL) (1998) *UK Telecommunications Industry Market Information 1992/3 to 1996/7*, OFTEL, London.

Office of Telecommunications (1999) *UK Telecommunications Industry Market Information 1993/4 to 1997/8*, OFTEL, London.

* Peake, S. (1994) *Transport in Transition: Lessons from the History of Energy*, Earthscan, London.

Piachaud, D. and Webb, J. (1996) *The Price of Food: Missing Out on Mass Consumption*, STICERD Occasional Paper 20, London School of Economics, London.

Plowden, S. (1972) *Towns Against Traffic*, Andre Deutsch, London.

Potter, S. (1997) *Vital Travel Statistics*, Landor Publishing, London.

Progress and Freedom Foundation (1998) Web page: http://www.pff.org

Root, A., Boardman, B. and Fielding, W. (1996) *The Costs of Rural Travel*, University of Oxford, Oxford.

Royal Society for the Prevention of Accidents (1998) *Paper at the Annual ROSPA Conference*, ROSPA, London.

Solomon, J. (1998) 'To drive or to vote? Young adults' culture and priorities 1998', *Chartered Institute of Transport Discussion Paper*, Chartered Institute of Transport, London.

Stokes, G. (1995) 'Assessing the effects of new transport policies on rural residents', *Transport Studies Unit Working Paper 836*, University of Oxford, Oxford.

Stokes, G., Goodwin, P. and Kenny, F. (1992) *Trends in Transport and the Countryside*, Countryside Commission Publications, Cheltenham.

Sustrans (1998) *Safe Routes to Schools Information Pack*, Sustrans, Bristol.

Taylor, B. (1997) 'Green in word', in Jowell, R. et al. (eds) *British Social Attitudes, the 14th Report*, Ashgate Publishing, Aldershot.

Turner, J. and Spencer, A. (1996) 'Selling sustainability! – cycle use in Asia and Africa', Paper presented to the Annual Conference of the British Association of Geographers, 4–7 January.

Weiland, S., Mundt, K., Ruckmann, S. and Keil, U. (1994) 'Self-reported wheezing and allergic rhinitis in children and traffic density on street of residence' *Annals of Epidemiology*, 4.

Whitelegg, J. (1993) *Transport for a Sustainable Future: The Case for Europe*, Belhaven Press, London.

Whitelegg, J. (1997) *Critical Mass: Transport, Environment and Society in the Twentieth Century*, Pluto Press, London.

World Energy Council (1995) *Global Transport Sector Energy Demand Towards 2020*, WEC, London.

Further reading

(In addition to the asterisked items in the References)

Augé, M. (1997) *Non-places: Introduction to an Anthropology of Supermodernity*, Verso, London.

Castells, M. (1997) The Information Age: Economy, Society and Culture, vols 1–13, Blackwell, Oxford.

Illich, I. (1974) *Energy and Equity*, Marion Boyars, London.

Plowden, S. and Hillman, M. (1996) *Speed Control and Transport Policy*, Policy Studies Institute, London.

Rayner, S. and Malone, E. (eds) (1998) *Human Choice and Climate Change*, vols 1–4, Battelle Press, Colombus, Ohio.

Smith, M., Whitelegg, J. and Williams, N. (1998) *Greening the Built Environment*, Earthscan Publications, London.

Vandenbroucke, F. (1998) *Globalisation, Inequality and Social Democracy*, Institute for Public Policy Research, London.

14
Housing

Alan Holmans

Welcome to our 'ovel.

Noel Coward, *Cavalcade*, 1930

A decent home for every family at a price within their means.

Fair Deal for Housing, 1971

The quotation from the *Fair Deal for Housing* White Paper (1971) summarizes an aspiration widely held in the twentieth century. It certainly did not describe housing conditions when the century began. It could not be said to be within reach when the twentieth century ended. But the story of British housing during the century is generally one of progress towards it, though with major interruptions due to the two world wars and their aftermaths. The forms this progress took, together with the setbacks along the way, are outlined in this chapter. The chapter concludes with a brief reflection on why nevertheless the quoted aspiration is still a long way from being attained, notwithstanding the quadrupling of real national income per head during the century.

The chapter summarizes the information about the number and type of households, which form the demand side of the housing system; the housing stock in terms of numbers, age and quality; housing conditions, in the sense of space, sharing and self-contained housing accommodation; housing costs and their financing and public expenditure on housing. For most of these topics information which spans the whole century is not available; the amount of detail about housing has grown through time. The amount of detail also varies between the constituent countries of the United Kingdom. Most of the data presented are therefore for England and Wales or just England, for reasons discussed at the end of the chapter.

Households

Households are the counting unit for the demand side of the housing system. The nomenclature has changed over time, but there is sufficient continuity for figures to be shown for the whole century. The population and its structure (discussed in Chapter 2) are the basic determinants of how many separate households there are. But, as will be shown, there have been considerable changes in the propensity to live as separate households and hence in the demand and need for separate dwellings (a convenient term to comprise houses and flats, though even in the 1990s, flats were only one-fifth of the total housing stock). Demand and need are inter-related but distinct: need is a

Table 14.1 Households, 1901–2001 (thousands)

	Households	Concealed families	Potential households	One-person households[a]
England and Wales				
1901	7007[b]	n/a	–	–
1911	8005[b]	n/a	–	–
1911	7943	(200)	8143	423
1921	8739	(550)	9289	527
1931	10233	(350)	10583	689
1939	11750	(250)	12000	n/a
1951	13259	935	14194	1403
1961[c]	14724	702	15426	2109
1971	16709	435	17144	3022
England				
1971[d]	15942	235	16177	2944
1981[d]	17306	166	17472	3932
1991[d]	19215	163	19378	5115
2001	21046	144	21190	6509

Notes: [a] An amendment was made in 1981 to the definition of a one-person household to require that to be counted a person must not only cater for him- or herself, but also not share the use of a sitting room or living room with anyone else. It is uncertain what difference was made to the census household count; the view of the Office of Population Censuses and Surveys (OPCS) was that the change brought the definition in line with what was already practice in the field, while an investigation by means of interview surveys estimated that if both definitions were correctly applied by interviewers, the change would reduce the estimated number of separate households by 108 000 in England in 1981 (Todd and Griffiths, 1986).

[b] 'Separate occupiers'. Three terms have been used in twentieth-century censuses: (i) 'separate occupiers'; (ii) 'private families'; and (iii) 'households'. Of these, (ii) and (iii) are identical in meaning, but (i) 'separate occupier', was different. The separate occupier concept was used in 1901 and 1911. An important feature of this concept which was carried over to the private family that someone who lived in the same habitation as another family was a separate occupier unless he 'boarded' with the main family; that is, ate meals with them. The 'private family' was a sub-category of separate occupiers, with institutions of various kinds and hotels excluded. The change was made in order to avoid analyses of the space available to families being distorted by institutions being included. The term 'private family' was replaced in 1951 by 'household', in recognition that an increasing number of census 'families' were not families in the ordinary sense.

normative concept that arises from policy objectives expressed in the form of 'a separate house for every family that wishes to have one' (1945) and 'a decent home for every family at a price they can afford' (1971 and 1977). Public subsidy extends the scope of demand for a separate dwelling to households without sufficient income to make their demand effective in the market and as well raises the standard of accommodation to which they have access. At the beginning of the twentieth century, large numbers of households did not have separate housing because their incomes were too low in relation to its cost. The comparative importance of rising real incomes and public subsidy as causes of improving housing standards is a key question about twentieth-century housing.

Private household population	Adult population	Persons per household All households	Persons per household Multi-person households
	18736	–	–
–	21653	–	–
34606	21653	4.36	4.55
36180	23883	4.14	4.41
38042	26998	3.72	3.91
39480	29129	3.36	n/a
41840	31362	3.19	3.45
44528	32340	3.02	3.36
48365	34152	2.89	3.31
45627	32246	2.86	3.28
46137	33414	2.67	3.16
47490	35973	2.47	3.01
49255	37354	2.34	2.94

[c] In 1961 a question about usual residence was introduced in an attempt to count households that were away from their residences on census date. Hitherto, the census was strictly a count of persons and households present; where everyone was away, no household was counted and the house or flat counted as 'vacant' or 'vacant, furnished'.

[d] The figures for 1971, 1981 and 1991 are derived from population estimates which include corrections for under-counting in the census, which was unusually large in 1991. How the under-count in 1991 was treated in estimating households is explained in Department of the Environment (DoE) (1995) Appendix to Annex B. The understatement of separate households because census enumerators did not always apply the household definitions correctly is discussed in OPCS (1994).

Sources: 1901–31: census enumerated figures, other than for concealed families and potential households which are the author's estimates (Holmans, 1987, Chapter III); 1939: author's estimates, except for adult population (aged 20 and over) which is official. This is included in order to distinguish between the effects of the building boom of the 1930s and then the effects of World War II (Holmans, 1987, Chapters III and IV); 1951 and 1961: census-based estimates (DoE, 1977, Chapter 1); 1971–2001: DoE (1995), Table I. The adult population in 2001 is from the official 1996-based projections (Office for National Statistics (ONS), 1999).

The number of separate households in total and relative to population is the starting point for an account of the demand side of the housing system. Table 14.1 shows the number of households, the private household population and the adult population and also average numbers of persons per household. The table also includes 'concealed families' and potential households. Concealed families are couples and lone-parent families who live as part of someone else's household; for instance, newly married couples living with in-laws. The number of concealed families varies with housing shortages and in particular rose steeply in both the 1914–18 and 1939–45 wars. They are a form of demand and need that went unmet. To provide a less distorted measure of demand to live separately, they are added to actual households to give totals of 'potential households'. Before 1951, only unofficial estimates of concealed families and therefore of potential households are available. They are subject to considerable uncertainty, but are nevertheless worth showing because if concealed families are ignored, a very misleading picture could be presented.

Over the century, the increase in the adult population (aged 20 and over) in England and Wales is put at 20.8 million, an increase of 111 per cent (see Chapter 2). The increase in the number of households is put at 15.3 million, far more than in proportion to population. Calculations are therefore made to show how much of the increase in the number of households can be explained arithmetically by the growth of the adult population, how much by changes in the age structure and marital status of the population and how much to increased propensities to live in separate households (higher headship rates). More adequate estimates can be given for the years after 1951 than for the first half of the century. Before 1931, we can only split the growth in the number of households into two parts: that increase which would result if the number of households rose at the same rate as the adult population (aged 20 and over), and the balance over and above this. This calculation is made for potential households in Table 14.1, even though the figures for concealed married couples in 1939 and earlier are unofficial and precarious, because shortages had such severe effects in 1921 and 1951. The number of couples able to live on their own instead of with in-laws when housing shortages eased needs to be distinguished for analytical purposes from other headship rate changes.

Household composition data make it possible to disaggregate the net increase in the number of households between two dates into the effect of the increase in the adult population, the change in its marital status and changes in household headship rates; that is, the proportion of members of a group defined by sex, marital status and age that head households. Table 14.2 gives only broad estimates; but they are sufficient to show that out of the total increase of over 15 million households between 1901 and 2001, about 9 million can be explained by the increase in the adult population and about 2.75 million by the changing age-structure and marital status of the adult

Table 14.2 Composition of net increases in potential households, 1901–2001 (thousands)

	Total increase	Pro rata to adult population	Age structure and marital status	Change in headship rates
England and Wales				
1901–11	+1000	+1100	−100	
1911–21	+1150	+840	+310	
1921–31	+1290	+1210	+80	
1931–39[a]	+1420	+840	+350	+230
1939–51[a]	+2190	+920	+775	+495
1951–61[a]	+1230	+440	+510	+280
1961–71[a]	+1720	+860	+330	+530
England				
1971–81	+1300	+590	+130	+580
1981–91	+1910	+1340	−90	+660
1991–2001	+1810	+740	+490	+580

Note: [a] The figures for 1931 to 1971 have been modified so as to work in terms of potential households and hence take the change in concealed married couple families out of the headship rate change.

Sources: 1931–71: DoE (1977), Table I.7; 1971–91 with a projection to 2001: DoE (1995).

population. Out of the total increase in households, some 12 million is attributable to non-demographic change and 3 million (about one-fifth) to higher proportions of men and women of given demographic status heading households. The largest component of the demographic increase in potential households was the very pronounced rise in the proportions of widows and widowers living alone instead of as members of someone else's household. But also important are an increase in the proportion of divorced men and women living independently and, in the last quarter of the century, a growth in independent living by single (in the sense of never married) non-cohabiting men and women in their twenties, thirties and forties. The pioneering analysis in the 1931 census housing report indicates that there was probably no significant change in headship rates between 1901 and 1931. The proportion of widows and widowers living alone appears to have begun to rise during the 1930s and has continued since then.

Dwellings: number, age and quality

The total stock

'Dwellings' is a convenient term to refer to houses and flats together and in concept denotes living quarters with the same degree of self-containment as a flat in a purpose-built block. It is not always an easy concept to apply in buildings which were once large single residences but have since been converted into two or more flats. In Table 14.3 the best approximation to a continuous series is used. The basic concept is that of the 'structurally separate dwelling'. It was introduced in 1921 and defined (census 1921, *General Report*, p. 34) as 'any room or set of rooms intended or used for habitation having separate access to the street or to a common landing or staircase to which the public have access'. It replaced the concept of a 'house', defined as 'a building used as a habitation'. As with households, there was sufficient information available from the 1911 census for an estimate to be made of the number of structurally separate dwellings. The main differences were that buildings not occupied by 'private families' were excluded and flats in blocks were counted individually instead of the whole block counting as one 'house'. For 1901 this information is not available.

Table 14.3 also includes the estimated number and proportion of vacant dwellings, as these are key quantities for analysing interactions between the number of households and the stock of dwellings. The proportion of the dwelling stock which is vacant is important, but a very difficult subject for a time-series. Figures for vacancies have been collected in all twentieth-century censuses, but with differing content. Also shown is the balance between the total

Table 14.3 Dwellings and the household/dwelling balance, 1901–91

	Dwelling stock (000s)	Vacant dwellings		Household/ dwelling balance[a] (000s)
		Number (000s)	Proportion (%)	
England and Wales				
1901	6710	n/a	n/a	−300
1911	7550	n/a	n/a	−455
1911	7691	(340)	(4.4)	−450
1921	7979	(120)	(1.5)	−1310
1931	9400	161	1.7	−1180
1939	11500	n/a	n/a	−500
1951	12530	138	1.1	−1660
1961	14646	314	2.1	−780
1971	17024	646	3.8	−120
England				
1971	16065	600	3.8	−112
1981	17912	740	4.1	+440
1991	19780	660	3.3	+400

Note: [a] Minus sign denotes more potential households than dwellings.

Sources: 1901–31: census enumerated figures, except for the figures for vacant dwellings in 1911 and 1921, which are the author's estimates; 1939: author's estimates; 1951 and 1961: DoE (1977), Chapter 1; 1971 and 1981: DoE *Housing and Construction Statistics* for the dwelling stock, and author's census-based estimate for dwellings; 1991: Holmans (1995), Annex A.

of potential households and the total of dwellings. How far the increase in the total stock of dwellings can be explained arithmetically just by the increase in the number of households is a question where history engages with controversies current at the time of writing (see, for example, Council for the Protection of Rural England (CPRE), 1995; Town and Country Planning Association, 1996.)

The dwelling stock in Wales grew by 225 000 between 1971 and 1991 (DoE, *Housing and Construction Statistics*). Thus overall, the housing stock in England and Wales grew by 14.1 million between 1901 and 1991. For comparison with the total increase in households over the whole century (Table 14.1) the housing stock must be run on to 2001, when it is likely to be approximately 16.0 million. Over the century the housing stock will have grown faster than the number of potential households, which is important evidence against the increase in households being to a significant degree a reflection of the increase in the dwelling stock.

As with households, so with dwellings: the time-series cannot measure changes exactly, but a picture can be presented in broad outline. The situation in 1911 warrants comment as the outcome of nearly a century of a free market in housing undistorted by war. The building boom at the end of the 1890s and the early years of the first decade of the twentieth century had fallen away and the high proportion of the housing stock that was vacant indicates that the reason was that the market was sated. Nevertheless, well over one million households shared a house (Table 14.9). In normative terms there were not enough houses for every household to have a house or flat to themselves, but in economic terms there was no shortage: effective demand for housing was met, with something left over; the vacancy rate (vacant dwellings as a proportion of the total stock) was higher than at any subsequent date. But many households had incomes too low in relation to rents to afford a separate dwelling. This was particularly so in London.

Until well into the 1960s, the principal influence on the housing stock in relation to potential households was the two world wars. In both (ten years in total) very few houses were built and in the second, the equivalent of a year's new build was destroyed by enemy action. With the number of households rising fast, the consequent shortages were long-lasting and were the dominant influence on housing policy in the inter-war years and the two decades after 1945. The shortfall in dwellings relative to potential households reached its all time high in the mid-1940s; it then diminished as the housing stock increased, until in the 1970s the total of dwellings exceeded potential households. That the number of dwellings exceeded the number of households did not mean that there was a surplus of dwellings in the sense of habitable houses standing empty because they could not be sold or let. The number of secondary residences was probably increasing and the growth of owner-occupation meant more that houses were vacant and for sale through the ordinary working of the housing market.

Age of the housing stock and components of change

The age-distribution of the housing stock is significant in several ways. Recently built houses and flats can incorporate the latest improvements in design of fittings and insulation and are often in better condition than older dwellings. In conjunction with the number of dwellings built period by period, the age-distribution shows the number and age of dwellings demolished and replaced. In Britain there is a particular interest as well in how high is the proportion of older houses that have been modernized instead of being replaced. A division of the housing stock into very broad age-ranges, pre-1914, inter-war and post-1945 can be made as far back as 1938; but a more detailed analysis of the age of the pre-1914 stock is available only from 1972. This division of the pre-1914 stock is important for studying the balance between demolition of old houses and modernization.

Table 14.4 Age of the housing stock, England, 1938–91 (millions)

Year			Year built			
	Pre-1870	1871–90	1891–1918	1919–44	1945 and later	Total
1938		7.1ᵃ		3.7	–	10.8
1960		6.5ᵃ		4.1	3.2	13.8
1972	1.5	1.7	2.4	4.0	6.7	16.3
1981	1.3	1.6	2.4	3.9	8.7	17.9
1991	1.3	1.6	2.4	4.0	10.4	19.7

Note: ᵃFigure covers pre-1870–1918.

Sources: 1938–72: estimates in Riley (1973) and Table I.23 of DoE (1977). 1981–91: DoE (1998c).

Important for the estimated age distribution of the housing stock and specifically the number of pre-1919 dwellings, is that converted flats are classified according to when the house was originally built, not when the conversions were done. The 1991 English House Condition Survey (EHCS) estimated that about 90 per cent of converted flats were in pre-1919 buildings. The same survey indicates that the average number of flats per converted house was just over three, so with 1.3 million converted flats in total in 1991, the pre-1919 stock is estimated to contain slightly under 1.2 million flats converted from rather less than 0.4 million houses. About 4.5 million houses built before 1919 were still standing in 1991.

Estimates of the number of dwellings built year by year before 1914 are not very precise, but are sufficient for a comparison with the number of pre-1914 dwellings still standing so as to calculate survival rates. For this calculation the net conversion gain has to be subtracted from the dwellings built pre-1870 and in 1871–90 and 1891–1918. In round terms, over half of houses and flats (in fact mostly houses) built between 1851 and 1870 were still standing in 1991 and nearly three-quarters of those built in 1871–90 and 1891–1918 (virtually all in 1914 or earlier). Houses built so long ago have remained in use as a result of very extensive modernization, which is discussed below. Since the stock in 1911 totalled 7.7 million (Table 14.3) and new building between then and 1914 was small, it can be inferred that about 1.1 million dwellings were demolished between 1851 and 1914. Slum clearance accounted for only a small proportion.

The changes in the age-composition of the housing stock are the outcome of additions by new building and conversions and deletions through demolitions and changes from residential to non-residential use. Estimates of these components of change are given in Table 14.5. The quality of the estimates of the gain to the stock from conversions and losses other than from slum clearance is not high, even in recent years.

Table 14.5 Components of change of the housing stock, 1911–90 (thousands)

	New building	Other gains (conversions)	Slum clearance	Other losses	Net increases
England and Wales					
1911–21[a]	292	–	–	–	288
1921–31	1605	–	15	169[b]	1421
1931–38	2088	200[c]	260	28[d]	2000
1938–50	1356	150[c]	96	280[d,e]	1130
1951–60	2550	99	363	167	2119
1961–70	3220	89	685	245	2378
England					
1971–80	2488	69	477	233	1847
1981–90	1780	187	104	107	1755

Notes: [a] No adequate basis for estimating components of change other than new building; slum clearance was small; a small number of dwellings were destroyed by enemy action.
[b] Other losses, net of conversion gains, derived as a residual.
[c] Sub-division between 1931–38 and 1938–51 uncertain.
[d] Derived as residuals.
[e] Includes 218 000 destroyed by enemy action, leaving 62 000 for other losses which is plausible.

Sources: The components of change of the housing stock up to 1970 are from DoE (1977), Table I.12; later figures are from the DoE's annual *Housing and Construction Statistics* volume, Table 9.2, various issues; the 'other losses' are as reported by local authorities, with an addition in 1981–90 to balance with the 1991 dwelling total.

Only a very broad picture of components of change of the housing stock can be drawn from Table 14.5, but again the outline is fairly clear. Demolitions are discussed first, along with improvements to the stock and then new building. Table 14.5 shows that in total some 2.0 million dwellings were removed from the housing stock by slum clearance after 1921. Virtually all were built before 1914, so about one quarter of the standing stock in 1914 was subsequently demolished through slum clearance. Another 1.2 million dwellings of all ages were demolished for other reasons (including 0.2 million due to enemy action in World Wars I and II). Demolitions ran highest in the decade 1961–70 when the peak of slum clearance coincided with large-scale urban road building. Slum clearance then fell away. Five-year totals show this more clearly than decade by decade: in 1971–75 the figure was 296 000; in 1976–80, 179 000; in 1981-85, 74 000, and in 1986–90, 30 000.

There were several reasons for the running down and then the virtual ending of slum clearance. In the first place, clearing the houses that were unfit by the standards of the 1950s and 1960s or even the 1930s, from the day they were built, was inherently a finite task. These were houses which could be dealt with by area clearance. Once they had gone, area clearance necessarily came to an end. The 1967 EHCS estimated that there were 1.1 million dwellings in actual or potential clearance areas. By 1986 that concept had disappeared from the EHCS. Unfitness due to disrepair could not be dealt with by area clearance and, in most instances, repair would be better than demolition. Also very important was the increase in the proportion of the older housing stock that was owner-occupied. The working doctrine of slum clearance grew up when the houses to be cleared were predominantly rented from private landlords; not until 1969 was market value compensation offered to owner-occupiers whose houses were compulsorily purchased as unfit. The market value of an unfit house would only buy another unfit house, so an owner-occupier whose house was caught by slum clearance could very well have to become a council tenant. That was usually acceptable or even welcomed in the first two decades after 1945 when a council tenancy was often seen as a prize; but when the reputation of council housing began to decline in the 1970s, owner-occupiers' resistance to clearance strengthened all the more. The diminishing reputation of council housing, particularly of some of that built by industrialized methods in the 1960s and 1970s, led to demolition and replacement of unfit dwellings being derided as 'new slums for old'.

Demolition of other dwellings has been incidental to other kinds of development, notably urban roads in the 1960s and 1970s, but also commercial development and higher density house building for sale on sites formerly occupied by houses with large gardens. This kind of activity is inherently small-scale. The prospect of large-scale replacement of older but not unfit houses was put forward in the 1960s as the stage that was to follow when slum clearance had been finished. The housing chapter of the *National Plan* in 1965 stated: 'Most houses are out of date, even if they are not entirely worn out, by the time they are 80 years old and if it were not for chronic and persistent shortages, one would expect most houses of that age to be replaced as the normal thing' (Cmnd 2764 (1965), p. 171). Views such as this led to very high figures for the houses that 'ought' to be replaced. Such figures for replacement were the basis of targets in the 1960s of 500 000 new houses a year, but not a very large increase in the number of households. How such a large-scale replacement of fit and older houses would be organized and financed was never seriously investigated and in the event nothing came of it. Instead the pre-1914 housing stock was modernized piecemeal, mainly by private initiative and finance. This modernization prevented pre-1914 dwellings from becoming out of date and largely explains the high proportion of the later nineteenth- century housing stock that has survived.

Modernization first took the form of installing the basic amenities (fixed bath or shower; hot water system; sink and WC within the dwelling) and subsequently central heating. Progress with the basic amenities is shown in Table 14.6. Not all of the reduction in the number of dwellings without them was due to modernization; some was due to demolitions. About 30 per cent of the reduction in dwellings without a fixed bath was due to demolitions; but 70 per cent (over 3 million) was due to bathrooms installed in houses built without one.

Table 14.6 Dwellings without basic amenities, 1947–96 (millions)

	England and Wales			England			
	1947[a]	1961[a]	1971	1971[b]	1981	1991	1996
Fixed bath or shower	4.8	3.2	1.5	1.6	0.5	0.1	0.1
Inside WC	n/a	n/a	1.9	2.0	0.6	0.1	n/a
Hot water supply to sink, bath and hand basin	7.4	n/a	2.2	2.4	0.7	0.2	0.2
One or more of the basic amenities	n/a	n/a	2.7	2.8	0.9	0.2	0.2

Notes: [a] Figures refer to households.
[b] The figures for England are higher than those for England and Wales because the 1971 and 1976 samples for England were grossed up by an improved method for comparability with the 1981 survey estimates.

Sources: 1947: *The British Household*, by the Government Social Survey; 1960: Government Social Survey (1962); 1971 onwards: House Condition Surveys.

The other form of modernization of older houses that can be monitored from survey data is the installation of central heating. As late as 1960, only about 0.8 million had central heating out of a total stock of 14.6 million. By 1971, the number of dwellings with central heating had risen to 4.6 million (England and Wales) and by 1991 to 16.5 million (England). The increase is partly the result of increasing proportions of new houses and flats built with central

heating and partly due to central heating being put into houses and flats originally built without it. Indications of the amount due to modernization can be
derived from the analysis by construction date from the 1991 EHCS.

**Table 14.7 Dwellings with central heating analysed by construction date,
England, 1991**

When built	All dwellings (000s)	With central heating (000s)	Proportion with central heating (%)
Pre-1918	5196	3287	74
1919–44	3891	3145	81
1945–64	4231	3447	81
1965–80	4694	4519	96
Post-1980	1713	1570	92
Whole stock	19725	16507	84

Source: DoE (1993a), Table A5.6.

In 1991, about 9 million dwellings built before 1960 had central heating,
compared with 0.8 million in 1960, so over 8 million houses and flats built
without it subsequently had it installed. The 1996 EHCS report suggests a
further 0.4 million between 1991 and 1996. In this respect, modernization was
on a very large scale. It was the next stage of upgrading the older housing stock
after the bathroom, inside WC and hot water system. By 1996, about 1.3
million dwellings built before 1960 had a second bathroom. By this means of
upgrading, obsolescence was kept at bay and demolition and replacement due
to obsolescence obviated, contrary to what was expected in the 1960s.

In the 1980s and 1990s, physically deficient housing was no longer a matter
of lack of basic amenities but, far more commonly, disrepair and poor environments. Discontinuities of definition and measurement between successive
EHCSs make it impossible to construct time-series for the numbers of dwellings
in different degrees of disrepair. Dwellings in poor environments were first
studied thoroughly in the 1991 EHCS.

New dwellings

From the inter-war years onwards, virtually all new dwellings were built with
an inside WC, hot water system and a fixed bath or shower (though in the
1930s some council houses were built with the bath in the scullery as an
economy measure). From the 1970s onwards, central heating became standard
for new houses and flats. In these respects the standard of new dwellings rose
through time, as it did in other ways such as fitted kitchens and more power
points. Dwelling size in terms of floor area and for houses the average plot size,
changed in ways that are harder to interpret in terms of quality. Information
was collected by the 1991 EHCS about average floor area and for houses

average plot size according to dwelling type and year of building. They are presented in Table 14.8 which can be read as a time-series, except that the pre-1914 dwellings are the survivors from the larger number originally built and so not necessarily representative of the size of all dwellings built before 1914. Too few dwellings built between the wars or after 1945 have been demolished for this to be a problem when looking at the size of dwellings built after World War I.

Table 14.8 Size of dwelling and plot area according to construction date, England, 1991

	Detached house	Semi-detached	Terraced house	Flat	Total
Floor area (average area, sq. metres)					
Pre-1918	158	101	79	66	89
1919–44	119	76	76	57	81
1945–64	111	74	71	57	77
1965–80	105	73	71	56	78
Post-1980	90	62	60	56	73
Plot size (average area, sq. metres)					
Pre-1918	1,209	446	160	...	376
1919–44	925	355	230	...	410
1945–64	823	341	243	...	411
1965–80	554	305	170	...	357
Post-1980	477	234	153	...	333

Source: DoE (1993a), Tables A3.4 and A3.8.

In the inter-war years, land for house building was plentiful and generally cheap, but after 1945 stricter controls and higher land prices can be seen to have led to smaller plot sizes (and to a lesser extent smaller floor areas) and higher densities. The average plot size for semi-detached houses built between 1914 and 1944 is equivalent to a density of about ten houses to the acre, with account taken of paths and roads. By the 1980s, the average density for semi-detached houses had risen by half. The effect on use of land of the reduction in average plot size for each type of house was partly offset by the rise in the proportion of houses that were detached, from 17 per cent for houses built between 1919 and 1944 and 20 per cent between 1945 and 1964, to 38 per cent of houses built between 1965 and 1980 and 54 per cent of houses built after 1980. Overall the average plot size for houses built after 1980 was nearly 20 per cent lower than for houses built in the inter-war years.

Concern about land for housing, particularly about building on 'greenfield' sites, grew strongly in the 1990s. It was given added impetus by the publication in 1995 of the Department of the Environment's estimate of a net increase of 4.4 million households between 1991 and 2016 (DoE, 1995). In annual terms, this is not materially higher than the increase since 1951 (Table 14.1). But the large number generated fears of large areas of countryside being built on and a consequent demand that many of the houses to accommodate these households should be built on reused urban sites, so-called 'brownfield' sites. The capacity of such sites in places where people would want to live was controversial; so too was the question of whether house buyers would be willing to risk their own money by buying houses on reused urban sites. The government's views are in *Planning for Communities of the Future* (Department of the Environment, Transport and the Regions (DETR), 1998b).

Housing conditions: sharing, crowding and 'under-occupation'

The size and composition of the housing stock and the number and type of households interact with the price of housing in relation to incomes, to determine how many households have a separate house or flat to themselves and how much space they have. Overcrowding was recognized in the nineteenth century as harmful. It was not always caused by sharing, but sharing owing to shortages or inability to afford separate housing came to be regarded as undesirable except possibly in the short term. 'A separate house for every family that wishes to have one', was stated as an aim of policy (by the war-time Coalition government) in 1945.

Progress towards this aim is shown in Table 14.9. The definition of sharing follows from the definitions of households and dwellings. All important is that two or more households can live in the same dwelling. That is not so according to the definitions used in some other countries, notably the US and France, where a household is defined as all residents of a separate dwelling. In Britain, however, changes in the number of sharing households are an important indicator of changes in housing pressure. 'Concealed families' are included as well as sharing households proper, because both are consequences of shortages and inability to afford separate housing and the distinction is sometimes a fine one. Being without even shared accommodation is the extreme consequence of inability to find housing that can be afforded. Homelessness came to prominence in the 1960s and 1970s through local authorities being given a statutory responsibility to provide housing for homeless families with children and certain other classes of priority need. The numbers rose during the 1980s and 1990s, but then fell. There are no comparable figures for earlier years. Causes include relationship breakdown and, in the early 1990s, mortgage defaults (Figure 14.1).

The quality of the figures in Table 14.9 is not good owing to the difficulty of applying the concept of the structurally separate dwelling in buildings

Table 14.9 Sharing and concealed families, 1911–91

	Sharing households (000s)	Concealed families (000s)	Sharing households + concealed families (000s)	Sharing households as proportion of all households (%)	Sharing households + concealed households as proportion of potential households (%)
England and Wales					
1911	(1200)	(200)	1400	15	17
1921	1732	(550)	2280	20	25
1931	1948	(350)	2300	19	22
1951	1872	935	2810	14	20
1961	886	702	1590	6	10
1971	780	435	1215	5	7
England					
1971	750	235	985	5	6
1981	440	166	605	3	3
1991	340[a]	163	500	2	3

Note: [a] Because of the uncertainties stemming from the under-count in 1991, the number of sharing households was taken from a survey source, the 1991 Labour Force Survey housing trailer, described in DoE, (1993b). The 1981 figure is the number of occupied non-self-contained household spaces, scaled up for the 40 per cent understatement found by the Post Enumeration Survey.

Sources: 1911: author's estimate; 1921–61: census enumerated figures; 1971 and 1981: census-based estimates; 1991: DoE (1993b).

where more than one household lives, but the picture they show is very clear. At the beginning of the century, sharing was very widespread, not because of physical shortages of housing (see the figures for vacant dwellings in Table 14.3) but because large numbers of households could not afford the rent of a separate house or flat. Increases in income and restriction of rents increased the proportion of households that could afford separate housing, but the wars held down the supply of housing, hence shortages in the physical sense. The large numbers of houses and flats built in the 1950s, 1960s and 1970s (Table 14.5) led to these shortages being much reduced, though not eliminated. Reducing shortages took much longer than anyone expected in the 1940s and the early 1950s because the increase in households (Table 14.1) was either not foreseen at all or heavily underestimated.

The amount of space available to households may be measured by rooms per person or persons per room from 1911 onwards and since 1960, by the number of bedrooms in relation to a standard. In other countries (notably Germany) floor area per person is frequently used; but in Britain surveys that collected data on floor area are too few for changes in the space available to households to be depicted in this way. Simple persons per room measures were soon criticized as not having regard to family composition and more sophisticated measures were discussed in the 1931 census *Housing Report*. Such measures became available not through the census but through housing surveys. In the 1960 housing survey, the Government Social Survey developed a 'bedroom standard' to measure density of occupation, which has been used in British housing surveys since then. It closely resembles the standard discussed in 1931: the 'standard' number of bedrooms is so calculated as to provide that not more than two people share a bedroom (for instance, a child should not have to sleep in the parents' bedroom); except for married couples (or living as married), persons of opposite sexes should not share unless both are under 10 years old; and that men and women aged 21 and over not living as a member of a couple should have a bedroom to themselves. Time-series are presented for both measures of density of accommodation. Statutory over-crowding (see DoE (1977), Chapter 1, for the definition) is not shown in time-series form because after 1960 it became too uncommon to register in a survey.

The number of rooms per person is necessarily related to household size: by definition a household must occupy at least one room, so for one-person households the minimum number of rooms per person is 1.0, and for a two-person household, 0.5. Table 14.10 shows the average number of rooms per person according to size of household from 1911 onwards. The comparison is not affected by whether separate dwellings were counted; the only discontinuity is in 1971, when the rule for counting kitchens as rooms was altered. The estimated effect was to increase the total number of rooms by about 4.8 million, equal to 0.1 rooms per person overall.

Table 14.10 Mean amount of household space, England and Wales, 1911–91 (rooms per person)

Size of household (persons)	1911	1921	1931	1951	1961	1971	1981	1991
1	2.84	2.92	2.99	3.32	3.66	3.92	3.97	4.14
2	2.08	2.01	2.07	2.06	2.19	2.37	2.41	2.52
3	1.54	1.47	1.49	1.46	1.55	1.70	2.41	2.52
4	1.23	1.18	1.18	1.15	1.22	1.35	1.41	1.48
5	1.02	0.98	0.98	0.97	1.03	1.12	1.19	1.24
6	0.88	0.84	0.83	0.84	0.89	0.96	1.01	1.05
7	0.77	0.73	0.73	0.74	0.78	0.83	0.88	0.84
8	0.69	0.65	0.65	0.66	0.70	0.74	0.78	n/a
9	0.63	0.60	0.60	0.60	0.63	0.67	0.71	n/a
10 or more	0.58	0.58	0.60	0.53	0.55	0.58	0.62	n/a
All households	1.10	1.10	1.21	1.36	1.50	1.71	1.86	2.06

Source: Census for each year shown.

Except for one-person households, the average number of rooms per person in 1951 was, if anything, lower than 40 years earlier in 1911. The overall increase of 24 per cent in rooms per person between 1911 and 1951 was due entirely to the change in the mix of sizes of households and in the increase in the average number of rooms occupied by men and women living alone, at this time mainly widows and widowers. After 1951, however, the average number of rooms per person increased at each census for all sizes of household.

The number of bedrooms in relation to the survey standard is in most respects a more meaningful measure of changes in the amount of space available to households than the average number of rooms per person, but is available for a much shorter period (from 1960 only) and only from surveys, not the census. Table 14.11 shows the estimated number of households with fewer bedrooms than standard, the standard number, one more than standard and two or more above standard. One more bedroom than standard normally implies that a household has a spare room, without which it would, by the standards of the later twentieth century, be regarded as short of space. Two or more bedrooms above standard has frequently been referred to in the later twentieth century as 'under-occupation'. This was not a source of concern earlier in the century; that worries about it should emerge owes something to the diminished prevalence of overcrowding, but also anxieties about the amount of land required to provide separate dwellings for the increasing number of households (Tables 14.1 and 14.3). A cross-analysis of tenure is shown in Table 14.11 because owner-occupation is all important for the causes of 'under-occupation'.

The figures in Table 14.11 are subject to sampling variation, but it is safe to conclude that since 1971 there has been only a modest fall in the number of households with fewer bedrooms than standard. But at the other end of the distribution, there has been a large and continuous increase in the number of households with two or more bedrooms more than the standard number for their household's size and composition. A man or woman living alone in a three-bedroom house has two more bedrooms than standard; so too does a couple by themselves in a three-bedroom house. This increase in households with two or more bedrooms more than standard has been concentrated among owner-occupiers. The number of tenant households with this many bedrooms was little different in the 1990s from what it had been in the 1960s, but there were 4 million more owner-occupiers with two or more bedrooms more than standard.

The main reason is the increase in the number of one-person households. Many are former members of couple households continuing to live in the same residence. Older owner-occupiers in this situation are usually outright owners and so are not under pressure from housing costs to move to a smaller house or flat. That they live in three-bedroom houses reflects choice rather than 'inefficiency in the use of the housing stock'. The number of older owner-occupiers who are couples by themselves or widows and widowers living alone

Table 14.11 Households according to bedroom standard and housing tenure, 1960–1996/97 (thousands)

| | England and Wales | | | England | |
	1960	1971	1981	1991	1996/97
Fewer bedrooms than standard					
Owner-occupiers	360	290	290	381	216
Local authority tenants	470	380	320	269	181
Housing association tenants			20	42	45
	770	320			
Other tenants			130	142	67
Total	1600	990	760	834	508
Bedrooms equal to standard or one above					
Owner-occupiers	4320	5,680	6400	7853	8026
Local authority tenants	2860	3600	4080	3050	2834
Housing association tenants			320	477	890
	3470	2560			
Other tenants			1380	1300	1627
Total	10650	11840	12190	12680	13378
Two bedrooms or more above standard					
Owner-occupiers	1310	2260	3160	4811	5366
Local authority tenants	200	650	700	550	466
Housing association tenants			30	44	76
	660	700			
Other tenants			390	382	352
Total	2170	3610	4270	5786	6261

Sources: 1960: Government Social Survey (1962); 1971: General Household Survey (see DoE, 1977, Table II.15); 1981 and 1991: Labour Force Survey housing trailers.

will continue to rise in future owing to the age-structure of owner-occupation. So the number of households with two or more bedrooms more than standard will continue to grow. Age structure effects of this kind, though, are not the only reason: for each type and size of household considered separately, the proportion of owner-occupiers that have two or more bedrooms above the standard number rises with income. More space (in terms of rooms) relative to household size is important among the forms in which a demand for better housing, generated by rising income, makes itself manifest.

Housing tenure

The changing distribution of households in Table 14.11 by number of bedrooms in relation to standard and household tenure reflects the change in the overall pattern of tenures. The reduction of just over one million between 1981 and 1991 in the number of local authority tenants with bedrooms equal to the standard number or one above it, for instance, was the result primarily of house-holds transferring from renting to owner-occupation through purchase as sitting tenants. The changing distribution of households and the housing stock between tenures is important in many other ways, not least private and public expenditure on housing (see below). The tenure of households and of dwellings is closely related, but not identical. A multi-occupied house let in rooms to four tenant households counts as one private-rented sector dwelling but is occupied by four private-rented sector households. When an owner-occupier rents out part of the house to a tenant, the house is still owner-occupied, but an owner-occupier and a private-rented sector tenant live there. When a household owns both the main residence and a second home, there is one owner-occupier house-hold and two owner-occupied dwellings. Apart from that, the relationship of owner-occupier households to owner-occupied dwellings is practically one to one and the same is true of local authority and housing association dwellings. With the reduction in sharing (Table 14.9), the difference between the tenure proportions in terms of households and dwellings has diminished. It is there-fore not necessary to show time-series for the tenure both of dwellings and of households. A time series for dwellings is shown here, primarily because there are official estimates from 1951 onwards.

The first year for which a reasonably firm estimate of the tenure of the housing stock in England and Wales can be made is 1938, thanks to information collected from local authorities (as rating authorities) by the Ministry of Health for an

Table 14.12 Tenure of the housing stock in England and Wales, 1938–96

	1938	1951	1961	1971	1981	1991	1996
Number (000s)							
Owner-occupied	3700	3900	6460	8870	11000	14040	14730
Local authorities and New Towns	1100	2200	3600	4800	5420	4130	3830
Housing associations	70	80	100	160	420	660	900
Private landlords and miscellaneous	6530	6350	4480	3190	2160	2020	2200
All tenures	11400	12530	14640	17020	19000	20860	21750
Proportions (%)							
Owner-occupied	32	31	44	52	58	67	67
Local authorities and New Towns	10	18	25	28	29	20	18
Housing associations	1	1	1	1	2	3	5
Private landlords and miscellaneous	57	51	31	19	11	10	10
All tenures	100	100	100	100	100	100	100

Sources: 1938: DoE (1977), Table I.12; figure for housing associations is author's estimate; 1951: the total is from DoE (1977), Table I.4, with the tenure distribution taken from DoE figures for 1950; 1961: DoE (1977), Table I.23; 1971 onwards: DoE, *Housing and Construction Statistics*.

inquiry into rating assessments of dwelling houses (the Fitzgerald Committee). The often quoted figure of 10 per cent as the proportion of households that were owner-occupiers in 1914, or the proportion of the stock owner-occupied, has no firm foundation, but is not inconsistent with the information about the tenure in 1938 of pre-World War I dwellings. In view of its doubtful status, it is not endorsed here. In 1914 dwellings belonging to organizations that would now be classed as housing associations numbered about 50000 and dwellings belonging to local authorities about 20000. What in the 1980s and 1990s came to be termed the 'social' rented sector amounted to about 1 per cent of the stock before 1914. Housing tenure was not asked for in the census until 1961.

Not all the figures in Table 14.12 can be relied on to the nearest 10000 to which they are shown, but the story that they tell is clear enough. Of the 3.7 million owner-occupied dwellings in 1938, some 1.8 million had been built after 1918. Together with the building of over 1 million houses and flats by local authorities, the housing boom of the inter-war years transformed the tenure of the housing stock. Nevertheless, the subsequent course of change was by no means continuously 'onwards and upwards' for owner-occupation. There was very little net increase in the owner-occupied housing stock between 1938 and 1951; and at the beginning of the 1990s, the growth of owner-occupation (measured as a proportion) was halted by the housing market slump. The owner-occupied housing stock grew partly from new building and partly from the sale for owner-occupation of dwellings (predominantly houses) that had previously been rented. The sales of dwellings from local authorities to owner-occupation in the 1980s through the Right to Buy are very well known; but sales for owner-occupation of hitherto rented dwellings by private owners in the 1950s and the first half of the 1960s were even more numerous. A total of 1.2 million houses and flats were sold by local authorities and New Towns for owner-occupation in 1981/82 to 1990/91; overall, from the mid-1960s to 1996/97 sales by local authorities and New Towns totalled between 1.8 million and 1.9 million, about one-eighth of the total owner-occupied housing stock in 1996. The number of houses rented from private owners that were sold for owner-occupation was, however, greater than this. Between the beginning of the 1950s and the end of the 1960s, some 2.3 million formerly rented dwellings were sold for owner-occupation and a further 0.8 million in the 1970s, and a few more in the 1980s. Almost one half of the increase in the owner-occupied housing stock in the 1950s and 1960s came from the private rented sector. This transfer within two decades of one-third of the private rented stock was made possible by nineteenth-century building for urban wage earners being terraced houses and not flats, except in parts of London, in contrast to the predominance of flats in continental cities and towns. Owner-occupation and purchase on mortgage is much simpler for terraced houses than flats. Sales of flats for owner-occupation first began to appear in significant numbers in the 1970s.

An essential part of the history of housing tenure in Britain and specifically of owner-occupation, is the housing market slump of the early 1990s. The fall in house prices in nominal and real terms is shown later in the chapter (Table 14.15). The surge in the number of mortgaged properties repossessed by lenders as a result of mortgage default is shown in Figure 14.1. For convenience, the number of owner-occupiers for whom part or all of their mortgage interest was paid from Income Support (Supplementary Benefit before 1988) is also shown as the increase in the 1990s shared the same causes.

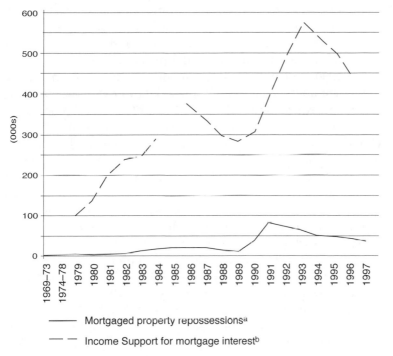

——— Mortgaged property repossessions[a]

— — Income Support for mortgage interest[b]

Figure 14.1 Mortgaged property repossessions (United Kingdom) and payments of mortgage through Income Support (Great Britain), 1969–97

Notes: [a]Lenders who are not members of the Council of Mortgage Lenders (CML) are not included; exactly how many mortgaged repossessions are missed as a consequence is not known, but the large lending institutions are CML members.
[b]The annual figures are the number at May of each year. The number of payments of Income Support for mortgage interest was affected by restrictions introduced in 1995, under which no payments are made in the first nine months of a claim (unless the claimant is aged 60 or over). 1985 Income Support for mortgage interest figure not collected owing to strike.

Sources: The figures for mortgaged property repossessions are from the quarterly publication *Housing Finance*, produced by the CML from information supplied by their members. The figures for mortgage holders receiving Income Support towards their mortgage interest are published in the annual volume *Social Security Statistics*, produced by the Department of Social Security.

The economic recession of the early 1980s did not leave owner-occupiers unscathed, but the impact of the recession of the early 1990s was far more severe. In the seven years from 1990 to 1996, almost 400000 mortgage holders lost their homes. 1997 was a year of recovery in the housing market, but even so the number of mortgaged properties repossessed was higher than in any year before 1990. The number of owner-occupiers receiving help from Income Support with their mortgages also rose fast. Most of the increase was in households receiving Income Support owing to unemployment. A considerable number of owner-occupiers unable to sell their houses and move owing to the slump rented them out; and as well as this there was a considerable amount of buying of formerly owner-occupied houses and flats for renting out. This was the source of the net increase of about a quarter of a million in the private rented housing stock between the late 1980s and 1996. Deregulation of new lettings in the private rented sector brought up the supply of housing to let by private owners; it also brought up rents and expenditure on Housing Benefit (see next section). From the late 1940s to the mid-1980s, the private rented sector reduced in size year by year. Slum clearance was one reason; but more important numerically were sales for owner-occupation. Between the end of the 1940s and the late 1980s, about 20 per cent of the private rented stock (broadly defined to include accommodation that went with the job or with business premises) was demolished through slum clearance and between 45 and 50 per cent sold for owner-occupation. The reason was not just that rent control and regulation made letting unprofitable; the demand for home ownership was at least as important.

The most rapid growth of the public sector (local authority and New Town) housing stock came in the 1950s. In the '300 000 houses a year' drive, the government of the day wanted houses built by anybody who could build them and local authorities had the organization to do so. Between 1952 and 1956, over 900 000 new dwellings were completed for local authorities and New Towns in England and Wales, more than in any other five-year period before or since. They were for the most part houses and not flats; together with the 700000 houses built for local authorities in 1946–51 they made up the bulk of the Right to Buy sales from the 1980s onwards. The public sector stock reached its greatest size in 1979 and after that diminished as new building was cut back and sales ran at high levels. At the end of the 1980s, new building by local authorities was brought to an end as an act of government policy and new building for letting at below market rents made a housing association function. That policy change, together with 'large-scale voluntary transfers' of local authority housing to housing association status for primarily financial reasons explains the increase of nearly 600 000 in housing association stock between 1981 and 1996 (Table 14.12).

The transfer of very large numbers of dwellings with their occupiers from renting to owner-occupation caused large changes in the circumstances of tenants. These changes took place at a time when social and labour market changes (outlined in Chapter 8), were leading to large increases in the number of non-earning households irrespective of tenure. As well as the increase in numbers unemployed, many more withdrew from the labour force through formal or informal early retirement: in 1976, 80 per cent of men aged 60–64 and 92 per cent of those aged 55–59 were economically active (in paid work or seeking it); in 1993 only 52 per cent and 75 per cent respectively. As a result

Table 14.13 Households analysed by tenure and number of earners, 1962–96[a]

	None	One	Two	Three or more	Total	Estimated number of households (000s)
			Number of earners[b] (%)			
Local authority tenants						
1962	11	34	33	22	100	3400
1971	23	34	38	15	100	4450
1978	30	30	28	12	100	5100
1982	44	30	19	7	100	4800
1990	60	23	12	5	100	3900
1993	66	21	11	3	100	3700
1996	64	23	11	3	100	3500
Owner-occupiers						
1962	17	45	28	9	100	6050
1971	19	38	36	7	100	7950
1978	19	30	40	11	100	9450
1982	21	34	36	9	100	10850
1990	24	29	38	9	100	13100
1993	29	28	35	7	100	13450
1996	27	28	36	9	100	13600
All tenures						
1962	16	42	29	13	100	14110
1971	22	36	31	10	100	15820
1978	25	30	35	10	100	16950
1982	30	32	29	8	100	17450
1990	34	28	30	8	100	19000
1993	39	27	28	6	100	19800
1996	36	28	29	7	100	20150

Notes: [a] The geographical area covered by the table differs over time. The 1962 and 1996 figures are for England. From 1971–93, the figures are sometimes for Great Britain and sometimes England and Wales. This differing geographic coverage introduces a degree of uncertainty, though small in proportion to the changes reported.
[b] 'Earners' are in receipt of income from employment and self-employment.

Sources: 1962: Cullingworth (1965); 1971–93: DoE, *Housing and Construction Statistics* (*Housing Statistics Great Britain* for 1971); 1996: DETR (1998c).

of these changes (and of the increase in the number of households with retired heads), there was a large increase in the number and proportion of households with no member in paid employment. In proportional terms this change was most pronounced among local authority tenants. But in absolute terms the number of owner-occupier households with no earning member rose by 2.4 million between 1971 and 1993, as compared with an increase of 1.4 million local authority tenant households with no member earning.

In the early 1960s, the children of many of the couples who had got council tenancies in the 1940s and early 1950s had left school and joined the labour force, hence the large number of tenant households with three earners or more. Their equivalents in the 1960s, 1970s and 1980s for the most part became owner-occupiers, with the result that a diminishing proportion of new local authority tenants were in paid employment. Households which exercised the Right to Buy were predominantly couple households with one or both members in paid work, which reduced still further the number and proportion of tenants in paid work. Local authority housing was always intended for households that could not afford adequate housing at market rents or prices; but the changes in tenants' circumstances in the 1980s and 1990s produced a concentration of households there with low incomes and therefore low rent-paying capacity, with important implications for subsidy policy. As housing associations took over from local authorities the provision of new social sector tenancies, they necessarily provided for tenants in the same circumstances as did local authorities.

Rents

Because changes in the quality of housing over the twentieth century were so marked, average rents or average mortgage outgoings overstate the 'true' rise in the price of housing, in the sense of what accommodation of constant quality would cost. Housing of 1914 'working class' standard no longer existed in the 1990s and so could not be priced. Three sets of information are available about the cost of housing to households: private sector rents; local authority rents and average mortgage interest payments. Average mortgage interest payments are a much smaller proportion of the outgoings of owner-occupiers than is rent for tenants; as well as mortgage interest, the home owner with a mortgage has to make repayments of mortgage principal and meet all the cost of upkeep and insurance, whereas for tenanted property these costs fall on the landlord to be recouped from the rent. These are not the only difficulties encountered when comparing the cost of renting with the cost of house purchase: the tenant is simply hiring the accommodation, but the owner-occupier with a mortgage is buying the asset as well as the use of the accommodation. How valuable is the asset is controversial, given that owner-occupiers as a group cannot realize the value of their dwellings by selling and renting or partially by selling and buying a cheaper house. That controversy cannot be pursued here. It was most prominent in the debates of the 1970s about equity between the tax treatment of owner-occupied housing and subsidies for local authority tenants (see DoE, 1977, Chapter 5).

Information about private sector rents is available for a much longer span of time than either mortgage interest or council rents. An inquiry by the Board of Trade into 'working class' living costs provides information about rents in 1912 and information collected in 1936 for the Inter-Departmental Committee on the Rent Restrictions Act gives an indication of rents in the inter-war years. Information about rents was collected again in 1957 to study the effect of the Rent Act of that year and concern about the way in which the rental market was working led to surveys in the early 1960s. The intervals between data points are too long and differences in the type of accommodation too great for a time-series; but they give a valuable guide to changes in rents in real terms and relative to income between pre- and post-World War I and pre- and post-World War II. Pre-1914 rent levels are important also because a substantial number of households could not afford a house to themselves at those rents and so had to share (Table 14.9).

'Working class' rents in 1912 averaged about 4s a week (net of rates), compared with average weekly earnings (of men in manual work) of about 32s. Domestic rates added about 1s 3d, so that rent plus rates amounted on average to 16 per cent of average earnings and rent exclusive of rates 12.5 per cent. The war brought about a rapid inflation both of earnings and prices; it was partly reversed by the post-war slump, but nevertheless both earnings and prices remained well above pre-1914 levels in nominal terms. Legislation in 1919 and 1920 permitted an increase in controlled rents of 40 per cent, from the 1914 base. In 1924, taken as a year when the post-war slump was over, prices were some 90 per cent above 1914 levels and earnings rather more. Rents were some 25–30 per cent lower in real terms than in 1914 and earnings slightly higher. Housing had become much more affordable and preferences for separate houses had become effective demand. But there was not sufficient supply to meet it, with pervasive shortages in consequence. World War II and its aftermath had a similar effect on rents in real terms. In 1939, about half of pre-1914 dwellings were let at controlled rents – for the most part 1914 rents plus 40 per cent – and half at market rents, which were about 25 per cent higher than controlled rents. Rent control was reimposed at 1939 levels at the outbreak of war. There was less inflation in 1939–45 than in 1914–18, but after 1945 there was no general increase in controlled rents, in contrast to after World War I. The general price level in 1950 was about 50 per cent higher than in 1939, so that rents fixed in cash terms were one-third lower in real terms. Rented housing had again become much more affordable, but at rents far too low to attract investment in new houses for rent. Provision of new houses for rent therefore became a local authority function, with a continuing and strong effect on council rents.

Rents charged for their houses by local authorities were not subject to rent control, but the way in which local authorities' housing finance worked had a similar effect in holding down rents in cash terms in the war and post-war years, with, in consequence, a steep fall in real terms. Rents were required to be set to cover costs, net of Exchequer and rate fund subsidies and in the 1930s averaged about 7s a week. This corresponded to controlled rents plus a differential for higher quality. The costs to be met from rents and subsidy comprised loan charges, repair costs and management costs, of which loan charges were the largest. They were set in money terms and during the war years fell slightly because the interest rates paid by local authorities during the 'three per cent war' enabled maturing debts to be refinanced at lower rates of interest. Repair costs and management costs rose, but not by much as shortages of materials limited the amount of work that could be done. Each authority pooled its housing costs and rental income, with the result that new building at higher costs increased average outgoings per dwelling from housing revenue accounts. Subsidies were not sufficient to meet the difference between the cost of new dwellings and rents in line with rents in the existing stock, so rents were raised across the board. Cross-subsidy between newer dwellings built at higher costs and the older stock built at much lower cost with smaller amounts of debt became the key to local authority housing finance in the 1950s and 1960s. The way in which it operated is summarized in the time-series in Table 14.14.

Thanks to the combined effect of inflation in reducing the real value of debts and loan charges, and very substantial subsidies under the 1946 and 1952 Housing Acts, rents on average were considerably lower in real terms in the mid-1950s than they had been in the 1930s. Exchequer subsidy for building for general needs was reduced in 1955 and abolished in 1956, on the grounds that many authorities had substantial capacity from cross-subsidy from older dwellings with low historic costs. In consequence, average rents rose by nearly 50 per cent in real terms in a decade. Subsidy was brought back, first in a small way (Housing Act 1961) and then on a large scale (Housing Act 1967), but under the combined impact of large building programmes, rising construction costs and land prices and higher interest rates, rents continued to rise in real terms. Local authority housing finance was reformed in 1972 by the ill-fated Housing Finance Act. It aimed to raise local authority rents to the same levels as registered fair rents in the private rented sector and concentrate subsidies on those who most needed them by a mandatory scheme of rent rebates related to income and household circumstances. Initially it worked as intended: between 1971/72 and 1973/74, average unrebated rents rose by 23 per cent in real terms, more than in any previous two-year period. The policy

Table 14.14 Average weekly local authority rents,[a] 1936–97[b]

	Cash	Constant (1997) value of money (£)
England and Wales		
1936	7s (approx)	13.00
1946	9s	10.20
1955/56	14s 6d	10.30
1960/61	20s 8d	13.00
1965/66	28s 7d	15.00
1971/72	£2.48	18.90
1973/74	£3.57	23.00
1975/76	£4.28	18.80
England		
1979	£6.40	17.80
1980	£7.70	18.10
1982	£13.48	26.10
1989	£20.70	28.30
1995	£38.31	40.50
1997	£41.18	41.20

Notes: [a]The rents are simple average rents for all types of dwelling, so changes through time do not take account of changes in the mix of types of dwelling or upgrading.
[b]Up to 1971/72 the rents are net of any rent rebates, but from 1973/74 figures are average unrebated rents. The break occurs because the Housing Finance Act 1972 required local authorities to have rent rebate schemes at least as favourable to tenants as the national model scheme prescribed by the Department of the Environment.

Sources: 1936: from a special return of stocks of dwellings and of rents called for from local authorities in England and Wales by the Ministry of Health, published in Cmd 5537 (1937); 1946 and 1955/56: author's estimates from rent income in aggregate housing revenue accounts; 1960/61–75/76: DoE (1977), Chapter 4; 1979 onwards: DoE, *Housing and Construction Statistics*.

was reversed by the Labour government that took office in 1974; rents were initially frozen for a year and then increased in cash terms by amounts too small to keep pace with very rapid inflation. The 1979 Conservative government returned to the policy of securing reductions in total subsidy by raising rents to shift the balance from general to means-tested subsidy. In two years (1980–82) average unrebated rents were raised by 75 per cent in cash terms and nearly 40 per cent in real terms, by more subtle means than in 1972. For several years after that, rents did little more than keep pace with prices; most authorities outside London were 'out of subsidy' in the sense of having had their Exchequer subsidies reduced to zero and so were not subject to pressure to make large rent increases. Local authority housing finance was reformed again in 1989 by the Local Government and Housing Act, which enabled the government to return to the policy of seeking subsidy savings by forcing up rents. Rents were raised in real terms by 40 per cent between 1989 and 1995.

But with many fewer tenants paying rent from their own funds (Table 14.17) the savings in total subsidy were much smaller than in the early 1980s and in 1995, the policy was effectively abandoned. Council rents entered the retail prices index (RPI) gross (that is, before deducting rent rebates) and the effect on National Insurance benefits, Child Benefit and other expenditure (including interest and principal of indexed National Savings Certificates) indexed to the RPI absorbed most of what savings there were on housing subsidies.

Housing association rents were released from the fair rent system for tenancies starting after the beginning of 1989 and rents were sharply raised in order to finance borrowing from private lending institutions for mixed funded developments. Average rents on new lettings (assured tenancies) were £29 a week in 1990 and £50.20 in 1996, an increase of almost 40 per cent in real terms. Nearly two-thirds of housing association tenants were receiving Housing Benefit, hence there was a very rapid rise in Housing Benefit for housing association tenants (Table 14.18). Concern about the growth of expenditure on Housing Benefit led, in the mid-1990s, to efforts to restrain the growth of housing association rents.

Private sector rents were similarly deregulated for lettings starting after the beginning of 1989 and rents rose rapidly in consequence. The average rent for assured shorthold tenancies, the principal form of deregulated tenancy, rose from £63 a week in 1990 to £94 in 1996/97, and the average rent for all private sector tenancies from £43 in 1990, to £76 a week in 1996/97, a 40 per cent increase in real terms. This likewise had a powerful effect on Housing Benefit expenditure (Table 14.18).

House prices, mortgage payments and interest rates

Changes in house prices can be shown in index number form from the 1930s onwards. The data from which the index is constructed are not wholly comparable, but a reasonably accurate picture is shown apart from the possibility that in the longer-term improvements in quality are not fully brought to account. Nor, however, are the reductions in plot sizes (Table 14.8). Also shown are average payments of interest to building societies. In the 1990s, several major building societies converted to banks; but there is no time-series for interest paid to all house purchase lenders, so the building society series is shown for continuity. The series is shown both gross and net of estimated tax relief on mortgage interest and (before 1983) option mortgage subsidy. Interest rates are similarly shown gross and net.

Table 14.15 shows a long-term upward trend in house prices in real terms, with sharp fluctuations round the trend. The years shown in the table are where possible cyclical peaks and troughs occur. The war years should

Table 14.15 House prices, mortgage interest rates, mortgage interest payments, UK[a], 1938–97

	House prices		Average payments of mortgage interest to building societies			Mortgage interest rates[b]		
	Nominal 1970 = 100	Real Terms	Gross	Net[c]	Net in 1997 prices	Gross	Net[d]	Net in 1997 prices[e]
1938	12.0	49	22	(22)	90	4.8	(4.8)	
1948	42.3	99	26	(26)	60	4.2	(4.2)	−0.4
1951	44.9	91	32	25	50	4.2	3.3	−0.6
1954	40.7	72	40	30	55	4.6	3.5	−0.7
1958	42.7	65	62	45	70	6.1	4.4	+0.9
1964	73.6	99	88	60	80	6.2	4.2	+2.2
1970	100	100	198	135	135	8.6	5.9	+0.9
1973	224	175	308	210	165	9.6	6.5	−1.3
1977	276	111	558	345	140	11.1	6.9	−9.8
1982	536	123	1260	880	200	13.3	9.3	−2.9
1989	1464	235	2835	2210	355	14.4	11.2	+4.0
1993	1337	176	2837	2380	315	7.9	6.6	+4.7
1997	1552	183	f	f	f	6.7	6.1	+3.1

Notes: [a] The figures for mortgage payments and interest rates refer to the United Kingdom; house prices are for England and Wales before 1966, United Kingdom after that.
[b] Average mortgage interest rate paid to building societies.
[c] Net of mortgage interest tax relief and (from 1967–83) option mortgage subsidy.
[d] Ratio of net to gross is the same as for mortgage payments.
[e] Net interest rate incomes year on year increase in the general price level.
[f] Series no longer published.

Sources: House prices: 1938–64 average prices recorded by the Inland Revenue Valuation Office for dwellings that had been sold less than five years before (see Holmans (1990) Annex A for further details); 1970 onwards: the house price index is the DoE's mix-adjusted index derived from the Building Societies Mortgage Survey and then the Survey of Mortgage Lending. This is published in the annual DoE's *Housing and Construction Statistics*; Average payments of interest: Council of Mortgage Lenders' *Compendium of Housing Finance Statistics* (Inland Revenue figures of mortgage interest tax relief have been deducted to give net interest payments); Mortgage interest rates: Council of Mortgage Lenders' *Compendium of Housing Finance Statistics* and *Housing Finance*.

probably be left out of the account of cyclical swings, because circumstances were so unusual. Those years apart, there were four house-price booms: from the end of the 1950s to the mid-1960s; the early 1970s (1970 to 1973); the late 1970s and 1980, and the boom of the late 1980s. This last was followed by a slump in house prices in cash terms, not quite 10 per cent overall, but much more pronounced in the south of England where the preceding boom had also been strongest. Falling house prices in cash terms had not been seen since the early 1950s. The fall in house prices in those years is shown in Table 14.15; it made far less impact than did the fall in house prices at the beginning of the 1990s, no doubt because far fewer households were owner-occupiers. The boom of the early 1970s was followed by a fall in house prices in real terms that was steeper than at the beginning of the 1990s. But so rapid was inflation in the 1970s, that house prices still rose in cash terms; since house-purchase debts are set in cash terms, the fall in prices in real terms in the 1970s did not produce the disruption experienced in the early 1990s. The long-term increase in house prices measured from peak to peak (1948–89) averaged 2.1 per cent a year in real terms; trough to trough (1958–93), 2.9 per cent a year. Taken together, these increases were about in line with the increase in real income. But since the average prices include an element of improvement in quality, it is likely that the 'true' increase in house prices was rather less than the increase in income, but nevertheless significantly positive in real terms.

Mortgage interest payments respond to increases in house prices with a considerable lag. On average, only about 10 per cent of the total stock of mortgages are taken out in the most recent year, so that in a period of rising house prices, the average new mortgage is much larger than the average of all outstanding mortgages. In real terms average interest payments were no larger in the mid-1950s than in the 1930s, but from then on the interacting effect of rising house prices (and therefore larger new mortgages) and higher interest rates pulled up mortgage interest payments very sharply. When inflation fell back in the 1990s and with it nominal interest rates, reductions in mortgage interest tax relief meant that net interest payments fell considerably less than did gross. Fuller detail about tax relief is given in Table 14.19.

Public funding for housing

Large-scale public funding for housing has good claim to be the greatest change in the housing area between the beginning and end of the twentieth century. Its only rival is large-scale long-term lending for house purchase. Exchequer subsidies for housing began in 1919 and have a continuous history since then. Contributions from local authorities' rate funds were compulsory from 1919–56; optional from 1956–72; compulsory again from 1972–75; optional again from 1975–90, and prohibited from 1990 onwards. With only rare exceptions, Exchequer subsidies were by far the larger. These subsidies from the Exchequer and the rate fund were for the purpose of enabling housing accounts (Housing Revenue Accounts from 1935) to balance with lower rents than would otherwise be required and so benefited all council tenants irrespective of income. Rents that were differentiated with respect to tenants' income and household circumstances were experimented with in the 1930s and came to the fore in the 1960s when the growing cost of subsidies led to attempts to restrain the increases by raising rents substantially (Table 14.15), but offering rebates according to income and household size. Until 1972, local authorities had powers to provide rent rebates, but not a duty. The Housing Finance Act 1972 imposed a duty to provide rent rebate schemes not less favourable to tenants than the national model scheme and also a parallel scheme of rent allowances for tenants of private landlords and housing associations. These schemes benefited tenants not receiving means-tested public assistance; public assistance (Unemployment Assistance from 1934, National Assistance from 1948, Supplementary Benefit from 1967 and Income Support from 1988) has always taken the form of a scale rate governed by the size and composition of claimants' households plus rent. For tenants receiving means-tested assistance, the rent was paid from public funds as part of social security expenditure. It was not separately distinguished as a category of expenditure until rent rebates and allowances were brought together with the rent element of Supplementary Benefit in 1982 and 1983 under the title of Housing Benefit. That title suggests it is a means-tested housing subsidy and so in a sense it is, but its existence has meant that scale rates of assistance could be set much lower than would be necessary if rent had to be paid from them. That is a source of saving in that a scale rate high enough to include rent would have to be paid to claimants of assistance who pay no rent or only very low rent. When Housing Benefit came into being, the rent element of Supplementary Benefit was the larger part of the total and it became the responsibility of the Department of Social Security. In consequence, Housing Benefit expenditure has tended to be looked at purely in social security terms, to the neglect of its interaction with private finance for housing associations and the meeting of housing needs in the private rented sector.

Subsidies to local authority housing are shown in Table 14.16. Although Housing Benefit was introduced in 1982/83, for continuity the term 'rent rebates' is used in the table, divided into rebates to tenants without and with Supplementary Benefit (subsequently Income Support). Figures for the rent element of Supplementary Benefit are estimates and not firm figures, but the picture they show is reliable enough.

General subsidy grew continuously in real terms from the end of World War I as a result of large building programmes (Table 14.12), and after World War II, rising costs of building and land and higher interest rates as well. In the first half of the 1970s the exceptionally rapid rise in costs, especially interest on loans, combined with rents being held down in 1974 and 1975 for counter-inflation reasons produced a steep rise in subsidy expenditure. From the end of the 1970s onwards the dominant theme was the shift from general subsidy to means-tested assistance with rents. In the first half of the 1980s, this policy achieved substantial savings in public expenditure, but in the early 1990s the savings were much less, as the proportion of tenants not receiving rebates was far lower.

The Right to Buy was taken up primarily by tenants not receiving Housing Benefit, which contributed substantially to the rise in the proportion (as distinct from the absolute number) of tenants receiving it.

Table 14.16 Subsidies to local authority housing including rent element of Supplementary Benefit for local authority tenants, England and Wales, 1935–97 (£ millions)[a]

	Exchequer[a]	Rate fund	Current prices Total general subsidy	Rent rebates not SB or IS
1935/36	11.8	3.5	15.3	–
1945/46	12.3	4.8	17.1	–
1955/56	45.4	18.2	63.6	–
1965/66	76.5	34.3	110.8	–
1970/71	159.0	55.8	214.8	(15)
1975/76	633	175	808	138
1979/80	1333	343	1776	196
1984/85	388	293	681	610
1989/90	651	83	734	827
1993/94	830	–	830	1192
1996/97	681	–	681	1048

Notes: [a] In 1993/94 and 1996/97 Exchequer subsidy is the sum of positive entitlements; negative entitlements are netted against rent rebates.
[b] Rent rebates became significant when rebate schemes were made mandatory by the Housing Finance Act 1972. Tenants receiving Supplementary Benefit (SB) received a scale rate plus rent. So that a tenant did not have to claim a rent rebate separately from his claim for SB, his SB amount was calculated from the unrebated rent. In 1982/83, the rent element of SB was combined with rent rebates into Housing Benefit. For comparability, estimates were made by the author of the rent element in SB expenditure in 1975/76 and 1979/80 from the number of local authority tenants receiving SB, the average local authority rent and the rates of average Housing Benefit for tenants receiving SB to the overall average rent in 1983/84. Housing Benefit was reformed in 1988 when Income Support (IS) replaced SB, which reduced the number of tenants receiving Housing Benefit.

Time-series of the same length are not available for tenants of housing associations and private landlords receiving Housing Benefit and its predecessors. Even a short time-series from 1988 is, however, valuable because housing associations have since then been the main providers of new social housing and a large number of dwellings were transferred from local authorities to housing associations. In addition, Housing Benefit enabled the private rented sector to accommodate in the region of a quarter of a million new tenants in housing need. How steep was the increase in expenditure on Housing Benefit for housing association tenants and tenants of private landlords is shown in Table 14.18: between 1988 and 1996/97 it more than trebled in real terms, from £1150 million to £3680 million at 1997 prices.

Owner-occupiers: mortgage interest tax relief and income support for mortgage interest

Until 1963, income tax was charged on the annual rental value of owner-occupied houses. As long as this was so, tax relief on mortgage interest was not

Rent rebates SB or IS	Total rent rebates[b]	Constant (1997) prices General subsidy	Rent rebates
–	–	585	–
–	–	405	–
–	–	905	–
–	–	1165	–
–	–	1790	–
265	403	3343	1770
415	611	4725	1625
1305	1915	1185	3340
1747	2474	985	3320
2482	3672	925	4085
2446	3494	695	3580

The Local Government and Housing Act 1989 reformed local authority housing finance by prohibiting rate fund contributions and provided that, where the housing revenue account was in surplus, the surplus should be used to help pay for Housing Benefit for local authority tenants. 'Positive subsidy entitlements' in 1993/94 and 1996/97 are payments of subsidy to authorities whose housing revenue accounts would otherwise be in deficit. Rebates are net of the other authorities' surpluses.

Sources: Exchequer subsidies and rate fund contributions to housing revenue accounts in 1965/66 and earlier are from *Local Government Financial Statistics* (annual); for 1970/71 onwards, the source is the DoE in *Housing Statistics, Great Britain* and then *Housing and Construction Statistics* (annual volume).

a special relief but part of ordinary tax principles, that expenses incurred in producing an income could be set off against it. Rental values for this purpose were as assessed in 1935; so the favourable tax treatment for owner-occupied housing was charging the tax on rental values well below the actual level. This charge (widely known as Schedule A) was abolished in 1963. In 1969 tax relief on interest on loans was withdrawn except for loans for business purposes and for house purchase. Mortgage interest tax relief thus became a special relief, tantamount to a subsidy. Recognition of this was given by provision of the equivalent of tax relief through the Option Mortgage Subsidy for owner-occupiers with incomes too low to benefit fully from tax relief. The growth of owner-occupation, rising house prices and higher interest rates led to a very large increase in the cost of mortgage interest tax relief. The maximum amount of mortgage debt eligible for relief (£30000 from 1983) gradually restrained the rise in real terms in the cost of the relief, as did reductions in income tax rates. In the 1990s, the relief was cut back first by confining it to the basic rate of tax and then reducing the relief below the rate of income tax. The motive for these restrictions of the relief was primarily fiscal, to increase revenue from income

Table 14.17 Local authority tenants receiving rent rebates:[a] England and Wales, 1970–96 (thousands)

	Receiving rebates, but not SB/IS	Receiving rebates, and SB/IS	Total receiving rebates[b]	Percentage of all tenants receiving rebates
1970	350	1023	1370	30
1975	940	1103	2040	41
1979	980	1266	2250	43
1983	1430	1580	3010	64
1987	1305	1705	3010	65
1988[c]	1070	1530	2600	58
1993	1050	1550	2600	66
1996	910	1540	2450	66

Notes: [a] Rent rebates became one category of Housing Benefit in 1982/83; rent allowances the other. Rent rebates are for local authority and new town tenants and are given by reductions off the standard (or unrebated) rent. Rent allowances are for tenants of private landlords and housing associations and for occupiers of certain other kinds of accommodation (for instance in hostels), who are not tenants in the strict sense.
[b] Strictly speaking, only tenants in the column headed 'Not SB/IS' received rent rebates before 1983, because tenants receiving SB received the equivalent of rebates through rent in the scale rate plus rent payment being based on unrebated rents.
[c] Reduction compared with 1987 due primarily to the reforms associated with Housing Benefit, though falling unemployment also contributed

Source: DoE's annual *Housing and Construction Statistics*.

tax without raising the 'headline' tax rate. Because interest rates were falling this could be done without increasing home-owners' outgoings. The final abolition of mortgage interest tax relief was announced in the 1999 budget.

The cost of mortgage interest tax relief is shown in Table 14.19. Also shown, because it grew so much in the economic recession of the first half of the 1990s, is expenditure on Income Support for mortgage interest. The rise in the number receiving it was shown in Figure 14.1. The increase in its cost was even greater owing to the steep rise in interest rates and the lagged effect of the house-price boom of the 1980s on the size of mortgages.

Payment of mortgage interest from Income Support (previously from Supplementary Benefit and before that, National Assistance) is historically a consequence of the way in which rent was defined when the amount of assistance is the scale rate plus rent. Until the 1980s, few owner-occupiers with mortgages qualified for National Assistance and then Supplementary Benefit: marital breakdown was the commonest reason and instances where unemployment was the cause were few. The situation changed radically in the 1980s and still more in the 1990s when, as noted above, the economic recession hit owner-occupiers very hard. The response of the government of the day to the steep increase in the cost was to restrict the availability of the assistance, in the

Table 14.18   Rent rebates and allowances in total, England, 1988–96/97

	Number (000s)				Expenditure (£ million)				Total at
	LA tenants	HA tenants	Private sector tenants[a]	Total	LA tenants	HA tenants	Private sector tenants	Total	1997 prices
1988	2600	295	400	3295	2290	320	460	3070	4525
1993/94	2600	470	640	3710	3670	930	1630	6230	6935
1994/95	2515	540	630	3685	3690	1175	1800	6665	7225
1995/96	2540	610	660	3810	3670	1425	2020	7115	7465
1996/97	2450	640	620	3710	3490	1560	2030	7080	7250

Note: [a] The numbers of private sector tenants receiving Housing Benefit as estimated from housing surveys fall far short of the figure published by the Department of Social Security (DSS) from returns by local authorities, which administer Housing Benefit. The difference is too large to be due to differences in coverage and, in the 1990s, fraud through fictitious tenancies was suspected, which would inflate the reported numbers of rent allowances paid. Reliance on survey sources means that estimates are subject to sampling variability. Another consequence is that the figures are of expenditure on rent allowances themselves, with costs of administration excluded.

Sources: Local authority tenants receiving rebate are from Table 14.8 and expenditure has been calculated by multiplying the numbers receiving rent rebates by the average weekly rebate and then multiplied by 52 for annual figures; for rent allowances to housing association tenants and private sector tenants, estimates are derived from housing surveys (the Private Rented Sector Survey for 1988 and the Survey of English Housing for 1993/94 and after).

expectation that mortgagors would insure their payments against sickness and unemployment.

Mortgage interest tax relief rose fast during the 1960s, but the surge in house prices and steep increase in interest rates (Table 14.15) produced an even larger increase in the first half of the 1970s. In the four years from 1971/72 to 1975/76, the cost almost doubled in real terms. It was this massive increase in the cost of tax relief that fuelled the controversies in the mid-1970s about the equity of the system of housing subsidies and tax reliefs. Mortgage interest tax relief survived those controversies apart from relief being limited to house-purchase loans up to £25 000 and withdrawn from loans on second homes, both with a six-year period of grace for loans already in being at the time of the 1974 budget when these restrictions were introduced. The £25 000 limit was raised to £30 000 in 1983, but was not further increased. But the house-price boom of the 1980s resulted in an increasing proportion of loans exceeding £30 000 and so attracting relief on only part of the interest paid. The 1990s saw relief restricted first to the basic rate and then to rates below the basic rate, with no period of grace – in this respect the Conservative government in the 1990s was more radical than the Labour government in the 1970s. These restrictions accounted for one-third of the reduction in the cost of the tax relief between the 1990/91 high point and 1996/97. The relief was further

Table 14.19 Mortgage interest tax relief and income support for mortgage interest, UK, 1963/64–1996/97 (£ millions)

	Current prices		Constant (1997) prices	
	Mortgage interest tax relief[a]	Income Support for mortgage interest	Mortgage interest tax relief[a]	Income Support for mortgage interest
1963/64	90	–	1030	–
1965/66	135	–	1420	–
1967/68	180	–	1785	–
1969/70	244	–	2180	–
1971/72	328	–	2500	–
1973/74	560	–	3610	–
1975/76	1004	–	4405	–
1977/78	1192	–	3975	–
1979/80	1639	31	4360	80
1981/82	2312	124	4745	255
1983/84	2792	150	5110	275
1985/86	4750	b	7815	b
1987/88	4850	335	7435	515
1989/90	6900	353	9260	475
1990/91	7700	553	9415	675
1991/92	6100	944	7125	1105
1992/93	5200	1143	5885	1295
1993/94	4300	1222	4785	1360
1994/95	3500	1057	3795	1145
1995/96	2700	1035	2830	1085
1996/97	2400	867	2460	890

Notes: [a] Includes Option Mortgage Subsidy.
[b] Information not collected owing to strike.

Sources: Mortgage interest tax relief is estimated by the Board of Inland Revenue and published annually in *Inland Revenue Statistics*; Income Support for mortgage interest is published by the Department of Social Security in the annual *Social Security Statistics*.

restricted to 10 per cent in 1998/99. The very muted complaint about this restriction conveyed the impression that the days of the tax relief on mortgage interest were numbered, and its abolition was announced in 1999.

Overview: the growth and decline in the role of government in British housing in the twentieth century

When the twentieth century began, the principal role of government in the housing system was one of regulating the physical standard of housing, setting minimum standards for new dwellings and exercising to some extent powers to close or demolish insanitary housing. There were powers to abate over-crowding, but they could be little exercised in practice because, for large numbers of households, crowded or shared accommodation was all that could be afforded. Those in the worst housing could not generally afford the houses and flats provided by the organizations that subsequently became known as housing associations. Overall their houses and flats, plus the even smaller number provided by local authorities, amounted to only 1 per cent of the total stock.

World War I and its aftermath brought about a very radical change. Exchequer subsidies for housing began in 1919; but a case can be made for regarding 1925 as the key year. The 1919 subsidy was a post-war emergency measure to cope with very high building costs and was brought to an end in 1921 for financial reasons; and the 1923 subsidy was initially for two years only and available to private enterprise as well as local authorities. The 1924 subsidy in contrast was for local authorities and had no time limit. It was enacted under the first Labour government very shortly before that government fell and was succeeded by a Conservative government with a very large majority. This government could have brought building by local authorities to an end by cancelling the subsidy except where contracts had already been let. It did not; the Prime Minister (Baldwin), according to his biographers, approved of the subsidy (Holmans, 1987). It remained in force until 1933 when it was replaced by a subsidy for rehousing people displaced by slum clearance. By the later 1930s local authority housing was a powerful going concern, which it remained for a further 50 years. It was the principal provider of new houses in the post-war decade and built on a large scale until the 1980s.

Rising real incomes and the development of long-term lending for house purchase generated a boom in owner-occupation in the 1920s and 1930s, which resumed in the 1950s and ran continuously until the beginning of the 1990s. Until the beginning of the 1970s, owner-occupation was a sector of housing that largely looked after itself as far as government was concerned; housing policy was primarily about local authority house building, subsidies and rents and about rent control in the private sector. Financial turbulence then led to governments (of both parties) taking a much more active role towards owner-occupation. There was a special short-term subsidy in 1973 and the £500 million loan (equivalent to £3 billion at 1997 money values) in 1974 to partially relieve an acute shortage of funds for mortgage lending. The government negotiated continually with building societies (then the dominant lenders for house purchase) to try to stabilize the supply of loans for house purchase. Owner-occupation appeared to have come within the active policy area along with both public and private renting. The cost of tax relief on mortgage interest grew until it was on a par with subsidies to local authority housing (Tables 14.16 and 14.19).

The end of the 1970s proved to be the second turning point. Cuts in total subsidy through a shift from general to means-tested subsidies (Table 14.16) and reductions in new building by local authorities were important in reducing public expenditure on housing. But more significant for the longer term was that the ease with which the government of the day could brush aside criticisms of the reduction in local authority house building showed that housing was no longer the make or break political issue that it had been thought to be from the end of World War II to the 1970s. This reduced political salience of housing was the key to the policy developments in the 1980s and 1990s. Without it, the government's refusal to countenance assessments of need for new house building could not have been sustained, nor would so limited a response to the mortgaged property repossession crisis as the 1991 'housing market package' have been tolerated.

There were three parts to the change of direction in housing policy. The first was the ending of new building for letting by local authorities, together with transfers by some authorities of their remaining rented stock (after the Right to Buy sales discussed above) to successor bodies that were organized as housing associations. The intention was to transfer other authorities' stocks to organizations which were formally private and so able to borrow to finance capital expenditure without it counting as public borrowing. New building for letting at sub-market rents was made a function of housing associations with mixed public and private funding. The second was the deregulation of private rented housing when newly let. The third was a sharp reduction of the rate at which mortgage interest tax relief was given, culminating in its abolition, and the curtailment of Income Support for mortgage interest (see above). There was a strong fiscal element in the first and the third. Financing capital expenditure on 'social' housing in ways that counted as private reduced public expenditure and borrowing. Reducing mortgage interest tax relief from the basic to a lower rate increased revenue from income tax without raising the 'headline' tax rate (the basic rate).

Transferring local authorities' housing stock to organizations that counted as private could be looked on either as getting round what had the appearance of arbitrary constraints on borrowing for investment in housing, or removing the ownership and management of housing from local authorities. The latter would probably have been the Conservative agenda if re-elected in 1997. If so, council housing would have been and gone within the twentieth century. Its substance of course, would still be there. With the announcment of the abolition of tax relief on mortgage interest, the end of the century sees owner-occupation fiscally on its own, as it was at the beginning of the century.

The great contrast would be in the very large amount spent on means-tested assistance with rents (Table 14.18), which had no counterpart at the beginning of the century. By the 1990s, this policy had become the principal governmental means of working towards the aim of 'a decent home for every family at a price within their means', as opposed to the state of affairs at the beginning of the century when large numbers of households shared multi-occupied houses because they could not afford a house or flat to themselves.

At the time of writing, means-tested assistance with rents was under heavy attack on grounds both of its cost and of alleged side-effects (impairing work incentives and providing inducements to cheat). Its cost was often criticized as part of 'welfare', which was supposedly becoming 'unaffordable'. If means-tested assistance with housing costs as it stood really was unaffordable, the implication would be that many more households would have to live in worse housing, probably having to share multi-occupied dwellings, instead of having a self-contained house or flat to themselves. That would be a retrogression towards the sharing and crowding with which the century began.

On a long time perspective one can ask why, as the twentieth century approached its end, 'a decent home for every family' might be deemed unaffordable when real GDP per head, and real personal disposable income per head, had both quadrupled since 1900. If the cause of poor housing was that good housing cost more in relation to income than many households could afford, why did not so large an increase in income solve the problem? This could be a question for prolonged, but probably inconclusive, debate; but it would be wrong to conclude a chapter on housing in the twentieth century without some suggestions at least:

(a) What would count as a solution to the problem of bad housing ('the housing question' in pre-1914 parlance) changed through time. At the beginning of the century, a self-contained house with piped water supply and an outside WC would suffice, provided the house was solidly built and in adequate repair. Over the years, the requirement changed very greatly to include a fixed bath or shower, a hot and cold water system and an inside lavatory and central heating or else individual heating with equivalent performance. This change could be seen as a consequence of rising income; but it offset part of what would otherwise have been the effect of rising income on the number of people not able to afford adequate housing.

(b) The number of households to be provided with self-contained housing rose much faster than the population (see Table 14.1). Real income per separate household rose by much less than did income per head of population. The quadrupling of real income per head of population is calculated from the whole population of all ages; per head of the adult population (who form households), the increase was rather less than triple. Per separate household, real income did not quadruple but only doubled.

(c) Even a doubling of real income per separate household is not to be despised. Its effect on ability to afford adequate housing was, however, partly nullified by the cost of housing (of a given standard) rising faster than the general level of prices. Rising income per household gave less of an increase in command over housing than over goods and services generally. The post-war years are covered in Table 14.15. Information about inter-war and pre-1914 rents discussed in Holmans (1987) indicates that a trend for the price of housing to rise faster than the general price level can be discerned far back into the nineteenth century and rents and house prices in the twentieth century continued this trend. The only clear exception was the inter-war period, which can be explained by improvements in rail and bus transport greatly increasing the supply of accessible land when there were only weak controls on building houses on it.

(d) Some of the public expenditure on housing can be seen, with hindsight, to have gone in ways that produced a poor return in improving conditions. That many of the worst housing areas are to be found in the local authority stock has been a severe disappointment. The reasons are complex and the parallels that can be seen in France and Germany (Emms (1990) and Power (1993)) tell against an explanation purely in terms of British misjudgements.

(e) Increased income inequality and higher unemployment in the 1980s and 1990s raised the number of working-age households with low earnings or no earnings at all, and hence in need of assistance with housing costs irrespective of what was happening to the general level of incomes. This increase in need for assistance, necessarily publicly funded, came at a time when resistance to public expenditure was strengthening and the scope for savings by better 'targeting' of assistance was substantially at an end.

Other reasons could, no doubt, be adduced; but the fact of numerous households not having a decent home at a price within their means at the end of the twentieth century is not in dispute.

Note on the geographical coverage of housing statistics

The United Kingdom is anything but united for most housing statistics. There have been separate population censuses in England and Wales and in Scotland since 1861, and the census in Ireland was separate from its inception. With separate census reports and tables on housing subjects for England and Wales and for Scotland, census-based time-series for Great Britain as a whole are very difficult to produce except for very straightforward topics. Up to 1961, 'national' tables were for England and Wales in total, with separate figures for Wales only as part of an analysis with figures for the English regions, or by adding figures for counties. From 1971 onwards, Wales has acquired a stronger statistical identity in census tabulations and in housing statistics more generally. Most of the powers over housing in Wales previously exercised by the Department of the Environment were transferred to the Welsh Office, which conducts its own housing surveys, sometimes in parallel with the Department of the Environment's surveys in England, but more often not. Housing in Scotland has always been the responsibility of the Scottish Office. The separate Scottish legal system has frequently made necessary separate legislation for housing in Scotland. The separate statistical identities for Scottish and more recently Welsh housing often leave no choice but to work with statistics for England and Wales or England, not Great Britain, and still less the United Kingdom. The separate government departments responsible for housing in England, Scotland, Wales and Northern Ireland produce their own figures for public expenditure on housing, which are often very difficult to add in any meaningful way.

Financial statistics relating to housing, especially house purchase loans, are different in that most are on a United Kingdom basis. The large building societies operating throughout the UK and the Bank of England collect banking and other financial statistics for the whole of the UK, which has one unified financial system. The national income accounts are also for the United Kingdom as a whole and are an important source for much of private expenditure and some categories of public expenditure.

Census-based time-series are shown for England and Wales or for England; to include Scotland and later Northern Ireland would add disproportionately to the length of the chapter, especially to the notes on sources and methods. The population of England even in 1901 was almost 80 per cent of the total for Great Britain and Northern Ireland; so a housing story told from figures for the whole could not be very different from one told from figures for England alone or England and Wales. Most time-series for housing surveys are for England.

References

Council for the Protection of Rural England (CPRE) (1995) *Circular Projections*, CPRE, London.

Cullingworth, J. B. (1965), *English Housing Trends*, Bell, London.

Department of the Environment (DoE) (various years) *Housing and Construction Statistics*, HMSO, London.

Department of the Environment (1977) *Housing Policy*, Technical Volume, HMSO, London.

Department of the Environment (1993a) *English House Condition Survey 1991*, HMSO, London.

Department of the Environment (1993b) *Housing in England Housing Trailers to the 1988 and 1991 Labour Force Surveys*, HMSO, London.

Department of the Environment (1995) *Projections of Households in England to 2016*, HMSO, London.

Department of the Environment, Transport and the Regions (DETR) (1998a) *English House Condition Survey 1996*, supplement issued, The Stationery Office, London.

Department of the Environment, Transport and the Regions (1998b) *Planning for Communities of the Future*, The Stationery Office, London.

Department of the Environment, Transport and the Regions (1998c) *Housing and Construction Statistics 1987–1997*, The Stationery Office, London.

Emms, P. F. (1990) *Social Housing – A European Dilemma*, School of Advanced Urban Studies, University of Bristol , Bristol.

Government Social Survey (1962) *The Housing Situation in 1960*, Central Office of Information, London.

Holmans, A. E. (1987) *Housing Policy in Britain: A History*, Croom Helm, London.

Holmans, A. E. (1990) *House Prices: Changes Through Time at National and Sub-National Level*, Government Economic Service Workshop Paper no. 110, Department of the Environment, London.

Holmans, A. E. (1995) *Housing Demand and Need in England 1991–2011*, Joseph Rowntree Foundation, York.

Office for National Statistics (ONS) (1999) *National Population Projections 1996-based*, The Stationery Office, London.

Office of Population Censuses and Surveys (OPCS) (1994) *Census Validation Survey Coverage Report*, HMSO, London.

Power, A. (1993) *Hovels to High Rise*, Routledge, London.

Riley, K. M. (1973) 'An estimate of the age distribution of the housing stock in Great Britain', *Urban Studies*, 10, pp.373–9.

Todd, J. E. and Griffiths, D. (1986) *Changing the Definition of a Household*, HMSO, London.

Town and Country Planning Association (1996) *The People: Where Will They Go?*, TCPA, London.

15
Social Services

Julia Parker and Josephine Webb

> It was with aspirations, with the enrichment of life, that the new welfare was concerned. Its institutions and services for education, health, housing, community development and assistance to the old, the children and the handicapped were ... highly valued and things to be proud of, unlike the Poor Law from which most of them had evolved.
>
> T. H. Marshall, 1981

In this chapter we trace the development of social services provided by public authorities for people whose families cannot supply the support or care they need and who are not able to make suitable arrangements privately. We deal separately with old people, with younger adults with physical or mental disabilities, and with children.

It is a complicated story. In so far as it rests on official statistics – the data most readily available – it is an incomplete and perhaps misleading account of changes in well-being over the last hundred years. The tale told by official statistics demonstrates the huge expansion of government activity since 1900, but its effects are hard to assess because statutory welfare services play only a small part in the lives of most individuals. Jobs, families, churches, community and kin networks and other institutions outside government are more important, but many have become less reliable during the twentieth century. So more public services may merely compensate for the weakening of other social relationships and other, perhaps more desirable, forms of care rather than add to the sum total of human welfare. On the other hand, they may represent a welcome alternative to enforced dependence on family support (Finch, 1995). Whatever the case, which will no doubt vary for different people, reliable judgements about the improvements brought by growing public provision would have to reflect measures of need in the population and of the satisfaction of people receiving services. There is very little information about either.

The concept and definition of need is notoriously elusive. Providers and receivers of services may have very different notions of requirements, which in any case change through time with increasing resources and rising expectations. The Victorian workhouse was a terrible symbol of degradation for those obliged to enter it, but for the Poor Law authorities it supplied paupers' essential needs. Present-day social services may have largely shaken off the deterrent image and stigma of the Poor Law but they remain preoccupied with economy and with rationing, and are not generally readily available except in times of crisis. Since 1948 the quality of residential accommodation has improved vastly but it may still be seen as threatening the independence and autonomy of frail old people, now increasingly claiming and accorded – in principle if not in practice – a right to live in their own homes with whatever domiciliary support is required. Similarly, institutions are no longer deemed suitable for children in public care, and tend to be the recourse for those too difficult for parents or foster parents to manage. Moreover, although local authority children's and old people's homes may have generally raised their standards, evidence of neglect and ill-treatment constantly recurs. And while changed conceptions of needs and entitlements may mean that support in the community in people's own homes or foster homes or some kind of sheltered accommodation has become the stated aim of government policy, the evidence available suggests that statutory domiciliary services are very deficient in both quantity and quality.

Nevertheless, the move from institutional to community care has been one of the most marked shifts in government policy during the twentieth century. In one sense it expresses the hope of enabling people to live as 'normal' and independent a life as possible rather than confining and segregating them in institutions. (A similar movement has developed in education over the last decades of the century in the transfer of children with learning difficulties or physical disabilities into 'mainstream' schools – see Chapter 5.) But it has also been driven by demographic change and the consequent anxiety about the high cost of residential accommodation for the rapidly increasing number of old people, as well as by greater understanding of the psychologically damaging effects of institutions. And it has been aided by advances in medicine that have made it possible to treat and control some forms of mental illness outside hospitals, thus appearing to offer a service both cheaper and more humane.

The shift to community care has also been a shift to family care. The government has been explicit that comprehensive public services for old people would be too costly (DHSS et al., 1981). But there is a dilemma here in that demographic and social changes have altered family roles and structure and reduced their ability to support either older or younger people. More old people live alone and a substantial number have no surviving children (Grundy, 1995), but public services have been slow to develop. Children themselves have attracted more public attention. 'Preventive work' with families received a boost in the 1940s and 1950s with the publication of psychological studies, notably by John Bowlby, emphasizing the importance of a secure family upbringing for the healthy physical and emotional development of young children (Bowlby, 1951). At the same time it was supposed that assisting parents to look after their own children would be a less expensive option than taking them into public care; a policy of 'support' rather than 'rescue' that was endorsed and elaborated in the Children Act of 1989 (Gibbons, 1992).

A further aspect of the development of welfare policy has been an increasing dependence on the market in that local authorities are encouraged to arrange to supply services through contracts with private and voluntary organizations, rather than provide them themselves. In one sense this is a curious reversal of the drive to expand state social services after World War II. On the other hand, it recognizes the many possible sources of support for vulnerable people and, in making local authorities responsible for determining 'need' and making plans to meet it, tries to overcome the failures in coordination and cooperation between different agencies that have bedevilled local social services since the 1940s.

In the following pages we examine the changes and developments that have occurred during the century. It will be clear that attempts to implement 'preventive work' and community care have been beset with difficulties. Responsibilities for complementary services have been split between different administrative bodies differently financed so that rational planning has been hampered. Geographical variations in definitions and measurement of need and in levels of public services persist. There are unavoidable problems in balancing the rights of parents against the needs of children for protection. And, most importantly, there is considerable danger that governments fail to grasp the magnitude of the cost that would be involved in fulfilling their stated aims. More in evidence at the end of the century is a preoccupation with reducing public spending, and a decline in collectivist values.

Old people

In 1900, old people – along with younger men, women and children who were destitute – were obliged to rely on the Poor Law or charity for support. Although under the Act of 1834 the famous principles of less eligibility and deterrence, operating through the workhouse test, had been designed to intimidate the able bodied and divert them from relief into employment, the severe and stigmatizing regime designed for people assumed to be voluntarily out of work pervaded the whole poor law system. Outdoor relief and the separate institutions for children and the sick and where the old might 'enjoy their indulgences without torment from the boisterous' (Webb and Webb, [1929]

1963, p.357, citing the Poor Law Report of 1834) were understandably slow to develop within a system designed to reduce the poor rates. Nevertheless, the regime was softened in many districts for the aged and infirm, as Macnicol has shown (Macnicol, 1998, Chapter 2). It was common practice in the middle of the century to give doles of one or two shillings a week, sometimes to supplement meagre earnings, to destitute old people who did not wish to enter the workhouse, though in the 1870s the Poor Law Inspectors were urging the local Guardians of the Poor to restrict relief to the institutions in order to induce families to support their older relatives. By the end of the century, however, policy had shifted to more lenient treatment of 'respectable' old people, and those who were both destitute and deserving were to be given adequate outdoor relief. The earlier period also witnessed sporadic attempts by the central department to improve conditions for old people within the workhouses as well as to liberalize outdoor relief. One very significant change, affecting old people as well as the sick, was the employment in some unions of qualified nurses in place of pauper attendants. But local practice remained very variable, and the advice appearing in Local Government Board circulars never became mandatory (Webb and Webb, 1963).

During the first half of the twentieth century an assortment of old age and unemployment insurance and assistance schemes developed outside the Poor Law, all brought together by Beveridge in his plan for social security in 1942 involving National Insurance to provide benefits as of right to cover the major predictable risks, and National Assistance dependent on a means test (the reformed Poor Law) to meet any remaining need. The move to establish old-age pensions outside the Poor Law was under way at the close of the nineteenth century and their growth over the last 100 years is detailed in Chapter 16.

Institutions

In 1900 there were 25 000 old people in the workhouses (Table 15.1). By the end of the century there were more than four times as many supported by local authorities in a variety of institutions, a further 137 000 financed by the Department of Social Security (DSS) and another 100 000 people paying for themselves (Table 15.2).[1] Also by the end of the century the character of the institutions had changed. The workhouses had gone – in name, at any rate. They were replaced by local authority 'residential accommodation' and by voluntary and private homes which, aided by public money, leapt from insignificance in the early years to help to meet the increasing demand for places and provided for three-quarters of all elderly residents in Great Britain by the 1990s (Table 15.3).

The steep rise in the number of the very elderly in institutions reflects the ageing of the population shown in Chapter 2, and particularly the increase in very old people who are more likely to be frail and dependent. At the same

Table 15.1 Elderly people supported in institutions[a] by the Poor Law, and by local authorities, 1900–95, England and Wales (000s)

	Poor Law institutions	Local authority homes	Voluntary and private homes	Total supported in institutions	Total supported in institutions per 1000 of the relevant age-group
England and Wales					
1900	25.0	–	0.2	25.2	28.4
1910	29.6	–	0.1	29.7	27.7
1920	20.6	–	0.1	20.7	15.9
1930	29.1	–	0.2	29.3	9.9
1938	25.0	–	1.4	26.4	b
1950	11.8	32.3	6.0	50.1	c
1960	–	64.5	9.4	73.9	13.5
1970	–	92.5	13.1	105.5	16.5
1980	–	109.9	16.4	126.3	17.0
1990	–	94.0	3.2	97.2	12.1
England only					
1990	–	87.7	3.2	90.8	12.0
1995	–	53.8	47.1	100.9	13.1

Notes: [a]Institutions include Poor Law mixed workhouses, voluntary homes for the handicapped and local authority welfare residential accommodation, but exclude Poor Law infirmaries and sick wards and institutions managed by hospital boards.
[b]Unavailable since no census around that time.
[c]Unavailable since in 1950 some younger handicapped people are included.
  Elderly people are defined as over 70 up to and including 1920; subsequently as over 65. Figures do not include people supported by local authorities in independent nursing homes, since information on these is unavailable until 1994. In 1995 they numbered 38 797 (in England), equivalent to 5 in 1000 of the population over 65. The increasing number of people supported by the Department of Social Security in the independent sector after 1980 are not included. They had reached 233 000 by 1993 (see Table 15.2) but funding was then transferred to the local authorities.

Sources: Halsey (1988), Table 12.4; *Health and Personal Social Services Statistics for England*, selected years; *Health and Personal Social Services Statistics for Wales*, selected years; Department of Health (1997) *Residential Accommodation: Detailed Statistics on Residential Care Homes and Local Authority-supported Residents*; Population figures come from CSO, *Statistical Abstract for the UK*, 1934; CSO, *Annual Abstract of Statistics*, 1962; and *Population Trends*, selected issues.

time the stigma of the Poor Law which deterred entry to the workhouse at the beginning of the century had faded by its close.

  The temporary drop in the number of old people in the workhouses after 1910 probably reflects the greater possibility of living independently after the introduction of state old-age pensions. In addition, conditions of full employment as existed during and immediately after World War I may well have made it easier for old people to find work and avoid poor relief (Macnicol, 1998, p.167). But the substantial change came after World War II when the

Table 15.2 Sources of finance for elderly and physically disabled residents in independent homes, 1986–95, Great Britain (000s)

	Private payers[a]	Income Support[b]	Local authority	NHS	Total
Feb 86	90	76	6	2	174
Nov 88	103	128	6	2	239
May 90	116	157	6	2	281
May 91	104	196	8	2	310
May 92	100	225	10	4	339
Feb 93	111	233	11	6	361
Feb 94	102	187	66	9	364
May 95	103	137	120	13	373

Notes: [a]Excludes third-party top-ups.
[b]Fees wholly or partly paid by the social security system. From 1993 this includes those with Preserved Rights.
    Figures are not comparable with Table 15.1 as they include disabled residents, refer to different geographical areas, different months and rely on different sources of information.

Source: Laing and Buisson, *Care of Elderly People: Market Survey*, 1995 and 1996.

Table 15.3 People aged 65 and over in residential accommodation for the elderly and/or younger physically disabled, 1970–95, England (000s)[a]

	Local authority	Voluntary	Private	Total
1970	86.9	23.3	18.1	128.2
1975	95.1	22.5	18.8	136.3
1980	102.9	25.4	28.9	157.2
1985	101.5	25.8	66.1	193.5
1990	89.3	26.6	119.9	235.9
1995	54.5	36.6	140.4	231.5

Notes: [a]Care homes registered as residential homes under the Registered Homes Act 1984 (including those dually registered as care homes and nursing homes) and establishments which are residential care homes within the meaning of the Act but exempt from registration.
    Figure for local authority homes includes homes jointly used by local authorities and hospitals, but owned by hospitals. From 1980, short-stay homes are included. From 1989, figures include residents whose age is not known in homes for elderly people. Figures for voluntary and private homes do not include those aged 65 or over in homes for people with mental illness or learning disabilities.

Sources: *Health and Personal Social Services Statistics for England*, 1977, Tables 7.1, 7.2 and 7.3; *Health and Personal Social Services Statistics for England*, 1985, Tables 7.1 and 7.2; *Health and Personal Social Services Statistics for England*, 1996, Table 5.49.

National Assistance Act of 1948 signalled the demise of the Poor Law and gave local authorities the duty of supplying residential accommodation for those in need of 'care or attention' not otherwise available to them. Residents able to do so would contribute to the cost and those without resources would be supported by the National Assistance Board, the body taking over the Poor Law responsibility for outdoor cash relief (Parker, 1965).

The duty to provide residential accommodation in response to 'need' rather than destitution was a departure from Poor Law principles, but in other ways the Poor Law traditions lingered in services for old people. In particular, the concern to foster family life evident in the Children Act of the same year was missing from the National Assistance Act, which made no attempt to provide any kind of substitute family care for elderly people without relatives to support them. The emphasis was firmly on institutions; local authorities were required to provide residential accommodation but only empowered to arrange domiciliary services or contribute to the funds of voluntary bodies developing welfare schemes or organizing meals or recreation for old or disabled people. The prominence accorded institutions and the neglect of domiciliary support was a pattern that persisted through the rest of the century, notwithstanding growing criticism, until the eventual shift in public policy to 'community care' in the National Health Service (NHS) and Community Care Act of 1990.

Nevertheless, although institutions were of first importance in 1948, the old workhouses were to be replaced by smaller homes for 30–35 residents, and local authorities were directed to have regard to the welfare of the people they were providing for. The emphasis on welfare and the development of more attractive homes may explain the sharp rise in the number of old people in institutions between 1938 and 1950 which continued more slowly in later years. As Titmuss has pointed out, war brought new demands for accommodation for old people. Elderly patients were discharged from hospitals to make room for expected war casualties; home care was less reliable as families were disrupted by war; air raids and bombing drove some old people into public shelters and others, who were evacuated but too frail to find billets in private households, into public assistance institutions or voluntary hostels. Overall, more elderly people from middle-class backgrounds were needing public services and demanding higher standards of care (Titmuss, 1950, pp.447–8; Means and Smith, 1983).

The number of smaller establishments increased from 63 to 699 during the five years after 1948 (Parker, 1965, p.109), and by 1960 housed 15 000 people, but the old workhouses remained the mainstay of local authority services for the handicapped and aged (Townsend, 1962, p.63). In later years the smaller and also the very large homes declined and most old people were to be found in medium-sized institutions for 35–70 residents.

Overall the number of elderly people supported in institutions by the local authorities more than doubled between 1950 and 1980. During the following decade Table 15.1 suggests a sharp fall, especially dramatic for residents in the voluntary and private sectors. But the figures are misleading as they exclude the rapidly growing number of people funded by the DSS[2] (Knapp et al., 1992; Joseph Rowntree Foundation, 1996). In fact, the total population of elderly people in residential care in Britain rose by nearly a half between 1980 and 1995. But while the number of people in local authority establishments fell by nearly half, residents in private and voluntary homes multiplied by three (Table 15.3).

After 1993 financial support for elderly people in private and voluntary accommodation was again channelled through the local authorities. By 1995 only a third of residents were supported by the DSS compared with two-thirds two years earlier, while local authorities' responsibilities increased tenfold. Meanwhile, the proportion of residents who were self-funding had fallen sharply, though the actual numbers remained fairly constant at just over 100000 (Table 15.2). The steep rise in the number of people in voluntary and private homes during the 1990s, while those in local authority accommodation were dwindling, reflects the growing importance of the market as the local authorities took on the job of purchasing rather than providing care (Audit Commission, 1997).

Meanwhile the reduction in long stay hospital beds has added to the number of people seeking places in local authority and private residential and nursing homes. This has underlined an anomaly in that while hospital beds are free of charge, patients in private nursing homes, in local authority accommodation, or receiving care in their own homes, generally have to pay. Disquiet over the financing of residential domiciliary care outside the NHS led to a Royal Commission, which recommended that 'pastoral care' and nursing be free to people needing it wherever it is provided and that it be funded from taxation (Sutherland, 1999). This proposal has been received by the government with muted enthusiasm.

At the end of the century, then, there were some 100000 elderly people supported in residential homes by local authorities and rather more financed by the DSS – representing an eightfold increase in numbers since 1900, but a similar proportion of the age-group. To that extent the chances of ending up in an institution, dependent on public funds, have barely changed. However, there were also more than 100000 residents in homes – mainly in the private sector – who were paying privately. So, in all, more than 350000 people were in long-term care. This represented a dramatic increase of over 100 per cent in the number of people over 65 in institutions, if hospitals and nursing homes are included, through the last two decades of the century alone (Table 15.2).

Community care

The major developments in statutory services for old people outside institutions – other than doles of poor relief – have come since World War II. The home help service, home nursing, health visiting and social work have all become established responsibilities of the public authorities; to begin with, scattered among the health and welfare departments and committees of local councils. Since the 1970s, nurses and health visitors have moved from local government to the health authorities, and the provision of 'temporary accommodation' for homeless people is now the job of local housing departments. More importantly, as we have noted, over the last two decades of the century and following the NHS and Community Care Act (1990), local councils have been encouraged and required to become 'purchasing' rather than 'providing' bodies, making arrangements with voluntary and private agencies to supply services. The new policies are supposed to cut costs, and to offer more choice to people needing help as independent organizations compete to provide it.

The growth of the various domiciliary services is clear enough. Table 15.4 shows the expansion of the home help service in the second half of the century, the number of people served increasing hugely and also representing a substantially larger proportion of the population. By 1980 almost 90 per cent of cases were people over 65 compared with two-thirds in the early 1950s (Dexter and Harbert, 1983, Appendix 1). So over time the focus of the service has changed, and also its nature. Originally mainly a matter of domestic assistance, home help has become more widely defined as 'home care' to accommodate the needs of the growing numbers of dependent old people who make up the majority of recipients.

Table 15.4 The home help service, 1950–95, England and Wales

		Number of home helps (000s)[a]		Total cases during year (000s)	Total cases as % of population
		actual	full-time equivalents		
England and Wales	1950	23.4	n/a	162.0	0.37
	1960	49.3	n/a	312.0	0.68
	1970	n/a	33.0	469.5	0.96
	1980	97.1	49.5	787.9	1.59
	1990	n/a	59.7	n/a	n/a
England only	1990	n/a	55.8	n/a	n/a
	1995	n/a	49.8	n/a	n/a

Note: [a]Excluding organizers of home helps.

Sources: Ministry of Health, *Annual Reports*, selected years; *Health and Personal Social Services Statistics for England*, selected years; *Health and Personal Social Services Statistics for Wales*, selected years.

Health visitors, too, have intermittently paid more attention to older people. The main focus of their work is still maternity and child welfare, but the number of children visited has fallen since the 1960s as births have fallen, while the number of older people visited rose rapidly through the 1960s and 1970s, though it then dropped back again (Table 15.5). A similar story can be told about domiciliary nursing, an important service for enabling people to stay in their own homes. There was a steady expansion over the post-war years, but a threefold increase in the number of elderly patients treated over the 1970s; since then provision appears to have stabilized (Department of Health, selected years; Welsh Office, selected years).

Table 15.5 Health visitors' cases by age and type, 1975–97/98, England (000s)

	Children born that year	Other children under 5	Persons aged over 5 and under 65	Persons aged 65 and over	Total cases attended
1975	618	1760	995	503	3877
1980	679	1651	1007	481	3817
1985	659	1672	1284	466	4080
1989/90	983	1332	1478	266	4058
1994/95	965	1287	1315	143	3711
1997/98[a]	n/a	n/a	n/a	n/a	3622

Notes: [a]Provisional figure.
 Figures refer to calendar years up to 1986, and financial years thereafter.

Sources: *Health and Personal Social Services Statistics for England*, 1987, Table 6.1; *Health and Personal Social Services Statistics for England*, 1993, Table 5.30; *Health and Personal Social Services Statistics for England*, 1996, Table 5.26; *Health and Personal Social Services Statistics for England*, 1998, Table B6.

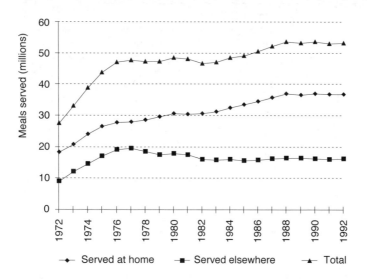

Figure 15.1 Meals services in Great Britain, 1972–92

Sources: *Health and Personal Social Services Statistics for England*, selected years; *Health and Personal Social Services Statistics for Wales*, selected years; *Scottish Abstract of Statistics*, selected years.

The meals service is an oddity in that in the early years it was entirely in the hands of the voluntary bodies – mainly the Women's Royal Voluntary Service and the Red Cross – and local authorities were not permitted to arrange services themselves until the early 1960s (Parker, 1965, p.127). The service grew during the 1970s but then, rather surprisingly, levelled off and, after a gentle rise to the end of the 1980s, levelled off again in the following decade (Figure 15.1). There is some evidence that direct provision is falling in the 1990s as the local authorities expand their links with private organizations (Table 15.6).

Table 15.6 Meals served in a survey week, 1992–97, England[a]

	No. of people receiving meals (000s)	No. of meals served (000s)	Meals served by type of provision (%)			
			Direct	Voluntary	Private	NHS
1992	275.7	776.7	60	35	4	1
1993	286.9	768.4	60	34	5	1
1994	300.4	794.1	56	36	8	1
1995	266.6	818.4	54	35	10	1
1996	251.8	771.0	56	35	9	0
1997	247.3	756.3	55	32	13	0

Note: [a]New statistical series. Survey week is during September/October.

Source: Department of Health, *Statistical Bulletin: Community Care Statistics* 1997.

The development of day centres is another indication of the move to provide more substantial support in the community and to defer or avoid the need for full institutional care. Local authorities nearly trebled the number of places they provided in the 20 years before 1990 (Figure 15.2). But thereafter, while they slowly increased their own provision – for old people and others with disabilities – the rapid growth came through arrangements with voluntary and especially private agencies (Table 15.7).

The significance of social work for elderly men and women is difficult to untangle. The increase in social work activity is obvious enough (Table 15.8). But as the profession has developed, hospital social work, work with offenders, with children and families and with the mentally ill have proved the most popular activities, and the ones for which professional training was established earliest; old people have been relatively neglected. Thus, while the new children's departments were able to recruit a scattering of newly qualified child care officers after 1948 (Packman, 1975, pp.9–12), the health and welfare departments relied largely on officers inherited from the Poor Law and untrained welfare assistants for work with old and disabled people (Parker, 1965, pp.111–13). In 1971, following the Seebohm Report and the subsequent

Table 15.7 Places at day centres purchased or provided by local authorities during a survey week, by client group and by type of provision, England (000s)

	1992	1993	1994	1995	1996	1997
Physically disabled	53.1	51.9	53.5	61.0	59.1	63.5
Learning disabilities	236.2	259.2	268.8	284.3	280.6	278.4
Mental illness	39.8	45.3	50.5	53.0	54.5	60.9
Over 65, all client groups	139.0	147.6	176.4	192.6	207.5	221.7
Other/unknown	41.1	20.9	20.1	11.1	7.6	7.4
Local authority	458.9	465.7	487.1	496.5	482.2	490.2
Voluntary	49.0	57.5	78.3	97.4	106.9	128.7
Private	1.4	1.8	3.8	8.2	20.1	13.0
Total	509.3	524.9	569.3	602.0	609.3	631.9

Sources: Department of Health, *Statistical Bulletin: Personal Social Services: Day and Domiciliary Services for Adults in England 1992*; Department of Health, *Community Care: Detailed Statistics on Local Authority Personal Social Services for Adults in England 1995*; Department of Health, *Statistical Bulletin: Community Care Statistics 1997*.

Table 15.8 Staff in local authority social services departments, 1973–97,[a] England and Wales, whole time equivalents

	1973
Management and supervisory, and senior social workers	3495
Social workers (including senior social workers and team leaders)	11137
Community workers	n/a
Trainee social workers	1535
Social work (welfare) assistants	1779
Total social work, headquarters and area office	17946
Other headquarters and area office staff	14376
Adult training centres	4968
Day centres for mentally ill, elderly and physically handicapped people	2623
Day nurseries and part-time nursery groups	7590
Home help service	42412
Residential accommodation for elderly, younger physically handicapped, etc.	45646
Homes and hostels for mentally ill people and people with learning disabilities	3156
Community homes for children and young persons in care	18827
All other staff	2125
Total staff	159670
Total staff, England only	151163

Notes: [a]Main series was discontinued in 1992 and replaced by a different one.
[b]Rounded figure.

Local Authority Social Services Act of 1970, most of the social work functions of local government were brought together to be administered through a single social services department with a chief officer responsible to a social services committee. The new arrangements were an attempt to improve planning and develop more effective coordination among a hitherto fragmented and diverse collection of activities. Social workers would work together more readily, it was supposed, if they belonged to the same department and were responsible to the same chief officer; and would be better able to tackle the problems of the people with whom they were confronted in relation to their family circumstances rather than being restricted by too narrow a definition of their professional duties. By this time the idea of the 'generic' social worker who would deal with a range of problems rather than specialize in work with children or the mentally ill, for example, had become fashionable and, reflected in new generic training arrangements, was seen by many as the way to improve the quality of what were coming to be termed the 'personal' social services.

All this might have meant that more qualified professionals would be in touch with elderly people, but this does not seem to have happened. The generally poor standards of services for the old and the disabled and the use of

1980	1985	1990	1992	1995	1997
3908	5251	7184	8654	n/a	n/a
19453	21717	25792	28089	n/a	n/a
607	1006	1975	2475	n/a	n/a
863	347	223	179	n/a	n/a
3301	3127	3332	3268	n/a	n/a
28132	31448	38505	42665	n/a	n/a
20209	20257	24425	25916	n/a	n/a
7370	9331	12496	13368	n/a	n/a
5499	7341	8504	8861	n/a	n/a
8565	9465	8976	7812	n/a	n/a
51854	58391	63852	62392	n/a	n/a
55936	61360	62814	53843	n/a	n/a
7198	10098	14267	16118	n/a	n/a
23199	17870	14471	12470	n/a	n/a
2881	4257	6229	6908	n/a	n/a
210841	299819	254540	250353	n/a	n/a
199529	217013	240342	235240	233862	229000[b]

Sources: *Health and Personal Social Services Statistics for England*, selected years; *Health and Personal Social Services Statistics for Wales*, selected years.

untrained volunteers who had only rather tenuous connections with statutory workers were evident in successive research studies and official reports through the 1970s and 1980s (Holme and Maizels, 1978, p.66; Audit Commission, 1985; 1986). However, the increasing emphasis on 'community care' as the more humane and cheaper way of supporting a larger elderly population as well as other vulnerable people has continued to stimulate further enquiries to determine how far it exists and how it might best develop (for example, Knapp et al., 1992; Lewis and Glennerster, 1996).

The way forward, outlined in the Griffiths Report in 1988, was to make local authorities responsible for discovering 'need' among their populations, for making plans for meeting it, and for monitoring the arrangements provided to see that they remained appropriate. The need for services was to be determined in consultation with the persons receiving them, their carers and their families. It was hoped that the local authorities would develop new and flexible forms of help in response to people's wishes rather than merely supply whatever happened to be already available. 'Care plans' were to be devised by 'care managers' and, as we have noted, local authorities were instructed to rely mainly on non-governmental agencies to provide whatever was deemed necessary. However, developing 'packages of care' seems to have been a slow and doubtfully satisfactory business (Audit Commission, 1997). One enquiry found little information about 'packages' available, but there were indications that the care provided by the public authorities was insufficient and there was little knowledge about how far people bought services privately (Joseph Rowntree Foundation, 1996, p.10).

Thus, by the end of the century 'quasi-markets' had been introduced into the social services as into other areas of social policy, with the public authorities responsible for identifying need and making plans to meet it, but buying in what they required from private and voluntary organizations (Le Grand and Bartlett, 1993). How far these arrangements will mean more opportunities for people using services to choose what they prefer, will lead to more flexibility and variety in the supply, and will prove cheaper and more efficient, remains to be seen, and must depend on the willingness and ability of the public authorities to pay for them. In the late 1990s there was mounting evidence that the local authorities were increasingly short of money, rationing their services and shifting the costs to consumers by charging for what they provided (Baldwin and Lunt, 1996; Phelps, 1997).

International developments

Britain is not alone in facing an ageing population. Between 1950 and 2050 most Organization for Economic Co-operation and Development (OECD) countries will find the proportion of elderly people of 65 and over in their populations doubling from 10 to more than 20 per cent, with a steeper rise in those over 75, who are likely to be the more dependent (OECD, 1994, Chapter 4). At the same time the ratio of those of working age to older people is shrinking, and more younger women are moving into paid employment. Moreover, family forms and living arrangements are changing in all the rich countries; there are more consensual unions, more divorces and more single-parent households. It is likely that in future more people will survive into old age without a partner and, under a regime of low fertility, more will be child-less and those with children may be geographically separated. So family care is likely to become less secure, and the aim of the governments of many devel-oped countries to increase it for the very old can only be a partial solution (United Nations, 1994, pp.5–6). The questions that all countries face are of how public services can best complement what families provide, and of how they can be planned to supply what people actually want (Sundstrom, 1994).

A report from the European Community (EC) claims that most member states appear to have been taken by surprise by the increase in their elderly populations. There is a huge gap between the demand and supply of care for elderly dependent people. Domiciliary services and long- and short-stay resi-dential homes are all deficient in both quantity and quality. Social policies for older people pay little attention to the family and, with the possible exception of Denmark (and more recently the UK), take little account of informal carers (Jani-Le Bris, 1993, p.119).

While community services are thin on the ground, the complexities involved in developing them are becoming increasingly evident in many OECD countries. Services tend to be inflexible, cooperation and coordination between the many agencies providing them poor, they frequently fail to reach people in greatest need, and they vary between different regions. As in the UK, a number of countries are experimenting with 'case management' schemes in the search for more effective and efficient arrangements (Davies, 1994).

Richard Hugman has produced an excellent analysis of the similarities and differences in the responses of European countries to their ageing populations, and he emphasizes a particular dimension of the discussion by insisting that future policies should not confine themselves to treating older people as dependants. The social contribution many make should also be recognized and supported and their 'social citizenship', the interests, needs and responsi-bilities shared with younger people, acknowledged (Hugman, 1994, pp.170–3).

Younger adults[3]

Services for younger people needing residential care or domiciliary support have followed a similar pattern to those for the elderly. Table 15.9 shows how the number of people of all ages registered as disabled has risen year by year.

Table 15.9 Persons registered as substantially and permanently handicapped, 1950–97, England and Wales (000s)

		General classes[a]	Blind	Partially sighted	Deaf	Hard of hearing
England and Wales	1950	n/a	81.3	n/a	n/a	n/a
	1955	47.4	94.7	18.1	16.4	10.3
	1960	93.4	97.5	24.2	21.3	14.2
	1970	251.1	103.1	37.4	25.6	17.7
	1980	961.6	115.1	55.3	31.5	36.2
England only	1980	900.7	107.8	51.4	29.7	35.1
	1982[b]	n/a	111.7	58.0	n/a	n/a
	1983	n/a	n/a	n/a	31.8	47.2
	1984	1107.7	n/a	n/a	n/a	n/a
	1985	n/a	n/a	n/a	n/a	n/a
	1986	n/a	120.6	71.1	34.1	63.4
	1987	1230.6	n/a	n/a	n/a	n/a
	1988	n/a	126.8	79.0	n/a	n/a
	1989	n/a	n/a	n/a	37.9	70.3
	1990	1265.6	n/a	n/a	n/a	n/a
	1991	n/a	136.2	93.8	n/a	n/a
	1992	n/a	n/a	n/a	44.0	99.3
	1993	1336.9	n/a	n/a	n/a	n/a
	1994	n/a	149.7	115.7	n/a	n/a
	1995	n/a	n/a	n/a	45.5	125.9
	1996	n/a	n/a	n/a	n/a	n/a
	1997	n/a	158.6	138.2	n/a	n/a

Notes: [a]General classes include the very severely handicapped, the severely or appreciably handicapped, other classified persons and the unclassified.
[b]From 1981, returns from each register were required every three years, a different register each year.

Sources: Ministry of Health, *Annual Reports*, 1951, 1955 and 1960; *Health and Personal Social Services Statistics for England*, selected years; *Health and Personal Social Services Statistics for Wales*, selected years; Department of Health, *Registered Blind and Partially Sighted People, Year ending March 1997*.

Institutions

Poor law statistics for the earlier part of the century do not distinguish younger disabled people, but later years show a steady fall in the number supported by the local authorities in institutions (Table 15.10). The local authorities, the main providers in the 1960s, have reduced their residents by two-thirds over the last 40 years so that by the end of the century most people with disabilities supported by local authorities in residential homes were in private or voluntary establishments. And while local authorities have increased their own accommodation for the mentally ill and people with learning disabilities, it is again the non-governmental sector that has grown most rapidly and which now dominates the market with roughly three-quarters of all places (Tables 15.11 and 15.12).

Table 15.10 Persons under 65 with physical or mental disabilities[a] in residential accommodation provided by or on behalf of local authorities, 1970–95, England

		Type of accommodation		
	Local authority[b]	Voluntary	Private & other	Total
1970	6023	4509		10532
1975	5840	4414		10254
1980[c]	4962	4074	285	9321
1985	4338	3547	208	8093
1990	3406	2784	356	6546
1995	2100	2400	2690	7200

Notes: [a]Includes the blind, deaf, epileptic, physically handicapped, mentally ill, people with learning disabilities and others.
[b]Includes homes jointly used by local authorities and hospitals.
[c]From 1980 short stay homes are included.

Sources: *Health and Personal Social Services Statistics for England*, 1978, Table 7.1; *Health and Personal Social Services Statistics for England*, 1991, Table 7.1; *Health and Personal Social Services Statistics for England*, 1993, Table 5.53; *Health and Personal Social Services Statistics for England*, 1996, Table 5.47

Table 15.11 Places in homes for mentally ill people, 1975–95, England

	Local authority	Voluntary	Private	Total
1975	2545		1366	3911
1980	3724		2142	5866
1985	4363	1952	1219	7534
1990	4349	2660	4697	11706
1995	3700	4600	6500	14800

Sources: *Health and Personal Social Services Statistics for England*, 1986, Table 7.3; *Health and Personal Social Services Statistics for England*, 1991, Table 7.3; *Health and Personal Social Services Statistics for England*, 1993, Table 5.56; *Health and Personal Social Services Statistics for England*, 1996, Table 5.50.

Table 15.12 Places in homes for people with learning disabilities, 1975–95, England

	Local authority	Voluntary	Private	Total
1975	7463		2885	10348
1980	12062		3746	15808
1985	15045	3991	3105	22141
1990	16886	7894	8382	33162
1995	13600	14300	12900	40800

Sources: *Health and Personal Social Services Statistics for England*, 1986, Table 7.3; *Health and Personal Social Services Statistics for England*, 1991, Table 7.3; *Health and Personal Social Services Statistics for England*, 1993, Table 5.56; *Health and Personal Social Services Statistics for England*, 1996, Table 5.50.

Community care

It is not possible to say very much about trends in community services for different groups of people as the statistics rarely distinguish the recipients. There has been a slight fall in places in centres for the physically disabled since 1975 (Figure 15.2), yet at the same time places have doubled for 'mixed client groups'. Establishments described as 'adult training centres' and 'special care centres' for people with learning disabilities have also increased rapidly. Some indication of earlier developments in community care for people with learning disabilities may be seen in the doubling of the numbers under local authority supervision between 1930 and 1970, and the great post-war expansion of numbers attending centres (Table 15.13).

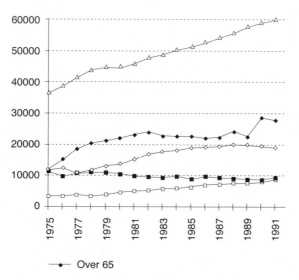

—♦— Over 65

—■— People under 65 with physical disabilities

—△— People with learning disabilities

—□— Adults with mental illness

—◇— Mixed client groups

Figure 15.2 Places in local authority day centres for various client groups, 1975–91, England and Wales

Sources: *Health and Personal Social Services Statistics for England,* selected years; *Health and Personal Social Services Statistics for Wales,* selected years.

The most dramatic increase in community services has been for the mentally ill and came after the 1959 Mental Health Act. In ten years the number under local authority supervision more than doubled and people attending day centres multiplied tenfold (Table 15.14); places in the centres nearly trebled again by 1990. There were three times as many social workers in day centres for the mentally ill and others by the end of the century (Table 15.8) and home help for all types of cases had increased substantially (Table 15.4).

Table 15.13 Local authority adult training centres and special care centres for people with learning disabilities, 1930–90, England and Wales[a]

	Cases under local authority supervision (000s)	Numbers attending occupation centres,[b] all ages (000s)	Local authority adult training centres[c]	
			Premises	Places (000s)
1930	46.7	n/a	10	n/a
1939	69.5	4244	69	n/a
1950	70.4	5340	n/a	n/a
1960	83.6	22041[d]	n/a	n/a
1970	104.1	48206	311	22.9
1975	n/a	n/a	415	36.3
1980	n/a	n/a	484	45.0
1985	n/a	n/a	541	52.0
1990	n/a	n/a	691	59.4

Notes: [a]For England, this series was discontinued after 1992.
[b]Includes both centres run by local authorities and those run by voluntary organizations.
[c]Training centres catering for both juniors and adults are excluded.
[d]1961 figure.

Sources: Board of Control, *Annual Reports*, 1930 and 1939; Ministry of Health, *Annual Reports*, 1950 and 1960; Department of Health and Social Security, *Digest of Health Statistics for England and Wales*, 1970; *Health and Personal Social Services Statistics for England*, selected years; *Health and Personal Social Services Statistics for Wales*, selected years.

Table 15.14 Local authority services for the adult mentally ill,[a] 1961–90, England and Wales[b]

	Number under local authority supervision (000s)	Local authority day centres	
		Number attending	Places
1961	40.0	354	n/a
1970	100.5	3644	2736
1975	n/a	n/a	3673
1980	n/a	n/a	5339
1985	n/a	n/a	6250
1990	n/a	n/a	7811

Notes: [a]Mentally ill and psychopathic aged over 16.
[b]For England, this series was discontinued after 1992.

Sources: Department of Health and Social Security, *Digest of Health Statistics for England and Wales*, 1970; *Health and Personal Social Services Statistics for England*, selected years; *Health and Personal Social Services Statistics for Wales*, selected years.

Nevertheless, concern was growing about mentally ill people in the community without effective support who were a danger to themselves or others. The reduction in hospital beds after the 1960s meant that vulnerable people were discharged and others never entered but were left without adequate alternative supervision. Eventually, in 1998, the Minister of Health made a statement in the Commons admitting that care in the community had failed, particularly for people with severe personality disorders, and that urgent changes were necessary to protect the safety of patients and the public. He promised an extra £700 million for the mental health services over three years for, amongst other things, more assertive 'outreach teams' and more day and respite care (*Independent*, 9 December 1998).

Services for the blind were fairly well established by the 1930s, and the number of blind people registered with the local authorities has since trebled to nearly 160 000 (Parker and Mirrlees, 1988, Table 12.15). Local registers, though notoriously incomplete, give some indication of the need for services, and people able to work could also register at the employment exchanges. The number of blind persons in workshops, occupied in home working schemes, or in outside employment has fallen slightly over the years, perhaps a result of the diminishing number of younger blind people. Home teachers have increased with the overall increase in blind persons registered, though after 1970 the statistics do not distinguish them from other workers in the local social services departments. The growth in the number of partially sighted people and of the deaf and hard of hearing on local registers may be seen from Table 15.9, but we have no statistics that distinguish the services they may have received.

Children

At the beginning of the century, there were over 57 000 children supported by the Poor Law, mainly in institutions and nearly half in the workhouses (Table 15.15). By 1938 the number of children maintained by the Poor Law authorities (now local government councils after the disbanding of the Boards of Guardians in 1929) had dropped by more than a third. The great majority were by this time in a variety of special children's homes, some in the voluntary sector, while 17 per cent were boarded out with foster parents. During the years before World War II the number of children fostered fluctuated, though it came to represent a rather higher proportion of all Poor Law children.

After the war, following the recommendations of the Curtis Committee (1946) which had been asked to consider how best to provide for children 'deprived of a normal home life with their own parents or relatives', the Children Act of 1948 established a new administrative framework for the child care service. Statutory children's departments were set up, headed by a

Table 15.15 Children^a under the Poor Law by type of accommodation, 1900–38, England and Wales (000s)

	1900^b	1910	1920	1930	1938
Poor Law establishments:					
Workhouses	23.5	15.8	6.0	4.7	2.3
Grouped cottage homes	}	11.6	11.7	9.5	8.6
Scattered homes	} 19.4	7.4	7.6	7.4	6.3
Other schools and children's homes	}	13.6	11.2	10.3	5.3
Other institutions:					
Voluntary homes for the sick and handicapped	0.2	1.3	2.2	1.5	1.1
Homes and hospitals for the mentally or physically handicapped	} 7.0	3.1	7.4	1.3	0.0
Training and industrial schools and other homes	}	9.1	7.5	6.8	5.2
Total in institutions:	50.1	62.0	53.6	41.4	28.7
Boarded out	7.4	8.8	9.4	8.2	6.0
Total supported by Poor Law	57.5	70.8	63.0	49.6	34.7
Children boarded out as % of all children supported by Poor Law	12.8	12.4	14.9	16.5	17.4

Notes: ^aChildren under 16.
^bIncluding children in Poor Law infirmaries and sick wards who were excluded in subsequent years. Numbers of those in voluntary homes for sick and handicapped have been retained because the sick and handicapped are not separated in the published Poor Law figures and it was considered that the majority in these establishments would have been handicapped rather than acutely sick. The latter we have excluded where possible.

Sources: Local Government Board, *Pauperism (England and Wales)*, 1900 and 1910; Ministry of Health, *Persons in Receipt of Poor-Law Relief (England and Wales)*, annually 1920, 1930 and 1938; Home Office, *Fifth Report on the Work of the Children's Branch, 1938*; Home Office, *Sixth Report on the Work of the Children's Branch, 1951*.

children's officer who was to be highly trained and carefully chosen to breathe 'warmth, love and skill' into the new arrangements (Packman, 1975, p.10). Under the Children Act local authorities had a duty to receive into care deprived children, those suffering cruelty or neglect, those deemed to be in moral danger and also those found guilty of an offence who might be committed to the care of the local authority by the juvenile courts (Heywood, 1978, p.151).

Public responsibilities under the Children Act were more generously defined than in earlier legislation, with the shades of 'less eligibility' lingering from the Poor Law finally officially rejected. Local authorities were required to further the best interests of children in their care and afford them opportunities to develop their character and abilities. Heywood contrasts this requirement, 'perhaps unmatched for its humanity in all our legislation', with the duty under the Poor Law that survived until 1948 to 'set to work or put out as apprentices' children whose parents were not able to keep them (Heywood, 1978, p.158). Under the Children Act local authorities were instructed to discharge their duties wherever possible by placing children with foster parents (Packman, 1975, pp.13–18), and during the following years the number of children fostered climbed to reach 37 000 in the 1990s, 65 per cent of those in care (Table 15.16). In fact, the proportion of children in care who were fostered had taken a downward turn after 1960, perhaps as skilled workers became more aware of the complex and delicate negotiations involved in successful fostering. But it had increased sharply again by the 1990s – no doubt in response to the drive to reduce public spending and Mrs Thatcher's 'rediscovery of family values' (Table 15.16).

Table 15.16 Children[a] in local authority care by type of accommodation, 1952–98, England and Wales (000s)

	England and Wales				England only			
	1952[b]	1960	1970	1980	1980	1990	1995	1998[c]
Placed with foster parents	26.3	28.7	30.3	36.9	35.2	34.5	32.1	35.2
Local authority homes	24.9	19.7	20.7	30.2	28.8	10.6	5.9	5.2
Hostels and voluntary homes	7.6	4.8	6.6	3.7	3.6	0.9 }	} 0.8	} 1.0
Schools for children with special educational needs	2.0	2.2	2.2	3.1	3.0	1.2 }		
Placed with parents	–	2.0	6.4	18.5	17.3	7.7	4.4	5.7
Lodgings or residential employment	–	1.7	1.7	1.9	1.8	1.7 }	} 6.8	} 6.6
Other accommodation	3.9	2.5	3.4	5.7	5.5	3.9 }		
Total in local authority care	64.7	61.7	71.2	100.2	95.3	60.5	49.9	53.7
Children fostered as % of all children in local authority care	40.6	46.5	42.5	36.8	36.9	57.0	64.3	65.6

Notes: [a]Children under 18.
[b]Detailed figures not available for 1950 because of changes following the Children Act of 1948.
[c]Provisional figures.

Sources: Home Office, *Children in the Care of Local Authorities in England and Wales*, 1952 and 1960; Home Office, *Children in Care in England and Wales*, 1970; *Health and Personal Social Services Statistics for England*, selected years; *Health and Personal Social Services Statistics for Wales*, selected years.

How far the high hopes of 1948 have been realized is another matter. By the end of the century evidence was mounting of widespread failure of the public authorities to secure the safety and well-being of children for whom they were responsible (Utting, 1997). Cases had emerged of children assaulted and ill-treated in foster homes and in institutions as well as in their own homes. Utting found only 8000 children in residential homes in 1995 compared with 40 000 20 years earlier and concluded that the swing away from institutions in favour of foster care had gone too far and had reduced residential accommo-dation below a level that could guarantee children's safety and allow reasonable choice in placing them (Utting, 1997, Chapter 2). Less than a year later the Social Services Inspectorate published a further damaging report claiming that local authorities were failing to provide proper care and protec-tion for vulnerable children (Department of Health, 1998a). The Department of Health responded immediately, announcing a three-year programme to 'transform' children's services by introducing a new special grant, setting objectives for local authorities and issuing guidance to councillors about their responsibilities (Department of Health, 1998b).

Much earlier, however, the ideological commitment to supporting the family, along with the desire to save money, combined to persuade local authority children's officers and local councillors, and later civil servants and ministers, that preventing family breakdown would be preferable to providing public care for children after it occurred (Parker, 1965, pp.48–58). So in 1963 the Children and Young Persons Act required local authorities to offer advice, guidance and assistance to families to reduce the need to receive children into or keep them in care, marking a move away from a 'paternalistic, protective child-centred attitude to positive and skilled family case work' (Heywood, 1978, p.191).

Thus the shift to prevention in the focus of the service was well under way. By the 1960s children supervised in their own homes already outnumbered those in care (Packman, 1975, p.72), and child care officers had embarked on their supremely difficult task of weighing the risk of physical or emotional harm for a child remaining with its parents against the likelihood of damage caused by separation. The dilemmas and tragedies attending these decisions, with little established and tested practice to guide them and which involve the most delicate balancing of rights and responsibilities against the need for protection, have beset the child care service ever since as public and profes-sional opinions have swung between emphasizing the supposed interests and well-being of parents or of children.

Through the 1970s public attention and anxiety switched to the danger of children being ill-treated in their own homes, and the number in public care rose to a record 100 000 in 1980 (Table 15.16). Then the pendulum swung back and numbers fell as evidence accumulated that long-term public care might also be damaging. The Children Act of 1989 attempted to strike a new balance between the rights of parents and of children. Local authority duties were reiterated and redefined to identify children in need, support them in their families and intervene to protect them if necessary. The legislation required that the child's welfare be paramount but also that parental responsibility be maintained (Gibbons, 1992). After the implementation of the Children Act in 1991 the number of children in care continued to fall and voluntary arrangements for respite care became more common (Kamerman and Kahn, 1997, p.89). It was this Act that first recognized family centres, listing them among the services local authorities were required to provide. The centres or 'family projects' take various forms. Generally to be found in poor neighbourhoods, they may provide for families where children are thought to be at risk, or act as community centres and meeting places offering a range of support to all local families as well as those in difficulties (Smith, 1996). There are no comprehensive national statistics but in 1993 there were about 500 members of the Family Centre Network (Ball, 1994, Table 3) and in 1997 the Department of Health estimated that there were 480 centres provided by local authorities (Department of Health, 1998c, Table 7). Some centres were run by health authorities, some by social services departments and some by voluntary bodies.

Meanwhile, from the early years of the century declining fertility, growing evidence of poverty and poor health, and increasing public awareness of the existence of child cruelty and neglect, led to the gradual development of services outside the Poor Law for all vulnerable children (Gilbert, 1966, Chapter 3). During the first decade of the century the school meals and medical services were introduced, marking the 'beginning of the construction of the welfare state' (Gilbert, 1966, p.102), and child protection legislation was consolidated and extended in the Children Act of 1908.

The move to feed children got off to a slow start, a highly contentious matter involving public intervention in family life to take over what many considered an essential parental responsibility (Gilbert, 1966, p.103). In the early years the service was heavily dependent on voluntary finance and support, but the steady increase in the number of children having meals in later decades may be seen in Table 15.17. It continued until the 1970s but since then government policies have led to a drop in the number of meals supplied, although the proportion of those provided free of charge to children from low-income families has risen.[4] A significant number of children also received school milk in the earlier years. Various schemes were in operation, and the statistics are confused and do not allow us to show trends, but milk virtually disappeared from the schools after the 1970s.

The maternity and child welfare service, offering health advice to women with young children, developed largely as a preventive measure though with some provision for the treatment of minor ailments (McCleary, 1935).The

Table 15.17 Provision of school meals, 1910/11–94/95, England and Wales[a]

	Number of main meals provided in a year (000s)	Number of main meals provided free (000s)	Number served as a % of population aged 5–14
1910/11	327	n/a	1.6
1920/21	11868	n/a	2.1
1930/31	16327	15184[b]	3.7[c]
1937/38	n/a	22691	10.0[c]

	Number served on a particular day (000s)	% of which provided free of charge	% of pupils on school roll taking meals[d]
1950/51	2745	n/a	50.4
1960/61	3408	n/a	52.4
1970/71	5148	12.2	67.9
1980/81	3770	20.7	48.3
1990/91	3192	27.6	42.9
1994/95	3504	39.7	44.5

Notes: [a]In maintained/local authority schools only, until the 1990s when grant-maintained schools are included. From 1910–38 main meals included breakfasts, dinners and teas; from 1950 onwards, dinners only. Population figures at census dates 1911, 1921, 1931 and for 1938 interpolated between 1931 and 1946. From 1950–51 to 1980–81 inclusive, figures refer to a selected day in autumn. From 1990–91 onwards, they refer to a selected day in January. After 1994–95, Welsh statistics no longer give figures for total pupils taking meals.
[b]Estimated.
[c]Includes both those served main meals and those served milk.
[d]English figures refer to number on school roll, Welsh figures refer to pupils present.

Sources: Board of Education (1911) *Report on the Working of the Education (Provision of Meals) Act 1906*; Board of Education, *Annual Reports* for 1920–21, 1931 and 1938; Ministry of Education, *Annual Report* 1950; Department of Education and Science, *Statistics of Education* 1963, 1975, 1981–82, 1991 and 1995; Welsh Office, *Statistics of Education in Wales*, 1981, 1993, 1997; Board of Trade, *Statistical Abstract for the UK*, selected years.

service worked through home visiting and local clinics, providing medical supervision for women before and after child birth and regular inspection of infants. At the beginning of the century voluntary organizations played a major part, employing nearly half the health visitors and running nearly half the clinics. By the 1930s, two-thirds of infants were receiving home visits, and all children under the age of one by the 1970s (Parker and Mirrlees, 1988, Table 12.22). The role of the voluntary organizations gradually diminished and by 1960 all health visitors were working for the local authorities, though a few voluntary clinics remained. In spite of the increase in work with old people since the 1960s, health visitors are still mainly concerned with maternity and child welfare (Table 15.5).

Social care for children outside their homes – apart from services linked to health or education or designed for young offenders – was largely a phenomenon of the post-war years, a response to the movement of women into paid employment detailed in Chapter 8. Both world wars produced pressure for public arrangements for child care to release women for industrial work. During World War I, 108 day nurseries were established, but this number had dwindled to 14 by 1940. It then increased to 1345 to supply places for 62 000 children by the end of World War II. This reflected the demand for women workers, including married women, in the factories; 'provision for the care of children is of first importance to the war effort' as Bevin remarked in 1941 (Kamerman and Kahn, 1997, pp.70–2). At the end of the war, however, as men returned from the forces and theories about the damaging effects on young children of separation from their mothers became more influential, policy shifted. Mothers of children under the age of two were discouraged from outside work and the number of nurseries had dropped to 900 by the end of the 1940s and halved again over the following 20 years with a corresponding diminution in the number of places (Table 15.18). After the 1970s the trend moved upwards again with the most marked expansion in the voluntary and private sectors, the registered nurseries and, especially, among child-minders.

Meanwhile, a rather different form of provision was growing in nursery classes and playgroups. In 1901, 43 per cent of three-year-old children were in the elementary schools, but they all but disappeared during the first decade of

Table 15.18 Day care for children, 1949–95, England and Wales

| | Places in nurseries (000s) | | Places in playgroups (000s) | | Places with registered child-minders (000s) |
	Local authority	Registered	Local authority	Registered	
England and Wales					
1949	43.2	n/a	n/a	6.9	1.7
1960	22.6	n/a	n/a	14.6	11.9
1965	21.4	n/a	n/a	54.9	n/a
1970	21.6	n/a	n/a	248.9	84.9
1975	26.0	27.1	3.0	349.1	100.0
1980	28.5	22.8	3.2	382.8	a
1985	29.1	26.3	3.1	419.3	146.3
1990	28.2	60.4	2.3	432.8	214.7
England only					
1990	28.0	57.7	2.0	409.6	205.6
1995	20.9	139.3	1.7	406.2	373.6

Note: [a]Figures not reliable.

Sources: Department of Health and Social Security, *Digest of Health Statistics for England and Wales*, 1969; *Health and Personal Social Services Statistics for England*, selected years; *Health and Personal Social Services Statistics for Wales*, selected years.

the century and it was only in the 1970s, after the Plowden Report, that government interest in the value of nursery education for encouraging the social development of young children revived at all strongly (Kamerman and Kahn, 1997, p.74). The most notable increase in provision, however, dating from these years and continuing to the end of the century, has been in play-groups in the private and voluntary sectors (Table 15.18).

In the 1990s, day care for children under school-age remains fragmentary – largely the responsibility of the voluntary and private sectors and very variable geographically. In 1968 day nursery places were restricted to children 'at risk' or with 'special needs' and to single parents, and most working women still rely on private and informal arrangements for day care (Kamerman and Kahn, 1997, pp.76–8). Through the 1990s governments have remained ambivalent about public funding. A 'child care disregard' was introduced in 1994 for working parents receiving Family Credit and in the following year a voucher scheme for nursery education (Kamerman and Kahn, 1997, p.75). More recently, the Labour government's emphasis on 'enabling' lone parents to move off benefits and into work is obviously dependent on expanding public day care arrangements. How far this will occur remains to be seen.

International developments

Social provision for children and young people in trouble through adverse family circumstances or their own behavioural problems, is moving along similar lines in European and other developed countries, and in the same direction as services for older people (Colton and Hellinckx, 1993; Kamerman and Kahn, 1997). There is a general decline in residential accommodation and a widely expressed intention to develop a range of community-based services, including more and earlier support for families to try to prevent the need to remove children from their homes. Services are also being increasingly supplied through voluntary and private agencies, albeit publicly financed, rather than directly through the public authorities, especially in Canada, the US, New Zealand and the UK. The trends reflect disillusion with residential care, distrust of government bureaucracy and the search for economy. But it is also increasingly widely recognized that fewer residential places may reduce the power to deal with more difficult or damaged children, and that alternatives to residential care are often poorly developed and can only achieve high standards if they receive substantial resources.

In their overview of foster and residential care for children in the European Community, Hellinckx and Colton (1993) identify six common developments. These include shrinking residential provision, a move to smaller homes and a tendency to greater variety in both residential and foster care and in other types of community arrangements. They also include a change in the characteristics of children coming into care. There are more children with severe problems; a reflection of changing family structures with more divorces and more broken relationships. A linked development, the authors claim, is the growing recognition among European countries that children can only be helped effectively if their family and cultural backgrounds are taken into account; and thus parents are encouraged to exercise their rights and take part in decisions about their children. Finally, they note a general move to greater professionalism of both foster parents and other care workers in most EC countries, though at the same time there remain severe shortages of adequately trained staff, particularly for residential work.

The cost of social services

Attempts to chart social services spending through the century should be treated with great caution. Costs relate to very different kinds of services at different periods. Before the 1940s they largely reflect indoor poor relief in a variety of institutions for destitute, old and disabled people, and for children. After the 1940s, expenditure covers residential homes and also an increasing range of domiciliary and community services which were supposed to advance 'welfare' and respond to need rather than to destitution. Nor are the figures over the years consistent. Spending on different services for different groups of people may be distinguished or not at different times. The most reliable figures are restricted to three periods for each of which it is possible to produce reasonably consistent trends but which are not properly comparable with one another.

Table 15.19 Expenditure[a] on indoor poor relief and selected welfare services, 1900/01–35/36, England and Wales[b]

	£m, cash terms	£m, 1997 prices	% of GDP
1900/01	5.9	354	0.41
1910/11	7.9	447	0.48
1920/21	20.1	441	0.43
1930/31	20.1	693	0.55
1935/36	18.0	686	0.49

Notes: [a]Expenditure (excluding that defrayed out of loans) on the maintenance of indoor paupers in Poor Law authority and non-Poor Law authority institutions, but excluding the maintenance of lunatics in institutions.
[b]From 1920/21 maternity and child welfare expenditure is included, and in 1930/31 blind welfare expenditure.

Sources: C. H. Feinstein (1972), *National Income, Expenditure and Output of the UK, 1855–1965*; Central Statistical Office, *Statistical Abstract for the UK*, selected years; Local Government Board, *Annual Reports*, selected years; Local Government Board, *Annual Local Taxation Returns*, selected years.

For the first period, up to World War II, the figures we have refer to Poor Law institutions, though they exclude the maintenance of 'lunatics' and the costs of children fostered. In 1930 and later years Poor Law hospitals and other special institutions are also excluded; from 1920 maternity and child welfare costs are counted in, and from 1930 those for blind welfare (Table 15.19). There appears to have been a fairly steady rise in spending in real terms, representing a pretty constant proportion of GDP. But the increase in spending is concealed as the years before 1930 included hospital costs.

The second period stretches from the welfare legislation of the late 1940s to the setting up of social services departments in 1971. After 1948 the Poor Law services other than cash relief were absorbed into the local health, welfare and children's departments while hospitals went to the newly formed Regional Hospital Boards. Local government remained responsible for the domiciliary and community health services; the home nurses, health visitors, and maternity and child welfare clinics. During the following 20 years, policy makers and social workers were endeavouring to find ways of responding to the many kinds of social need which confronted them and to establish social work as a profession with shared and coherent aims, principles and methods of work. But developments in this very varied collection of services were slow; expenditure in real terms barely changed through the 1950s, though it began to rise gently during the 1960s.

It was only in the 1970s, the beginning of the third period, that the growth rate increased sharply (Table 15.20), and the upward trend in spending, though temporarily reversed in the mid-1970s and again in the early 1980s, continued to the close of the century. The share of GDP accounted for by local welfare services, more commonly termed personal social services after 1970, remained pretty constant at only a fraction of 1 per cent before the 1970s, but thereafter

Table 15.20 Expenditure on the personal social services, 1950/51–96/97, United Kingdom[a]

	£m, cash terms	£m, 1997 prices	% of GDP at market prices
1950/51	29	547	0.21
1960/61	60	754	0.23
1970/71	274	2281	0.52
1980/81	2230	5102	0.94
1990/91	5626	6881	1.01
1996/97	10318	10566	1.37

Note: [a]Excludes expenditure on welfare foods, school milk and school meals.

Sources: Central Statistical Office (selected years), *Annual Abstract of Statistics*; Office for National Statistics (1997), *Economic Trends Annual Supplement*.

rose steeply through the decade, fell back through the 1980s, and rose again more slowly in the 1990s. Even so, little more than 1 per cent of the national wealth went to the personal social services in the late 1990s (Figure 15.3).

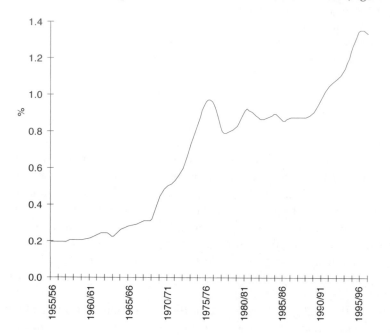

Figure 15.3 Expenditure on personal social services as a percentage of GDP, United Kingdom, 1955/56–96/97

Sources: Central Statistical Office (selected years), *Annual Abstract of Statistics*; Office for National Statistics (1997), *Economic Trends Annual Supplement.*

Three stages of welfare?

The century has witnessed three important stages in the development of collective responsibility for welfare. The rhetoric about the extent and nature of that responsibility has moved towards a more generous conception, and there has been a more gradual shift in the character of public services. State intervention during the last 30 years, however, has tended to be checked by alarm at rising public spending and by fears of the costs of dependency of an increasingly elderly population, neither necessarily well founded (Hills, 1997).

The first half of the century was marked by the haphazard development of public services outside the Poor Law – school meals and milk for children and insurance and assistance for unemployment, sickness and old age. The Poor Law remained very important with its minimal provision and stigmatizing associations, though institutional provision, for children particularly, was improving.

After World War II the Poor Law was repealed. It was replaced by a national scheme designed to guarantee a minimum income to the majority of people as of right, and a collection of welfare services run by local authorities. The crucial change here was that local services, whether for old or disabled people or for children, were no longer regarded as minimal provision for the destitute. They were supposed to offer high standards of comfort, support and security and opportunities for occupation or training that would allow people to live as normal a life as possible (Marshall, 1965). Views changed about the best strategies, with increasing emphasis through the 1960s on 'community care' and maintaining people in their own homes rather than in public institutions.

The third stage of welfare involved the insistence that high standards would not be achieved through the plans and decisions of bureaucrats and professionals alone. Planning must be more democratic and officials and services answerable and responsive to the wishes of the people who used them. Thus, community health councils were established early in the 1970s which were supposed to give local people a voice in the running of health services and the Seebohm Report urged that the new social services departments of local authorities be 'community based'. More recently, through the last two decades of the century, government has adopted the idea of 'case management' in the personal social services whereby local authorities are instructed to assess need and make plans to meet it in consultation with the people concerned. All this reflects the belief that people relying on public services should have some choice in what they receive.

However, there was another strand in the move to individual choice which gave more weight to individual responsibility: Mrs Thatcher's ambition to attack the supposed dependency culture and to 'roll back the frontiers of the state'. An important government aim since 1979 has been to curtail the activities of allegedly wasteful and inefficient public bodies and revert to a pluralist system of welfare where markets and voluntary organizations and families play a larger part, and competing agencies offer wider choice. The emphasis on individual choice and responsibility, mistrust of government bureaucracy and anxiety to limit public spending have all combined to curtail state welfare services at the end of the century.

The mixed economy of welfare is nothing new. People needing support have always received it mainly from their families, their local communities, churches, philanthropic and self-help groups, and the market. We do not have the statistics to measure in any precise way the extent and character of voluntary effort in welfare matters, though voluntary organizations have been particularly active in developing a variety of services for children through the nineteenth and early twentieth centuries. After the 1940s their position was strengthened rather than weakened by the emergence of the Welfare State, as the public authorities tended to use the voluntary bodies as agents to perform

the new statutory duties; and the 1990s saw still closer links, with local authorities contracting with voluntary bodies as well as with private agencies for the
supply of services.

Nor do we have any precise measure of family or informal care. It is assumed
that parents look after their children but responsibility for older or for disabled
people is more problematic (Finch, 1989). We have no quantitative measures for
most of the century. Recent enquiries confirm that both women and men give
regular help to one another if they are living together, and that families are by
far the most usual source of help for vulnerable people (OPCS, 1996). Various
estimates for the 1990s point to round about two and a half million adults
looking after others – apart from child-rearing – in or outside their homes. One
attempt to calculate the replacement costs of this informal care puts it at £35
billion, or 5 per cent of GDP – a sum many times greater than the total amount
spent by the state through the NHS, DSS and local authorities (Evandrou and
Falkingham, 1998, pp.242–5). How far government efforts to limit public
services will lead to a shift to greater family responsibility can only be established by future surveys. But given demographic and social trends, any such
move would impose considerable burdens on younger people. And, as Evandrou
and Falkingham observe, it remains to be seen whether the duty of local authorities under the 1995 Act to assess the needs of carers when deciding on claims
for services will lead to more support for those looking after others.

The more general aim of encouraging people who use services to take part
in assessing their own needs and deciding how they should be met seems to
be rarely realized and may indeed be impossible to achieve. The Social Services
Inspectorate point out that it is the more confident and assertive people who
become more involved in planning; many do not even know whether they
have been 'assessed' or whether they have a 'care manager' whom they can
contact (Department of Health, 1998d, p.23). In any case, local authority
resources are limited, so the extent to which they can respond to the wishes or
preferences of consumers is bound to be restricted.

The problem is to devise an equitable rationing system within a range of
services where the needs of vulnerable children, of adults with different
disabilities and of frail elderly people are all competing for attention. Much
must depend on the skill and commitment of local authority staff but the
personal social services are in a weak position compared with health or education. As we have seen, they claim less than 2 per cent of national resources and
professional workers are thin on the ground. 'The majority of staff employed
in social service departments and the independent sector have no qualifications' (Department of Health, 1998d, p. 62). It is hardly surprising that efforts
to encourage participation and develop responsive services have had only very
limited success and vary greatly among local authorities – as indeed is the
tradition in local government activities.

The government has not been able to ignore the evidence of widespread failure in the social services and has promised reform. In November 1998 the Minister of Health announced a 'radical overhaul' of the social service system (Department of Health, 1998e). He proposed a 'General Social Care Council' to supervise the regulation and training of all social care workers and also regional 'Commissions for Care Standards' to inspect all care services, whether provided in people's own houses, by independent agencies or in residential homes. Only the twenty-first century can show where these good intentions lead.

Notes on sources

The statistics we have used to illustrate the development of institutional and domiciliary social services for different groups of people must be interpreted very cautiously. We have tried to present trends but the tables are often incomplete and we deal almost entirely with statutory services as there are no comprehensive statistics for voluntary bodies.

Institutions

Figures for the population in public institutions come from the annual returns on persons receiving poor relief, the annual reports of the Local Government Board, the Ministry of Health, the Home Office and the Ministry of Education and for later years from the Department of Health and Social Security (DHSS) and the Department of Health. There are no reliable statistics for the population of institutions for the years before World War II. Inmates were differently classified in different years and sometimes categories overlap – the old with non-able-bodied and able-bodied adults, for instance. In the early years sick children are not distinguished from healthy ones, and sick old people are not always distinguished from other sick adults. Therefore it is not possible to construct tables showing the numbers of people in particular categories in institutions at different times. Nor can we always distinguish the type of accommodation; there are no consistent figures showing the proportion of the sick in infirmaries or special sick wards, nor the number of old people and children in different kinds of public accommodation since 1948.

Domiciliary welfare services

In some cases government departments have published statistics which indicate the development in domiciliary services for different groups of people, such as the blind or the mentally ill; but generally the figures are incomplete. In other cases we can gain some idea of the growth of particular services, even though we may not be able to say how far the services benefited particular people. Some services, such as welfare clinics and occupation centres for people with learning disabilities, were started by voluntary organizations, then supplemented by local authorities under permissive legislation and later in some cases taken over entirely by the local authorities as legislation became obligatory. Consequently figures sometimes distinguish voluntary organization workers or clinics at first and later drop the distinction. Furthermore, statistics may relate to visits in one year and cases served in another, as with the home nursing service. At best, and even if they are consistent, the statistics give only a rough guide. They do not reveal the amount of attention given to each person in relation to need, so there is nothing to show how adequately individuals have been served.

Recent sources

The main sources of social services statistics for the period since about 1960 are the publications *Health and Social Services Statistics*, produced separately by the Department of Health for England and by the Welsh Office for Wales. Since 1997, the English publication has been slimmed down considerably and detailed statistics appear instead in diverse small reports and bulletins, indicated in the sources to tables. The Welsh statistics have not appeared since 1994, and although the Welsh Office has indicated that the series will be resumed in the near future, this had not happened at time of going to press. Therefore the Welsh statistics have not been included in the bulk of the tables since we wanted to make the tables as consistent over time as possible. Statistics on the Scottish social services can be found in the *Scottish Abstract of Statistics* but unfortunately are rarely comparable with those for England and Wales.

Notes

1   These figures include physically disabled residents in independent homes as well as those over 65.
2   Residents in local authority homes have contributed to the cost of their accommodation since 1948, if judged able to do so by the local authority. People in private or voluntary homes have been eligible for board and lodging allowances from the DSS. Before 1980 such payments were negligible, but the growing number of dependent old people, and the closing of long-stay hospital beds, resulted in a huge increase in people in nursing and residential homes in the private and voluntary sectors. DSS payments were determined locally to reflect local costs and varied between £51.00 and £215.00 a week for residential care in 1983 (House of Commons, Fourth Report, 1991). Expenditure increased dramatically through the decade, from £10 million in 1979 to £1390 million in 1990 as the number of claimants rose from 12 000 to 199 000 (House of Commons, 1991, Appendix). Nor was the increase in public spending the only problem. People were supported by the DSS in residential accommodation without any inquiry as to how far it might have been cheaper for them to

live in their own homes with domiciliary services. The government therefore decided to introduce a unified budget to cover the cost of social care, whether in a person's own home or a residential or nursing home. The budget was to be managed by the local authorities, who would be in a position to make the best use of any money available in the light of an assessment of individual needs. The new arrangements were introduced in the NHS and Community Care Act of 1990 and came into operation in 1993, though people already in institutions continued to be funded by the DSS.

3   The terminology used to describe younger adults in various categories has changed over the years, which can cause confusion. The term 'mentally ill' has recently been replaced by 'people with mental health problems', while those who used to be known as the 'mentally handicapped' have become 'people with learning disabilities'. The 'physically handicapped' are now more commonly referred to as 'people with physical or sensory disabilities'.

4   After 1971 local authorities were no longer required to provide milk for children over the age of seven. In 1980 nutritional standards for meals were scrapped and local authorities left to act according to their discretion. Free meals still had to be provided for children from families on Supplementary Benefit (now Income Support) or receiving Family Income Supplement (now Family Credit).

References

Audit Commission (1985) *Managing Social Services For the Elderly More Effectively*, HMSO, London.

Audit Commission (1986) *Making a Reality of Community Care*, HMSO, London.

Audit Commission (1997) *The Coming of Age: Improving Care Services For the Elderly*, Audit Commission, London.

Baldwin, Sally and Lunt, Neil (1996) *Charging Ahead: The Development of Local Authority Charging Policies for Community Care*, Policy Press, Bristol.

Ball, Christopher (1994) *Start Right: The Importance of Early Learning*, Royal Society of Arts, London.

Bowlby, John (1951) *Maternal Care and Mental Health*, World Health Organization, Geneva.

Colton, M. and Hellinckx, W. (eds) (1993) *Child Care in the EC*, Arena, Aldershot.

Davies, B. (1994) 'Improving the case management process', in OECD, *New Orientations for Social Policy*, Social Policy Studies no. 12, OECD, Paris.

Department of Health (1998a) *Someone Else's Children*, Report from the Social Services Inspectorate, Department of Health, London.

Department of Health (1998b) *Quality Protects: Transforming Children's Services*, press release.

Department of Health (1998c) *Personal Social Services, Local Authority Statistics Children's Day Care Facilities at 31 March 1997, England*, Government Statistical Service, London.

Department of Health (1998d) *Social Services Facing the Future, The Seventh Annual Report of the Chief Inspector, Social Services Inspectorate 1997/98*, The Stationery Office, London.

Department of Health (1998e) *Modernising Social Services*, The Stationery Office, London.

Department of Health (various years) *Health and Personal Social Services Statistics for England*, HMSO, London.

Department of Health and Social Security (DHSS) et al. (1981) *Growing Older*, Cmnd 8173, HMSO, London.

Dexter, Margaret and Harbert, Wally (1983) *The Home Help Service*, Tavistock, London.

*Evandrou, Maria and Falkingham, Jane (1998) 'The personal social services', in Glennerster, Howard and Hills, John (eds) *The State of Welfare*, Oxford University Press, Oxford.

Finch, Janet (1989) *Family Obligation and Social Change*, Polity Press, Cambridge.

*Finch, Janet (1995) 'Responsibilities, obligations and commitments', in Allen, Isobel and Perkins, Elizabeth (eds) *The Future of Family Care for Older People*, HMSO, London.

Gibbons, Jane (ed.) (1992) *The Children Act 1989 and Family Support: Principles Into Practice*, HMSO, London.

Gilbert, Bentley B. (1966) *The Evolution of National Insurance in Great Britain*, Michael Joseph, London.

Griffiths, Roy (1988) *Community Care: Agenda for Action*, HMSO, London.

Grundy, Emily (1995) 'Demographic influences on the future of family care', in Allen, Isobel and Perkins, Elizabeth (eds) *The Future of Family Care for Older People*, HMSO, London.

Hellinckx, W. and Colton, M. (1993) 'Residential and foster care in the EC', in Colton, M. and Hellinckx, W. (eds), *Child Care in the EC*, Arena, Aldershot.

Heywood, Jean S. (1978) *Children in Care: The Development of the Service for the Deprived Child*, Routledge and Kegan Paul, London.

Hills, John (1997) *The Future of Welfare: A Guide to the Debate*, Joseph Rowntree Foundation, York.

Holme, A. and Maizels J. (1978) *Social Workers and Volunteers*, British Association of Social Workers, London.

House of Commons (1991) Social Security Committee, Fourth Report, *The Financing of Private Residential and Nursing Home Fees*, HMSO, London.

Hugman, Richard (1994) *Ageing and the Care of Older People in Europe*, Macmillan, Basingstoke.

Jani-Le Bris, Hannelore (1993) *Family Care of Dependent Older People in the European Community*, European Foundation for the Improvement of Living and Working Conditions, Shankill.

*Joseph Rowntree Foundation Inquiry (1996) *Meeting the Costs of Continuing Care,* Joseph Rowntree Foundation (Chairman Sir Peter Barclay), York.

*Kamerman, Sheila B. and Kahn, Alfred J. (eds) (1997) *Family Change and Family Policies in Great Britain, Canada, New Zealand, and the United States*, Clarendon Press, Oxford.

Knapp, Martin et al. (1992) *Care in the Community: Challenge and Demonstration*, PSSRU, Ashgate.

Le Grand, Julian and Bartlett, Will (eds) (1993) *Quasi-Markets and Social Policy*, Macmillan, Basingstoke.

*Lewis, Jane and Glennerster, Howard (1996) *Implementing the New Community Care*, Oxford University Press, Oxford.

McCleary, George Frederick (1935) *Maternity and Child Welfare Movement*, King and Son, London.

Macnicol, John (1998) *The Politics of Retirement in Britain, 1878–1948*, Cambridge University Press, Cambridge.

*Marshall, T. H. (1965) *Social Policy*, Hutchinson, London.

Marshall, T. H. (1981) 'Value problems of welfare capitalism', in *The Right to Welfare and Other Essays*, Heinemann, London.

Means, R. and Smith, R. (1983) 'From public assistance institutions to "sunshine hotels": changing state perceptions about residential care for elderly people, 1939–48', *Ageing and Society*, 3, Part 2.

Office of Population Censuses and Surveys (OPCS) (1996) *Living in Britain: Results from the 1994 General Household Survey*, HMSO, London.

Organization for Economic Co-operation and Development (OECD) (1994) *New Orientations for Social Policy*, Social Policy Studies no. 12, OECD, Paris.

*Packman, Jean (1975) *The Child's Generation*, Blackwell, Oxford.

Parker, Julia (1965) *Local Health and Welfare Services*, Allen and Unwin, London.

Parker, Julia and Mirrlees, Catriona (1988) 'Welfare' in Halsey, A. H. (ed.) *British Social Trends Since 1900*, Macmillan, Basingstoke.

Phelps, Liz (1997) *Rationing Community Care*, National Association of Citizens' Advice Bureaux, London.

Smith, Teresa (1996) *Family Centres: Bringing Up Young Children*, HMSO, London.

Sundstrom, G. (1994) 'Care by families: an overview of trends', in OECD, *New Orientations for Social Policy*, Social Policy Studies no. 12, OECD, Paris.

Sutherland, Stewart (1999) *With Respect to Old Age: Long Term Care – Rights and Responsibilities: a report by the Royal Commission on Long Term Care*, The Stationery Office, London.

Titmuss, R. M. (1950) *Problems of Social Policy*, HMSO/Longman, Green and Co., London.

Townsend, Peter (1962) *The Last Refuge: A Survey of Residential Institutions and Homes for the Aged in England and Wales*, Routledge & Kegan Paul, London.

United Nations (1994) *Ageing and the Family*, United Nations, New York.

Utting, William (1997) *People Like Us: The Report of the Review of the Safeguards for Children Living Away from Home*, The Stationery Office, London.

Webb, Sidney and Webb, Beatrice (1963) *English Poor Law History Part 2, Vol. 1*. Frank Cass, London (first published 1929).

Welsh Office (various years) *Health and Personal Social Statistics for Wales*, Welsh Office, Wales

Further reading

The asterisked items in the References are valuable sources for further reading.

16
Social Security

Josephine Webb

> However abundant goods may be, when every man tries to get as much
> as he can for his own exclusive use, a handful of men end up sharing the
> whole pile, and the rest are left in poverty ... But in Utopia, where every-
> thing belongs to everybody, no man need fear that, so long as the public
> warehouses are filled, he will ever lack for anything he needs ... in Utopia
> no men are poor, no men are beggars, and though no man owns
> anything, everyone is rich.
>
> Thomas More, *Utopia*, 1516

Introduction and definitions

This chapter charts the development and expansion of social security provision in Britain during the twentieth century. For our purposes, the term 'social
security' is taken to refer to cash benefits provided by the state to individuals
and families.[1] Three broad categories of benefit can be distinguished:

- social insurance benefits, paid to those with a sufficient record of contributions. In Britain these are also often referred to as National Insurance (NI)
  benefits
- social assistance benefits, paid after a means test
- benefits which are neither contributory nor means-tested, but are paid to
  people who fall into a specified category. These will be referred to as contingency benefits.[2]

Tax allowances, although treated differently in the government accounts from
cash benefits, will also be considered, since they have the same effect of
increasing the individual's disposable income.

After a brief historical overview, each main group of benefit recipients will
be considered in turn: children, lone parents and widows, the unemployed,

the low paid, the sick and disabled and their carers, and the elderly.[3] Then we can put the pieces of the jigsaw together and look at the overall picture; how the balance has shifted between the different groups of recipients and the different types of benefit, and what has happened to total expenditure on social security.

Historical overview

The origins of social security

In the late nineteenth century, the only poverty relief provided by the state was through the Poor Law, administered at the local level. If those in need had no alternative form of provision (such as assistance from their families, philanthropic gifts, or benefits provided by friendly societies), this was their last resort. The 1834 Poor Law treated the destitute punitively, working on the principle of 'less eligibility', which meant that recipients of poor relief should be worse off than the lowest paid worker, to preserve the incentive to work. Relief was either administered inside workhouses ('indoor relief') or was given in the form of allowances to people living outside the workhouse ('outdoor relief').

At the beginning of the twentieth century, evidence from social surveys increased awareness of the extent of poverty (see Chapter 10). The inadequacy of the Poor Law was increasingly recognized, and a Royal Commission reported on the subject in 1909. In the event, the Liberal government allowed the Poor Law to linger on, but introduced a variety of reforms to narrow its scope, including an old-age pension and limited unemployment and health

Table 16.1 Number of people receiving outdoor relief under the Poor Law, England and Wales, 1900–48 (000s)[a]

	Adults[b]	Children[c]	Total	% of population
1900	421.8	158.2	580.0	1.80
1910	360.4	184.1	544.5	1.52
1920	167.5	138.4	305.8	0.82
1930	528.7	338.3	867.0	2.19
1939	678.5	261.7	940.2	2.28
1948	231.6	110.2	341.8	0.80

Notes: [a]Numbers receiving relief on 1 January each year.
[b]Figures for adults include the insane and casual paupers receiving outdoor relief.
[c]Children defined as under 16.

Sources: Local Government Board, *Pauperism (England and Wales) Half-yearly Statement*, Jan 1900 and 1910; Ministry of Health, *Persons in Receipt of Poor-Law Relief (England and Wales)*, 1921, 1930, 1939 and 1948; percentage of population calculated from figures from Board of Trade, *Statistical Abstract for the UK*, selected years.

insurance schemes. In the inter-war period, these schemes were consolidated and expanded, but remained fragmented. Table 16.1 shows how the numbers forced to resort to Poor Law outdoor relief fell as a percentage of the population between 1900 and 1920 but then increased again with the Depression. (For the numbers receiving indoor relief, see Chapter 15.)

The Beveridge Report

In 1941, the government asked Beveridge to chair an inquiry into the insurance system, in response to complaints from trade unions about its complexity (Abel-Smith, 1994, p.13). The inquiry's terms of reference were 'to undertake, with special reference to the inter-relation of the schemes, a survey of the existing national schemes of social insurance and allied services, including workmen's compensation, and to make recommendations' (Beveridge, 1942, para. 1). In 1942 the Beveridge Report was published, and made a huge impact on popular opinion and the policies of the time. Beveridge proposed an integrated compulsory social insurance system covering retirement, unemployment, sickness and disability, and widowhood. He argued that 'benefit in return for contributions, rather than free allowances from the State, is what the people of Britain desire' (Beveridge, 1942, para. 21). When the post-war legislation was introduced, the first sentence of the National Assistance Act of 1948 stated that 'the existing poor law shall cease to have effect' and this was regarded as an important symbolic act.

Beveridge wanted benefits to be paid at a flat rate, set at subsistence level, to last as long as the need existed, and with allowances for dependants. He assumed that most married women would not work, and designed the scheme so that their entitlement to benefits would depend on the contributions made by their husbands. For people who could not be fitted into the insurance scheme, such as lone mothers and disabled people unable to work, there was means-tested social assistance to fall back on.[4] But this was deliberately made a second-rate benefit: assistance 'must be felt to be something less desirable than insurance benefit; otherwise the insured people get nothing for their contributions' (Beveridge, 1942, para. 369).

Despite its euphoric reception, in practice many of the recommendations in the Beveridge Report were never implemented, such as the principle of subsistence benefits (Lowe, 1994, p.120). Beveridge's plan has also gradually become outdated as changes have occurred which he did not anticipate, such as the increase in the number of women working, the proliferation of insecure employment, and the rise in the number of lone parents (Baldwin and Falkingham, 1994). In responding to these developments, the social security system has moved away from his blueprint. From the 1950s to the 1970s, piecemeal changes were made to the system, such as an experiment with earnings-related supplements to National Insurance benefits between 1966 and 1981, and the introduction of several new benefits, including the first to be aimed specifically at low-paid workers, and a number of contingency benefits designed to help disabled people.

The Fowler review and the 1990s

In the 1980s the Conservative government attempted to cut social security spending. One of its first acts was to change the basis on which benefits were uprated. Until that point, benefits had been increased in line with prices or earnings, depending on which was higher (usually earnings), but from now on, the assumption was that they were to be increased in line with prices only. This move was followed by the 'Fowler review' of social security[5] which took place in 1985 and claimed to be 'the most fundamental examination of our social security system since the Second World War' (Department of Health and Social Security (DHSS), 1985a, preface). Many reforms were subsequently implemented in 1988, simplifying some benefits and removing various anomalies. Overall, there were gainers and losers, and the net effect on expenditure was small (Evans, et al., 1994, pp.79–83; p.91).

Between 1988 and 1997, more incremental changes were made to the system; new benefits were introduced, others abolished or replaced, and eligibility criteria for some benefits were altered. The most notable trend in this period was the marked shift from social insurance to means-tested benefits, discussed below. But since the election of the new Labour government in May 1997, the prospects for social security have been uncertain. 'Welfare reform' is currently high on the agenda, and at the time of writing (April 1999) many new measures were being piloted or proposed. The principle behind most of these reforms is that the system 'should help and encourage people of working age to work where they are capable of doing so' (Department of Social Security (DSS) 1999, p. 11).

Children

Large family size in relation to wages was one of the main causes of poverty in the first half of the century, as shown in Chapter 10. A child tax allowance scheme was introduced in 1909 but this only assisted the small and relatively affluent section of the population who paid income tax, and in the inter-war period a campaign for family allowances was led by Eleanor Rathbone (Macnicol, 1980, pp.23–24). The campaign was finally successful in 1945 when the Family Allowances Act was introduced, and these allowances began to be paid in 1946. They were not means-tested and did not require a contribution record. Initially, they were not paid for the first child in a family, but only for the second and later children, and they were not paid at subsistence level despite Beveridge's recommendations.

Child tax allowances continued to operate in parallel with family allowances, and cost more in terms of forgone revenue – the Inland Revenue estimated that the child tax allowance cost £1.25 billion in 1975/76, more than twice the expenditure on family allowances in that year (Inland Revenue, 1978, Table 1.5). The allowance was eventually phased out between 1977 and 1979, which helped the government pay for the introduction of Child Benefit in 1977. Child Benefit was essentially the same family allowance scheme but with benefit extended to the first child in each family. The numbers receiving it almost doubled, causing a large jump in expenditure, as can be seen in Table 16.2.[6] The value of the benefit continued to rise until 1987, when it was frozen in cash terms and the government put more resources into means-tested benefits for families with children instead. In 1991 Child Benefit was unfrozen again, but subsequent increases were not large enough to make up for the lost ground, until 1998 when it was announced that it was to be given a large boost. In 1999 the rate of the benefit was raised even further and, so far, it has not been taxed, despite some earlier indications that this was being considered (Department of Social Security (DSS), 1998a, p.58). A pilot Educational Maintenance Allowance scheme for those aged 16–18 was also announced, which is to be means-tested and, if considered successful, will replace Child Benefit for those staying in education after the age of 16 (HM Treasury, 1998b, p.44).

Table 16.2 Family allowances, Child Benefit and One Parent Benefit, Great Britain, 1950–97[a]

	1950	1955	1960	1965
Family allowances/Child Benefit				
Children attracting benefit (000s)	4756	5114	5764	6423
Families receiving benefit (000s)	3050	3278	3569	3869
Weekly rate: 1st child	–	–	–	–
Weekly rate: 2nd child[b]	£0.25	£0.40	£0.40	£0.40
Expenditure (£m)	62	107	131	146
Expenditure (£m, 1997 prices)	1170	1520	1647	1536
One Parent Benefit				
Children in families receiving benefit (000s)	–	–	–	–
Families receiving allowances (000s)	–	–	–	–
Weekly rate	–	–	–	–
Expenditure (£m)	–	–	–	–
Expenditure (£m, 1997 prices)	–	–	–	–

Notes: [a]Includes payments for children overseas. Numbers relate to 31 December each year, except for 1955 and 1960 when they relate to 31 January of the following year
[b]From April 1997, One Parent Benefit was incorporated into main Child Benefit rates. The rate for the eldest qualifying child of a lone parent was £17.10. 1956–75: rate for third and subsequent children was slightly higher than that for the second child.

Lone parents and widows

Widows

Under the Poor Law, widows were expected to work, even if they had dependent children. Lloyd George wanted to provide for them in his 1911 social insurance scheme, but backed down in the face of opposition from the commercial insurance societies, and they were left to rely on the Poor Law until 1925. The Widows', Orphans' and Contributory Old Age Pensions Act of that year established pensions for all widows of insured men with allowances for dependent children, and for some 'pre-Act' widows for whom it was too late for contributions to be made. However, benefit rates were low and some widows still had to apply to the Poor Law for extra assistance (Richardson, 1984, pp.15–20).

Beveridge included widows in his insurance scheme (1942, para. 346), and in 1946 several benefits for them were introduced. These included an allowance paid on widowhood, a widowed mother's allowance for those with dependent children, and a widow's pension for women widowed at the age of 50 or over with no dependent children. This scheme remained in place for the second half of the century, and Table 16.3 shows how the number of widows receiving benefits gradually fell over time. Expenditure in real terms rose up to the early 1980s, as benefits were increased in line with earnings, but has fallen

1970	1975	1980	1985	1990	1995	1997[b]
6955	6824	13092	12148	12079	12698	n/a
4249	4458	7141	6784	6707	6996	n/a
–	–	£4.75	£7.00	£7.25	£10.40	£11.05[b]
£0.90	£1.50	£4.75	£7.00	£7.25	£8.45	£9.00
339	532	2944	4468	4591	6332	7063
2823	2333	6736	7350	5615	6642	7007
–	–	684	862	1186	1597	–
–	–	438	576	773	994	–
–	–	£3.00	£4.55	£5.60	£6.30	–
–	–	61	134	229	312	–
–	–	140	220	280	327	–

Sources: Report of the Ministry of Pensions and National Insurance for the year 1953, p.71; 1956, p.64; 1961, p.90; *Annual Report* of the Department of Health and Social Security for the year 1970, Table 147; *Social Security Statistics*, 1975 and 1978, Tables 30.30 and 44.01; *Social Security Statistics*, 1995, Tables G1.03, G1.05, G1.11 and G1.12; *Social Security Statistics*, 1997, Tables G1.08 and G1.09; *Social Security Statistics*, 1998, Tables G1.03 and G1.05.

since. In 1998 changes were proposed to modernize the system and ensure that
widows and widowers receive equal treatment.

Table 16.3 Benefits for widows, Great Britain, 1950–95[a]

	Number of widows receiving benefits (000s)[b]	Expenditure (£m) cash terms	1997 prices
1950	446	21.7	409
1960	543	65.5	823
1970	542	168	1399
1979[c]	452	563	1498
1990	354	889	1087
1995	314	1016	1066
1997	284	1010	1002

Notes: [a]Numbers in receipt relate to March 1950, December 1960 and
1970, November 1979, and September 1990, 1995 and 1997. Expenditure
relates to financial years beginning in year shown. Figures include
payments to widows overseas.
[b]Excluding widows' allowances (known as widows' payments after 1988).
[c]1980 data not available.

Sources: Report of the Ministry of National Insurance for 1951, p.45 and
p.60; Report of the Ministry of Pensions and National Insurance, 1961,
p.92 and p.137; *Social Security Statistics*, 1975, Tables 11.30 and 44.02;
Social Security Statistics, 1985, Tables 11.30 and 44.04; *Social Security
Statistics*, 1995 and 1998, Tables G3.01 and G3.03.

Lone parents

Before we look at how the benefit system has treated this group, the term 'lone
parent' requires some attention. One issue concerns the marital status of lone
parents: they can be unmarried, divorced, separated or widowed. The term
'single parent' is particularly open to misconstruction - sometimes it is used to
denote unmarried parents in particular and sometimes is just used as a
synonym for 'lone parent' generally. Second, readers should be on their guard
against the careless use of 'lone parents' and 'lone mothers' as synonyms.
Although the social security system now treats lone fathers and lone mothers
equally, in 1995 only 1.8 per cent of families with dependent children were
headed by a lone father, compared with 20 per cent of such families headed by
a lone mother (Haskey, 1998, p.8), and lone fathers' working patterns and
incomes are generally very different from those of lone mothers.

In the first half of the century, most lone parents were widows, but there
were also deserted and separated wives with children, unmarried mothers,
widowers, and so on. No provision was made for these groups until Beveridge's
review, and he had trouble fitting them into an insurance system (Beveridge,
1942, paras 346; 347). Eventually they were left to rely on less generous
National Assistance and its successors. They have not been required to be avail-

able for work, but can claim benefit until their youngest child reaches the age of 16. Some regard this situation as an anachronism left over from the days when married women with children did not work, and question whether it is appropriate in today's society (Commission on Social Justice, 1994, p.240), although others believe that bringing up children is a sufficiently important social contribution that society should provide lone parents with a genuine option to stay at home. Table 16.4 shows how in the second half of the century, the number of lone parents claiming social assistance shot up; in 1955 55 000 were claiming but by 1993 this had risen to over a million.

Table 16.4 Income Support for lone parents, Great Britain, 1970–97[a]

	Number of lone parents on Income Support (000s)	Number of dependants provided for (000s)	Percentage of lone parents receiving benefit for two years or more	Average weekly payment cash terms	1997 prices
1970	191	374	40.8	£8.96	£74.60
1975	276	534	44.6	£21.05	£92.33
1980	316	559	52.2	£37.78	£86.44
1984[b]	492	832	54.7	£40.06	£69.82
1990	793	1384	57.0	£56.09	£68.60
1995	1040	1927	61.4	£76.63	£80.38
1997	982	1824	62.2	£79.21	£79.21

Notes: [a]Figures relate to November 1970, December 1975, 1980 and 1984, May 1990 and 1995 and November 1997. Lone parents classified under a different premium heading (e.g., disabled) are excluded.
[b]1985 figures are unavailable.

Sources: Department of Health and Social Security, *Annual Report* 1970, Tables 112, 113 and 118; *Social Security Statistics*, 1975, 1981 and 1986, Tables 34.31, 34.38 and 34.89; *Social Security Statistics*, 1991, Tables A2.09, A2.12 and A2.34; *Social Security Statistics*, 1996, Tables A2.06, A2.09 and A2.32; *Social Security Statistics*, 1998, Tables A2.05, A2.06, A2.09 and A2.29.

This rise has occurred partly due to demographic changes described in Chapter 2. Evidence from the General Household Survey also indicates that since the early 1980s lone mothers have become gradually less likely to work full-time than in the past, and more likely to depend partly or entirely on benefit. This is consistent with the findings of Disney and Webb (1990, pp.17–19), who discuss how the rise in unemployment in the 1980s discouraged many lone parents from seeking work.

Towards the end of the century, the Labour government has tried to encourage lone parents to work, setting up the New Deal for lone parents in 1997 (extended to all lone parents in October 1998). This programme gives them the opportunity to see a personal advisor, get information about job vacancies and child care options, and find out whether they would be better off in work. A preliminary evaluation of the pilot scheme concluded that 'the New Deal programme has had a positive effect, consisting of a reduction of between 1 and 2 per cent in the overall number of lone parents on Income Support by the end of March 1998' (Hales, et al., 1998, p.1). So far it has not been compulsory for lone parents to attend a New Deal interview, although the indications are that it will become so in future. Even if this does happen, it seems unlikely that lone parents will actually be compelled to take paid work against their wishes.

Another benefit for lone parents was introduced in 1977. This was a non-contributory benefit called One Parent Benefit which took the form of a supplement to Child Benefit, and was paid for the first child only. Table 16.2 shows how the number of families receiving this more than doubled between 1980 and 1995, as did expenditure in real terms. One Parent Benefit was phased out in 1997 on the grounds that it gave lone parents more generous treatment than married couples with children.[7] This caused unease among many MPs and went against evidence that the cost of bringing up children is relatively higher for lone-parent families than for two-parent families (Dickens et al., 1996, p.55).

Apart from earnings and benefits, another potential source of income for lone parents is maintenance from the absent parent. The 1974 Finer Report recommended a Guaranteed Maintenance Allowance, but it was never introduced (Kiernan, Lewis and Land, 1998, pp.177–8), and maintenance was left to the courts to decide. However, evidence accumulated that in many cases it was paid irregularly, or not at all, and the issue was taken up again with the launch of the controversial Child Support Agency (CSA) in 1993. The CSA is supposed to assess how much maintenance absent parents ought to pay for their children and ensure that they pay it, but attracted widespread criticism for delays and mistakes (Hutton et al., 1998, pp.27–8) and reforms intended to simplify the system were put forward in 1998.

The unemployed

At the end of the nineteenth century, politicians began to accept the idea that unemployment was at least partly a structural problem, and in 1911 the National Insurance Act was passed. Part II of this introduced an experimental unemployment insurance scheme, which covered a limited number of industries where employment was generally high but vulnerable to occasional fluctuations. Benefits, set well below subsistence level, began to be paid in 1913 and unemployment was lower than expected, so the fund soon showed a handsome surplus (Gilbert, 1966, p.285).

In the inter-war period, high unemployment undermined the contributory basis of the scheme (Gilbert, 1970, pp.75–80). The government was forced to abandon the insurance principle and introduced a 'genuinely seeking work' test and also a means test for some claimants in 1922, to reduce costs and prevent abuse (Deacon, 1976, pp.21–6). In 1931 the scheme was restructured and put back on to a contributory basis. From now on, those without sufficient contributions to qualify could apply instead for 'transitional payments' subject to a households means-test which many considered intrusive. The generosity of the Public Assistance Committees which administered these payments varied from place to place, causing resentment and unrest (Deacon and Bradshaw, 1983, pp.14–22).

The Unemployment Act of 1934 restructured the system and created the dual approach which is still with us today. It set up one body, the Unemployment Insurance Statutory Committee, to deal with unemployment insurance and keep its finances healthy, and established the Unemployment Assistance Board to handle claims from workers for means-tested assistance. This caused an outcry to begin with since there were more losers than gainers from the new national rates of payment, but the rules were relaxed in response to the protests and crisis was averted (Gilbert, 1970, pp.179–92; Deacon and Bradshaw, 1983, pp.22–6). Table 16.5 shows the increase in the numbers of unemployed and expenditure on them, and the shift towards assistance which occurred between 1930 and 1935.

Table 16.5 Benefits for the unemployed, United Kingdom, 1920–35

	1921	1925	1930	1935
Number of insured persons registered as unemployed (000s)[a]	2038	1243	2500	1858
Expenditure on unemployment insurance (£m), cash terms[b]	52848	43658	71929	40065
Expenditure on unemployment insurance (£m), 1997 prices[b]	1424	1364	2479	1528
Expenditure on unemployment assistance (£m), cash terms[b]	–	–	19247	42423
Expenditure on unemployment assistance (£m), 1997 prices[b]	–	–	663	1618

Notes: [a]Numbers registered at December each year
[b]Expenditure figures exclude administration costs and relate to insurance years (July to July) beginning 1921 and 1925, and financial years beginning 1930 and 1935.

Source: *Statistical Abstract for the UK*, 1935, Tables 101 and 104.

In his report, Beveridge made it clear that he believed it was the duty of government to ensure full employment; only then could an unemployment insurance scheme operate successfully (Beveridge, 1942, para. 440).[8] Beveridge wanted unemployment insurance, now known as Unemployment Benefit, to be unlimited in duration, but this recommendation was never implemented. Instead, a limit was set, initially at 7 months (with the possibility of extension in some circumstances) and increased to 12 months in 1966. After that, the unemployed could move on to means-tested benefits if they satisfied the eligibility criteria. Thus the dual system of 1934 was retained.

Table 16.6 Benefits for the unemployed, Great Britain, 1950–97[a]

	1950	1960	1970	1980	1990	1995	1997
Numbers of unemployed people receiving benefits (000s)							
Social insurance[b]	209	177	302	940	343	386	180
Social assistance[c]	70	107	200	825	1029	1635	1049
Both social insurance and social assistance	37	31	58	161	60	120	25
Total receiving at least one unemployment-related benefit	242	253	443	1604	1312	1901	1204
Expenditure (£m), cash terms							
Social insurance[c]	17	30	150	1280	870	1102	570
Social assistance	n/a	n/a	n/a	794	2945	4823	3359
Total[d]	n/a	n/a	n/a	2428	5318	8643	6149
Expenditure (£m), 1997 prices							
Social insurance[b]	321	379	1252	2929	1064	1156	565
Social assistance[c]	n/a	n/a	n/a	1817	3602	5059	3332
Total[d]	n/a	n/a	n/a	5555	6504	9067	6100

Notes: [a]Figures refer to December 1950 and November from 1960 onwards. Before 1979, figures for social assistance do not distinguish assistance to the unemployed separately.
[b]Insurance benefits for the unemployed were Unemployment Benefit from 1948–96 and contributory Jobseeker's Allowance thereafter.
[c]Assistance benefits for the unemployed were National Assistance from 1948–66, Supplementary Benefit from 1966–88, Income Support from 1988–96 and income-based Jobseeker's Allowance thereafter.
[d]Total expenditure on the unemployed is greater than the sum of expenditure on UB and IS since it includes expenditure on other benefits received by unemployed people, such as Housing Benefit.

Sources: Report of the National Assistance Board for 1950, p.34; Report of the Ministry of National Insurance for July 1949–December 1950, page 54; Department of Employment and Productivity (1971), *British Labour Statistics Historical Abstract 1886–1968*, Tables 176 and 177; *Social Security Statistics*, 1975, Tables 1.32 and 44.02; *Social Security Statistics*, 1995, p.3, Tables A2.03, C1.01 and C1.02; *Social Security Statistics*, 1998, p.3, Tables A2.03, C1.01 and C1.03.

Table 16.6 shows how the total number of unemployed people receiving benefits and expenditure on them increased in line with unemployment (see Chapter 8 for figures on this), shooting up in the 1980s. Figure 16.1 presents the same information in graph form for the period since 1970, and reveals some striking trends about the types of benefits received by unemployed people. The numbers receiving Unemployment Benefit have dropped since the early 1980s and the numbers receiving means-tested Income Support and its predecessors have soared. In November 1980, slightly more unemployed people were receiving Unemployment Benefit than Income Support, but by November 1995, four times as many people were on Income Support as were on Unemployment Benefit.

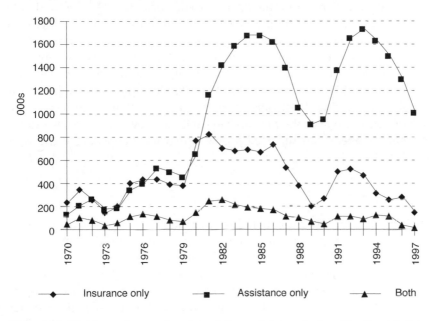

Figure 16.1 Numbers of unemployed receiving social security benefits, Great Britain, 1970–97

Notes: Figures refer to November except 1981 and 1976 where this was unavailable due to industrial action, so February 1982 and May 1976 figures have been used respectively.

Sources: *Social Security Statistics*, 1976, 1983 and 1988, all Table 1.32; *Social Security Statistics*, 1992, 1995, 1996 and 1998, all Table C1.01.

There are two explanations for the change. First, the great rise in unemployment in the early 1980s meant that many people were unemployed for over a year and therefore exhausted their entitlement to Unemployment Benefit; those who qualified could then transfer to Income Support instead. (This is similar to what happened in the 1930s.) Second, over the 1980s the government made eligibility criteria and contribution conditions for Unemployment Benefit progressively more stringent (Atkinson and Micklewright, 1989, pp.127–33) so fewer people qualified for it in the first place.

The blurring of the boundaries between unemployment insurance and social assistance culminated in 1996 when Jobseeker's Allowance was introduced. There are two 'routes' into Jobseeker's Allowance: a contributory route and a means-tested route (so it is in effect two different benefits under the same name). Contributory Jobseeker's Allowance replaced Unemployment Benefit and is similar to it, but only lasts for six months rather than a year. 'Income-based' (that is, means-tested) Jobseeker's Allowance replaced and is similar to Income Support for the unemployed.[9] Jobseeker's Allowance should in theory cost less than the old system since it shifts the unemployed off contributory benefit more quickly, continuing the trend towards means-testing. The government expected the introduction of Jobseeker's Allowance to reduce expenditure on benefits for the unemployed by around £60 million in 1996–97 and £240 million in 1997–98 (DSS, 1997, p.52). Spending on the unemployed did indeed fall subsequently but it is not possible to say how much of this was due to the rule change itself and how much was due to the fall in the number of unemployed people which was happening at the same time (DSS, 1999, p.84).

The low paid

Beveridge did not recognize that low pay might be a problem for some workers, since he expected family allowances to take care of the problem of large families. However, family allowances were not introduced at subsistence level as he had proposed, and were not nearly high enough to cover the costs of children. In the 1960s poverty was 'rediscovered', especially that of low-paid families with children, and in 1971 the government introduced a means-tested in-work benefit to help them, Family Income Supplement. It argued that this would be better targeted than an increase in family allowances across the board (Deacon and Bradshaw, 1983, pp.79–80).

The way in which Family Income Supplement was calculated was complicated, and take-up was very low at first. The benefit was also criticized for exacerbating what came to be known as the poverty trap (Field and Piachaud, 1971, pp.772–3): the situation where an increase in a person's earnings leads to little or no increase in income, since the person loses benefit and at the same time may have to pay higher taxes. In 1988 Family Income Supplement was replaced by a more generous scheme called Family Credit. Table 16.7 shows how expenditure increased, partly due to more families receiving Family Credit and partly to higher average amounts being paid. In the 1990s the government relaxed many of the eligibility rules for Family Credit, in an attempt to encourage parents to make the transition from depending entirely on benefit to working and using Family Credit to top up their income. These efforts appear to have met with some success; Table 16.7 shows that the number of families receiving Family Credit roughly doubled between 1990 and 1997.

Table 16.7 Family Income Supplement and Family Credit, Great Britain, 1971–97[a]

	Numbers receiving benefit (000s)			Average amount (£ per week)		Expenditure (£m)	
	Couples	Lone parents	Total	cash terms	1997 prices	cash terms	1997 prices
FIS							
1971	32	15	47	£1.73	£13.18	4	30
1975	26	31	57	£2.82	£12.37	12	53
1980	38	50	88	£7.85	£17.96	42	96
1985	117	81	199	£12.20	£20.07	130	214
FC							
1990	193	122	314	£27.40	£35.51	494	604
1995	340	268	608	£50.17	£52.63	1740	1825
1997	406	342	748	£57.84	£57.84	2338	2319

Note: [a]1971 figure refers to August; 1975–90 figures refer to April; 1995 and 1997 figures refer to May.

Sources: *Social Security Statistics*, 1977, Tables 32.10 and 44.01, *Social Security Statistics*, 1984 and 1988, Table 32.10. *Social Security Statistics*, 1991, Table A1.06; *Social Security Statistics*, 1995, Table A1.02; *Social Security Statistics*, 1998, Tables A1.01, A1.02 and A1.05.

In September 1999, Family Credit was replaced by a yet more generous scheme called the Working Families Tax Credit (HM Treasury, 1998a).[10] The aim of this scheme is to 'make work pay' for families with children, and to remove from them the stigma associated with claiming benefit, since it will be paid to workers through the pay packet instead. However, critics have argued that this will increase the administrative burden on (especially small) employers, who may then be reluctant to employ workers eligible for the tax credit. The fact that it is more generous and more families can claim it also has the side-effect that more will be drawn into the poverty trap, standing to lose the tax credit if they later increase their earnings.

Another development has been the pilot testing since 1996 of Earnings Top-Up, an in-work benefit aimed at low-paid workers without children, both single people and couples. They are a group who have not so far been eligible for social security benefits. The pilots are to last for three years, and if the results are considered successful, Earnings Top-Up will be introduced nation-wide.

The sick, disabled and injured

Industrial injuries and war pensions

From the beginning of the century, industrial and war injuries were treated separately from civilian disabilities, and under the post-war legislation these two groups have continued to receive more generous benefits than other disabled people. The first piece of social security legislation was the Workmen's Compensation Act of 1897, which introduced limited compensation for injured workers, and in 1916 a Ministry of Pensions was created to pay out war pensions to people disabled in war and the widows and other dependants of servicemen who were killed. Table 16.8 shows the numbers receiving these, which jumped up again with World War II, but have since fallen over time, until 1991 when they started to rise again. The DSS has suggested that this was due to more World War II veterans retiring, and also an increase in claims for hearing loss, closely associated with age.[11]

Table 16.8 War pensions, United Kingdom, 1920–97[a]

| | Beneficiaries of war pensions (000s)[b] | | | Expenditure (£m)[c] | |
	Disablement	Widows and dependants	Total	cash terms	1997 prices
1920	n/a	n/a	3345	85	1856
1930	494	876	1370	49	1686
1940	418	433	851	37	1102
1950	725	323	1047	78	1474
1960	522	202	724	96	1200
1970	384	136	519	128	1066
1980	266	88	354	424	970
1990	192	56	248	815	997
1995	264	51	315	1258	1320
1997	262	59	321	1281	1271

Notes: [a]Figures differ slightly from those in Table 16.14 due to minor methodological differences.
[b]Beneficiary figures refer to March from 1920–50, and to December from 1960 onwards.
[c]Expenditure figures relate to the financial year beginning in the year shown.

Sources: Ministry of Pensions report, 1919–20, p.11; 1921–22, p.19; 1929–30, p.1; 1931–32, p.1; 1939–48, p.33; Ministry of Pensions and National Insurance, *Annual Report*, 1953, p.70; 1962, p.91; *Social Security Statistics*, 1975, Tables 36.30 and 44.01; *Social Security Statistics*, 1995 and 1998, Tables F1.01 and F1.03.

Sickness and disability

Part I of the National Insurance Act of 1911 introduced a number of contributory benefits for sick workers, administered by 'approved societies', mutual friendly societies and trade unions approved by the government (Gilbert, 1966, p.349). The statistics do not show how many people actually received such benefits, but the numbers covered by the insurance scheme and expenditure on the benefits gradually increased over time. This scheme continued to operate until 1948.

Beveridge included sickness and disability in his plan for social insurance; he wanted a subsistence level disability benefit to be paid for as long as necessary until the recipient was able to return to work, with allowances for dependants.

Such a benefit was eventually introduced, called Sickness Benefit. For those without a sufficient contribution record and those with extra needs such as special diets, social assistance was available (Beveridge, 1942, para. 371).

Several important changes to the system were made in the 1970s. In 1971, Invalidity Benefit was introduced which was like a more generous version of Sickness Benefit paid after 28 weeks. Table 16.9 shows the statistics for both benefits combined from this point onwards. Also in 1971, an official survey of disabled people in England and Wales was published (Harris et al., 1971), which drew attention to their poverty and led to the introduction in the mid-1970s of several new contingency benefits for disabled people, such as the benefits which are now known as Severe Disablement Allowance and Disability Living Allowance. (The publication *Social Security Statistics* contains information on all of them.)

Table 16.9 Benefits for the sick and disabled, Great Britain, 1950–97/98[a]

	Recipients (000s)	Expenditure (£m) cash terms	1997 prices
1950[b]	908	69	1294
1955[b]	921	100	1416
1960[b]	896	135	1697
1965/66[c]	900	248	2614
1970/71	922	374	3112
1975/76	998	873	3829
1980/81	1043	1804	4128
1985/86	1137	2625	4318
1990/91	1678	4647	5683
1995/96	2406	7906	8293
1997/98	2341	7421	7362

Notes: [a]Figures relate to Sickness Benefit, Invalidity Benefit and Incapacity Benefit (see text for more details).
[b]For 1950–60, figures refer to average of monthly claims throughout year, and financial years beginning in the stated year.
[c]For 1965 onwards, claimant figures refer to claimants incapacitated at the end of the statistical year (June, from 1965/66–80/81, and April from 1985/86 onwards) and expenditure figures relate to financial year.

Sources: Ministry of Pensions and National Insurance, *Annual Report*, 1963, p.146; *Social Security Statistics*, 1977, Tables 3.40, 44.02 and 44.04; *Social Security Statistics*, 1995, Table D1.04; *Social Security Statistics*, 1996, Table D1.06; *Social Security Statistics*, 1998, Tables D1.03 and D1.04.

In 1983, the government introduced Statutory Sick Pay, a system whereby employers administer sick pay for their employees and are reimbursed through the National Insurance system. Only those who had recently made contributions but were not in employment at the time of falling sick remained eligible for Sickness Benefit.

The general trend has been for more people to be in receipt of sickness and invalidity benefits; the numbers stayed roughly constant between 1950 and 1980, but since then have more than doubled. This pattern is not unique to Britain and appears to be correlated with the increase in unemployment (Lonsdale and Seddon, 1994, p.154). One explanation is that in a time of high unemployment, it may be easier for people with partial disabilities to claim benefit as a disabled person than as an unemployed person, and disability benefits are also more attractive since they tend to be paid at a higher rate. An alternative theory is that in a recession, employers can be more selective and employ able-bodied people instead, and the evidence suggests that the growth was caused not by a rise in the number of initial claims, but rather by existing claimants staying on benefit longer (Berthoud, 1998, p.30).

The government clamped down on this in 1995 when it replaced both Sickness Benefit and Invalidity Benefit with a new benefit called Incapacity Benefit, which has a stricter qualifying test and is less generous than Invalidity Benefit in a number of ways (Ward, 1997, p.9). Table 16.9 indicates that there was subsequently a small drop in numbers receiving the benefit which fed through to expenditure. Further reforms were proposed in 1998 which, if implemented, will require people of working age applying for disability benefit to attend an interview with a personal advisor, to see whether it would be possible for them to work instead.

Carers

Since the 1970s, there has been growing recognition of the costs incurred by those who look after the sick and disabled, such as forgone earnings and extra expenses related to care-giving. In 1975 Britain introduced a contingency benefit aimed directly at carers of the severely disabled, called Invalid Care Allowance, although it is paid at a rate below Income Support and suffers from a number of other shortcomings (McLaughlin, 1990, pp.50–1). Initially,

Table 16.10 Invalid Care Allowance, Great Britain, 1980–97

| | Allowances current at end of year (000s) | | | Expenditure (£m) | |
	Men	Women	Total	cash terms	1997 prices
1980	n/a	n/a	7	5	11
1985	6	4	10	13	21
1990	24	110	134	208	254
1995	74	242	316	617	647
1997	94	280	374	745	739

Sources: *Social Security Statistics*, 1995 and 1998, Tables E4.02 and E4.04.

married women were not eligible for Invalid Care Allowance on the grounds that they were likely to be at home anyway. However, after a judgment by the European Court of Justice in 1986 the government was forced to extend eligibility to them, which explains the large rise in the number of women receiving it after that point, shown in Table 16.10.

Carers are also eligible for means-tested Income Support, provided that the person they care for receives certain specified disability benefits.

The elderly

In the late nineteenth century, the issue of old-age pensions was highly contentious and they were opposed by many factions (Macnicol, 1998, Chapters 4 and 5). Yet the labour movement managed to persuade the Liberals of their case, and after workmen's compensation, the next serious departure from the Poor Law came with the Old Age Pensions Act of 1908. This introduced a means-tested pension for people over 70, although recipients had to satisfy certain conditions to ensure that they were of suitably good character: for example, an applicant had to prove that he had been 'habitually' employed in his trade. Pensions began to be paid in January 1909, and proved to be very popular (Gilbert, 1966, p.226). In March 1909, 484 000 pensions were being paid in Great Britain, a figure which had nearly doubled to 917 000 by 1924 (Board of Trade, 1912, p.317; 1928, p.60). In 1925, contributory old-age pensions were introduced. Those who had made sufficient contributions received this between the ages of 65 and 70; then they moved on to the other, non-contributory pension but did not have to take a means test. Unfortunately this administrative procedure renders the statistics available for both pensions for these years fairly meaningless, so they are not presented here. Benefit rates were set at a relatively low level and large numbers of elderly people were still forced to resort to the Poor Law (Gilbert, 1970, p.253). Although the poverty surveys conducted in the inter-war period found that unemployment was the chief cause of poverty, as we would expect, old age remained an important reason too (Macnicol, 1998, Chapter 12).

Beveridge proposed a new scheme of contributory retirement pensions, to be paid at a flat rate. This was introduced but, contrary to his wishes, the system was made 'pay-as-you-go' from the beginning and has been ever since (that is, the contributions of the present generation of workers pay for the pensions of the present generation of pensioners).

In 1961, graduated (earnings-related) pension was introduced, which required workers earning over a certain level to make extra contributions and in return gain a top-up to their basic pension. This scheme never properly got off the ground and in 1975 legislation bringing in the more extensive State Earnings Related Pension Scheme (SERPS) was passed, which replaced it.[12] SERPS provided

Table 16.11   Retirement pensions,[a] Great Britain, 1950–97

	Contributory/Retirement Pension			Additional Pension (SERPS)		
	Number receiving[b] (000s)	Expenditure (£m)[c] cash terms	1997 prices	Number receiving[b] (000s)	Expenditure (£m)[c] cash terms	1997 prices
1950	4162	249	4692	–	–	–
1960	5563	677	8509	–	–	–
1970	7363	1778	14802	–	–	–
1980	8918	10518	24065	298	8	18
1990	9956	21973	26873	3066	726	888
1995	10427	27740	29099	4585	2222	2331
1997	10709	30382	30139	5317	3119	3094

Notes: [a]Including pensions paid to residents overseas but excluding old person's pension.
[b]Numbers in payment figures relate to end of March 1950, end of December 1960 and 1970, November 1970 and September 1990 and 1995.
[c]Expenditure figures relate to financial year beginning in year shown.

Sources: Ministry of National Insurance report for 1951, p.45 and p.60; Ministry of Pensions and National Insurance report for 1961, p.93 and p.137; *Social Security Statistics*, 1975, Tables 13.30 and 44.02; *Social Security Statistics*, 1985, Table 13.30; *Social Security Statistics*, 1995, Tables B1.01, B1.03 and B1.11; *Social Security Statistics*, 1998, Tables B1.01, B1.03 and B1.10.

an earnings-related pension based on the best 20 years of earnings, as a second tier (the first tier being the flat-rate basic state pension). Benefits began to be paid in 1979 but the scheme was due to take 20 years to mature, and people could opt out into occupational schemes as long as they satisfied certain criteria.

One of the main concerns of the 1985 Fowler review was the future cost of pensions, given the ageing population (see Chapter 2). The government proposed to abolish SERPS, but after consultation decided to retain it but make it less generous in various ways; for example, by basing it on lifetime earnings rather than an individual's best 20 years of earnings (DHSS, 1985b, p.13). It was estimated that these modifications would almost halve the future cost of SERPS (DHSS, 1985b, p.20). At the same time, tax incentives were provided to encourage people to 'contract out' of SERPS and instead contribute more to occupational pensions, or set up personal pensions, a relatively new form of provision (ibid., p.15).[13]

The abolition of the link between benefit rates and earnings hit pensioners' incomes hard, as Table 16.17 below shows. Yet for many people the decline in the state pension was offset to some extent by the growth of occupational and personal pensions, as shown in Table 16.12 and Figure 16.2, encouraged by tax reliefs. The Inland Revenue estimated the value of relief to occupational schemes in 1997/98 at £8.9 billion (Inland Revenue, 1998, p.75), and the higher the pension contribution, the greater the relief. Looking at state provision in isolation would therefore give a misleading picture of what has been happening to the living standards of a large number of (although by no means all) pensioners.

Table 16.12 Membership of occupational pension schemes, United Kingdom, 1936–91

	Membership (millions)	Members as % of those employed		
		Men	Women	Total
1936	2.6	–	–	–
1953	6.2	34	18	28
1956	8.0	43	21	35
1963	11.1	63	21	48
1967	12.2	66	28	53
1971	11.1	62	28	49
1975	11.4	63	30	49
1979	11.6	62	35	50
1983	11.1	64	37	52
1987	10.6	60	35	49
1991	10.7	57	37	48

Sources: Government Actuary, *Occupational Pension Schemes 1975*, Table 3.2; Government Actuary, *Occupational Pension Schemes 1991*, Table 2.1.

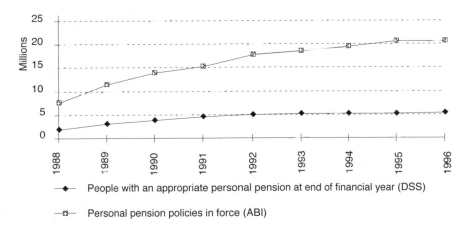

—◆— People with an appropriate personal pension at end of financial year (DSS)

—▫— Personal pension policies in force (ABI)

Figure 16.2 Personal pension statistics, United Kingdom, 1988–96

Sources: Association of British Insurers: *Insurance Review Statistics*, 1988–92, p.18; 1989–93, p.18; and 1990–94, p.18; Association of British Insurers (1997), *Insurance: Facts, Figures, Trends*, p.12; *Social Security Statistics*, 1997 and 1998, Table H2.02.

Statistics on the ownership of personal pensions are complex. The DSS publishes figures for the numbers owning an 'appropriate' personal pension (the type introduced in 1988) but these exclude the self-employed and people who own other types of personal pension. Meanwhile, the Association of British Insurers (ABI) publishes figures for the number of personal pension policies in force, but since it is possible to own more than one policy, these do not give the whole picture either. Figure 16.2 compares the two series, and the actual number of people owning personal pensions lies somewhere between them. It is clear that this form of provision has expanded since 1988, and also that the rate of increase slowed in the early 1990s; according to the ABI, this was due partly to the economic recession and partly to adverse publicity surrounding personal pensions as a result of the mis-selling scandal which afflicted the industry.

Who are the owners of these second-tier pensions? Evidence from the 1996 General Household Survey (ONS, 1998, Table 6.7) indicates that 75 per cent of men working full-time have a supplementary pension, either occupational or personal. This compares with 65 per cent of women working full-time, and just 33 per cent of women working part-time. At the end of the century, as Titmuss (1958, p.74) warned, we have a situation where there are 'two nations in old age': some pensioners face a reasonably prosperous retirement due to their personal and occupational pensions, while others have to rely on the basic state pension topped up with Income Support; not a cheerful prospect.

In December 1998, the government published its proposals for pension reform in a Green Paper (DSS, 1998b). It proposed to abolish SERPS and to replace it with a flat-rate 'Second State Pension' which would be more generous than SERPS for those on low incomes. A minimum income guarantee would be introduced which the government would aim to increase in line with earnings, and low-cost 'stakeholder pensions' for those on middle incomes would also be established. It remains to be seen how workable or effective these proposals will be.

The overall picture

Moving on to the wider picture, in this section two trends will be examined: first, the shift towards means-testing; and second, the rise in spending on social security.

Shift towards means-testing

At the beginning of the century, the only benefits available were in the form of public assistance. Gradually new benefits were introduced, as we have seen, and social insurance began to play a much larger role. By the 1920s roughly half of all social security expenditure went on social insurance benefits, and by the end of the 1930s they accounted for about 60 per cent (Beveridge, 1942, Table XVIII). Beveridge intended this pattern to continue, and social assistance was expected to decline in importance. But this never happened; Figure 16.3 indicates how the proportion of the population receiving means-tested Income Support has shot up since 1951.[14] Since every person receiving benefit may have dependants, the total number of people for whom benefit is being paid is much higher than the recipient count alone.

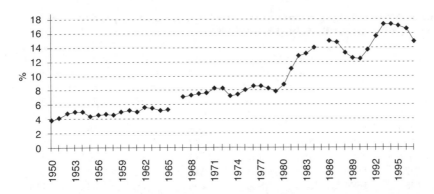

Figure 16.3 Proportion of the population dependent on Income Support and its predecessors, Great Britain, 1951–97

Notes: Population figures are mid-year estimates. Figures for recipients and their dependants relate to September in 1950, November or December from 1951–84, February in 1986 (hence no figure for 1985), May from 1987–96 and November 1997. 1997 figure includes beneficiaries of income-based Jobseeker's Allowance, which replaced Income Support for the unemployed.

Sources: NAB, *Annual Reports*, 1950–65; Ministry of Social Security, *Annual Report*, 1966, p.55; 1967, Table 31; DHSS, *Annual Reports*, 1968–71; *Social Security Statistics*, 1972, Table 34.29; *Social Security Statistics*, 1973–88, all Table 34.31; *Social Security Statistics*, 1989, Table 37.13; *Social Security Statistics*, 1995–97, all Table A2.01; *Social Security Statistics*, 1998, Table A2.01 and C1.11; *Annual Abstract of Statistics*, 1952, Table 6; 1977, Table 2.1; 1996, Table 2.1; *Population Trends*, 94, Winter 1998, Table 2.

Social insurance appears simply to have broken down. This is partly due to social changes which have occurred (Baldwin and Falkingham, 1994), but many now take the view that the system was flawed all along (Glennerster and Evans, 1994). Beveridge, as a liberal, believed that the state should leave room for voluntary supplementation. He wanted benefits to be paid at a flat rate that was minimal but also adequate – an impossible balancing act. In practice social insurance benefits were set too low from the beginning and while the better-off could afford supplementation through private insurance, the rest could not. Instead they often had to resort to means-tested assistance to top up the social insurance benefits, defeating the whole point of social insurance, which was to avoid the need for means-testing. Thus, as Glennerster and Evans point out, 'as a flat-rate poverty-based scheme, it never had a hope of securing the support of the middle class as social security had done in the US' (Glennerster and Evans, 1994, p.70). Table 16.13 breaks down the recipients of Income Support according to their 'client group'. It shows big increases particularly amongst lone parents and the unemployed, but all along, apart from the recessions of the early 1980s and 1990s, the largest group receiving social assistance has been pensioners. In most cases they claim relatively small amounts of means-tested benefits to top up their inadequate contributory state retirement pension.

Table 16.13 Numbers receiving Income Support and its predecessors by client group, Great Britain, 1950–97 (000s)

	Elderly[a]	Lone parents	Unemployed	Sick or disabled	Widows	Others	Total receiving IS
Sept 1950	795	35	66	218	98	73	1285
Dec 1955	1152	55	61	246	75	24	1612
Dec 1960	1309	71	128	268	65	18	1857
Dec 1965	1420	108	112	287	55	15	1997
Nov 1970	1902	191	239	323	63	20	2738
Dec 1975	1679	276	541	242	30	24	2793
Dec 1980	1694	316	854	205	15	34	3118
Dec 1984	1683	492	1952	273	20	188	4609
May 1990	1675	793	1063	330	319		4180
May 1995	1770	1040	1717	716	363		5606
May 1997	1720	1014	1224	827	398		5183

Notes: In 1983 a new unified Housing Benefit scheme was introduced. Prior to that, some people received Supplementary Benefit purely to help with their housing costs. The statistics do not distinguish how many. (See Chapter 14 for more information on Housing Benefit.)

In 1996, income-based Jobseeker's Allowance replaced Income Support for the unemployed. The May 1997 income-based JSA figure is included in this table to make it comparable with earlier years.
[a]Elderly defined as over 60.

Sources: Report of the National Assistance Board for 1950, p.6; 1955, p.6 and 1960, pp.8–10; *Social Security Statistics*, 1972, Table 34.30; *Social Security Statistics*, 1976, 1981 and 1986, Table 34.31; *Social Security Statistics*, 1996, Table A2.05; *Social Security Statistics*, 1998, Tables A2.05 and C1.02.

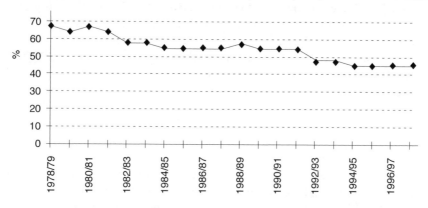

Figure 16.4 Proportion of benefit expenditure taken by contributory benefits, Great Britain, 1978/79–97/98

Sources: Data provided by the Department of Social Security; *Social Security Statistics*, 1998, p.3.

During the 1960s and 1970s, the proportion of expenditure on social insurance rose slightly as more people became eligible, but the proportion going on contingency benefits declined and means-testing began to play a bigger role (Atkinson, 1989, pp.110–12). Since 1980, the trend has accelerated. Figure 16.4 shows the great decline in the proportion of spending taken by contributory benefits, which in 1992/93 fell below 50 per cent for the first time since the 1920s. The proportion of spending taken by non-contributory benefits, most of which are means-tested, has conversely increased.

Rise in expenditure on social security

Moving on to aggregate expenditure, the social security system has been described as 'a leviathan almost with a life of its own' (DHSS, 1985a, p.45), but this is a misleading image since spending is in fact largely determined by exogenous economic and demographic trends. Table 16.14 shows how expenditure gradually rose in the first half of the century, and Table 16.15 shows the level of spending since 1950 (Figure 16.5 gives the same data as a percentage of GDP). It can be seen that spending dropped back in the late 1980s as the country came out of recession.

Table 16.14 Expenditure on social security benefits, United Kingdom, 1920–38 (£m)

	1920[a]	1925	1930	1935	1938
Poor relief	6.4	17.7	14.3	25.9	21.8
Sickness benefits	11.2	18.5	23.2	21.2	22.2
Contributory pensions	–	–	31.9	43.9	47.0
Unemployment benefits	4.5	46.5	75.2	44.5	52.7
Non-contributory old-age pensions	23.6	27.6	37.6	44.2	48.7
War pensions, etc.	92.3	62.2	49.8	41.2	37.9
Unemployment and retraining[b]	20.9	0.1	0.1	43.3	37.4
Total expenditure (£m)	158.9	172.6	232.1	264.2	267.7
Total expenditure, 1997 prices (£m)	3478	5330	7998	10079	9345

Notes: [a]Includes Southern Ireland.
[b]Grants for resettlement and training of demobilized men in 1920, and unemployment transitional payments or unemployment assistance benefits in 1935.

Sources: Feinstein (1972) *National Income, Expenditure and Output of the UK, 1855–1965*, Table 4.4; Peacock and Wiseman (1961) *The Growth of Public Expenditure in the UK*, Table A22.

But spending has resumed its climb since then, and social security is now the largest single item of government expenditure. Why has the cost of social security increased so much? Four main determinants of expenditure can be distinguished.

1   The number of benefits in existence. The introduction of new benefits to deal
    with contingencies not previously catered for has added to the overall cost of
    the system. There are currently over 30 different benefits, compared with just
    7 before the Beveridge reforms, excluding health insurance (Beveridge, 1942,
    Table XVIII). The precise effect of the introduction of a new benefit is diffi-
    cult to quantify since many people who begin to claim it might previously
    have been claiming other benefits instead. For example, when Invalidity
    Benefit was introduced, it floated many disabled people off supplementary
    means-tested assistance, reducing expenditure on that. For our purposes, it is
    the *net* expenditure of the introduction of new benefits which matters.

**Table 16.15 Expenditure on social security benefits, United
Kingdom, 1950–95**

	£m, cash terms	£m, 1997 prices	% of GDP
1950	0.67	12.7	5.8
1955	0.99	14.3	5.8
1960	1.49	18.8	6.5
1965	2.41	25.6	7.6
1970	3.92	33.3	8.9
1975	8.91	41.0	9.3
1980	25.44	59.9	12.7
1985	46.25	77.0	15.0
1990	62.93	78.6	13.1
1995	103.62	109.5	17.0

Sources: Central Statistical Office, *National Income and Expenditure* (*The Blue Book*),
1961–97; *Economic Trends Annual Supplement 1997*, Table 1.2.

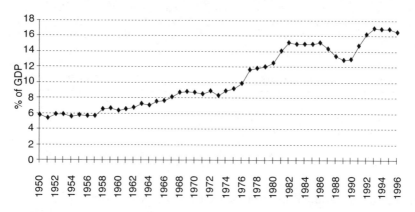

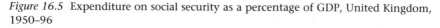

Figure 16.5 Expenditure on social security as a percentage of GDP, United Kingdom,
1950–96

Sources: Central Statistical Office, *National Income and Expenditure* (*The Blue Book*), 1961–97;
Economic Trends Annual Supplement 1997, Table 1.2.

2 The number of people receiving each particular benefit. In turn, this depends on several factors:

a) demographic and economic trends, which determine how many people meet given eligibility criteria for a particular benefit. For instance, if there are more lone parents due to higher divorce rates, then more are likely to qualify for means-tested Income Support.

b) eligibility criteria which the government can tighten or relax. For example, when Child Benefit was extended to families with only one child, more families became eligible to receive it.

c) levels of take-up. Not everybody who is eligible for a particular benefit necessarily claims it, and this appears to be a problem particularly associated with means-tested benefits. Table 16.16 presents official take-up statistics for two of the main means-tested benefits. (There are two main ways of measuring take-up: expenditure refers to the amount of benefit

Table 16.16 Take up of selected social security benefits, Great Britain, 1975–96/97

Supplementary Benefit/Income Support		
Expenditure	Caseload	
	Pensioner	Non-pensioner
1975	n/a	74%	75%
1981	85%	67%	75%
1985	91%	84%	
1990	85%–96%	74%–88%	
1994/95[cd]	88%–92%	76%–83%	

Family Income Supplement/Family Credit	
Expenditure	Caseload
1978/79[a]	55%	50%
1985–86[b]	54%	48%
1990–91[b]	68%	62%
1994/95[d]	82%	69%
1996/97[d]	84%	72%

Notes: [a]October 1978 to September 1979.
[b]Calendar years 1985 and 1986 combined.
[c]More recent figures for Income Support have been published but are not presented here since it was announced in December 1998 that an error had been discovered in these estimates and they were going to be revised (DSS press release, 11 December 1998). The new estimates were not available at the time of going to press, but should be ready in late 1999.
[d]Financial year.

Sources: Supplementary Benefits Commission, *Annual Report*, 1978, p.103; *Social Security Statistics*, 1983, p.261; 1989, pp.450–1; Department of Social Security (1994), 'Income Related Benefits: Estimates of Take-Up in 1990 and 1991', p.5; Department of Social Security (1996), 'Income Related Benefits: Estimates of Take-Up in 1994/95', p.3; Department of Social Security, press release, 1 October 1998.

claimed, while caseload refers to the number of people eligible. Since people are more likely to claim if they are entitled to a larger amount, take-up measured by expenditure is usually higher than when measured by caseload.) The table suggests that there may have been some improvement in take-up rates for Family Credit over time, but it is hard to discern a clear pattern for take-up of Supplementary Benefit and Income Support, because the range of estimates is so wide.

d) levels of fraud. Governments have been increasingly concerned about this problem but it is notoriously difficult to quantify, and official estimates are fraught with difficulties (Sainsbury, 1998, pp.3–6). If, as seems likely, means-tested benefits are more susceptible to fraud than other types, then it is plausible that the shift towards means-testing has been accompanied by higher levels of fraud, but there is no hard evidence to support this.

3 The duration spent on benefit. The longer each individual claimant remains on benefit, the greater the cost, and durations on benefit are now longer

Table 16.17 Weekly rates for selected benefits, 1948–97

	1948	1955	1961	1965
National Assistance/Supplementary Benefit[b]				
£ per week, cash prices	£1.20	£1.88	£2.68	£3.80
£ per week, 1997 prices	£23.92	£27.09	£32.78	£40.39
% of average earnings, all workers	–		–	–
Income Support				
£ per week, cash prices	–	–	–	–
£ per week, 1997 prices	–	–	–	–
% of average earnings, all workers	–	–	–	–
Retirement Pension				
£ per week, cash prices	£1.30	£2.00	£2.88	£4.00
£ per week, 1997 prices	£25.91	£28.82	£35.22	£42.52
% of average earnings, all workers	–	–	–	–
Unemployment Benefit/Jobseeker's Allowance				
£ per week, cash prices	£1.30	£2.00	£2.88	£4.00
£ per week, 1997 prices	£25.91	£28.82	£35.22	£42.52
% of average earnings	–	–	–	–
Sickness Benefit				
£ per week, cash prices	£1.30	£2.00	£2.88	£4.00
£ per week, 1997 prices	£25.91	£28.82	£35.22	£42.52
% of average earnings	–	–	–	–

Notes: Rates of SB and rates of IS cannot be directly compared since they vary for different family types – see Evans et al. (1994).

Average earnings are taken from the New Earnings Survey estimates of earnings for all adults.

Average earnings for months other than April are interpolated from the NES figures for the previous and the following April.

All benefit rates refer to single individuals, on their own insurance where applicable. Retirement pension figures are for a man or woman under 80. Income Support figures are for a single person over 25.

than in the past. Again, this is due to demographic and economic trends, such as increased longevity and long-term unemployment.

4 Rates of benefit in real terms. Britain has never had an official poverty line, and governments have always been reluctant to spell out exactly what items of expenditure are supposed to be covered by benefits. Post-war benefits were set below Rowntree's scale, and uprating them has been a thorny issue (Bradshaw and Lynes, 1995, pp.13–15). In the 1950s it was accepted that recipients should share in national prosperity, and benefits were uprated in line with prices or earnings, whichever was higher. This increased the overall cost of the system in real terms, until the link with earnings was cut in 1980. Since then, most benefits have been uprated in line with prices, so they have stayed roughly constant in real terms and fallen as a proportion of average earnings, as shown in Table 16.17.[15] Benefit levels are certainly not generous; recent research has shown that they are significantly below what would be required for even a low-cost budget (Yu, 1993, pp.28–9).

1971	1975[a]	1980	1985	1990	1995	1997
£5.80	£9.60	£21.30	£29.50	–	–	–
£49.30	£44.25	£50.18	£49.12	–	–	–
19.6	17.9	17.7	16.5	–	–	–
–	–	–	–	£36.70	£46.50	£49.15
–	–	–	–	£45.84	£49.15	£49.15
–	–	–	–	13.9	13.8	13.4
£6.00	£11.60	£27.15	£38.30	£46.90	£58.85	£62.45
£51.00	£53.46	£63.97	£63.77	£58.58	£62.20	£62.45
20.3	21.6	22.6	21.4	17.8	17.5	17.0
£6.00	£9.80	£20.65	£30.45	£37.35	£46.45	£49.15
£51.00	£45.17	£48.65	£50.70	£46.65	£49.10	£49.15
20.3	18.2	17.2	17.0	14.2	13.8	13.4
£6.00	£9.80	£20.65	£29.15	£35.70	£44.40	£47.10
£51.00	£45.17	£48.65	£48.53	£44.59	£46.93	£47.10
20.3	18.2	17.2	16.3	13.6	13.2	12.8

[a]April. There was another uprating of benefits in November.
[b]Ordinary rate has been used where more than one rate applied.

Sources: *Social Security Statistics*, 1988, Table 34.01; DSS (1997), *Abstract of Statistics for Social Security Benefits and Contributions*, Tables 6.1, 6.3, 6.4 and 6.8.

Rising social security expenditure does not necessarily indicate that the system is failing in some way, or out of control. The question is whether it is achieving as much as it should, given the level of expenditure. This is difficult to answer, since the objectives of the system are far from clear. Many would regard relief of poverty as being the principal objective, but there is more to it than this; for example social security also serves to insure against risks and to redistribute income over a person's life-cycle (Barr and Coulter, 1990, p.275). This makes evaluation of the system much more difficult; we cannot simply define success as the proportion of benefits going to the bottom half of the income distribution, for example, because this would be to ignore the other functions of social security. Figure 16.6 shows how many benefits go to the relatively well-off as well as the poor; this is in the nature of a system which includes many non-means-tested benefits.

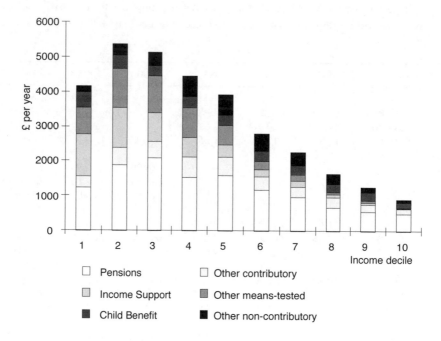

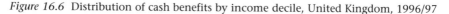

Figure 16.6 Distribution of cash benefits by income decile, United Kingdom, 1996/97

Notes: Both contributory and income-related Jobseeker's Allowance are included in the figure for other contributory benefits.

Source: Stuttard, Nigel (1998), 'The effects of taxes and benefits on household income, 1996–97', in *Economic Trends*, 533, pp.33–67.

Social security spending has undoubtedly been affected by unemployment and family breakdown, and if these problems could be ameliorated then the cost would fall, yet Figure 16.7 shows that the bulk of spending goes on the elderly and disabled. The system ought to provide people in these categories with an adequate minimum level of income, and a standard of living in line with contemporary norms. By international standards, the UK does not stand out as being especially generous, as Table 16.18 shows.

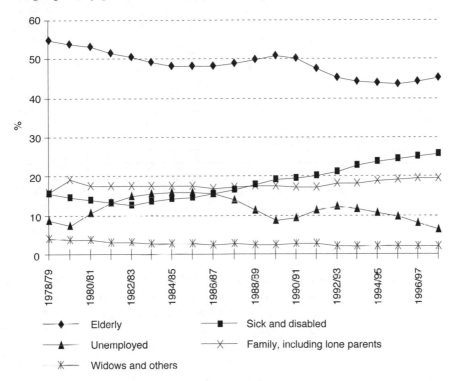

Figure 16.7 Proportion of benefit expenditure taken by different client groups, Great Britain, 1978/79 to 1997/98

Sources: Information provided by the Department of Social Security; *Social Security Statistics*, 1998, p.3.

To sum up, in this chapter we have seen how the benefit system developed steadily over the century, becoming gradually more comprehensive and generous as the country grew more affluent, up to 1980. Since then, persistent efforts have been made to reign back spending and discourage the 'dependency culture'. At the end of the century, social insurance is in decline, means-tests prevail once again, and those able to afford it make private provision for themselves. State-provided social security has largely become a residual measure for those with no alternative.

Table 16.18 Social security transfers^a as a percentage of GDP, 12 selected OECD countries, 1960–93

	1960	1968	1974	1985	1990	1993
Australia	5.5	5.1	7.0	9.5	9.8	11.6
Canada	7.9	7.3	9.2	12.2	12.9	16.0
France	13.5	17.0	15.5	22.1	21.2	23.6
Germany (West)	12.0	13.7	14.6	16.2	15.2	15.9
Ireland	5.5	6.5	11.4	16.5	14.1	15.4
Italy	9.8	12.6	13.7	17.2	18.2	19.5
Japan	3.8	4.5	6.2	10.9	11.5	12.1
Netherlands	n/a	16.2	20.7	26.2	25.8	26.7
Spain	2.3	8.1	9.5	16.0	15.9	18.4
Sweden	8.0	10.6	14.3	18.2	19.5	25.0
United Kingdom	6.8	8.7	9.2	13.5	11.6	15.6
United States	5.0	6.4	9.5	10.9	11.2	13.2

Note: ^aSocial security transfers consist of social security benefits for sickness, old age, family allowances, etc., social assistance grants and unfunded employee welfare benefits paid by general government

Source: OECD (1996), *Historical Statistics 1960–1994*, Table 6.3.

Notes on sources

Sources of statistics for the period before World War II can be found in various annual reports. These include the annual reports of the Local Government Board, which give information on the Poor Law, those of the Ministry of Pensions which contain statistics on war pensions, and those of the Unemployment Assistance Board which give information about its activities. Two more general sources are the *Abstract of Labour Statistics* produced by the Board of Trade and later by the Ministry of Labour, and the *Statistical Abstract for the UK*, the precursor of the *Annual Abstract of Statistics*.

For the period from the 1940s to the 1960s, the best sources of statistics are the annual reports of the difference administrative bodies, listed below. The dates given refer to the time period covered rather than the actual date of publication, which is often a year or two later.

- National Assistance Board annual reports 1944–65. The NAB then became the Supplementary Benefits Commission, which produced annual reports from 1975–79.
- Ministry of National Insurance annual reports 1944–52, followed by Ministry of Pensions and National Insurance annual reports 1953–65.
- Ministry of Social Security annual reports 1966–67. The Ministry then became the Department of Health and Social Security which produced annual reports from 1968–71.

From the 1970s to the end of the century, the main source is *Social Security Statistics*, published annually since 1972, initially by the Department of Health and Social Security but since the 1988 reorganization, by the Department of Social Security. Information on expenditure is available in the Treasury publication, the *Government's Expenditure Plans* (especially in volume II) published annually between 1977 and 1990; since 1991 the DSS has published its own annual department report, called the *Government's Expenditure Plans*, which contains the same information in greater detail. Finally, the Analytical Services Division of the DSS also publishes an annual *Abstract of Statistics* which provides information on benefit rates in relation to prices and earnings, and benefit expenditure in relation to GDP.

Acknowledgements

I am very grateful to A. B. Atkinson, David Piachaud, A. H. Halsey, Julia Parker and George Gillham for their helpful comments.

Notes

1   This chapter does not cover Housing Benefit since this is dealt with in Chapter 14, but expenditure on Housing Benefit is included in the tables and figures presented here.
2   Elsewhere they are sometimes called non-contributory benefits but this creates potential for confusion since means-tested benefits are also non-contributory.
3   This is not a comprehensive list of groups who may be entitled to benefits; the aim in this chapter is to provide a broad overview. Some of the groups mentioned may overlap, of course.
4   Since World War II, the main means-tested assistance benefit has gone through three incarnations. It began as National Assistance, then in 1966 became Supplementary Benefit and finally in 1988 was turned into Income Support. The fine details of all these schemes differ, but they have served the same essential function, of providing a minimum income for various categories of people.
5   Named after the Secretary of State at the time, Norman Fowler.
6   Throughout the chapter, where tables give expenditure figures they are for the financial year beginning in the year shown; for example, 1990 corresponds to financial year 1990/91.
7   Lone parents already receiving One Parent Benefit when it was abolished still get it, under the new title of Child Benefit (Lone Parent).
8   His calculations assumed an unemployment rate amongst insured employees of 8.5 per cent (Beveridge, 1942, para. 41).
9   The published figures for the number of people on Income Support are now lower since those unemployed people who under the old system would have received Income Support now receive income-based Jobseeker's Allowance instead. In the relevant tables presented here, these unemployed people are added to the Income Support figures to make the totals as comparable as possible.
10   It should be noted that since this will be a tax credit rather than a cash benefit as such, expenditure on it will no longer be counted as part of the DSS budget.

11   The law was subsequently changed in 1996 so that war pensions are no longer increased to reflect any rise in overall hearing loss after leaving service.

12   People who contributed to graduated pension during these years still receive it when they retire, and information about it is still published in *Social Security Statistics*; in 1997 roughly three-quarters of pensioners received it, but the average extra amount was just £2.36 a week (*Social Security Statistics*, 1998, table B1.11).

13   Under a personal pension scheme, an individual pays contributions into a fund which he or she owns, but which is managed by a financial institution. When the person retires, the fund is used to buy an annuity to provide him or her with a pension.

14   There have been significant changes in the structure of this benefit over time. In 1983, a unified Housing Benefit was introduced; prior to this, some people received Supplementary Benefit purely to cover their rent (see Chapter 14 for more on this). Given that they will have dropped out of the statistics after 1983, this makes the increase even more striking. Furthermore, big changes were made to the structure of the benefit in 1988 when it became Income Support; see Dilnot and Webb (1988) or Evans et al. (1994) for more detail.

15   As Bradshaw and Lynes (1995, pp.47–8) point out, the impression gained from such a comparison depends partly on the choice of earnings index. In the earlier period, benefit rates were conventionally compared with average male manual earnings, but since 1970 it has been possible to compare them with average earnings of both sexes, which seems preferable. These average earnings figures are derived from the New Earnings Survey estimates of the earnings of all full-time adult workers whose earnings are unaffected by absence.

References

Abel-Smith, Brian (1994) 'The Beveridge Report: its origins and outcomes', in Hills, John, Ditch, John and Glennerster, Howard (eds), *Beveridge and Social Security: An International Retrospective*, Clarendon Press, Oxford.

*Atkinson, A. B. (1989) *Poverty and Social Security*, Harvester Wheatsheaf, London.

Atkinson, A. B. and Micklewright, John (1989) 'Turning the screw: benefits for the unemployed 1979–1988', in Atkinson, A. B., *Poverty and Social Security*, Harvester Wheatsheaf, London.

*Baldwin, Sally and Falkingham, Jane (eds) (1994) *Social Security and Social Change: New Challenges to the Beveridge Model*, Harvester Wheatsheaf, London.

Barr, Nicholas and Coulter, Fiona (1990) 'Social security: solution or problem?', in Hills, John (ed.) *The State of Welfare: The Welfare State in Britain since 1974*, Clarendon Press, Oxford.

*Berthoud, Richard (1998) *Disability Benefits: A Review of the Issues and Options for Reform*, York Publishing Services, York.

*Beveridge, William H. (1942) *Social Insurance and Allied Services*, Cmnd 6404, HMSO, London.

Board of Trade (1912) *Fifteenth Abstract of Labour Statistics*, HMSO, London.

Board of Trade (1928) *Statistical Abstract for the UK for the years 1912 to 1926*, HMSO, London.

Bradshaw, Jonathan and Lynes, Tony (1995) *Benefit Uprating Policy and Living Standards*, SPRU Social Policy Report 1, University of York, York.

Commission on Social Justice (1994) *Social Justice: Strategies for National Renewal*, Vintage, London.

Deacon, Alan (1976) *In Search of the Scrounger: The Administration of Unemployment Insurance in Britain 1920–1931*, Occasional Papers on Social Administration 60, Social Administration Research Trust, London.

* Deacon, Alan and Bradshaw, Jonathan (1983) *Reserved for the Poor: The Means Test in British Social Policy*, Blackwell, Oxford.

Department of Health and Social Security (DHSS) (1985a) *Reform of Social Security, Vol.1*, Cm. 9517, HMSO, London.

Department of Health and Social Security (1985b) *Reform of Social Security: Programme for Action*, Cm. 9691, HMSO, London.

Department of Social Security (DSS) (1997) *Social Security Departmental Report: The Government's Expenditure Plans 1997–98 to 1999–2000*, Cm. 3613, The Stationery Office, London.

*Department of Social Security (1998a) *New Ambitions for Our Country: A New Contract for Welfare*, Cm 3805, The Stationery Office, London.

Department of Social Security (1998b) *A New Contract for Welfare: Partnership in Pensions*, Cm 4179, The Stationery Office, London.

Department of Social Security (1999) *Social Security Department Report: The Government's Expenditure Plans 1999/2000*, Cm 4214, The Stationery Office, London.

Dickens, Richard, Fry, Vanessa and Pashardes, Panos (1996) *The Cost of Children and the Welfare State: an Empirical Analysis Based on Consumer Behaviour*, Department of Economics Discussion Paper 466, University of Essex, Essex.

Dilnot, Andrew and Webb, Steven (1988) 'The 1988 social security reforms', in *Fiscal Studies*, 9(3), pp. 26–53.

Disney, Richard and Webb, Steven (1990) 'Why social security expenditure in the 1980s has risen faster than expected: the role of unemployment', *Fiscal Studies* 11(1), pp.1–20.

Evans, Martin, Piachaud, David and Sutherland, Holly (1994) *Designed for the Poor – Poorer by Design? The Effects of the 1986 Social Security Act on Family Incomes*, STICERD Welfare State Programme Discussion Paper WSP/105, London School of Economics, London.

Feinstein, C. H. (1972) *National Income, Expenditure and Output of the United Kingdom, 1855–1965*, Cambridge University Press, Cambridge.

Field, Frank and Piachaud, David (1971) 'The poverty trap', *New Statesman*, 3 December, pp.772–3.

*Gilbert, Bentley B. (1966) *The Evolution of National Insurance in Great Britain*, Michael Joseph, London.

Gilbert, Bentley B. (1970) *British Social Policy 1914–1939*, Batsford, London.

Glennerster, Howard and Evans, Martin (1994) 'Beveridge and his assumptive worlds: the incompatibilities of a flawed design', in Hills, John, Ditch, John and Glennerster, Howard (eds), *Beveridge and Social Security: An International Retrospective*, Clarendon Press, Oxford.

Hales, Jon, Shaw, Andrew and Roth, Wendy (1998) *Evaluation of the New Deal for Lone Parents: A Preliminary Assessment of the 'Counterfactual'*, Department of Social Security In-House Report no. 42, Department of Social Security, London.

Harris, Amelia et al. (1971) *Handicapped and Impaired in Great Britain*, Office of Population Censuses and Surveys, London.

Haskey, John (1998) 'One-parent families and their dependent children', *Population Trends no. 91*, Spring, pp.5–14.

HM Treasury (1998a) *The Working Families Tax Credit and Work Incentives*, HM Treasury, London.

HM Treasury (1998b) *Modern Public Services for Britain: Investing in Reform*, The Stationery Office, London.

*Hills, John, Ditch, John and Glennerster, Howard (eds) (1994) *Beveridge and Social Security: An International Retrospective*, Clarendon Press, Oxford.

Hutton, Sandra, Carlisle, Jane and Corden, Anne (1998) *Customer Views on Service Delivery in the Child Support Agency*, Department of Social Security Research Report no. 74, The Stationery Office, London.

Inland Revenue (1978) *Inland Revenue Statistics 1978*, HMSO, London.

Inland Revenue (1998) *Inland Revenue Statistics 1998*, The Stationery Office, London.

*Kiernan, Kathleen, Lewis, Jane and Land, Hilary (1998) *Lone Motherhood in Twentieth-Century Britain: From Footnote to Front Page*, Clarendon Press, Oxford.

Lonsdale, Susan and Seddon, Jennifer (1994) 'The growth of disability benefits: An international comparison', in Baldwin, Sally and Falkingham, Jane (eds), *Social Security and Social Change: New Challenges to the Beveridge Model*, Harvester Wheatsheaf, London.

Lowe, Rodney (1994) 'A prophet dishonoured in his own country? The rejection of Beveridge in Britain, 1945–1970', in Hills, John, Ditch, John, and Glennerster, Howard (eds), *Beveridge and Social Security: An International Retrospective*, Clarendon Press, Oxford.

McLaughlin, Eithne (1990) *Social Security and Community Care: The Case of the Invalid Care Allowance*, Department of Social Security Research Report no. 4, HMSO, London.

Macnicol, John (1980) *The Movement for Family Allowances, 1918–45: A Study in Social Policy Development*, Heinemann, London.

Macnicol, John (1998) *The Politics of Retirement in Britain, 1878–1948*, Cambridge University Press, Cambridge.

Office for National Statistics (ONS) (1998) *Living in Britain: Results from the 1996 General Household Survey*, The Stationery Office, London.

Peacock, Alan T. and Wiseman, Jack (1961) *The Growth of Public Expenditure in the United Kingdom*, Oxford University Press, London.

Richardson, Ann (1984) *Widows Benefits*, Policy Studies Institute, London.

Sainsbury, Roy (1998) 'Putting fraud into perspective' in *Benefits* 21, pp.2–6.

Stuttard, Nigel (1998) 'The effects of taxes and benefits on household income, 1996–97', in *Economic Trends*, 533, pp.33–67.

Titmuss, Richard M. (1958) 'Pension systems and population change', in *Essays on the Welfare State*, Allen and Unwin, London.

Ward, Sue (1997) *An Unfit Test: CAB Clients' Experience of the Medical Test for Incapacity Benefit*, National Association of Citizens' Advice Bureaux, London.

Yu, Autumn C. S. (1993) 'A low cost budget', in Bradshaw, Jonathan (ed.) *Household Budgets and Living Standards*, Joseph Rowntree Foundation, York.

Further reading

In addition to the asterisked items in the References, four further books may be of interest:

Atkinson, A. B. (1995) *Incomes and the Welfare State*, Cambridge University Press, Cambridge, contains several essays on the development of social security and possible future policy options.

Brown, Joan C. (1984) *The Disability Income System*, Policy Studies Institute, London, provides an authoritative account of the development of benefits for the disabled.

Hill, Michael (1990) *Social Security Policy in Britain*, Edward Elgar, Aldershot, provides a general review of social security policy up to 1989.

Hills, John (1997) *The Future of Welfare: A Guide to the Debate*, Joseph Rowntree Foundation, York, explains why the Welfare State is not in crisis.

Part VI
Social Order and Social Control

17
Volunteers and Voluntarism

Brian Harrison and Josephine Webb

The Public Authority and the salaried official can only do the work in gross; they are apt to be blunt and obtuse; to have no fingers, but only thumbs ... We need the voluntary worker to be the eyes and fingers of the Public Authority ... as the circumference of Public Authorities is extended the greater becomes the periphery.

Eleanor Rathbone, quoting Sidney Webb,
House of Commons debates 30 April 1936

Definition and scope

The USSR's collapse has recently highlighted democracy's dependence on 'civil society', whose weakness threatened Russia's attempt in the 1990s to establish democratic structures. Integral to civil society is voluntarism, which the *Oxford English Dictionary* defines as 'the principle of relying on voluntary action rather than compulsion'. Its first citations come from the US, where it is stronger than in Britain. Its first British citation in this broad sense (1973) occurs in inverted commas, and the word first appears in a trade union context; indeed, the Trades Union Congress (TUC) membership (6.7 million in 1998) surpasses that of even the largest voluntary society in Britain. Yet the reality of voluntarism had been growing for centuries in Britain, embracing at its widest extent any coordinated initiative within the community that is not prompted by the state. Not till the 1970s did Britain require a term to capture diverse attitudes so readily taken for granted: that is, to denote formal and informal variants of 'self-help', together with the mutual help, self-defence and spontaneous initiative that are nourished by charity, foundation, pressure group and 'think tank'. The term was needed only when such attitudes and institutions seemed under threat.

Diversity is voluntarism's strength. For lawyers a charity is a non-political organization which tangibly benefits a significant number of people without distributing profits (Ware, 1989, pp.77–9). Its neutrality is perpetually at risk

587

when collaborating with government, and in the 1970s Oxfam and other prominent charities acknowledged the dangers of becoming politically partisan. By no means all voluntary organizations are charities; conversely, some organizations technically known as charities are peripheral to the voluntary sector. The 'foundation', for decades prominent in American life, is a sub-category of charity whose importance is growing in Britain. The term 'pressure group', also American in origin, did not enter general use in Britain till the 1960s. Defined by the *Oxford English Dictionary* as 'a group or association of people representing some special interest, who bring concerted pressure to bear on public policy', its sub-categories are diverse. Of these, the 'interest group' or 'lobby' (the Engineering Employers' Federation, for example) operates continuously and usually unobtrusively to represent people whose material interests interact with government policy. It will usually be self-interested, though self-interest and the national interest may coincide. By contrast, the 'opinion group' or 'cause group' (the Campaign for Nuclear Disarmament, for example) is self-consciously altruistic, though it may nourish subtle variants of self-interest within its crevices. It operates more openly because its strength lies in its supporters' voting power. The distinction between 'interest' and 'opinion' group is not clear-cut, and some groups (the trade-union movement in the 1960s and 1970s, for example) may straddle the divide.

Some pressure groups seek to supersede the state, some aim to be captured by it. For example, the Family Planning Association's aim was realized in 1975 when the state assumed its role of advising on birth control. Such groups diverge, too, on where and how they apply their pressure, and on how they relate to political party. A pressure group can sometimes become a political party, or at least claim to be doing so; it was from the trade union movement that the Labour Party emerged, and environmentalists hope that by mobilizing themselves in the 'Ecology Party' they will force the other parties to listen. On the other hand, in a simple-majority electoral system a party cannot become a pressure group without endangering its mass electoral support; hence the Labour Party's wariness since the 1970s in its relations with the trade unions. The 'think tank' (the Institute of Economic Affairs, for example) has been increasingly prominent in Britain since the 1960s, and resembles the foundation in its breadth of concern. Unlike the 'opinion group' it works up a range of practicable policy proposals from other people's ideas instead of pioneering and campaigning on a single issue. Unlike the foundation and pressure group, it positively courts partisan alignment. Through the Fabian Society it became integral to Labour's twentieth-century policy making, and through the Centre for Policy Studies it helped transform the Conservative Party's agenda in the 1970s.

A non-governmental activism so pervasive and diverse can be discussed only selectively here. Charities are prominent in what follows partly because they are at the voluntarist end of the interventionist spectrum that runs from the individual to the state, but also because their fund-raising role furnishes statistics which can clarify trends. There is something paradoxical about the fact that as voluntarism became less salient in national policy between the 1880s and the 1970s, reliable and consistent runs of statistics on voluntary activity improved. For it is the state that collects and systematizes statistics, and exclusive reliance upon them may conceal voluntarism's importance before World War II. Braithwaite, a pioneer in tracing charitable trends, used income figures in the Charity Organisation Society's annual register, and found that between 1908 and 1927 major changes in welfare, warfare, taxation policy and the economy had not greatly altered the level of charitable funding. Data on charities in Liverpool showed that their total income advanced between 1923 and 1933, benefiting from falling prices and charging more for services. She estimated the total income of all charities in England and Wales at £42.5 million in 1934, a year in which central government was spending a total of £150.7 million on social insurance and old-age pensions (Braithwaite, 1938, pp.109, 115–16, 163; Mitchell, 1988, p.590). The Charities Act (1960) made more systematic information available, though some charities were not required to register. In the early years many of the charities on the Act's public register of charities for England and Wales were not new; by 1970 the register included 76 648 charities, of which only 10 444 had been set up during the previous ten years. By 1998 the register included 188 476 charities, and thousands were being added annually. Some are subsidiaries of other charities, and defunct charities are gradually weeded out. Most charities are very small; in January 1998 the 70.5 per cent of registered charities whose annual incomes were under £10 000 accounted for only 1.5 per cent of charities' total annual income. Conversely, the annual incomes of 248 charities (0.15 per cent of the total) each exceeded £10 million, accounting for two-fifths of the total income of all charities (Charity Commission Website).

Table 17.1 Number of charities in England and Wales registered with the Charity Commission, end of year, 1961–98

1961	1182
1965	57530
1970	76648
1975	119978
1980	136048
1985	154135
1990	171434
1995	181467
1998	188476

Source: *Annual Reports of the Charity Commissioners for England and Wales*; Charity Commission Website.

Grants made by the top 400 charitable foundations (Table 17.2) have increased markedly in real terms since the mid-1980s, although the aggregated statistics are inevitably rough and ready.

Table 17.2 Grants made by top charitable foundations in the UK, ranked by grants given, 1987–96

| Year | Grants made by top 20 (£m) | | Grants made by top 400 (£m) | |
	Cash terms	1997 prices	Cash terms	1997 prices
1987	106.3	164	204.2	316
1988	117.6	173	234.8	346
1989	143.3	196	282.8	387
1990	193.1	241	348.8	436
1991	236.5	279	437.6	516
1992	269.0	306	481.1	547
1993	582.0	652	792.2	887
1994	441.9	483	692.7	757
1995	602.1	636	901.6	953
1996	824.9	851	1157.2	1193

Sources: Charities Aid Foundation, *Charity Trends* for years 1988–93; Charities Aid Foundation: *Dimensions of the Voluntary Sector* for years 1995–98.

Rare indeed is the charity or pressure group which declares itself redundant, and given volunteers' responsiveness to new needs, voluntary bodies proliferate. Corporately jealous of their independence, they tend also to mobilize independent-minded people who feel strongly about things. Splits within voluntarist bodies are not necessarily damaging: they often reflect growth and commitment, and can even be amicable and deliberate. For example, the Royal Society for the Prevention of Cruelty to Animals (RSPCA) encouraged the National Society for the Prevention of Cruelty to Children's (NSPCC) formation in 1884 to counter the reproach that animal lovers do not like children. Such splits can also generate creativeness, energy and cash. In the 1980s the Cancer Research Campaign and Imperial Cancer Research Fund argued that their joint presence in the field boosted overall revenue for cancer research; besides, according to *The Times* on 4 October 1983, a coordinating committee fostered an informal mutual division of labour. On the other hand, such splits inconvenience governments, and on 4 November 1997 the *Financial Times* reported that John Prescott was pressing the water companies to amalgamate their two competing organizations – the Water Services Association and the Water Companies Association – into a single lobby group.

Coordination can also come from within the voluntarist world, often through pragmatic and informal collaboration between quite distinct organizations; the National Trust, for instance, takes a pride in conservation work which recruits volunteers from the Prince's Trust and the Scout Associations.

More formal is the collaboration promoted by confederal voluntarist structures like the TUC, the Confederation of British Industry (CBI) and the Institute of Directors. Attempts have also been made formally to coordinate charities. From 1869 the Charity Organisation Society (COS) tried to boost charity as a cure for poverty, primarily within London, by attacking fraud, removing duplication and coordinating philanthropy with the state's Poor Law structure. But the relevant charities were sectarian, the Society acquired a rather censorious image, and its resolute pragmatism distanced it unduly from twentieth-century economic theory. So despite being rechristened 'Family Welfare Association'(FWA) in 1946, its influence drained away. Still, its demise should not be antedated. Though after 1918 it showed none of its late-Victorian vitality, the number of its applicants kept up well until the 1950s, and the proportion assisted (financially or otherwise) rose to more than half between the wars and fell only slowly thereafter.

Table 17.3 Cases dealt with by District Committees of the Charity Organisation Society, London, 1900–59

	Applications made	Applications withdrawn	Applications assisted
1900	16631[a]	n/a	n/a
1905	19631[a]	n/a	n/a
1910	22320	3540	8463
1914	19074	3714	7508
1920	13240	2403	7169
1925	14574	2484	7840
1930	14876	2450	8010
1935	15856	3378	8114
1940	16352	2932	10101
1945	15163	2500	9988
1950	11075	n/a	6352
1955	4477	n/a	2524
1959	2912	n/a	n/a

Note: [a]Applications decided. The number of applications made is unavailable for these years, but the experience of other years suggests that it was probably a thousand or so above the number of applications decided.

Sources: Annual reports of the COS, 1900–46; FWA, 1946–59.

The COS kept alive the ideal of personal service, and in strongly emphasizing the importance of well documented casework it helped to pioneer the growing twentieth-century profession of 'social worker'. In seeing the family whole instead of despatching its various problems to separate specialisms, it seemed both administratively and intellectually backward between the wars, but in the 1960s social workers came to regard this integrating outlook more favourably. By then, however, the FWA was in serious decline, nor would its founders have relished its increasingly centralized structure, let alone its mounting reliance on local authority funding. Yet its continuing influence extends still further: it simultaneously responded to new needs and concealed its resourcefulness from posterity by encouraging new voluntarist offshoots, such as the Citizens' Advice Bureaux. Besides, its earlier decentralized and participatory structure made it an airport lounge through which influential people travelled to other destinations, selected partly because the COS's pragmatic emphasis continuously exposed its unfashionable theories to the facts.

Add to this the contribution made by the COS's Birmingham supporters towards creating a further voluntarist cooperative venture, broader in outlook, launched in 1919: the National Council of Social Service (NCSS). It encouraged people to fill the gaps in voluntary provision, and provided specialist knowledge on shared problems such as taxation and legal advice. It fostered village halls, community centres, Citizens' Advice Bureaux, Young Farmers' Clubs, youth hostels, boys' clubs and welfare structures for old people. Its expenditure rose very fast after 1932 because government backed its efforts to help the unemployed. Government provided 35 per cent of its income in 1941/42, 44 per cent in 1951/52, 60 per cent in 1970/71 and its support retained that high level in the 1980s. By then government was assigning it special tasks such as 'Opportunities for Volunteering', whereby unemployed people were enlisted into voluntary work in welfare projects; this explains the peak in its funding during that decade.

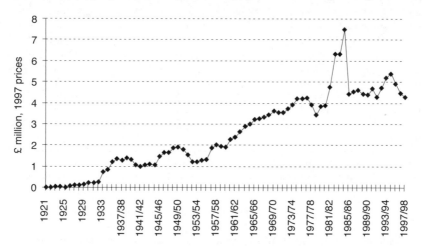

Figure 17.1 Expenditure of National Council for Voluntary Organisations, 1921–97/98

Notes: NCVO was known as the National Council of Social Service until 1980. The way in which the statistics are calculated was changed in 1976/77, 1978/79, 1982/83, 1987/88, 1988/89, 1994/95 and 1996/97. In each case the figure calculated under the new procedure is shown.

Sources: Morgan (1947), p.81; NCVO annual reports.

In 1980 the NCSS was rechristened 'National Council for Voluntary Organisations' (NCVO) to avoid confusion with the statutory social services, and its annual report for 1980/81 lists its re-stated aims: 'to extend the involvement of voluntary organisations in responding to social issues', 'to be a resource centre for voluntary organisations', and 'to protect the interests and independence of voluntary organisations'. Since then it has coordinated the voluntary sector's response to such contemporary developments as the changing role of the state and the impact of the National Lottery. Its published expenditure figures seem mutually consistent up to the mid-1970s, but thereafter their basis often changes. This partly reflects the NCSS's maternal role, for, like the RSPCA in the nineteenth century, it benevolently edged its fledgelings (Age Concern in 1970, the Charities Aid Foundation in 1974, the Citizens' Advice Bureaux in 1977) into leaving the nest. But it also reflects NCVO willingness in the 1980s to supply services in response to government funding. In its annual report for 1988/89 its Director says that 'whereas a decade ago, voluntary organisations were perceived largely as an adjunct of the state, now they are increasingly seen as equal and independent partners working alongside the public and private sectors'.

Information about giving by individuals comes from two main sources, each with strengths and weaknesses: the Family Expenditure Survey (FES) and the Individual Giving Survey (IGS), previously known as the Charity Household Survey. The government-run FES is an annual survey which asks a random sample of about 7 000 people to record two weeks' total expenditure; it defines charitable giving relatively narrowly, with little guidance on how to answer questions. The IGS, conducted by the Charities Aid Foundation between 1985 and 1993, defines giving more broadly, and confines its questions to charitable giving and volunteering. It asks its small quota-sample of about 1 000 people about their gifts during one month, and jogs memories with prompts. The longest time-series of FES data available shows (Table 17.4) that between 1974 and 1993/94 the proportion of households giving to charity fell, but because the mean size of weekly donations increased in real terms, total household donations to charity rose in real terms, though when related to the growth of incomes they fell slightly. This decline may stem partly from younger generations' diminished tendency at all ages to give by comparison with their elders (Banks and Tanner, 1997, pp.19–20).

The IGS run of data is much shorter and, though more comprehensive than the FES, suffers from two problems: the survey design has changed (for example, in 1992 the unit of analysis changed from the household to the individual adult) and the small size of the sample means that the estimates are very rough. Overall, the IGS estimates suggest that total giving in real terms did not change significantly between 1987 and 1993 (Halfpenny and Lowe, 1994, p.7). A survey comparing patterns of donation in Spain, France, Britain, the US and

Canada during 1991 showed that for the proportion of the adult population giving, Britain (65 per cent) surpassed all except Spain (71 per cent), and that Britain's mean donation per person surpassed all but Canada and the US; but it also revealed Britain's typical donation per donor per month as by far the lowest of the five (Charities Aid Foundation, 1994, pp.11; 83).

Table 17.4 Charitable giving, UK households, 1974–93/94 at 1996 prices

	% of households giving	Mean amount given per week (giving households)	Median amount given per week (giving households)	Mean amount given per week (all households)
1974	34.3	£2.48	£0.84	£0.86
1980	32.3	£2.11	£0.72	£0.70
1985	30.8	£3.61	£0.91	£1.11
1990	28.6	£3.87	£1.20	£1.11
1993/94	29.1	£4.11	£1.23	£1.18

Source: Analysis of Family Expenditure Survey by Banks and Tanner (1997), p.38.

The volunteers

It is difficult to count volunteers because there are major problems of definition and no long runs of comparable data. The General Household Survey (GHS), an annual national official survey of people aged 16 and over, investigated levels of volunteering on five occasions (Table 17.5). Its definitions were narrow in 1973 and 1977, but widened in 1981 to include 'all work for which people were not paid and which was of service to others apart from their immediate family and personal friends'. So the Survey included 'not only voluntary work carried out through an organisation of some kind ... but also things which people did on their own initiative and not through any formal organisation': that is, activities such as helping neighbours (but not friends), running sports clubs or music societies, and conducting political or trade union business. Not surprisingly, the percentage rose substantially. Yet it remained identical in 1987, when the definition once more narrowed – this time to denote 'unpaid work, except for occasional out-of-pocket expenses, which is done through a group or on behalf of an organisation of some kind', and involves 'service or benefit to other people or the community and not only to one's immediate family or personal friends'. Perhaps informants interpreted definitions technically different as meaning the same thing. The GHS surveys of 1987 and 1992 are comparable because they used the same definition; they show a small but statistically significant increase in the proportion doing voluntary work, which stems entirely from an increase among women (Matheson, 1990, p.5; Goddard, 1994, p.16).

Table 17.5 General Household Survey statistics on volunteering, Great Britain, 1973–92

Year	Definition	% volunteering in past 4 weeks, total	% volunteering in past year Men	Women	Total
1973	Narrow	7.3	–	–	–
1977	Narrow	8.6	–	–	–
1981	Broad	15.3	21.4	23.5	22.5
1987	Narrow	14.5	21.4	25.2	23.4
1992	Narrow	13.8	21.4	26.6	24.2

Sources: Calculated from Office of Population Censuses and Surveys: *General Household Survey 1973*, Table 4.4a; *General Household Survey 1977*, Table 7.6; *General Household Survey 1981*, Tables 8.1 and 8.10; Matheson (1990), Tables 4b and 16; and Goddard (1994), Table 9.

The National Centre for Volunteering (till 1996 known as the Volunteer Centre UK) conducted surveys in 1981, 1991 and 1997. All define voluntary work very broadly as 'any activity which involves spending time, unpaid, doing something which aims to benefit someone (individuals or groups), other than or in addition to close relatives, or to benefit the environment'. The resulting figures are much higher than those of the GHS, and show an increase between 1981 and 1991 but a slight fall in 1997.[1]

Table 17.6 National Centre for Volunteering statistics on volunteering, Great Britain, 1981–97

Year	% volunteering in the past year Men	Women	Total	% volunteering in the past month, total
1981	43	45	44	27
1991	50	53	51	31
1997	48	48	48	29

Source: Davis Smith (1998), Tables 1.4 and 2.3.

Informal mutual help between friends and neighbours should not be forgotten. The National Centre for Volunteering's surveys also asked about neighbourhood care such as visiting an elderly or sick person, shopping for someone, and baby-sitting. In 1997, 22 per cent claimed regular involvement in informal activity, and 74 per cent had helped in the past year, mostly irregularly (Davis Smith, 1998, pp.147; 149). Many more people therefore provide neighbourhood care than do formal voluntary work.[2] Britain was compared with Belgium, Bulgaria, Denmark, Germany, Ireland, the Netherlands, Slovakia and Sweden on the proportion of respondents who volunteered during 1993/94, 'volunteering' being defined as 'time given freely and without pay to any organisation which has the aim of benefiting people or a particular cause'. Here Britain surpassed all but the Netherlands and Sweden, but came bottom of the list for the proportion volunteering at least once a month; so it seems that the volunteering culture spreads relatively widely but less deeply in Britain (Gaskin and Davis Smith, 1995, p.x; Davis Smith, 1996, pp.180–3). On the other hand, a survey of volunteering (defined as participating in a formal voluntary sector organization) in 1991 showed that for the proportion of adults volunteering during the past month and for average hours of volunteering per month, Britain surpassed France and Spain but was thoroughly outclassed by Canada and the US (Charities Aid Foundation, 1994, pp.13, 80).

Who, then, are the volunteers in Britain? They include people who give not just money, but also time, effort and thought. Voluntary bodies are not staffed entirely by volunteers. The National Trust, for example, sees the volunteer as its 'life blood', but volunteering within the Trust occurs at several levels: the Trust is itself a voluntary organization, funded by voluntary subscription, participatory in structure through its many committees recruited from volunteers, resting on 190 Associations, and drawing upon about 30 000 member and non-member volunteers to run its day-to-day activities, but also upon 6 000 regular staff (National Trust, 1995, p.1). So volunteers are enlisted at several levels and are guided by paid full-timers. 'Nowadays many of the most active voluntary organizations are staffed entirely by highly trained and fairly well-paid professional workers', wrote Bourdillon in 1945. 'The distinctively "voluntary" character of such bodies is the product, not of the kind of workers they employ, but of their mode of birth and method of government' (Bourdillon, 1945, p.3). In 1990 the 171 434 registered charities employed between 438 000 and 482 000 people – 2 per cent of total employment in Britain if part-timers are included – and deployed them overwhelmingly in health and the social services (Posnett, 1995, p.5). Most volunteers, however, are unpaid, and until 1911 these included MPs. Town and County Councillors remain unpaid, and government still relies heavily on volunteering by Justices of the Peace and participants in public inquiries.

Volunteering was built into the life-style of the privileged classes before democracy's advent, and the royal family is still prominent in the charitable world. Through charity and voluntary work, marginalized religious or ethnic groups have long bought themselves social acceptance. Beveridge recognized, however, that the twentieth century has distributed leisure 'more widely, in smaller parcels', making it hard to get 'from the many the voluntary service which used to come before from some of the few, and without which a good society cannot be made' (Beveridge, 1948, p.222). For a time, the relatively well-to-do leisured woman helped to fill the gap. There was a long interval between women getting the vote and their rejecting the separation of spheres between breadwinning husband and domesticated wife. Even in the type of unpaid work she undertook, the woman volunteer reflected this persisting separation, for women were noticeably prominent in religious and cultural organizations, whereas men predominated in sports clubs, trade and professional associations and ex-servicemen's organizations (Bottomore, 1954, p.355; Harrison, 1978, pp.83–4; 111–12). By the 1970s, however, such women were taking up paid careers, which often meant that the state paid them for work hitherto done voluntarily: running crèches, old people's homes and institutional care outside the family. Even in the 1980s, though, women were more likely than men to do voluntary work, and volunteers came disproportionately from women who were working, especially from part-timers (Matheson, 1990, pp.6, 9).

Membership figures for women's organizations are at first sight puzzling, for they suggest decline in the 1960s, precisely when feminism was emerging from its trough-period since the late 1920s. The explanation is twofold. First, the women's organizations in Table 17.7 catered for a non-feminist outlook among women: that is, for a continuing separation of spheres whereby women's role remained largely domestic and recreational. Within the Townswomen's Guilds, wrote Mary Stott in 1978, 'the derogatory description "women's lib" is enough to put an end to the mere possibility of co-operation, in many traditional Guilds' (Stott, 1978, p.214). But, second, the newer type of feminist structure was often relatively informal, sometimes on principle, and relied on statistically elusive 'networking'. The playgroup movement, for

Table 17.7　Selected women's organizations, 1900–98

Year	Members of Mothers' Union[a] (000s)	Members of National Federation of Women's Institutes[b] (000s)	Number of Townswomen's Guilds[c]
1900	169.9	–	–
1911	362.6	–	–
1920	386.0	–	–
1930	510.1	291.6	4 (1929)
1940	510.2	291.0	544 (1939)
1950	492.2	446.7	n/a
1960	453.2 (1961)	444.7	2028 (1958)
1970	334.1 (1971)	436.4	n/a
1980	214.7	384.3	n/a
1990	173.4	318.7	n/a
1998	146.0 (1995)	265.4 (1996)	1900

Note: [a]Mothers' Union statistics relate to the UK and Ireland.
[b]NFWI statistics relate to England, Wales, Jersey, Guernsey and the Isle of Man.
[c]Townswomens' Guild statistics relate to the UK.

Source: Information from organizations concerned.

instance, launched in 1961, generated many unofficial structures. By 1968 there were 5 802 registered child-minders, yet legislation in that year was followed by a fourfold increase in their number within two years – a change which must merely reflect child-minders' shift from unofficial to official categories (Jackson and Jackson, 1979, p.174). Equally informal were other voluntary movements inspired by 1960s values: gay and lesbian liberation structures, for instance, and community action groups. The Townswomen's Guilds, an urban equivalent of the Women's Institutes launched in the late 1920s, were at first much smaller than the other two bodies, but grew in relative numerical significance. The 535 Guilds in 1939 had about 54 000 members, rising to 105 000 in the United Kingdom by 1990 (*Townswoman*, July 1939, p.90; *Social Trends*, 1992, Table 11.7).

Surveys repeatedly show that social status regardless of gender helps to prompt volunteering. Professional people offer specialized skills, and with better education comes self-confidence. This carries the danger that welfare policies will reflect only attitudes far removed from those of the beneficiary, whether on child care, housing or family relationships generally. Beveridge in 1948 saw 'the business motive' as 'in continual or repeated conflict with the Philanthropic Motive' and as 'a good servant but a bad master' (Beveridge, 1948, p.322). Yet voluntarism and entrepreneurship are closely linked, and this became more obvious in the 1960s and 1970s when fund-raising was commercialized. Charitable advertising and fund-raising methods became more professional, and philanthropic professionalism increasingly entailed not just expertise in the subject area, but skill at publicity and money making. The Salvation Army's campaign in 1967 to raise £1 million was a landmark here, with its slogan, 'For God's sake, care'. The late 1960s saw a huge expansion in charities' share of the Christmas card market, and in 1970 Shelter launched Shelter Shops, a home-order postal service. On 6 October 1972 *The Times* reported that Oxfam's 430 gift shops had raised nearly £1 million in the previous year through selling cheap second-hand clothing and furniture. By 15 December 1998 the *Guardian* could record more than 6500 charity shops in Britain, with Oxfam as the country's fifth largest retailer. Many of the British foundations originated in business profits (Table 17.17), and were reinforced by the American foundations (Rockefeller; Ford) which were also influential in Britain.

A further link with business comes through corporate funding. Between 1979 and 1987 the top 200 corporate donors increased their donations (whose percentage of profits ranged between 0.17 in 1977 and 0.24 in 1982) by over 50 per cent in real terms (Charities Aid Foundation, various years). Some companies also provide voluntary bodies with professional services or facilities; IBM in the early 1990s, for instance, seconded valuable business expertise and provided equipment (Fogarty and Legard, 1993, pp.8–12). Many firms in the 1980s realized that sponsorship, especially of cultural and sporting events, brought cheap publicity or benefited the firm's workforce or locality, though the growth of large firms with headquarters in far-off places eroded such local loyalties. The attempt to revive such involvement led Michael Heseltine, the then Secretary of State for the Environment, to enlist leading businessmen for his famous bus tour of Liverpool in August 1981 after the Toxteth riots. A year later 'Business in the Community' arose to propagate this sense of responsibility. Donations and other types of support collectively make up what is known as 'community contribution'. During the six years between 1990/91 and 1995/96 the charitable donations of the top 400 corporate donors averaged at 0.26 per cent of pre-tax profits, community contribution at 0.42 per cent, though these figures should be interpreted cautiously because such expenditure is not recorded in any standardized way (Brown and Smyth, 1997, p.9; Tuffrey, 1997, p.114).

Yet to focus on formal voluntary structures risks neglecting the sort of volunteer who made the influential *Good Food Guide* possible. With no premises, subscriptions or paid officials, the Good Food Club was, said its editor in 1961, 'the creation, and the creature, of its members. It depends wholly upon their reports, and without these it would not even exist' (Postgate, 1961). Also sometimes forgotten is the mutual help that occurs within the less formal and more humbly patronized pubs and clubs. Still, the *Observer* on 3 August 1975, discussing the Claimants and Unemployed Workers' Union, said it could mobilize the unemployed into about 70 branches nation-wide,[3] which shows how even the least privileged groups can organize themselves.

Aims and destinations

Voluntarist concern is wide and ever-widening. Information about charities improved considerably in 1977 when the Charities Aid Foundation (CAF) began producing *Charity Statistics*, later renamed *Charity Trends* and now *Dimensions of the Voluntary Sector*. At first it covered only the top 200 fund-raising charities, but it has become progressively more detailed and now includes the top 500. The data on the top 200 are imprecise, if only because charities do not submit their accounts simultaneously, and coverage includes only charities required to register. To incorporate the large incomes of some omitted charities – universities, for example – would greatly change the picture. Furthermore, the series ranks charities only by voluntary income; a rank order by total income would look very different. Voluntary income consists of donations, legacies, covenants, Gift Aid, income from charity shops and fund-raising, whereas total income would add income from trading, sale of goods and services, rent, investments and income from government. Yet these categories are not clearly distinct; the National Trust's membership subscriptions, for instance, could be viewed as trading income because in effect they constitute an entry fee to Trust properties (Ware, 1989, p.75). Table 17.8 demonstrates remarkable stability. Oxfam, the National Trust and the Imperial Cancer Research Fund have been outstandingly successful; two others regularly appear among the top five, but some (the RSPCA, for example) feature regularly only in the bottom half of the list.

Table 17.8 Number of appearances (maximum 20) in the top 20 fund-raising charities in the UK, ranked by voluntary income, 1977–96/97

	Top 20	Top 5	Top 1
Oxfam	20	20	8
National Trust	20	18	7
Imperial Cancer Research Fund	20	19	2
Royal National Lifeboat Institution	20	16	1
Cancer Research Campaign	20	13	0
Save the Children Fund	20	5	1
Barnardo's	20	4	0
Salvation Army	20	1	0
Christian Aid	19	0	0
Royal National Institute for the Blind	20	0	0
Royal Society for the Prevention of Cruelty to Animals	20	0	0
Guide Dogs for the Blind Association	19	0	0
Help the Aged	19	0	0
National Society for the Prevention of Cruelty to Children	19	0	0
Scope (formerly Spastics Society)	18	1	0
British Red Cross Society	17	0	0
Marie Curie Cancer Care	15	0	0
ActionAid	14	0	0
British Heart Foundation	14	2	0

Sources: Charities Aid Foundation (various years), *Charity Statistics, Charity Trends* and *Dimensions of the Voluntary Sector.*

Figure 17.2 shows an increase since 1977 in the top 200 charities' real income, both voluntary and non-voluntary. The rise in non-voluntary income reflects growing government grants and fees in exchange for services. Well before 1979, central government provided voluntary bodies with a mounting proportion of their funds; in the 1930s the Ministry of Labour funded unemployment relief schemes through the National Council of Social Service. Still, between the mid-1970s and mid-1980s government funding of charities rose sixfold; by 1992 the Spastics Society, for example, received much more from central government fees and grants than from voluntary donations, and Barnardo's almost as much.

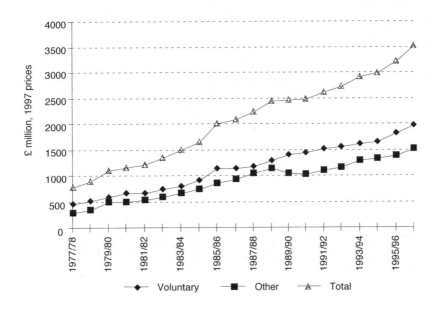

Figure 17.2 Income of the top 200 registered fund-raising charities in the UK, 1977/78–96/97

Note: The discrepancy in the CAF series between the 16th edition of *Charity Trends* in 1993 and the first edition of *Dimensions of the Voluntary Sector* in 1995 can be discounted because the last *Charity Trends* statistics relate mainly to 1992, whereas the first *Dimensions* statistics relate mainly to 1993.

Sources: Charities Aid Foundation (various years), *Charity Statistics, Charity Trends* and *Dimensions of the Voluntary Sector.*

Charities' incomes since 1977 have increased in real terms, but Figure 17.3 shows that the total income of the top 200 charities has also almost trebled as a proportion of GDP.

Since 1991/92 the Office for National Statistics survey of charities has supplemented earlier sources. It combines information from Scotland and Northern Ireland with data from the Charity Commission's register, and shows charity income's percentage of GDP as rising from 1.82 per cent in 1991/92 to 2.18 per cent in 1995/96 (calculated from Ward et al., 1996, p.43), whereas in 1934 Braithwaite's estimate was only 1.22 per cent of GDP for England and Wales (Braithwaite, 1938).

How has the balance changed between different types of charity? Table 17.9 shows the present-day ranking, but in similar analyses a century ago, service-men's welfare and religious work would have been more prominent. In 1860 the 101 London religious charities accounted for 58 per cent of the total raised by London charities from voluntary contributions, but medical causes were advancing, and in 1907 two-fifths of voluntary donations went to urban English medical charities (Lascelles, 1934, pp.320–1; Owen, 1965, p.479).

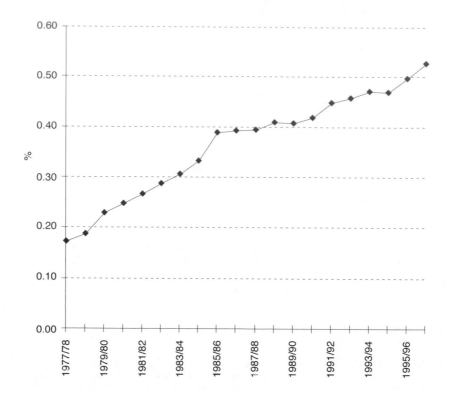

Figure 17.3 Income of the top 200 registered fund-raising charities in the UK as a percentage of GDP at factor cost, 1977/78–96/97

Sources: Charities Aid Foundation (various years), *Charity Statistics, Charity Trends* and *Dimensions of the Voluntary Sector.*

Table 17.9 The preponderance of different types of fund-raising charity in the top 500, 1996/97

Type of charity	Number of charities in the top 500	Voluntary income of sector (£m)	% of voluntary income of the top 500
Medicine and health	213	816	36.5
General welfare	115	582	26.1
International aid	53	380	17.0
Animal protection	26	169	7.6
Heritage/environment	18	118	5.3
Religious/missionary	41	89	4.0
Arts/recreation	14	40	1.8
Youth	13	29	1.3
Education	7	10	0.5

Source: Charities Aid Foundation (1998), *Dimensions of the Voluntary Sector*, p.151.

Twentieth-century warfare has advanced both state and voluntary activity. Modern warfare compelled governments to mobilize society and the economy comprehensively, which entailed collaborating more closely with many types of voluntary body. In World War I the huge number of volunteers postponed conscription till 1916, and for long afterwards ex-servicemen's organizations, such as the British Legion (Table 17.10), remained salient.

Table 17.10 Royal British Legion statistics, 1921–95

	Branches	Members, (000s)		Total	Sum raised from Poppy Appeal, (£000s)	
		Ordinary and associates[a]	Women's section		Cash terms	1997 prices
1921	1478	–	–	18	106	2550
1930	4679	299	108	407	525	18092
1940	6177	352	101	452	577	17218
1950	8556	764	243	1008	880	16606
1960	8103	c.750[b]	c.250[b]	c.1000[b]	954	12068
1970	7092	c.530[b]	c.220[b]	c.750[b]	1201	10209
1980	5987	752	164	916	4902	11549
1990	5349	716	117	833	12826	16020
1995	4831	613	96	708	16370	17303

Notes: [a] Associate members are not ex-service, and in 1995 numbered 228000 – about a third of total membership; their numbers are gradually increasing.
[b] Membership figures for 1955–70 are contemporary approximations; accurate records were not then needed.

Source: Information from the Royal British Legion.

Nor did conscription in World War II dispense with volunteering among servicemen, for volunteers were still required for dangerous jobs with the Royal Air Force (RAF) or in submarines. Furthermore, both world wars freed women to exploit the separation of spheres in a non-feminist way by carrying out a distinctive welfare and charitable role. The Women's Royal Voluntary Service exemplifies this. Created by the government in 1938, government funded, and structured around local authorities, it organized a nucleus of paid full-timers who at the war-time peak mobilized over a million women volunteers, tackling the tasks the government prescribed. Like the Citizens' Advice Bureaux, it did not disband after the war and in 1990 claimed 160000 members, a tenth of them men. With subsequent major organizational change, its volunteers were down to 125600 by 1996, but it still made itself useful in numerous ways: mobilizing volunteers behind delivering half the country's meals on wheels, helping out in hospitals, and responding rapidly with help in emergencies and disasters.

Annual reports, the source for Figure 17.4, clarify growth patterns within individual charities, and incidentally show how long-run real income statistics can conceal pronounced annual fluctuations.[9] Each voluntary organization knows best how to measure its changing fortunes; the National Trust, for instance, could assess its prosperity by acreage owned, by membership, by visitors to its properties or by the number of full-time employees.

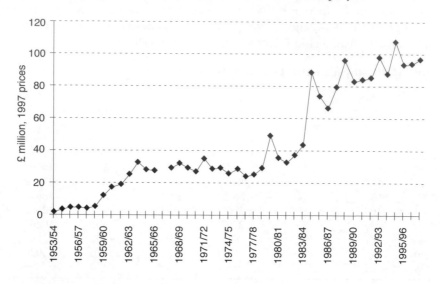

Figure 17.4 Annual income of Oxfam, 1953/54 to 1997/98

Note: Gap in graph for 1966/67 is due to change in accounting year. Until 1966 this began in September, but in 1967 it changed to April.

Source: Oxfam, annual reports.

Voluntarism was nowhere more salient in 1900 than in the individual's self-protection against future mishap. In 1899 Seebohm Rowntree found that about one-seventh of York's population aged 15 and above had joined friendly societies. With more than 11 million members in that year, they surpassed trade unions in their hold on working people (Rowntree, 1901, pp.8, 350, 357, 360). Friendly society statistics must be interpreted cautiously because registration with the Registrar of Friendly Societies was voluntary, and because friendly societies were so diverse (Hanson, 1972, pp.118–27).

Indeed, trade unions themselves performed important friendly society functions. Between 1912 and 1945 registered trade unions' proportion of total expenditure on approved society benefits reached a plateau, and by 1938 trade unions accounted for only a twelfth of those who were insured in approved societies.[4] By then insurance firms (with 47 per cent) and friendly societies (with 45 per cent) were dominating the field. Friendly societies' overall membership fell markedly after World War II (Beveridge, 1948, pp.77, 94). Beveridge hoped that their role might broaden out from mutual insurance into locally based social service agency, but we now know that centralized and taxpayer-funded public welfare undermined their social function.

Table 17.11 Friendly societies in the UK, 1910–95 (excluding collecting societies)

Number of societies, Orders and branches	Number of members (000s)	Members as a % of the total population	Total benefits paid, (£m)	
			Cash terms	1997 prices
1910	26776	6328	14.1	5.7	325.4
1920	23286	7217	15.5	6.1	133.2
1930	21339	7524	16.4	10.1	348.6
1940	19267	8363	17.3	13.0	388.3
1950	15226	6980	13.8	15.1	284.1
1960	10814	5991	11.4	18.5	233.9
1970	6962	4751	8.6	26.8	228.0
1980	4242	3596	6.4	48.0	113.1
1990	1887	3186	5.5	199.7	249.4
1995	1307	2951	5.0	470.3	497.2

Sources: Board of Trade (various years); Central Statistical Office (various years); Registry of Friendly Societies (various years).

Other well established mutual institutions have also declined or changed. In the late 1990s the Freemasons, who are involved in charitable as well as ceremonial activities, were having trouble in recruiting, although there were still 350 000 Masons in England and Wales in 1999 (*Independent*, 23 January 1999). Many building societies have become banks, and enterprising supermarkets have overtaken relatively conservative cooperative retail societies. With the Friendly Societies Act (1992), however, and the associated coordination of friendly societies into the Association of Friendly Societies after 1995, a renaissance may be in prospect, especially given the all-party search for new ways of funding welfare. Furthermore, some new forms of mutual institution have emerged. Credit unions resemble banks but are run by and for those on low incomes. Members contribute small savings which gradually accumulate and are spent in times of crisis, making high-cost credit unnecessary. Late in 1998 the government's supportive consultation paper noted that 'credit unions have been doing invaluable work encouraging people to save money by providing savings facilities, low cost credit, and financial education to the less well off, giving them the chance to build up a good credit record' (HM Treasury, 1998). Local Exchange Trading Systems (LETS), which took off in Britain from 1992, are essentially local barter systems. Members boost their income by trading services such as dog-walking or hairdressing, priced in local currency.

Table 17.12 Credit unions in Great Britain and LETS in the UK, 1980–98

Year	Number of credit unions	Number of LETS
1980	57	0
1985	82	1
1990	275	5
1995	531	350
1998	624	450

Sources: Registry of Friendly Societies (1993, 1996 and 1998);
Information from Letslink UK

The Welfare State never dispensed with the volunteer. Indeed, the term 'voluntarism' was originally used in Britain to denote 'the involvement of voluntary organizations in social welfare', broadly defined, and in this specialist sense came into general use from the late 1950s; volunteers guided the citizen towards state benefits. The National Council of Social Service, justifying continued voluntarist influence in its annual report for 1945/46, pointed out that 'as the State becomes more and more the public's school-master, employer and landlord, so it will become increasingly necessary for the citizen to have independent advice on his relationships with the State'. Citizens' Advice Bureaux grew fast during World War II, and instead of disbanding thereafter

Table 17.13 Number of Citizens' Advice Bureaux and enquiries received, 1940–96/97

	Number of advice centres	Number of enquiries during year (millions)
1940	433	–
1948	572	–
1953	477	–
1960	416	1.1
1965	n/a	1.3
1970	n/a	n/a
1975	674	2.7
1980	879	4.1
1985	937	6.3
1990	n/a	7.1
1995	1781	6.5
1996/97	1746	6.4[a]

Note: [a] Problems rather than enquiries; the classification has changed, but these are roughly comparable.

Sources: Citron (1989), pp.3–4; Richards (1989), pp.4–6; National Association of Citizens' Advice Bureaux annual report, 1996/97.

they were propped up by local authorities and charities and survived a withdrawal of state funds which proved only temporary. The Bureaux' expanding clientele reflects the growing administrative complexities of modern life. To quote Beveridge, they 'explain the working of public authority to the citizen'. The authority is then seen 'as something not alien and hostile to himself but something for which he may be responsible' (Beveridge, 1948, pp.284–5). As *The Economist* pointed out on 30 August 1952, they were 'a very English way of meeting ... the challenge of bureaucracy'.

Volunteers did more than merely advise people in trouble. They often themselves offered services to them and to local and central government, thereby enhancing the weight of their advice on public policy. Until the 1980s voluntary organizations concerned with welfare were increasingly influential, not to mention pressure groups like the trade union movement which include welfare in their agenda. Political parties, too, derive ideas, recruits and energy from welfare pressure groups – Conservatives favouring the less statist variety, Labour the more interventionist. Many more (Shelter, Age Concern, Help the Aged, for example) could be added to Table 17.14.

Table 17.14: Membership of voluntary organizations relevant to public welfare (000s), Great Britain, 1971–92

	1971	1981	1992
British Red Cross Society	172	112	90
National Association of Leagues of Hospital Friends[a]	250	475	350
Pensioners' Voice	600	113	25
Mencap	40	50	55
St John Ambulance Brigade[b]	91	77	50
National Association of Round Tables of Great Britain and Ireland[c]	29	30	20

Notes: [a] Volunteers.
[b] England and Northern Ireland.
[c] Includes Republic of Ireland.

Source: Central Statistical Office (1994), *Social Trends 1994*, Table 11.4.

Other volunteers integral to public welfare were blood donors, whose numbers quadrupled between the late 1940s and the late 1960s (Table 17.15). For Titmuss, blood donation exemplified the superiority of altruism over the private market; the good society must therefore leave room for altruistic conduct (Titmuss, 1973, pp.270–7).

Since World War II volunteers have recognized the need for face-to-face consolation and encouragement in misfortune. The advance of the Samaritans, Cruse, Alcoholics Anonymous, Relate and ChildLine, not to mention the many organizations for those who suffer from particular diseases and disabilities, shows the volunteer assuaging miseries largely beyond material remedy. In an increasingly secular and atomized society, many such organizations offer help once provided by neighbours, religious organizations and the extended family. The Marriage Guidance Council's change of name in 1988 to Relate – symbolizing its decision to cater for divorced, cohabiting and same-sex couples – epitomizes voluntarist adaptability.

Table 17.15 Blood donations and donors, England and Wales, 1950–97/98

	Blood donations received (000s)	Effective civilian blood donors (000s)
1950	523	428
1955	760	591
1960	1024	854
1965	1270	1091
1970	1509	1418
1975	1769	1780
1980	2019	2206
1985	2044	n/a
1989/90	2147	n/a
1994/95	2303	2222
1997/98	2245	1925

Sources: Titmuss (1973), p.50; Department of Health (various years), *Health and Personal Social Services Statistics for England*; National Blood Authority, *Annual Reports*, 1995 and 1998.

Table 17.16 Other advisory and counselling services: clients (000s), UK, 1971–97

	1971	1981	1991	1997
Relate[a]	22	38	70	70
Alcoholics Anonymous	6	30	45	50
Samaritans[b]	n/a	1713	2554	2886
ChildLine[c]	–	–	55	103
Cruse Bereavement Care	n/a	n/a	69	100[d]

Notes: [a]Before 1988, National Marriage Guidance Council.
[b]UK and Republic of Ireland. Statistics refer to calls where verbal contact was made.
[c]Clients calling ChildLine for the first time in that year.
[d]Approximate figure.

Sources: Central Statistical Office, *Social Trends*, 1996, Table 8.11; information from organizations concerned.

Twentieth-century voluntarism reflects the diffusion of leisure and culture. British and American foundations significantly advance academic research, the arts and intellectual life. From 1913 the Carnegie United Kingdom Trust was prominent during its first half-century for its educational and cultural projects; of the £5.5 million it spent on grants, one-third went to educational purposes and one-eighth to the arts (Robertson, 1964, pp.270–1). In the 1960s a Nuffield Foundation project profoundly influenced science teaching in schools, and without grants from the foundations, the Royal Society could not have occupied its new home in Carlton House Terrace. By 1997 the Wellcome Trust's expenditure on research on medicine and its history ran at almost 75 per cent of the Medical Research Council's expenditure, and a higher proportion of its expenditure represented 'free money' in the sense of not being pre-empted by ongoing research structures. For research in the humanities, the Leverhulme Trust's scholarships are of major national importance. Table 17.17's statistics can be compared to the Economic and Social Research Council (ESRC) expenditure of £65 million in 1996/97 and the British Academy's of £23.3 million.

Voluntary bodies contribute significantly to education in a broader sense. Whereas the early twentieth century came to think of poverty as curable and the mid-twentieth century came to see affluence as attainable, voluntary bodies helped the late-twentieth century increasingly to recognize the tension between affluence, environment and health. The environment was a fast-growing voluntarist cause (Table 17.18), the World Wide Fund for Nature (WWF) appearing twice among the top 20 fund-raising charities since 1977. A combination of recreational opportunity and conservationist zeal now invalidates Beveridge's complaint that 'for cultural purposes, such as the National Trust' money 'hardly came at all' (Beveridge, 1948, p.302). Among the many outdoor recreational organizations, only the cyclists have declined.

These movements tightened the growing ethical constraints upon commercial concerns, and promoted such causes as organically grown food, non-animal cosmetics, non-fur clothes and ethical investment policy. In 1986 anti-apartheid university students deployed their latent banking power to force Barclays Bank to withdraw investments from South Africa. A related development was the consumer movement's second phase since 1945. Its first phase assumed that nationalization and rationalization would benefit the consumer through economies of scale and through inculcating a sense of public service. By 1957 these benefits were proving elusive, and in that year the Consumers' Association was launched, on American precedents, to counterbalance producer power. Its growth, initially very fast, seems now to have reached a plateau (Table 17.19). In the mid-1970s the Labour government reinforced consumerism by subsidizing the consumer advice centres that were spontaneously appearing, but in 1979 the Conservatives, seeing the free market as the consumer's best friend, abolished them and assigned their residual role to the Citizens' Advice Bureaux, whose government grant was increased.

Table 17.17 Expenditure or grant allocation[a] of charitable foundations specializing in research (£m), 1940–97

Year ended	Leverhulme Trust Expenditure		Nuffield Foundation Grant allocation	
	cash terms	1997 prices	cash terms	1997 prices
1940	0.03	0.98	–	–
1950	0.04	0.74	0.51	9.66
1960	0.18	2.26	1.77	22.43
1970	0.72	6.15	1.41	11.97
1980	2.29[b]	5.39	3.88	9.14
1990	9.70	12.11	5.63	7.03
1997	16.05	16.05	6.40	6.40

Notes: [a]Expenditure relates to the particular year shown, whereas grant allocation refers to grants approved in that particular year but which may be distributed over a period of years.
[b]Commitments rather than expenditure.
[c]The Joseph Rowntree Foundation began life as the Joseph Rowntree Village Trust, established in 1904 to look after the Garden Village of New Earswick. In 1959 its objectives expanded to cover research and development; it was known as the Joseph Rowntree Memorial Trust until 1990. It is quite separate from the Joseph Rowntree Charitable Trust and the Joseph Rowntree Reform Trust Ltd.

Table 17.18 Membership of environmental groups, 1900–98 (000s)

	1900	1910	1920
Royal Society for the Protection of Birds, adult members, UK	26[a]	n/a	n/a
Greenpeace, members, UK	–	–	–
Friends of the Earth, supporters, England, Wales and N. Ireland	–	–	–
Ramblers' Association, members, Great Britain	–	–	–
Council for the Protection of Rural England, members	–	–	–
National Trust, members, England, Wales and N. Ireland	0.3	1	1

Notes: [a]1899 figure. Membership was defined differently in later years.
[b]1939 figure.
[c]Membership in the mid-1960s was 15000, and in the mid-1970s, 30000 (CPRE annual report for 1979, p.21).

Table 17.19 Consumers' Association membership, 1960–98

	March 1960	March 1970	March 1980	March 1990	March 1998[b]
Members (000s)	170	–	–	969	750
Which? circulation (000s)	–	600	677	875	584
Subscriptions to other CA products[a](000s)	–	–	–	–	437

Notes: [a]Consisting of *Gardening Which?*, *Holiday Which?*, *Drug and Therapeutics Bulletin*, *Health Which?* and legal services.
[b]Figures up to 1990 include subscribers having a free trial; figures after 1990 exclude them.

Sources: Consumers' Association: *Which?*, selected years; information from Consumers' Association.

J. Rowntree Foundation[c] Grant allocation		Wolfson Foundation[e] Grant allocation		Wellcome Trust[e] Expenditure	
cash terms	1997 prices	cash terms	1997 prices	cash terms	1997 prices
–	–	–	–	0.06	1.85
–	–	–	–	0.06	1.17
0.05[d]	0.67[d]	0.55	6.96	0.60	7.59
0.26	2.23	1.66	14.11	2.89	24.57
0.91	2.14	3.04	7.16	10.34	24.35
5.61	7.00	9.80	12.24	70.00	69.19
6.09	6.09	18.00	18.00	227.00	227.00

[d]1959 figure. Includes expenditure on maintaining parks and open spaces.
[e]The Wellcome Trust figures are for expenditure on research into medicine and its history. The earlier reports of both the Wellcome Trust and the Wolfson Foundation provide aggregate figures for several years at a time, so an annual average has been calculated.

Sources: Annual reports of and information provided by organizations concerned; Waddilove (1983), p.216; Briggs (1991), pp.65, 82, 107, 221

1930	1940	1950	1960	1970	1980	1985	1990	1995	1998
n/a	5[b]	6	11	67	329	390	483	515	581
–	–	–	–	–	n/a	n/a	283	229	194[e]
–	–	–	–	–	n/a	n/a	226	200	200
–	n/a	9	11	22	36	50	79	112	124
n/a	n/a	n/a	n/a[c]	n/a[c]	n/a	n/a	30[d]	n/a	47
2	7	23	97	226	949	1323	2032	2285	2410

[d]1989 figure.
[e]1997 figure.

Sources: Organizations concerned; Samstag (1988), pp.40, 42, 149.

Late-Victorian and Edwardian religious and semi-military commitment boosted organizations for children, yet these are surprisingly resilient in a decolonized and relatively secular world. Earlier maturing and teenage consumerism help to explain the slow-down among organizations for teenagers; membership of the Combined Cadet Force (CCF), Boys' Brigade, Boy Scouts and Girl Guides peaked in the 1960s. Organizations for younger children, however, fared better, with Cub Scouts going from strength to strength and Brownie Guides keeping up their numbers (Central Statistical Office, *Social Trends*, 1994, Table 11.5).

Voluntarists have strong international links. Nineteenth-century British humanitarianism rested upon an Anglo-American philanthropic network, and

Table 17.20 Membership of selected organizations for young people, UK, 1900–98 (000s)

	1900	1910	1920	1930
Boys Brigade[a]	41	62	58	121
Scouts[b]	–	107	325	438
Girl Guides[c]	–	8	184	561
Youth Clubs UK	–	–	n/a	n/a
Combined Cadet Force	–	–	–	–
Duke of Edinburgh's Award[d]	–	–	–	–

Notes: [a]UK and Ireland.
[b]Figures include Beaver Scouts, Cub Scouts, Venture Scouts, Instructors and Leaders as well as Scouts.
[c]All figures include adults and Brownies, and from 1960 onwards, British Guides in foreign countries.
[d]Figures relate to number of awards (bronze, gold and silver) gained in each year, rather than number of participants.
[e]1941 figure.
[f]Includes adults.

twentieth-century British social policy reflects a continuous tension between the competing ideals of individualist US and interventionist USSR. British domestic cause groups – from free trade to the attack on state-regulated prostitution, from anti-slavery to birth control, from feminism to pacifism – all instinctively moved beyond national frontiers. Monarchs touring the empire left a trail of hospitals, schools and charities in their wake (Prochaska, 1995, p.120), and there were increasing inter-war efforts to reconcile empire with internationalism. Youth movements once semi-militarist in mood began to present their internationalist and even multi-cultural face (MacKenzie, 1984, pp.256–7), and pressure groups like the League of Nations Union promoted internationalism more directly. Volunteers fought in Spain, cared for Basque refugees and camped with the unemployed. After 1945 charities such as Oxfam and pressure groups like the Campaign for Nuclear Disarmament harnessed to secular causes much of the international idealism that had earlier boosted missionary work, and after 1958 Voluntary Service Overseas mobilized youthful idealism behind alleviating poverty abroad.

This voluntarist internationalism had its practical as well as idealistic aspects. Pressure groups, like heat-seeking missiles, lock on to the locations of power, and these were increasingly outside Britain. After 1945 non-governmental organizations clustered around the United Nations, leading some critics of famine relief organizations to emphasize their widening distance from their beneficiaries. Some even pronounced them unaccountable and their 'disaster pornography' and 'disaster tourists' counter-productive (De Waal, 1995, pp.15–17). Edward Heath set up the Women's Consultative Council in 1962 to disseminate information about the European Economic Community (EEC), but seven years later United Nations pressure led Harold

1940	1950	1960	1970	1980	1990	1998
113	145	161	137	156	106	85[g]
343	472	588	539	641	672	607
400[e]	435	595	745	859	694	733[h]
n/a	153	173	302	765	567	650
30	60	74	46	56	41[f]	42[f]
–	–	n/a	n/a	n/a	40	50

[g]1997 figure.
[h]1995 figure.

Sources: Halsey (1972), p.568; Central Statistical Office, *Social Trends 1976*, Table 10.12; *Social Trends 1983*, Table 11.1; *Social Trends 1992*, Table 11.12; information provided by organizations concerned.

Wilson to replace it with the Women's National Commission. And although it was governmental initiative from 1961–73 that prompted Britain's bid to join the EEC, the National Referendum Campaign and the 'Get Britain Out' Referendum Campaign produced in 1975 something of the clash between self-organized opinion groups that had invigorated nineteenth-century political debate. After Britain joined the EEC in 1973, British pressure groups – humanitarians, environmentalists, feminists, farmers, trade unionists and employers – found Brussels fertile territory. In the late-twentieth-century global economy, British volunteers and voluntarism, still lively at home, seemed also very much for export.

Impact

Voluntarist political salience has fluctuated quite markedly during the twentieth century. Liberty and pluralism were central to nineteenth-century Liberal values, which assumed that citizens would become increasingly adept at managing their own affairs, whether corporately or individually, whereas twentieth-century Liberals have sought to reconcile the 'positive' and 'negative' variants of liberty. The twentieth century came to expect more of politicians and civil servants, liberty's dependence on political pluralism was neglected, local self-government went out of fashion, and the link between prosperity, democracy and spontaneous non-governmental initiatives was played down. The Soviet Union's supposedly humane and rationalistic progressivism swelled the charms of central 'planning'. Perhaps this is why volunteers and voluntarism received no chapter in this book's first two editions. Progressive people in the 1930s dismissed the 'do-gooder' as amateur, inefficient and probably also class-prejudiced. The volunteer's locally based, insensitive and even churchy intrusiveness seemed destined to succumb before a centralized, professional, expert and state-funded welfare service. On 30 April 1946 Bevan told the House of Commons he would 'rather be kept alive in the efficient if cold altruism of a large hospital than expire in a gush of warm sympathy in a small one', and as late as 2 July 1975 Barbara Castle was 'firmly convinced' that 'a valid social democracy' should show 'a toughness about the battle for equality rather than do-goodery' (Castle, 1980, p.144).

Yet the advance of the state does not require the volunteer to retire; in the twentieth century both have advanced together. Volunteers extended the state's frontiers at many points, exposing new needs and devising new remedies. In the nineteenth century, voluntary tax contributions anticipated the income tax, voluntary restraints on factory hours preceded the Factory Acts, specialized and non-profit-making employment agencies foreshadowed the labour exchange, and Andrew Carnegie was John the Baptist for the public library. In the twentieth century, war-time voluntary rationing schemes prepared the way for compulsion; friendly societies and trade unions pioneered the mutual insurance against sickness and ill-health that the Welfare State later rendered universal. Nor did twentieth-century interventionism cause Liberals and Labour to repudiate libertarian attitudes; both parties knew it was both prudent and desirable to work with the grain of public attitudes and traditions. Douglas Jay's idea that 'the gentleman in Whitehall really does know better what is good for people than the people know themselves' embarrassed the Attlee government (Jay, 1937, p.317), for British political theorists have embraced concepts of 'the state' only hesitantly. British governments have long assumed that when in difficulties they can enlist the citizen volunteer. Voting in Britain has never been compulsory, and political parties have refrained from milking the taxpayer for funds. As for military service, it took a major threat to national security and a major political crisis in 1916 before Britain nerved itself to conscription even in war-time, and (unusually in Europe) peace-time conscription existed only briefly: for a few months during 1939 and from 1945 to 1960. The well known inter-war cartoonist Strube portrayed John Citizen as innocent victim of bureaucrats and politicians, just as cartoonist Giles's family man in the 1950s was plagued by the Inland Revenue. Orwell in 1940 saw the British people as valuing 'the liberty to have a home of your own, to do what you like in your spare time', and thought 'the most hateful of all names in an English ear is Nosey Parker' (Orwell, 1970, p.78). Hitler and the Kaiser if anything reinforced such attitudes; 'the example of Germany', wrote Beveridge in 1948, 'shows the vital necessity of not allowing youth organisation to become a function of the State' (Beveridge, 1948, p.142).

Until the 1970s the advance of public welfare and economic planning was promoted by that most influential of think tanks, the Fabian Society; and by pressure groups like the Family Endowment Society, the Socialist Medical Association or Shelter. Yet in the 1960s doubts about statism emerged inside the Labour camp, and by 1973 R. H. S. Crossman was urging the labour movement to reconsider its inter-war contempt for 'do-good volunteering'. For him, altruistic feeling needed an outlet, and public welfare demanded the volunteer's initiative and personal touch (Crossman, 1976, pp.13, 20–1, 24). Such ideas had long been influential in a think tank whose methods (but not whose ideals) were decidedly Fabian: the Institute of Economic Affairs, which in the mid-1970s helped to nourish free market ideas within the Conservative Party. Even Heath's government of 1970–74 made an appointment which Beveridge had earlier pronounced 'a contradiction in terms' (Beveridge, 1948, p.313): a minister for voluntary organizations. Voluntarism was soon carried much further. Private health care, private house ownership, private education, even private policing had for some time been spontaneously gaining ground even during periods of Labour government, and after 1979 Thatcher played up the voluntarist dimensions of Beveridge's war-time welfare vision; his report, she claimed, had 'a Thatcherite ring to it' (Thatcher, 1995, p.120). With corporatism abandoned, trade-union power scaled down, privatization leaping forward and welfare pressure groups in eclipse, free market voluntarism in the 1980s advanced rapidly.

Four successive election defeats edged the Labour Party in the same direction. In 1994 its leader could 'begin to see a new and exciting role for the voluntary sector' (Prochaska, 1995, p.272), and five years later was telling the NCVO's annual conference that those who believe in community should 'reclaim the idea of doing good and wear it as a badge of pride' (*Guardian*, 22 January 1999). Ample Labour voluntarist traditions were there for the asking, for the right had never monopolized the British tradition of public service. R. H. Tawney, who exemplified that tradition, pointed out in 1912 that in curing poverty there would be no direct line of progress from COS to socialism; there must be a third phase whereby a change in the outlook of each individual citizen would reinforce the efforts of the state. 'In the third stage', he wrote, 'one realises that the attitude of the state is just the attitude of countless individuals', for no state 'can apply ideas which do not exist in society' (Tawney, 1972, p.45; cf.76). By 1996 the Labour MP Frank Field, influential on his party's welfare policy, was articulating growing concern about public welfare's impact upon character. Declaring that 'self-interest, not altruism, is mankind's main driving force', he contrasted the welfare structures which had emerged after 1945 with the early labour movement's institutions; these reflected its 'much more rounded view based upon a clear reading of human character' (Field, 1996, p.15).

No voluntarist tide swept through the general public in the 1980s. A much discussed opinion survey of 1988 was interpreted to show that 'after nine years of Thatcherism the public remained wedded to the collectivist, welfare ethic of social democracy' (Crewe, 1989, p.243). The British Social Attitudes Survey revealed a discriminating public, alert to inefficiency and undue duplication among charities, and conservative on their role. Between 1987 and 1990, respondents agreeing that 'the government has a basic responsibility to take care of people who can't take care of themselves' increased from 80 to 91 per cent, whereas those agreeing that 'the government ought to help more and not rely on charity to raise needed money' rose from 80 to 88 per cent (Taylor Gooby, 1993, p.7). In this situation the National Lottery's impact on voluntarism was inevitably controversial. It raised large sums for good causes without troubling the taxpayer, yet this huge state-sponsored fund-raiser, created somewhat paradoxically by a Conservative government, simultaneously put voluntarist fund-raising at risk. In 1995 the NCVO investigated individual giving. Its survey, designed to be comparable with the IGS, found that people giving to charity during the last month had fallen from 81 per cent in 1993 to 70 per cent in 1995. Charitable giving had dropped by 6.6 per cent in real terms, and the Lottery had cut charitable income by £339 million. In the same period the National Lottery Charities Board had allocated only £264 million for distribution, thus allegedly denying charities £75 million (NCVO, 1996, pp.2, 9). The Lottery's patrons seem, however, to come from groups which had always been less likely to give to charity, so the charities' losses may have been exaggerated (Banks and Tanner, 1997, p.31). Another disruption to the charitable world occurred in 1997 with the death of Diana, Princess of Wales. Her memorial fund had raised a huge sum, £85 million by August 1998, although less than some wild initial estimates (*Financial Times*, 7 October 1997; *Guardian*, 26 August 1998). The Band Aid precedent in 1985 suggests that its long-term impact on charitable giving will be ephemeral. None the less, voluntarism and the volunteer remained closer to the centre of public debate during the 1990s than anyone would have anticipated 30 years earlier.

Acknowledgements

We asked many charities and voluntary organizations for information, and we gratefully acknowledge here the generous help they gave us.

Notes

1   The Charities Aid Foundation's IGS between 1987 and 1993 also covered volunteering, defined similarly to the GHS, but the wide confidence intervals and short time-series limit its usefulness.
2   Care carried out within the family is also very important; see Chapter 15 for more on this.
3   See also the Newton Abbot experience in Jordan (1973).

4 Approved societies were those societies approved by the government to administer health and unemployment insurance schemes on its behalf.

References

*Banks, James and Tanner, Sarah (1997) *The State of Donation: Household Gifts to Charity, 1974–96*, Institute for Fiscal Studies, London.
*Beveridge, William (1948) *Voluntary Action: A Report on Methods of Social Advance*, Allen and Unwin, London.
Board of Trade (various years) *Statistical Abstract for the UK*, HMSO, London.
Bottomore, T. (1954) 'Social stratification in voluntary organisations', in Glass, D. V. (ed.) *Social Mobility in Britain*, Routledge and Kegan Paul, London.
Bourdillon, A. F. C. (1945) *Voluntary Social Services: Their Place in the Modern State*, Methuen, London.
*Braithwaite, Constance (1938) *The Voluntary Citizen*, Methuen, London.
Briggs, Asa (1991) *The Story of The Leverhulme Trust*, Leverhulme Trust, London.
Brown, Paul and Smyth, John (eds) (1997) *Guide to Company Giving 1997–98*, Directory of Social Change, London.
Castle, Barbara (1980) *The Castle Diaries 1974–76*, Weidenfeld and Nicolson, London.
Central Statistical Office (various years) *Annual Abstract of Statistics*, HMSO, London.
Charities Aid Foundation (CAF) (1994) *International Giving and Volunteering*, Charities Aid Foundation, Tonbridge.
*Charities Aid Foundation (various years) *Charity Statistics*, Charities Aid Foundation, Tonbridge.
*Charities Aid Foundation (various years) *Charity Trends*, Charities Aid Foundation, Tonbridge.
*Charities Aid Foundation (various years) *Dimensions of the Voluntary Sector*, Charities Aid Foundation, West Malling.
Charity Commission for England and Wales Website: http://www.charity-commission.gov.uk
Charity Commission for England and Wales (various years) *Annual Report*, HMSO, London.
Citron, Judith (1989) *The Citizens Advice Bureau: For the Community by the Community*, Pluto Press, London.
Crewe, Ivor (1989) 'Values: the crusade that failed', in Kavanagh, Dennis and Seldon, Anthony (eds) *The Thatcher Effect: A Decade of Change*, Clarendon Press, Oxford.
*Crossman, R. H. S. (1976) 'The role of the volunteer in the modern social service' [Sidney Ball lecture, 1973] in Halsey, A. H. (ed.) *Traditions of Social Policy: Essays in Honour of Violet Butler*, Blackwell, Oxford.
Davis Smith, Justin (1996) 'Volunteering in Europe', in Charities Aid Foundation (1996) *Dimensions of the Voluntary Sector 1996*, Charities Aid Foundation, West Malling.
Davis Smith, Justin (1998) *The 1997 National Survey of Volunteering*, National Centre for Volunteering, London.
De Waal, Alexander (1995) 'Compassion fatigue', *New Statesman*, 17 March.
Field, Frank (1996) *How to Pay for the Future: Building a Stakeholders' Welfare*, Institute of Community Studies, London.
Fogarty, Michael and Legard, Robin (1993) *More than Money: How Businesses and Voluntary Organisations can Work Together*, Joseph Rowntree Foundation, York.
Gaskin, Katharine and Davis Smith, Justin (1995) *A New Civic Europe?: A Study of the Extent and Role of Volunteering*, Volunteer Centre UK, London.

*Goddard, Eileen (1994) *Voluntary work: A Study Carried Out on Behalf of the Home Office as Part of the 1992 General Household Survey*, HMSO, London.

Halfpenny, Peter and Lowe, Debbie (1994) *Individual Giving and Volunteering in Britain*, Charities Aid Foundation, Tonbridge.

Halsey, A. H. (ed.) (1972) *Trends in British Society since 1900*, Macmillan, London.

Hanson, Charles (1972) 'Welfare before the Welfare State', from Hartwell, R. M. (ed.) *The Long Debate on Poverty*, Institute of Economic Affairs, London.

Harrison, Brian (1978) *Separate Spheres: The Opposition to Women's Suffrage in Britain*, Croom Helm, London.

HM Treasury (1998) *Proposed Amendments to the Credit Unions Act 1979: A Consultation Document*, HM Treasury, London.

Jackson, Brian and Jackson, Sonia (1979) *Childminder. A Study in Action Research*, Routledge, London.

Jay, Douglas (1937) *The Socialist Case*, Faber, London.

Jordan, Bill (1973) *Paupers: The Making of the New Claiming Class*, Routledge and Kegan Paul, London.

Lascelles, E. C. P. (1934) 'Charity', in Young, G. M. (ed.) *Early Victorian England 1830–1865*, Oxford University Press, Oxford.

MacKenzie, John M. (1984) *Propaganda and Empire: The Manipulation of British Public Opinion, 1880–1960*, Manchester University Press, Manchester.

Matheson, Jil (1990) *Voluntary work: A Study Carried Out on Behalf of the Home Office as Part of the 1987 General Household Survey*, HMSO, London.

Mitchell, B. R. (1988) *British Historical Statistics*, Cambridge University Press, Cambridge.

Morgan, John (1947) 'The National Council of Social Service with appendix on work in rural areas', in Mess, Henry A. (ed.) *Voluntary Social Services since 1918*, Kegan Paul, London.

National Council for Voluntary Organisations (NCVO) (1996) *Charity and the Lottery: The Competition for Loose Change*, National Council for Voluntary Organisations, London.

National Trust (1995) *The National Trust and Volunteers*, Leaflet no. 10, National Trust, London.

Orwell, George (1970) 'The Lion and the Unicorn', in *The Collected Essays, Journalism and Letters*, *vol. II*, Penguin, Harmondsworth.

Owen, David (1965) *English Philanthropy 1660–1960*, Harvard University Press, Cambridge, Mass., and London.

Posnett, John (1995) 'The Resources of registered charities in England and Wales 1990/1', in *Researching the Voluntary Sector*, first edition, Charities Aid Foundation, Tonbridge.

Postgate, Raymond (ed.) (1961) *The Good Food Guide 1961/62*, Consumers' Association, London.

Prochaska, Frank (1995) *Royal Bounty: The Making of a Welfare Monarchy*, Yale University Press, New Haven, and London.

Registry of Friendly Societies (various years) *Report of the Chief Registrar of Friendly Societies*, HMSO, London.

Richards, Jean (1989) *Inform, Advise and Support: The Story of 50 Years of the Citizens' Advice Bureaux*, Lutterworth, Cambridge.

Robertson, William (1964) *Welfare in Trust: A History of the Carnegie United Kingdom Trust 1913–1963*, Carnegie United Kingdom Trust, Dunfermline.

Rowntree, B. S. (1901) *Poverty: A Study of Town Life*, Macmillan, London.

Samstag, Tony (1988) *For Love of Birds: The Story of the Royal Society for the Protection of Birds, 1889–1998*, RSPB, Sandy.

Stott, Mary (1978) *Organization Woman: The Story of the National Union of Townswomen's Guilds*, Heinemann, London.

Tawney, R. H. (1972) *Commonplace Book* (ed. Winter, J. M. and Joslin, D. M.), Cambridge University Press, Cambridge.

*Taylor Gooby, Peter (1993) *The Future of Giving: Evidence from the British Social Attitudes Survey*, Charities Aid Foundation, Tonbridge.

Thatcher, Margaret (1995) *The Path to Power*, HarperCollins, London.

Titmuss, Richard M. (1973) *The Gift Relationship: From Human Blood to Social Policy*, Penguin, Harmondsworth.

Tuffrey, Michael (1997) 'Getting the measure of corporate involvement', in Charities Aid Foundation, *Dimensions of the Voluntary Sector 1997*, CAF, West Malling.

Waddilove, Lewis E. (1983) *Private Philanthropy and Public Welfare: The Joseph Rowntree Memorial Trust 1854–1979*, Allen and Unwin, London.

Ward, Roger et al. (1996) 'Charities' contribution to gross domestic product: the results of the 1996 ONS Survey of Charities' in *Economic Trends*, 517, November.

*Ware, Alan (1989) *Between Profit and State: Intermediate Organisations in Britain and the United States*, Polity Press, Cambridge.

Further reading

(In addition to the asterisked items in the References)

Beveridge, William and Wells, A. F. (1949) *The Evidence for Voluntary Action*, Allen and Unwin, London.

Finlayson, Geoffrey (1994) *Citizen, State, and Social Welfare in Britain 1830–1990*, Clarendon Press, Oxford.

Prochaska, Frank (1988) *The Voluntary Impulse: Philanthropy in Modern Britain*, Faber, London.

Rooff, Madeline (1972) *A Hundred Years of Family Welfare: A study of the Family Welfare Association (formerly Charity Organisation Society) 1869–1969*, Michael Joseph, London.

Wolfenden, Lord (1978) *The Future of Voluntary Organisations: Report of the Wolfenden Committee*, Croom Helm, London.

18
Leisure

Jonathan Gershuny and Kimberly Fisher

> After dinner, he may find himself drinking Brazilian coffee, smoking a
> Dutch cigar, sipping a French cognac, reading *The New York Times*,
> listening to a Brandenburg Concerto and entertaining his Swedish wife –
> all at the same time, with varying degrees of success.
>
> Staffan Linder, *The Harried Leisure Class*, 1970

Leisure started the century as the name of a class, and ends it as a category of
consumption. Leisure was once assumed to be an attribute of the progress of
civilization, in which we move, step by step, from a primitive world of
unremitting toil toward a future of uninterrupted play. At earlier stages of civilization, leisure was the exclusive perquisite of the rich, progress, through the
automation of production would mean that an ever-increasing proportion of
the population of developed societies would achieve this desirable state, while
the working hours of the remaining part would continuously decline. The
Sabbath day of rest was considered to be a foretaste of this paradisial state of
society, and indeed the Babylonian Talmud identifies the start of the messianic
era with the point in history that all abstain from work on one particular
Saturday.

However, more recently – indeed almost immediately after the announce-
ment (by the French sociologist Joffre Dumazedier) of the imminent arrival of
the leisure society in the mid-1960s – some quite strongly dissenting views
emerge. Does work time *necessarily* decline with technological progress and
economic growth? Does leisure really 'trickle down' from superordinate classes
to subordinate? What, anyway, is meant by the word 'work' in this context?
In particular, what happens to those sorts of 'work' that have been traditionally carried out by women? Similarly, what is *not* leisure? Some people (indeed,
a growing part of the population, as unskilled jobs disappear and the majority
of women enter the labour force), may view their work as a major source of
interest and recreation, and consider their nominally 'free' time as hopelessly

compromised by family requirements (this is the central thesis of Hochschild, 1997). Work *becomes* leisure, and leisure, work.

In what follows we shall examine the (surprisingly limited) statistical basis for the consideration of these competing assertions. But before the empirical evidence, let us consider, in a little more detail, the nature of the theoretical arguments.

Leisure theories and concepts

Three fundamentally important concepts in the nineteenth-century discussions of leisure (whose echoes are still very present in the twentieth century) are the *saturation of wants*, the *exploitation* of a subordinate class by a superordinate, and the *diffusion* of leisure habits from the superordinate to the subordinate.

The first of these notions is most clearly articulated by John Stuart Mill in the chapter in his *Principles of Political Economy* (1871) entitled 'On the possible futurity of the labouring classes'. He makes a number of remarkably modern-sounding (or at least 1960s-sounding) claims about the prospects for the saturation of wants. He asserts, quite straightforwardly, that the growth of productive capacity means that all the material wants of the next generation of the whole populations of modern economies could be fully satisfied. Hence, there is a very serious prospect of substantial reductions in hours of paid work.

The second of these notions, rather more clearly *political* economy, comes from Marx's *Capital*. (1867 [1967]) Marx defines exploitation in terms of the employer's ability to force his workers to contribute work time over and above the level necessary to maintain and reproduce their own labour power. The capitalist's profit results directly from his ability to enforce long working hours, and the ratio of this 'surplus' labour to total work time is Marx's 'rate of exploitation'. Reducing the rate of exploitation reduces profit and hastens the final crisis of capitalism. The reduction of working hours was thus advanced from the status of the pipe-dream of liberal triflers, to a major goal of socialist politics.

In short, both the 'positive' analysis of the liberal economists and the policies of the socialists were united in the view that 'progress' involved the reduction of working hours for the 'labouring classes'.

A somewhat similar expectation, though stemming from an utterly different analytical perspective, emerges from Thorstein Veblen's 1899 (1953) sociological classic *The Theory of the Leisure Class*. Here the mechanism for the diffusion of leisure through the social classes was to be through a process of 'emulation'. Leisure, in Veblen's analysis, had been in medieval times and previously, the exclusive right of feudal proprietors. These first deployed their own and their dependants' expertise in the 'leisure pursuits' of hunting and fighting, to maintain and extend their landed possessions. 'Exploits' (Veblen's ironic term for the participation in these violent activities of a 'leisured' retinue of armed men) were a mechanism for exploitation and expropriation by the superordinate class. Over time the 'leisurely' characteristics of the dominant class and their hangers-on become reduced to mere *symbols* of social dominance; the landed rich come gradually to maintain not just themselves, but also large retinues of dependants, in an idle state, as a *demonstration* of their social pre-eminence. And so too (runs Veblen's argument) do those of lesser social status who aspire to greater, seek to emulate the idleness of their betters in the hope they may be mistaken for them. Not merely the lesser gentry but also the urban bourgeoisie seek spare time in which to demonstrate leisureliness. Thus, it is through the social-positional, rather than the intrinsic, characteristics of the relevant activities (so Veblen argued) that leisure becomes desirable, and 'trickles down' through the social orders.

Keynes' (1928 [1972]) essay 'Economic Possibilities for our Grandchildren' bears strong similarities to Mill's chapter of 50 years before (though it is not specifically cited as a source). He argues that technological progress works like compound interest, to increase productivity against a background of needs that can be satisfied. Keynes' major original addition to the line of argument in this essay is in fact the identification of a new sort of 'leisure problem': how are the working classes to use their leisure? Keynes' somewhat patrician view is that, having little experience of free time, the newly leisured classes won't know what to do with their leisure hours. Hence, he implies, a need for education for leisure, a need for mass training in leisure consumption (his views here prefiguring aspects of the discussion of the impact of human capital in the formation of consumption habits found in Pierre Bourdieu's (1979) *Distinction*).

All this discussion so far relates to the historical evolution of paid work time in the money economy. The classical economists assumed that 'work' was coterminous with paid employment. Some sociologists, even in the 1930s, took a broader view, to include unpaid work, cooking and cleaning within the household. But as with paid work so with unpaid; the rate of technical progress in household production would outstrip the rate of growth of household wants. The dominant view in the 1930s was that automation would reduce the burden of domestic chores. The Lynds (1937), for example, in their classic *Middletown* study, provided an extensive statistical account of how housework time had been reduced by the acquisition of new items of domestic equipment.

Bertrand Russell's 'In Praise of Idleness' (1960) followed this trend of argument about the *possibility* of the coming mass leisured state, adding to it an almost moral sense of its *desirability*. And more than a century of enlightened argument from liberal and progressive thinkers reached its apogee in the optimistic 1960s, during which Dumazedier's (1967, 1974) *Society of Leisure* was seen as an almost inevitable correlate of the unavoidable coming of Bell's *Post-Industrial Society* (1976).

It would have been nice. But unfortunately, there is a trend of counter-argument that specifically denies the inevitability of a leisurely future, and suggests that perhaps the future will turn out to be even busier than the present. The argument starts from the evidence of economic anthropologists who observe that in fact the least economically 'developed' cultures tend to have the least work time. Marshall Sahlins' hugely entertaining *Stone Age Economics* – which in 1972 propounded an image of a Neolithic leisure society in contrast to the then more prevalent assumption that this was a post-industrial phenomenon – is perhaps the best introduction to this literature. But the foundations of the counter-thesis date from around the same time that Dumazedier proclaimed the leisure millennium, social historians (for example, Thompson, 1973) and sociologists (for example, Wilensky and Lebeaux, 1965) were suggesting that the primary effect of industrialization was in fact to *increase and intensify* labour time.

A substantial theoretical argument to the same effect was not long in following. In 1970 Staffan Linder's *The Harried Leisure Class* presented a full-blown argument explicitly reversing Veblen's, portraying the whole of the development process as involving increase in work pressures, and also growing pressures of consumption. Based on a rather simple 'marginalist' proposition, Linder argues that a rational individual will maximize the return on the marginal moment in each activity. There is a continuous growth of productivity of work in the money economy, and hence there must be tendencies either (i) to shift time towards paid work, or (ii) to increase the intensity of leisure consumption so as to increase its marginal productivity – so even leisure becomes unleisurely.

A distinct strand in this counter-thesis is the explicit discussion of unpaid work. Two different arguments disturb the cosy image of leisure growth from the reduction of domestic work time.

The first relates to the supposedly labour-saving characteristics of domestic equipment. Joann Vanek (1974) observed that in the US, housewives' daily domestic work time total had not reduced at all between the late 1920s and the mid-1960s. In her own and in others' subsequent work, it has emerged that part at least of this surprising effect is to be explained by the virtual disappearance of private paid domestic service over this period. But despite this, and despite also the gathering body of international evidence that there is indeed some quite substantial historical reduction in domestic work time associated (at least temporally) with the diffusion of domestic equipment, it is still widely believed that domestic work time does not reduce in this way.

The second relates specifically to the gendered distribution of unpaid work. It has been clear that the various categories of unpaid 'housework' have, with just a few minor exceptions, been carried out predominantly by women. If those women who specialize in unpaid work are not also employed in the money economy, there is the possibility of a degree of symmetry between men's role in the workplace and women's in the home. But through much of the second part of this century, women have been entering the workforce in increasing numbers. First Young and Willmott, in *The Symmetrical Family* (1973), then Meissner et al. (1975) demonstrated conclusively that the consequence of this has been the accumulation of a dual burden of paid and unpaid work which specifically reduces *women's* leisure. Subsequent work in this area through the 1980s and 1990s (Hochschild, 1989; Gershuny et al., 1994; Gershuny, 1995) produces the slightly less pessimistic conclusion that there is gradual change, as women reduce and men slightly increase their unpaid work in response to changes in the gender distribution of paid work. But aspects of this dual burden phenomenon persist and remain important.

So, while our progressive forebears in the nineteenth century, and the earlier part of the twentieth, confidently looked forward to a continuous growth of free time, this prospect is no longer uncontested. Juliet Schor's 1993 *Overworked American* – subtitled 'The Unexpected Decline of Leisure' – combines most of the distinct lines of the counter-thesis; increasing paid work time, women's dual burden, less, and more hurried, leisure. It is by no means uncontroversial, even in the US context (see for example, Robinson and Godbey, 1997), but it stands nevertheless as a not-implausible description of the UK position.

Definitions of leisure

From the literature, we can distinguish three distinct approaches to a definition: leisure as a series of recreational categories; leisure as an aspect of consumption; and leisure as the residual category of what is left as 'free' time once 'work' is completed. The last of these is by no means non-problematic, but is used as the organizing principle for the evidence provided in this chapter. The former two have considerable appeal, nevertheless.

Young and Willmott (1973) encourage us to take the strongly principled view that leisure is whatever people consider it to be. In the time-use diary they gave to their survey respondents, they asked, throughout the day, what activities were taking place, and then quite separately, whether their respondents considered each of these activities to be work, or leisure, or neither, or both. This discussion was not in fact taken very far in the text itself, but the data show fairly clearly that even within the quite narrowly selected group of 25–45-year-old Home Counties couples, quite a wide range of different perceptions of what activities were or were not leisure activities emerged. To choose just two examples, some considered their paid employment as leisure, while others excluded watching television from their list of leisure activities. This sort of finding has theoretical implications that would take us well outside the scope of this chapter. But it is also true that this same data source provides a reasonable level of agreement that *most* people take leisure to consist of a limited (and predictable) set of recreational activities, extending from relatively passive home-based activities such as watching television, via out-of-home spectator or audience activities, to active participation in hobbies and sports. It is possible to go further, and distinguish among these categories according to some supposed functional significance (for example, Parker, 1976). Perhaps some are seen as being involved in physical recuperation from work stress and strain, others in providing an alternative source of personal identity (as where the office worker becomes a cricketer), or as the literal re-creation of the spirit (where a consciousness inured to the drabness of industrial surroundings is reawakened by exposure to beautiful sights or sounds). But genuine evidence to support any such attributions of purpose to people's play is in very short supply.

The second definition relates to the use of leisure in assertions of social status or of social differentiation. In this view, leisure is pretty well coterminous with consumption, and includes, in addition to explicitly recreational activities, acts of domestic eating and drinking, the wearing of particular clothes, and also the use of particular sorts of domestic equipment. The 'trickle down' model in which the leisure/consumption habits of higher status groups are emulated subsequently by lower, stems most recently from Veblen, and certainly forms a substantial part of Linder's 'harried leisure' argument, as it does of Hirsch's (1977) *Social Limits to Growth*, with its darkly pessimistic view of economic 'development' as the endless increase of consumption in the ultimately unachievable pursuit of individual social advancement.

Perhaps the most interesting modern use of this second definition is that of Bourdieu in *Distinction*. In this account, status, or at least distinctiveness, is not achieved by emulation of a social superior, but through the establishment of a style of leisure consumption, based on a combination of cultural knowledge ('human and social capital') with financial resources, to establish patterns of daily activity which assert the individual's 'distinction'. The Anglophone trickle-down model implies a strong unidimensional hierarchy of social statuses. In helpful contrast, this Gallic view of leisure as the means through which the individual deploys various different personal resources to construct a distinctive life-style, and hence asserts a distinctive social position, implies a more realistic-seeming complex, multiple and ambiguous status order. Leisure, for Bourdieu, is the means for asserting individuality in a modern society.

Residual definition

But perhaps the most appropriate conceptualization of leisure, for present purposes at least, is simply as the *free time* remaining once all work – in the broadest sense – is accomplished. The inclusive use of 'work' to cover all work-like activities, whether paid-for or unpaid, is of some importance in this context. The alternative 'leisure equals consumption' approach of course includes much of what might alternatively be considered as 'domestic production'. Status asserted through life-style, demands the Aga as well as the Opera. By contrast, the residual definition concentrates exclusively on acts of *final* consumption, on the meal as opposed to the cooking.

The straightforward statement of this approach is in the so-called 'third person criterion' (Hawrylyshn, 1978). Leisure, in this view, is 'activity that could not be undertaken by someone else without losing the essential intrinsic benefit accruing from it'. Hence leisure, in what follows, is equivalent to 'free time', time outside paid and unpaid work obligations. Also, though this is a matter of convention and certainly does not follow from the Hawrylyshn rule, sleep time is customarily excluded from this notion of leisure!

Sources of leisure data

In the remainder of this chapter, we shall be considering data from three distinct sources.

The first category of evidence is, paradoxically, on employment (often, though not necessarily, deriving from administrative sources). These are, of course, in themselves not leisure statistics at all. But, given the 'residual' nature of our conceptualization of leisure, and in combination with evidence on unpaid work (see below), work time statistics provide us with evidence about a precise complement to our subject, and hence by subtraction, evidence on the subject itself. The evolution of employment patterns and of changing work time is discussed more fully by Gallie in Chapter 8 of this book.

However, employment statistics also provide evidence on leisure in a very different, considerably less direct, but still quite obvious manner. There is employment in those industries which produce the goods and services used in leisure consumption – what we might call 'leisure jobs'. Change in employment levels in these particular sectors provides an indirect indicator of change in rates and levels of leisure participation. Somewhat more directly, the official sources also give us information collected for administrative purposes on holiday entitlements.

A second general category of evidence, output or consumption indicators, also sometimes is collected for administrative purposes. This category includes 'pure' output indicators (for example, Board of Trade statistics on film attendance), and also statistics on consumption expenditures. Expenditure on particular categories of leisure-related commodities offers a more direct indicator than employment in these leisure industries. In combination series of data on price levels, data from the Family Expenditure Survey (collected on a national scale for the first time in 1951, and subsequently on a continuous basis since 1954) give us a picture of changing rates of purchase of leisure-related commodities, both goods and services. We can, to a limited degree, tell from these categories of leisure expenditure – and also from statistics from this and similar sources of ownership of leisure goods – something about the distribution of leisure activities across the population.

But of course, expenditure is not itself strictly consumption. Commodities may be purchased, and then stored rather than used. An increased rate of expenditure on sports equipment, for example, might almost as well be a symptom of a short-term reduction in leisure time – as where the increasingly time-pressured executives purchase their golf clubs as a symbol of their thwarted *intent* to increase their recreation. Strictly speaking, 'consumer' expenditure even on leisure commodities is only evidence of consumption in that limited number of examples of short-term perishable services such as restaurant meals or seats at the theatre. Otherwise, like those hoards of unused book tokens, leisure expenditures, strictly interpreted, yield information only on projected leisure, and not on actual leisure practices.

The essence of consumption is ultimately as a category of personal experience. The act of purchasing something is of course itself a leisure or consumption experience. But when we buy the golf clubs, what we experience is shopping, not golf. We experience golf only when we play golf. There is ultimately, therefore, no real substitute for the third category of evidence: direct indication of leisure consumption activities from specific individual survey data. There are two distinct sorts of evidence that fall into this category. First, there is questionnaire-based evidence on rates of participation in leisure activities (as, for example, provided by the General Household Survey (GHS) at irregular intervals since 1973 – though as we shall see in a moment, even this evidence is only of limited use as a time-series), which establishes frequencies or rates of participation in leisure. And there is also a second category of evidence, on the time devoted to leisure activities as revealed by the nationally representative time-diary (or 'time-budget') surveys.

These two sorts of population activity indicators might fit together straightforwardly into an overall national-level system of accounting of leisure or leisure change. If the questionnaire-based participation data were sufficient to establish reliable population-level estimates of participation frequency (that is, the mean time between acts of participation in specific leisure activities), then the frequency multiplied by the mean duration of each particular class of leisure event (as estimated from the time-diary data) would give the average time devoted by the population to the category of event. Or alternatively, we can calculate population mean time even if the questionnaire evidence is only sufficient to establish a participation rate (for example, the proportion of the population who might be expected to participate in the activity in a given week), as long as we can establish the amount of time devoted to the activity in the given week by those who participate in it.

P mean participation rate over a period
F mean frequency of participation over a period
D mean duration of each instance of participation
T' mean time spent in an activity by participants
T mean time spent in an activity by population
T=P.T'
T=F.D

In other words, by combining the results of quite simple questions carried in large sample surveys of the sort employed from time to time in the GHS ('How often do you go to the cinema? – once per week/month/three months?') with evidence from even quite small time-diary surveys, it would in principle be possible to construct quite substantial and well founded accounts of leisure use patterns. In this chapter however, while we present both kinds of data separately, we do not take the final step of bringing them together to produce this sort of integrated leisure time use account.

An aside on the official treatment of leisure statistics in the UK

The ambiguities in the construction of an operational definition of leisure pursuits are highlighted in the shifting opinions towards leisure statistics adopted by the compilers of *Social Trends*. The first six editions included a leisure section following the employment section, identifying the leisure statistics as a 'complementary extension of the data on people's working lives' which 'can only be understood in relation to time spent in employment, whether paid or unpaid' (No. 4, 1973, p.94). In its early editions, *Social Trends* concentrated on paid holidays from work, holiday destinations, and reading activities. By 1976, editorial staff at *Social Trends* elected to move the leisure to follow the 'environment' section later in the volume. The seventh issue redefines leisure to encompass 'the complete area in which an individual can exercise choice over his activities – including the working environment' (No. 7, 1976, p.173). Accordingly, the leisure statistics for that year included more references to club and society membership, and participation in physical activities, as well as updating the previous offerings. From 1977–87, the table of paid holiday entitlements was moved to the 'employment' section, yet was returned to the 'leisure' section from 1988. From 1981, statistics of membership in organizations appear in several sections. The publication was reorganized for the 1996 edition, and since that year no longer includes a 'leisure' section. Most statistics relating to product ownership (cars, video machines, televisions, and so on), organization membership, and non-work activities now appear in a 'lifestyles' chapter, which also includes statistics on voting trends and affiliations to religions and political parties.

Paid work, free time and holidays

In this section, we consider leisure from the vantage point of the residual definition; leisure time viewed as, in effect, the *outcome* of the evolution of unpaid and paid work over the century. Gallie, in Chapter 8, has highlighted a substantial growth in the rate of women's participation in paid employment. By contrast, over most of the century, while men's labour market participation rate increased during the mid-part of life (25–55), it has actually fallen at the start of the working life (that is, ages 14 to 24, because of growth of educational participation) and at end (that is, 55+, because of earlier retirement).

Women now constitute nearly half of the paid workforce, yet around 40 per cent of all employed women work part-time. Women thus supply considerably less than half of all paid work time. By contrast, while the percentage of employed men working part-time quadrupled between 1961 and 1991, this percentage none the less accounts for about only 4 per cent of employed men, around one-tenth of the equivalent women's rate. The official employment hours statistics show reductions in work-hours for both full-time men (from 47.7 hours/week in 1938 to 42.8 hours/week in 1997) and full-time women employees (from 49.3 to 39.2 hours per week). In summary, we can say that from the point of view of the official statistics: (1) for men, the reduction in working hours, a small growth in part-time work, and a small overall decline in participation rate, mean that the paid work week has become considerably shorter over the century; (2) for women, the overall increase in the participation rate, combined with the general reduction in working hours, probably means a small increase in paid work time.

We cannot draw any direct inference about leisure from these data since we need also to know what happened to unpaid work over the same period; and the official statistics are entirely mute on this subject. Fortunately, there is an alternative source of data. The best way of estimating of how people spend their time is through a 'time-budget' or 'time-diary' survey, in which a sample of individuals is asked to maintain a complete schedule of all their activities for a given period (usually one day, but in the case of most of the surveys used here, a complete week). The UK government (unlike most other European administrations) has never yet conducted a full-scale national time-diary study (though a national study is planned for the year 2000). Nevertheless, other organizations have conducted large-scale, nearly national studies since the early 1960s. The British Broadcasting Corporation (BBC) Audience Research Department conducted what it called 'viewer/listener availability studies' in 1961 and 1974/75 (published in 1965 and 1978 respectively) using a seven-day diary method and a national sample, and the Economic and Social Research Council (ESRC) funded comparable (not strictly national, but reasonably representative nevertheless) studies, in 1984, and again in 1987, as part of its 'Social

Change and Economic Life Initiative' (SCELI) (these two are combined to produce a synthetic '1985' in what follows) (SCELI, 1984; 1987). And the Institute for Social and Economic Research (ISER) at Essex University, in conjunction with the Office of National Statistics (ONS), conducted a small national one-day diary study in 1995. (Note that these studies are all based on samples of people based at home: the time use of people away from home – notably those on holidays – is not included.) We can combine the results of these studies to give a more general picture of change in work patterns than we get from the official statistics.

These studies provide a mass of information about the time-use patterns of different sorts of people at different sorts of time. To simplify the presentation of this complex evidence we use a straightforward statistical technique, multiple classification analysis (MCA) (which is in fact just a simple way of presenting multiple regression results: Andrews et al., 1967). Table 18.1 presents MCA models of the paid work time of British adults aged 20–60, at four historical time-points, broken down by sex, age and family status and employment status (these are the variables known to be the main determinants of paid work time (Gershuny et al., 1994; Gershuny, 1995)). The 'grand mean' statistics give estimates of the overall average time spent in paid work by British adults at each time-point. The remaining coefficients show the effects of belonging to particular sub-groups of the population, controlling for all of the other categories (in a manner analogous to partial regression coefficients).

Table 18.1 Average minutes spent in paid work per day by British adults, 1961–95

		1961	1975	1985	1995
Grand mean =		296	271	250	246
Family status					
	Aged <40, no children	1	3	25	20
	Co-resident child under 5	5	1	–11	–8
	Co-resident child under 15	–6	–5	–8	6
	Aged 40+, no children	0	3	–4	–15
Employment status					
	Full-time	140	133	96	118
	Part-time	–108	–83	–52	–56
	Other, non-employed	–277	–245	–183	–205
Sex					
	Man	23	23	24	19
	Woman	–23	–23	–24	–18

Sources: BBC Audience Research, 1965; 1978; SCELI, 1984; 1987; ISER and ONS, 1995.

The table can be read in a very simple manner. Take, for example, the 1961 column: we can straightforwardly estimate, to choose a specific case, the average daily paid work time of a man employed full-time with a small child. This is the grand mean (296 minutes) plus the small-child effect (5 minutes) plus the full-time employment effect (140 minutes) plus the male effect (23 minutes), giving a total of 464 minutes. By contrast, the same sum for 1995 gives a total of 375 minutes, meaning, over the 35-year period, a reduction of about 90 minutes per day – rather more than the approximately 60 minutes per day reduction that we would have expected from the official figures. This modelling technique ignores interaction effects – the fact that, for example, part-time jobs have different effects for men and women – but the consequences are relatively unimportant for this particular analysis (since virtually all of the part-time workers *are* women).

The table shows an overall, though not an entirely regular, decline in paid work time. Full-time workers experienced a reduction in working time from the 1960s to the 1980s, then faced some increases in hours again through the mid-1990s. Even so, full-time workers of the 1990s worked fewer hours than their counterparts in the 1960s. Women's part-time work held approximately constant at around 165 minutes throughout the period (though the numbers of part-time workers have increased dramatically over the period). What is important about Table 18.1, however, is that it provides a series of estimates that we can add to the parallel changes in unpaid work over the period, so as to calculate leisure time as the residual category.

Holiday entitlements

However, before we do so, we should note briefly that these reductions in weekly paid work time have been accompanied by a growth in holiday entitlements. In 1938, 40 per cent of employees in the UK had some form of paid holiday entitlement; this rose to 91 per cent in 1950, and 95 per cent in 1970. Subsequently this total has if anything fallen slightly, leaving approximately 10 per cent of employees without such entitlements in the early 1990s (*Ministry of Labour Gazette*, 1938; 1952; *Employment Gazette*, 1981; 1993).

How long are these holidays? Historical statistics in this field are in short supply. But an indication of the extent of growth of these entitlements is given by Table 18.2 which shows the changing distribution of holiday entitlements for full-time manual workers covered by national agreements on terms of service. Even by 1990, only half of all employees were covered by such agreements, and the coverage was substantially lower in the 1950s, so the sample is undoubtedly a biased one. Nevertheless, the table does give some indication of the very substantial increase in the level of holiday entitlement considered appropriate by employers over the last half-century.

Table 18.2 Paid holiday entitlement for full-time manual workers covered by national agreements, 1951–90

	1951	1955	1960	1965	% 1970	1975	1980	1985	1990
<2 weeks	31	1	0	0	0	0	0	0	0
2 weeks	66	96	97	75	41	1	0	0	0
2+ to 3 weeks	2	2	2	22	59	18	2	0	0
3+ to 4 weeks	1	1	1	3	0	81	43	17	9
4+ to 5 weeks	0	0	0	0	0	0	55	63	64
5 weeks up	0	0	0	0	0	0	0	20	27

Sources: *Social Trends*, 1971, no. 2, p.64; *Employment Gazette*, December 1981, vol. 89 (12), p.534; April 1985, vol. 93 (4), pp.154–6; April 1990, vol. 98 (4), p.228; April 1992, vol. 100 (4), p.152.

By 1996, all European Union (EU) states had passed statutory entitlements for paid holidays for their workforces except Italy and the UK. *The Working Time*

Table 18.3 Time spent on unpaid work, 1961–95

minutes per day	Shopping, domestic travel 1961	1975	1985	1995
Grand mean	25	35	46	49
Aged <40, no children	–1	–3	–9	–2
Co-resident child under 5	–1	1	7	8
Co-resident child under 15	2	4	4	9
Aged 40+, no children	1	–4	–3	1
Full-time	–10	–11	–7	–9
Part-time	6	8	5	7
Other, non-employed	21	19	14	14
Man	–7	–7	–7	–9
Woman	7	6	7	8

minutes per day	Other unpaid work (odd jobs, garden) 1961	1975	1985	1995
Grand mean	35	31	39	35
Aged <40, no children	–12	–1	–9	–8
Co-resident child under 5	3	–2	–7	–7
Co-resident child under 15	9	0	5	–5
Aged 40+, no children	4	3	9	14
Full-time	–5	–8	–5	–11
Part-time	9	6	2	–2
Other, non-employed	8	13	10	23
Man	17	17	13	12
Woman	–17	–17	–13	–12

Sources: BBC Audience Research, 1965; 1978; SCELI, 1984; 1987; ISER and ONS, 1995.

Directive Research Report released to the Commons in November 1996 concluded that enacting paid holiday legislation in the UK would not significantly affect employment or the economy (Lourie, 1996), and in October 1998, British workers, with some limited exceptions, gained the right to four weeks' annual paid holiday (*Labour Market Trends*, 1998).

In summary, the reduction in weekly work hours, which excludes holiday time, certainly underestimates the overall reduction in the annual total of paid work undertaken in Britain over the century. However, in the discussions of time use that follow, we shall simply ignore this fact, and concentrate specifically on changes in time use in 'normal' (that is, non-holiday) weeks.

Unpaid work

Table 18.3 gives the breakdowns for the unpaid work of the working-age population, summarized in exactly the same form as in Table 18.1. The usefulness of the modelling is perhaps more limited in this case, because here the inter-

Cooking				Other domestic work (cleaning, laundry)			
1961	1975	1985	1995	1961	1975	1985	1995
63	59	56	48	55	47	44	47
−16	−14	−14	−15	−18	−9	−14	−17
6	−1	2	5	12	1	4	8
14	6	3	6	14	2	6	8
3	6	8	5	1	3	2	3
−24	−17	−12	−11	−21	−17	−13	−12
22	9	18	15	14	5	18	18
48	34	18	13	41	33	19	15
−37	−36	−22	−13	−33	−30	−23	−25
37	35	21	12	32	28	24	24

Child care				All unpaid work			
1961	1975	1985	1995	1961	1975	1985	1995
13	15	25	39	191	187	210	218
−8	−8	−20	−32	−55	−35	−66	−74
33	27	54	85	53	26	60	83
2	−5	−8	14	41	7	10	32
−13	−14	−21	−33	−4	−6	−5	−10
−6	−6	−5	−8	−66	−59	−42	−51
−3	−2	−8	5	48	26	35	43
14	15	14	14	132	114	75	79
−6	−5	−10	−11	−66	−61	−49	−46
6	5	10	10	65	57	49	42

action effects are important. We know, for example, that the relationship between having small children and various sorts of domestic work is quite different for men and for women. Nevertheless, the grand means, employment and sex effects are reasonably representative of the actual differences between the various groups. (A more detailed discussion of trends in unpaid work in a number of countries can be found in Gershuny, 1995.)

Consider first the means. Shopping and domestic travel time have been increasing (because of the growth of self-service shopping and the fact that the bigger the shop the more distant it must be from its average customer). Cooking time has decreased (partly because of lighter, and more pre-cooked, meals, but also because of a particular leisure trend that we shall turn to in a moment). 'Easy care' domestic materials have reduced other domestic work such as house cleaning. Time devoted to other non-routine domestic jobs has remained reasonably constant over the period. And time devoted to child care (as a 'main activity') has increased regularly and substantially through the period (partly because of perception of increasing dangers to children; partly because of new child-raising concepts like 'quality time'; and partly because the reduction of core housework and cooking time allows the conversion of formerly 'secondary' child care activities – for example, preparing the supper *while* supervising the toddler – into primary activities). Add together these five categories of unpaid work, and we find an increase in the total of domestic work of the order of half an hour per day, over the period.

Now consider the influence of gender. The gender effects for shopping remain roughly constant – which, given the doubling of the total time devoted to this activity, implies a convergence in the proportions done by the two sexes. A similar gender convergence emerges with 'odd jobs'. For cooking and housework, the gender gap declines. Despite the absolute increase in the gender gap for child care, the overall increase reported is such than men were doing a larger proportion of the child care in the mid-1990s than they were in the early 1960s. Overall, the absolute gap between men's and women's unpaid work was around 130 minutes in 1961, and has decreased by reasonably regular steps to 90 minutes in 1995. Add the gender effects to the means to see changes controlling for employment and family effects, and we find men's unpaid work increasing substantially from 125 minutes per day to 172, while women's remains pretty much unchanged at 256 minutes per day in 1961, 260 minutes in 1995. Women still do more unpaid work, but the gap has narrowed.

Now we can make the final step, and put together the paid and unpaid work into a single total, shown in Table 18.4. The total work burden dropped about 30 minutes between 1961 and 1975, then inched upward by increments of a few minutes over the subsequent decades. Now add in the gender differential. When we take all sorts of work together, we find what the standard sociological notion of 'the dual burden' would lead us to expect, women do substantially more work than men. Over the period, the differential substantially declines from about 85 minutes to about 50 minutes. Overall, men, worked a total of 445 minutes per day in 1961, and, controlling for changes in the distribution of employment and family status, around 440 minutes per day in 1995. Women respectively worked 530 and 488 minutes.

Table 18.4 Time spent on all paid and unpaid work, 1961–95

	1961	1975	1985	1995
Grand mean	487	458	460	464
Aged <40, no children	−54	−32	−41	−54
Co-resident child under 5	58	27	49	75
Co-resident child under 15	35	2	2	38
Aged 40+, no children	−4	−3	−9	−25
Full-time	74	74	54	67
Part-time	−60	−57	−17	−13
Other, non-employed	−145	−131	−108	−126
Man	−43	−38	−25	−27
Woman	42	34	25	24

Sources: BBC Audience Research, 1965; 1978; SCELI, 1984; 1987; ISER and ONS, 1995.

Assuming (as in fact the evidence approximately confirms) that sleep remains unchanged, then the residual, leisure time, has increased overall across the population by just about 20 minutes over the last 35 years. But when we add in the gender effects, we find that men's leisure time stays pretty much unchanged, varying only by a few minutes, as their reduction in paid work time is taken up by their increase in unpaid work. Women gained some 40 minutes per day of extra leisure time, though, in absolute terms, they still have some 50 minutes less leisure per day than men. None the less, something approaching half of the gender differential has disappeared over the last third of a century.

Leisure participation: alternative indicators

In this section we turn our attention to some other indicators of leisure participation.

Employment in leisure industries

As we suggested previously, there are some grounds for scepticism about the use of output or expenditure data as indicators of consumption (since the producers may stockpile or the purchasers may store). But in a sub-set of the cases (which in fact corresponds precisely to the economists' definition of a 'final service', which is 'consumed directly as it is produced'), evidence of economic activity is also evidence of consumption: restaurant meals, purchase of tickets to live performances, hotel bedrooms taken for the night, may be reliably assumed to have been consumed by their purchasers. The Family Expenditure Survey yields data on these categories of expenditure back to the early 1950s. In fact we can compile a comparative data series going back considerably further if we concentrate on employment data. (Indeed, on the assumption that productivity growth in these final service industries is inconsiderable, this is the preferable of the two approaches, since it avoids the important problem with the expenditure data, of coping with changes in relative prices over the period.)

Table 18.5 Numbers employed in leisure services, 1930–97 (000s)

	Catering, hotels, restaurants, pubs, clubs, etc.	Entertainment, sports and recreation
July 1930	351	78
July 1939	507	157
Dec 1950	629	212
Nov 1960	562	220
Dec 1970	568	242
June 1980	922	299
Dec 1990	1219	469
Dec 1997	1285	515

Sources: *Ministry of Labour Gazette*, January 1931, vol. 30 (1), pp.27–8; January 1940, vol. 48 (1), pp.22–3; January 1952, vol. 60 (1), pp.15–16; January 1962, vol. 70 (1), pp.15–16; *Employment Gazette*, February 1971, vol. 79 (2), pp.161–3; January 1981, vol. 80 (1), pp.S11–13; May 1991, vol. 99 (5), pp.S12–13; *Labour Market Trends*, April 1998, vol. 106 (4), pp.S12–13; Jones (1986).

Table 18.6 Percentage of workforce in leisure industries, 1930–97

	Catering, restaurants and hotels	Entertainment, sports and recreation	% employed in leisure
July 1930	2.8	0.6	3.5
July 1939	3.4	1.0	4.4
Dec 1950	2.9	1.0	3.9
Nov 1960	3.9	1.5	5.4
Dec 1970	4.6	1.9	6.5
June 1980	4.2	1.4	5.6
Dec 1990	5.5	2.1	7.6
Dec 1997	5.7	2.3	8.0

Sources: *Ministry of Labour Gazette*, January 1931, vol. 30 (1), pp.27–8; January 1940, vol. 48 (1), pp.22–3; January 1952, vol. 60 (1), pp.15–16; January 1962, vol. 70 (1), pp.15–16; *Employment Gazette*, February 1971, vol. 79 (2), pp.161–3; January 1981, vol. 80 (1), pp.S11–13; May 1991, vol. 99 (5), pp.S12–13; *Labour Market Trends*, April 1998, vol. 106 (4), pp.S12–13; Jones (1986).

The question of productivity in the leisure services is of very considerable importance. To the extent that we can accept the traditional assumption that there is effectively no growth in productivity over time in final services, Tables 18.5 and 18.6 showing a more than doubling of the proportion of employees in various categories of leisure services, provide us with altogether the clearest and most unambiguous empirical evidence of the growth of leisure over the century. If, under this assumption, a larger proportion of the working population is employed in leisure production, then a larger part of the society's consumption must, *in some sense*, be devoted to these specific leisure activities.

The exact meaning of 'a larger part' in this case, depends on what sort of productivity change, if any, is taking place. There is, first, the sort of productivity change that allows the same, or an equivalent, quality of service to be provided with fewer labour inputs. For example, a new larger and more automated theatre may produce the same play, to the same or a higher standard, for a larger audience, and employ fewer stagehands. With this sort of productivity growth, the same employment would provide services to more people, and more of the society's time would be devoted to leisure consumption – and in this case, an increase in labour would imply an unequivocal increase in the 'leisureliness' of the society – simply *more* consumption of the same leisure services.

There is, however, a second sort of productivity growth, in which the nature of the service is changed, generating more complex consequences. The emergence of fast-food restaurants provides one obvious example. In this case, the labour of a leisure-service worker provides for more consumers per unit of labour time. There are more leisure consumers per leisure-service worker, but what happens to the society's leisure time depends on the relationship of the change in employment level to the change in consumer time per unit of output (that is, if the meal takes half the time to eat, but there are twice as many restaurant workers, the time the society devotes to eating out remains unchanged). We then would face the Linder/Hirsch question of whether the society is in fact more leisurely when twice as many people dine out, but diners eat twice as fast. Ultimately, such changes in leisure provision and consumption raise political questions. Sympathizers with the *ancien régime*, as Hirsch himself appears to have been, might well consider this simply a loss of true leisureliness. Alternatively, one might view such change as creating wider access to new leisure.

And the reality is of course that accompanying the growth in the number of leisure-service workers there has been some of both sorts of productivity growth – an increase in the number of traditional restaurants as well as in fast-food joints. We will turn in a moment to look more directly at the evolution of leisureliness in terms of the time devoted to different sorts of leisure activity. Before this, we should consider some more potential indirect indicators.

Provision and use of leisure facilities

Table 18.7 Service establishments, 1980–94

	Number of businesses			
	1980	1985	1990	1994
Hotels and pubs	54889	55061	54599	48593
Camps & caravan sites	1587	1571	2027	2038

Source: *Annual Abstract of Statistics* 1988; 1992; 1998, Table 11.4.

Curious trends in the numbers of various types of establishments emerge. The number of hotels and pubs, for example, has fallen (Table 18.7) during the same period that the numbers of people employed in such facilities has increased substantially – which suggests a growing scale, if not necessarily scale economies. During the 1980s, the number of camping and caravan sites grew considerably. These new sites undoubtedly created some of the jobs identified in the previous section, though on a much smaller scale, since the leisure consumers in this case provide most of the leisure services themselves. This is an example of the second sort of productivity growth mentioned above, which has involved an increase of leisure consumer's time (in something quite akin to unpaid work) and a relatively small growth in paid work.

Table 18.8 Cinemas and admissions, 1937–96

	No. of cinemas		Admissions (millions)
1937	4734	1950	1396
1939	4901	1955	1182
1944	4728	1960	510
1949	4659	1965	327
1954	4509	1970	193
1959	3414	1975	116
1964	2057	1980	96
1969	1581	1987	67
1974	1535	1990	79
1979	1564	1995	97
1983	1432	1996	112
1989	481	n/a	n/a
1994	505	n/a	n/a
1996	495	n/a	n/a

Sources: *Annual Abstract of Statistics* 1937–47, Table 79; 1938–49, Table 96; 1957, Tables 90 and 91; 1967, Table 84; 1977, Table 10.72; 1984, Table 10.40; and 1998, Table 19.3.

Cinemas provide something of a paradigm case of this sort of change, in which paid service work progressively disappears, as consumers move to new 'self-servicing' or 'do-it-yourself' modes of provision of services (Gershuny, 1983). The 1930s to the 1990s saw a tenfold reduction in the number of cinemas, and an even larger fall in the number of admissions (Table 18.8) – pretty clearly associated with the spread of television in the 1950s and 1960s, and later of pay-per-view downloading from phone lines, video recorders, and new delivery routes for broadcast television programming. Here home-based provisions replace job-creating service consumption outside the home.

Another example of what was previously large-scale leisure provision outside the home, is professional football. Table 18.9 tells two different stories. Overall, there is a substantial reduction in 'live' attendance at matches. But the decline is concentrated at the bottom end of the league: attendance at Fourth Division matches is reduced by nearly one half from the 1951/52 season to the 1993/94 season. By contrast, Division 1 (now the Premier League) attendance is also reduced, but only by 10 or 20 per cent. Our conjecture is that we see here a consequence of the developing mixture of 'modes of provision' of this particular leisure service. Fewer people attend the lower divisions of the league – because of the availability of televised broadcasts of matches among Premier League clubs on television. There is a vastly larger audience for football overall (TV + live attendance) than there was previously; and the large television audience in turn feeds the enthusiasm of fans of the leading clubs, who as a result travel to attend matches in hardly reduced numbers.

Table 18.9 Average number of fans attending football matches, Football League (England and Wales) 1961/62–93/94

	1961/62	1966/67	1971/72	1976/77	1980/81	1986/87	1990/91	1993/94
Division 4	6060	5407	4981	3863	3082	3100	3253	n/a
Division 3	9419	8009	8510	7522	6590	4300	5208	n/a
Division 2	16132	15701	14652	13529	11202	9000	11457	11752
Division 1[a]	26106	30829	31352	29540	24660	19800	22681	23040
Totals	57717	59946	59495	54454	45534	36200	42599	34792

Note: [a] Now the Premier Division; Division 2 is now Division 1, and so on.

Source: *Social Trends*, 1992, no. 22, Table 10.19.

We might guess that similar processes affect all live leisure-service provisions, not just sport, but also music, dance, and theatre. The broadcast of matches or performance on television does directly deplete the live audience, but brings a much larger number into indirect contact with the performance – which in turn influences and educates tastes, for a much wider group than just those who previously attended live, and as a result indirectly feeds back into the future audience for the live performance.

Ownership of leisure equipment

The other side of this complex evolution of leisure consumption activities outside the home is the development of leisure facilities within the home. Of these, radio was the very first widely diffused example. Radio (or 'wireless', a term that carries an indirect reference to the 1920s competitor technology for broadcast entertainment – sound diffused by cable), and subsequently television licences provide a simple indirect way of tracking the long-term spread of these activities – covering, indeed, the whole of the period since their very first introduction in the UK. By the mid-1950s, virtually every household in the country had either radio or television, and by the mid-1970s, virtually all households had television. (The totals slightly above 100 per cent in Table 18.10 in the 1950s and 1960s probably reflect the very rapid spread of television ownership requiring a small number of households to buy two licences within one year.)

Table 18.10 Broadcast licences as a percentage of the number of census households, 1926–97

	1926	1937	1947	1957	1967	1977	1987	1997
Wireless	24.7	79.2	87.1	52.2	15.5	n/a	n/a	n/a
B&W TV	0.0	0.0	0.1	48.1	88.1	44.2	12.4	2.1
Colour TV	0.0	0.0	0.0	0.0	0.0	54.4	84.8	97.2

Sources: *Annual Abstract of Statistics* 1937–47, Table 232; 1938–50, Table 262; 1957, Table 257; 1962, Table 258; 1968, Table 261; 1973, Table 271; 1984, Table 10.38; 1994, Table 10.37; 1997, Table 10.33; 1998, Table 10.32; Jones (1986).

Table 18.11 Percentage of General Household Survey respondents living in a household containing leisure equipment, 1973–97

	1973	1980	1983	1987	1990	1993	1997
Satellite dish	–	–	–	–	–	–	22
Home computer	–	–	–	25	28	31	34
CD player	–	–	–	–	24	45	67
Video recorder	–	–	23	56	75	82	89
Phone	48	75	79	85	88	91	95
Car	61	67	66	69	74	75	78

Source: General Household Survey.

Table 18.11 uses the General Household Survey to chart the diffusion of various kinds of home leisure facilities over a somewhat shorter period. By 1997, around one-third of the population lived in a home containing a computer. The rate of growth in this proportion, from 25 per cent in 1987, may seem surprisingly slow; but in fact the majority of those reporting computer ownership in 1987 were referring to machines rather less powerful than the basic personal computer, and many of those households have subsequently purchased more powerful equipment. The telephone is now the second most widely diffused item of equipment after the television, and the great majority of households now have CD and video players. The GHS data indicate that more than 20 per cent of the British population live in households without cars. Particularly for the elderly, rural dwellers, and the poor, lack of access to a car can greatly restrict possibilities for leisure (Chapter 13 discusses transport in greater detail).

General Household Survey leisure participation evidence

Table 18.12 Participation rates in various sporting activities in the past month, General Household Survey sample members aged 20–40, 1977–97

	Walking	Team sports	Tennis, badminton	Skiing, skating	Cycling, running	Swimming, sailing	Non-comp. sports	All non-team sport
Mean	0.28	0.07	0.09	0.01	0.06	0.17	0.06	0.29
Men	0.27	0.14	0.11	0.01	0.08	0.17	0.09	0.34
1973	0.06	0.10	0.06	0.01	0.01	0.12	0.07	0.22
1977	0.18	0.12	0.14	0.01	0.03	0.16	0.07	0.32
1980	0.19	0.11	0.14	0.01	0.04	0.16	0.06	0.32
1983	0.16	0.10	0.11	0.01	0.06	0.16	0.05	0.29
1986	0.25	0.10	0.10	0.01	0.07	0.17	0.06	0.31
1987	0.35	0.22	0.13	0.01	0.10	0.19	0.09	0.37
1990	0.36	0.17	0.13	0.02	0.12	0.21	0.13	0.40
1993	0.38	0.16	0.10	0.02	0.15	0.21	0.14	0.42
1997		0.17	0.09	0.02	0.17	0.20	0.13	0.42
Women	0.29	0.01	0.06	0.01	0.05	0.16	0.03	0.24
1973	0.06	0.00	0.03	0.01	0.00	0.06	0.01	0.11
1977	0.20	0.01	0.07	0.01	0.01	0.10	0.02	0.18
1980	0.21	0.00	0.08	0.01	0.02	0.14	0.02	0.22
1983	0.17	0.00	0.07	0.01	0.03	0.15	0.01	0.21
1986	0.32	0.01	0.06	0.01	0.03	0.16	0.02	0.23
1987	0.33	0.04	0.07	0.01	0.08	0.19	0.03	0.29
1990	0.35	0.01	0.07	0.02	0.07	0.21	0.06	0.32
1993	0.34	0.01	0.05	0.01	0.08	0.21	0.06	0.31
1997		0.01	0.06	0.02	0.11	0.24	0.07	0.36

Source: General Household Survey.

The GHS periodically includes questions about respondents' leisure activities, providing, at least in principle, a unique long-term view of changing rates of participation in various sports over the last third of the century. These data have not been used widely, however, perhaps because the form of the questions and the range and specificity of the classification varies on every occasion. Nevertheless, with some caution, it is possible to construct a set of 'lowest common denominator' estimates of the distribution of sports participation in a given four-week period.

Table 18.12 considers people aged between 20 and 40, and shows how participation in some broad groups of activities has evolved from 1973 onwards. (We should say that, wherever we find substantial disjunctions between successive estimates, we assume that this results from differences in the form of the question, and striking leaps should be seen as artefactual. So the overall growth over the period in the activities covered by the first two columns, which show just such effects from 1983–87, probably do not adequately reflect long-term trends, and are for this reason excluded from the more aggregated analysis in the following table.)

Walking is the most widespread activity. The predominance of men playing football accounts for the high gender divisions in team sports. Participation in tennis and badminton appears to have declined quite substantially over the period. Skiing and ice skating increased, albeit from a very low level. Swimming and sailing (very largely swimming) increased among both young men and young women, but with a much larger rate of increase among the women, who by 1997 constituted the majority of participants in this activity. Golf, ten-pin bowling and bowls have grown markedly. And finally, the overall rate of monthly participation in the sports, which we take to be the most reliable of the indicators, seems to have risen reasonably regularly from about 32 per cent of young men in 1977 to around 42 per cent in 1997, and from 18 per cent to 36 per cent of young women over the period. Clearly some gender convergence has occurred.

Table 18.13 looks at this aggregate sports participation rate, broken down further by age and social class. For each of the separate age, class and gender groups, we see the same phenomenon of substantial growth in participation. In each of the class and age-groups, we find that the growth for women has been rather faster than that for men. And while it remains true that the members of the professional classes are still substantially more likely to take exercise than are members of the working classes, the *rate of growth* in participation among the working classes has been generally much higher than among the professional classes. Therefore, in short, at the end of the century, British society as a whole was converging on higher levels of participation (in, at least, the non-team sports) than it had 30 years ago.

Table 18.13 Participation rates in non-team sports in the past month, General Household Survey sample members, by age, class and sex, 1977–97

General Household Survey sample members ages 20–39

	Men			Women		
	Professional	Intermediate	Working	Professional	Intermediate	Working
1973	0.29	0.23	0.15	0.14	0.12	0.05
1977	0.45	0.32	0.23	0.26	0.20	0.10
1980	0.48	0.32	0.23	0.29	0.25	0.14
1983	0.46	0.33	0.28	0.34	0.25	0.14
1986	0.47	0.33	0.29	0.37	0.26	0.21
1987	0.52	0.41	0.37	0.45	0.34	0.29
1990	0.57	0.46	0.38	0.44	0.39	0.23
1993	0.56	0.46	0.43	0.40	0.36	0.28
1997	0.51	0.43	0.33	0.45	0.37	0.30

General Household Survey sample members aged 40–59

	Men			Women		
	Professional	Intermediate	Working	Professional	Intermediate	Working
1973	0.25	0.14	0.08	0.09	0.07	0.03
1977	0.31	0.19	0.11	0.08	0.11	0.04
1980	0.34	0.19	0.14	0.15	0.12	0.05
1983	0.32	0.20	0.16	0.18	0.11	0.10
1986	0.38	0.21	0.18	0.23	0.19	0.09
1987	0.39	0.31	0.25	0.29	0.22	0.17
1990	0.45	0.31	0.25	0.27	0.27	0.15
1993	0.44	0.33	0.28	0.33	0.29	0.18
1997	0.42	0.29	0.27	0.31	0.26	0.16

General Household Survey sample members aged 60–79

	Men			Women		
	Professional	Intermediate	Working	Professional	Intermediate	Working
1973	0.15	0.06	0.05	0.04	0.02	0.01
1977	0.15	0.08	0.06	0.05	0.03	0.01
1980	0.16	0.06	0.06	0.07	0.04	0.02
1983	0.21	0.10	0.06	0.08	0.05	0.02
1986	0.22	0.12	0.07	0.08	0.07	0.03
1987	0.24	0.17	0.18	0.26	0.21	0.16
1990	0.28	0.16	0.16	0.15	0.12	0.07
1993	0.31	0.20	0.17	0.19	0.15	0.07
1997	0.27	0.19	0.14	0.21	0.15	0.08

Source: General Household Survey.

Leisure time use

Gender, family and employment status effect

Finally, we turn to the most comprehensive picture of the distribution of leisure across British society: that of how leisure time is used. For convenience, we again adopt the MCA technique discussed earlier. Table 18.14 shows the changing pattern for a number of leisure or consumption activities.

The first of these is eating at home. We find a remarkable – if entirely expected – reduction of 45 minutes per day in the time devoted to eating meals and snacks at home. This decline is by regular decrements through the decades. The underlying regression models for all four time-periods are very similar, showing exactly the expected pattern (for example, no gender difference, full-

Table 18.14 Leisure activities, eating and socializing, 1961–95

| | Eating meals and snacks at home | | | |
	1961	1975	1985	1995
Grand mean	96	79	69	52
Aged <40, no children	−2	−5	−15	−8
Co-resident child under 5	−1	−4	−4	−1
Co-resident child under 15	3	0	5	3
Aged 40+, no children	0	9	11	5
Full-time	−13	−6	−8	−8
Part-time	11	3	5	5
Other, non-employed	25	12	16	14
Man	−1	1	1	1
Woman	1	−1	−1	−1

| | Sports, walking | | | |
	1961	1975	1985	1995
Grand mean	9	10	14	10
Aged <40, no children	5	3	2	4
Co-resident child under 5	−2	0	−1	−3
Co-resident child under 15	−1	−1	0	1
Aged 40+, no children	−3	−1	−1	−2
Full-time	−1	−3	−1	0
Part-time	−2	3	0	4
Other, non-employed	3	4	2	−1
Man	3	4	4	4
Woman	−3	−4	−4	−3

Sources: BBC Audience Research, 1965; 1978; SCELI, 1984; 1987; ISER and ONS, 1995.

time employed people spending less time, older people spending more time). This, we can conclude, is a reliable trend: eating remains a substantial activity within the home – but occupies barely more than half the time it did two generations ago.

By contrast, activities in public service arenas – just as we were led to suspect by the 'provision' evidence – have been substantially rising. This trend is not quite so regular, since it is itself the aggregate of a number of conflicting trends over different parts of the period (pub-going rising through the 1960s and 1970s, cinema declining in the 1960s, restaurants growing through the 1980s, and so on). The gender gap remains substantial in this case: men having fully 25 minutes per day more of this sort of leisure than women do. Again, the underlying structures of the regression result are rather similar for the four,

Eating out, pubs, cinema, theatre, etc				Socializing			
1961	1975	1985	1995	1961	1975	1985	1995
28	47	42	61	35	42	35	40
15	14	21	24	11	9	7	16
−11	−11	−17	−21	−3	3	1	−3
−8	2	−2	−3	−8	−8	−5	−14
−4	−4	−3	−4	−4	−1	−1	−2
−1	−2	−1	−3	−8	−7	−5	−14
4	−1	0	3	−1	2	4	1
2	5	3	5	17	16	9	27
5	11	5	13	−2	−5	−5	3
−5	−11	−5	−12	2	5	5	−3
Other leisure at home				TV and radio			
1961	1975	1985	1995	1961	1975	1985	1995
74	79	84	65	139	128	135	129
7	−2	2	10	−13	−10	−2	−10
−13	−11	−15	−22	−15	−7	−7	−5
−6	−2	2	−14	3	4	2	7
5	16	10	14	21	10	6	7
−21	−15	−12	−17	−11	−14	−15	−17
7	8	6	14	−5	1	−4	−23
44	28	23	26	25	30	35	47
9	1	−2	2	17	17	19	8
−9	−1	2	−2	−16	−16	−19	−7

entirely separate surveys, and we can be reasonably confident that there has been a real change in the society. The meal at home provides an opportunity for one sort of sociability that has declined by 45 minutes per day. Participation in eating, drinking and collective spectacles provides the opportunity for another sort of leisure – sociability, which has increased, over the same period, by more than 30 minutes per day.

'Socializing' – visiting, or being visited by – members of other households, has remained roughly constant over the period, at an average of 35–40 minutes per day. Perhaps surprisingly, given the evidence in the previous section of the increased rates of monthly participation in various sports over the quarter-century, *time* devoted to playing sports does not appear to have increased at all. There is in fact no necessary contradiction here: we have evidence (Gershuny 1986) that in cases where the range of different types of leisure participation increases, the average amount of time spent in each of these activities decreases (since the day has a fixed 24 hours, if more activities are to fill it, each of them must take less time).

'Other home leisure' (games, hobbies, reading) shows no particularly clear trend, though overall it falls a little, from 74 minutes per day in 1961, to 65 minutes in 1995. Perhaps most surprising of all of these results, time devoted to radio and television (as a main activity) has not changed much over the whole of this period. A larger proportion of this was radio in 1961. Nevertheless, as we saw earlier, by 1961 three-quarters of the households in the UK possessed televisions. And it may well be that as the substantially higher 'audience research' estimates of lengths of time the television is switched on, irrespective of whether anyone is actively watching it, this sort of statistic underestimates the pervasive nature of the television. But nevertheless, though television watching is by far the largest single activity within the household in terms of time use, at the end of the television century it shows no sign of progressively taking over all life outside paid work.

National time accounts

We can now add up the different sorts of time use, to get an overall picture of the changing place of leisure in the society's day. Paid work time (among the 20–60-year-olds covered in this comparative analysis) has declined substantially, by 50 minutes per day. But more than half of the potential gain in free time has been taken up by the growth in unpaid work, whether because of the increase in 'self-servicing' (as in the case of shopping) or, to put it at its lowest interpretation, 'defensive time use' (part at least of the explanation of the growth in child care time). Women's unpaid work time has declined, and men's has increased. So virtually the entire net 20-minute decline in the work total has accrued to women.

Quite the largest proportional changes are found in the growth in out-of-home leisure service consumption activities. The remaining leisure activities show small and irregular changes, to give a small net increase that pretty well mirrors the decline in work time. In both cases, the major gross shift happened in the 1960s and early 1970s.

And once we add the declining total of 'eating at home' to the residual – that, like non-social eating, could be described as 'reproductive activity' – sleeping, resting doing nothing, bathing and other personal care, we find a remarkable overall stability: these two categories overall vary by only a few minutes, by hardly 1 per cent of their total over the entire period.

So if there is any simple single conclusion to be drawn about what are in detail quite complex trends in leisure patterns over the last part of the century, it must be this: for that part of the twentieth century for which we have consistent and comprehensive evidence, it seems as if the more optimistic prophecies of the nineteenth-century writers are coming, slowly, to pass. By the end of the 1990s, British people had decreased their mid-century working hours by 23 minutes per day, or two hours 40 minutes per week, and gained two hours and 20 minutes more leisure per week over 34 years. We might perhaps define this change as *progress* – at a rate of seven extra weekly hours of leisure per century? There is a long way to go; but this is not grossly inconsistent with the view of the future set out in the first paragraph of this chapter.

Table 18.15 National time accounts, 1961–95

Activities	1961	1975	1985	1995
Paid work	296	271	250	246
Cooking	63	59	56	48
Cleaning, laundry	55	47	44	47
Other domestic work	35	31	39	35
Child care	13	15	25	39
Shopping, domestic travel	25	35	46	49
All work	487	458	460	464
Eating out, cinema, pubs, etc.	28	47	42	61
Socializing	35	42	35	40
Sports, walking	9	10	14	10
TV and radio	139	128	135	129
Other leisure at home	74	79	84	65
All specific leisure activity	285	306	310	305
Eating at home	96	79	69	52
Sleep, personal care, etc.	572	597	601	619
All reproductive activity	668	676	670	671
Work + leisure + reproduction	1440	1440	1440	1440

Sources: BBC Audience Research, 1965; 1978; SCELI, 1984; 1987; ISER and ONS, 1995.

References

Andrews, F., Morgan, J. and Sonquist, J. (1967) *Multiple Classification Analysis: A Report on a Computer Program for Multiple Regression Using Categorical Predictors*, Ann Arbor, Survey Research Center, Michigan.

Bell, Daniel (1976) *The Coming of Post-Industrial Society: A Venture in Social Forecasting*, Penguin, Harmondsworth.

Bourdieu, Pierre (1979) *Distinction: A Social Critique of the Judgement of Taste*, Routledge and Kegan Paul, London.

British Broadcasting Corporation (BBC) (1965) *The People's Activities*, BBC, London, data archived at the Institute for Social and Economic Research, University of Essex, Wivenhoe Park, Colchester CO4 3SQ, UK.

British Broadcasting Corporation (1978) *The People's Activities and The Use of Time*, BBC, London, data archived at the Institute for Social and Economic Research, University of Essex, Wivenhoe Park, Colchester CO4 3SQ, UK.

Dumazedier, Joffre (1967) *Toward a Society of Leisure*, Free Press, New York.

Dumazedier, Joffre (1974) *Sociology of Leisure*, Elsevier Scientific Publishing Company, Amsterdam.

Employment Gazette (1981) 'Recent changes in hours and holiday entitlements', vol. 89 (4), pp.183–4.

Employment Gazette (1993) 'Working time and holidays in the EC: how the UK compares', vol. 101 (9), pp.395–403.

General Household Survey, collected by the Office for National Statistics, London, 1973, 1977, 1980, 1983, 1986, 1987, 1990–91, 1993–94, 1996–97. Data supplied by The Data Archive, University of Essex, Wivenhoe Park, Colchester CO4 3SQ, UK.

Gershuny, Jonathan I. (1983) *Social Elevation and the Division of Labour*, Oxford University Press, Oxford.

Gershuny, Jonathan I. (1986) 'Leisure: feast or famine', *Society and Leisure*, vol. 9 (2), pp.431–54.

*Gershuny, J. (1995) 'Economic activity and women's time use', in Niemi, I. (ed.) *Time Use of Women in Europe and North America*, UN/ECE, Geneva.

*Gershuny, Jonathan, Godwin, Michael and Jones, Sally (1994) 'The domestic labour revolution: a process of lagged adaptation', in Anderson, Michael, Bechhofer, Frank and Gershuny, Jonathan (eds) *The Social and Political Economy of the Household*, Oxford University Press, Oxford.

Hawrylyshn, O. (1978) *Estimating the Value of Household Work in Canada 1971*, Statistics Canada, Ottawa.

Hirsch, Fred (1977) *Social Limits to Growth*, Routledge and Kegan Paul, London.

Hochschild, Arlie (1989) *The Second Shift: Working Parents and the Revolution at Home*, Piatkus, London.

Hochschild, Arlie (1997) *The Time Bind: When Work Becomes Home and Home Becomes Work*, Metropolitan Books, New York.

Institute for Social and Economic Research (ISER) and Office for National Statistics (ONS) (1995) *Time Use Study*. Data archived at the Institute for Social and Economic Research, University of Essex, Wivenhoe Park, Colchester CO4 3SQ.

*Jones, Stephen G. (1986) *Workers at Play: A Social and Economic History of Leisure 1918–1939*, Routledge and Kegan Paul, London.

Keynes, John Maynard (1972) 'Economic possibilities for our grandchildren', in *Essays in Persuasion: The Collected Writings of John Maynard Keynes, Vol. IX*, Macmillan, London (first edition 1928).

Labour Market Trends (1998) 'Work and Leisure Time', vol. 106 (11).

Linder, Staffan Burenstam (1970) *The Harried Leisure Class*, Columbia University Press, New York.

Lourie, Julia (1996) *The Working Time Directive: Research Paper 96/10*, House of Commons Library, London.

Lynd, Robert S. and Lynd, Helen Merrell (1937) *Middletown in Transition*, Harcourt, Brace, New York.

Marx, Karl (1967) *Capital*, International Publishers, New York, (first edition 1867).

Meissner, M. et al. (1975) 'No exit for wives: sexual division of labour and the cumulation of household demands', *Canadian Review of Sociology and Anthropology*, vol. 12, pp.424–39.

Mill, John Stuart (1871) *Principles of Political Economy: With Some of Their Applications to Social Philosophy*, seventh edition, Longmans, Green, Reader and Dyer, London.

Ministry of Labour Gazette (1938) 'Collective agreements providing for payment of wages for holidays', vol. 46 (3), pp.86–9.

Ministry of Labour Gazette (1952) 'Payment of wages for holidays', vol. 60 (5), pp.157–61.

Parker, Stanley (1976) *The Sociology of Leisure*, Allen and Unwin, London.

*Robinson, John P. and Godbey, Geoffrey (1997) *Time for Life: The Surprising Ways Americans Use Their Time*, Pennsylvania State Press, University Park.

Russell, Bertrand (1960) *In Praise of Idleness: and Other Essays*, Allen and Unwin, London.

Sahlins, Marshall (1972) *Stone Age Economics*, Aldine-Atherton, Chicago, Ill.

*Schor, Juliet (1993) *Overworked American: The Unexpected Decline of Leisure*, Basic Books, New York.

Social Change and Economic Life Iniative (SCELI), data collected by the Economic and Social Research Council in 1984 and 1987, and archived at the Institute for Social and Economic Research, University of Essex, Wivenhoe Park, Colchester CO4 3SQ, UK.

Thompson, Allan (1973) *The Dynamics of the Industrial Revolution*, Edward Arnold, London.

Vanek, Joann (1974) 'Time Spent in Housework' *Scientific American*, December, pp.116–20.

*Veblen, Thorstein (1953) *The Theory of the Leisure Class*, The New York American Library, New York, (first edition 1899).

Wilensky, Harold L. and Lebeaux, Charles N. (1965) *Industrial Society and Social Welfare: The Impact of Industrialization on the Supply and Organisation of Social Welfare Services in the United States*, Free Press, New York.

Young, Michael, and Willmott, Peter (1973) *The Symmetrical Family*, Routledge and Kegan Paul, London.

Further reading

In addition to the asterisked items in the References.

Pronovost, Gilles (1998) 'Trend report: the sociology of leisure', special edition of *Current Sociology*, July, vol. 46 (3).

Rojek, Chris (1985) *Capitalism and Leisure Theory*, Tavistock, London.

Veal, A. J. (1987) *Leisure and the Future*, Allen and Unwin, London.

19
Religion

Peter Brierley

> God is losing market share, awareness, trial and repeat purchase.
>   Luke Skywalker, 'Ethics in Business', 1998

> There is no logical quantitative connection between the number of
> people who go to church and those who recognize within themselves a
> spiritual need, even if it surfaces only occasionally. You might as well say
> that the only people interested in politics are those who go to meetings
> or are members of a political party.
>   Robert McLeish, 'Public Broadcasting: Servant or Leader?' in Porter,
>   David (ed.) *Word on the Box*, 1996

Introduction

The first quotation gives the false impression that religion, or at least
Christianity, the majority religion, is about to fade out in Britain. It misleads
because it gives no indication of the huge numbers of people who profess to
be religious, nor does it indicate that the *rate* of change is relatively small.
There are far more Christians around than the reader may think, and likely to
be so for the foreseeable future.

'Religion' is a comprehensive word which can stir the deepest emotions –
witness Northern Ireland. At the same time it can stretch the finest intellect –
'theology', it used to be said, was 'the queen of the sciences'. Durkheim offers
three aspects of religion – belief, practice and affiliation; we will look at all
three in this chapter. The first is internal, measured usually by asking people
individually; the second and third are external and, at least theoretically,
measured by observation.

Religious statistics are relatively few, and are not spread equally across these
three measures, nor uniformly through the century. Since the observable
presence of religions other than Christianity has only been a phenomenon of

recent decades, most of the data relate to Christianity. In addition, key data are missing for some years, and are estimated here where necessary usually using linear regression techniques. Nor are the data comprehensive – some denominational data, especially for the many smaller denominations, are simply not available for early decades. Some data, like that on membership, are collected according to different definitions,[1] or at different times of the year.[2]

In addition attitudes about collecting data vary. Some clergy feel that collecting data is unscriptural, and quote the story of King David being punished for counting his people.[3] Others feel the emphasis should be on quality not quantity, and there are reports of clergy falsely boosting numbers in order to have the psychological satisfaction of thinking they minister to more than they actually do. It should, however, be clearly said that the majority of clergy at the end of the twentieth century firmly recognize the value of comprehensive, well-founded and relevant statistical information, needed for their work just as data are required in every other branch of modern life.

Measuring religious people: community

There are three broad ways of counting religious people – their community, their membership and their attendance. The first two would both come under Durkheim's concept of affiliation. Looking first at community, this is taken as all those who belong, or are affiliated, or in any way associated, however vaguely, to a religion. It would include those baptized as babies, for example, even if they have nothing to do with a church subsequently in later life.[4] We here focus mainly on data for the Trinitarian churches.[5] Table 19.1 gives estimated figures for the Trinitarian church community, made up of the baptized population of the Anglicans and Roman Catholics and estimates for the other denominations, and for all other religions (Jews, Hindus, Muslims, Sikhs and others) and Non-Trinitarian churches. There is one other source for the total religious picture for 1900, but not, unfortunately, for intermediate years – David Barrett's *World Christian Encyclopedia*. He suggests a higher number of Anglicans (25.1 million) and a higher total figure for Protestants (9.5 against 7.2 in Table 19.1) making Christians 97 per cent of the population (Barrett, 1982, p.699). This appears unreasonably high.

Table 19.1 indicates that there are a considerable number of Christians in the United Kingdom, and that although their percentage of the population has decreased throughout the century, their actual numbers remain large. The critical estimates in the table are for the Church of England – its baptized population is very difficult to assess. The table suggests a two million drop in the last 20 years to 64 per cent. Note also the growth of Catholics in the last 50 years, due to immigration, and the small but real impact of the New Churches in the 'Other' row for 1990 and 2000.

Table 19.1 Christian and religious community in the UK, 1900–2000 (millions)

Year	1900	1910	1920	1930
Anglican	23.1	25.4	56.3	27.1
Roman Catholic	2.5	2.7	2.9	3.2
Presbyterian	3.2	3.4	3.5	3.5
Methodist	1.7	1.8	1.7	1.8
Baptist	0.7	0.8	0.8	0.8
Others[b]	1.6	1.8	1.8	1.8
Total Christian: number	32.8	35.9	37.0	38.2
Total Christian: % of pop.[c]	86	85	84	83
Other Religions	0.2	0.3	0.4	0.5
Total number	33.0	36.2	37.4	38.7
Total % of pop.[c]	86	86	85	84

Notes: [a]Revised figure.
[b]Independent, Orthodox, Pentecostal, New and Other Churches.
[c]Including Northern Ireland population prior to 1921.
[d]Estimated figures.

The rise of the other religions in the last third of the twentieth century makes the number of religious people in the population almost static. Thus the record does not suggest the demise of religion in the UK, but rather a slow change to include faiths other than Christianity and a relatively stationary number of religious people which is not growing as the population increases. The percentages given are similar to the percentages who say they believe in God (see Table 19.9 below).

Measuring religious people: membership

Unlike the religious community, there is much information on church membership, almost too much. In 1996 there were 243 different denominations in the UK, a figure which has considerably increased since the first count of 97 in 1977 (Brierley, 1997a, Table 8.14.3). As just three of these – the Church of England, the Roman Catholic Church in England and the Church of Scotland – accounted for 64 per cent of total membership in 1995, it may be seen how relatively small are the other 240, yet cumulatively important. (It also may be seen how *institutional* church life stands in the UK, part of the culture we share with Europe, the only continent where it is so, reflecting perhaps our history of empire – institutionalism in essence – through the last two millennia.[6])

Part of the problem of measuring across the century is that many of the smaller denominations did not publish figures of membership in early years; they have been assessed comprehensively only since 1970, but Robert Currie is an excellent source for many of the detailed figures, and not just for the twen-

1940	1950	1960	1970	1980	1990	1995	2000[d]
27.6	28.5	28.4[a]	28.2[a]	27.7	26.6	26.1	25.6
3.5	4.0	4.8	5.4	5.7	5.6	5.7	5.8
3.5	3.5	3.5	3.1	2.8	2.7	2.6	2.6
1.7	1.7	1.7	1.5	1.4	1.4	1.3	1.3
0.8	0.7	0.6	0.6	0.6	0.6	0.6	0.5[a]
1.8	1.7	1.7	1.6	1.6	1.7	1.8	1.9
38.9	40.1	40.7	40.4	39.8	38.6	38.1	37.7
82	80	77	72	71	67	65	64
0.7	0.8	1.1	1.9	2.6	3.6	4.1	4.5
39.6	40.9	41.8	42.3	42.4	42.2	42.2	42.2
83	81	79	76	75	73	72	71

Sources: Brierley (1995a), Table 11; Brierley (1997a), Table 16.

tieth century (Currie et al., 1974). A summary of the main figures was given in the previous edition of this volume (Brierley, 1988a). One attempt has been made to fill in these gaps (Hadaway and Marler, unpublished), and use has been made of that in compiling the following table. The Roman Catholics do not have figures corresponding to membership. They call their community figures 'membership', so their numbers below relate to Mass attendance, a convention long followed in the *UK Christian Handbook*, initially at their request.

Table 19.2 shows that church membership is always much less than the community figure, and fell from 37 per cent at the beginning of the century to 20 per cent at the end. The pattern is typical, however, of most individual denominations – membership grew in absolute terms from 1900 to the 1930s, despite World War I. It dropped a little in the Depression of the 1930s, and World War II (despite the thesis that war often helps people turn to God) in the 1940s, but recovered a little (mostly because of immigration) in the 1950s. The really big drops occurred in the 'Swinging Sixties' and the 1970s, though perhaps half a million of this is definitional change,[7] since when the decline has continued at a high but slightly lesser pace. The growth of 'Other Churches' in the latter part of the century is clear but, though important, is not of sufficient magnitude to offset large losses elsewhere. Why the decline was so great in the 1970s is not known; it could be partly age (a lot of older members died), it might have been a disillusionment because of educational changes, or a loosening in the loyalty of the middle classes, the impact of widespread television on leisure habits, or the increase in sporting events (which has certainly been one cause of the decline in the later decades). Likewise, the growth of other religions is

Table 19.2 Christian and religious membership in the UK, 1900–2000 (000s)

Year	1900	1910	1920	1930
Anglican	3237	3876	3820	4172
Roman Catholic	1607[a]	1699[a]	1795[a]	1909[a]
Presbyterian	1703	1820	1867	1879
Methodist	794	868	826	868
Baptist	366	418	405	406
Others[b]	624	708	755	845
Total Christian: number	8331	9389	9468	10079
Total Christian: % of pop.[c]	32	32	30	29
Other Religions	164	179	194	209
Total number	8495	9568	9662	10288
Total % of pop.[c]	33	33	30	29

Notes: [a]Estimate.
[b]Independent, Orthodox, Pentecostal, New and Other Churches.
[c]Adult population, including Northern Ireland population prior to 1921.
[d]Increase due to gradual build-up of electoral roll before its six-year culling in 1996.

Table 19.3 Membership of other churches in the UK, 1900–2000 (000s)

Year	1900	1910	1920	1930
Christian Brethren	44	51	58	65
Other Independent	15	18	21	27
Congregational	437	495	487	490
Orthodox	0	0	0	20
Salvation Army	85	93	131	170
Pentecostal	0	1	6	21
Religious Society of Friends	17	20	19	19
Four smaller denominations[a]	19	24	26	26
New Churches[c]	0	0	0	0
Other Denominations	7	7	7	7
Total	624	708	755	845

Notes: [a]Churches of Christ, Church of the Nazarene, Seventh-Day Adventists, and the Moravians.
[b]This decline is partly due to a change of definition. In 1972 the United Reformed Church (URC) began which included many of the Congregational Churches. The URC is included in Table 19.2 under Presbyterian; the figures presented here are for the continuing Congregational Churches.
[c]Also known as House Churches.
[d]Estimated figures.

1940	1950	1960	1970	1980	1990	1995	2000[a]
3908	3441	3341	2994	2179	1728	1785[d]	1584
1998[a]	2223[a]	2626[a]	2714	2457	2201	1915	1784
1877	1860	1868	1666	1438	1214	1100	987
830	772	766	642	520	452	401	367
382	337	318	269	240	231	223	220
816	801	848	837	719	866	937	1001
9811	9434	9767	9122	7553	6692	6361	5943
27	24	24	21	17	14	13	13
244	270	421	736	1094	1532	1817	2028
10055	9704	10188	9858	8647	8224	8178	7971
27	25	25	23	19	18	17	17

Sources: All the early figures (1900–60) are based substantially on Currie et al. (1974); figures for 1970 are from Brierley (1995a), Table 16; and 1980–2000 are from Brierley (1997a), Tables 2.8 and 2.10.

1940	1950	1960	1970	1980	1990	1995	2000[d]
69	67	68	70	72	69	63	61
32	37	41	46	51	63	65	69
452	391	357	284	108[b]	89	74	66
52	104	158	183	203	266	289	320
127	106	104	92	72	60	57	51
31	40	60	94	127	162	196	211
20	21	21	22	19	18	18	19
25	21	22	23	27	29	30	32
0	0	0	0	10	77	110	135
8	14	17	23	30	33	35	37
816	801	848	837	719	866	937	1001

Sources: Christian Brethren figures are from Summerton, Neil (1990) 'The Christian (Open) Brethren in the British Isles in Numerical Context', unpublished paper, but see Summerton, Neil (1996) *Local Churches for a New Century: A Strategic Challenge*, Partnership Publications, London. Orthodox Churches: figures are estimates of the membership of the Greek Orthodox Church, which began in the UK in 1922. They have no records except that in 1922 they had 4 parishes, increasing to 11 by 1964, with 108 estimated in 2000. Other Orthodox churches developed in the UK through immigration after World War II. Salvation Army: records for the early part of the century were destroyed by bombing in World War II, but some estimates exist for the 1920s which have been used here. Other estimates for 1970 are from Brierley (1988b). All other figures for 1900–60 come from Currie et al. (1974) or Brierley (1989). All other figures for 1970 are from Brierley (1995a), and 1980–2000 are from Brierley (1997a).

obvious in the last half of the century; again, mainly through immigration. This increase does not, however, totally offset the decline in the Christian churches.

It is important to realize that this decline in membership parallels the decline in membership of many other institutions in the latter part of the twentieth century. Thus while the Christian church membership in the UK may have decreased by 21 per cent between 1980 and 2000, the decline in the trade union movement over the same period was 55 per cent (Brierley, 1997a, Table 5.9.1, see also Chapter 8 in this volume). Dr Grace Davie subtitles her book 'Believing without Belonging' to describe this societal, not just religious, change (Davie, 1994). It is, she says, 'the most significant feature of British, and indeed European, religion at the turn of the millennium' (Brierley, 1997a, Foreword, page 0.3).

The 'Other Churches' total in Table 19.2 is here published for the first time for the earlier years of the century. The composition of that total is given in Table 19.3.

It is immediately obvious from Table 19.3 that some denominations have remained fairly static over the twentieth century, others have decreased, and three especially have grown – the Orthodox, New (House) Churches and Pentecostal Churches. All three have seen the starting of many new congregations in the last 30 years, all have small congregations with often authoritative leadership unburdened by a dominant hierarchy in terms of local freedom for action, and each has a specific spirituality.

The 'church planting' phenomenon has been a key emphasis of many denominations in the 1990s, partly stimulated by organizations outside the denominational structure like the British Church Growth Movement and Challenge 2000, as well as being seen as of increasing importance within the denominations. For example, when the Decade of Evangelism began in January 1991, the Archbishop of Canterbury, George Carey, gave a public commendation to Church of England 'plants', and the number of such in the mid-1990s was estimated at 30 a year (Lings, 1994, Appendix). There are different types of 'plant' – pioneer planting where no church has been previously; replacement planting when an older building is replaced by a new one; sectarian planting when a particular denomination starts a new church irrespective of how many other churches there may already be in the neighbourhood; and saturation planting, when churches are started because the density of churches to population is deemed too low (Murray, 1998).

Measuring religious people: attendance

A visible behavioural manifestation of a person's religious belief is their attendance at religious services or meetings. Attendance has not been measured very often, although numbers of communicants for the Anglican and

Presbyterian churches are available since 1900 (see, for example, Brierley, 1989). The first count of attendance was in 1851 as part of the Census of Population in England and Wales; depending on how the figures are taken, the percentage attending church that day was 39 per cent, *including* those who went two or three times (Mann, 1854; census, 1851). (If the same percentage of 'twicers' which were counted in 1903 applied in 1851, then this figure would reduce to 24 per cent of the population in church that Sunday). Robin Gill has analysed these figures in detail (Gill, 1993).

One major large scale study of London was undertaken by the *Daily News* between November 1902 and November 1903 (Mudie-Smith, 1904). This sought to count everyone entering every place of worship in a specific Borough of London for every service, counting a different Borough each week. The conclusion of the report's author is: 'The outstanding lesson of the Census is that the power of preaching is undiminished. Wherever there is the right man in the pulpit there are few, if any, empty pews' (Mudie-Smith, 1904, p.7). *Excluding* twicers, the percentage of the population who attended church in London was 19 per cent each Sunday, 43 per cent of whom were Church of England, 43 per cent Free Churches, 8 per cent Roman Catholic, and 6 per cent 'other services'. Whether this 19 per cent applies throughout the whole country is not known.

A Mass Observation survey in 1948/49 found that 15 per cent of the population attended church (*British Weekly*, January/February 1949). In 1979 the English Church Census found 11 per cent of adults and 14 per cent of children (aged 14 or under) attended in an average week (Brierley, 1980; 1983); and the 1989 census, 10 per cent of adults and 14 per cent of children (Brierley, 1991a). The Welsh Church Census of 1982 found 13 per cent of adults and 21 per cent of children (Brierley and Evans, 1983); the Welsh Churches Survey of 1995, 9 per cent of adults and 8 per cent of children (Gallacher, 1997). In Scotland in 1984, 17 per cent of adults and 19 per cent of children attended weekly (Brierley and Macdonald, 1985); by 1994 this was 14 per cent and 18 per cent respectively (Brierley and Macdonald, 1995). No survey of church attendance has been undertaken in Northern Ireland.

These studies indicate that Scotland was more religious than Wales (if church attendance is the judge of religiousness), and Wales more than England in the 1980s but not the 1990s. The figures as a whole indicate that there has been a decline in church attendance over the century, but this decline is very small and slow (if the London figure of 1903 is taken for the whole country). To fall from 19 per cent in 1903 to 15 per cent in 1951 to 11 per cent in 1979 to 10 per cent in 1989 and an estimated 8 per cent in 2000 is a decline of 0.6 per cent compound per annum (Brierley, 1997a, Table 2.12.1). However, at current attendance levels, that is still a decline of over 400 people per week, most of whom are under 20 years of age (Brierley, 1991a, Table 36).

To illustrate the range of material available, the following tables give the number of adult church attenders in England by various control variables (Brierley, 1991b; 1997a, Tables 2.12.1 and 2.17.2). Similar information is available for children, church members, and for Scotland and Wales. Little information has been collected about attendance at Non-Trinitarian churches[8] or at services of other religions, though mosque attendance was surveyed in 1986 (Holway, 1986, p.150).

Table 19.4 Percentage of English adult attenders by denomination, 1980–2000

Year	1980	1990	1995	2000[a]
Anglican	25.4	26.1	26.7	27.2
Baptist	5.3	5.6	6.1	6.3
Catholic	42.0	38.3	34.4	31.8
Independent	4.3	5.1	5.8	6.2
Methodist	11.5	11.3	11.0	10.5
New	1.3	3.2	4.9	6.4
Orthodox	0.2	0.3	0.3	0.4
Pentecostal	3.8	4.7	5.4	5.8
United Reformed Church	3.6	3.0	3.0	3.0
Others	2.6	2.4	2.4	2.4
Total number (= 100%)	3814200	3512200	3197800	3061800

Note: [a]Estimated figures.

Sources: Brierley (1991b; 1997a).

Table 19.5 Percentage of English adult attenders by churchmanship,[a] 1980–2000

Year	1980	1990	1995	2000[c]
Anglo-Catholic	3.7	3.6	3.8	4.0
Broad	9.4	9.1	9.4	9.5
'Catholic'[b]	44.8	41.7	38.1	35.6
Evangelical: Broad	8.6	9.0	9.3	9.6
Evangelical: Charismatic	9.3	11.3	12.9	14.1
Evangelical: Mainstream	6.4	7.2	8.0	8.6
Liberal	10.4	10.6	10.8	10.9
Low Church	5.9	5.9	6.0	6.0
Others	1.5	1.6	1.7	1.7
Total number (= 100%)	3814200	3512200	3197800	3061800

Notes: [a]Churchmanship is the name given to a type of theological position; the various choices were self-made by the minister of each church on a form where the words were deliberately not defined.
[b]In inverted commas to indicate that not all of these are Roman Catholic.
[c]Estimated figures.

Sources: Brierley (1991b; 1997a).

Table 19.6 Percentage of English adult attenders by church environment, 1979–2000

Year	1979	1989	2000[a]
City centre	5.9	5.4	4.7
Inner city	10.5	10.0	9.6
Council estate	8.0	8.0	8.1
Suburban fringe	34.6	34.3	33.9
Separate town	14.9	16.0	17.2
Other built-up area	4.5	4.5	4.5
Rural: commuter	10.7	10.8	10.9
Rural: other	10.9	11.0	11.1
Total number (= 100%)	3814200	3512200	3061800

Note: [a]Estimated figures.

Source: Brierley (1991b).

Table 19.7 Percentage of English adult attenders by age-group and gender, 1979–2000

Year	1979	1989	2000[a]
Under 15	26	25	23
15–19	9	7	7
20–29	11	10	9
30–44	16	17	18
45–64	20	22	23
65 or over	18	19	20
Male	45	42	40
Female	55	58	60
Total number (= 100%)	3814200	3512200	3061800

Note: [a]Estimated figures.

Source: Brierley (1991b).

Tables 19.4 to 19.7 show that the main decreases in English Christian Church attendance are in the numbers of Catholics, those in city centres and inner city areas, men and those under 30. The increasing numbers are of New Church attenders, Evangelicals (especially charismatics), those in towns, women and those over 30 years of age. Some of these movements are linked, as, for example, many Catholics live in urban areas.

These figures are based on *counts* of people attending church. However, one series of data has been collected looking at whether people *say* they attend church or religious service/meeting (unpublished British Social Attitude surveys data, collected by Social and Community Planning Research (SCPR) and summarized in Brierley, 1997a, Table 2.13.1). Some 70 per cent of the population say they do. Of these, consistently from 1983 to 1996 the average percentage saying they attended weekly was 18 or 19 per cent, that is, about double the percentage actually counted. The detailed census material described above did not take frequency of attendance into account, other than those who attended twice on a Sunday. The SCPR data are important therefore in showing how people regard their church attendance, and show that far more think they attend weekly. Only 35–40 per cent of those who say they belong to a religion say they *never* attend a religious service or meeting. Thus between 60 and 65 per cent who belong say they attend at least occasionally, or 40–45 per cent of the population, percentages which are a substantial proportion of the Christian community in Table 19.1 in 1990 and 2000. We cannot conclude that the number of people attending church sometime is decreasing, only that the *frequency* of attendance is decreasing, and with that the number present on an average Sunday.

A number of studies in the 1990s have focused on the reasons why people join or leave churches. An overview of changes across the whole country in 1992/93 was published in 1996, showing that moving house was a key reason (Brierley, 1996). A third of those who attend a church in their new location do not take out membership. Detailed surveys on why people left reveal other reasons. In 1993, 62 per cent said they had left because church had become irrelevant to them (Fanstone, 1993) while in 1996 and 1998, unfulfilled expectations, changes in life and loss of faith emerged as the top three reasons (Kay and Francis, 1996; Richter and Francis, 1998).

Another survey published in 1993 looked at the beliefs of those who leave church and later return; the average time before returning was eight years (Gibbs, 1993). *Finding Faith in 1994* confirmed the ages at which people joined, left and rejoined (40 per cent return) the church (Brierley, 1995b). It also confirmed John Finney's earlier study on how recent converts found faith (Finney, 1990). A large-scale survey on conversion was undertaken in 1967 looking at the causes of finding faith (Scripture Union, 1968; Hill, 1986, Chapter 8). Several general overviews of the church have been published, such as by David Perman (1977) and David Winter (1988).

Of great importance in earlier years were the numbers attending Sunday School, which reached their peak in the 1880s (Laquer, 1976). 'In 1957, 76 per cent of those over 30 had at some time attended Sunday School' (Martin, 1967, p.42); in 1992 it was 41 per cent, 'many of whom would now be over 50' (Brierley, 1993b). Historical figures across the century have been collated (Brierley, 1989, pp.41–50). The 1989 English Church Census collected Sunday School figures by denomination and county, showing about 7 per cent of children then attended (Brierley, 1991b). Many studies have been undertaken by Leslie Francis on young people (Francis, 1984; Francis and Kay, 1995; Francis et al., 1995).

Measuring religious people: putting it together

The last 20 years have seen a plethora of quantitative studies on religious people. In terms of the population, they are perhaps best summarized in a diagram (see Figure 19.1).

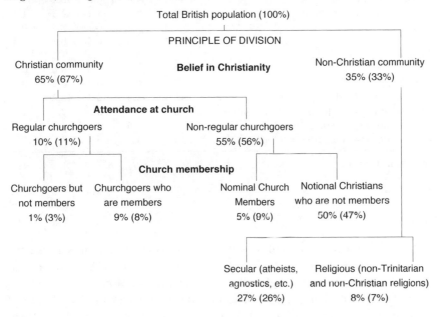

Figure 19.1   Religious structure of the population in Great Britain, 1980 and 1990

Note: Figures in brackets give 1980 percentages.

Source: Adapted from Brierley (1997a), Table 2.2.

This chart introduces the terms 'nominal' (people who are church members but who do not attend church at least once a month), and 'notional' (people who say they are Christian but are neither church members nor regular attenders).

The chart also includes the Non-Trinitarian churches and other Religions. The two largest Non-Trinitarian churches are the Mormons (Church of Jesus Christ of Latter-Day Saints) and the Jehovah's Witnesses. The former have been in the UK since the turn of the century, and with 185 000 estimated members in 2000, are larger than the latter with 147 000 who started here just before World War I.[9] Whilst there have been Jews in the UK for many centuries, most of the other non-Christian religions have come since World War II. As is clear from Tables 19.1 and 19.8, the numbers of both Non-Trinitarians and other religions are growing rapidly, increasing as Christianity declines. The total number of religious people in the population is just over 42 million, a figure which has remained constant over the last 30 years.

Table 19.8 Size of the Christian and non-Christian community in the UK, 1970–2000 (millions)

Year	1970	1980	1990	1995	2000[a]
Christian (Trinitarian)	40.4	39.8	38.6	38.1	37.7
Christian (Non-Trinitarian)	0.7	0.8	1.1	1.3	1.4
Hindu	0.3	0.4	0.4	0.4	0.5
Jew	0.4	0.3	0.3	0.3	0.3
Muslim	0.3	0.6	1.0	1.2	1.4
Sikh	0.1	0.3	0.5	0.6	0.6
Other Religions	0.1	0.2	0.3	0.3	0.3
Total including Christians: number	42.3	42.4	42.2	42.2	42.2
Total including Christians: % of population	76	75	73	72	71
Total excluding Christians: number	1.9	2.6	3.6	4.1	4.5
Total excluding Christians: % of population	3	4	6	7	7

Note: [a]Estimated figures.

Source: Brierley (1997a).

Belief

Religion is notoriously difficult to define but at its most basic it is a system of beliefs and practices in response to God or gods (Smart, 1983; Barker et al., 1992). The core of much religious literature is a description of or an exhortation to belief, but attempting to measure what is believed and by whom only began in any coherent way with the development of the market research industry just before World War II. A list of all the studies which included religious questions has been compiled (Field, 1987), and analysed according to whether they were answered positively or negatively (Gill et al., 1997). Table 19.9 extracts both sets of answers for data measured first in the 1940s/50s.

Much could be written about these figures; they suggest that what has happened since World War II is not so much a relatively small decline of religious belief in Britain but rather a much greater increase of disbelief. This supports the thesis of this chapter that Christianity is more widely spread in the population than is commonly supposed, but also indicates that the divide between Christian and non-Christian is becoming sharper.

Other measurements of belief have been largely confined to the European Values Systems Study in 1981 (Abrams et al., 1985; Harding and Phillips, 1986), and 1990 (Barker et al., 1992; Ester et al., 1994). Their results are not dissimilar to Table 19.9, but include like measurements for other countries in Europe and beyond.

It could be argued that belief is reflected in the number of baptisms, confirmations and church marriages. Some of the relevant data on baptisms are available across the century, and are given in Table 19.10. The figures show

Table 19.9 Religious belief and disbelief in Britain since 1940, adults

Decade	1940s/50s	1960s	1970s	1980s	1990s
% who believe in:					
God	81	78	70	71	70
God as personal	43	40	32	32	30
God as spirit	38	38	38	39	40
Jesus as Son of God	68	62	n/a	47	n/a
Life after death	49	49	37	43	43
Devil	24	28	20	24	26
Exchange of messages with the dead	15	n/a	11	14	14
Ghosts	15	n/a	19	27	31
% who do not believe in:					
God	n/a	10	15	18	27
Jesus as Son of God	18	22	n/a	39	n/a
Life after death	21	23	42	40	41
Devil	54	52	70	64	67
Exchange of messages with the dead	59	n/a	79	77	80
Ghosts	64	n/a	73	65	62

Source: Gill et al. (1997).

that over three-quarters of infants were baptized up to 1960. This percentage had slipped to just under half by 1990, rose to 50 per cent for the years 1993–95 (Brierley, 1997a, Table 2.5.1) and then fell to 49 per cent in 1996. The size of these percentages indicates a considerable residue of Christian and other religious belief.

Confirmation figures for the Church of England suggest that 6 per cent of 15–19-year-olds were confirmed up to 1960, with a decreasing percentage thereafter (Brierley, 1989, Table 13). About 40 per cent of those baptized were confirmed about 15 years later, a percentage which again held up to 1960, but decreased to half that figure by the end of the century.

Belief may also be said to be imperfectly reflected in the proportions getting married in a religious building, invariably a church or synagogue prior to 1980. Certainly, the importance of the church as a social institution can be measured in this way. 85 per cent of all marriages in England and Wales had a religious ceremony in 1900, a percentage which had declined to 74 per cent by 1930, 70 per cent by 1960, 53 per cent by 1990 and an estimated 40 per cent by 2000 (Brierley, 1989, Table 30; 1997a, Table 4.8.1), but is likely to be lower in the event owing to the 1995 Marriage Act allowing marriages in 'approved premises' other than a registry office. The increasing incidence of divorce, and the fact that many divorcees remarrying either cannot or do not wish to remarry in church, reduce the proportion of religious marriages. In 1993 for instance 64 per cent of those marrying for the first time were married in church. The majority of religious marriages are Church of England (79 per cent

Table 19.10 Infant baptisms (000s) by denomination and as a percentage of births, 1900–2000, UK

Year	1900	1910	1920	1930
Church of England	564	573	604	424
Other Anglican churches[a]	14	14	15	10
Methodist[b]	48	52	50	53
Church of Scotland	60[c]	51[c]	54[c]	38
Other Presbyterian churches[d]	20	20	18	14
Roman Catholics, England and Wales	55	60	101	83
Roman Catholics, Scotland and N. Ireland[e]	32	34	54	40
Total	793	804	896	662
Percentage of births	73	78	91[f]	91

Notes: [a]Church in Wales, Episcopal Church of Scotland and Church in Ireland; figures estimated pro rata from Communicants, Permanent Numbers and Community respectively from Church of England electoral roll and baptism figures.
[b]Estimated by taking 6.2% of the Community Roll from 1900–20, 6.3% for 1930–60 and 2000, and actual figures for 1970–90, these percentages being linear regression estimates from the actuals for 1970–90. Figures are not available prior to 1968.
[c]Including United Free Church of Scotland which merged with the Church of Scotland in 1929.
[d]Presbyterian Church in Wales, Presbyterian Church in Ireland and, up to 1972 when it merged with the United Reformed Church, the Presbyterian Church in England; figures estimated by taking pro rata membership to Church of Scotland membership and baptisms.

in 1900; 64 per cent in 2000), followed by the Roman Catholics (5 per cent in 1900; 19 per cent in 2000). About 7 per cent are Methodist, 2 per cent Baptist, 2 per cent Congregational, 2–4 per cent Other Protestants, and 1 per cent Jewish. Detailed historical figures are available (Office for National Statistics, 1993, Table 3.8a), as are figures for Scotland (Brierley, 1989, Table 31) and Northern Ireland (see, for example, Brierley, 1994, Table 23).

At death, 71 per cent of people are cremated, virtually all with a religious ceremony (Brierley, 1997a, Table 4.7.2). Most of the other 29 per cent are buried likewise.

A number of studies have looked at young people's beliefs. Leslie Francis has surveyed 500 secondary school pupils every four years by asking them 24 questions about Christianity; some positive and some negative (Finney, 1990; Kay and Francis, 1996, Table 4.2). They show fewer agreements with positive statements on the church (27 per cent in 1974; 14 per cent in 1994), prayer (44 per cent and 27 per cent) and God (42 per cent and 26 per cent), but decline in belief that Jesus was the Son of God was less marked (32 per cent to 25 per cent).

Religious literature

The number of religious books is another guide to the extent of religious belief. There has been a dramatic increase in the mid-1990s: 2600 were published in 1993; 3300 in 1994; 4400 in 1995 – falling back slightly to 4300 in 1996 and

1940	1950	1960	1970	1980	1990	1995	2000[g]
365	441	412	347	266	229	186	199
8	10	9	7	5	4	4	3
51	47	46	39	30	30	23	22
35	43	51	35	23	15	14	8
12	13	13	10	7	5	4	4
87	92	123	108	76	80	75	72
39	40	43	34	23	26	24	23
597	686	687	580	430	389	330	331
90	88	74	64	57	49	45	45

[e]Roman Catholic Churches in Scotland and Northern Ireland; estimated pro rata to Catholic population in England and Wales.
[f]This total probably represents some catching up on baptisms from the years of World War I, and will probably have included some older than infants.
[g]Estimated figures.

Sources: Church of England, Church of Scotland and Roman Catholic figures are estimated or taken from Currie et al. (1974) for 1900–60, and Brierley (1995a; 1997a) for later years.

4100 in 1997. This rise totally outpaces the proportionate increase in other categories of book such as children's books (from 7000 in 1992 to 8000 in 1996), fiction (8100 to 9200) or political science (5100 to 6800). However, religious books have not always seen such increases, as Table 19.11 indicates. Also, the large increase just described did not bring the religious books' percentage of all titles published as high as in the 1930s, 1940s or 1950s. (The number of titles was not published prior to 1928.)

The most popular religious book, the Bible, has continued to be published and translated into languages all over the world. The total is given in Table 19.11, and shows the impact in the last 50 years of the work of such organizations as the Wycliffe Bible Translators and the Bible Societies.

Christian organizations

Christian agencies, often called 'para-church agencies', come in many varieties. These are organizations which undertake either religious work or are registered as religious charities. Some are companies limited by guarantee. In the 1998/99 edition of the *UK Christian Handbook*, some 5500 addresses were given; more than double the 2400 listed in the first full edition in 1983 (Brierley, 1997a, pp.18–19). Altogether, 17 per cent were established before 1920, and still exist; some are over 300 years old. However, a third (32 per cent) have only been set up since 1985, evidence of a considerable vitality in

Table 19.11 Religious books published, Bible translations and number of Christian agencies started which still survive, 1900–2000, UK

Year	1900	1910	1920	1930
Total titles published	n/a	n/a	n/a	15494
Total religious titles	n/a	n/a	n/a	857
Religious as % of total	n/a	n/a	n/a	5.5
Occult as % of religious	n/a	n/a	n/a	7
Languages of Bible translations[a]	621	725	825	975
No. of agencies started in decade	106	77	127	112

Notes: [a]Number of languages into which at least one book of the Bible has been translated.
[b]Up to 1995 only.
[c]The number of religious books published in 1995 was an all-time high, and rose faster in the period 1993–95 than any other category.

this sector. Three-fifths (59 per cent) are registered charities, and one-fifth (20 per cent) work with only volunteer unpaid staff. Those with paid staff average 16 people; 12 per cent are Anglican, 9 per cent Roman Catholic, 18 per cent other denominations, and the remainder are interdenominational or ecumenical. Together they have a gross turnover/income of £1.8 billion. Every week, four more such organizations are started in the UK (Brierley, 1997a, Table 5.11). The number which were established in each decade this century and are still in existence is given in Table 19.11; this excludes those which have subsequently closed. It also excludes the 649 which began prior to 1900. The type of organization has been analysed, with growth seen especially in the services sector (Brierley, 1993a, Table 1; 1997a, pp.5.10 and 5.11).

Church buildings

Two other church series are of interest – the number of church buildings and the number of clergy. Both of these come from the sources already mentioned (Currie et al., 1974; Brierley, 1989; 1993a; 1994; 1995a); we have space only to look at the numbers of churches (or congregations where groups do not meet in an ecclesiastical building[10]).

Table 19.12 shows a remarkable consistency in the number of churches in the UK in the twentieth century, the number varying between 49 000 and 57 000, and reaching a peak in 1930. The increase due to the New and Pentecostal Church planting philosophy may be seen in the later years in the 'All Others' column. Whilst the number of churches has not kept up with population growth, the average church size kept above 150 people for the first 80 years, only dropping in the 1990s as societal disaffection with membership began to make inroads on church membership also. These figures, and the earlier ones, do not support Bryan Wilson's secularization thesis of behaviour without belief; rather, belief persists even if some religious behaviour

1940	1950	1960	1970	1980	1990	1995	2000[e]
11053	17072	23783	33489	48158	63980	95064	101600
519	971	1247	1245	1725	2360	4442	3900
4.7	5.7	5.2	3.7	3.6	3.7	4.7[c]	3.8
8	6	6	13	15	17	11	15
1053	1197	1426	1657	1710	1946	2123	2300
167	247	436	802	1345	630[b]	102[d]	n/a

[d]1996 and 1997 only.
[e]Estimated figures.

Sources: Brierley (1989; 1997a).

decreases. They do, however, support David Martin's forecast in the rise of small denominations and an increase in implicit religion.

Many sociologists argue for secularization. Bryan Wilson talks of 'societalization' in which 'life is increasingly enmeshed and organized, not locally but societally (that society being most evidently, but not uniquely, the nation state)' (Wilson, 1982, p.154). Bruce explains this as meaning that 'the society rather than the community has increasingly become the locus of the individual's life, so religion has been shorn of its functions' (Bruce, 1998, p.7). He also mentions the impact of social differentiation (society breaking up into competing groups), rationalization (the impact of the scientific method) and cultural diversity (democracy removing churches from the centre of public life). As a consequence, Bruce says, quoting Peter Berger (1980), while believers still believe, they cannot avoid the knowledge that many people (including many like themselves) believe other things (Bruce, 1998, p.15). Whilst all this may be true, it does not stop people still counting themselves as Christian. Similar arguments for secularization are given by Peter Ester (Ester et al., 1994, pp.9–11). This chapter is not the place for a detailed argument for or against the secularization of religion, which has undoubtedly happened to some extent, but simply a statement that the statistics show, as in one recent book's title, *The Church is Bigger than You Think* (Johnstone, 1998). The impact of the death of Diana, Princess of Wales, for example, needs to be considered in this context.

Full-time church officials

The number of full-time clergy across all denominations in 1900 is not known. In 1980 there were 35 700, the same as the estimated total in 2000 (Brierley, 1997a, Table 2.6). As well as those serving the church in the UK there were also 8200 missionaries of all denominations serving overseas in 1980, with an

Table 19.12 Estimated number of church buildings or congregations by denomination, 1900–2000, UK

Year	1900	1910	1920	1930
Church of England	17468	18026	18270	18417
Church of Scotland	3458	3188	3186	2920
Congregational[a]	5226	5288	5098	5048
Presbyterian Church of Wales[b]	1353	1528	1664	1601
Roman Catholic[c]	2259	2552	2741	3058
Baptist[d]	3203	3567	3541	3646
Methodist[e]	12353	12504	12851	13504
All others	7370	7738	7884	8888
Total number	52690	54391	55235	57082
Total per 10000 pop.	13.8	12.9	12.5	12.4
Total members per church	158	173	171	175

Notes: [a]Including the figures for United Reformed Churches (usually included under Presbyterian) of 1936 churches in 1980, 1800 in 1990 and 1700 in 2000, and an estimate prior to 1980 for the Congregational Union of Ireland of 24 churches between 1900 and 1970 (their 1980 figure).
[b]The figures for 1900–60 have been reduced by 1600 each year from those given in Currie et al. (1974) as Currie's series includes chapels and other buildings, and all other figures in this table relate to churches only.
[c]Including estimates for Northern Ireland based on their mass attendance. There were a number of closures in England and Wales in the early 1970s accounting for the drop between 1970 and 1980.

estimated total of 9000 by 2000; 36 per cent of these serve in Africa, 20 per cent in Europe and 17 per cent in Asia (Brierley, 1997a, Table 3.5 and Figure 3.3.2).

8 per cent of the ministers were female in 1990, 13 per cent in 1994, against 58 per cent of missionaries in 1991 and 57 per cent in 1995 (Brierley, 1988b, Tables 8b and 34; 1993a, Table 9b; 1995a, Table 3.10), reflecting something of the desire for women to serve even if unable to enter the ordained ministry in the UK. It will be interesting to see whether these proportions change subsequent to the ordination of women by the Church of England in 1994. The age of clergy in the Church of England is available for various years (Brierley, 1988a, Table 13.18, for example). In 1984, 5 per cent were in their twenties, 22 per cent in their thirties, 28 per cent in their forties, 28 per cent in their fifties, 15 per cent in their sixties, and 2 per cent in their seventies.

Britain and its world context

In 1990[11] the world had 1512 million Christians; 28 per cent of the population. In addition 18 per cent were Muslim, and 13 per cent Hindu (Barrett, 1995, p.25). This century, Christianity in Europe has dramatically declined, and equally dramatically grown in South America, Asia and Africa, as may be seen in Table 19.13 below.

It has already been noted that UK church life is remarkably institutional; the same is true of all the Western world (top half of the Table), as may also be seen

1940	1950	1960	1970	1980	1990	1995	2000[f]
18666	18220	17973	17760	16884	16380	16255	16110
2483	2340	2093	2119	1852	1685	1616	1533
4972	4637	4247	3765	3187	2969	2906	2789
1595	1439	1410	1300	1169	1025	939	867
3451	3827	4822	5096	4160	4339	4286	4282
3728	3804	3744	3678	3317	3588	3448	3427
12913	12010	11917	9988	8481	7562	7092	6636
9143	9420	9959	9824	10866	11941	12490	12904
56951	55697	56165	53530	49916	49489	49032	48548
11.9	11.1	10.7	9.6	8.9	8.6	8.4	8.2
172	169	174	170	151	135	130	122

[d]Including estimates for the Strict and Particular Baptists, Baptist Union of Ireland and Old Baptist Union for years prior to 1970, ranging in total from 518 churches in 1900 to 529 in 1960.
[e]Actual numbers 1970–2000; 1900–60 pro rata to 1970 on membership, with adjustment for 1910.
[f]Estimated figures.

Sources: Brierley (1989; 1997a).

in Table 19.13. Furthermore, over the 30 years 1960–90, that institutionalism has not changed, whereas it has reduced in the Third World (bottom half). This is because of the rapid growth world-wide of the smaller denominations, including Pentecostalism; this last has increased from 1 per cent of Christendom in 1960 to 6 per cent in 1990, and is forecast to grow to 8 per cent by 2010.

The differences between the institutional Christianity of the Western world and the expansionist Christianity in the Third World in the latter part of the twentieth century are readily portrayed in the last section of Table 19.13. The number of churches increased 28 per cent from 1960–90 in the Western world, but 362 per cent in the Third World. As a consequence, their number per 10000 population greatly rose: fourfold in Africa, fivefold in Asia, but sixfold in South America. Pentecostalism has replaced some Roman Catholicism in Latin America, seen in this table by the huge number of churches they have started, and the subsequent large fall in numbers per church; a change which David Martin (1990) observes with great perceptiveness.

As far as the UK is concerned it may be seen by comparison with Table 19.12 that in 1990 it had 15 per cent of Europe's churches, but twice as many per 10000 population than across Europe as a whole. They are, however, only a fifth (1960) or a sixth (1990) of the size of a European church, reflecting the Protestant heritage of the UK, and the relatively small proportions of Catholics, Lutherans and Orthodox Christians.

Table 19.13 Christian community and churches across the world in 1900, 1960 and 1990

Continent	Community			% of which are in institutional denominations[a]	
	1900	1960	1990	1960	1990
Europe	71	46	30	98	97
North America	11	23	21	67	68
Oceania[c]	1	1	1	80	80
Africa	2	7	15	76	63
Asia	4	7	14	80	55
South America	11	16	19	97	86
Total (= 100%)	554m	924m	1512m	88	78

Notes: [a]Anglican, Catholic, Lutheran, Orthodox or Presbyterian. An institutional denomination is one where in at least one country in the world it is the State Church.
[b]Not the community; in 1960 members were 50% of the community, in 1990 they were 56%.

It may be seen from Table 19.13 that South American churches are the largest in the world; this is due to their large proportion of Catholic churches. The same is true in the UK. By comparing Tables 19.2 and 19.12, it may be seen that in 1990 the Catholics had a mass attendance in the UK averaging 507 people per church, the Presbyterians a membership of 221, Anglicans 105, and all others 74.[12]

What of the grandchildren?

What kind of Christian heritage will be left in 2040? The Christian scene could well be characterized as follows:

- There will still be many churches (30000+) in evidence in the UK, and some of the 5000 rural Norman churches will still be open.
- Spirituality will not be dead (religious community still 50 per cent of the population), but its Christian proportion will be less, as the non-Christian religions will have a significant share.
- The basic doctrines of Christianity will be believed less, and there will be many who actively do not believe them. Tensions between believers and non-believers could become acute.
- There will be many nominal Christians, perhaps a third of the population, and implicit religion will flourish.
- Church membership will probably have hit an all time low, possibly below the 5 per cent critical mass, as society continues to move away from commitment of any kind.
- Average Sunday attendance at church, especially in the non-institutional churches, will be higher than membership. Church attendance may well be

| Number (000s) | | Churches/congregations Per 10000 pop. | | Members per church[b] | |
1960	1990	1960	1990	1960	1990
302	325	4.6	4.1	811	786
346	493	12.8	11.6	393	402
21	38	13.3	14.1	215	219
126	476	4.5	7.4	272	228
104	529	0.6	1.7	322	200
35	220	2.4	7.5	2656	806
934	2081	3.1	3.9	585	410

[c]Mainly Australia and New Zealand.

Sources: Barrett (1982) for 1900 figures; Brierley (1997b) for 1960 and 1990.

on a midweek evening rather than Sunday morning. New traditions will replace old traditions, with flexibility and time, not money, new key values (Barna, 1990, p.33).

- Congregations will be smaller than they are now, but the charismatic churches will continue to start new ones. Urban congregations will struggle more than rural ones.
- Christianity will continue to exert an influence on the life of the nation's peoples, though baptism and marriage in church will be much less. Funerals however will continue to be times of spiritual reality.
- There will still be many Christian organizations (3000+), but probably far fewer, if any, Christian bookshops as literature (including religious material) will be available through electronic means.

In summary, then, a smaller Christian core valuing integrity (Barna, 1990), and a continuing wider, but vaguer, Christian penumbra, with a religious fringe beyond that including the other religions. Belief will be real for the few, but disappearing among the many. It will be a different world from the one grandfather even imagined, but still one where faith is worth having!

Notes

1. Thus, for example, the Church of England electoral roll, used here as a proxy for membership, is measured by the number of people who have signed the roll, the qualifications being that they have lived in the parish (or attended the church) for at least six months and are over 15 years of age (it used to be 16 years). Baptist membership, on the other hand, counts, in the main, those adults who have been baptized by immersion. Pentecostals ask for evidence of a person being born again, living an upright Christian life for at least six months, and speaking in tongues. The same kinds of variation may be seen between the different religions (see note 4 below).

2 Thus the Church of England collects attendance figures usually in May, or May and other times of the year; the Roman Catholics use the last Sunday in October, and the Methodists the end of the year (though since 1990 they have used October also). Whilst these are real differences, the speed at which religious statistics normally change is sufficiently slow for these timing differences to be inconsequential.

3 See 2 Samuel 24, but note also the parallel account in 1 Chronicles 21 where verse 1 makes it clear that David was tempted by Satan to do his census. In any case it is David's *motive* which is crucial. Counting people as such is not wrong, otherwise God would not have asked Moses twice to count the people of Israel (at the beginning and end of their wilderness wanderings), nor would there be a book in the Bible called *Numbers*!

4 Such christened infants are taken as members of the Christian community. Those born into Muslim families are taken – not necessarily with any external ceremony – as being Islamic. Likewise the Hindu, Sikh, and so on, communities are defined by the number of families, while Jews count households. In some instances, though perhaps less so in Britain, race is equated to religion.

5 Trinitarian churches are those which accept the historic formulary of the Godhead as the three eternal persons, God the Father, God the Son and God the Holy Spirit, in one unchanging Essence. Groups not included are listed in Brierley (1997a), pp.10.2–5.

6 This is followed through in more detail in Brierley (1998).

7 A major component of the decline in the 1970s was the decrease in the Church of England membership. These figures, based on the electoral roll, went through a key definition change in 1972, whereby all on the roll had to sign afresh after every six years. This meant that those who had moved away or deceased were automatically taken off. This pruning was especially marked when it first took place in 1972.

8 Sometimes in the literature referred to as 'Marginal Protestants'.

9 Details of both the New Church and Theosophists, and many other like groups, are in Brierley (1989) for the years 1900–60, based on Currie et al. (1974). For 1980–2000, see Brierley (1997a).

10 Many of these initially started in houses and were therefore called House Churches. However, outgrowing people's homes has meant that they now meet in schools, public halls, and so on. They are now collectively called New Churches.

11 In 1992, the UN changed its definition of the continents, following the split-up of the old USSR, which had always been counted as part of Europe. Now instead only the six most western countries are part of Europe and the rest are in Asia, creating a discontinuity for some religious groups, like the Orthodox Church. As a consequence, for simplicity, the text uses the year 1990 to enable the same definitions to be applied throughout.

12 In the 1989 English Church Census (Brierley, 1991b), some denominations had an attendance larger than membership – Baptists (85 average attendance to membership of 73), Independents (including the New Churches) (71 to 51), and Pentecostals (95 to 72).

References

*Abrams, Mark, Gerard, David and Timms, Noel (eds) (1985) *Values and Social Change in Britain*, Macmillan, Basingstoke.

Barker, David, Halman, Loek and Vloet, Astrid (1992) *The European Values Study 1981–90*, Summary Report, Gordon Cook Foundation.

Barna, George (1990) *The Frog in the Kettle*, Regal, Ventura, California.

Barrett, David (1982) *World Christian Encyclopedia*, Oxford University Press, Oxford.

Barrett, David (1995) 'Status of global mission', *International Bulletin of Missionary Research*, Connecticut, January.

Berger, Peter L. (1980) *The Heretical Imperative*, Collins, London.

Brierley, Peter W. (1980) *Prospects for the Eighties*, Volume 1, Bible Society, London.

Brierley, Peter W. (1983) *Prospects for the Eighties*, Volume 2, MARC Europe, London.

Brierley, Peter W. (1988a) 'Religion', in Halsey, A. H. (ed.) *British Social Trends since 1900*, Macmillan, Basingstoke.

Brierley, Peter W. (1988b) *UK Christian Handbook 1989/90*, MARC Europe, London.

Brierley, Peter W. (1989) *A Century of British Christianity*, MARC Monograph no. 14, MARC Europe, London.

*Brierley, Peter W. (1991a) *'Christian' England*, MARC Europe, London.

Brierley, Peter W. (1991b) *Prospects for the Nineties*, MARC Europe, London.

Brierley, Peter W. (1993a) *UK Christian Handbook 1994/95*, Christian Research, London.

Brierley, Peter W. (1993b) *Reaching and Keeping Teenagers*, Monarch Publications, Crowborough.

Brierley, Peter W. (ed.) (1994) *Irish Christian Handbook*, 1995/96 edition, Christian Research, London.

Brierley, Peter W. (ed.) (1995a) *UK Christian Handbook*, 1996/97 edition, Christian Research, London.

Brierley, Peter W. (ed.) (1995b) *Finding Faith in 1994*, Report by Christian Research for Churches Together in England.

Brierley, Peter W. (ed.) (1996) *Changing Churches: An Analysis of Some of the Movements in the Contemporary Church Scene*, Leaders Briefing no. 3, Christian Research, London.

*Brierley, Peter W. (ed.) (1997a) *Religious Trends*, no. 1, 1998/99 edition, Christian Research, London.

Brierley, Peter W. (1997b) *World Churches Handbook*, Christian Research, London and Lausanne Committee, Edinburgh.

Brierley, Peter W. (1998) *Future Church*, Monarch Publications, Crowborough.

Brierley, Peter W. and Evans, Byron (1983) *Prospects for Wales*, Bible Society and MARC Europe, London.

Brierley, Peter W. and Macdonald, Fergus (1985) *Prospects for Scotland*, MARC Europe, London, and the National Bible Society of Scotland, Edinburgh.

Brierley, Peter W. and Macdonald, Fergus (1995) *Prospects for Scotland 2000*, Christian Research, London, and the National Bible Society of Scotland, Edinburgh.

Bruce, Steve (1998) *Conservative Protestant Politics*, Oxford University Press, Oxford.

*Currie, Robert, Gilbert, Alan and Horsley, Lee (1974) *Churches and Churchgoers*, Oxford University Press, Oxford.

*Davie, Grace (1994) *Religion in Britain since 1945*, Blackwell, Oxford.

Ester, Peter, Halman, Loek and de Moor, Ruud (eds) (1994) *The Individualizing Society: Value Change in Europe and North America*, Tilburg University Press, the Netherlands.

Fanstone, Michael (1993) *The Sheep That Got Away*, Monarch Publications, Crowborough.

Field, C. D. (1987) 'Non-recurrent Christian Data', in Maunder, W. F. (ed.) *Reviews of United Kingdom Statistical Sources: Religion*, Volume XX, Pergamon Press, Oxford.

Finney, John (1990), *Finding Faith Today*, Bible Society, Swindon.

Francis, Leslie J. (1984) *Teenagers and the Church*, Collins, London.

Francis, Leslie J. and Kay, William K. (1995) *Teenage Religion and Values*, Gracewing, Leominster.

Francis, Leslie J. et al. (eds) (1995) *Fast-moving Currents in Youth Culture*, Lynx, Oxford.

Gallacher, John (1997) *Challenge to Change: The Results of the 1995 Welsh Churches Survey*, Bible Society, Swindon.

Gibbs, Eddie (1993) *Winning Them Back: Tackling the Problem of Nominal Christianity*, Monarch Publications, Crowborough.

*Gill, Robin (1993), *The Myth of the Empty Church*, SPCK, London.

Gill, Robin, Hadaway, C. Kirk and Marler, Penny Long (1997) 'Is Religious Belief Declining in Britain?', unpublished draft.

Hadaway, C. Kirk, and Marler, Penny Long, 'The Measurement and Meaning of Religious Involvement in Great Britain', paper unpublished at time of writing.

Harding, Stephen, and Phillips, David (1986) *Contrasting Values in Western Europe*, Macmillan, Basingstoke.

Hill, Monica (ed.) (1986) *Entering the Kingdom*, MARC Europe, London.

Holway, Jim (1986) 'Mosque Attendance', in Brierley, Peter (ed.) *UK Christian Handbook*, MARC Europe, London.

Johnstone, Patrick (1998) *The Church is Bigger than You Think*, Christian Focus Publications, Fearn and WEC, Gerrards Cross.

*Kay, William K. and Francis, Leslie J. (1996) *Drift from the Churches*, University of Wales Press, Cardiff.

Laquer, Thomas (1976) *Religion and Respectability*, Yale University Press, London.

Lings, George (1994) *Breaking New Ground*, General Synod Report, Church House.

McLeish, Robert (1996) in Porter, David (ed.) *Word on the Box*, Paternoster Publishing, Carlisle.

Mann, Horace (1854) *Religious Worship in England and Wales*, Routledge, London.

Martin, David (1967) *A Sociology of English Religion*, SCM Press, London.

Martin, David (1990) *Tongues of Fire*, Blackwell, Oxford.

Mudie-Smith, Richard (1904) *The Religious Life of London*, Hodder and Stoughton, London.

Murray, Stuart (1998) *Church Planting*, Paternoster Publishing, Carlisle.

Office for National Statistics (ONS) (1993) *Marriage Series*, FM2, no. 16, Government Statistical Service, London.

Perman, David (1977) *Change and the Churches: An Anatomy of Religion in Britain*, Bodley Head, London.

Richter, Philip, and Francis, Leslie J. (1998) *Gone but Not Forgotten: Church Leaving and Returning*, Darton, Longman and Todd, London.

Scripture Union (1968) *Background to the Task*, Scripture Union, London.

Skywalker, Luke (1998) 'Ethics in Business', in *Ethos*, April/May.

Smart, Ninian (1983) in Richards, Alan and Bowden, John (eds) *A New Dictionary of Christian Theology*, SCM Press, London.

Wilson, Bryan R. (1982) *Religion in Sociological Perspective*, Oxford University Press, Oxford.

Winter, David (1988) *Battered Bride? The Body of Faith in an Age of Doubt*, Monarch, Eastbourne.

Further reading

The asterisked items in the References are valuable sources for further reading.

20
Crime, Sentencing and Punishment

Roger Hood and Andrew Roddam

The ordering of these returns [on convictions for crime] is a measure of excellent use in furnishing data for the legislator to go to work upon. They will form altogether a kind of political barometer, by which the effect of every legislative operation relative to the subject, may be indicated and made palpable.

Jeremy Bentham, *A View of the Hard Labour Bill*, 1778

Introduction

As the twentieth century opened the number of crimes[1] recorded by the police in England and Wales and the proportion per head of population were at their lowest point since the first national criminal statistics were published in 1857. In that year there had been 475 recorded crimes per 100000 population. Yet by 1900 there were only 300 per 100000, the vast majority of which were petty thefts.

Recorded crime had fallen despite the fact that the collection of criminal statistics had been improved in 1895 and even though the increase in the size and competence of police forces might have been expected to have produced more reports of crime. Alongside the decline in recorded crime the convict prison population had been reduced by almost 60 per cent since 1869 (Radzinowicz and Hood, 1986, pp.113–29; 567; 775–8). The view was widely held in Edwardian England that, except for pockets of resistant 'habituals', crime was being defeated by material and moral progress. Even though recorded crime began to rise after World War I, the proportion of convicted offenders sentenced to custody and the number of long-term prison sentences were further reduced. This was a product of a policy aimed at the general 'abatement of imprisonment'.[2] By the mid-1930s confident penal administrators began to claim that the supply of recidivists could be 'cut off at the roots' and the whole prison system reduced to a minor arm of the state's apparatus of social control (Ruck, 1951, pp.55; 62). In 1937 about 10 500 persons were residing in the prisons of England and Wales, of whom only 850 were serving sentences of penal servitude or preventive detention of over three years and only 300 were serving more than five years.

In the second half of the century the number of recorded crimes increased dramatically and so did the number of persons convicted of the more serious offences. So substantial was the growth in crime that, despite continuing attempts to restrict the use of custodial sentences, the daily average population of prisoners both grew and changed in character. By 1997 there were 61 000 people in prison including 24 000 serving sentences of three years or longer.

This chapter explores the relationship between the changing volume and seriousness of crime, the number of persons convicted or cautioned, the venue of trial, sentencing policies and practices, and the size and nature of the penal population.[3]

Statistical caveats

Criminal statistics have long been recognized as 'the most difficult and certainly one of the most imperfect branches of [official] statistics in general, difficult to compile, difficult to comprehend and difficult to interpret' (Radzinowicz, 1945a, p.193).[4] They are especially difficult to interpret when used as a barometer of changing morality or respect for the law. This is because the extent to which events are interpreted as criminal victimizations and reported to the police, the extent to which they are recorded as crimes of various types by the police, the extent to which such crimes are cleared up, and the use by police and prosecutors of their discretionary powers to bring offenders to justice, are all affected by the very moral and social changes which the statistics seek to illuminate.

It is well known that at least 80 per cent of crimes officially recorded by the police result from complaints made by victims or witnesses rather than events discovered by the police themselves. If the proportion of crimes committed which were reported to and recorded by the police had remained constant over time there would be no problem in using 'crimes recorded by the police'[5] as an indicator of changing criminality during this century. But there is every reason to believe that this has not been the case. For example, it is notorious that the line between what is regarded as a socially acceptable recourse to force and what is considered criminal violence has shifted over time: for example, in relation to domestic violence and rape. Even if the victim considered the harm caused to be a crime, it may not have been a matter which was regarded as appropriate to report to the police. As recent 'victimization surveys' have shown, crimes may not be reported because they are regarded as too trivial; or because the victim believes that nothing can be done by the authorities to bring the perpetrator to book; or, at the extreme, because the victim fears retaliation or other social consequences of doing so.[6] Furthermore, social changes such as increased telephone ownership and the spread of insurance cover have affected both the ability and necessity to report crime (Lewis, 1992, p.16).[7]

Even when citizens have reported crime to the police, there has been no strict obligation on the police to record the event as a crime. Officers have to decide whether the incident constitutes a crime and if so under which legal heading to record it. Again it is notorious that police practices in these matters have changed over time, sometimes dramatically. Indeed, earlier in this century the police were inclined only to record complaints as crimes if they believed there was a good chance of clearing them up: 'Why should I show a crime committed without a chance of showing a prisoner against it?', was the response of a Chief Constable to the Chief Inspector of Constabulary in 1921 (Mannheim, 1941, p.39). Sometimes such crimes were dealt with by recording them as 'non-crimes'. A well known example was the practice in the Metropolitan Police before 1931 of using a 'Suspected Stolen Book' in any case 'where there was any doubt as to whether a crime had been committed'. When the use of this book was discontinued the total number of crimes recorded by the Metropolitan Police surged upwards, from (in round figures) 15 300 in 1927, to 26 200 in 1931, to 83 000 in 1932. 'It was estimated that had the 1931 figures been returned on the same basis as those for 1932, the figure for the former year would had been 79 000' (Ruck, 1935, p.350). In recent years the police have been under pressure to change their attitudes towards complaints of domestic violence and rape, with a marked effect on the number of such offences officially recorded as crimes (Lloyd and Walmsley, 1989; Smith, 1989).

Of course, some types of crime are greatly under-represented in the official criminal statistics because they occur far from the public gaze or have no easily identified 'victim' to make a complaint to the police. The most numerous are those offences that take place as part of business activity, including serious 'white-collar' crimes, as well as breaches of regulations protecting health and safety and the environment. Furthermore, many such offences are regulated by agencies other than the police, such as the Inland Revenue, Customs and Exercise, the Factory Inspectorate and the Health and Safety Executive. They, much more frequently than the police, seek to obtain desistence from offending by warnings or by imposing their own penalties, thus bypassing the criminal process. In addition there are crimes recorded by other police forces such as the British Transport Police which do not find their way into the official Home Office *Criminal Statistics for England and Wales*.[8]

Time-series analyses of trends in crime are made difficult by changes in the way in which the official *Criminal Statistics* have been compiled and presented (Walker, 1995; Coleman and Moynihan, 1996). As regards the figures for crimes recorded by the police, these have been affected by the reclassification of some crimes from indictable to summary non-indictable offences,[9] and the inclusion of some summary offences as 'notifiable' – such as criminal damage of less than £20 since 1977. More important in many ways is the problem of comparing the relative seriousness of offences recorded at different periods of time. It goes without saying that, as expensive consumer goods have become more widely available, the value of the property stolen – often for resale – has increased. In the case of property crimes value can be linked, of course, to other economic indices. It is far more difficult to judge whether the 'quality' of violent or sexual acts reported and recorded is comparable over longer periods. Attempts to tackle this problem through the development of 'crime indices' based on the numerical scoring of various aspects of the circumstances involved in and the harm caused by the offence, or by constructing a 'situational classification' based on the relationship between the parties and the motivation of the offender, were widely discussed in the 1960s (Sellin and Wolfgang, 1964; Rose, 1970, pp.33–52). In 1967 the Departmental Committee on Criminal Statistics (the Perks Committee) rejected these approaches as too controversial (Departmental Committee on Criminal Statistics, 1967; McClintock, 1974, pp.28–42). Nevertheless, the fact that the classification of crime under five main headings (Table 20.1) has remained virtually unchanged for 100 years has obviously had some advantages from the point of view of assessing trends.

As Thorsten Sellin put it, over 60 years ago: 'The value of a crime rate for index purposes decreases as the distance from the crime itself in terms of procedure increases' (Sellin, 1931, p.346). This is because the only official data available about 'offenders' relates to those who are proceeded against either in the courts or – in more recent years – by way of a formal police caution. Unlike the United States, there are no statistics relating to persons arrested. Much therefore depends on the ability and desire of the police to bring offenders to formal justice. This will vary according to age, gender, social class, ethnicity, type of offence and type of policing – whether it is reactive to citizens' complaints or proactive in seeking to arrest suspects, such as those involved in trading in illegal drugs. Some crimes are much easier to clear up than others. In the case of most violent crimes the offender has usually been seen and is often known to some extent by the victim. When burglaries occur there are rarely witnesses to the crime and thus the police have to rely on other clues, the most common of which is their knowledge of likely perpetrators – 'round up the usual suspects!'

For reasons already alluded to, certain types of persons who commit offences are much less likely to be processed by the agencies of criminal justice. The 'policed' are considerably more likely to belong to the least economically and socially powerful groups including ethnic minorities, particularly people of Afro-Caribbean descent. As a result of ethnic monitoring, it has been established that black people are, on the whole, five times more likely to be stopped and searched than white people and then more likely to be arrested. Discriminatory practices in targeting such groups as suspects may, in some circumstances, interact with social disadvantage to create a greater propensity to commit crimes of various kinds. Thus, discriminatory policies contribute, to some extent, to the substantial over-representation of Afro-Caribbean citizens in the criminal justice system of England and Wales (Hood, 1992; Fitzgerald, 1993; 1995; Smith, 1997; Home Office, 1998).

The categorization in the *Criminal Statistics* of persons found guilty and sentenced to various measures has also changed over time. It was only towards the end of the 1930s that a possible distinction was drawn between the penalties imposed on the three main age-groups: those aged 16 and under, those aged 17 and under 21, and those 21 and over, but not for males and females separately. This only became possible after World War II. Changes in the law, particularly in relation to the age of criminal responsibility and the powers of the Juvenile Court (established in 1908), have had an impact on the categorization of statistics. Thus, the age of criminal responsibility was raised first from 7 to 8 and later from 8 to 10 by the Children and Young Persons Acts of 1933 and 1963 respectively. At the other end of the scale, the upper age-limit for the Juvenile Court was raised first from 16 to 17 in 1933 and then from 17 to 18 by the Criminal Justice Act 1991 and the court renamed the Youth Court. Also, the introduction (and often subsequent demise) of new types of punishment makes it difficult to maintain consistent categorizations of offenders receiving various penalties. As the lengths of custodial sentences imposed by the courts have changed (see below) so has the way in which lengths of sentences have been grouped in both criminal and prison statistics, again making comparisons over time more difficult.

Assuming that a prosecution goes ahead, the impact of the case on the criminal justice process and the institutions of punishment will depend to a considerable extent on how the facts of the case are legally classified (McConville, et al., 1991).[10] Some indictable offences can only be tried summarily at a Magistrates' Court; others are 'indictable only' and must be tried in the Crown Court. Most indictable offences are 'triable either way'. This means that they may be tried at either venue depending on decisions made by the defendant or by the magistrates who first hear the case. These courts have very different powers, magistrates being limited to a maximum penalty of six months' imprisonment (or for more than one offence a maximum of twelve months consecutively). During this century there have been substantial changes in the classification of offences and in the policies of prosecutors and magistrates (sometimes guided by the Court of Appeal) in deciding what is the appropriate venue for trial, all of which have had an impact on the type and severity of penalties imposed. Many offences have been downgraded from triable only on indictment to triable either way and from triable either way to triable summarily only. For example, the Criminal Justice Act 1925 made malicious wounding and committing actual bodily harm, which made up the bulk of violent offences against the person, triable either way instead of on indictment only (*Criminal Statistics, 1927*).

The inventory of crime

Trends in officially recorded crime

In 1997 the number of crimes recorded by the police was 57 times greater than in 1900, having risen from just under 78000 to around 4460000. Expressed as a proportion per 100000 population over the age of 10, it was 29 times higher in 1997 than in 1900: rising from around 300 to 8576.

It has been said by the Home Office that the sharp upward curve of recorded crime (Figure 20.1) after 1957 is deceptive. It is only a reflection of the exponential increase that occurs when constant percentage increases are based on ever higher numbers. And it is true that if one views the trend on a logarithmic scale 'since 1918 the increase in recorded crime has been extremely consistent, about 5 per cent per year' (Barclay, 1995, p.8). On the other hand, the 'man in the street' is an 'absolutist', not a 'relativist'. He is more concerned with the actual rise in the volume of crime. In any case, the logarithmic way of presenting the trend masks some important fluctuations in the level of crime over shorter periods.

In 1920 (in relation to the population over the age of 10) recorded crime was only 5 per cent above the level it had been in 1900 and it hardly increased over the next seven years. However, from 1927–37, the years of depression, it more than doubled and had nearly doubled again by the time the war was over. In the decade immediately after the war, recorded crime per head of population increased by only 5 per cent, having at first given the impression that it would continue to fall from its war-time peak. It was after 1957 that 'the emergence of the affluent society' was 'accompanied by a further increase in recorded crime ... higher than ever before, remaining fairly constant at 10 per cent each year' (McClintock et al., 1968, pp.18–19). Indeed it shot upwards by 121 per cent between 1957 and 1967 and similarly doubled over the next decade. From the end of the 1970s to the early 1990s the rate of increase slowed: recorded crime was 50 per cent higher in 1987 than ten years earlier.[11] But, just as in other decades since the war, this hid some sharp fluctuations in the rate of both property and personal crime associated with changes in economic prosperity.[12] Since 1992 the number of recorded crimes has fallen each year – the first time for over a century. However, it should not be forgotten that crime figures were still 20 per cent higher in 1997 than they had been in 1987 (*Criminal Statistics, England and Wales, 1997*, p.23).

Underlying trends in criminal victimization

Since 1982 the British Crime Survey (BCS) has conducted regular sweeps of a sample of households in order to reveal the underlying trends of victimization. Respondents have been asked to report to the survey offences that have been committed against them during the past year and to say whether they have reported them to the police. The crimes covered involve, of course, only those in which there has been a personal victim, thus excluding 'victimless' crimes such as illegal drug use, and almost all 'white collar' or business crimes. Apart from this, the BCS has made it possible to make a broad comparison between events experienced and defined as crimes by citizens and the number of similar offences recorded by the police.

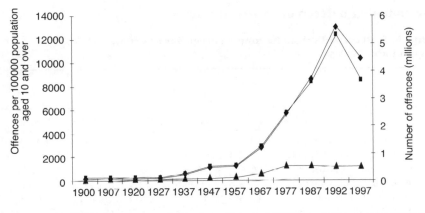

—■—   Notifiable offences recorded by the police per 100000 population aged 10 and over
—◆—   Notifiable offences recorded by the police – actual numbers
—▲—   Total found guilty or cautioned for indictable offences

Figure 20.1 Changes in recorded crime[a] and persons found guilty or cautioned for indictable offences, 1900–97, England and Wales

Note: [a]Does not include criminal damage of less than £20 (which was first included as a recorded crime in 1977).

Source: Annual *Criminal Statistics, England and Wales.*

For example, the findings suggest that although recorded crime fell by 8 per cent between 1993 and 1995, the number of victimizations reported to the 1996 BCS for similar offences rose by 2 per cent. However, between 1995 and 1997, victimizations have fallen at the same rate as recorded crime (Mirrlees-Black et al., 1988, pp.23–4).

However, whatever may be said about the relationship between the underlying trend of victimizations and the trend of recorded crimes, no one now seriously doubts that the number of crimes actually committed has increased over the century. The increase is much less than the official statistics portray, but has nevertheless been considerable.[13] Thus, in 1981, 28 per cent of respondents to the British Crime Survey reported that an adult or household had that year been the victim of a crime covered by the survey (the majority of course not being very serious). Fourteen years later, in 1995, the proportion reporting a crime had risen to 39 per cent.[14] This may have been partly due to changing attitudes to offences such as domestic violence leading to greater disclosure of such incidents, but this is not the whole story for over the same period acquisitive crimes had also doubled. As a leading Home Office analyst of crime trends has said, it all adds up to a 'striking picture of consistent long-run growth in crimes whose origins are diverse' (Field, 1990, p.4).[15]

The changing pattern of recorded crimes

Table 20.1 Recorded crime by major categories of offence, 1900–97, England and Wales

	1900	1907	1920	1927	1937
All notifiable offences	77934	98822	100697	125703	266265
Violence against the person	1908	1940	1546	1846	2723
As a percentage of all offences	2.4	2.0	1.5	1.5	1.0
Most serious violent crime	664	669	607	535	664
As a percentage of all violence	34.8	34.5	39.3	29.0	24.4
Less serious violent crime	1244	1271	939	1311	2059
As a percentage of all violence	65.2	65.5	60.7	71.0	75.6
Sexual offences	1582	1976	2940	3533	4646
As a percentage of all offences	2.0	2.0	2.9	2.8	1.7
Burglary	7493	11470	15596	19481	45131
As a percentage of all offences	9.6	11.6	15.5	15.5	16.9
Burglary in the home	3812	6243	6893	8390	18959
As a percentage of all burglaries	50.9	54.4	44.2	43.1	42.0
Robbery	271	275	267	110	209
As a percentage of all offences	0.3	0.3	0.3	0.1	0.1
Theft, handling, fraud, forgery	64090	79398	78014	97179	208989
As a percentage of all offences	82.2	80.3	77.5	77.3	78.5
Theft of/from a vehicle	0	0	0	0	23919
As a percentage of all thefts	0.0	0.0	0.0	0.0	11.4
Other indictable offences	2590	3763	2334	3554	4567
As a percentage of all offences	3.3	3.8	2.3	2.8	1.7
Criminal damage[a] and arson	444	535	329	281	533
As a percentage of other offences	17.1	14.2	14.1	7.9	11.7

Note: [a]Excludes criminal damage under £20 from 1977 (which was first included as a recorded crime in 1977).

Remarkable changes in the pattern of offences recorded by the police have occurred during the century (Table 20.1).

- *Offences of personal violence* have remained a small proportion of all crime throughout the century, although more than doubling from 2.4 per cent in 1967 to 5.6 per cent in 1997. The homicide rate fell from 10 per million population at the beginning of the century to about 7 per million in the early 1960s. It then began to rise but has remained between 10 and 13 over the decade 1987–97, one of the lowest homicide rates in the world.[16]
- As the number of recorded *violent crimes* has increased during the century the proportion of them which were of the less serious kind (actual bodily harm) also increased: from 65 per cent in 1900 to 91 per cent in 1997. This suggests a much greater propensity for citizens to report less serious violent

| | | | | | | % change | |
1947	1957	1967	1977	1987	1997	1900–37	1957–97
498576	545562	1207354	2463025	3708994	4460629	242	718
4508	10960	29048	82190	141042	250827	43	2189
0.9	2.0	2.4	3.3	3.8	5.6		
1155	2291	4127	5825	10998	23570	0	929
25.6	20.9	14.2	7.1	7.8	9.4		
3353	8669	24921	76365	130044	227257	66	2521
74.4	79.1	85.8	92.9	92.2	90.6		
9899	18635	22501	21313	25154	33165	194	78
2.0	3.4	1.9	0.9	0.7	0.7		
111789	105042	266385	604050	900104	1015075	502	866
22.4	19.3	22.1	24.5	24.3	22.8		
34284	32686	90635	262606	483001	519265	397	1489
30.7	31.1	34.0	43.5	53.7	51.2		
979	1194	4564	13730	32633	63072	–23	5182
0.2	0.2	0.4	0.6	0.9	1.4		
363910	400528	872211	1608141	2184981	2299350	226	474
73.0	73.4	72.2	65.3	58.9	51.5		
38122	62455	201787	605705	1048153	1117572	–	1689
10.5	15.6	23.1	37.7	48.0	48.6		
7491	9203	12645	133601	425080	799140	76	8583
1.5	1.7	1.0	5.4	11.5	17.9		
2860	2965	10695	123881	412945	739344	20	24836
38.2	32.2	84.6	92.7	97.1	92.5		

Source: Annual *Criminal Statistics, England and Wales.*

attacks and for the police to record them.[17] It may well also be that during the last decade the police began to record some victimization in the more serious categories of violence than formerly, because over this period violent offences involving more serious harm increased at a substantially faster rate (10 per cent a year) than the less serious ones (6 per cent a year). Thus, according to the BCS, violent victimizations rose by 31 per cent between 1981 and 1995 (from 1.3 to 1.7 per cent of all victimizations) but the number recorded by the police rose at a much faster rate, almost doubling (Mirrlees-Black et al., 1996). Since then, recorded woundings have increased by 18 per cent whereas the BCS figure for victimizations had fallen by 17 per cent (Mirrlees-Black et al., 1998, p.24).

- *Sexual offences* have remained rare in relation to the total amount of recorded crime, and have proportionately decreased since 1957. This is because they have increased at a slower rate than other categories of crime – by 78 per cent over the last 40 years. During the last decade recorded rapes have increased by about 10 per cent a year, but again much of this increase appears to be the result of changes in police recording practices. A Home Office report showed that in several areas there had been 'dramatic' increases in the number of rapes recorded by the police (50 per cent in two years) even though fewer had been reported to them (Smith, 1989, pp.1; 24). However, there is evidence to suggest that more women have begun to report rapes committed by persons already intimately known to them than was the case in earlier years.[18]

- *Robbery with violence*, although remaining comparatively rare, accounting in 1997 for a mere 1.4 per cent of all recorded crimes, increased from 1200 in 1957 to 63000 in 1997 (5000 per cent). This enormous numerical increase yet again reflects to some extent police recording practices, for between 1981 and 1995 the number of recorded robberies rose twice as fast as the number of underlying victimizations (*Criminal Statistics*, 1996, p.40). But of course this accounts for only a fraction of the growth of robberies. Firearms have been relatively rarely used in robberies and even more rarely fired. There was only one case in London in 1950 and two in 1957 (McClintock and Gibson, 1961, pp.29; 111). Although a more recent study showed that the number of armed robberies in London had markedly increased, a firearm was discharged in only 4 per cent of incidents, almost all of them without causing physical injury (Morrison and O'Donnell, 1994, pp.1; 3; 36).

- *Burglary*, both of the home and of other premises, which accounted for one in ten recorded crimes at the beginning of the century, took on a greater significance as the century progressed. No doubt this was connected with the greater opportunities for financial reward as transferable possessions increased. Other factors included a large increase in the number of homes left unguarded as more women went to work, the fragmentation of established communities, and greater mobility connected with the development of transport.[19] Household burglary has grown both absolutely and in proportion to population. In 1900 it accounted for 5 per cent (roughly 4000) of all recorded crime, was only 6 per cent in 1957, but 12 per cent (approximately 520000) in 1997. The General Household Survey combined with the British Crime Survey has shown that from the early 1970s to the mid-1980s the number of recorded burglaries rose eight times faster than the number of households reporting a burglary to the surveys. This was attributed both to the increased rate of reporting burglaries to the police, necessitated by the growth of household insurance, and to the police improving their recording practices. However, since then, the underlying rate of burglaries has risen at a faster pace than crimes recorded by the police, this time linked to a fall-off in insurance claims and perhaps a growing sense of realism that the police are not able to clear up most of the burglaries reported to them (*Criminal Statistics*, 1997, p.41).[20]

- At the beginning of the century *thefts, handling stolen goods, frauds and forgeries* made up over 80 per cent of all recorded crime: but by the end just over half. Even more significant has been the shift in the object of thefts, the spread of ownership of motor vehicles having an enormous impact. In 1937 thefts of or from a vehicle accounted for 9 per cent of all recorded crime (about 24000 recorded offences). In 1997, they made up 25 per cent (nearly 1 120 000 offences), half of all the thefts recorded by the police. As with burglary, the BCS has shown that acquisitive crime as a whole increased between 1981 and the mid-1990s at a considerably faster rate than such crimes officially recorded. There seems to have been less of an incentive to report them.

- *Drug trafficking* (supplying illegal drugs) was not made a notifiable offence until 1982. Between 1987 and 1997 these offences, which are regarded as serious by the courts, have increased threefold: from just over 7000 to over 23 000. In addition, the spread of drug dependency has had a vast impact on the amount of acquisitive crime, including robbery. A recent study estimated that 'use of heroin and crack cocaine may be responsible for inflating criminal involvement by as much as one-third' (South, 1997; Bennett, 1998, p.47).

- The offences loosely classified as *'other offences'*, the bulk of which are criminal damage, have increased very substantially since World War II. They accounted for 17 per cent of all recorded crime in 1997 as compared to an average of 2 per cent until the 1970s. Yet, this is still the tip of an iceberg. The number of offences of vandalism recorded by the police in 1997 was still only 15 per cent of the number estimated by the 1998 BCS (Mirrlees-Black et al., 1998).

- Figures for *non-indictable (other than motoring) offences* exist only for those who have been proceeded against, found guilty or cautioned (there are no national statistics of such offences reported to or recorded by the police). Table 20.2 shows that from 1900 until World War II the number of persons convicted for non-motoring non-indictable offences diminished substantially.

Table 20.2 Non-indictable offences other than motoring offences, all ages, 1900–97, England and Wales

	Found guilty			Found guilty and cautioned		% cautioned	
	Total	Males	Females	Males	Females	Males	Females
1900	580885	n/a	n/a	–	–	–	–
1910	497805	n/a	n/a	–	–	–	–
1920	459026	n/a	n/a	–	–	–	–
1927	330385	n/a	n/a	–	–	–	–
1937	244118	n/a	n/a	–	–	–	–
1947	174044	n/a	n/a	–	–	–	–
1957	302645	261150	41495	312489	49340	16.4	15.9
1967	336881	304116	32765	324778	39748	6.4	17.6
1977	419941	369846	50095	396632	57737	6.8	13.2
1987	426000	315700	110300	389400	123300	18.9	10.5
1997	416500	313100	101200	388800	118200	19.5	14.4

Source: Annual *Criminal Statistics, England and Wales*.

Immediately post-war the number was even lower, but rose by 75 per cent over the next decade as the number of regulations increased and they were more rigorously enforced. Since 1957, the number of women found guilty or cautioned for regulatory offences has increased by 240 per cent compared to an increase of 120 per cent for men. This may reflect the much larger proportion of households for which women have become responsible.

Early in the century, prosecutions for drunkenness – simple and with aggravation (the majority) – accounted for four out of ten convictions in Magistrates' Courts. By 1937 drunkenness cases were only 10 per cent of summary non-motoring convictions. After rising to just over 25 per cent during the more prosperous mid-1970s, convictions declined again to around 7 per cent in 1997.

- Barbara Wootton was fond of saying that the typical criminal in England and Wales was *the motoring offender* and certainly there is no doubt that these offences predominate in the work of the Magistrates' Courts. Table 20.3 shows that there were a mere 562 convictions in 1900. By 1952 convictions had increased sixfold to around 375 000. But since then, with the tremendous growth in road traffic, the number has escalated, reaching 1.5 million convictions plus over 6 million fixed penalties in 1990. By 1996, for reasons which are not obvious, fixed penalties had fallen to just over 3.25 million, with convictions remaining at just under 1.5 million.

Table 20.3 Offences involving motor vehicles, 1900–96, England and Wales

Year	Convictions	Obstructing the highway	Written warnings	Fixed penalties
1900	562[a]		n/a	–
1910	11048	15522[b]	n/a	–
1920	62663	27083[b]	n/a	–
1930	170963	26037[b]	n/a	–
1952	375329[c]	–	170025	–
1960	765365[c]	–	245102	–
1970	1419670[c]	–	238172	1519076
1980	2238000[d]	–	304000	3622000
1990	1501000[d]	–	218000	6298000
1996	1492000[d]	–	188000	3352000

Notes: [a]Although the Locomotives Act 1896 placed restrictions on the use of 'light locomotives' on the highways (including a speed limit of 14 mph) it was the Motor Cars Act 1903 which introduced the twentieth-century system of control, with licences for drivers and new offences of driving recklessly, negligently and dangerously. The *Criminal Statistics, 1900* shows only 562 offences by 'locomotives', without stating their nature.
[b]An increasing number of these offences would nowadays probably be called 'parking offences'.
[c]The source for these figures is the Home Office's post-war series of *Offences relating to Motor Vehicles*, which for the first time showed figures for written warnings (the equivalent of cautions for other types of offences), as well as more detailed sub-divisions of offences leading to convictions. Later the series showed figures for fixed penalties.
[d]The series *Offences relating to Motor Vehicles* has by now been replaced by special issues in the series *Home Office Statistical Bulletin*, from which these figures are taken.

Source: Adapted and updated from Walker (1988), p.624.

Trends in convictions and cautions

As a larger proportion of citizens have come to report offences and the police have recorded more of them as crimes, the gap between crimes recorded and persons convicted or cautioned has grown ever wider (Figure 20.1).

The impact of cautioning

Before World War II cautioning of offenders arrested for indictable offences was a very rare occurrence. But after the war, cautioning began to be used as a means of steering juveniles arrested for minor offences away from the court. Indeed, as Table 20.4 shows, by 1997 as many as 83 per cent of males and 95 per cent of females aged 10–14 who were officially processed by the criminal justice system were cautioned. The cautioning of young offenders aged 14–17 also increased dramatically, and by the 1980s this method of dealing with offenders began to be taken seriously for both 17–21-year-olds and adults.

It was often argued, when the practice of formally cautioning offenders began to become more widespread, that it would lead to 'net-widening' (Cohen, 1985; McMahon, 1990). In other words, rather than replacing findings of conviction, formal cautions would be used to draw more and more offenders previously dealt with informally by the police into the 'net' of the criminal justice system. As Table 20.4 shows, the number of young persons found guilty by the courts continued to increase until 1977, despite the increase in the number of cautions. However, over the last 20 years of the century a major change occurred under the influence of Home Office Circulars and changing police practices, including the spread of informal warnings and other measures of censure for petty offending (Audit Commission, 1996, pp.20–1). Both the number of young offenders found guilty and the number cautioned have fallen and the total number of adults found guilty or cautioned has risen very little. The evidence (Table 20.5) does not support the prediction that the use of cautioning would, in the longer term, bring many more persons into the criminal process.

The sex ratio

The ratio of adult males to females found guilty or cautioned per 100 000 of the population has remained remarkably stable for many years: at about 6:1 (Table 20.4). But amongst juveniles there has been an extraordinary change from 18 males for every female aged 10–14 in 1937 to 3 males for every female in 1997; and from 13 males for every female aged 14–17 down to just 4. It does not appear therefore that the changing pattern of adult women in the workplace and other aspects of adult female 'emancipation' led to a larger increase in adult female convictions than in male convictions. However, social changes do appear to have had a differential impact on the amount of known delinquency among younger females relative to young males.[21]

Recidivism

With the development of better statistical records, and in particular the system known as the Offenders' Index, it has become possible to chart all convictions for 'standard list offences'[22] against every member of the population from the age of criminal responsibility onwards. This shows that the proportion of men with a conviction by the age of 23 was considerably lower in the 1973 birth cohort (20 per cent) than in the 1958 cohort (29 per cent). In part this is almost certainly a reflection of the increase in the use of cautions for young offenders since that time. But it is also due to the general decrease in the rate of findings of guilt and cautions for the younger age-group per 100 000 population referred to above.

Venue of trial, numbers sentenced and penalties imposed

Venue of trial and numbers sentenced

The number of adults sentenced for indictable offences has greatly increased over the century, but at a faster rate in the Crown Court[23], with its greater sentencing powers, than in Magistrates' Courts, despite the downgrading of

Table 20.4 Persons found guilty or cautioned and percentage cautioned for indictable offences per 100,000 in each age-group, and the ratio of males to females found guilty and cautioned, 1930–97, England and Wales

Age-group	Found guilty		Cautioned		Found guilty and cautioned			% cautioned	
	Males	*Females*	*Males*	*Female*	*Males*	*Females*	*Ratio M:F*	*Males*	*Females*
10–14									
1930[a]	518	30	–	–	518	30	17	–	–
1937[b]	1222	67	–	–	1222	67	18	–	–
1947[b]	1140	96	–	–	1140	96	12	–	–
1957[b]	1071	75	423	50	1494	125	12	28.3	40.2
1967	1623	199	864	187	2487	386	6	65.2	51.6
1977	1258	159	2532	899	3790	1058	4	67.2	85.4
1987	351	26	2123	648	2477	676	4	85.8	96.2
1997	214	23	1041	421	1255	444	3	82.9	94.7
14–17									
1930	708	63	–	–	708	63	11	–	–
1927	1125	89	–	–	1125	89	13	–	–
1947	1515	178	–	–	1515	178	8	–	–
1957	2058	198	342	54	2400	252	10	14.2	21.9
1967	3342	479	648	160	3890	639	6	19.9	25.0
1977	5278	681	2717	929	7995	1610	5	34.4	58.0
1987	2281	211	3192	998	7385	1638	5	47.6	72.7
1997[c]	2861	423	3080	1068	5941	1491	4	51.8	71.7
17–21									
1930	622	70	–	–	622	70	9	–	–
1937	800	101	–	–	800	101	8	–	–
1947	1023	180	–	–	1023	180	6	–	–
1957	1555	182	84	19	1639	201	8	5.1	9.5
1967	3024	346	175	26	3199	372	9	5.5	7.0
1977	6434	896	220	46	6654	942	7	3.3	5.3
1987	8172	1051	1171	359	7084	1069	7	12.5	25.5
1997[d]	5257	724	2737	655	7995	1379	6	34.2	47.5
21+									
1930	228	37	–	–	228	37	6	–	–
1937	238	44	–	–	238	44	5	–	–
1947	380	67	–	–	380	67	6	–	–
1957	387	58	13	6	401	64	6	3.3	9.1
1967	688	121	21	14	710	135	5	3.0	11.1
1977	1126	253	38	29	1164	282	4	3.7	10.2
1987	1145	169	134	66	1279	234	5	10.5	28.0
1997	1006	153	339	108	1345	262	5	25.2	41.4

Notes: [a]Age-group is actually 7–13 inclusive.
[b]Age-group is actually 8–13 inclusive.
[c]Age-group is actually 14–17 inclusive.
[d]Age-group is actually 18–20 inclusive.

Source: Annual *Criminal Statistics, England and Wales*.

Table 20.5 Numbers for sentence and the sentences imposed for indictable offences, all adults,[a] Crown and Magistrates' Courts, 1900–97, England and Wales

	1900[b]	1907[b]	1920[b]
CROWN COURT			
Number for sentence[c]	7975	10382	7225
Punishments imposed as % of those for sentence			
Custody[d]	90.2	86.1	76.5
Suspended sentence			
Fine	1.1	0.5	0.0
Probation/supervision orders[e]	0.5	0.0	8.2
Community service orders			
Nominal penalties[f]	7.8	12.4	13.4
Otherwise disposed of[g]	0.4	1	1.9
	1900[h]	1907[h]	1920
MAGISTRATES' COURT			
Number for sentence[i]	35284	39893	32942
Punishments imposed as % of those for sentence			
Custody[d]	47.1	49.8	31.7
Suspended sentence			
Fine	26.7	23.6	38.6
Whipping[j]	9.0	5.1	0.1
Probation/supervision orders[e]	14.0	17.6	11.3
Community service orders			
Nominal penalties[f]	2.9	3.8	17.3
Otherwise disposed of[g]	0.3	0.1	1.0
ALL COURTS			
Percentage to custody	55.5	57.3	39.8
Percentage given community sentence	11.7	14.0	10.7
	1900[h]	1907[h]	1920
COMPARATIVE ANALYSIS			
Percentage sentenced at Crown Court	18.4	20.7	18.0
Custody, % at Crown Court	30.0	31.1	34.6
Community sentences, % at Crown Court	0.8	0.0	13.7
Burglaries, % sentenced at Crown Court[k]			
Woundings[l], % sentenced at Crown Court[k]			
Thefts/frauds, % sentenced at Crown Court[k]			
Total number of persons cautioned			
% Custody of all sentenced and cautioned	55.5	57.3	39.8

Notes: [a]Until 1933, persons aged 16 were tried as adults. From 1933–91 it relates to persons aged 17 and over. From 1992 it relates to persons aged 18 and over. It also includes a number of juveniles tried for homicide or jointly with adults, for example, as their accomplices.

1927[b]	1937	1947	1957	1967	1977	1987	1997
6062	7439	17301	19926	34592	65496	90712	71738
75.0	65.9	67.1	54.3	60.1	48.5	52.4	60.9
					18.2	14.6	3.1
0.0	1.5	0.0	11.7	16.5	15.4	7.7	3.6
9.0	15.6	13.7	21.7	16.5	7.1	9.0	15.0
					4.7	10.1	12.2
13.2	16.0	17.0	8.0	4.7	5.0	4.8	3.2
2.8	1.0	2.2	4.3	2.2	1.1	1.4	2.0
1927	1937	1947	1957	1967	1977	1987	1997
38952	40634	62677	65887	147422	268117	251650	199491
27.0	23.0	20.2	14.9	12.1	6.2	7.3	11.1
					6.4	5.0	0.3
32.8	30.4	49.0	51.0	62.8	64.6	51.8	39.7
17.8	21.1	10.6	13.9	12.4	7.0	11.1	16.5
					1.2	8.0	8.6
21.3	24.4	19.0	15.0	11.7	12.6	14.7	20.4
1.1	1.1	1.2	5.2	1	2	2.1	3.4
33.5	29.7	30.4	24.0	21.2	14.5	19.2	24.3
16.6	20.3	11.3	15.7	13.2	8.9	19.2	22.1
1927	1937	1947	1957	1967	1977	1987	1997
13.5	15.5	21.6	23.2	19.0	19.6	26.5	26.4
30.2	34.4	47.8	52.5	53.8	65.7	72.2	66.4
7.3	11.9	26.3	32.2	23.8	26.0	26.4	28.0
		100.0	100.0	50.9	68.5	78.0	73.1
		26.8	26.6	37.5	59.9	71.5	37.5
		22.6	20.6	19.3	47.5	60.4	18.1
			4060	9039	16100	56200	115600
33.5	29.7	30.4	22.9	20.2	13.8	16.5	17.0

[b]Includes persons under the age of 16, as the *Criminal Statistics* for these years did not provide any breakdown by age.

continued

Table 20.5 (*cont...*)

cIncludes those committed for sentence from Magistrates' Courts to the Higher Courts.
dIncluding imprisonment, penal servitude (abolished in 1948), preventive detention and corrective training (replaced in 1967 by extended sentences), committal to an industrial or reformatory school (replaced in 1933 by approved schools), remand homes (abolished in 1963), borstals and detention centres (abolished in 1988) and young offender institutions.
eFrom 1970 probation orders for children under the age of 16 were replaced by supervision orders. Includes combination orders (a combined probation and community service order) introduced by the Criminal Justice Act 1991.
fMainly consisting of absolute and conditional discharges, recognizances and bind-overs.
gIncludes a small number of persons sentenced to death until the abolition of capital punishment in 1965, persons not finally disposed of, committals to institutions for the mentally disordered, committals to inebriate reformatories and other miscellaneous numerically unimportant disposals.
hIncludes persons under the age of 16, as Juvenile Courts were not established until 1908
iExcludes those committed for sentence from the Magistrates' Courts to the Higher Courts.
jAll these persons would have been males under the age of 14. Whipping was abolished by the Criminal Justice Act 1948.
kThis relates only to males aged 17 and over.
lOffences of grievous bodily harm, Section 20 of the Offences Against the Person Act 1861. The more serious woundings under Section 18 of the Act (grievous bodily harm with intent) are not included as they are triable on indictment only at the Crown Court.

Source: Annual *Criminal Statistics, England and Wales: Supplementary Tables*, vols 1 and 2.

Table 20.6 Numbers for sentence and the sentences imposed for indictable offences, all juveniles,a Juvenile Courts, 1920–97, England and Wales

JUVENILE COURTS	1920	1927	1937
Number for sentence	12919	11037	28992
Punishments imposed as a percentage of those for sentence			
Custodyb	10.9	8.1	10.1
Attendance centre ordersc			
Fine	17.2	6.8	6.7
Whippingsd	9.9	2.0	0.4
Probation/supervision orderse	31.3	49.5	49.6
Community service orders			
Fit person order/care order	0.0	0.1	0.5
Nominal penaltiesf	30.1	33.0	31.4
Otherwise disposed ofg	0.6	0.5	1.3

Notes: aFor the age-ranges of offenders who could be dealt with in the Juvenile (now Youth) Court.
bIncluding committal to an industrial or reformatory school (replaced in 1933 by approved schools), remand homes (abolished in 1963), borstals, detention centres (abolished in 1988) and young offender institutions.
cAttendance centres (and detention centres) were introduced by the Criminal Justice Act 1948, although it was not until 1950 that the first one was opened and not until 1954 that the number of committals reached a thousand.
dAbolished by the Criminal Justice Act 1948, but by then very infrequently used.

many indictable offences so as to make them triable only in Magistrates' Courts[24] (Table 20.5). Earlier in the century – for example, in 1937 – fewer than one in six indictable cases were sentenced in the Higher Courts, but in 1997 it was one in four.[25] In real terms, this was a nearly tenfold increase from around 7450 to 71750 cases.

Penalties imposed in the Juvenile Courts

The trends in the punishment of juveniles (Table 20.6) show:

- A decline in the proportionate use of custodial measures until 1997, after which they began to be used more frequently (Allen, 1991; Godfrey, 1996).
- A sharp decline in corporal punishment until its abolition in 1948.
- The popularity of probation orders in the 1930s, a subsequent decline in their use in the 1970s, and a revival when more intensive forms of supervision were introduced in the 1980s.
- A substantial fall-off in the use of fines in the 1990s compared with the 1970s.
- Throughout the century, a substantial use of nominal penalties despite the vast increase in the use of cautions.
- In recent years, the number of juveniles sentenced in the Crown Court has greatly increased, reaching 4900 in 1997, 45 per cent of whom were sentenced to custody and over 700 to long terms of detention, compared to only 42 in 1977.[26]

1947	1957	1967	1977	1987	1997
35013	44335	60397	91647	40245	46300
10.4	8.3	8.0	5.0	8.3	11.4
	3.5	7.5	10.0	15.7	10.6
11.8	15.0	27.8	35.6	22.9	10.8
0.0					
42.3	36.5	28.9	17.7	18.2	25.9
				3.7	6.5
0.9	1.5	1.9	6.0	1.6	
33.2	34.5	25.4	25.6	28.7	31.3
1.4	0.7	0.5	0.1	0.9	3.5

[e]From 1970 probation orders for children and young persons under the age of 16 were replaced by supervision orders. Includes combination orders (a combined probation and community service order) introduced by the Criminal Justice Act 1991.
[f]Mainly consisting of absolute and conditional discharges, recognizances and bind-overs.
[g]Includes cases which were not finally disposed of, committals to institutions for the mentally disordered, committals to inebriate reformatories and other miscellaneous but numerically unimportant disposals.

Source: Annual *Criminal Statistics, England and Wales: Supplementary Tables*, vols 1 and 2.

Penalties imposed on adults

Table 20.5 shows the main trends in the penalties imposed between 1900 and 1997 on adults over the age of 17 for indictable offences by both Magistrates' and Crown Courts.[27]

- There was a great decline in the use of custodial measures. Just under 50 per cent of all adults sentenced in Magistrates' Courts and 90 per cent at the Higher Courts before World War I were sent to prison. In the inter-war years the proportion given a custodial sentence as well as the use of both very long and very short sentences fell substantially (Radzinowicz, 1945b, p.120; 1999, pp.86–90). Indeed, in 1936 only one person was sentenced to more than ten years. By 1992 the custody rate in the Crown Court had fallen to 40 per cent and in Magistrates' Courts to a mere 4 per cent, despite the increased use of cautions for less serious offences. Since then the use of custody has increased dramatically to 61 and 11 per cent respectively, although it should be recognized that the proportion sentenced to custody of all adults convicted or cautioned for an indictable offence was still lower in 1997 (17 per cent) than it had been prior to World War II (30 per cent).
- Suspended imprisonment, introduced in 1967, fell into disuse and is used now only in exceptional circumstances.
- Probation, which was quite popular with the Magistrates' Courts before World War II, steadily lost favour until attempts were made in the late 1980s to find acceptable alternatives to imprisonment by making probation and community sevice more rigorous and demanding 'punishments in the community'.[28] By 1997, about a fifth of sentenced adults in Magistrates' and Crown Courts received a 'community sentence'. However, there is strong evidence to suggest that they were being used not solely in place of custody, but for offenders who previously would have been subjected to less controlling measures (Ashworth, 1995).
- By the 1970s fines had become the most frequently imposed penalty in Magistrates' Courts, accounting for two-thirds of all those sentenced. However, in the difficult economic climate of the 1980s and early 1990s, their use fell to 40 per cent, and in the Crown Court to a mere 4 per cent.
- The periodic downgrading of offences from Crown Court to Magistrates' Court jurisdiction has meant that few of those convicted in the Crown Court now receive nominal penalties, although they are still applied to a quarter of adults sentenced by magistrates,[29] despite the fact that there has been an increase in the use of cautions (see above).

An upsurge of imprisonment

Understandably, a great deal of attention has recently focused on the *proportionate* use of custody, especially in the Crown Court, over the last decade of the century. Nevertheless, the decline in the number of adults over the age of 18 sentenced by these courts (from 91 000 to 72 000 between 1987 and 1997) meant that the *number* sentenced to custody by the Crown Court actually fell by 9 per cent over this period. For the same reasons, the number committed to custody by Magistrates' Courts for indictable offences increased very little (Table 20.5).

Why, then, did the total number of persons over the age of 18 sentenced to custody increase by 21 000 between 1987 and 1997? The answer lies in the very substantial increase in the use of custody for non-indictable offences, especially for motoring offences in the Magistrates' Courts. The number sentenced to imprisonment for such offences rose by 16 600 over this period, accounting for 79 per cent of the total increase in custodial sentences. But, as most of these sentences were short, this cannot be the explanation for the increase in the average size of the sentenced prison population of 9500 prisoners over the same period (see below). Indeed, the daily average population of male and female prisoners serving 12 months or less *declined* by 2750, while the population serving three years or more *rose* by 10 750 (82 per cent).

Clearly, any attempt to reduce the prison population at the end of the century needs to focus on those who receive longer terms of custody. Only a general reduction in the number of persons convicted of serious crimes in the Crown Court, and/or a change in sentencing policy relating to the length of prison sentences and the amount of time to be spent in custody, would be likely to have a marked impact on the size of the prison population.

Penal institutions

Figure 20.2 shows the number of *receptions under a custodial sentence*.[30] The main points to note are:

- At the beginning of the century there were about 150 000 receptions a year into penal institutions, rising to 180 000 in 1907. This number was largely made up of very short-term prisoners committed for petty offences who were unable to pay fines. As a result of the Criminal Justice Administration Act 1914, which gave people time to pay their fines, the number of receptions fell precipitously to about 25 000 in 1920 and remained close to that level until the outbreak of World War II.
- Because the increase in the numbers convicted in the post-war years far outstripped the *proportionate* decline in the use of custody, receptions steadily rose until they reached 62 000 in 1987. Following a fall to around 45 000 in 1993 as a result of the Criminal Justice Act 1991, the number rose again.

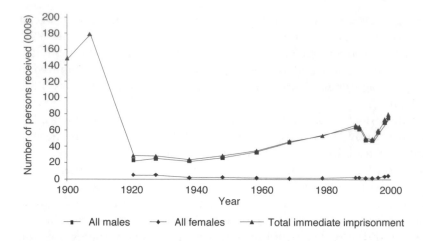

Figure 20.2 Changes in receptions into prisons[a] under a custodial sentence, all ages, males and females, 1900–96, England and Wales

Note: [a]Including borstal, detention centres and young offender institutions.

Source: The Annual *Report of the Prison Commissioners* for England and Wales (from 1963 the Prison Department), or, since 1970, the separately published *Prison Statistics, England and Wales*.

Figure 20.3 shows the size of the *population in penal institutions* for males and females. It should be noted that:

- The total population in custody fell from 18 000 in 1907 to an average of around 10 000 throughout the inter-war years. The number of women prisoners declined from nearly 3 000 at the beginning of the century to under

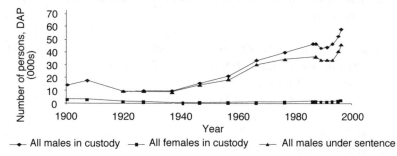

Figure 20.3 Changes in the daily average population of prisons,[a] all ages, males and females, 1900–96, England and Wales

Note: [a]Including borstal, detention centres and young offender institutions.

Source: The Annual *Report of the Prison Commissioners* for England and Wales (from 1963 the Prison Department), or, since 1970, the separately published *Prison Statistics, England and Wales*.

700 in 1937 (Sutherland, 1956). From the end of World War II the average prison population rose steadily (although of course there were fluctuations associated with legislative and administrative interventions such as those affecting the length of remission and parole). The prison population reached a peak of around 48 000 in 1987 before falling to 45 000 in 1993, only to surge ahead in 1997 to 62 000 and even higher to 64 000 at the end of March 1999. It has been estimated that, if present trends continue (although there is no reason to assume that they necessarily will), the prison population in the year 2005 may be as high as 82 800.[31]

- There has been an ever-widening gap, especially noticeable since the early 1970s, between the total prison population and number who were 'under sentence'. This mirrors the substantial increase in the population of prisoners on remand awaiting trial as a result of the increase in the proportion of cases committed to the Crown Court for trial.

- There were, on average, 1000 women prisoners in 1947 and the number did not exceed 2000 until 1996. But this is not an indication that women began to be treated comparatively more harshly than men. Indeed, the proportion of women to men in prison has fallen from 6.3 per cent in 1937 to 4.4 per cent in 1997.

- Prior to their abolition by the Children and Young Persons Act 1969, there existed a network of institutions outside the penal system for juvenile offenders and young people considered by the Juvenile Court to be in need of care and protection. The reformatory and industrial schools founded in the mid-nineteenth century were transposed into Home Office approved schools by the Children and Young Persons Act 1993.[32] Table 20.8 shows the extensive use of this form of detention under the administration of local authorities and voluntary bodies. Despite the movement to try to make less use of these institutions, which gathered support at the end of the nineteenth century (Radzinowicz and Hood, 1986, pp.220–4), there were in 1900 still 19 000 boys and girls in reformatory and industrial schools. By 1927 the population had been cut by a third to just over 6000. Yet 40 years later there were still 5000 young people in these quasi-penal institutions. The abolition of approved schools in 1969 and their replacement by community homes with educational facilities virtually extinguished the use of long-term custody as a sentence for convicted young offenders outside the penal system.

- In the post-war years, the increase in serious crime and the rise in the number of such cases sentenced at the Crown Court (see above) have had a tremendous impact on the nature of the prison population. In 1972, 75 per cent of the daily average population of prisoners had been sentenced by the Crown Court, a proportion which had risen to 88 per cent by 1997. Moreover, whereas in 1937 the 800 male prisoners serving over three years

Table 20.7 Receptions and population of schools for young offenders, 1913–67, boys and girls, England and Wales

| | Receptions | | Population | |
	Boys	Girls	Boys	Girls
1913[a]	4632	1112	14642	4274
1920[a]	2440	354	12076	2391
1927[a]	1343	195	5193	1067
1937[b]	2330	700	5377	1445
1947[b]	2631	772	5621	1531
1957[b]	2982	695	3862	923
1967[b]	4340	824	4044	829

Notes: [a]Reformatory and industrial schools.
[b]Approved schools.

Source: *Report on the Work of the Children's Department* (of the Home Office) (nine were published, at irregular intervals, from 1923).

of penal servitude or preventive detention accounted for 9 per cent of the daily average sentenced population of 9000 males, in 1997 the 23 000 male prisoners serving over three years accounted for about half of the 46 700 men under sentence, of which over 3500 were serving a sentence of life imprisonment. A prison system which had housed predominantly short-term prisoners was transposed into one in which the majority of prisoners were serving medium and long sentences. A system which had dealt mainly with property offenders became one in which the majority were serving sentences for violence, sexual offences, robbery with violence or trading in drugs (Morgan, 1997, pp.1151–62).[33] Even within the period 1987–97 the proportion of the daily average male population serving a sentence for one of these serious offences rose from 46 to 58 per cent. This mirrors the changing pattern of cases dealt with in the Crown Court and clearly has implications for prison management in maintaining security and order.

- Yet, even though the prison population of England and Wales has expanded so greatly in the second half of the century, its size has, in fact, diminished when seen in relation to the number of recorded crimes and those found guilty or cautioned (Figure 20.4). Had it not been for policies which success-fully diverted many offenders from stringent criminal processes and custodial penalties, the prison population would have been very much larger. Even taking into account the increase in the prison population after 1993, the number of prisoners in relation to the total amount of recorded crime and, more pertinently, to those found guilty or cautioned, was still somewhat lower in 1997 than it had been in 1937.[34] Similar trends of a falling ratio of prisoners to recorded crimes have been observed in France, New Zealand, West Germany and the Netherlands (Young and Brown, 1993).

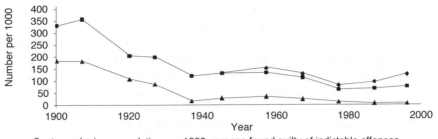

Sentenced prison population per 1000 persons found guilty of indictable offences
Sentenced prison population per 1000 persons found guilty or cautioned for indictable offences
Sentenced prison population per 1000 recorded offences

Figure 20.4 Changes in the relationship between the sentenced prison population (all ages, males and females) and various measures of crime, 1900–96, England and Wales

Source: Annual *Criminal Statistics, England and Wales*; the annual *Report of the Prison Commissioners* for England and Wales (from 1963 the Prison Department), or, since 1970, the separately published *Prison Statistics, England and Wales.*

Prison populations are, of course, affected not only by the proportion of defendants sentenced to custody but also to a much greater extent by the length of sentences imposed and served. The trends are best extracted from the data on receptions into penal institutions because sentence lengths were not given separately in *Criminal Statistics* in relation to age and gender before World War II.

- The outstanding feature of the 1930s was the decrease in the use of both long and very short terms of imprisonment. Thus: 'out of every 100 prisoners sentenced to imprisonment in 1900 72 served sentences of less than 4 weeks, while the corresponding figure for 1936 was only 35' (Radzinowicz, 1945b, p.119). In the post-war period, the distribution of lengths of prison sentences changed remarkably. For example, in 1997, 20 per cent of those received were serving over 18 months and up to three years and 11 per cent longer than three years, compared to only 8 and 3 per cent respectively in 1957.
- To some extent, this obviously reflects the types of case dealt with in the courts. It was hardly surprising that the increased proportion of serious cases appearing in the Crown Court between 1987 and 1997 should have led to an increase in the average length of custodial sentences imposed (from 19 to 24 months). But it also reflects what seems to be a changing attitude towards the use of long-term imprisonment. Whereas, as we have noted, sentences of over three years were rare prior to World War II, courts at the end of the century were less reluctant to impose long prison sentences: 385 prisoners were received with sentences of over ten years in

1997. This has been interpreted as a policy of 'bifurcation', or downgrading of punishment for less serious offences balanced by severe penalties for those considered to be dangerous to the community (Bottoms, 1957). Undoubtedly what Tony Bottoms has called 'popular punitiveness' has also been a factor (Bottoms, 1995). Willingness to impose longer sentences may also reflect changing perceptions of the pain associated with a prison sentence as prisoners' conditions and rights have improved.

- There have also been a number of changes during the century which have affected the proportion of the sentence which a prisoner has had to serve in custody. Remission, which began as 'ticket of leave' in the convict system of the nineteenth century, became established early in the twentieth century first at one-sixth of the sentence for prisoners sentenced to imprisonment and one-quarter for those sentenced to penal servitude. During World War II, due to pressures on the system it became fixed at one-third of the sentence for all prisoners. Parole, introduced in 1967, made it possible for prisoners sentenced to more than 18 months to be released after serving one-third of their sentence, subject to supervision until they reached the two-thirds point of the sentence, when all control over them expired. In the late 1980s it was estimated that in the previous 20 years the system had allowed 'over 12 000 prisoners to be released from custody earlier than would otherwise have been the case' (Carlisle Committee, 1988, para. 184). The Criminal Justice Act 1991 introduced release on supervision at half the sentence for all prisoners serving less than four years, subject to supervision until the three-quarter point of the sentence, after which they were at risk of having to serve the remaining quarter if they reoffended. Those sentenced to a determinate period of four years or longer could earn discretionary release after serving a half (rather than a third) of their sentence. Since 1993, the criteria for parole have been made progressively more stringent, with the result that the proportion of prisoners serving four years or more who have been granted early release has declined from about 54 per cent under the 'old parole system' to about 35 per cent in 1997 under the new Discretionary Release System. This, of course, has been another factor responsible for the increase in the prison population since the early 1990s.[35]

Some international comparisons

The problem of providing reliable internationally comparable criminal and penal statistics, so avidly pursued in the nineteenth century, remains as acute as ever (Radzinowicz and Hood, 1986, pp.94–103). Nevertheless, such broad comparisons as have been made of offences recorded by the police in various countries suggest that crime has increased over the ten years 1987–97 at a faster rate in England and Wales than it has in Northern Ireland and Scotland, and faster than in several European nations, including France, the Netherlands, Sweden and Switzerland (Table 20.8). However, the international criminal victimization survey carried out in 1989 and 1992 showed that the proportion of persons victimized in England during those years was lower than in the Netherlands; on a par with Italy and Spain; just above Germany (West) and Sweden; but considerably higher than in France, Belgium, Finland, Norway, Switzerland, Scotland, and especially Northern Ireland.

Table 20.8 Crime and prison population rates: international comparisons, 1987–97

Country	% Change 1987–97		Prison population per 100000 population 1997	Rank	Prison population per 100000 crimes 1997	Rank
	Crime rate	Prison population				
England and Wales	18	31	120	8	1347	16
Northern Ireland	1	−15	95	12	2541	8
Scotland	−11	12	119	9	1446	13
Austria	23	−6	86	17	1443	14
Belgium		27	84	18	1041	19
Czech Republic	17	−24	209	3	5341	2
Denmark	1	−1	60	22	597	21
Finland	19	−30	58	25	796	20
France	10	8	90	14	1558	11
Germany	5		87	15		
Greece	25	46	53	26	1476	12
Hungary	173	−41	132	7	2606	7
Ireland (Eire)	6	25	67	21	2667	5
Italy	31	46	87	16	2057	9
Netherlands	3	140	75	20		
Norway	22	29	59	23		
Poland	95	−40	149	4	5787	1
Portugal	5	68	142	5	4405	4
Russia	121	44	686	1		
Spain	−7	59	108	11	4625	3
Sweden	9	8	59	24	433	22
Switzerland	15	73	84	19	1562	10
Australia	23	48	95	13	1329	17
Canada	7	27	113	10	1350	15
Japan	20	−8	40	27	2664	6
New Zealand	28	65	137	6	1088	18
US	0	101	645	2		

Source: *Criminal Statistics, 1997, England and Wales.*

In recent years comparisons have been made between the size of the prison populations of various countries (Table 20.8). These are particularly hazardous because the basis for counting is not always the same. To give just two examples: the figures for some countries include a much larger proportion of remand rather than sentenced prisoners, and some countries include juveniles in institutions while others do not. Furthermore, as two leading commentators have rightly pointed out, 'better comparisons would take account of admissions and sentence lengths for both remand and sentenced populations and would take account of some or all of crime rates, prosecutions, convictions and sentences' (Young and Brown, 1993, p.1).

These figures show that at the end of 1997 England and Wales, Scotland, and Northern Ireland all had higher prison populations per 100 000 of their populations than did most Western European countries, only Portugal having a higher rate of prisoners. The rate was however considerably lower than Eastern European countries and very much less than the prisoner ratio in Russia and the United States. Looked at in relation to the amount of recorded crime (and always remembering that this may be counted differently) the rate of prisoners in England and Wales was lower than in Scotland and approximately half that in Northern Ireland (where the figures include those serving sentences for politically motivated crimes). It was also considerably lower than the rate in France, Ireland, Italy, Portugal and Spain.

Notes on sources

The main sources on which this chapter has drawn have already been cited in the references and endnotes to the text, Figures and Tables. There follows a note on the main sources of official statistics and related research studies.

Criminal Statistics, England and Wales (published annually since 1857 but subject to regular revisions in format, style of presentation and informational content). Since 1980 the detailed annual figures relating to proceedings in courts and recorded offences have been made available separately in four volumes of Supplementary Tables. Vol. 1, Proceedings in Magistrates' Courts; Vol. 2, Proceedings in Crown Court; Vol. 3, Recorded offences and court proceedings by police force area, cautions; Vol. 4, Proceedings in Magistrates' Courts – data for individual Petty Sessional Divisions.

Prison Statistics England and Wales (published annually since 1962, but subject to various changes in style, format and content). Before 1962, the statistics were published in the annual *Reports of the Prison Commissioners* – and prior to 1948 in the *Reports of the Commissioners of Prisons and Directors of Convict Prisons*.

Annual Report of the Parole Board for England and Wales (from 1968: parole was introduced by the Criminal Justice Act 1967).

Probation Statistics England and Wales (since 1977). The *Report on the Probation and After-care Statistics* was published in 1975 and 1976 but, before that, statistics relating to the use of probation had to be gleaned from the annual *Criminal Statistics, England and Wales*. There was no generally available data relating to the population on probation or to the manpower of the Probation Service.

Home Office Statistical Bulletins. This series of statistical reports published by the Government Statistical Service is available from the Home Office Research and Statistics Directorate. The series, which began in 1980, provides a wide variety of information on many aspects of criminal justice, including: Summary Probation Statistics; Firearm Certificate Statistics; Statistics of Drug Addicts Notified to the Home Office, United Kingdom; Police Complaints and Discipline; Statistics of Mentally Disordered Offenders; Motoring Offences, England and Wales. Synopses of the main trends in Notifiable Offences Recorded by the Police and of Cautions, Court Proceedings and Sentencing are published as *Bulletins* in advance of the annual *Criminal Statistics*. The latest report on the 1998 British Crime Survey and other non-routine statistical surveys have also been published in the *Bulletin* series.

Home Office Research Studies (before 1969 *Home Office Studies in the Causes of Delinquency and the Treatment of Offenders*) provides reports on many empirical studies, including, for example, M. Hough and P. Mayhew (1983) *The British Crime Survey*, HO Research Study, no. 76. Since 1995, the Home Office Research and Statistics Directorate has published a series of *Research Findings*. These provide brief but informative reports on studies commissioned by the Home Office, some of which are later published more fully as a Home Office Research Study.

A valuable review and discussion of all branches of statistics relating to the criminal justice and penal systems is to be found in Walker (1995).

Acknowledgements

We would like to thank Professor Andrew Ashworth and David Faulkner for several very helpful suggestions. We have found Professor Nigel Walker's excellent treatment of the subject in earlier editions of this book especially helpful.

Notes

1   The term 'crime' refers to acts which are proscribed by criminal law. They vary from those known as 'indictable' offences (which are recorded by the police) to offences, often but not solely of a regulatory nature, which are non-indictable and can only be dealt with summarily at Magistrates' Courts. The range of behaviours subject to criminal sanctions has changed over time – some acts have been decriminalized while others have been criminalized – and in the way they have been classified as indictable or non-indictable. In reality, what citizens define as crime and think

worthy of bringing to official notice, has been affected by changing social definitions of behaviour.

2   A term first used during Winston Churchill's brief tenure as Home Secretary in 1910
in relation to an 'Abatement of Imprisonment Bill', see Radzinowicz and Hood
(1986), pp.650–1.

3   We chose to look at this data in some depth rather than attempt to repeat and
update the survey, which included police and probation manpower statistics,
carried out by Professor Nigel Walker in his chapter on 'Crime and Penal Measures'
in previous editions of this book. We have drawn on Nigel Walker's helpful notes
relating to some of the statistical tables.

4   On nineteenth century views of the value of criminal statistics, see Radzinowicz
and Hood (1986), pp.107–12.

5   Changes have been made in the description of the data recorded as crimes. 'Crimes
known to the police' became 'Serious offences recorded by the police' in 1978 as a
result of the Criminal Law Act 1977. In 1981 this was changed to 'Notifiable
offences' because it was thought that 'serious offences' was a misleading description
for a list which included some which would not normally be considered 'serious'.

6   Since 1982 the Home Office has conducted seven 'sweeps' of the British Crime
Survey, 'a large household survey of people's experiences and perceptions of crime
in England and Wales'. Nearly 15 000 adults were interviewed in the survey carried
out in 1997. See Mirrlees-Black et al. (1998).

7   According to the British Crime Survey, the proportion of households with home
contents insurance policies stabilized during the 1990s at about four-fifths,
although the economically disadvantaged and those living in deprived areas were
considerably less likely to be insured; see Budd (1999).

8   Maguire estimates that in recent years some 80 000 offences have been recorded
annually by the British Transport Police, the Ministry of Defence Police and the
Atomic Energy Authority Police. Some overlap with the police figures due to joint
operations, but by no means the majority. See Maguire (1997), p.149.

9   For example, common assault was made a summary offence in the Criminal Justice
Act 1988 and no longer 'notifiable'. However, unauthorized taking of motor
vehicles, which was also downgraded by the Act, remains a 'notifiable' offence.

10   It should be noted that the responsibility for prosecutions was transferred from the
police to the Crown Prosecution Service in 1986 under the Prosecution of Offences
Act 1985.

11   For an interesting discussion of changes in crime rates during the period 1981–87,
see Farrington and Langan (1992). For a more recent comparison, see Langan and
Farrington (1998).

12   For an excellent study which slows clearly the *negative association* between
consumption growth and property crime and the *positive association* between crimes
against the person and consumption growth in the period since World War II, see
Field (1990).

13   It is much greater than the increase in the number of police officers available to deal
with and process it. In 1921 there were nearly 57 000 police officers. By 1996 there
were about 127 000, an increase of 123 per cent: only a fraction of the increase in
recorded indictable offences and well below the increase in the number of persons
found guilty or cautioned. The police remain largely a male force, but the number
of women has increased at a far greater rate than the number of men. Whereas in
1921 there were only 31 women police officers, by 1996 they numbered nearly
18 000, some 15 per cent of all officers. See, in general, Heidensohn (1992).

14 It should be noted, however, that there is probably a great under-reporting of domestic violence and sexual offences by respondents to victimization surveys. Also, the likelihood of victimization is greatly skewed by multiple victimization. It has been suggested that 4 per cent of victims experience 44 per cent of all crimes. (Zedner, 1997, p.592; Pease 1997, pp.974–6). For an attempt to understand changing experiences of victimization and commission of crime since the 1930s, see Hood and Joyce (1999).

15 However, the 1998 British Crime Survey revealed that the proportion of house-holds/adults who had been a victim had fallen to 34 per cent by 1997 (Mirrlees-Black et al., 1998, p.55).

16 Lewis notes that improvements in medicine have reduced the death rate from serious violence while on the other hand advances in forensic science may have led to more deaths being identified as homicide (Lewis, 1992, p.18).

17 See Walmsley (1986), who noted that between 1974 and 1984 the largest increase has been in the 'less serious' category of violence against the person (85 per cent) rather than in the more serious felonious woundings (18 per cent).

18 See Lloyd and Walmsley's comparison of reported rapes in 1973 and 1985, which found that in certain respects the offences reported in 1985 were 'nastier' than those reported in 1973 (Lloyd and Walmsley, 1989, p.46).

19 This was recognized by the late 1920s as a potent factor: 'whereas the number of recorded crimes against property with violence had increased in the Metropolitan Police District between 1911 and 1928 by 10.6 per cent, the increase in the Outer Home Counties over the same period had been 437.8 per cent (more than fourfold)'. See *Criminal Statistics for 1928*, pp.xii–xiii.

20 The clear-up rate for burglaries fell from about 33 per cent in 1977 to 23 per cent in 1997.

21 A recent self-report study of offending showed that the size of the sex ratio was lowest amongst 14–17 year olds (1.4:1 males to females) but by age 22–25 it had increased to a ratio of 11:1; see Graham and Bowling (1995). For a concise and balanced analysis of trends in female as compared with male crime, see Heidensohn (1997), especially pp. 764–8; also Heidensohn (1996).

22 See 'Criminal history studies based on the Offenders Index' in *Criminal Statistics, England and Wales, 1997*, pp.192–209. Standard list offences are defined as 'all indictable and triable either way cases plus a few of the more serious summary offences'.

23 The Higher Courts (Assizes and Quarter Sessions) were renamed the Crown Court by the Courts Act 1971.

24 See Garland, who suggests that criminal justice systems have responded to high crime rates by 'defining deviance down' in order to limit the burden on the system (Garland, 1996, pp.456–7). Appendix 2 of the annual *Criminal Statistics, England and Wales* provides a useful summary of changes affecting mode of trial.

25 The majority of triable-either-way cases which go to the Crown Court do so because Magistrates commit them there, rather than the defendant electing trial at Crown Court. This is because the Mode of Trial Guidelines laid down by the Lord Chief Justice (for example, in relation to charges of possessing drugs with intent to supply) urge them to do so. See Hedderman and Moxon (1992).

26 Under Section 53(2) of the Children and Young Persons Act 1993. The figure for 1997 to some extent reflects the fact that since 1992 the Act has applied to 17-year-olds.

27 Aged 16 and over before 1934, and aged 18 and over after 1992.

28 See the Government White Papers with their telling titles: *Punishment, Custody and the Community*, Cm. 424, 1988; *Supervision and Punishment in the Community: A Framework for Action*, Cm. 966, 1990; *Strengthening Punishment in the Community: A Consultative Document*, Cm. 2780, 1995. For a useful review of probation statistics, see Hine (1995).

29 If an offender commits another offence during the period of conditional discharge – usually 12 months – he or she will be liable to be sentenced for the original offence as well as the new offence. The explanation of the relatively frequent use of this measure in the 1990s given by some magistrates was that in some cases a conditional discharge was likely to be more effective than a fine. This was both because it acted as a 'sword of Damocles' and because some offenders could not afford to pay a realistic fine. See Flood-Page and Mackie (1998), pp.53–4.

30 This is not the same as the number of persons received each year, because a person may be received more than once. The greater the number of short sentences imposed the more the figure for receptions will have exaggerated the number of persons involved (as at the beginning of the century). The figures refer to receptions into all kinds of prison service institutions, including borstals, detention centres and young offender institutions.

31 See White and Powar (1998). The authors show that using alternative scenarios the prison population could vary between 64 400 and 92 600 by the year 2005.

32 Bailey (1987) contains much useful statistical information.

33 It should be noted that the ethnic composition of the prison population has changed as one would expect given a more ethnic diverse society. Nevertheless, Afro-Caribbean offenders are greatly over-represented in relation to their number in the population at large. In 1997 the number of Afro-Caribbean prisoners per 100 000 of the black population was 1249. This compares with 150 and 176 per 100 000 for the South Asian and white populations respectively. See *Prison Statistics England and Wales 1997* (1998) Cm. 4017, Chapter 6, at pp.112–13.

34 For a similar analysis for the years 1950–91, coming to similar conclusions, see Nuttall and Pease (1994).

35 See *Annual Report of the Parole Board for England and Wales 1997*, and Hood and Shute (1996). They estimated that the more stringent criteria introduced in 1992 would add at least 1000 to the prison population. Since then the criteria have become even more stringent.

References

Allen, Rob (1991) 'Out of jail: the reduction in the use of penal custody for male juveniles 1981–1988', *Howard Journal*, vol. 30, pp.30–52.

Ashworth, Andrew (1995) *Sentencing and Criminal Justice*, second edition, Butterworth, London.

Audit Commission (1996) *Misspent Youth: Young People and Crime*, Audit Commission, London.

Bailey, Victor (1987) *Delinquency and Citizenship: Reclaiming the Young Offender, 1914–1948*, Oxford University Press, Oxford.

Barclay, Gordon (1995) *A Digest of Information on the Criminal Justice System*, third edition, Home Office Research and Statistics Department, London.

Bennett, Trevor (1998) *Drugs and Crime: The Results of Research on Drug Testing and Interviewing Arrestees*, Home Office Research Study, no.183, HMSO, London.

Bottoms, Anthony E. (1957) 'Reflections on the renaissance of dangerousness', *Howard Journal*, vol. 16, pp.70–96.

Bottoms, Anthony E. (1995) 'The philosophy and politics of sentencing', in Clarkson, C. and Morgan, R. (eds) *The Politics of Sentencing Reform*, Oxford University Press, Oxford, pp.17–49.

Budd, Tracey (1999) *Burglary of Domestic Dwellings: findings from the British Crime Survey*, Home Office Statistical Bulletin 4/99, Government Statistical Service, London.

Carlisle Committee (1988) *The Parole System in England and Wales*, Cm 532, HMSO, London.

Cohen, Stanley (1985) *Visions of Social Control*, Polity Press, Cambridge.

Coleman, Clive and Moynihan, Jenny (1996) *Understanding Crime Data: Haunted by the Dark Figure*, Open University Press, Buckingham.

Departmental Committee on Criminal Statistics (Perks Committee) (1967) *Report*, Cmnd. 3448, HMSO, London.

Farrington, David P. and Langan, Patrick A. (1992) 'Changes in crime and punishment in England and America in the 1980s', *Justice Quarterly*, vol. 9 (1), pp.5–46.

Field, Simon (1990) *Trends in Crime and their Interpretation: A Study of Recorded Crime in Post-War England and Wales*, Home Office Research Study, no. 199, HMSO, London.

Fitzgerald, Marian (1993) *Ethnic Minorities and the Criminal Justice System*, Royal Commission on Criminal Justice Research Study, no. 20, HMSO, London.

Fitzgerald, Marian (1995) 'Ethnic differences', in Walker, Monica A. (ed.) *Interpreting Crime Statistics*, Oxford University Press, Oxford, pp.158–74.

Flood-Page, Claire and Mackie, Alan (1998) *Sentencing Practice: An Examination of Decisions in Magistrates' Courts and the Crown Court in the mid 1990s*, Home Office Research Study, no. 180, HMSO, London.

Garland, David (1996) 'The limits of the sovereign state: strategies of crime control in contemporary society', *British Journal of Criminology*, vol. 36, pp.445–71.

Godfrey, David (1996) 'Lost in the myths of crime: the use of penal custody for male juveniles, 1969 to 1993', *Howard Journal*, vol. 35, pp.287–98.

Graham, John and Bowling, Benjamin (1995) *Young People and Crime*, Home Office Research Study, no. 145, Home Office, London.

Hedderman, Carol and Moxon, David (1992) *Magistrates' Court or Crown Court? Mode of trial decisions and their impact on sentencing*, Home Office Research Study, no. 125, HMSO, London.

Heidensohn, Frances (1992) *Women in Control? The Role of Women in Law Enforcement*, Oxford University Press, Oxford.

Heidensohn, Frances (1996), *Women and Crime*, second edition, Macmillan, Basingstoke.

Heidensohn, Frances (1997) 'Gender and crime', in Maguire, M., Morgan, R. and Reiner, R. (eds) *The Oxford Handbook of Criminology*, second edition, Oxford University Press, Oxford, pp.761–98.

Hine, Jean (1995) 'Community sentences and the work of the Probation Service', in Walker, Monica A. (ed.) *Interpreting Crime Statistics*, Oxford University Press, Oxford, pp.61–90.

Home Office (1998) *Statistics on Race and the Criminal Justice System*, Home Office, London.

Hood, Roger (1992) *Race and Sentencing: A Study in the Crown Court*, Oxford University Press, Oxford.

Hood, Roger and Joyce, Kate (1999) 'Three generations: oral testimonies on crime and social change in London's East End', *British Journal of Criminology*, vol. 39 (1), pp.136–60.

Hood, Roger and Shute, Stephen (1996) 'Parole criteria, parole decisions and the prison population: evaluating the impact of the Criminal Justice Act 1991', *Criminal Law Review*, pp.77–87.

Langan, Patrick A. and Farrington, David P. (1998), *Crime and Justice in the United States and England and Wales, 1981–96*, US Department of Justice, Washington, DC.

Lewis, Chris (1992) 'Crime statistics: their use and misuse' *Social Trends*, HMSO, London.

Lloyd, Charles and Walmsley, Roy (1989) *Changes in Rape Offences and Sentencing*, Home Office Research Study, no. 105, HMSO, London.

McClintock, F. H. (1974) 'Facts and myths about the state of crime', in Hood, Roger (ed.) *Crime, Criminology and Public Policy: Essays in Honour of Sir Leon Radzinowicz*, Heinemann, London, pp.33–46.

McClintock, F. H., Avison, N. H. and Rose, G. N. G. (1968) *Crime in England and Wales*, Heinemann, London.

McClintock, F. H. and Gibson, E. (1961) *Robbery in London*, Macmillan, London.

McConville, M., Sanders, A. and Leng, R. (1991) *The Case for the Prosecution*, Routledge, London.

McMahon, Maeve (1990) 'Net widening: vagaries in the use of a concept', *British Journal of Criminology*, vol. 30, pp.121–49.

Maguire, Mike (1997) 'Crime statistics, patterns, and trends: changing perceptions and their implications', in Maguire, M., Morgan, R. and Reiner, R. (eds) *The Oxford Handbook of Criminology*, second edition, Oxford University Press, Oxford, pp.135–88.

Mannheim, Hermann (1941) *Social Aspects of Crime in England between the Wars*, George Allen and Unwin, London.

Mirrlees-Black, Catriona, Budd, Tracey, Partridge, Sarah and Mayhew, Pat (1998) 'The 1998 British Crime Survey England and Wales', *Home Office Statistical Bulletin*, Issue 21/98, Government Statistical Service, London.

Mirrlees-Black, Catriona, Mayhew, Pat and Percy, Andrew (1996) 'The 1996 British Crime Survey', *Home Office Statistical Bulletin*, Issue 19/96, Home Office, London.

Morgan, Rod (1997) 'Imprisonment: current concerns', in Maguire, M., Morgan, R. and Reiner, R. (eds) *The Oxford Handbook of Criminology*, second edition, Oxford University Press, Oxford, pp.1137–94.

Morrison, S. and O'Donnell, I. (1994) *Armed Robbery: A Study in London*, Oxford Centre for Criminological Research, Occasional Paper no. 15, Oxford.

Nuttall, Christopher and Pease, Ken (1994) 'Changes in the use of imprisonment in England and Wales 1950–1991', *Criminal Law Review*, pp.316–23.

Pease, Ken (1997) 'Crime prevention', in Maguire, M., Morgan, R. and Reiner, R. (eds) *The Oxford Handbook of Criminology*, second edition, Oxford University Press, Oxford, pp.974–6.

Radzinowicz, Leon (1945a) 'English criminal statistics', in Radzinowicz, L. and Turner, J. W. C. (eds) *The Modern Approach to Criminal Law*, Macmillan, London, pp.174–95.

Radzinowicz, Leon (1945b) 'The assessment of punishments by English courts', in Radzinowicz, L. and Turner, J. W. C. (eds) *The Modern Approach to Criminal Law*, Macmillan, London, pp.110–22.

Radzinowicz, Leon (1999) *Adventures in Criminology*, Routledge, London.

Radzinowicz, Leon and Hood, Roger (1986) *A History of English Criminal Law*, vol. 5, *The Emergence of Penal Policy*, Clarendon, Oxford.

Rose, G. N. G. (1970) 'The merits of an index of crime of the kind devised by Sellin and Wolfgang', in *The Index of Crime: Some Further Studies, Collected Studies in Criminological Research*, vol. 7, Council of Europe, Strasbourg, pp.33–52.

Ruck, S. K. (1935) 'Crime', in Llewellyn Smith, H. (ed.) *The New Survey of London Life and Labour, vol. 11, Life and Leisure*, P. S. King, London.

Ruck, S. K. (ed.) (1951) *Paterson on Prisons*, Frederic Muller, London.

Sellin, Thorsten (1931) 'The basis of a Crime Index', *Journal of Criminal Law and Criminology*, vol. 22, pp.335–56.

Sellin, Thorsten and Wolfgang, Marvin (1964) *The Measurement of Delinquency*, John Wiley, New York.

Smith, David (1997) 'Ethnic origins, crime, criminal justice', in Maguire, M., Morgan., R. and Reiner, R. (eds) *The Oxford Handbook of Criminology*, second edition, Oxford University Press, Oxford, pp.703–59.

Smith, Lorna (1989) *Concerns About Rape*, Home Office Research Study, no. 106, HMSO, London.

South, Nigel (1997) 'Drugs: use, crime and control', in Maguire, M., Morgan, R. and Reiner, R. (eds) *The Oxford Handbook of Criminology*, second edition, Oxford University Press, Oxford, pp.925–60.

Sutherland, Edwin (1956) 'The decreasing prison population of England', in Cohen, Albert, Lindesmith, Alfred and Schuessler, Karl (eds) *The Sutherland Papers*, Indiana University Press, Bloomington (written 1934), pp.200–26.

Walker, Monica A. (ed.) (1995) *Interpreting Crime Statistics*, Oxford University Press, Oxford.

Walker, Nigel (1988) 'Crime and Penal Measures', in Halsey, A. H. (ed.) *British Social Trends since 1900*, Macmillan, Basingstoke, pp.616–44.

Walmsley, R. (1986) *Personal Violence*, Home Office Research Study, no. 89, HMSO, London.

White, Philip and Powar, Iqbal (1998) 'Revised projections of long term trends in the prison population to 2005', *Home Office Statistical Bulletin*, Issue 2/98, January.

Young, Warren and Brown, Mark (1993) 'Cross-national comparisons of imprisonment', in Tonry, M. (ed.) *Crime and Justice: A Review of Research*, vol. 17, University of Chicago Press, London, pp.1–49.

Zedner, Lucia (1997) 'Victims', in Maguire, M., Morgan, R. and Reiner, R. (eds) *The Oxford Handbook of Criminology*, second edition, Oxford University Press, Oxford, pp.577–612.

Appendix 1: Price Indices

The problem of converting prices into their current equivalents has recurred throughout this book, and the purpose of this appendix is to explain the details of the price index we have used.

The official price series takes the Cost of Living Index from July 1914 to June 1947, the Interim Index of Retail Prices from June 1947 to January 1956, and the Retail Price Index thereafter. The figures for these indices up to 1990 have been published by the Central Statistical Office (1991) and the more recent figures can be found in the *Economic Trends Annual Supplement*.

However, an important criticism has been made of the official series. It has been argued that during World War II the official Cost of Living Index understated the rise in prices, because the weights used by the index were based on an inquiry into working-class budgets in 1904 and had not been revised (Seers, 1948). There was a similar controversy during World War I (Winter, 1986, Chapter 6). Throughout this book, therefore, for the period 1900–52 we use the index published by Charles Feinstein (1972, Table 65), and the official price series thereafter.

Applying the indices over a period of time requires various calculations to be made, since from time to time the indices are rebased. We have constructed a 'ready reckoner', shown in the table below. For any given year, to convert into 1997 prices, all that needs to be done is to multiply the price by the figure shown for that year. For example, to find out what £50 in 1930 would be worth in 1997 prices, we multiply by 34.46, giving a result of £1723. The calendar years refer to annual averages, and we have also made the relevant calculations for financial years (this was only possible from 1952 onwards); these refer to the average indices for the months April–March of the years shown.

References

Central Statistical Office (1991) *Retail Prices 1914–1990*, HMSO, London.

Feinstein, C. H. (1972) *National Income, Expenditure and Output of the UK 1855–1965*, Cambridge University Press, Cambridge.

Seers, D. (1948) 'The increase in the working class cost of living since before the war', *Bulletin of the Oxford University Institute of Statistics*, vol. 10, pp.140–61.

Winter, J. M. (1986) *The Great War and the British People*, Macmillan, London.

Calendar years

1900	60.02	1950	18.87	**Financial years**	
1901	60.70	1951	17.18	1952/53	15.63
1902	60.70	1952	15.80	1953/54	15.29
1903	60.02	1953	15.33	1954/55	14.91
1904	59.35	1954	15.06	1955/56	14.21
1905	59.35	1955	14.41	1956/57	13.59
1906	58.70	1956	13.72	1957/58	13.12
1907	57.44	1957	13.23	1958/59	12.78
1908	58.70	1958	12.85	1959/60	12.79
1909	58.06	1959	12.77	1960/61	12.57
1910	56.83	1960	12.65	1961/62	12.09
1911	56.23	1961	12.23	1962/63	11.64
1912	54.51	1962	11.73	1963/64	11.46
1913	53.42	1963	11.50	1964/65	11.01
1914	52.89	1964	11.14	1965/66	10.52
1915	44.15	1965	10.63	1966/67	10.14
1916	37.35	1966	10.23	1967/68	9.907
1917	30.88	1967	9.981	1968/69	9.390
1918	26.84	1968	9.533	1969/70	8.931
1919	25.32	1969	9.041	1970/71	8.326
1920	21.89	1970	8.500	1971/72	7.620
1921	24.06	1971	7.766	1972/73	7.116
1922	29.84	1972	7.253	1973/74	6.443
1923	31.24	1973	6.642	1974/75	5.465
1924	31.06	1974	5.724	1975/76	4.386
1925	30.88	1975	4.609	1976/77	3.804
1926	31.61	1976	3.954	1977/78	3.337
1927	32.57	1977	3.413	1978/79	3.081
1928	32.77	1978	3.153	1979/80	2.661
1929	33.18	1979	2.780	1980/81	2.288
1930	34.46	1980	2.356	1981/82	2.052
1931	36.84	1981	2.106	1982/83	1.916
1933	38.99	1982	1.939	1983/84	1.831
1934	38.71	1983	1.854	1984/85	1.743
1935	38.15	1984	1.766	1985/86	1.645
1936	37.09	1985	1.665	1986/87	1.594
1937	35.14	1986	1.610	1987/88	1.533
1938	34.91	1987	1.546	1988/89	1.447
1939	33.81	1988	1.474	1989/90	1.342
1940	29.84	1989	1.367	1990/91	1.223
1941	27.11	1990	1.249	1991/92	1.168
1942	25.44	1991	1.180	1992/93	1.132
1943	24.62	1992	1.137	1993/94	1.113
1944	24.06	1993	1.120	1994/95	1.084
1945	23.64	1994	1.093	1995/96	1.049
1946	22.63	1995	1.057	1996/97	1.024
1947	21.45	1996	1.031	1997/98	0.992
1948	19.93	1997	1.000		
1949	19.42				

Appendix 2: Censuses and Surveys

One strand which unites the chapters in this book is that they all refer to census or survey data. Social surveys have a long tradition in Britain stretching back to the Domesday Book of 1086. In the first half of the twentieth century, they tended to focus on relatively small areas such as York, Merseyside or London, and looked at local conditions in detail. The development of sampling made such surveys much more affordable and they flourished in the inter-war years (Abrams, 1951). During and after World War II, the government began to develop national sample surveys for official purposes. In many cases, these cover a specific subject area, such as the New Earnings Survey, the National Travel Survey or the British Crime Survey. Other surveys are more general, and in this appendix we provide a brief guide to three of these, and the census.

The census

The main distinction between a census and a survey is that participation in the census is obligatory. Population censuses have been carried out in Britain every ten years since 1801, with the exception of 1941 when it was prevented by World War II (and in 1966 there was an additional sample census). Naturally, there have been some changes in the design of the questionnaire over this period, but the fact that census data are available for the whole of the twentieth century means that long-term trends can be measured. The main geographical unit in the census is Great Britain, although there are some small differences in procedure between the constituent countries, England, Wales and Scotland. Since 1926, a census has also been separately conducted in Northern Ireland but its questions are rather different (Hakim, 1982, p.28).

The census is a particularly valuable resource for a number of reasons. First, its coverage is very good since it aims to cover the whole population. For various reasons this is difficult to achieve: not all residential accommodation may be identified, a household may be absent on census day and mistakenly recorded as vacant, incorrect information may be supplied by the people filling in the forms, and so on. In 1981 the level of under-coverage was 2.3 per cent and in 1991 it was 2.2 per cent, a slight improvement. Men aged 20–34 and women aged 85 and over were particularly likely to be missed out (Office of Population Censuses and Surveys, 1995, Table 10.5). Nevertheless, by comparison with surveys this is a very high level of coverage, and means that very detailed information about small groups and local areas is available.

The census also provides a great variety of information about the population. Topics covered include marital status, housing tenure and conditions, occupation and industry, hours worked, educational qualifications, and car ownership, and in 1991 a question on ethnicity was included for the first time. Questions which are particularly onerous to code are processed only for a 10 per cent sample of returns. Further information on the 1991 census can be obtained from the census report (Office of Population Censuses and Surveys, 1995), while the Website of the Office for National Statistics gives some details of the forthcoming 2001 census (http://www.ons.gov.uk).

713

Family Expenditure Survey

The Family Expenditure Survey (FES) has been carried out each year since 1957 (there was also a one-off study in 1953/54). It is a survey of a random sample of private households in the UK, which asks questions about household expenditure and income. The basic unit of the survey is the household, defined as a group of people living at the same address and sharing household expenses such as food and bills. Each adult (aged 16 or over) in the household is asked to keep records of expenditure for two weeks, and is also interviewed. (Since 1995/96, children aged 7–15 have also been asked to complete expenditure diaries.) In 1997/98, 6409 households took part, and the response rate was 62 per cent in Great Britain and 60 per cent in Northern Ireland. The survey is continuous; that is, interviews are spread evenly across the year so that seasonal expenditure changes are covered.

There is some evidence to suggest that the households which refuse to participate are different in some respects from those which do take part, implying that their patterns of expenditure and income may also differ. Factors associated with higher non-response include the household being located in Greater London, the household containing three or more adults, the household head being born outside the UK or a member of an ethnic minority group, and the household head having no post-school qualifications, being self-employed, or being in a manual social class group. Another problem is that certain items, such as tobacco, alcohol, confectionery and National Lottery spending, are also under-reported. Further information about the FES can be found in the annual publication, *Family Spending* (Office for National Statistics, 1998a).

General Household Survey

The General Household Survey (GHS) is also a continuous survey, but of more recent origin. It has been running since 1971 and is based each year on a sample of the general population living in private households in Great Britain. Since the 1988 survey, the fieldwork has been conducted on a financial rather than calendar year basis. In 1996/97, interviews were obtained with 17043 adults, either in person or occasionally by proxy, in 9158 households throughout the country. Partial responses are accepted (some people decline to answer all the questions, and people being interviewed by proxy are not asked all the questions) which means that the response rate can be calculated in several ways. In 1996/97, if partial responses are included, the response rate was 77 per cent, while if they are excluded then it was 66 per cent. The middle response rate, which accepts some of the partial responses, was 76 per cent, the lowest in the history of the GHS.

Each year the GHS includes questions on population and fertility, family and household information, housing, health, employment and education. Other subjects are covered periodically and new questions are occasionally introduced. For example, the 1996 survey asked about smoking, drinking, sport and leisure activities, burglary, mobility and membership of personal and occupational pension schemes, in addition to the core topics.

There are some indications that the GHS tends to over-represent children and to under-represent adults in their twenties and early thirties, and Londoners. Further information about the GHS can be found in the annual report *Living in Britain* (Office for National Statistics, 1998b).

Labour Force Survey

The Labour Force Survey (LFS) was established in 1973 and was conducted every two years until 1983. Between 1984 and 1991 it was annual, and since 1992 it has been quarterly. It asks questions about labour force participation and earnings, and also covers personal information such as ethnicity and marital status. Over time, various changes have been made to the definitions used and questions asked (see Office for National Statistics, 1997) The sample is about 120 000 adults (aged 16 or over) living at 60 000 private addresses in the UK, which makes it by far the largest sample survey. Each household is interviewed five times; once every three months. The response rate for the first interview in the spring of 1998 was 78 per cent (Office for National Statistics, 1998c, p.24).

Non-respondents tend to be younger than the population as a whole and more likely to live in urban areas, but a grossing system is used which attempts to counterbalance this. Another distinctive feature of the LFS is that about 30 per cent of its responses are collected by proxy, and the proportion is much higher for some groups, especially young people. The proxy data vary in accuracy; for characteristics such as employment the information is fairly good, but for data which the proxy is less likely to know well, such as detailed estimates of hours worked and earnings, the match is poorer (Office for National Statistics, 1998c, Section 11). Further information about the background and methodology of the LFS can be obtained from Volume 1 of the *Labour Force Survey User Guide*.

Other surveys

Two other surveys of note have not been used much in this book, since they were established relatively recently, but for those interested in social trends, they should become increasingly useful in future.

British Household Panel Survey

This is an annual study which follows the same sample of individuals – the panel – over a period of years. It began in 1990 and each year's survey is referred to as a 'wave'. The Wave 1 panel consisted of 5500 households in Britain containing 10 300 individuals; every adult member of sampled households is interviewed. The same people are re-interviewed in successive waves and, if they split off from original households, all adult members of their new households are also interviewed. Children in each household are interviewed once they reach the age of 16. Topics covered by the survey include household structure, labour market position, income and wealth, household finances, housing, health and caring, and values and opinions. For further information, see Buck (1994).

British Social Attitudes Survey

This annual survey was established in 1983, and looks at the attitudes, values and beliefs of the British public. In 1996, interviews were conducted with 3662 individuals in Britain and the response rate was 68 per cent (Jowell et al., 1997, p.219). The subjects covered by the surveys are wide-ranging and vary from year to year, but include attitudes to housing, work and unemployment, health care, education, social security and dependency, tax and spending, transport, the environment, constitutional reform, law and order, civil liberties, religion, family obligations, and many others. A report on the survey is published every year; for more information, see Brook et al. (1992).

References

Abrams, Mark (1951) *Social Surveys and Social Action*, Heinemann, London.

Brook, Lindsay, et al. (1992) *British Social Attitudes Cumulative Sourcebook: The First Six Surveys*, Gower, Aldershot.

Buck, N. H. (1994) *Changing Households: The British Household Panel Survey 1990 to 1992*, ESRC Research Centre on Micro-Social Change, Colchester.

Hakim, Catherine (1982) *Secondary Analysis in Social Research*, Allen and Unwin, London.

Jowell, Roger et al. (eds) (1997)*British Social Attitudes: The 14th report*, Ashgate, Aldershot.

Office for National Statistics (1997) *Labour Force Survey Historical Supplement 1997*, The Stationery Office, London.

Office for National Statistics (1998a) *Family Spending: A Report on the 1997–98 Family Expenditure Survey*, The Stationery Office, London.

Office for National Statistics (1998b) *Living in Britain: Results from the 1996 General Household Survey*, The Stationery Office, London.

Office for National Statistics (1998c) *Labour Force Survey User Guide*, Volume 1, ESRC Data Archive, Colchester (Website address http://dawww.essex.ac.uk).

Office of Population Censuses and Surveys (1995) *1991 Census: General Report, Great Britain*, HMSO, London.

Index